PHILOSOPHY OF ŚRĪ MADHVĀCĀRYA

PHILOSOPHY OF
ŚRĪ MADHVĀCĀRYA

B. N. K. Sharma

MOTILAL BANARSIDASS PUBLISHERS
PRIVATE LIMITED • DELHI

4th Reprint: Delhi, **2014**
Revised Edition: Delhi, 1986
First Edition: Delhi, 1962

ISBN: 978-81-208-0068-7

MOTILAL BANARSIDASS
41 U.A. Bungalow Road, Jawahar Nagar, Delhi 110 007
8 Mahalaxmi Chamber, 22 Bhulabhai Desai Road, Mumbai 400 026
203 Royapettah High Road, Mylapore, Chennai 600 004
236, 9th Main III Block, Jayanagar, Bengaluru 560 011
Sanas Plaza, 1302 Baji Rao Road, Pune 411 002
8 Camac Street, Kolkata 700 017
Ashok Rajpath, Patna 800 004
Chowk, Varanasi 221 001

Printed in India

by RP Jain at NAB Printing Unit,
A-44, Naraina Industrial Area, Phase I, New Delhi–110028
and published by JP Jain for Motilal Banarsidass Publishers (P) Ltd.
41 U.A. Bungalow Road, Jawahar Nagar, Delhi-110007

स्वतन्त्रं परतन्त्रं च द्विविधं तत्त्वमिष्यते

Dedicated to

ŚRĪ MADHVĀCĀRYA
(Ānandatīrtha Bhagavatpāda)

Who showed how philosophy can fulfil its purpose and attain its goal by enabling man to realize the eternal and indissoluble bond of Bimba-Pratibimba-bhāva that exists between the Infinite and the finite.

ABBREVIATIONS

AA	Aitareya Āraṇyaka
Ait Up	Aitareya Upaniṣad
AB	Aitareya Brāhmaṇa
ABMM	Akhila Bhārata Mādhva Mahāmandal (Udipi).
adhi	adhikaraṇa
AV	Anu-Vyākhyāna
Bhag	Bhāgavata Purāṇa
BORI	Bhandarkar Oriental Research Institute, Pune
Brh Up	Bṛhadāraṇyaka Upaniṣad
BS	Brahmasūtras
BSB	Brahmasūtra Bhāṣya
BSPC	Brahmasūtras and Their Principal Commentaries
BT	Bhāgavata-Tātparya
Chan Up	Chāndogya Upaniṣad
Cri. Sur. I. Phil.	Critical Survey of Indian Philosophy
DMS	Daivī Mīmāṁsā Sūtras
Epil	Epilogue
fn	footnote
GB	Gītā Bhāṣya
GBt	Gītā Bhāṣya Tīkā
GK	Gauḍapāda Kārikās
GOS	Gaekwad Oriental Series
GT	Gītā Tātparya
GTt	Gītā Tātparya Ṭīkā
HDSV	History of Dvaita School of Vedānta and Its Literature
I. Phil.	Indian Philosophy
KN	Karma Nirṇaya
KNt	Karma Nirṇaya Ṭīkā
MBSB	Madhva: Brahmasūtrabhāṣya

MGB	Madhva: Gītā Bhāṣya
MahNUp	Mahānārayaṇa Upaniṣad
MS	Manuscript
MSS	Madhvasiddhāntasāra
Mbh	Mahābhārata
MbhTN	Mahābhārata Tātparya Nirṇaya
MVij	Madhva Vijaya
Man Up	Māṇḍūkya Upaniṣad
Mith. Kht.	Mithyātvānumānakhaṇḍanaṭīkā
Mund Up	Muṇḍaka Upaniṣad
Nym	Nyāyāmṛta
NS	Nyāya Sudhā
N.S. Press	Nirnayasagar Press (Bombay)
NV	Nyāya Vivaraṇa
OL	Oriental Library
Pan	Pāṇini (Sūtras)
PL	Pramāṇa Lakṣaṇa
PLt	Pramāṇa Lakṣaṇa Ṭīkā
PMS	Pūrva Mīmāmsā Sūtras
PP	Pramāṇa Paddhati
RGB	Rāmānuja: Gītā Bhāṣya
RV	Ṛg Veda
SBSB	Śaṅkara: Brahmasūtrabhāṣya
SNR	Sannyāyaratnāvalī
Svet Up	Śvetāśvatara Upaniṣad
TA	Taittirīya Āraṇyaka
TB	Taittirīya Brāhmaṇa
TC	Tātparya Candrikā
TD	Tattvapradīpa
Tg	Taraṅgiṇī
Tdy	Tattvodyota
Tdyt	Tattvodyota Ṭīkā
TP	Tattvaprakāśikā
Taitt Up	Taittirīya Upaniṣad
Tr	Translation
TS	Tattva Saṅkhyāna
TSt	Tattvasaṅkhyāna Ṭīkā
TT	Tarka Tāṇḍava

TV	Tattva Viveka
TVt	Tattvaviveka Ṭīkā
Up	Upaniṣad
UpKh	Upādhi Khaṇḍana
UpKht	Upādhi Khaṇḍana Ṭīkā
VTN	Viṣṇu Tattva Nirṇaya
VTNt	Visṇutattvanirṇaya Ṭīkā
VS	Vaiśeṣikasūtras

CONTENTS

IV. THE WORLD OF EXPERIENCE

V. DOCTRINE OF ĀTMAN

VI. DOCTRINE OF BRAHMAN

VII. SĀDHANA-VICĀRA

VIII. DOCTRINE OF MUKTI

BIOGRAPHICAL NOTE

Śrī Madhvācārya (1238-1317) was the historical founder of the Dvaita system, which is one of the three principal schools of Vedānta. He was a native of Tuḷunāḍu in Karnataka. Pājakakṣetra, eight miles south-east of the modern town of Udipi, on the West coast of S. India, was the village of his birth. He lived seventynine years.

He appeared on the Indian philosophical scene after the systems of Śaṅkara and Rāmānuja had been well established. The reasons which led him to propound a new system of Vedānta were his doctrinal differences and ideological dissatisfaction with contemporary trends and schools of thonght within and without Hinduism and particularly with the system of Śaṅkara which was the dominant philosophy of the time. In spite of the Theistic revolt against Śaṅkara led by Rāmānuja, Madhva could not agree with him on many points of Theistic doctrine. So he felt called upon to give a new lead in thought to his countrymen.

Madhva called his system 'Tattvavāda' (realism). It is described by Vidyāraṇya in his *Sarvadarśanasaṅgraha* as "Pūrṇaprajñadarśana". Pūrṇaprajña and Ānandatīrtha are other names of Madhvācārya. All the three names have been found used by him in his works. He is now more widely known by the last name of Madhva or Madhvācārya.

While yet in his teens, the call of the spirit took him to Acyutaprajña, an ascetic of the Ekadaṇḍi order, belonging to the Sanaka, Ekānti or Brahmasampradāya. He received initiation from him, as a Sannyāsin. After this, Madhva studied the classics of the Advaita school, such as the *Iṣṭasiddhi*. Later, he began to expound the Prasthānatrayī, independently and from a new standpoint, laying bare the defects in the current interpretations of Śaṅkara and his school. Sometimes, he used to enter into scholastic disputations with the veteran scholars of the day. Mention has been made in his biography of Buddhisāgara, Vādisiṁha and Bhānu Paṇḍita. He toured all over India several times and visited Badarikāśrama, Bengal, Bihar and Banaras in the north and many centres of learning on the *Godāvarī* and important places like Goa. Śrīraṅgam, Rāmeśvaram and Kanyākumarī in the south.

Madhva has left thirtyseven works in all. They include : (i) Daśa Prakarṇas or ten philosophical monographs expounding his logic and metaphysics and critiques of Advaita doctrines of *upādhi*, *māyā* and *mithyātva*; (ii) commentaries on the ten Principal Upaniṣads; (iii) commentaries on the *Gītā* and the *Brahmasūtras*; (iv) a brief commantary on the first forty Sūktas of the *Ṛgveda*; (v) an epitome of the *Mahābhārata* in verses; (vi) brief notes and comments on the *Bhāgavata*; and (vii) miscellaneous works comprising stotras, poems and works on worship and ritual. His greatest work is the *Anu-Vyākhyana*, a critical exposition of the philosophy of the Brahmasūtras. It is a metrical work and is his masterpiece. It was commented upon by Jayatīrtha, in his famous work, the *Nyāyasudhā*.

Madhva's writings are characterized by extreme brevity of expression and compression of thought. They need the help of a very good commentary to be understood in their fulness of thought and depth of meaning and intention. His commentator Jayatīrrtha has infused into them the necessary amplitūde of utterance and expansiveness of thoguht and wealth of details.

Madhva was endowed with a fine magnetic personality. He was a born leader of men. As a creative thinker, he cared little for the conventions of fashionable belief and interpretation. He was not cowed down by the mere technical display of learning. His logic was as inexorable as his faith in Theism was unshakable. He made a deep impression on his contemporaries. Some of his eminent disciples like Trivikrama Paṇḍita. Padmanābha Tīrtha and Narahari Tīrtha were distinguished scholars of Advaita and other systems before they became converted to his views. They belonged to different parts of India and spoke different languages. After establising his system on firm foundations, Madhva installed the idol of Bālakṛṣṇa secured from Dvārakā at his Mutt in Udipi, in 1285. He made Uḍipi the spiritual centre of his school and entrusted the worship at the Maṭha of Śrīkṛṣṇa to eight ascetic disciples. Their line of successors and those of other disciples, all entrusted with the work of propagating his system, are flourishing to this day.[1] According to tradition, Madhva disappeared from men's vision and retired to Badarikāśrama in his seventyninth year. Nārāyaṇa Paṇḍita, the son of one of his direct disciples, Trivikrama Paṇḍita, wrote Madhva's biography in a Sanskrit Kāvya of sixteen cantos known as *Madhva-Vijaya.* It is the main source of Madhva's life and activities.

Madhva went directly to the fountainheads of ancient thought,—the source-books of Hindu philosophy, to draw his inspiration from them. He followed the streams of thought and interpretation emerging directly from them and flowing though the Epics, Purāṇas and Pañcarātras and other interpretive literature of more ancient standing than the interpretations of later day commentators, however eminent. There was a strong note of Mystic fervor in his thought and writings. His arguments were often so intimately connected with the authorities he had so diligently collected for himself from forgotten and fading sources as to appear to be almost entirely dependent on them. It was Jayatīrtha who successfully brought out the inherent logical strength behind his authorities. There were certain great ideas behind Madhva's writings,—ideas of tremendous philosophical power, significance and potentiality—such as the conception of *Sākṣi*, the doctrine of *Svatantratattva*, *Viśeṣas* in relation to the concept of identity and difference,—and creation in the new sense of *Parādhīnaviśeṣāpti.* With these fruitful ideas, which he derived partly from his study of his sources and partly from his own cogitations based on them, Madhva built up a cogent and independent system of Theistic philosophy and worked out its details and put it on a firm and enduring basis of textual sanctions and logical satisfyingness. He urged the necessity of adopting a fresh attitude of mind and a new set of fundamental concepts and categories in place of the old and worn out ideas of the fashionable schoolmen, including those of the latest in the field. Once the metaphysical necessity of

1. The genealogical Tables of these lines have been given in my *HDSV*.pp. 201-209.

discarding the outmoded ideas and the need to go in for more effective theories and newer modes of approach to the problems of philosophy were established, the whole course of philosophical inquiry was bound to take a new turn and enter upon a new terrain. Providence blessed Madhva with two great assets—an interpreter of such outstanding eminence as Jayatīrtha and a dialectical expositor of the calibre of Vyāsatīrtha, whom it harnessed to the cause of expounding his system to posterity.

JAYATĪRTHA (1345-88)

Jayatīrtha is Madhva's Commentator *par excellence*. According to tradition, he was the son of a nobleman of Mangalavedha, now in the Maharashtra State. As a chieftain's son he was given training in riding and the use of arms. For a full account of his life see my *HDSV*. Chap. XXI. As a young man, he renounced the pleasures of married life and became a disciple of Akṣobhya Tīrtha, one of the four direct disciples of Madhva. This Akṣobhya was himself a redoutable scholar and is reported to have engaged the famous Vidyāraṇya in a historic disputation over the 'Tattvam asi' text, at which the celebrated follower of Rāmānuja, Vedānta Deśika, is reported to have acted as the umpire and given his verdict in favor of Akṣobhya :

असिना तत्त्वमसिना परजीवप्रभेदिना ।
विद्यारण्यमहारण्यं अक्षोभ्यमुनिरच्छिनत् ॥

(Quoted in *Mūvāyirappaḍi Guruparamparāprabhāvam* of Brahmatantra Svatantra Jeer).

Jayatīrtha studied Madhva's works under Akṣobhya Tīrtha and later succeeded him as Pontiff of his Mutt in 1365. He toured all over India and propagated Madhva's philosophy by writing commentaries on most of the important works of Madhva. He seems to have spent the major part of his life at Eragola and partly at Malkheḍ or Mānyakheṭa, the historic capital of the Rashtrakuṭas of Karnataka, now in the Culbarga district of Karnatka state.

Later, he seems to have moved south towards Ānegondi (Hampi) and passed away there in 1388. There is reason to believe that his mortal remains were laid to rest facing the tomb of Padmanābha Tīrtha himself on the island, which later came to be known as Navabrindavana, on the *Tungabhadrā* river.

The Brindāvana Samādhi of Śrī Jayatīrtha (1365-88) facing that of Śrī Padmanābha Tīrtha (1317-24) in the Navabrindāvana island in the Tuṅgabhadrā river near Ānegondi, the ancient capital of the Vijayanagar Empire.

The tomb facing Padmanābha Tīrtha's bears on its front two figures carved on it, one of an ascetic in standing position holding a *daṇḍa* and a *Kamaṇḍalu* in his hands flanked by the figure of a crossbelted soldier with a drawn sword held in the left hand, the right forefinger pointing to the ascetic. These figures are obviously intended to record and commemorate the earlier and later phases of life of the prince Jayatīrtha who renounced family life and a military career and became a Paramahamsa.

Jayatīrtha has left us commentaries on most of the important works of Madhva. He has also left two independent works, one on logic (*Pramāṇa-Paddhati*) and another on metaphysics (*Vādāvali*). All his works have been printed. His greatest work is the *Nyāyasudhā* a commentary on Madhva's *Anu-Vyākhyāna. It is a work of monumental erudition in philosophy.*

Jayatīrtha standardized Madhva's thought and its interpretation. He was a born stylist. His style is noted for its elegance, lucidity, brilliance and felicity. His arguments are most scholarly and penetrating and his dialectic superb. His writings are characterised by an extreme orderliness of thought and presentation. He brings out the architectonic unity of Madhva's philosophical system and the grandeur of his metaphysical ideology of the *Svatantra-Tattva*, impressively. He has placed Madhva's philosophy and his interpretation of the Vedanta on a self-sufficient basis in respect of both its Adhikaraṇa Prasthāna and its Vāda-Prasthāna. For these remarkable services to the system posterity and tradition have honored him with the title of "Ṭīkācārya" or 'Commentator *par excellence.*

VYĀSATĪRTHA (1460-1539)

About a century after Jayatīrtha came Vyāsatīrtha, the Prince of dialecticians in the Dvaita system. He was born in Bannūr in the Mysore district of Karnataka. He become a Sannyāsin while still in his teens. He studied logic and Madhvaśāstra under the celebrated Mādhva Saint and Scholar Śrīpādarāja of Mulbāgal (near Kolār). Earlier, he is reported to have studied the classics of the Advaita, Viśiṣṭādvaita and Mīmāṁsā systems at Kāñcīpuram in Tamilnāḍu. He succeeded to the Pontifical seat of his Guru Brahmaṇya Tīrtha in 1478 AD and held sway for a long period of sixtyone years.

Vyāsatīrtha had many sides to his personality. He became the leader of the devotional movement of the Haridāsa Kūṭa of Karnataka, after Śrīpādarāja. The famous Purandara Dāsa, Kanaka Dāsa and others were his disciples. The illustrious writers VijayīndraTīrtha and Vādirāja Tīrtha were also his disciples. He was the religious adviser and spiritual Guru of Emperor Kṛṣṇadeva Rāya of Vijayanagar[1] and was held in the greatest honor and esteem at the Court of Vijayanagar by the kings of the second and third dynasties of Vijayanagar. We have a full account of Vyāsatīrtha's glorious life and career in the *Vyāsa-yogicarita*, a fine Campū Kāvya in Sanskrit, by Poet Somanātha. Vyāsatīrtha passed away in 1539 AD at Vijayanagar (where he lived for the major part of his life) and his mortal remains lie entombed in Nava Bṛndāvana, an island near Ānegondi on the Tuṅgabhadrā river.

Vyāsatīrtha wrote ten works in all.[2] The most famous of these are the *Nyāyāmṛta*, *Tarkatāṇḍava* and *Tātparya Candrikā*. They show his encyclopaedic range of knowledge of contemporary thought and philosophical literature and an astonishingly brilliant intellect of great clarity and penetration, rarely to be met with in one man. He had the ability to marshal vast quantity of factual material and extraordinary ramifications of thought into half a dozen propositions couched in terse and telling terms. His works embody the highest achievements of Mādhva philosophy, in the spheres of constructive exposition of the siddhānta and polemical refutation of other views and reinforcement of the siddhānta. Dasgupta has paid him the

1. See : उत्साहं मम वीक्ष्य मद्गुरुरसौ
श्रीव्यासतीर्थो मुनिः ॥

(MS of *Kṛṣṇadevarāyakṛti*, Madras GOL D. No. 18279).

2. Besides the *Sattarkavitāsa*, he mentions on p.385 on his *Upadhikhaṇḍana—Mandāramanjarī* another work of his own entitled *Bheda-Sanjīvini*, which appears to be different from his *Bhedojjīvana*. No MSS of *Sattarkovilāsa* and *Bhedasanjīvini* are, however, known so far.

highest tribute saying that "the logical skill and depth of acute dialectical thinking shown by Vyāsatīrtha stands almost unrivalled in the whole of Indian thought (*His of I. Phil.* iv. p. viii). The *Advaitasiddhi* of Madhusūdana Sarasvatī is a criticism of Vyāsatīrtha's *Nyāyāmṛta*. This was refuted by Rāmācārya-Vyāsa in his *Taraṅgiṇi*.

PREFACE TO THE SECOND EDITION

This book "Philosophy of Śrī Madhvācārya' was first published in 1962, by the Bharatiya Vidya Bhavan, Bombay. It was awarded the D. Litt. degree in Philosophy by the Bombay University in 1968.

The work has been out of print for many years now. There has been a persistent demand for its republication, from various parts of the country and from abroad, as it happens to be the only exhaustive standard work of reference and consultation on the subject, fully documented and with fiirst-hand inside knowledge of the texts and traditions of the Dvaita school in its authentic milieu, written in lucid lively English.

Dr. K. Narain's 'Outlines of Madhva Philosophy' (Udayana Publications, Allahabad) appeared almost at the same time as the first edition of this book. Though it covers similar ground, my work differs from his in its insightful approach to the seminal contributions of this school of Vedānta to the distinctive problems of Indian Philosophy and in its selection of topics and their comprehensive coverage, with copious discussion and assessment.

Dr. Narain's other work : '*A Critique of the Mādhva Refutation of Śaṅkara Vedānta* (Allahabad, 1964) requires separate attention. I have, however, thought it fit to take note of his criticisms of such of Madhva's positions as fall within the scope of my present work. I have also taken passing note of some of the adverse comments on the treatment of the *Advaita Śrutis* in Madhva's philosophy, contained in Dr. Krishnakant Chaturvedi's book in Hindi, entitled *Dvait Vedānt Kā Tāttvik Anuśilan* (Delhi, 1971).

The structural pattern of the work remains the same. But a great deal of fresh matter in the light of further reading and cogitation has gone in, while revising and enlarging the work for the second edition. These additiona are mostly expository and partly discursive. The ramifications of topics like the classification of Adhikārins for Brahmavidyā, Dhyāna, Guṇopasamhāra, phases of Aparokṣa-Jñāna, Utkrānti, Laya and Bhoga, falling under the scope of the Sādhana and Phala Adhyāyas of the Brahmasūtra have been only briefly dealt with here. They will be found exhaustively dealt with in the *third volume* of my *Brahmasūtras and Their Principal Commentaries* (Bharatiya Vidya Bhavan, Bombay, 1978).

I am deeply thankful to M/s Motilal Banarsidass, Delhi, for following up their publication of the revised edition of my *History of Dvaita School of Vedanta and Its Literature*, with the revised edition of this book which is its indispensable companion velume.

4/2 Shah Building
Bhagat Road
Bombay 400 016
June 9th, 1986

B.N.K. Sharma

PREFACE TO THE FIRST EDITION

This is the first complete, critical and comparative exposition of Śrī Madhvācārya's Philosophy in English. I am indeed very happy that it has been possible for me to bring out this work, which I had promised my readers in the Preface to the first volume of my *History of Dvaita School of Vedānta and Its Literature* (1960), so expeditiously. I earnestly hope that the present work, together with its companion volumes on the *History of the Dvaita school will* place in the hands of the reading public ample materials for a close and intensive study of Madhva's philosophical system, as a whole, in its historical and doctrinal aspects.

Works written on the subject of Madhva's philosophy, years ago, by pioneers in the field have now become outmoded, naturally. Of more recent ones, in the field, Dr. R. Nagaraja Sarma's *Reign of Realism in Indian Philosophy* (Madras, 1937) is restricted to an exposition of the ten small philosophical monographs of Madhvācārya. It does not draw upon Madhva's major works like the *Brahmasūtrabhāṣya* or the *Anu-Vyākhyāna*. It is not, therefore, a complete and organic presentation of Madhva's philosophy. H.N. Raghavendrachar's *Dvaita Philosophy, Its Place in the Vedānta* (Mysore Uni. 1941) has erred in representing Madhva's thought as a pure Monism in principle. This is a novel and a revolutionary interpretation, which is opposed to the established traditions of the system. It has not only *not* found any wide acceptance among scholars; but has evoked refutations from orthodox spokesmen. His advocacy of what he calls "Svarūpa-Sṛṣṭi" or creation of the essence of Souls in Madhva's philosophy is, indeed, a very unfortunate misinterpretation of Madhva's position, as it has been explained in the works of accredited exponents of the Siddhānta. Moreover, the doctrine of Creation as "Parādhīnaviśeṣāpti", specially formulated by Madhva, would lose its point, if Raghavendrachar's interpretation is accepted. This point has been dealt with in the present work.

The treatment of Madhva's philosophy in Dr. Radhakrishnan's *Indian Philosophy* (1927) has been "brief and summary". We have a more detailed and sympathetic treatment of Madhva's thought in Dasgupta's *History of Indian Philosophy*, Vol. IV (1949). But it has not taken any notice of the new issues raised by Raghavendrachar's book. Apart from this, Dasgupta's treatment of the subject is by no means exhaustive. Obviously, it could not be expected to be exhaustive as his object was not to write an independent treatise on Madhva's philosophy; but simply to deal with it as part of the general and larger movement of thought known as 'Indian Philosophy'. It is but natural then, that he should have passed over many important aspects of Madhva's thought. His method of approach has been more or less descriptive in that he does not attempt any expression of opinion on the issues involved or any evaluation of doctrines.

My aim in writing this book is to give a complete, copious, critical and comparative exposition of Madhvācārya's system of philosoyhy, bringing out its logical strength and metaphysical consistency and satisfyingness. It is intended to be an organic presentation of the system in all its essential aspects. It differs from all the other works in the field, including Dasgupta's, in showing how the concepts and categories of Madhva's philosophical thought have been conceived and formulated and have been put into a coherent system and in what relation they stand to those of other allied and rival systems. It brings out the special significance and interconnections of Madhva's doctrines and the architectonic unity of his system in relation to its parts. The reader is enabled to see for himself and appreciate the precise value and significance of some of Madhva's distinctive contributions to the perennial problems of religion and philosophy—particularly 'Indian Philosophy', for which he can justly claim credit—such as for example the doctrine of Sākṣī, Svatantra, Viśeṣa, Saviśeṣābheda and Creation as Parādhīnaviśeṣāpti. Dr. Jvala Prasad, who deplores in his *History of Indian Philosophy* (1956) that "*there has been no original contribution to Indian Philosophy for centuries*" has probably had no access to or inward knowledge of the works of Madhva, Jayatīrtha or Vyāsatīrtha.

Not only is such a systematic and critical exposition of Madhva's philosophical system called for, but *it has long been overdue*. Metaphysically, it embodies the most powerful and sustained refutation of Vedāntic monism. It has produced front-rank thinkers like Madhva, Jayatīrtha and Vyāsatīrtha. It has an extensive philosophical literature of rare philosophical penetration, in Sanskrit. It has influenced the philosophical thought of Caitanya and his followers in distant Bengal. It has given birth to a Devotional Movement of the Haridāsa Kūṭa from within; which in its turn has enriched the literature of one of the major languages of South India. It has become the living faith of a large section of the Indian people speaking seven different languages of present-day India.

In its own right, then, this system deserves much more attention than has been given to it by our modern scholars and writers on Indian philosophy. They have done it an injustice by classifying it under 'minor religious systems' belonging "more to the religious history than to the philosophical development of India" Every system of philosophy, in India, not excluding the Advaita, has its own religious basis and development. It is an error of judgment to suppose that the religious and theological aspects have over-shadowed the philosophical in Madhva's system, while it (the latter) stands in undiminished brightness in the systems of Śaṅkara and Rāmānuja. The cult of the Saguṇa-Brahman has invaded a large part of the philosophical territory of Advaita. The recognition given to such aspects as Pañcāyatanapūjā and Tāntric forms of worship of Śrī-Cakra and Goddesses like Rājarājeśvarī among Advaitins shows that the religious element is by no means negligible in Advaita. As for Rāmānuja's system, he "attempts a harmonious combination of absolutism with Personal Theism",—to quote a modern authority. To quote another, "Rāmānuja's beautiful stories of the other world, which he narrates with the confidence of one who has personally assisted at the origination of the world, carry no conviction. The followers of Rāmānuja move with as much Olympian assurance through the chambers of the Divine mind as Milton through the halls of Heaven" (Radhakrishnan, *I. Phil.* ii, p. 720).

There is much of substantial philosophical thought in Madhva's system, as there is in those of Śaṅkara and Rāmānuja. Failure to recognize this simple fact for want of first-hand acquaitance with the works of the three great master-minds of the system, Madhva, Jayatīrtha and Vyāsatīrtha, does not entitle responsible authors and writers on Indian philosophy to pronounce *ex cathedra* judgments on the philosophical status of Madhva's system or dispose of it in a few pages summarily. The progress of philosophy is generally due to a powerful attack on currrent traditions, when men feel compelled to go back upon received opinions and raise once more the fundamental questions which their predecessors had disposed of on the basis of some older schemes of thought. The movement of thought initiated by Madhva constitutes a new era in Vedāntic thought in India. It *relaid the foundations of philosophy at a much deeper level of philosophical certitude open to man viz., the Sākṣi* and thereby opened up a new line of *Samanvaya* between authority and experience; *Śruti* and *Anubhava* (See pp. 154, 168-69) For this reason alone, if not for any other, his philosophy deserves to be carefully read by all lovers of thought as a fresh adventure of the philosophical spirit.

Freedom of opinion and independence of thought are the birthright of every philosopher. In opposing Śaṅkara's philosophy, Madhva has but exercised this right of a philosopher. There is no point, then, in pompously accusing him for this, as a "born foe of Śaṅkara" and make it an excuse for dismissing his philosophy in *three and a half pages*, as has been done in a reputed work on Indian Philosophy claiming to be a "Critical Survey of Indian Philosophy" *written by an Indian scholar.* One is amazed at the wrong sense of 'values' shown by some of our living philosophers, which makes them forget the claims and importance of *living* systems of Indian thought and lavish their attention on those that are dead and have often no more than a purely antiquarian, technical or academic interest today. Without disputing their right to recognition, I will only say that *our living systems deserve more attention from our philosophers.* In this sense, the University of Bombay has given the right lead to the reorientation of philosophical studies in independent India by making suitable provision for the study of Madhva's philosophy in its curricula. I would fain hope that this example will be followed by other Universities in our country and abroad. The honor our temples of learning can show to the thinkers of this country lies in providing facilities for our young men and women to study their contributions to human thought.

Materials from the original Sanskrit texts and sources of the system have been presented here, in a modern garb, keeping in view the modern philosophical temper and its likes and dislikes, in the selection of materials and emphasis on problems. Doctrinal fidelity has been scrupulously observed, side by side with fairness and impartiality of judgment.

The special merit of the work lies in its being designed to be the most fully documented work so far published on Madhva's philosophy, quoting profusely from the accredited works and original sources of the system, for purposes of elucidation and authentication. For this reason, the Sanskrit quotations have been freely introduced within the body of the reading matter in English in many places. So much textual matter could hardly have been pressed within the limits of a few footnotes here and there. On the other hand, the full weight, significance and bearing of the quotations on the doctrines at issue and the effectiveness of their contextual appeal, as intended by their particular interpretations could hardly have been conveyed to the reader, in full force, if the quotations had all been relegated to a separate section, at the end of the book. In these circumstances, a *via media* had to be found. I hope the general reader will see the point and pardon me for the inconvenience that may be caused by this arrangement. I have, however, tried to introduce the texts in a way that would allow the general reader to skip over them, if necessary, without much interruption to thought or intellectual appeal. These quotations have not, however, been translated, *as a rule*, as that would have increased the bulk of the work, But their general purport has been sought to be brought out by the trend of the discussion or exposition. These quotations are also intended to serve as a corpus of reference-material (which will be welcomed by many, as the old editions of the original works of Mādhva philosophy are themselves now out of print and very difficult to obtain) for those interested in pursuing specialized study of the system and to stimulate their interest in going to the originals for further light.

I have gone to the standard works of the different systems of Indian philosophy, in Sanskrit, for purposes of comparing and contrasting the views of Madhva and his commentators with those of the other schools, wherever necessary. I have consulted and have often quoted from the works of several modern Indian and Western writers, in English, on Eastern and Western thought. My obligations to these distinguished writers and their works have been acknowledged in the body of the work and in the footnotes.

This is also the first modern work, in English, on Madhva's system, to present adequate collateral evidence from the standard works of the Advaita, Viśiṣṭādvaita and other schools, for purposes of intelligent criticism, comparison and evaluation. In drawing attention to the value and significance of Madhva's contributions to the various problems of religion and philosophy, I have invited attention to striking parallelisms of thought between Madhva and some Western philosophers including Christian thinkers like St. Thomas Aquinas, Ralph Cudworth, Dawes Hicks, Albert Schweitzer, Alexander Cambell Fraser and' others. I have also drawn attention to those aspects of Madhva's thought which strike a modern note or are strikingly in advance of his times and the views of his predecessors and contemporaries. (See his views on Avyākṛta-Ākāśa, the validity of Memory, etc.) So far as I am aware, these aspects of his thought have *not* been touched upon or adequately emphasized or evaluated by any of the modern scholars who have written on the subject of Madhva's philosophy till now.

For reasons explained in the Biographical Note I have incorporated substantial material both interpretive and dialectical, from the works of Jayatīrtha and Vyāsatīrtha. Further materials from the works of Vyāsatīrtha have been reserved for another work I have in view.

In discussing doctrinal and philosophical issues, I have generally confined myself to the problems germane to Madhva's philosophy alone,—except where a further examination or criticism of their counterpart doctrines pertaining to other schools was felt to be desirable or necessary in the interest of elucidation or reinforcement of Madhva's own doctrines. That is why I have not entered into any elaborate polemical discussion of such doctrines of the Advaita school as *Mithyātva*, the nature of *Avidyā*, its definition and proofs, *Adhyāsa*, *Ekajīvājñānavāda*, *Śabdāparokṣa*, *Pratikarmavyavasthā* and others, as falling outside the scope of the present work.

Ruparel College,
Bombay-400 016
1st March, 1962.

B.N.K. SHARMA

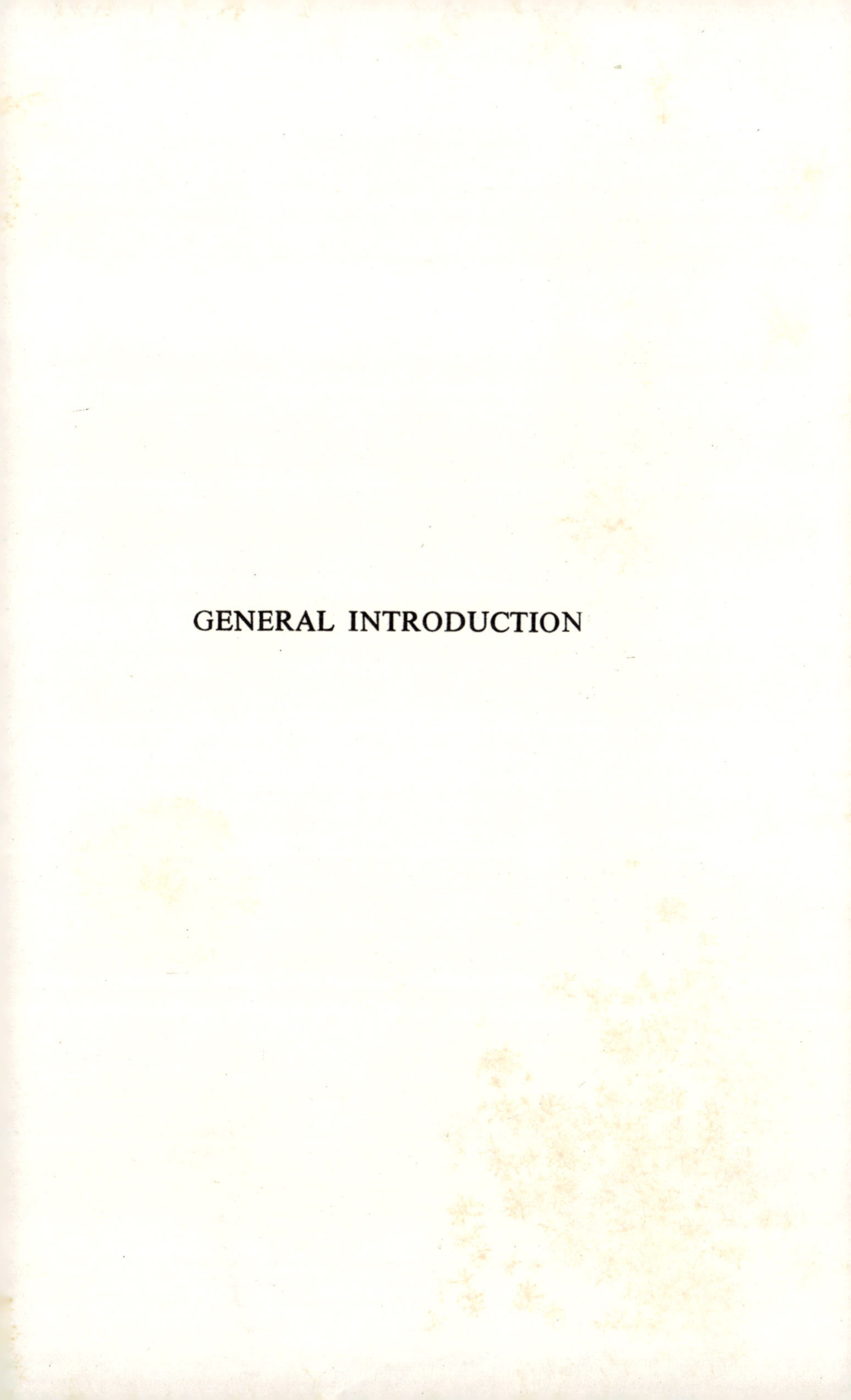

GENERAL INTRODUCTION

CHAPTER I

THE FUNCTION AND GOAL OF PHILOSOPHY

THERE are no people who could be impervious to the demands of this world for an explanation of its apparent chaos and contradictions. Only an all-embracing explanation of life, consistent with experience, would satisfy the requirements of reason, man's highest instrument for the regulation of life. For this reason, philosophy cannot be a mere exercise of the intellect or a pursuit for sheer aesthetic interest or curiosity. It must have a spiritual *raison d'etre* and must satisfy man's spiritual need. It must deal with problems which force themselves on our thought and press for a solution viz., what man is, why he is conditioned as he is, what his goal is and how he is to attain it.

The question is not, therefore, merely one of philosophy or no philosophy; but one of a good philosophy or a bad one. Every rational being, then, has a philosophy of his own, whether he knows it or not. It is the business of an earnest aspirant to go through the entire process of thought under proper spiritual guidance and find a solution of the problems which vex him. The Śāstras are there to guide him on right lines.

"From time immemorial, various schools of thought have been flourishing in the world. There can be no total extinction of any system. All the same, Bādarāyaṇa-Vyāsa has taken the trouble in his Brahma-sūtras, of refuting the various defective systems, so that the good souls, eligible for Divine grace, may have their doubts cleared, their ignorance destroyed and their knowledge improved by sound reasonings based on the Śruti and attain enlightenment.[1]"

---

1. Cf. अनादिकालतो वृत्ताः समया हि प्रवाहतः ।
न चोच्छेदोऽस्ति कस्यापि समयस्येत्यतो विभुः ।

Philosophy asks for a conceivable unity in place of the confusing multiplicity. But neither a pure abstraction of being nor a mere totality or aggregate of beings can give us a true unity. Some community or reciprocity there must be. "The question is how little would suffice. It seems clear that either each must be connected with all, in at least one way; or that all must be connected with some *one*. There must be a universal principle directly relating all; or a Supreme Individual to which all are related. The latter would imply the former, insofar as through their common relation to the Supreme One, all would be related, though only indirectly, to each other.[2]"

Madhva finds such a principle of unity in the unity of government, sustenance and control of the universe by Brahman. He finds this idea tellingly expressed in the Śruti text :

विश्वमेवेदं पुरुषः तद्विश्वमुपजीवति[3]

(*MahNUp* xi. 2)

"The Supreme Puruṣa is verily the Universe (all this); *for it depends upon Him for its sustenance*". The Supreme and Independent Brahman is not so much the cause *in time* of the dependent realities as the logical and metaphysical explanation of all else that is. Hence the definition of the one independent principle in Madhva's system :

स्वरूपप्रमितिप्रवृत्तिलक्षणसत्तात्रैविध्ये परानपेक्षम्

(Jayatīrtha's Tsṭ)

"The independent principle is that which does not depend on

....

तथापि शुद्धबुद्धीनामीशानुग्रहयोगिनाम् ।
सुयुक्तयस्तमो हन्युरागमानुगताः सदा ।
इति विद्यापतिः सम्यक् समयानां निराकृतिम् ।
चकार निजभक्तानां बुद्धिशाणत्:सिद्धये ॥

(Madhva, *AV* ii.2.1)

2. James Ward : *Pluralism and Theism*, p. 42. An identical view has been propounded by Jayatirtha in his commentary on Madhva's *TS*. See fn 7.

3. Madhva paraphrases this with special reference to the purport of the 'Tat tvam asi' text as. तत्तन्त्रत्वादैतदात्म्यम्.

any other for its own nature and existence, self-awareness or for becoming an object of knowledge to the selves and for the free and unfettered exercise of its own powers."

As Cook Wilson says, "There are certain facts of immediate certainty which cannot be doubted or called into question, such as the reality of the external world, the principle of causality, the existence of other minds and of our own selves and God. Experience is the immediate datum from which one has to philosophize and philosophy is under a moral obligation to explain the conditions indispensable for its possibility. *The worth of a philosophical system is to be judged by the extent to which it is able to explain experience, rather than explain it away*".

Reality presents to an inquiring mind three primary data: the thinking self, a world of external realities and indications of an Infinite Power rising above them. Though these three data are commonly postulated as distinguishable essences, terms like 'reality', 'substance' or 'existence' *are not* applied to all of them in the same sense by all persons in all stages of spiritual or philosophical development. It has happened time and again in the history of Philosophy, both in the East and in the West, that the one or the other of them has been raised to a position of greater prominence than the rest. Such shifting of emphasis has led to the emergence of several forms of materialistic, pan-egoistic and monistic heresies which, in the history of speculation, are quite familiar. Justifications for each point of view could easily be found. The Self is the immediate starting point of all experience. It is so borne in upon us as to easily usurp the place of honor. The existence of things outside of us in time and space and even the reputed existence of a Deity are, after all, secondary, being reached only through acts of private consciousness and may, for aught we know, be illusory or at any rate, not so irrefragably real as the self. From an opposite point of view, matter which can be moved and measured and is therefore tangible, could be set up as a sterner reality than either God or the souls, who seem to shrink into shadowy abstractions by its side. To the mystics, on the other hand, the Infinite Being *alone*, conceived as :

नित्यशुद्धबुद्धमुक्तसत्यसुखाद्वयप्रत्येकपूर्णम् ।

(*DMS* quoted by Madhva in *BT* XI.11.5)

is so all-absorbing as to transcend all and constitute the sole reality of all that there is or can be.

An unbalanced exaltation of any one of these three data over the rest, in the realm of thought, feeling or action, is the cause of much false philosophy and bad morals. The more pretentious philosophies of ancient and modern times, which have sought to resolve the three data into one, have failed inexorably in the end or have been obliged to make compromises, or concede some sort of a "conditional" or "phenomenal" reality to the other data. If the material world, which fills the horizon of senses, is taken to be the single reality that matters most, it would lead us to a materialism of the West or the Cārvāka philosophy of the East. The ego-centric explanation would land us in a panegoism, solipsism or subjective idealism, *ekajīvavāda* and the like; while the theocentric attitude would end in an absolutism, deism or pantheism.

But the true function of philosophy, aided by reason and experience, is to determine by what relationship of the three-fold data of experience can man's thirst for an ultimate explanation of the enigma of existence be really and fully satisfied. Reason seeks to interpret the plurality of things and processes which constitute the world as a system of parts evolved or conditioned by one Universal Power or Mind so as to be factors of one whole and subject to one universal reason. As a true philosopher, Madhva ignores neither of the three data of experience; nor does he exaggerate the claim of any one of them at the expense of the others. The changeable no less than the unchangeable, the independent no less than the dependent is an ultimate component of Reality as a whole:

द्विविधं हि प्रमेयं, स्वतन्त्रमस्वतन्त्रं च

(*NS* p. 286 b)

This is one of the profoundest conclusions of Dvaita metaphysics reached by the evidence of *pratyakṣa, anumāna and śabdapramāṇa*. It would not be possible to understand or explain the universe if we are indifferent to matter and spirits, much more so to the Deity. One must face facts established by our own knowledge and be guided by them in interpreting them philosophically.

"Philosophy is not a quest for unity *regardless of facts of logic.*

It is a quest for such unity as the facts of logic admit of" (E.S. Brightman, *Philosophy of Religion*).

The fact of knowledge is indisputable. And as there can be no knowledge without a knower, a known or knowable object;[4] the reality of the knower and the objects of knowledge must be accepted. Whatever else one may choose to admit or reject, absolute scepticism as to the possibility of knowledge of any kind is unsustainable. Even supposing that all our knowledge of reality so far has been proved to be contradicted, the possibility of knowledge has still to be admitted. One cannot deny the possibility of knowledge and yet claim that knowledge has been proved to be contradicted. Madhva says well, referring to Śrīharṣa's dogged scepticism regarding the acceptance of *pramāṇa-vyavasthā*:

> यदि नाङ्गीकृतं किंचिदनङ्गीकृततापि हि ।
> नाङ्गीकृतेति मूकः स्यादिति नास्मद्विवादिता ॥
>
> (*AV* i.4.11)

At the worst, thinking or the mind would still survive as the residuum of universal doubt.

Starting then from knowledge as one of the uncriticized certainties of life, we are faced with a plurality of objects and with other thinking beings like ourselves[5]. We think and reason, feel pleasure and pain. Can any of these states be *less evident to us than our own existence*? In conceding then the existence of our own good selves, we are also forced to admit the reality of our most intimate and poignant experiences of pleasure and pain, in short—the joys and sorrows and limitations of life. That is why Madhva tells us:

> न दुःखानुभवः क्वापि मिथ्यानुभवतां व्रजेत् ।
> कोऽपि ह्यर्थो न निश्चेतुं शक्यते भ्रमवादिना ।
> **भ्रमत्वमभ्रमत्वं च सर्वं वेद्यं हि साक्षिणा ।**
> शुद्धः साक्षी यदा सिद्धो, दुःखित्वं वार्यते कथम् ?
>
> (*AV* ii.3.28)

---

4. न च स्वरूपमन्यद्वा ज्ञेयं ज्ञातारं च विना दृष्टम् । न च ज्ञातृज्ञेयरहितं ज्ञानं क्वापि दृष्टम् (Madhva, *VTN* i)

5. चेष्टालिंगेन सात्मत्वे परदेहस्य साधिते
. . . . (Madhva, *UpKh* 12)

"Never can the experience of pain and suffering in the world by the souls be dismissed as 'false experience'. The illusionist philosopher can never hope to establish anything for certain, even in the realm of the so-called empirical reality. Whether a given experience is true or false, has to be adjudged by the Sākṣī in the last analysis. If the impeccability of the Sākṣī is accepted, how can one deny that our experience of happiness or sorrow is real or contend that it is imagined or superimposed ?"

The fact of knowledge, again, establishes the presence of many more things and persons besides ourselves. Reality is not apprehended as one but as many and there is no reason to reject the apprehension of the many as an 'appearance' only. For things will not *cease to be* simply because the law of parsimony may be violated:

कल्पनागौरवादेव पदार्था न स्युरेव हि[6]

It is at this point that Madhva introduces the philosophical distinction between the Independent Real and the dependent reals. The reals cannot all of them be independent, lest there should be chaos and strife. Neither can *all* be dependent without an independent principle to relate and regulate them. The dependents cannot obviously control one another, without a *higher* principle to connect them. Otherwise, there would be a regress of strife and opposition through which they would destroy one another and perish in the transaction and there would be no reality left in the end. It is thus very necessary to dichotomize reality into *Svatantra* and *Paratantra*.[7]

---

6. *Contrast* : एकेनैव सर्वानुगतेन सर्वत्र सत्प्रतीत्युपपत्तौ ब्रह्मवत् प्रपंचस्य प्रत्येकं सत्स्वभावताकल्पने मानाभावात् (*Advaitasiddhi*, 1.3)

7. एके तु एकमेव तत्त्वमिति मन्यन्ते । तदसत् । प्रत्यक्षादिविरोधात् । सर्वस्य स्वतन्त्रत्वे, नित्यसुखादिप्रसंगः । अस्वातंत्र्ये, च न कस्यापि प्रवृत्तिः । अन्धपंगुवत् स्यादिति चेन्न । प्रत्यासत्तेरेवानुपपत्तेः । यदि सर्वमेव स्वतंत्रं स्यात्, तदा पारतंत्र्यादिप्रतीतिविरोधः । नित्यसुखादिप्रसंगश्च । यदि वा परतंत्रमेव तत्त्वं भवेत्, अनवस्थितेरसंभवाच्च न कस्यापि सत्तादिकं स्यात् ।

(Jayatīrtha, *Tsṭ*)

"Some philosophers hold that there is only one single reality in the universe. That is *not* correct, as it goes against the evidence of perception and other sources of knowledge. So there must be more than one real. However, if all these reals are to be taken to be equally independent, there will have to be eternal happiness for all. But such is not the actual fact. If

Experience shows that human souls and their material environments are not independent.

न च कर्मविमामलकालगुणप्रभृतीशमचित्तनु तद्धि यतः ।

(Madhva, *Dvādaśa Stotra iii*. 6)

Were human beings independent masters of their own destiny, we should expect to find peace and plenty and bliss unalloyed in human life. We should lack nothing and have everything for the asking. But we know only too well that it cannot be:

आत्माप्यनीशः सुखदुःखहेतोः ।

(*Svet Up* i.2)

This shows that things are directed by an unknown agency, which for want of a better name all the world agrees to designate as "God" or *Paramātman* or the Supreme Being.

In this way does Madhva establish the existence and reality of matter, souls, *svabhāva*, *kāla*, merit and demerit and other eternal verities under the control of one Supreme Being. The *svatantra* and the *paratantra* are thus the fundamental presuppositions of his system. The dependence of the finite reals is proof of the existence of the Deity, according to the great Nyāya philosopher Udayana too:

सापेक्षत्वादनादित्वात् वैचित्र्याद्विश्ववृत्तितः ।
प्रत्यात्मनियमात् भुक्तेरस्ति हेतुरलौकिकः ॥

(*Nyāya-Kusumāñjali* 1.4)

---

all the reals are to be put down as equally dependent, with no Independent Being anywhere in the Universe, all movement of the dependent reals would be rendered impossible—because all of them are 'dependent' and cannot direct one another. If their movement is claimed to be possible like the coming together and co-operative movement of the lame man and the blind man, we have to point out that there being no independent princip e to direct them, the dependent reals because of their *very dependence*, canno't come together. If all are to be conceived as independent, there will be violation of the experience of dependence and other characteristics of finitude. If all are to be equally dependent, with no Independent Principle, there will be a regress of dependence (A depending on B, B on C and so on *ad infinitum*). There will be instability all around with the result that everything will lose its reality in the end."

"From dependence, from eternality, diversity, universal practice and from the apportionment to each individual self of its own joys and sorrows of mundane life, it follows that there is a supernatural cause (viz. *adṛṣṭa*)". Explanation: By establishing, in the first place, the existence of such a supernatural cause not open to the senses, in the form of merit and demerit, it will follow that God is established as the superintendent thereof" (*Siddhe ca tasmin tadadhiṣṭhātṛtayā Īśvarasiddhiḥ*).

The aim of philosophy, then, would be not merely to realize the distinction between 'appearance' and 'reality' but to *understand and realize the still more important distinction between the Independent Real and the dependent realities*. Madhva is not, therefore, an uncritical realist who takes everything to be real; nor a sentimental idealist who would deny all but one reality. He is for a rational realism which would admit whatever is established on the un-contradicted evidence of the *Pramāṇas*, the senses, the mind and the *Sākṣi*, in addition to reason and revelation. He introduces a new element of value into the discussion of the problem of *Pramāṇas*, in the form of the concept of *Sākṣi*, whose nature and scope will be explained in its appropriate place. The *Sākṣi* is man's highest instrument of all valid knowledge and experience. It is on its evidence that we become conscious, however dimly, of the existence of a higher power than ourselves, in this vast and mysterious universe.

It will, therefore, be seen that any other approach to the problem of philosophy and any other analysis of the reals or the data of experience into 'positive' and 'negative' reals (*bhāva* and *abhāva*) as in Nyāya thought, or as *cit* and *acit* (as in Jain or Rāmānuja view) would be irrelevant to the aim and purpose of religion and philosophy, which is to evaluate phenomena and enable man to get out of the bondage of life which is the outcome of a misplaced assumption of his independence (*svātantryābhimāna*) in it.[8]

---

8. यद्यपि भावाभावतया चेतनाचेतनतया वा, नित्यानित्यतया वा द्वैविध्यं शक्यते वक्तुं, तथापि तस्य वैयर्थ्यादियमेव विभागो न्याय्यः। परतंत्रप्रमेयं स्वतंत्रप्रमेयायत्ततया विदितं निःश्रेयसाय भवति। अन्यथा, गङ्गावालुकापरिगणनवत् इदं तत्त्वसंख्यानमपार्थकं स्यात्। (*ibid*)

CHAPTER II

MADHVA'S THOUGHT IN RELATION TO EARLIER AND CONTEMPORARY SCHOOLS

THE system of Madhva is founded on the continuous authority of a wide range of religious and philosophical literature of India which has been the main source of Indian thought in its widest sense. The history of the evolution of Madhva's thought from these source-books of his system and the history of its development at the hands of Madhva and his numerous commentators and expositors have been dealt with by me in my *History of the Dvaita School of Vedānta and Its Literature* (Motilal Banarsidass Delhi 1981, 2nd Edn.).

The present work aims at a fairly complete and comprehensive critical exposition of Madhva's philosophy, as presented in his own works and as further interpreted and elaborated by his illustrious commentator Jayatīrtha in the first instance and by the famous dialectician of the Mādhva school, Vyāsatīrtha, who came a hundred and twentyfive years after the former.

If Indian philosophy is to be accepted as much more than an interpretation of certain basic texts and traditions, though not as completely detached from them, attempts should be made to present the various systems of thought and their logical, epistemological and ontological foundations and their metaphysical superstructures, in their architectonic unity. The philosophical system of Madhva and his commentators has not received adequate attention from this point of view.

No doubt, Indian philosophers, particulatly the Vedāntins, have stressed the limitations of discursive thought and shown the possibilities of spiritual intuition in understanding the nature of reality, urging the necessity to correct and supplement the conclusions of pure logic and metaphysical speculations with the help of one's own intuitions and those of bygone generations, handed down through the Scriptures and intended to be recaptured in our own religious and spiritual experiences and discoveries. But this is not to say that reason has had no part to play in the evolution of their thought. Philosophy, as an interpretation of reality, cannot spin out its theories *in vacuo*, away from the world of experience. As Dr. Radhakrishnan puts it, perhaps a little too extravagantly, "the Indian philosophers first arrive at a system of consistent doctrine and then look about for texts of an earlier age to support their position. They either force them into such support or ingeniously explain them away" (*I. Phil.* i, p. 130).

All schools of Indian philosophy, save the Cārvāka, have two main aspects in their system-building: one rational or philosophical and the other a dogmatic, textual, revelatory or authoritarian aspect. The former examines the fundamental presuppositions of thought and constructs a metaphysical theory on certain *a priori* epistemological and ontological foundations of its own, on which they erect a full-fledged system and correlate it to the interpretations of texts which have come to be regarded as ultimate sources of philosophical knowledge and inspiration in the land and community of their birth and invested with special authority and sanction on problems of philosophy. While accepting the judgments of established traditions and authority, on such problems, the Indian philosophers have, to an equal extent, used the methods of reasoned thought and criticism, to examine the presuppositions of their textual systems and the nature and constitution of their categories of thought in the light of independent proofs.

In doing so, they have always tried to make out a case for their respective theories before the bar of reason, on such unexceptionable criteria of system-building as adherence to a strictly philosophical method and outlook, sound logical deductions and analysis of principles, consistency of thought and faithfulness to experience. It is the business of philosophy to look at experience as a whole and take note of the suggestions forced upon it by the mind of man and confirm them as theories if they have the requisite explanatory value.

Such is the essence of the Hindu method of *Tattvanirṇaya* (truth-determination). In the body of any Siddhānta, then, there is a good deal of critical analysis and exposition of the principles of epistemology, logic and metaphysics of one's own school, together with a reasoned examination of those of other schools. As a modern writer[1] puts it, "Philosophy is essentially a collective and co-operative business. Effective co-operation consists in disagreement. The true process of philosophy, as a science, is that of a Platonic dialogue, in which the propositions, objections and rejoinders of numerous interlocutors are found focussed upon a given question and the argument shapes itself through its own immanent dialectic, to a conclusion." The *Vikalpa* method of *Śāstric* discussion in Sanskrit philosophical writings is nothing more than the Platonic dialogue in its perfect form. Every important doctrine of logic, epistemology and metaphysics, of the different schools of Indian philosophy, has been developed on the same lines. They are the result of a long and arduous process of thought-dissection. No doctrine or strand of philosophic belief can thus be put down as absolutely original, isolated from or uninfluenced by contemporary opinion or as devoid of a nexus with the past.

So closely are the two aspects of rational thought and textual interpretation and synthesis intertwined in most of the Indian schools that it is often difficult to pronounce any opinion whether they are actuated more by a predominantly philosophical purpose or an authoritarian outlook. They disclose both kinds of leanings and it is often a question of emphasis whether a given system is to be treated as being more speculative and rational than dogmatic and textual. Western scholars have generally held that the philosophy of the Vedānta is essentially *dogmatic*, being nothing more than a clever, ingenious and elaborate system of textual interpretation of the *Prasthānas*, doubtless with a good deal of philosophic insight and acumen. But its achievement cannot be accepted as truly philosophical, insofar as the pursuit of philosophy is not the outcome of a disinterested love of thought or a quest of truth, but has been undertaken to

1. Arthur O. Lovejoy, *The Revolt of Dualism*, Open Court Publishing Company, America.

achieve individual salvation. Others regard the Vedānta as a truly philosophical system in conception, method and execution. That it is bound up with the interpretation of sacred texts is only circumstantial in that, true to Indian traditions, it has merely used material handed down by former generations, and built on its foundations a new and vigorous system of thought, reserving the fullest right of selection, emphasis, alteration and criticism, in the name of interpretation (*Vyākhyāna*). It embodies the greatest independence of thought and originality of conceptions under the guise of reconciliation with the help of canons of interpretation. The commentators are seldom obliged to call a halt to philosophic speculation when faced with a trying or obscure text or with contradictory ones. They exercise their reason to synthesize and extract sense out of seeming enigmas and contradictions. In this they bid fair to direct the authorities, instead of their letting them direct their thoughts.[2] In this sense, then, Indian philosophy can claim to be as genuinely philosophical in spirit as any other attempt made elsewhere, on the basis of pure reason. It is thus a purely *historical accident* that has made Indian philosophy textual though some are inclined to view it as incorrigibly text-ridden. *The supreme place Madhva has assigned to the Sākṣi as "Upajīvyapramāṇa" of Scripture, in the event of the latter encroaching on the legitimate jurisdiction of the former is a striking example of the unflinching rational outlook of Mādhva thought.* But with all the limitations imposed on the free movement of thought by the respect for texts and traditions, the Indian philosophers have shown themselves to be actuated by a genuine philosophic spirit like their compeers in the west and have risen to great heights in the art of philosophizing, which for alertness of mind, acuteness of thought and boldness of ideas, cannot be rivalled by others claiming to be more scientific or free from dogmas. The achievements of Indian thought cannot, therefore, be said to be lacking in merit or devoid of a true philosophic spirit; though these are often hidden from view by the trappings of authority in which they are often clothed and concealed.

2. Cf. Madhva's plea for interpreting "Tattvam asi" in conformity with Upajīvyapramāṇas. See my *HDSV*, pp. 360-62.

Criticism is the life-breath of Indian philosophical systems, as philosophic life, like biological, is governed by the same law of strife and survival of the fittest. Each of the older systems of thought should thus have contributed something to Mādhva thought also, at least negatively, by way of material for criticism. It is not as if his system alone grew up *in vacuo*, without *reference* to anything that went before. Historical interpretation must admit, here as in other cases of contact of minds, the impact of contemporary thought, and echoes of forgotten schools which though, then out of court or not "living" must still have continued to exercise a great deal of intellectual influence on successive thought-currents by their technique and methods of treatment—in short, by laying down the high-ways and byways of thought along which all current ontological and epistemological progress had to be made with freedom to differ in details and conclusions.

The critical side of Madhva's system, consisting partly in its dialectical struggles with earlier schools both major and minor, shows how it was able not only to avoid their pitfalls and mistakes but also to absorb some of their good points, or improve upon them or tianscend them in a higher system. That such impact of ideas is by no means denied in Madhva's case is clear from the description of his commentary on the *Brahmasūtra* as a critique of twentyone earlier ones in the field. A critic is not an iconoclast out and out. He receives ideas while in the act of demolishing older opinions. The contact of minds is a very subtle affair. Deeper things there happen than meet the surface. As Vijayīndra Tīrtha observes in his *Madhvādhva-Kaṇṭakoddhāra*, as an exponent of a new Prasthāna, Madhva exercised his right to agree with or differ from his compeers to the full and in doing so rejected much that was cumbersome, or effete in the older theories and used whatever ideas were fundamentally sound though not in the same place or within the same design. Often in his criticisms, he rescued and rehabilitated ideas of permanent significance from the ill-balanced views of earlier and contemporary schools and realigned them to better advantage.

The Cārvāka system is condemned outright for its unmitigated hedonism. But its faith in the reality of experience and of sense-awareness as the pivot of realism is accepted by Madhva.

The Cārvāka is condemned, unreservedly, for his hedonism, for his atheism and for his materialism (*Dehātmavāda*) but not for his bold stand for the supremacy of *Pratyakṣa Pramāṇa*. Only, he had stopped short at *Pratyakṣa*, refusing to go beyond, which is rather unphilosophical, in that there are more things in the universe than could be measured by *Pratyakṣa* alone. Enjoyment of life is no sin. One need not, like the Buddhist, give a counsel of despair to shun the world, abhor life and court gradual suicide or extinction. कुरु भुङ्क्ष्व च कर्म निजं नियतम्—says Madhva, with the salutary advice : हरिपादविनम्रधिया सततम्[3], for one should not, like and Mīmāṁsakas, surrender the aim of life to a mess of pottage, Ṣvarga, understood in the transient sense of a limited pleasure: अपाम सोममममृता अभूम (*RV* VIII.48.3). To take such a view of life's purpose is to miss the true goal of the Vedic philosophy of Karma, says Madhva. The Vedas enjoin the performance of sacrifices with set rewards, not from the highest point of view, but only in a limited sense. Karma-phala, attractive as it is, is not the ultimate intention or message of the Scripture. It is only an inducement to effort of the right kind[4] with a view to raising the spiritual standard of man higher and higher and taking him on the upward march, by stages. Karma is only a step in the ladder though a necessary one. It is not the be-all and end-all of scripture as the Mīmāṁsakas would have it. The best Karma is that performed without attachment and for the sake of no other reward than the satisfaction of God and as His worship : तत्कर्म हरितोषं यत् (*Bhāg* iv.29.40) ; वृणीमहे ते परितोषणाय (iv.30.40); एतं ह्येव वीणायां गायन्ति (*ChānUp* i. 7.6). While accepting the Mīmāṁsaka doctrine of *Svataḥprāmāṇya* of *Śabda*, Madhva emphasized that the highest subject-matter of the Veda is God and not merely a round of duties or acts of sacrifice.[5]

---

3. Do your work as it has devolved upon you and enjoy its rewards with constant devotion to the Lord (*Dvādaśastotra*, iii. 1 ab)

4. रोचनार्था फलश्रुतिः (*Bhāg* xi.3.46)
यथा भैषज्यरोचनम् (xxii.21.23)
कर्ममोक्षाय कर्माणि विधत्ते ह्यगदं यथा । (xi.3.44)

5. कार्यं साधनमिष्टस्य भगवानिष्टदेवता
मुख्येष्टं वा सुमनसां 'प्रेयस्त'दिति च श्रुतेः (*AV* i.1.1).

Jaina philosophy and moral code have some affinity to Madhva's thought. The new type of Vedic sacrifices with flour-made animals (*Piṣṭa-paśu yajñas*)[6] instead of living animals, introduced by Madhva as a much-needed reform in Brahmanical society, was in all probability, partly due to the moral pressure and influence of Jaina ideas. A powerful community of Jainas inhabited the S. Kanara district then, as now. It was also under Jaina rule in the twelfth and thirteenth centuries. Madhva's views on some questions of logic, epistemology and ontology show many striking parallels to and affinities with corresponding Jaina theories, notably on the nature of the Universal (*Jāti*) and in the theory of the self as an object of its own perception (*Aham sukhī*) which is denied by the Advaitin. The recognition of certain types of cognition like *Manaḥparyaya* and *Kevala* in Jaina philosophy, corresponds, in a measure, to the *Yogipratyakṣa* and *Kevala-Pramāṇa* of Madhva. The self-revelatory capacity of knowledge of the perceiver (ज्ञातुरात्मनः स्वप्रकाशत्वम्) is based on the triunity of *Jñātṛ*, *Jñeya* and *Jñāna*, all of them being admitted to be revealed in knowledge. So also, the Jaina conception of substance in relation to its attributes, as a *distinction of reference and not of existence*: अनन्तधर्मात्मकं वस्तु, as Haribhadra Sūri puts it, is perfected by Madhva, by formulating the doctrine of *Saviśeṣābheda* to hold the substance and attributes together in one integrated mould. The further distinction of qualities or attributes as *Paryāya* and *Svabhāva* in Jaina ontology is parallel to Madhva's distinction of attributes into *Ayāvad-dravyabhāvi* and *Yāvad-dravyabhāvi*. The Jaina dichotomy of reality into *Jīva* and *Ajīva* appears in the form of *Svatantra* and *Paratantra*, with greater philosophical aptness and justification, as pointed out by Jayatīrtha. The Jainas have classified reality as Jīva and Ajīva.[7] In this classification, Jīva or sentient reality admittedly holds a position superior to insentient reality. While the distinction between Jīva and Ajīva is worth

---

6. The *MVij* (IX.44-50) refers to an actual performance of a *Piṣṭapaśuyāga* under Madhva's direction and the opposition he had to encounter. For a work in defence of Piṣṭapaśuyajña see under Vijayīndra Tīrtha in my HDSV p. 411.

7. संक्षेपतस्तु द्वावेव पदार्थौ जीवाजीवाख्यौ (*SBSB* ii. 2.33)

making, we should not stop merely with such a dichotomy in philosophy. It would be more pertinent to the evaluation of the position and status of the reals in a philosophical system to introduce a classification of a different kind viz. the one into *Svatantra* and *Paratantra*, as Madhva has done. That Jayatīrtha is thinking on these lines may be gathered from his remarks quoted *earlier* in Chap. I, fn. 8. The peculiar doctrine of the Jainas that the whole universe is filled with Jīvas is also shared by Madhva:

परमाणुप्रदेशेषु ह्यनन्ताः प्राणिराशयः (*VTN*)

Madhva is not enamoured of the extreme realism of the Mīmāṁsakas. He recognizes the need for periodical creation and dissolution of the universe. He also sets right the extreme epistemological realism of the Prābhākaras and admits the possibility of error in human cognitions. He is for calling error by its proper name and not for confusing the issue by using misleading terms like *Akhyāti*, *Akhyātisaṁvalitasatkhyāti* and so on. But his realism does not demand that *the object presented in illusions must have a reality of its own elsewhere* (*anyatra sat*) as the Nyāya Realists would have it. If experience is any test, the object presented in illusory perception is an absolute unreality. At the same time, Madhva takes care to state that no illusion can be explained without the acceptance of two necessary reals—a substratum (*adhiṣṭhāna*) and a *Pradhāna* (prototype) of the superimposed object.[8]

Madhva has rejected much that was defective and outmoded in the conceptions, categories, definitions and methodology (*prakriyā*) of the older schools of Nyāya, Mīmāṁsā and Vedānta. The interpretational principle of *Upakramaprābalya* of the Pūrva Mīmāṁsakas is set aside by him in favour of the more logical *Upasaṁhāraprābalya*, on the authority of the *Brahmatarka*[9]. He has

---

8. अधिष्ठानं च सदृशं सत्यवस्तुद्वयं विना ।
न भ्रान्तिर्भवति क्वापि स्वप्नमायादिकेष्वपि । (*VTN*)

9. Madhva refers to the thesis of *Upasaṁhāraprābalya* in his *AV*:
उपक्रमादिलिंगानां बलीयो ह्युत्तरोत्तरम् ।

The question has been discussed fully, refuting the view of *Upakramaprābalya* of Advaita, in Vyāsatīrtha's *TT* and in Vijayīndra Tīrtha's special work *Upasaṁhāravijaya*. For a summary of their arguments see my *HDSV* pp, 309-11 and 408-10.

given us his own views about the Vedāntic concepts of *Sākṣi*, *Svaprakāśatva*, *Bhāvarūpājñāna*, *Māyā*, *Pratibimba*, etc. He has propounded a fresh doctrine of the validity of knowledge with special reference to the principle of *Sākṣi as a corrective* to all the earlier theories on the subject. Though traceable to some of the older sources referred to by him, the merit of these new doctrines lies in the precise and forceful way in which he has developed their potentialities and fitted them into their proper places, in his own realistic metaphysics and elucidated their bearings upon the different aspects of his thought. Similarly, his revised definition of 'Pramāṇa' as "*yathārtham*", so as to embrace all types of valid knowledge and its instruments and to ensure the validity of memory is a significant departure and advance in contemporary thought.

But, though open to the ideas of the older systems and their thought-patterns, Madhva has made many striking contributions of his own, in many important respects. It is these that entitle him to a place of honor in Indian Philosophy. He has drawn the attention of the philosophical world to the imperative need for going in for a new set of concepts and categories like *Svatantra* and *Paratantra*, *Sākṣi*, *Viśeṣas*, *Bheda* as *dharmisvarūpa* and as *saviśeṣābhinna* from it, *Svarūpabheda* and *Svarūpatāratamya* among selves, *Biṁbapratibiṁbabhāva* relation between *Brahman* and *Jīvas* and eternal creation through *Parādhīnaviśeṣāpti*. These ideas were so radically different from those till then entertained in dealing with philosophical questions, that if their necessity was demonstrated, the whole treatment of the problems of philosophy would change its course and enter upon a fresh terrain. We shall see something of these new aspects and direction of thought, developed by Madhva in the chapters that follow.

Madhva's Influence on other Schools and Commentators

Notwithstanding Madhva's powerful attack on various shades of (*Jīveśvara-*) *bhedābhedavāda* and *Brahmapariṇāmavāda*, many of the post-Madhva commentators on the Vedānta Sūtras were still reluctant to shake off their fascination for the language and ideology of *Brahmapariṇāmavāda* or Brahman's material causality of the world, which had come down to them from the earlier line of Pantheistic commentators like Bhāskara and Brahmadatta and which had a semblance of support in the sūtras such as *Prakṛtiśca* (1.4.23). This is best illustrated in the case of Nimbārka, who ostensibly holds that between Jīva and Brahman the relation of difference and identity are *both equally true and real*. This is opposed to Madhva's view. But then, when Nimbārka defines what he means by identity and difference we find that his view of difference and identity is virtually the same as Madhva's though his way of phrasing them is different. For, according to Nimbārka 'difference' means dependence of the Jīva on Brahman, while 'identity' stands for *lack of independent existence and functioning on the part of the Jīva* (See Ghate, *The Vedanta*, p. 29). Thus, in Nimbārka's view, the Jīva's difference from Brahman and his identity with it would point to *the same fact* of dependence on Brahman. His view that the description of the Jīva in the Upaniṣads as being identical with Brahman is to be understood in the sense that the former is dependent for ever on Brahman for his existence and functioning, is nothing new or unacceptable to Madhva and has been most tellingly emphasized by him in his writings:

यदधीना यस्य सत्ता तत्तदित्येव भण्यते ।
विद्यमाने विभेदेऽपि मिथो नित्यं स्वरूपतः ।।
'सर्वं खल्विदं ब्रह्म' इत्युच्यते—तदधीनसत्ता-प्रवृत्तिमत्त्वात्;
न तु सर्वस्वरूपतः

(*MGB* iv. 14)

Thus, the *Bhedābhedasiddhānta* of Nimbārka is nothing more than a high-sounding paraphrase of Madhva's position and cannot, therefore, be treated as falling outside the scope of its influence. There are also other evidences of the influence of Madhva's works on Nimbārka and his commentator Śrīnivāsa. The untraceable Śruti *Atha kasmād ucyate Brahmeti bṛhanto hyasmin guṇāḥ* cited by Madhva in his *NV* on *BS* i.1.1 is found quoted by Nimbārka (in a slightly different form) : *Bṛhanto guṇā asmin iti Brahma* in his commentary on *BS* ii.3.28. His interpretation of the Utpattyadhikaraṇa of the *BS* in terms of the refutation of the Śākta system follows Madhva. Several untraceable Śrutis *cited only by Madhva,* for the first time, so far as we know, have been cited by Nimbārka's commentator Śrīnivāsa. The idea that the second Pāda of the third Adhyāya of the Sūtras is to be connected with the theme of Bhakti was mooted by Madhva for the first time in the tradition of interpreting the Sūtras :

भक्तिरस्मिन् पाद उच्यते । भक्त्यर्थं भगवन्महिमोक्तिः

(*MBSB* iii. 2.1)

It appears from Nimbārka's introductory remark to this Pāda that he was much impressed by this point of view, though in the actual working out of the interpretations of the various *adhikaraṇas* of this Pāda, he has not been able to establish *so close a structural alignment of each of the adhikaraṇas with the theme of Bhakti,* as Madhva has been able to do (See my *BSPC,* Vol. III, Pāda 2). Nevertheless, Nimbārka's statement :

भक्त्युद्रेकसिद्धये तद्गुणाश्चोच्यन्ते recognises the force of Madhva's stand.

Madhva's influence on Vallābha has *not been any the less.* The way in which Vallabha has raised the *Bhāgavata Purāṇa* to the position of a fourth Prasthāna and commented on it may be attributed to the example set by Madhva, the first known Vaiṣṇava Ācārya and Bhāṣyakāra to have written a commentary on that Purāṇa and drawn upon it a great deal in his interpretation of the Sūtras and the *Gitā.* The distinction accepted by Vallabha between the fruits of Jñānamārga and Bhaktimārga[10] in *mokṣa* rests squarely on the doctrine of *Tāratamya* of bliss in *Mokṣa* among Jīvas, which is a distinctive doctrine of Madhva's philosophy and is *not* found in any other school of Vedānta.

---

10. ज्ञानमार्गभक्तिमार्गयोरनावृत्तौ तुल्यत्वेऽपि, **फलप्राप्तौ वैलक्षण्यम्।**

(Vallabha iv.4.22)

मुक्तेरपि भक्तिमार्गीयतदीयत्वमेव ज्यायः । नहि, मुक्तानां कश्चन **भगवदुपयोगो** ऽस्तीति भावः । (iii.4.48)

उक्तभगवदीयत्वं न साधनरूपम् 'मुक्तानामपि सिद्धानां कोटिष्वपि" ।

(*Bhâg* vi.14.5) (Vallabha *BSP* iii.4.39)

Lastly, Vallabha has *borrowed, without acknowledgement*, the verse :

> भ्रान्तिमूलतया सर्वसमयानामयुक्तितः ।
> न तद्विरोधाद् वचनं वैदिकं शङ्क्यतां व्रजेत् ॥

from Madhva's *Aṇubhāṣya*—a short metrical digest of the BS, in his '*Aṇubhāṣya*' on BS ii.2.11. In holding that the fruits of Bhaktimārga are superior to and sweeter than those of Jñānamārga in Mokṣa, Vallabha observes that for Jñānins God's grace and favor last only upto the time of their release. This grace and favour are showered upon the Bhaktas to a greater extent and throughout Mokṣa. Though Madhva does not recognise any exclusiveness between Bhakti and Jñāna,[11] he recognises gradation of intrinsic bliss among the released according to their natural fitness. Vallabha's distinction in the *fruits* of Bhakti and Jñāna presupposes the presence of Tāratamya in the fruits of Mokṣa. In his commentary on *Gītā* II.52 Madhva quotes *Bhāgavata Purāṇa* in support of Ānandatāratamya there. Vallabha's son has quoted from Madhva's *BSB* ii.4.29 in his *Vidvanmaṇḍanam*.

The influence of Madhva's philosophy has been most prominent and pronounced on the Caitanya school of Bengal Vaiṣṇavism. The growth of this influence can be traced in the works of Rūpa Gosvāmī, Sanātana Gosvāmī and Jīva Gosvāmī. It reached its zenith in the writings of Baladeva Vidyābhūṣaṇa (1720-80). His *Govinda Bhāṣya* on the *BS* is *heavily indebted* to Madhva's, as I have shown with copious details in my *HDSV*, Appendix V. Baladeva's *teacher* Rādhā-Dāmodara also quotes from Madhva in his *Vedāntasyamantaka*. The doctrine of Viśeṣas has been taken over *bodily* from Madhva's philosophy and from the works of Vyāsatīrtha by Rādhā-Dāmodara, from whom Baladeva takes it over.

While noticing often Baladeva's divergences in the interpretation of the *BS* from Śaṅkara and Rāmānuja in his edition of the *BS* with English translation, Dr. Radhakrishnan has failed to show how a considerable part of Baladeva's divergences from Śaṅkara and Rāmānuja is, in reality, derived from Madhva.

---

11. See Chapter XLVIII, fn 13.

Had it been done, it would have underlined the extent of Madhva's influence on one of the leading exponents of the Caitanya school. Some distinctive textual interpretations and sources cited by Madhva have found their way into the later commentaries of the Śaṅkara and Rāmānuja schools, notably Śrīdhara Svāmī and Raṅgarāmāṇuja and the author of the Advaita commentary on the *Viṣṇusahasranāma* by a *later* Śaṅkarācārya.

CHAPTER III

MADHVA'S SAMANVAYA OF UPANIṢADIC PHILOSOPHY

LABELS are convenient as a rule, though they might mislead at times. Insofar as Madhva admits a plurality of selves, for ever distinct from Brahman, though always subject to and guided by it, his system may be tentatively regarded as a pluralistic theism. But it would not express the whole truth about the system, *in its highest reach*. There has been a persistent tendency, however, to represent the philosophy of Madhva as an "absolute dualism". This has naturally prevented the system from getting its meed of recognition, as a sound philosophical system in the first place and a Vedāntic one at that; for most people have an aversion for the term "dualism" which has some unpleasant associations. That apart, "dualism" signifies the recognition of "*two independent principles*"[1]. Madhva is *not* certainly a dualist *in this sense*. It will be shown presently that neither the term "dualism" nor its Sanskrit equivalent "dvaita" is commensurate with the highest metaphysical ideology of Madhva's thought, which consists in the acceptance of *One Independent Transcendent-cum-Immanent Being as the source and explanatian of all finite existence*.

There is a fundamental difference in outlook between the 'dualism' of Madhva and those of the Sāṁkhya-Yoga and Nyāya-Vaiśeṣika schools. Dualism has as much to do with the question of the *status of the reals* recognized as with their *number*. Neither the *Puruṣas* nor the *Prakṛti* have, in Madhva's system, an *independent status* or functioning-capacity as in the Sāṁkhya :

शरीरेन्द्रियादिसंबन्धोत्पत्तौ या शक्तिः, सा-बीजशक्तिः ।
जीव एव तद्वानिति ब्रूते (साङ्ख्यः) न तु तदीयां बीजशक्तिं तत्त्व-
वादिन इव भगवदधीनाम् : (*NS* p. 329)

1. See Dogbert D. Runes, *Dictionary of Philosophy*, p. 84

Nor does it ascribe to God the position merely of an Onlooker (Draṣṭā) or a *deus ex machina,* or even of a co-operating force in the cosmic evolution, as is done by the Nyāya and Yoga schools. Mere Deism has no attraction for Madhva. God is not only above the universe but *in it.* By virtue of these two aspects He becomes the very ground of the reals,[2] the giver of their reality to them.

One distinguishing mark of the Vedānta in all its forms is the fundamental belief that everything in the universe has to be traced to an absolute principle which is the ultimate source and explanation, both logical and ontological, of all else (सर्वसत्ता-प्रतीति-प्रवृत्तिनिमित्तम्). Nothing in the world is self-explained or self-explicable. Brahman is the only self-explained reference of all. Such a transcendent reference is denied by the Sāṁkhya :

या जगदुपादानं सा प्रकृतिरेवोपादानत्वशक्तिमती इति ब्रूते । न पुनः वेदवादिन इव तामपि शक्तिमीश्वरायत्ताम् । (*NS* p. 329)

Its acceptance is by no means a strict metaphysical necessity in the Nyāya-Vaiśeṣika or Yoga systems. The Vedānta, on the other hand, traces the world of matter and souls to Brahman, which is the cause of the world and gives *meaning* to its being and becoming.

The metaphysical dependence of the universe on Brahman is differently conceived in the different systems of Vedānta. Śaṅkara equates it with an appearance (*adhyāsa*). The world of appearance, which is superimposed on Brahman, would not be there but for the reality of Brahman. It has no existence outside or apart from Brahman :

तदनन्यत्वं तद्व्यतिरेकेणाभावः । (S*BSB* ii. 1.14)

Śrīdhara explains the significance of this statement by saying—

---

2. Cf. तदनुप्रविश्य सच्च त्यच्चाभवत् । (*TaittUp* ii.6)
प्रकरोतीति प्रकृतिः । (*MBSB* i.4.27)
स जीवनामा भगवान् प्राणधारणहेतुतः । (Madhva's Commentary on *ChāndUp*)

"in virtue of whose reality, even the unreal creation appears to be real" : यत्सत्यतया मिथ्यासर्गोऽपि सत्यवदवभासते ।

(Commentary on *Bhāgavata* i.1.1)

Rāmānuja, on the other hand, views the dependence of the world of matter and souls on God, on the analogy of the dependence of the human body on the soul, for its subsistence. God is the soul (*ātmā*) of the world. When the soul departs, the body perishes. So it would be, in the case of the world and the souls. While it remains perfectly true that our bodies cannot exist and function in the absence of the life-giving capacity of the soul, Madhva finds this analogy misleading insofar as the soul is not bound to the body as the Viśiṣṭādvaitic theory of Brahman would appear to assume. The relation of body and soul does not also do complete justice to the more or less derivative being of matter and souls that is admitted in that system[3]. It is all very well to say that identity means *Apṛthaksiddhi* or inseparable existence. But it would cut both ways. That seems hardly fair. The dependence due to *Apṛthaksiddhi* between God and His 'body' (or attributes) viz., matter and souls cannot be *of the same kind or order*, as exists or may be said to exist between God and His essential attributes of reality, knowledge and bliss. It is the inevitable implication of Rāmānuja's position that the Infinite cannot exist without its attributes of *Cit* and *Acit*, which are necessary to It. Yet, Rāmānuja himself is unable to concede so much in view of the many texts to the contrary, especially *Gītā* IX.4, wherein he admits frankly that *Cit* and *Acit contribute in no way to the existence of the Deity* : मत्स्थितौ तैर्नं कश्चिदुपकारः (*RGB*). Here, for once, Rāmānuja gives up his theory of reciprocal dependence and equates inseparable existence (*avinābhāva*) as 'dependence':

अविनाभावश्च नियाम्यतयेति 'मत्तः सर्वं प्रवर्तते' इत्युपक्रम एवोदितः ।
(*RGB* x.21).

The logical consequence of such a view would be that the world of matter and souls is immaterial and non-essential to God in

---

3. Cf. सहकारिभिरारम्भे न स्वातंत्र्यं विहन्यते ।
तत्सद्भावप्रवृत्त्योश्च स्वाधीनत्वव्यवस्थितेः ॥
(Vedānta Deśika, *Tattvamuktākalāpa*, p. 255.)

the end. Such a view is, however, inconsistent with Rāmānuja's general position *that it has its basis in the nature of God.* It is also difficult to conceive how Brahman could be said to be unchanging in view of the changing nature of its *Viśeṣaṇas* (*Cit* and *Acit*). The modes change from subtle to gross state and *vice versa.* If these changes of the modes make no substantial impression on Brahman, they cannot be said to be *grounded in its nature.* But Rāmānuja nevertheless concedes that Brahman is subject to *change of some sort* in and through these changes of the modes themselves :

> उभयप्रकारविशिष्टनियंत्रंशे तदवस्थातदुभयविशिष्टतारूपविकारो भवति । (*Śribhāṣya* ii.3.18)

"Unless Rāmānuja is willing to explain away the immediate perfection of the Absolute and substitute for it a perpetually changing process, a sort of progressing perfection, he cannot give us any satisfactory explanation of the relation of the soul of the Absolute *to its body*" (Radhakrishnan, *I. Phil.* ii, p. 716). That is why Madhva abandons the metaphor of 'body and soul' and the doctrine of 'reciprocal dependence' and the 'contribution theory', which it implies.[4]

In his view, the world of matter and souls has come out and exists only as a result of an act of Will of God, which is its *nimittakāraṇa.* It cannot exist without His sufferance. This is the meaning of texts like: इच्छामात्रं प्रभोः सृष्टिः (*ManUp* 8) ; द्रव्यं कर्म च कालश्च... (*Bhāg* ii.10.12). But the existence of matter and souls is, in the last analysis, immaterial to God : नहि जीवप्रकृतिभ्यामीश्वरस्यार्थः (Madhva, *BT* ii. 9. 31). It is the world that is bound to God, not He to it. The Universe is thus dependent on Brahman (ब्रह्मसापेक्ष) neither in the Advaitic nor in the Viśiṣṭādvaitic sense of the term, but as existing and functioning at God's will. The self-existent being of God would in no way have been affected if

---

4. पारार्थ्यलक्षणं हि शेषत्वम् । अतः शेषभूतो मुक्तः स्वप्रयुक्तेन केनचिदतिशयेन हि शेषिणं संयोजयति । **अकिंचित्करस्य शेषत्वानुपपत्तेः ।**

(*Nītimālā*, X, p.74, Annamalai Uni. Skt. Ser., 1940)

The 'Contribution theory' would also have to concede that "*God is not absolute actuality, but is Himself in the making*" (Radhakrishnan, ii. p. 715) [Italics mine].

the world had never existed at all. The relation in which the world stands to Brahman is, thus, neither superimpositional as in Advaita, nor physical and intra-organic as in Viśiṣṭādvaita, but a trans-empirical one, symbolized by the idea of *Bimba-Pratibīmbabhāva*, in which *Bimba* is defined as that which determines the *sattā*, *pratīti* and *pravṛtti* of the *Pratibimba*, as will be made clear in Chapter XXXVI. The statement that the world cannot exist without God means that it owes its very power of existence, functioning, etc., to God and derives them from Him : तदधीनसत्ताप्रतीतिप्रवृत्तिमत्. The entire universe is thus an expression of the Divine will.[5] It is in His absolute power. He can make and unmake it all at will. His power over it is absolutely unrestricted.[6] Alone among Indian philosophers, Madhva would concede that, *theoretically*, there is nothing impossible or absurd in agreeing that God *can* create a world out of nothing, that He *could* bring into existence a universe not unlike the one with which we are now familiar, without the aid of a pre-existent matter or souls. But the *fact remains* that He has *not*, in His infinite wisdom, *chosen to do so*. And all our philosophy has necessarily to take note of this and respect it. Similarly, He does not choose to destroy the eternal existence of matter and souls and other entities, even though they are all dependent on Him :

तदधीनसत्ताकमपि तेन नोत्साद्यते (*Tdyṭ* p. 9).

Madhva introduces the symbolism of *Bimbapratibimbabhāva*, (Original and Reflection) in place of *Adhiṣṭhānāropyabhāva*, and *Śarīraśarīribhāva* of the Advaita and Viśiṣṭādvaita, to illustrate the true nature of the dependence of selves on God. It is intended to avoid the defects of assuming *an unreal or a reciprocal dependence* and establish in their stead, a real but unilateral dependence of all finite reality on the Independent principle, for its existence, knowledge, knowability and activity (*sattā*, *pratīti* and *pravṛtti*).

On the Advaita view of *āropa* (superimposition) the substratum (*adhiṣṭhāna*) *does not and cannot confer any true reality on the super-*

5. स्वमतिप्रभवं जगदस्य यतः (*Dvādaśa-Stotra*, iv.2).
6. भस्म कुर्याज्जगदिदं मनसैव जनार्दनः (*Mbh.* v.66.8).

imposed or sustain it, of its own free will as God does in respect of the world[7]. Creation, then, would be completely mechanical and unregulated by a purposive will. The knowledge of the substratum, on the Advaitic view, far from sustaining the superimposed object would *destory it at once*. Hence the relation between the world, God and the souls *would not be a* true and permanent relation, as it appears from texts like : *Satyasya satyam* (*BrhUp* ii.3.6) and *Nityo nityānām* (*Kaṭha Up* ii.2.13), in the Upaniṣads, on this view. But the Original (*Bimba*) as conceived by Madhva, *does sustain* the reflection (*pratibimba*) while maintaining its own transcendence and without making the *Pratibimba* an intra-organic part of its own being. The relation of *Bimbapratibimbabhāva* as conceived by Madhva would be permanent and *true of all states of the Jīvātman and not merely* a passing one, true of Saṁsāra alone, as their *adhiṣṭhāna-āropyabhāva* would make it in the Advaitic view. There will be no destruction of the *Pratibimba* so long as the contact of the *Upādhi* is intact. The function of an *Upādhi* (medium) is to manifest the Pratibimba. In the present case, it is the pristine nature of the *Jīvasvarūpa* itself as *Cit* that would suffice, according to Madhva, to manifest itself to itself in its true nature of metaphysical dependence on Brahman and of being endowed with a measure of similarity of attributes (as part of the meaning of the word *pratibimba*) with its Original (Brahman) without calling to aid the sarvices of any external medium (*bāhyopādhi*) :

Svayam evātra pradarśakaḥ cittvāt (*MGB* ii. 18).

This power self-revelation is hidden in the Jīva in the state of Saṁsāra (*BS* iii.2.5 and iii.2.19).

Hence, *Bimbapratibimbabhāva* between God and Soul, though a fact, always, is not realized in full in bondage. It is by means of its internal *Svarūpaviśeṣas* that the Soul acts as its own reflecting medium (*upādhi*) in realizing its true relation of dependence etc., to the Supreme. It is in this sense that an *Upādhi* is at all called for to manifest to the individual soul its own *Svarūpa* and its relation to God. As this true *Svarūpa* free from all impurities con-

7. गतिर्भर्ता प्रभुः साक्षी निवासः शरणं सुहृत् । (*Gītā* ix. 18)
गामाविश्य च भूतानि धारयाम्यहमोजसा । (*Gītā* xv. 13).

stitutes the essence of the Jīva, it is termed *Svarūpa-upādhi*, in Madhva's terminology. The term *Pratibimba* would be misleading, if it is understood in its popular sense of an appearance brought about by a material and *an external medium*. This is *not* the sense in which the figure of *Pratibimba* as applied to the Jīva is used and is meant to be understood in Madhva's Siddhānta (See his *BSB* iii 2.18; See also Chapter XXXVI).

Madhva takes us to the highest limit of Divine transcendence. The Supreme is independent of all accessories in creation :

शक्तोऽपि भगवान्विष्णुरकर्तुं कर्तुमन्यथा ।
स्वभिन्नं कारणाभिन्नं भिन्नं विश्वं करोत्यजः ॥

(*AV* ii.1.19)

Though capable of doing without accessories or making such changes in them as He pleases, God, out of His own free will, has made the world different from Himself and partly different and partly identical with its material cause (*Prakṛti*). Jayatīrtha, in explaining this point, shows how the practical and theoretical aspects of God's omnipotence are to be reconciled, in accordance with the Śruti.[8]

Taking his stand on *Bimbapratibimbabhāva* as the only satisfactory metaphysical relation that would do full justice to and correctly represent the natural relation (*Svābhāvika-sambandha*) between God and the souls, Madhva finds the key to the reconciliation of the *Bheda* and *Abheda* Śrutis in the twin ideas of *Svatantra* and *Paratantra* that underlies the very conception of *Bimbapratibimbabhāva*. The *Bheda-Śrutis* bearing testimony to the reality of the world of matter and souls speak the truth from the

---

8. "**अन्यथा**" कारणैर्विना कर्तुं शक्तोऽपि हरिः कारणान्तराण्युपादायैव करिष्यामीति स्वेच्छानियतः कारणैरेव जगत्सृजति । एवं "**अन्यथा**" प्रकृत्या अहंकारमहंकारेण महान्तमित्येवं, तथा प्रकृतिं निमित्तीकृत्य कालादिकं चोपादानीकृत्य कर्तुं शक्तोऽपि, एतेनैवेदमुपादानीकृत्यैवेदं स्रक्ष्यामीति स्वेच्छानियतो "**नियतैः**" क्लृप्तैरेव स्वनियतसत्ताशक्त्यादिमद्भिरेव, तथा "**नियतैः**" स्वनियतसत्ताशक्त्यादिमद्भिरेव कारणान्तरैरिदं जगत्करोतीति योजना ।

इदमुक्तं भवति—यदुक्तमीश्वरस्य कारणोपादाननियमोऽस्ति न वेति, तन्नास्तीति ब्रूमः । तथा च प्रकृत्यादीनां कारणत्वं युक्तम् । स च नियमो न कुलालादेरिव तान्यपहाय व्यत्यस्य वा करणे शक्त्यभावनिबन्धनः । येन, तस्य स्वातंत्र्यमन्येषां पारतंत्र्यं च न स्यात् । किं नाम, स्वेच्छानियमत एव । (*NS*, *II* p. 299)

point of view of factual existence and dependence of all finite reality on God. The *Abheda-Śrutis* speak the truth from the point of view of the utter transcendent majesty and independence of the one Supreme Principle. There is no essential contradiction in accepting the equal reality of both these truths. The mistake lies in pressing for a *Svarūpaikya* (identity of essence) by abolishing the finites (as unreal) or in treating them as intraorganic part of the Infinite, which would destroy its homogeneity. The *Svatantra-tattva* of Madhva is not a mere theological concept into which all plurality is sacrificed. It is a philosophical idea corresponding to the Spinozistic conception of 'substance' defined as *res completa* "complete in itself, determined by itself and capable of being explained entirely by itself". Such substantiality is possessed only by Brahman. *The Pratibimba cannot be complete in itself, is not determined by itself and is not capable of being explained by itself* (without reference to the *Bimba*).

The true reconciliation of the finite and the infinite must be based on this basic fact. Hence, Madhva holds that God or Brahman is the *only independent Reality* or the highest reality, so to speak (*Advaitam nāma yad ucyate tat Bhagavadapekṣayetyarthaḥ* —Madhva's *ChānUp Bhāṣya*). Everything else, Prakṛti, Puruṣas Kāla, beginningless merit, etc., is *ex hypothesi* dependent on Brahman for its very existence and functioning, though not created by Brahman *de novo*. As dependent reals they do *not constitute a 'challenge'* to the Absolute or a limitation to it. Their existence is not irreconcilable with the existence of Brahman in any metaphysical sense. Madhva thus rises to the highest pitch of Transcendentalism while keeping his feet firmly on the *terra firma* of observed facts, without sacrificing the reality of the world and its values or abolishing the individuals, *in the last analysis*. If philosophy is to be an interpretation of reality as a whole, it must have relation to the facts of life and experience. However high and for however long the philosopher may choose to soar on the naked peaks of the Absolute, he must at last set his feet on hard earth. *We cannot deny this world to have the other*. Madhva indicates the right 'angle of Brahman' (*brahmadṛṣṭi*) from which the philosopher should look at the world of matter and souls :

द्रव्यं कर्म च कालश्च स्वभावो जीव एव च ।
यदनुग्रहतः सन्ति न सन्ति यदुपेक्षया ॥ (*Bhāg* ii 10 12)

इदं हि विश्वं भगवानिवेतरो यतो जगत्स्थाननिरोधसंभवः ।

(*Bhāg* i.5.20)

नहि जीवप्रकृतिभ्यामीश्वरस्यार्थः । (*BT* ii.9.34)

यदधीना यस्य सत्ता तत्तदित्येव भण्यते ।

विद्यमाने विभेदेऽपि मिथो नित्यं स्वरूपतः । (*BT* ii.5.2)

देवतानां स्वभावोऽपि स्वरूपमपि सर्वदा ।

तदधीनं यतो यामी * * * ॥

स्वभावसत्तादातृत्वं यंतृत्वमिति कीर्त्यते ।

(*Commentary on BrhUp*. iii.7.23)

काल आसीत् पुरुष आसीत् परम आसीत् तद्यदासीत् तदावृतमासीत् तदधीनमासीत् अथ ह्येक एव परम आसीत् यस्यैतदासीत् । न ह्येतदासीत् ।

(*Śruti quoted in BSB* ii.1.17)

नहि तदधीनं पृथगित्येवोच्यते । (*Commentary on BrhUp*. ii.4.14)

अद्वैतं परमार्थतः । (*MānUp*. i.17)

यदद्वैतं नामोच्यते तत् "परमार्थतः" भगवदपेक्षयेत्यर्थः ।

(*Commentary on ChānUp* ii.21)

In his *Bhāgavata Tātparya*, rising to the highest peak of transcendentalism, Madhva distinguishes the highest reality from mere existence. What is truly real is what has being in itself and for itself. Such reality is possessed only by Brahman:

पारमार्थिकसत्यत्वं स्वातंत्र्यमभिधीयते ।

तद्विष्णोरेव नान्यस्य **तदन्येषां सदास्तिता** ॥

(*BT* XI.24.17)

The others, especially Prakṛti and Puruṣas, insofar as they depend for their very existence and activity on the Supreme, merely *exist* from eternity. They cannot lay claim to any *independent* reality. In a hypothetical sense then, it is permissible sometimes to speak of them "*as if not existing*" or "other than real[9]".

9. Cf. न ह्येतदासीत् (Quoted by Madhva in *BSB* ii.1.17); द्वैतमिव भवति (BrhUp iv.5.15)

Also : *Qua comparata nec pulchra sunt, nec bona sunt, nec sunt* (St. Augustine Con. xi.4)

यदाविरासीद् **अनृतस्य** सर्वम्

(Śruti quoted by Madhva in *BSB* i.1.1)

Here '*anṛtam*' is used in the sense of 'changing' (अनृतं परिणामतः— Madhva in *Tdy*)

Such descriptions in the Śrutis should not blind us to *the fact* of their actual existence, distinct from Brahman and in complete dependence upon it. We are welcome to hold that dependence signifies want of substantiality in the Spinozistic sense of the term. Madhva would not be perturbed by this and would accept the contention. But it does not deprive a thing of its reality. Reality, in other words, is not the same as substantiality in the highest philosophical sense of that term. It is just uncontradicted existence (*anāropitam pramitiviṣayaḥ*). We have no right to deny reality to the world of matter and souls, simply because they are *not independent* or do not always exist *in the same form*. But they *are there*, *have been there and will be there* though ever changing and depending on Brahman. Even the eternal substances, as we have seen, are not exempt from creation in the sense of *Parādhīnaviśeṣāpti* in Madhva's philosophy. Such creation is the badge of the finite :

तद्वशत्वज्ञापनार्थमेव सृष्ट्युक्तिः ।

(Madhva's Commentary on *ChānUp*)

Why there should at all be such a world of matter and souls, or why God should *tolerate* their existence, is more than what any philosophy could answer. Nor is it its business to do so. The only plausible theistic answer to such a query is that given by Jayatīrtha.

ननु, शक्तस्यापि परमेश्वरस्य तन्नियमानुसरणेच्छा कुत इति चेत्; किं कारणं पृच्छसि, उत ज्ञापकम् ? आद्ये स्वभावोऽयमिति ब्रूमः । द्वितीये, श्रुतिप्रसिद्धेरिति । (*NS* p. 289)

Though Brahman can do very well without Prakṛti or Puruṣas, it prefers, in its infinite glory and inexorable will, *to do with them.* Such dependence (*apekṣā*) of Brahman on things which are in themselves dependent on It, is no mark of inferiority or limitation. It is, at the most, a self-limitation and even that attests and enhances its majesty :

साधनानां साधनत्वं यदात्माधीनमिष्यते ।
तदा साधनसम्पत्तिरैश्वर्यद्योतिका भवेत् ॥

(*MBSB* ii.1.15)

The dependent is often treated as of "no consequence" and having no separate existence :

नहि तदधीनं पृथगित्येवोच्यते ।
(Madhva's Commentary on *BrhUp* ii.4.14)

यदधीना यस्य सत्ता तत्तदित्येव भण्यते । (*BT* ii.5.2)

न वै वाचो, न मनांसि इत्याचक्षते, 'प्राणा' इत्येवाचक्षते ।
(*Chān Up* v.1.15)

All this will show that Madhva has given earnest thought to the position and status of the reals in his system with the insight and imagination of a *level-headed philosopher*. He has substituted a Brahman-centric view for the ego-centric interpretation of Upaniṣadic thought. It is a pity that missing this distinction of Madhva's philosophy, some historians of Indian philosophy should have tried to dismiss him as belonging "*more* to the religious history than to the philosophical development of India".

He has shown that if we are to avoid *playing tricks with evidence*, the only satisfactory synthesis of the conflicts between the *Dvaita* and *Advaita Śrutis* in the Upaniṣads would be in the adoption of the idea of the one Independent Transcendent-cum-Immanent Reference of all finite reality. He has no sympathy with the reckless monism of Śaṅkara which is indifferent alike to the hopes and aspirations of man and reduces the panorama of creation to a random illusion of which no questions ought to be asked or need be answered.[10] At the same time, he is not for ascribing false perfection of any kind to the world of matter and souls. The world and the souls are given just what is their due and nothing more. They are real in that they are not the result of any superimposition (*anāropita*). *Independent* they are not and God is greater than His creation[11] and is immanent in it. Such in a

---

10. Cf. अपि च नेयं पारमार्थिकी सृष्टिः । नहि द्विचन्द्रालातचक्रगन्धर्वनगरादिविभ्रमा समुद्दिष्टप्रयोजना भवन्ति भ्रान्तानाम् । (Bhāmati ii.1.33).

न ह्ययं सृष्ट्यादिप्रपंचःप्रतिपिपादयिषितः । न हि तत्प्रतिबद्धः कश्चित्पुरुषार्थो दृश्यते, श्रूयते वा । (S *BSB* i.4.14).

11. सारतो जगतः कृत्स्नादतिरिक्तो जनार्दनः । (*Mbh* V. 66.7)

nutshell is the position of Madhva. When we emphasize the existence of subordinate reals side by side with the independence of Brahman, we have a dualism or more properly a theistic realism. When we think exclusively of the transcendence of Brahman and isolate or abstract It from everything else, we may and do sometimes resort to the 'language of monism'. Such according to Madhva and Jayatirtha is the summit level of Upaniṣadic thought. Jayatīrtha has expounded this ultimate synthesis of Upaniṣadic thought with his characteristic clarity and brilliance :

सर्वाण्यपि हि वेदान्तवाक्यानि असंख्येयकल्याणगुणाकरं सकलदोषगन्धविधुरं एकरूपमेव परं ब्रह्म * * * प्रतिपादयन्ति। किंतु, १) कानिचित् सर्वज्ञत्वसर्वेश्वरत्वसर्वान्तर्यामित्वसौन्दर्यौदार्यादि-**गुणविशिष्टतया**; २) कानिचित् अपहतपाप्मत्वनिर्दुःखत्वभौतिकदेहरहितत्वादि**दोषाभावाविशिष्टतया**; ३) कानिचिदतिगहनताज्ञापनाय **अवाङ्मनसगोचरत्वाकारेण**; ४) कानिचित् सर्वपरित्यागेन तस्यैवोपादानाया**द्वितीयत्वेन**; ५) कानिचित् सर्वसत्ताप्रतीतिप्रवृत्तिनिमित्तताप्रतिपत्त्यर्थं **सर्वात्मकत्वेन**, इत्येवामाद्यनेकप्रकारैः परमपुरुषं बोधयन्ति। ततो व्याकुलबुद्धयो गुरुसंप्रदायविकलाः सर्वत्राप्येकरूपतामननुसन्दधाना वेदं छिन्दन्ति। (*NS* p. 123)

"All Upaniṣadic texts, without exception, speak of the glory of Brahman as the abode of infinite perfections and attributes and free from all imperfections. Of these, some (i) represent It as endowed with attributes like omniscience, lordship, inner rulership, munificence, beauty, goodness, etc. (ii) Others represent It as free from all such limitations as sin, suffering, liability to physical embodiment and so on. (iii) Yet others describe Brahman as lying beyond the reach of mind and speech, in order to bring home to us Its comparative inaccessibility. (iv) Others depict It as *the only one that exists*—in order that we may all seek It, to the exclusion of everything else. (v) Others represent It as the self of all so that It may be understood to be the source of all existence, knowledge and activity in the finite world. But confused heads, missing this central unity of Vedic teaching in and through a multiplicity of inter-connected approaches, *mar the unity of their teaching by introducing artificial distinctions of standpoints of Saguṇa and Nirguṇa, Vyavahāra and Paramārtha and so forth, in interpreting the message of the Upaniṣads*".

This new synthesis of Upaniṣadic philosophy propounded by Jayatīrtha in the light of Madhva's interpretation of the Vedānta will be seen to be more satisfying than the characterless monism (*nirviśeṣādvaita*) of Śaṅkara on the one hand and the intraorganic monism (*viśiṣṭādvaita*) of Rāmānuja, on the other, which hardly allows Brahman to exist by itself. *Svatantra-Advitīya-Brahmavāda*,[12] if we may so agree to designate the philosophy of Madhva, would appear to be logically the more consistent and philosophically the more commensurate solution of the problem of the finite and the infinite. The Advaitin altogether ignores the relative aspect and existence of the world of matter and souls for all time; while the Viśiṣṭādvaitin detracts from the self-sufficiency of God by his intraorganic conception of their relationship. The new synthesis put forward by Madhva has the advantage of preserving these two vital elememts in proper blend under the terms of

द्रव्यं कर्म च कालश्च स्वभावो जीव एव च ।
यदनुग्रहतः सन्ति, न सन्ति यदुपेक्षया ।। (*Bhāg* ii. 10.12)

which is the corner-stone of Madhva's philosophical synthesis. Brahman as the *Svatantratattva* is implied in the very existence of the relative and the *Paratantra*.

Prof. V. B. Inamdar, writing in *Homage to Dr. T. G. Mainkar* (ed. by C. R. Deshpande, Bombay, 1982) has rejected the alternative title I have suggested as "clumsy and not quite suitable, as it can also describe the Advaita of Śaṅkara, as his Brahman also is Svatantra" (*Op. cit.* p. 111). There is no denying the fact that the terms 'Dvaita' and 'Dualism', in their commonly accepted sense of a philosophical system committed to the

12. This new designation was first suggested by me in 1936. It received the approval of the late Satyadhyāna Tīrtha, Svāmiji of the Uttarādi Muṭṭ, the greatest authority on Dvaita philosophy in the present century. It was later adopted as the title of one of my works, published in 1942. Dr. Radhakrishnan refers to "the implicit monism" of Madhva (*I.Phil.*i.p.40). H.N. Raghavendrachar has claimed that Madhva's philosophy rightly be called "Brahmādvaita" and that Madhva is a monist in the truest sense of the term. Alur Venkatarao of Dharwar gave Madhva's philosophy the name of "Pūrṇabrahmavāda". All this is a sign that philosophical interest among the followers of Madhva is very much alive and resurgent.

acceptance of *two independent reals or principles* is inapplicable and inappropriate to Madhva's view. Hence the need to think of a more suitable title which would be commensurate with its actual teaching about the status of the 'tattvas' accepted in Madhva's system. As no single compact word satisfies this requirement, a little diffuseness has got to be put up with in the interest of finding a name which would dispel outright and effectively bar all avoidable misconceptions regarding the status of the reals in the system. For, it is not only the number of the reals in the system that is involved in this question but the relative status of the Tattvas.

Prof. Inamdar's contention that Śaṅkara's Brahman too is 'Svatantra' is unsustainable. To Śaṅkara his Brahman is 'Nirviśeṣa' (without *any* characteristic). It is not both Saviśeṣa and Nirviśeṣa. (See his comment on *BS* iii. 2. 11 of the Ubhayaliṅgādhikaraṇa.) To declare Śaṅkara's Brahman to be "Svatantra" is to deprive it of its 'Nirviśeṣatva' and make it 'Saviśeṣa'. Śaṅkara would hardly be disposed to thank the Professor for such a suggestion. In any case, the Svatantratattva, as shown by Jayatīrtha, to be *meaningfully so*, must be independent of any other (existing) principle in respect of its being, its awareness of its own self or being and its activity. *Śaṅkara's Brahman has no self-awareness and cannot have it.* For, in his philosophy, to talk of Brahman being conscious of its own being or conceive of its being so would be to court the fallacy of the overlapping of the subject and the predicate in the same act (*kartṛkarmavirodha*). Nor can a Nirviśeṣa-Brahman have any self-directed activity.

Inamdar's next objection is that the term 'advitīyam' in the *ChāndUp* has been interpreted in the sense of having no equal or superior "*by none except Madhva*" (*op. cit.* p. 11). This is not correctly informed. For, more than two centuries before Madhva, the same meaning has been accepted for the term by Rāmānuja's predecessor Yāmunācārya, in his *Siddhitraya*, while discussing the interpretation of the Śruti text. He has also driven home his interpretation with an effective analogy:

यथा चोलनृपः सम्राडद्वितीयोऽद्य भूतले ।
इति तत्तुल्यनृपतिनिवारणपरं वचः ।

न तु तद्भृत्यतत्पुत्रकलत्रादिनिवारकम् ॥

(*Siddhitraya*, Ubhayavedāntagranthamālā, Book Depot, Madras, 1972)

Prof. Inamdar has also argued that the next sentence in the *ChanUp* says, "the original principle wished to be just many', which leaves no room to think of a rival or superior in that context". But a comparison of that text with another of the same type in the same context af creation from the *AitUp* "the Ātman alone existed in the beginning and nothing else whatever winked" (*nānyat kiñcana miṣat* i. 1. 1), meaning that nothing else was active (*vyāpāravat*) then, as everything else was in an undeveloped state and inactive—shows that the statement in the *ChanUp* has to be understood as a *significant negation*, in keeping with the principle of 'Ekavākyatā' (consistency) of Śrutisiddhānta. From this point of view, there is nothing to object to Madhva's and Yāmuna's interpretation of the word 'advitīyam', which emphasizes the aspect of Brahman's supreme independence. 'Svātantrya' or independence is far too positive a characteristic that can be meaningfully ascribed to Śaṅkara's Nirviśeṣa-Brahman. It can neither have *a will to create* nor a wish to become many except through Adhyāsa (superimposition). But the Nirviśeṣa is logically *prior to Adhyāsa.*

The Professor's last objection is that the title 'Svatantra-advitīya-Brahmavāda' "covers only half the field as the chief emphasis would be only on the supremacy of Brahman, ignoring the other important aspect of Madhva's doctrine viz., the reality and the non-identity with Brahman of the other categories of existence as opposed to the Māyāvāda. In fact, *the latter was the mainspring* of Madhva's theory and the chief aim was to demolish Monism" (*Op. cit* p. 112).

I have anticipated this objection while drawing attention to Madhva's "Sat-siddhānta",[13] quoting Jayatīrtha's clarification as to how 'Sat-siddhānta' consists of *two aspects* of Para and Apara Siddhānta (main and subsidiary doctrine) relating to the Para-tattva (the supreme knowable) and the Apara-tatta (the dependent knowable) or the Aparaprameya, respectively, The Para-Siddhānta relates to the supreme Brahman, its independence,

13. See Chapter IV, fn. 4.

infinitude and freedom from all imperfections (*nirdoṣāśeṣasadguṇam*). Everything which pertains to finite reality (viz. the world of matter and souls) constitutes the 'Aparasiddhānta' (subsidiary doctrine). For, the Paratantra-Prameya (dependent knowable) is not something set over and against the Svatantra, in Madhva's system. *They are not on a par.* The concept of "*Ekavijñānena sarvavijñānam*" (knowing the many by knowing the One) from the *ChanUp* has also been explained by Madhva accordingly (See Chapter XXVIII), from the point of view of the primacy of the Svatantratattva. It is thus the supremacy of Brahman with its transcendental attributes that is the mainspring of Madhva's philosophy:

सर्वंत्राखिलसच्छक्तिः स्वतन्त्रोऽशेषदर्शनः ।
नित्यातादृशचिच्चेत्ययन्तेष्टो नो रमापतिः ॥
(Madhva, *Tdy*, Introductory verse)

That is the prime import (*mahātātparya*) of all Śāstra and all the rest of the teaching relating to the finite reality is the subsidiary import (*avāntaratātparyam*) of Śāstra:

सर्वोत्कर्षे देवदेवस्य विष्णोः
महातात्पर्यं नैव चान्यत्र सत्यम् ।
अवान्तरं तत्परत्वं तदन्यत्
सर्वागमानां पुरुषार्थः ततोऽतः ॥ (Madhva, *VTN*)

Madhva's approach to the thesis of *Ekavijñānena sarvavijñānam* in the *ChānUp* rests on the same premise of the knowledge of the chief leading to the knowledge and fulfilment of the purpose of the subsidiary:

Pradhānavijñānād apradhānam jñātaphalam bhavati.

The concluding words of Jayatīrtha in his commentary on Madhva's *TS* emphasize the same truth (See Chapter I, fn 7.).

I readily agree with Prof. Inamdar that "any name therefore which we may give for this system must have a clear and direct bearing on the fundamental aspect of Madhva thought" (p. 112). Since Madhva's "Para-Siddhānta" must naturally and necessarily be deemed to be the fundamental aspect of his teaching, it will not be difficult any more to realize that notwithstanding a little diffuseness in the phrasing, the alternative title of 'Svatantra-Advitīya-Brahmavāda' suggested by me brings it out clearly and directly without the vagueness and other shortcomings of the commonly current title of "Dvaita".

CHAPTER IV

MADHVA'S CONTRIBUTION TO INDIAN THOUGHT

MADHVA'S philosophical categories differ much in their scope and function from those of contemporary schools. Sometimes the nomenclature is retained but the conception is different. In other cases everything including the names is different. Madhva is generally allergic to over-elaboration of details and picturesque Prakriyās in the establishment of his theories. A robust commonsense and a rigid adherence to the tests of truth characterize his logic and epistemology. He does with the barest minimum of metaphysical presuppositions. His theories disclose both realistic and idealistic trends in important respects. He does not shrink from them because of their scholastic affiliations with this or that system of contemporary philosophy. His acceptance of 'Sa-viśeṣābheda' (identity-in-difference) between substance and attributes (in certain cases) and between 'difference' and its substratum (*dharmi*) shows a strong idealistic bent. On the other hand, his rejection of the universal (*sāmānya*) shows an extreme realistic attitude, undreamt of in the Nyāya-Vaiśeṣika and Mīmāṁsā realisms. There is, therefore, little truth in the assumption that "the philosophical side of Madhva's teaching is mainly based on the pre-Madhva Realisms like those of the Nyāya-Vaiśeṣika and Pūrva Mīmāṁsā" or that "he makes a clever use of Nyāya-Vaiśeṣika categories in the development of his views".

Madhva is original in his ontological theory of Svatantra and Paratantra which is the keynote of his philosophy and in his philosophical ideology of a Svatantra Advitīya Brahman, to which it leads. The concept of "Difference" is given an entirely new orientation by the acceptance of "Viśeṣas". Of course, categories and concepts like substance, quality, generality, existence, time, space, causation and the like are the common property of all schools of philosophy. But it is the distinctiveness and merit of their conceptions that mark one philosopher from another. So it is with Madhva. His views on the nature of substance and its relation to the qualities "possessed" by it and on space and time are quite different from those of the Nyāya-Vaiśeṣika and Mīmāṁsā Realists and are in many respects strikingly modern and far ahead of contemporary views. He has four new categories viz. Viśiṣṭa, Aṁśi, Śakti and Sādṛśya, not recognised by the Nyāya-Vaiśeṣika realists. He rejects the Samavāya (inherence) of the Nyāya-Vaiśeṣika realism *in toto*. He makes his Viśeṣas do duty for Samavāya. But his Viśeṣas have nothing *save their name* in common with those of the Nyāya-Vaiśeṣika. Though a Bhedavādin, Madhva does not subscribe to the Nyāya-Vaiśeṣika or the Viśiṣṭādvaitic view that substance and attributes should be absolutely different or externally related (by Samavāya, as in Nyāya). Nor does Madhva accept the Bhāṭṭa view of their identity-cum-difference (bhedābheda) *in all cases*. He dismisses the dogma of *Guṇe guṇānaṅgīkāraḥ*—that a quality cannot reside in another quality—as unproved.[1] He has no use for the universal essence (Jāti) and *anugatasattā* of the Mīmāṁsā and Nyāya schools. He holds a position akin to that of Nominalists that difference and resemblance (*sādṛśya*) are both unique and *sui generis* in each particular, though perceived through a counter-correlate (*pratiyoginirūpya*), thus effectively barring the argument from universals to Monism. He is as much opposed to the Satkāryavāda of the Śāṅkhyas as to the Asatkāryavāda of the Nyāya. He does not agree with the Nyāya that the mind is only inferentially established through non-simultaneity of cognitions.[2] It is to him intuitively established (*sākṣivedya*)—which has great psychological significance.

There are fundamental differences between Madhva and other Realists in respect of the theory of Knowledge and Error, on the question of the sources of validity of knowledge, the

---

1. अस्मत्पक्षे गुणाद्याश्च तद्वन्तो हि विशेषतः । (*AV* ii.2.14)
2. युगपज्ज्ञानानुत्पत्तिर्मनसो लिङ्गम् । (*Nyāyasūtra* i. 1.16)

status of memory as a valid source of knowledge, on the admissibility of indeterminate perception, the nature of the soul, self-consciousness, God and ultimate release. His conception of Śākṣī as the ultimate criterion of all knowledge and its validity is essentially built on Vedāntic foundations. He is concerned more with the philosophical status of the world and the selves than with any qualitative or quantitative analysis of phenomena and their properties as in the Nyāya-Vaiśeṣika or with their physical and intellectual classification of Padārthas. He sets himself, in the spirit of a true philosopher, to discover and elucidate the nature of the highest principle behind the cosmos. The Universe is not self-sufficient or self-important to a Vedāntin, as it may be to a Sāṅkhya or a Naiyāyika. There is nothing to be gained by too much preoccupation with it. It would be enough if it is realised as being at all times dependent on Brahman and controlled by It in all stages of its being and becoming.[3] This is the main point emphasized by all schools of Vedānta from different angles. Madhva also approaches the Universe from this particular angle. The doctrine of the world is only an 'Apara-Siddhānta' or a subsidiary truth (*ānuṣaṅgika*) to the doctrine of Brahman, says Madhva.[4] His system, therefore has its roots in the Aupaniṣada standpoint and cannot be treated as divorced from it. It is true that Vedāntic systems have made extensive use of the categories and thought-measuring devices of the Logical Realism of the Nyāya-Vaiśeṣika. But the metaphysical bearings of Madhva's system cannot be grasped except as a reaction against the different types of Monism which preceded it, such as the pure Monism of Śaṅkara (*nirviśeṣādvaita*), the correlative or intra-organic monism (*viśiṣṭādvaita*) of Rāmānuja and the transmutative Pantheism (*Brahmapariṇāmavāda*) of Vṛttikāra, Bhāskara, Brahmadatta, Yādavaprakāśa and others, within a strictly Vedāntic set-up. Madhva's agreement with non-Vedāntic realisms is in respect of the general principles of empirical realism such as the acceptance of the reality of the world, of difference, the possibility of knowledge,

3. ईशावास्यमिदं सर्वं यत्किंच जगत्यां जगत् । (ĪśaUp 1)

4. **द्विविधः सत्सिद्धान्तः । परापरभेदात्** * * * अनेनापरसिद्धान्तान्तरमाह * * * **उपलक्षणं चैतत् । प्रपंचसत्यत्वादिकमपि ग्राह्यम् ।** (NS p. 518b)

the scheme of Pramāṇas and the dualism of matter and spirit. But the conception, aim and philosophical significance of his categories are quite different from the scholastic tradition of these schools. These have been evolved by Madhva as a result of independent cogitation and critical analysis of the principles and categories of contemporary Vedāntic schools, in the light of materials gathered from an older school of Vedāntic Realism, traces of which are found in the texts from *Brahmatarka* and other sources cited by him. For purposes of logical refutation of other schools, including the Vedāntic, Madhva and his followers have freely drawn upon the dialectical machinery of the Nyāya-Vaiśeṣika and other schools. They have utilized it in self-defence against the Advaita and in refuting the criticisms of the Advaitins themselves on all earlier forms of realistic thought as reoriented in the light of their own special theories. They have also used it in the constructive exposition of their own Siddhānta. This excessive use of Nyāya-Vaiśeṣika methodology of logical dialectics, in the later phases of the Madhva school, *tended, in popular estimation, to give it an air of being an absolute 'Dualism'*, fighting for the reality of every human being and particle of matter in the Universe, *as their birth-right* and *as being of the same* staus as that of the Supreme Being. But the keynote of Madhva's philosophy has always been the acceptance of the ONE INDEPENDENT REAL as the "Parasiddhānta" and all the rest as of secondary importance :

अतो भगवदुत्कर्षं एव सर्वागमानां महातात्पर्यम् । (*MGB* ii. 24)

By applying the doctrine of Saviśeṣābheda to Brahman Madhva preserved its complete homogeneity, without sacrificing the infinite richness of its qualitative content, thereby introducing a more dynamic, colorful conception of Brahman through the doctrine of identity-in- difference, *for the first time in Indian thought*. His theory of "Viśeṣas" is the life-breath of the doctrine of identity-in-difference. Without it, it would be impossible to conceive of an identity-in-difference, *in any school of thought ancient or modern*. Since no other school has accepted "Viśeṣas", the credit for the philosophical conception of "identity-in-difference" should also go to Madhva. This theory of Viśeṣas is his most outstanding contribution to the stock of philosophical ideas in

Indian thought. Its elasticity and resilience to admit of internal distinctions of reference, without the disadvantage of "difference", "difference-cum-identity", "Samavāya" or "fictitious difference" (*kālpanikabheda*), through the inner resources of the substance itself, replaces many worn-out and outmoded conceptions of time, space, causation and creation by more satisfactory ones. This is no small contribution to thought. This will be made clear in appropriate contexts.

In the field of epistemology also Madhva's contributions have been outstanding and in some respects far ahead of his time. His comprehensive definition of 'Pramāṇa' and its clear distinction into 'Kevala' and 'Anu' and, above all, his conception of Sākṣī as the ultimate criterion of all knowledge and validity are front-rank contributions to epistemology. *There is nothing approaching it in any other system of Indian philosophy.* It remains Madhva's unique contribution to the theory of knowledge. Its repercussions on realism in modern thought are sure to be fruitful, if properly exploited. His own realism is thereby established on the firm philosophical foundation of intuitionism instead of an empiricism pure and simple. Similarly, his thesis of *Bimbapratibimbabhāva* between God and soul is a new conception that goes beyond all contemporary attempts to solve the problem of the relation between God and the finite selves. *Bheda* (difference), in the sense of pure exclusion, between Jīva and Brahman has no attraction for Madhva. He is *not satisfied* with a mere external master-and-servant relation between God and soul[5]. God cannot be excluded from the Jīva at any stage of its being. Nor can the individual be completely merged in the Supreme. The only way in which he could retain his individuality of orbit and yet be bound to the Supreme by a natural attraction of being is through the (symbolic) relation of *Bimbapratibimbabhāva*. It is not extinction of individual consciousness in Mokṣa but its sublimation in tune with the Infinite[6] that is at the root

5. Cf. पारतंत्र्य**मात्रो**क्तौ तु राजपुरुषवदेव प्रतीतिः स्यात् ।
(*Jayatīrtha*, *Tdyt* p. 29)

6. Cf. कामेन मे काम आगात् । (*TA* iii.15.2)
नित्यसिद्धत्वात् सादृश्यस्य नित्यानन्दज्ञानादेः, न भक्त्यादिना प्रयोजनमित्यतो ब्रवीति–

of the conception of *Bimbapratibimbabhāva* between the Supreme and the individual. *This touches mysticism at a crucial point.*

It will be seen that Madhva's views on *Svarūpabheda*, *Tāratamya* and *Traividhya* among souls make important contributions to the problem of evil, freedom and freewill. Madhva does not promise *Sarvamukti*. But as a broad hypothesis of human nature and destiny in the widest sense, his views on these questions are not without their strong points, though there may be many other philosophers who may not be disposed to take such a rigid view of the diversity of human nature and destiny. Madhva for his part would argue that the business of philosophy is to tell the truth, whether it pleases or irritates, and not simply to indulge in pious platitudes and pleasant imaginings. His theory of *Jīva-traividhya* is a logically derived conclusion. It goes beyond the commonly accepted explanations of the theory of karma in Vedānta, as an ultimate explanation of the inequalities of life. It points out that if these inequalities of life are to be explained satisfactorily, the theory of Karma, which is supposed to explain such inequalities in equipment and opportunities, must in the last analysis take its stand on certain basic differences in the nature (*svabhāva*) of the souls themselves. The plurality of selves which is experienced by us will have to be grounded in something that is *more fundamental than Prākṛtic vestures and influences including Karma. If that something is not there,* the law of Karma itself would be a cruel joke on humanity. It is *Svarūpabheda* alone that would supply the missing link in the theory of diversity of individual Karma *ab initio*[7]. Madhva has shown great boldness of spirit in detecting the weak point in the conventional theory of Karma as generally advanced in Hindu philosophy and rectifying the deficiency by *filling the gap* in the theory with his doctrine of *Svarūpabheda*, *Tāratamya* and *Traividhya* among souls. Considering the importance of the theory of Karma in Hindu

---

अम्बुवदग्रहणात्तु न तथात्वम् (*BS* iii.2.19) अम्बुवत् स्नेहेन । ग्रहणं ज्ञानम्। भक्ति विना न तत् सादृश्यं सम्यगभिव्यज्यते । (Madhva, *BSB*)

7. सिद्धौ हि कर्मभेदस्य स्यादुपाधिविभिन्नता।
तत्सिद्धौ चैव तत्सिद्धिरित्यन्योऽन्यव्यपाश्रयः।
आत्मस्वभावभेदस्य निर्दोषत्वेन. . . . . . ॥ (Madhva in *UpKh* 10-11)

philosophy, Madhva's emphasis on *Svarūpabheda* of souls as *the* determining factor in the differentiation of their karmas from time immemorial would be seen to put the whole theory of karma in a better and more intelligible light, *for the first time in Indian thought.*

II. ONTOLOGY

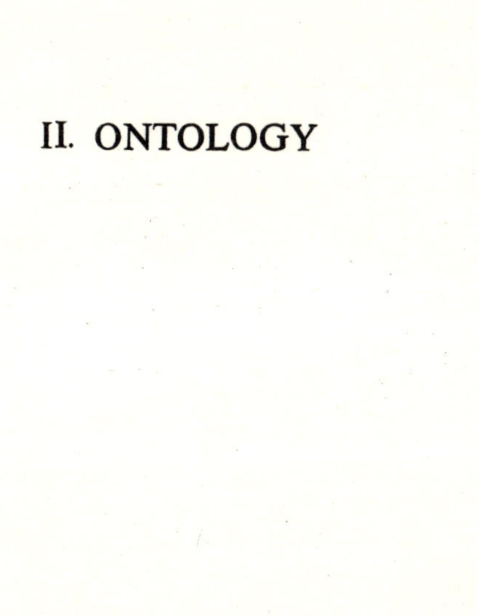

CHAPTER V

MADHVA'S ONTOLOGICAL THEORY

AS already pointed out, in the General Introduction, Madhva's ontology turns upon the two principal ideas of being—reality and independence. The former presents the idea of reality expressed in space-time relations, pertaining to the world of matter and souls. The latter is the higher aspect of reality which is characteristic of the Deity alone. Reality in the ordinary sense of the term may consist in one or more of the three aspects of existence, consciousness and activity:

स्वरूपप्रमितिप्रवृत्तिलक्षणं सत्तात्रैविध्यम्

as Jayatīrtha refers to them. The idea is found in other systems also as in Advaita where existence (*asti*), consciousness (*bhāti*), and bliss (*priyam*) are appropriated to Brahman (*brahmarūpam*)[1] or in Buddhism which defines phenomenal reality (*paratantra-satyam*) in terms of practical efficiency (*arthakriyākāritvam*).

CRITERION OF REALITY

The criterion of reality according to Madhva is that it should be unsuperimposed and given as an object of valid knowledge, as existing at some point of time and in some place.[2]

The tortoise's hair, though unsuperimposed and unsuperimposable for want of its prototype, is not however a reality as it is not presented as existing at some time or place, to anybody's valid knowledge. The two ideas, of being unsuperimposed and

---

1. अस्ति भाति प्रियं रूपं नाम चेत्यंशपञ्चकम् ।
आद्यं त्रयं ब्रह्मरूपं जगद्रूपं ततो द्वयम् ॥ (*Dṛgdṛśyaviveka*, 20)

2. अनारोपितं प्रमितिविषयः । प्रमितिशब्देन सत्त्वाकारोल्लेखित्वमत्र विवक्षितम् ।
(Vyāsatīrtha, *TV Mandāramañjarī*, p. 2)

being given as an object of valid knowledge as existing in some place and time, are thus complementary and are implicit in Madhva's definition of reality (*tattvam*) given by him as '*Prameyam*'[3] in his *TV* as explained by Jayatīrtha in his Commentary on it.

Vyāsatīrtha points out in his *Mandāramañjarī* how the condition of being unsuperimposed is sufficient to preclude the objective content of an erroneous experience such as that of silver in shell from being admitted to be 'real':

प्रतीयमानत्वसामान्यस्य अनारोपितपदसन्निधानात् निषिद्धभ्रान्तिविषयत्वरूपविशेषपर्यवसानायोगात्, प्रमाविषयत्वरूपविंशेषपर्यंवसानात् ।

Dr. K. Narain's finding in his work entitled *A Critique of the Mādhva Refutation of Śaṅkara-Vedānta* (Udayana Publications, Allahabad, 1964), p. 15 that "the criterion of reality according to Madhva always consists in being an object of experience" or that his definition of reality is "extensive to include the facts of illusion which nevertheless are objects of experience" and that "Madhva's criterion of reality, originally contemplated as consisting in objectively to experience, has been slightly modified by Vyāsatīrtha" *are all due to a complete misunderstanding of Madhva's correct position and reading his own ideas into Madhva's words.*

In the first place, it will be seen from the opening words of Madhva in his *TV* that he proposes to equate 'tattvam' and 'prameyam'. And *pramā* is universally understood in the sense of valid knowledge or valid experience and to *exclude invalid knowledge and experience.* When *the same Madhva* defines 'tattvam' in his other work (the *TS*) as 'anāropitam' he should naturally be understood to mean by it what is an object of valid knowledge (*pramitiviṣayaḥ*), consistent with his other rendering of *tattvam as prameyam.*[4]

Dr. Narain's confusion of thought is probably due to his allowing himself to be carried away by the superficial sense of

---

3. प्रमेयं द्विविधं मतम् । (Madhva in *TV*)

4. यदि नाम कूर्मरोमादिकमप्यनारोपितं, किं तावता "तत्त्वम्" स्यादित्यतः **प्रतीतौ सत्यामिति** वाच्यम् । तच्च 'प्रमेयम्' इति च एकोऽर्थः ।

(Jayatīrtha in *Tvt*, p. 1).

the adjunct '*pratīti*' used by Jayatīrtha in his commentary "*pratītau satyām iti vācyam*", and drawing the hasty conclusion from it that Madhva is or was at any time satisfied with the criterion of reality as consisting in merely being an object of experience, without taking care to define whether the said experience is a valid one or *not* and remaining unmindful of his definition becoming "extensive to include the facts of illusion, which nevertheless are objects of experience".

Dr. Narain could have avoided this pitfall, *if, instead of following his own light*, he had allowed himself to be guided by Vyāsatīrtha as to how in the context of Madhva's definition, the adjunct *pratīti-viṣayatvam* supplied by Jayatīrtha, has necessarily to be interpreted in the sense of *pramāviṣayatvam* or being the object of a *valid knowledge or experience.*

The purpose of Vyāsatīrtha's suggesting a negative definition of reality (in his *Nym*) is *not*, therefore, to save Madhva's definition of '*anāropitam pramitiviṣayaḥ*' from any overpervasion in respect of objects of erroneous experience, as Dr. Narain persists in supposing but quite a different one, viz. to formulate an alternative definition of reality from Madhva's point of view, which would bring it under the scope of the criterion of "non-contradiction", also, thereby establishing that the criterion of reality as uncontradictedness is not the exclusive property or monopoly of the Advaitavādin and that it is perfectly applicable to Madhva's criterion of reality too, in terms of *trikāla sarvadeśīyaniṣedha-apratiyogitvam*".[5]

Advaita talks of *Bādha* or contradiction of experience of the world in terms of *traikālika-niṣedhapratiyogitvam*. Madhva has given his own definition of *Bādha* which is purely epistemological :

विज्ञातस्यान्यथा सम्यग्विज्ञानं ह्येव तन्मतम् ।

or as a correct cognition of what has been known *otherwise than* as it is (*anyathā vijñātasya samyag vijñānam bādhaḥ*)—i.e. to say a correct knowledge replacing an earlier distorted one.

Explaining this Jayatīrtha writes in his *Vādāvali* that such correcting knowledge is possible in Dvaita philosophy in respect

5. which signifies : not being the counter-correlate of a negation of the thing in question, with reference to all the three periods of time and all places.

of the misconception of the world's nature as 'indescribable' (*anirvacanīya*) as contended by the Advaitin, coming to be corrected by the true knowledge of its nature as a reality existing in time and space, though, not for ever. But Dr. Narain goes beyond this and speaks, with a knowing air, of "a belief in Mādhva philosophy" that "the transitory knowledge of the world is *contradicted* and removed by the eternal knowledge of the Lord and other entities" (*op. cit.* p. 14). This astonishing statement is probably due to a (bad) rendering of Jayatīrtha's words :

क्षणिकत्वादिना विज्ञातस्य प्रपंचस्य, अक्षणिकत्वादिना बाधकज्ञान-विषयत्वस्य अस्माभिरङ्गीकारात्।

But they do not lend themselves to the translation given by Dr. Narain. What Jayatīrtha has actually said is that the definition of Bādha in terms of *Anyathā vijñātasya samyag vijñānam* can be applied to the misconception of the world as being momentary (*kṣaṇika*) or unreal (*mithyā*) engendered by the propaganda of Nihilists and Monists, when such distorted knowledge comes to be set aside by the correct knowledge of its being *not* momentary (*akṣaṇika*) and *not* unreal (*amithyā*) but durable (*sthira*) and real (*satya*). That the contradicting knowledge (*bādha*) here does not *annul* the object of misconception would follow from Jayatīrtha's clear explanation of Madhva's words : *Vijñātasya anyathā samyag vijñānam bādhaḥ.* The correcting knowledge in regard to the misconception of the world in the instances cited could not affect the *reality* of the world or the Jīvas, as such, in Madhva's philosophy. That is what the Advaitin is bent upon establishing. Dr. Narain's attempts to make it appear that Bādha or contradiction *in the Advaitic sense is acceptable to Mādhva philosophy* is a lamentable distortion of the truth. Had Dr. Narain looked up Rāghavendra Tīrtha's commentary on Jayatīrtha's *Vādāvali* he would have known the correct position:

अनिर्वाच्यत्व-क्षणिकत्व-ब्रह्माकार्यत्वादिना पूर्वं विज्ञातस्य, विशेषदर्शनानन्तरं सत्यत्व-ध्रुवत्व-ब्रह्मकार्यत्वादिना ज्ञातत्वांगीकारात् ।

Dr. Narain, however, *repeats* his finding in the third paragraph of p. 14 of his book about "the transitory existence of the world being contradicted in the philosophy (of Madhva) by the right and eternal knowledge of the Lord". He should know that in the Advaita theory, *Bādha* as applied to the world involves liquidation of the world (*dharmi*) as such.[6] But in the Dvaita view there is no liquidation of the world by the knowledge of Brahman, but only a correct assessment of its *status* as a reality depending on Brahman for its existence, activity and cognisedness, as along as it lasts in space and time.

In this connection Dr. Narain has torn one of Madhva's statement in his *Tdy*:

प्रत्यक्षबाधितं च जगन्मिथ्यात्वम्; सदिति प्रतीयमानत्वात् ।

from its context and has proceeded to read his own meaning into it, *viz.* that the criterion of reality according to Madhva always consists "in being the object of experience". The statement quoted from Madhva is neither a definition of reality nor does it make it "extensive to include the facts of illusion which are nonetheless objects of experience" (*op. cit.* p. 15). Such a fallacious contention is the outcome of not taking into account the distinction so clearly drawn in Madhva's philosophy between valid and invalid experience.[7] For, further down in his *Tdy* Madhva goes on (by way of explaining his earlier statement : *Na ca pratyakṣadṛṣṭam anyena kenāpi bādhyam dṛṣṭam* quoted by Dr. Narain) to point out :

चन्द्रप्रादेशत्वादिविषयं तु, दूरस्थत्वादिदोषयुक्तत्वादपटु । न च जगत्प्रत्यक्षस्यापटुत्वे किंचिन्मानम् ।

that a perception can only be corrected by a more powerful valid perception. This recognises the existence of superficial perceptions (such as the perception of the limited size of the moon) which are erroneous. But there is no reason to doubt the soundness of our perceptual experience of the reality of the world. Thus, Madhva's definition of reality as *anāropitam* culminating in *pramitiviṣayaḥ* or being an object of valid knowledge does not require to be modified by Vyāsatīrtha to prevent its over-pervasion or "extensiveness to include the facts of illusions" as Dr. Narain persists in thinking and trying to make out.

---

6. अविद्या सह कार्येण नासीदस्ति भविष्यति ।

7. Even the *Tarkasaṅgraha* of Annambhaṭṭa writes:
स (अनुभवो) द्विविधः, यथार्थोऽयथार्थश्च ।

The *Advaitasiddhi* has objected to Vyāsatīrtha's definition of the real त्रिकालसर्वदेशीयनिषेधाप्रतियोगित्वम् on the technical ground that the counterpositive of an absolute negation for all time and space as envisaged by his definition is beyond the range of human perception. The absence of such a negation, in its turn, must be still more so.

The *Nyāyāmṛta-Taraṅgiṇī* has, in reply, cited the perceptual judgment *Ghaṭe ākāśatvābhāvaḥ* in support of the possibility of such a cognition without the perception of the counterpositive of the negation. The absence of negation with reference to *Trikālasarvadeśa* (the three periods of time and all space) can certainly be perceived in the world *in the sense of* difference or reciprocal negation (*anyonyābhava*). In such a case, the perception of the locus (*adhikaraṇa*) of the absence in question is sufficient for the perception of the absence of the thing negated, as in 'the pillar is *not* the ghost (*stambhaḥ piśāco na*) :

निषेधाप्रतियोगित्वमित्यत्र अन्योन्याभाव एव नञर्थतया विवक्षितः। एवं च, प्रकृते, अन्योन्याभावाधिकरणस्य घटादिजगतो योग्यत्वात् तन्निष्ठं सार्वदैशिकसार्वकालिकनिषेधप्रतियोगिभिन्नत्वरूपं सत्त्वं **प्रत्यक्षयोग्यमेव**, इति न कोऽपि दोषः। (Śrīnivāsa : Commentary on *Nym* 1.9)

Thus, both the terms in the definition of *Tattvam*, are necessary to have an adequate conception of the real. The second term bars the possibility of a real existing somewhere, without being given as an actual psychological fact in immediate apprehension, such as "a comet rushing through, space, entirely unbeheld". For, Madhva, like Bradley, would argue that the real is present to the mind of God as a system of presentations, even when our perception of it is suspended or is not there or even in respect of realities which no human subject perceives.[8] Madhva derives this doctrine from his interpretation of the Upaniṣadic text *Tam eva bhāntam anubhāti sarvam* (*MundUp* ii.2.10). This is the implication of his doctrine that all acts of consciousness (*pramiti*) by the dependent selves are ultimately dependent on God's (*pramitau parādhīnam*). He would not, therefore, agree with the view of modern realists that the fundamental characteristic of what is real lies in its independence of

---

8. विश्वमीश्वरः सदा पश्यति, तेनेदं न मायेत्यवधार्यताम् । (Madhva, *Tdy*).

all relation to the experience of a subject. That is the reason why Madhva rejects the definition of Svayamprakāśatva in Advaita as 'unknowability as an object of knowledge" (*avedyatvam*). The existence of the Ātman must be a part of an experience of the Ātman itself: *Na ca svaprakāśatvam api vinā mānaṃ siddhyati*. The failing of intuitionism is that it offers no account of the way in which things are known. The addition of the explanatory adjunct "intuitively" (*svaprakāśatvena*) seems only to deny an explanation though seeming to give one.

प्रमाणाभावे, सत्यत्वं न स्यादित्यस्य, 'प्रमाणेन विना सिद्ध्यती'त्यस्यानुत्तरत्वात्; सिद्ध्युपायान्तरस्यानुपन्यस्तत्वात्। (*VTNt* p. 96 b)

To the contention that the reality of a thing cannot be established in the absence of any proof of its reality, it is no answer to say that it is established without the aid of any source of knowledge. Even 'self-evidence' as self-evidence, must admit of a subject-object relationship in its operation. And that will confirm the position that the self is open to Sākṣi-Pratyakṣa (which is one of the Pramāṇas).

APPEARANCE AND REALITY

Madhva's definition of reality raises the question of the nature and implications of "reality". Is mere existence 'reality' ? Or is real existence in space and time; or else real existence *for all time* and through all space ? It is here that the issue assumes its familiar philosophical aspect. We have here one of the dividing lines of philosophical systems which splits them into different schools. Śaṅkara's approach to metaphysics is said to lie in his making *a philosophical distinction* between existence and reality, as against the commonsense view that accepts surface phenomena as real. "If all that occurs or what we perceive were true, there, would be no false appearances. Dissatisfaction with the first view of things is the mother of all philosophy. While commonsense accepts surface-phenomena as real, reflective thinking asks if the first view is also the final view. The purpose of philosophy is to distinguish the unreal from the real, the transient from the eternal".[9] This distinction between the existent and the real is the point of departure between physics and metaphysics. The Platonic distinction of the

9. Dr. S. Radhakrishnan, *I Phil.* II, p. 527

actual and the ideal, the matter of the Milesians, Empedoclean element, Pythagorean numbers, all these represent the persistent attempts of philosophers all through the ages, to locate the real behind the apparent. No philosopher would be worth his salt, if he did not undertake such an analysis into the nature of being. Modern philosophy has been dallying with the same problems for centuries, under different names. Descartes and Spinoza were both obsessed with it. Wolff and Kant merely changed the names and opposed 'phenomena' to 'noumena'. Hegelian philosophy distinguished 'being' from 'existence'. Modern Science also has its own theories of phenomena as the splitting up of electric energy.[10]

The distinction is not, however, the monopoly of idealistic thinkers. Madhva, as a result, readily admits the criticism of Bradley that between recognizing a datum and blindly recognizing its content as a reality, there is a world of difference. There is room in experience for both truth and illusions[11]. Our senses need not always be veridical.

Appearance is not reality. But there is no reason why existence should not be. Even the critical philosopher like Kant, in holding that the thing-in-itself cannot be objectively known, would appear to recognize objective experience as a reality. To say that the objects do not *exist* simply because they do not *persist*, is an unwarranted perversion of logic. It involves a confusion between opposites and distincts. Distinction is not denial. If an object perceived in a given setting does not exist at another place and time, we cannot rush to the conclusion that it is unreal. Existence, then, *is* a test of reality. Madhva would define "satyam" as existence at (some) time and place (किंचित्कालसंबन्धित्वं) and not necessarily as *existence for all time and throughout space* (सर्वदेशकालसंबन्धित्वं). *Actual existence* at some time and place is sufficient to distinguish the real from the unreal (त्रैकालिकनिषेधप्रतियोगि) which cannot be said to *really exist* at the time and place of its

10. *op. cit.* II. p. 521.

11. cf. भ्रमेऽप्यभ्रमभागोऽस्ति । (*AV* iii.4.41)
अनादौ संसारे, इन्द्रियलिंगशब्दजन्येषु ज्ञानेषु द्वयीं गतिमनुसन्दधत्....।
(*NS* p. 218 b)

appearance (or at any other), save in our distorted imagination. The unreal has no *actual existence* in time or space, though it may *appear* to have it. Such an appearance is indeed the characteristic mark of unreality :

असतः सत्त्वेन प्रतीतिर्हि भ्रान्तिः ।

The Advaitic dialecticians are disloyal to experience in denying that the unreal *can* appear *as the real*, immediately *in error*. We can have no conception of the unreal in error, apart from such appearance:

असतः ख्यातिं निषेधतः तत्ख्यातिरभूत् न वा; यद्यभूत् न तत्ख्यातिनिषेधः । यदि नाभूत् तथापि । (Madhva, *GT* ii. 26)

We are, however, concerned here with actual facts. Saṅkara admits that the illusory snake in the rope has no actual existence at any time: **नहि** रज्ज्वां भ्रान्तिबुद्धया कल्पितः सर्पो **विद्यमानः** सन् निवर्तते (Commentary on *GK*, i, 17).

Illusions, then, arise when the non-existent appears as existent and *vice versa* : यदविद्यमानं रूपं, तस्य सत्त्वेन प्रतीतेरेव भ्रान्तित्वात् । (Madhva, *GT* ii.26)

This is borne out by own experience and no useful purpose will be served in trying to escape it by dialectic ingenuity.

The second test of reality recognized by Madhva is: *arthakriyākāritvam* (practical efficiency). One cannot make vessels out of the illusory silver in the nacre. Even where an illusory appearance of a snake in the rope is found to produce certain reactions of fear and the like, there is always a definite modicum of reality behind it:

सर्पभ्रमादावपि हि ज्ञानमस्त्येव तादृशम् ।
तदेवार्थक्रियाकारि तत् संदेवार्थकारकम् ॥ (*AV* i. 4. 11)

It is not the "snake" that causes the fear or worse reactions; but the "consciousness" of there being a snake due to the rope itself mistaken for a snake, forming the qualifying adjunct of the psychosis. So far as that particular psychological experience is concerned, there is not the slightest difference in the intensity of feeling between it and that of an actual experience of a snake in daylight. The "snaky-feeling" may be overcome soon afterwards; but it exists for the time being and that alone is the cause of fear, not the non-existent *snake*.[12]

The real, then, is neither necessarily momentary (*kṣaṇika*) nor necessarily eternal, as the Buddhists and the Advaitins assume, in their respective theories of truth (यत्सत् तत्क्षणिकम्; अबाधितं सत्यम्). Śaṁkara posits that the real must be so *for all time*. This is metaphysically-motivated. It is not an epistemological or a logical deduction:

नहि सता सकलदेशकालसता भाव्यमिति नियामकमस्ति ।

(*NS* p. 207b)

This is the Madhva view of the matter and it cannot be dismissed as unreasonable. As a matter of fact, even those entities whose reality is *limited* to a particular period of time or place, can be reckoned to be real within the meaning of the dictum : त्रैकालिकनिषेधाप्रतियोगित्वं सत्त्वम्, for, what actually is at a given time and place, cannot admit of *absolute negation with reference to all periods of time and all places*: नहि विनाशो बाधः, अपितु, कालत्रयसत्तानिषेधः । न ह्येकस्मिन् काले सतः, स सम्भवति । (*VTNt* p. 95)

Its present existence must be admitted; though it may cease to exist the next hour or day. The Mādhva doctrine of truth reminds us of the timelessness of truth as a logical content propounded by Plato. Reality, then, consists simply in actual 'relation to time and place': 'वास्तवदेशकालसंबन्धित्वम्, which cannot be predicated of unrealities like hare's horn. The Mādhva conception of reality is thus a *via media* between the extreme momentariness (*kṣaṇikatva*) of Buddhists and the eternalism of Advaitins. Madhva endorses the Nyāya view that a thing is real so long as it is assignable to a definite space-time setting and not simply so long as it *appears to be*. The immediate corollary of such a position is that the doctrine of tripartite classification of reality (Sattātraividhya) in Advaita, into absolute, practical and apparent (पारमार्थिक, व्यावहारिक, and प्रातिभासिक), is a myth. The Mādhva definition of reality as Anāropitam (अनारोपितम्) is intended to show that the so-called Vyāvahārika and

---

12. **तज्ज्ञानस्यैव** भयकंपादिजनकत्वात् । सर्पतया ज्ञातरज्जोरेव विशेषणत्वेन, व्यभिचाराभावात् । सर्पाजन्यत्वाच्च । (*Vādāvali*, p. 49)
Cf. also Śaṅkara.

यद्यपि, स्वप्नदर्शनावस्थस्य सर्पदर्शनोदकस्नानादिकार्यंजातमनृतं तथापि **तदवगतिः सत्यमेव ।**

(*BS* ii.2.14)

Prātibhāsika are *not realities* in the true sense of the term. All existents that are not superimposed (*anāropitam*) are absolutely real (पारमार्थिकसत्य). The "Vyāvahārika" and the "Prātibhāsika" 'reals', are both admittedly falsifiable (*bādhya*), the one earlier and the other later :

न च वियदादिप्रपंचस्याप्यात्यन्तिकं सत्त्वमस्ति। प्राक् तु ब्रह्मात्मदर्शनात् वियददादिप्रपंचो व्यवस्थितरूपो भवति। सन्ध्याश्रयस्तु प्रपंचः प्रतिदिनं बाध्यत इति। (Śaṅkara, *BSB* iii.2.4).

They are, as such, both equally unreal and have no common ground with the Pāramārthika, which is *never sublated.* As Kumārila puts it, there can be no common ground between the false and the true, to justify the distinction of degrees between them or their being brought under a single category of thought :

सत्यत्वं न च सामान्यं मृषार्थपरमार्थयोः। (*Ślokavārtika*)

We may speak of the *opposition* of real and the unreal; but *not* of internal degrees of *reality* between the real and the unreal. We may speak of a man and his shadow; but not of a real man and a shadow man. It would be as ridiculous, if not more, to speak of the truly real, the falsely real (*vyāvahārika*), and the still more falsely real (*prātibhāsika-satya*).

There being then, only two possible modes of predication acceptable to logic, Madhva is unable to concede any *tertium quid* between reality and unreality. X is either real or unreal. It is a misuse of language to call it provisionally real (व्यावहारिक) : कालान्तरेऽप्यमानं चेदिदानीं मानता कुतः ? asks Madhva. The unreal cannot, by any stretch of the imagination, be accepted as real, in serious thought : *Nāsato vidyate bhāvaḥ.* Such an attempt can only be treated as a piece of sophistry or a perversion of thought calculated to mislead the unwary :

सत्या चेत् संवृतिः केयं मृषा चेत् सत्यता कथम् ?
सत्यत्वं न च सामान्यं मृषार्थपरमार्थयोः।
वञ्चनार्थमुपन्यासो लालावक्त्रासवादिवत्॥

(Kumārila, *Ślokavārtika*)

Madhva therefore rejects the concept of "Mithyātva" as a *tertium quid* as quite unproved and equates it with absolute negation or unreality :

Mithyāśabdastvabhāvavācyeva. Tadanyatra pramāṇābhāvāt. (*KN*)

The Advaitins have from the beginning been trying to distinguish between the two; but to Madhva it is a distinction without a difference.[13]

Gradation of Reality

Though existence is thus 'reality', Madhva recognizes that its highest expression must be metaphysical independence of every other form of existence in finite reality, in respect of its being, powers and activity. The reason for this has already been made clear. Everything in finite reality is therefore grounded in the Independent Reality, known as Brahman and needs it for its being and becoming. For this reason, the Independent Real has been described in the Vedānta as "the Real of the reals" (*satyasya satyam—BrhUp* ii. 3) and *Nityo nityānām*—Eternal of the eternals" (*KaṭhaUp* ii. 2.13).

Existence is but one aspect of reality. It does not exhaust it. Nor is it the highest or fullest expression of it. As Dawes Hicks puts it so well, "There is no mystery whatsoever about the notion of pure being. Being is simply the fundamental category of thought which denotes everything and cannot, therefore, specially denote anything,—in other words, connotes nothing. That which every entity is, cannot be a property by which one entity could be distinguished from the others. God, whatever else He is, must certainly *be*. But so must a triangle or a pebble in the street, a planet or the Sun. In short, there is no being which is simply and purely, being. It is what God is *over and above mere being* that is of primary significance to the religious consciousness" (*Philosophical Bases of Theism*. p. 117).

While existence in space and time is thus reality and is possessed by the world of matter and souls, there must be something more than mere existence, having metaphysical independence or substantiality in its own right which we may agree to designate as the highest real or the philosophical Absolute which would be the ultimate explanation of all else. Such independent reality

---

13. तस्मात् स्वरूपेण त्रैकालिकनिषेधप्रतियोगित्वे, अत्यन्तासत्त्वं दुर्वारम् । (*Nym* i.1) For a full disscussion of this question see *NS* and *Nym* and my *HDSV* pp. 350-51.

should be immanent in the universe, whence the latter could derive and draw its sustenance. Without presupposing such a basic and transcendental reality that would have to be immanent in the world, there would be chaos and disorder in the universe. Madhva makes a strong plea for recognizing such a principle :

1. अधिष्ठानमिति प्राहुर्मूलाधारं विचक्षणाः ।
यत्स्थितं दृश्यते वस्तु संस्थानं तदुदीरितम् ।
उभयं हरिरेवास्य जगतो मुनिपुङ्गव ॥ (*BT* ii. 5.2)

2. द्रव्यं कर्म च कालश्च स्वभावो जीव एव च ।
यदनुग्रहतः सन्ति न सन्ति यदुपेक्षया ॥ (*Bhāg* ii.10.12)

3. स्वभावसत्तादातृत्वं यन्तृत्वमिति कीर्त्यते । (*BrhUp* iii.7)

4. सत्ता प्रधानपुरुषशक्तीनां च प्रतीतयः ।
प्रवृत्तयश्च ताः सर्वा नित्यं नित्यात्मना यतः ।
शक्तीस्ताः प्रेरयत्यंजः तदधीनाश्च सर्वदा ॥ (*AV* ii.2.5)

5. कालकर्मस्वभावादि नित्ययेश्वरेच्छया ।
प्राप्तमेव विशेषेण सृष्ट्यादावुन्नयत्यजः ॥ (*BT* ii.5.21)

6. यद्यपि नित्यत्वं जीवस्याप्यस्ति, तथापि सर्वप्रकारेण
अविनाशित्वं विष्णोरेवेति । (*GT* ii.7)

7. दधिस्थघृतवत् काष्ठे वह्निवच्च जनार्दनः ।
देहेन्द्रियासुजीवेभ्यो विविच्य ज्ञायते न तु ॥ (*BT* vii. 1.9)

This is quite a new point of view in the interpretation of Upaniṣadic thought, for which Madhva should get due credit. It is not, of course, new in the sense of its having been unknown to the Upaniṣadic tradition. What is meant is that Madhva was the pioneer to penetrate into the tangled mass of Vedic and Post-Vedic literature and rediscover, refine and rehabilitate the point of view and give it a proper exposition.

सत्त्वं स्वातंत्र्यमुद्दिष्टं तच्च कृष्णे न चापरे ।
अस्वातंत्र्यात् तदन्येषामसत्त्वं विद्धि...॥ (*BT* XI.19.16)
वस्तु स्वतंत्रमुद्दिष्टं अस्वतंत्रमवस्तु च
स्वाधीनं सदिति प्रोक्तं पराधीनमसत् स्मृतम् ॥ (*BT* XI.26.2)

Such statements as the above are not intended to deny the reality of the world in the actual sense of the word. They are intended to emphasize the dependent nature of everything in the cosmos on Brahman.[14] It is a mystic approach and parallels to it can be found in the writings of mystics all over the world. St. Augustine's famous pronouncement in this strain has already been quoted in Chapter III. They show how monistic descriptions in exuberant language are to be understood and interpreted. Independence is philosophical "self-determination" which is explained almost in the same terms as the substantiality of Spinoza, as a *res campleta* which gives meaning and completion to everything else. This idea is contained in the classical definition of "Svatantra" put forward by Jayatīrtha :

स्वरूपप्रमितिप्रवृत्तिलक्षणसत्तात्रैविध्ये परानपेक्षम् ।

Madhva says that from the highest point of view, even sentience is synonymous with independence :

स्वेच्छानुसारितामेव स्वातंत्र्यं हि विदो विदुः । (*AV* ii.2.1)

inasmuch as "self-determination" is the real mark of sentience:[15]

चेतनत्वं स्वतंत्रं स्यात् स चैको विष्णुरेव हि । (*BT*)

The insentient (*jaḍa*) is so because it cannot act of its own accord (स्वतःप्रवृत्त्यशक्त). Inasmuch as the human souls are *not independent* existents, knowers and agents, in a philosophical sense, they are regarded by Madhva as so many "Reflections", Images, or "Ābhāsas" of the Supreme Reality, in the sense that all their powers are rooted in the Supreme Source and derived from it, (नहि प्रतिबिंबस्य क्रिया, स हि बिम्बक्रिययैव क्रियावान्[16]—*GB* ii. 19) like the reflected light of the moon.[17]

---

14. Cf. न राजादीनामिव **नियामकत्वमात्र**मन्तर्यामित्वम् अपितु, सत्तादिप्रदत्वमित्युक्तं भवति । (*NS* p. 166)

15. Cf. ज्ञानमेव हीच्छाजनकम् । सेच्छं चेदंगीकृतं तदा तदचेतनं किं? चेतनमेवेत्यर्थः । अचेतनमपि प्रधानं स्वातंत्र्येण प्रवृत्तिमदस्त्विति वदता अचेतनमिच्छावत् अस्त्वित्युक्तं स्यात् । स्वेच्छानुसारित्वस्य स्वातंत्र्यशब्दार्थंतया सर्वसंमतत्वात् ।अचेतनस्येच्छावत्त्वमंगीकुर्वाणेन चेतनत्वमप्यंगीकर्त्तव्यं स्यात् । (*NS*)

16. Meaning : बिंबाधीनक्रिययैव ।

17. Cf. को ह्येवान्यात् कः प्राण्यात् यदेष आकाश आनन्दो न स्यात् ?
TaittUp (ii.7) ; *Gīta*, xv.12

While the Independent Real is thus the ultimate presupposition of all philosophy, the dependent reals embody the justification and proof of the independent. Though the independence of God is not seriously disputed by other schools of thought, its significance and philosophical necessity have not been so well brought out, as in the system of Madhva. It is not as a concession to religious prejudice or a fashionable belief that Madhva accepts the Svatantra as the highest expression of reality. It is the warp and woof of all metaphysics. The Advaitic Brahman, being *ex hypothesi* attributeless (*nirdharmaka*) and static, could not be spoken of as "Svatantra" within the definition of

स्वरूपप्रमितिप्रवृत्तिलक्षणसत्तात्रैविध्ये परानपेक्षम् । (*TSt*)

The Viśiṣṭādvaitic Brahman being *ex hypothesi* an intra-organic unity (*Viśiṣṭaikyarūpa*) cannot be shown to be superior to its modes of Cit and Jaḍa or *independent of them* (*Parānapekṣa*), so long as the system is committed to their reciprocal dependence of Śeṣaśeṣibhāva and its corollary of the "contribution theory" of mutual advantage between the two[18], held by at least a section[19] of the Rāmānuja school. Rāmānuja himself rises above such necessity in one context (under *GB* ix. 4) and Vedānta Deśika openly endorses Madhva's view, as already pointed out and thus abandons the position believed to be characteristic of the Rāmānuja school that "the difference of parts of God, as matter and souls, always existed and there is no part of Him which is truer *and more ultimate than this*" (Dasgupta, *I. Phil.* iii, p. 200). If this is so, Madhva's stand would by no means be redundant or superfluous.

The independence of God and His freedom from all imperfections is very much compromised in the Pantheistic philosophies of Bhāskara, Yādavaprakāśa and Nimbārka, so long as these systems adhere to the actual transformation of the Brahman-stuff, whether wholly, directly, or in part, or indirectly, even, through its existential aspect (*sacchakti*) or energy-aspect (*cicchakti*). They lead to a great disruption of moral experience of

---

18. *Tattvamuktākalāpa*, p. 255.

19. Teṅgalais. See also passage from *Nītimālā* quoted *ante* Chapter III. fn. 4

remorse and responsibility. Logical Pantheism is inconsistent with our ideals of goodness and evil. God is perfect. As His personal effects, whatever and whoever exists must also be perfect. But such pantheistic unity is disproved by the inevitable presuppositions of human life. Our instincts refuse to accept that evil is good and to see the Deity in disorder, virtue in crime, truth in error. Nor can our evaluations of truth and error be dismissed as illusory. If the events of the world are the modes of God, how can they be illusory ?

We find the same inability to rise and stick to the high level of the independence of God or the Absolute and the necessary dependence of the entire Universe on God , in the non-Vedāntic Theistic systems like the Nyāya-Vaiśeṣika and Yoga. Their limitations in this respect have already been made clear (See reference in *NS* p. 329, quoted *ante* in Chapter III). Even the eternality of the atoms, admitted by the Nyāya-Vaiśeṣikas, could not be exempted from the sway of the Deity.

There is no need to suppose that what is eternal cannot possibly be 'dependent' on another. Let us take a non-eternal object like a pot. It is not a matter of 'accident' that such objects are non-eternal. Their non-eternality or impermanence is 'determined' by some reason. Otherwise, they may as well be destroyed the very next moment after coming into being. Similarly, what is wrong if one should suppose that the eternality of eternal substances is also 'determined' by a governing principle or power. Surely, we do not find the non-eternal objects forgoing their non-eternality and becoming eternal just because their non-eternality is *determined* by another principle. It is the nature of the non-eternal to be destroyed sooner or later. In the same way, even where an eternal substance is 'determined' by another, there is no fear of its losing its eternality and becoming non-eternal by the caprice of the determining principle. For the governing principle will maintain and guarantee the *status quo* of the other as an eternal entity for all time. There is, therefore, nothing illogical or inconceivable in maintaining that eternal Padārthas (entities) also are dependent on God just like the non-eternal or impermanent entities.[20]

---

20. नित्यस्य पराधीनतासंभवादित्यत आह—**नित्यमिति** । यथाहि घटादयोऽनित्यस्वभावा

The reality of the universe is thus, in Madhva's opinion, an important philosophical accessory (*ānuṣaṅgika*) to the realisation of the ideology of the Svatantratattva. He cannot, therefore, be charged with an obsession for the reality of the world and of five-fold difference (*pañcabheda*), as some critics have done. Jayatīrtha puts Madhva's attitude to the world in its proper perspective, by referring to the doctrine of the reality of the world as a "subsidiary metaphysical doctrine" or "Aparasiddhānta" (*NS* p. 538 b).[21] The world is not important *in itself* to the Dvatia philosopher.

परतंत्रप्रमेयं हि स्वतंत्रायत्ततया विदितं निःश्रेयसाय भवति । अन्यथा, गंगावालुकापरिगणनवत् इदं तत्त्वसंख्यानमपार्थकं स्यात् । (*TSt*)

Madhva is no theological dualist. There is no place in his new creation theory of "Sadasatkāryavāda" or 'eternal creation' through "Parādhīnaviśeṣāpti" for the "Oriental Augustinian monarchotheistic" idea of creation at a certain date by the sheer fiat of God out of fathomless *nothing*.

Paradoxically enough, Madhva admits the creation of eternal substance also in a *Pickwickian sense* of "Parādhīna-Viśeṣāpti", which will be explained later. Real creation, in his view, means such an *eternal dependence* of the world of matter and souls on God, as would involve their non-existence in the event of God's Will to that effect. His Will is the essential condition and sustaining principle that invests them with their reality and without which they would be but void names and bare possibilities. The scientific value of Madhva's doctrine of "Parādhīna-Viśeṣāpti" will be evident when it is contrasted, for a moment, with the fact that Biblical Chronology in the West fixed the date of Creation of the world at 4004 B.C. Geology has since vastly extended cosmic time. But although the actual date may be pushed back indefinitely, the view of creation as an event

---

अपि नाकस्मादनित्या भवन्ति । तथा सत्युत्पत्त्युत्तरक्षण एव विनाशप्रसंगात् । एवं नित्यस्यापि नित्यता यदि पराधीना, तदा को दोषः ? न चानित्यता पराधीनेति कदाचित् घटादेर्नित्यता प्राप्ता ! विनाश-कारणोपनिपातध्रौव्यात् ! तथा, नित्यस्य नित्यतायाः पराधीनत्वेऽपि न जात्वनित्यताप्रसक्तिः । तन्नियमननियमादिति । तदिदमुक्तं नित्यं चेति । (*NS* p. 330)

21. द्विविधः सत्सिद्धान्तः, परापरभेदात् ।...अनेनापरसिद्धान्तमाह...। उपलक्षणं चैतत् । प्रपञ्चसत्यत्वादिकमपि ग्राह्यम् ॥

in time, at some indefinite period in the past still continues to lurk in many quarters and even eminent theologians like Flint have clung to it heroically. But thanks to the stupendous advance of science in recent times, such crude notions have no place in serious thinking, quite apart from the difficulty of having to answer the question of why the Deity should have chosen a particular time to create, after having kept in its shell all along before. It will be clear then that the dependence of even the eternal entities on God and their creation or evolution through "Parādhīnaviśeṣāpti" brings out the independence of God all the more prominently.

The supremacy of God as the immanent-cum-transcendent Principle of the universe introduces order and unity in the cosmos, in spite of its internal differences and ramifications. The multiverse of reals becomes a universe in that it owes allegiance to a single source and derives its strength, power and reality, beauty, goodness, etc., now and for ever from the One.

तत्तंत्रत्वादैतदात्म्यम्। सर्वमेतत् ब्रह्मेत्युच्यते । तदधीनसत्ताप्रतीतिमत्त्वात्,
नतु, तत्स्वरूपत्वात्। उक्तं हि पाद्मे—
त्वदधीनं यतः सर्वमतः सर्वो भवानिति।
वदन्ति मुनयः सर्वे न तु सर्वस्वरूपतः ॥ इति ॥

(*Madhva*, *GB* iv. 24)

Thus, Madhva's chief ontological classification of being into Svatantra and Paratantra does full justice to the three primary data of philosophy in the light of the requirements of religious consciousness and speculative reason.

CHAPTER VI

MADHVA'S ONTOLOGICAL SCHEME

Brahman as the only Independent Real is the highest ontological principle of Madhva's philosophy. It is Infinite (पूर्ण), of perfect bliss (भूमा, संप्रसाद), the Real of reals (सत्यस्य सत्यम्), the Eternal of eternals (नित्यो नित्यानाम्), the Sentient of all sentients (चेतनश्चेतनानाम्), the source of all reality, consciousness and activity (सत्ताप्रतीतिप्रवृत्तिनिमित्तम्) in the finite.

Dependent reality (पराधीनप्रमेयम्) consists of Cetana and Acetana. The subdivisions of the Cetanavarga are, to some extent, theological in character. The special place is given there to Śrītattva as the presiding deity (principle) over the entire domain of Jaḍa-Prakṛti. Śri or Lakṣmī is, for this reason, designated as Cetana-Prakṛti. Similar presiding principles (Abhimāni-Devatās) are accepted for other material principles like Mahat, Ahaṁkāra, Bhūtas, Indriyas, etc. on the clear authority of the *Upaniṣads*, *Brahmasūtra* (ii.1.6)[1] and the *Pañcarātras*. The Śrītattva ranks next to the Supreme Being, *qua* Paratantra. But it is not without a partial parity of status with the Supreme in virtue of being co-pervasive in time and space and being ever-free from bondage (*nityamuktā*) and therefore designated as "Sama-nā" (*BSB* iv.2.7). Śrī is placed in the *īśvarakoṭi* and has cosmic sway[2], accordingly, over the destinies of the souls and the modifications of matter. An analogous position,

---

1. Śaṅkara also admits as a Siddhānta view the existence of Abhimāni-devatās. (See *BSB* i. 3. 33.)

2. See *Ambhṛṇī Sūkta*, *RV* X. 125.

विश्वस्थितिप्रलयसर्गमहाविभूति—
वृत्तिप्रकाशनियमावृतिबन्धमोक्षाः ।
यस्या अपाङ्गलवमात्रतः (*Dvādaśa-Stotra* vii,1)

with some difference in details, is given to Śrī, in tne theology of Rāmānuja also.

The rest of the Cetana-varga, is subject to the bondage of Prakṛti and is further subdivided into "released' and "unreleased". There is an intrinsic gradation among the released and unreleased alike, Hiraṇyagarbha among the released (and in Saṁsāra too) occupying a privileged position as Jīvottama. Unlike Rāmānuja, Madhva accepts an innate distinction among (released) souls into Deva, Ṛṣi (Pitṛ, Pa) and Naras. The Devas are *Sarva-prakāśa* (fit to realize God as pervasive), the Sages are *Antaḥprakaśa* and the rest *Bahiḥprakāśa*[3]. The non-released are again classified as salvable (*mukti-yogya*), ever-transmigrating (*nityasaṁsārin*) and the damnable (*tamo-yogya*). This tripartite classification of Souls is unique to Madhva theology[4]. Its ethical and philosophical merits will be discussed later.

The Acetana section falls into two categories of positive (*bhāva*) and negative (*abhāva*). Three kinds of negation (*abhāva*) are accepted—*prāgabhāva* (antecedent negation), *pradhvaṁsa-abhāva* (subsequent negation) and *Sadābhāva* (absolute negation). The mutual or reciprocal negation of Nyāya philosophy is equated with "Difference" and is not considered a mere negation as it does not involve negation of existence in the very first act of perception. The conception of *atyantābhāva* differs radically from the Nyāya view in that its counter-correlative (*pratiyogi*) has no factual existence (*aprāmāṇika*). (See Chapter XIII.)

In the domain of positive reals, we have both the eternal and the non-eternal. If everything is eternal, static and uncreated, causation would cease to have any meaning. Even if it were interpreted in terms of manifestations, the question would still arise about the manifestation itself—whether it is caused or uncaused. In the former case, the question will be continuously

3. 'अन्तःप्रकाशा बहिःप्रकाशाः सर्वप्रकाशाः । देवा वाव सर्वप्रकाशाः, ऋषयोऽन्तःप्रकाशाः, मनुष्या एव बहिःप्रकाशा' इति चतुर्वेदशिखायाम् (Madhva, *BSB* iv.3.16)

4. See my *BSPC* ii. pp. 226-27

repeated involving a regress. In the latter case, the same redundancy of causal effort will be there.

It would also be impossible to account for creative evolution, dissolution, etc. in the absence of some enduring stuff out of which things can be created and into which they can be resolved and returned. The doctrine of momentary creation (*kṣaṇikavāda*) and dissolution cannot be accepted by a reflective mind, as it is disproved by our experience (*Pratyabhijñā*) and conviction of the continuity of objects.

There is, thus, a clear case for the acceptance of both eternal and non-eternal Bhāvas. Space, time, the Vedas, the subtle aspects of the elements, senses, Āhaṁkārika Prāṇa, Mahat, Ahaṁkāra and the qualities of Sattva, Rajas and Tamas, are deemed to be eternal. The grosser developments of these are non-eternal. Where the substances show both the aspects, as far example, time viewed as an eternal process and as a succession of moments, each aspect would be referred to its appropriate category and the substance itself be spoken of as "Nityānitya".

The world of attributes comprising qualities (primary and secondary), actions, Sattā, Śakti, Sādṛśya, etc., are regarded by Madhva as constituting the very essence of the substances themselves.[5] They need not, then, be regarded as having a separate existence of their own, requiring independent enumeration or classification. But where they are conceptually distinguished from their substances, by the power of (internal Viśeṣas) they could certainly be enumerated, classified, and studied separately[6]. Madhva, however, puts forward a twofold classification of attributes in general as (i) *yāvad-dravyabhāvi* (coeval) and (ii) *ayāvad-dravyabhāvi* (changing). The former type of attributes or properties, being coessential, is *identical* with the substances themselves. The latter are to be considered

5. द्रव्यमेव ततोऽनन्तविशेषात्मतया सदा ।
नानाव्यवहृतेर्हेतुरनन्तत्वं विशेषतः ॥ (*AV* ii.2.13)

6. It is from this standpoint that the conventional classification of Padārthas (into *ten* categories) in *Madhvasiddhāntasāra* and other works is to be understood.

as partly different and partly identical (*bhinnābhinna*) with their substances, in an equal measure.[7] This relation applies in respect of the pairs : (1) cause and effect, (2) temporary qualities of substances and their substratum, (3) genus and species, (4) Viśiṣṭa and Śuddha (the thing-in-itself and the thing as qualified), and (5) part and whole etc.

7. In respect of permanent attributes the relation is taken to be one of 'colorful identity' (*saviśeṣābheda*) rather than absolute identity (*nirviśeṣābheda*) which would make them tautologous. This clear and unequivocal stand has to be kept in mind in interpreting Madhva's doctrine of creation of eternal substances like Jīva, Prakṛti, Avyākṛtākāśa etc., in terms of what has been defined by him as "Parādhīna-Viśeṣāpti".

CHAPTER VII

THE CONCEPT OF VIŚESAS

THE relation between substance and attributes is one of the intriguing problems of philosophy. It has well-nigh taxed the ingenuity and resources of philososphers in the East and in the West. Madhva's contribution to the solution of this problem is both original and significant. *He has actually contributed a new idea—the concept of Viśeṣas—to the treatment of this philosophical problem.* It is an outstanding discovery of his. Madhva accepts a relation of 'colorful identity' (सविशेषाभेद) in respect of coessential attributes and difference-cum-identity (भेदाभेद) in the case of transient attributes:

खण्डिते भेद ऐक्यं च; यावद्वस्तु न भेदवत् । (*TV*)

He has thus made a striking effort to rise above the 'dualism' of substance and attributes and combine them into a homogeneous whole that admits, however, of logical, conceptual and linguistic distinction, wherever necessary, through the self-differentiating capacity of substances themselves, to be known as "Viśeṣas" or relative particulars.

These Viśeṣas are ubiquitous and are not confined to material substances. They exist among sentients as well, including the Supreme Being. In sentient beings, these Viśeṣas, whether manifested or not, are identical with their substrata; while in regard to insentients, attributes which are co-eval would be identical with the substances (and distinguishable by Viśeṣas); while changing or impermanent ones would be different-cum-identical with their substances. The whole question has been very clearly expounded by Jayatīrtha in his commentary on the *GT* xi. 15, p. 184.

"Viśeṣa also is of two kinds as pertaining to a Cetana. Some of these are 'produced' and some are 'eternal'. Though the

Viśeṣa as constituting the nature of a sentient person is eternal, it is spoken of as being 'produced' by reason of its becoming manifested at times and remaining unmanifested at other times. In the same way, Viśeṣas pertaining to insentient things are also twofold in their nature. The substance as such is the material cause of the Viśeṣas in an insentient thing. Though Viśeṣas co-exist with the substance, as partaking of its nature, still a distinction can be made of them. In respect of insentient reals some Viśeṣas are produced as effects and some others last as long as the thing itself lasts. To illustrate, in the statement 'the nature of the sentient being *is*', the Viśeṣas such as sentiency, thingness and 'having a nature' are always manifested. In an example like 'The sentient person is doing this' or is engaged in eating, going, etc., "the eating", "the doing" and such other Viśeṣas are subject to manifestation and non-manifestation (as actions). Both these types of Viśeṣas in a sentient object are completely identical with their substratum.

So also, in the statement 'the mango fruit is', the traits of mangoness, fruitness, etc., are co-eval with the substance and are, therefore, entirely identical with it. In the statement 'The mango is yellow or ripe', the traits of ripeness and yellowness are transitory and are, therefore, to be regarded as being *both* identical with the substance in one sense and different from it, in another."[1]

The argument for the acceptance of Viśeṣ as thus presented by Trivikrama Paṇḍita. The conception of the relation between substance and attributes is a very difficult one. If they are identical, the distinction of 'substance' and 'attributes' is meaningless.

---

1. चेतने कश्चिद्विशेषो जायते कश्चिन्नित्य इति एवं विशेषोऽपि द्विविधो भवति । चेतनद्रव्यात्मकत्वेन नित्यस्यापि विशेषस्य व्यक्तिविशेषविवक्षया जननोक्तिसंभवात् । अचेतने विशेषिद्रव्यस्यैव विशेषोपादानत्वात्, उपादानविशेषिद्रव्यात्मना यावद्द्रव्यभाव्यपि, कार्यरूपेण कश्चिद्विशेषो जायते कश्चित् यावद्द्रव्यभावीति द्विविधो विशेष इति भावः । चेतनवस्तुस्वरूपमस्तीत्यत्र चेतनत्ववस्तुत्वस्वरूपत्वास्तित्वविशेषाः नित्याभिव्यक्ताः। चेतनः करोति, भुङक्ते, गच्छतीत्यत्र करणगमनभोजनविशेषाः व्यक्त्यव्यक्तियुताः (शक्तिरूपेण नित्या, व्यक्तिरूपेण जायन्ते) ते द्विविधा अपि विशेषिणा अत्यन्ताभेदिनः ।

तथा, चूतफलस्वरूपं अस्तीत्यत्र चूतत्वफलत्वादिविशेषा; यावद्द्रव्यभाविनो विशेषिणात्यन्ताभिन्नाः । पीतं चूतफलमित्यत्र पीतत्वादिविशेषाः कादाचित्का, विशेषिणा भिन्नाभिन्ना इति भावः ॥

We would have substance alone or attributes alone, in that case and not *both* of them. If the two are different, their relation becomes a purely external one. If they are related internally by Samavāya, this relation itself has to be related to the terms and so on *ad infinitum*. The difficulty will persist even if substance and attributes are treated as partly identical and partly different. The only way in which a regress can be avoided, on any one of these alternatives, would be by agreeing to invest the first relation itself with a certain capacity to take care of itself, explain itself, and relate itself to the relata, without waiting to be explained or related to its terms by another relation. Since an appeal has thus ultimately to be made to the self-explicability of the relation, it will be wiser, more economical and expedient, to invest the substance itself with such an intrinsic capacity of integrating its attributes into a homogeneous whole, with itself, without prejudice to their distinction of references according to exigencies, and without the need for any external *relation*. This intrinsic capacity of substances is proposed to be called "Viśeṣas"—a very appropriate name,[2] so far as any one could see, *and one which could not be improved upon.* We have, here, in the Viśeṣas of Madhva, a remarkable anticipation of the Hegelian doctrine of "internal relations".

Experience shows that the various qualities of a thing are not the fictions of the mind. The temporal, spatial, qualitative, quantitative and causal characteristics of objects that we see are not altogether the fancies projected by the mind; for there is no reason why and how *all minds* should or could project alike and carry on with a sense of pre-established harmony of world-building impressions. But there are attributes like the "light of the Sun" and the 'primary qualities' which could not be perceived apart from the objects possessing those qualities. The idea of a triangle as a three-sided plane figure implies the other idea of the sum of its angles being equal to two right angles. The two ideas are not however the same though they involve each other. There are a number of practical difficulties which stand in the way of an *absolute identity* of the two: substance and attributes.

2. अभिन्नेऽपि विशेषकत्वात् विशेषः । (*Tg* p. 333)

Jayatīrtha draws attention to some important considerations of this kind which justify a certain measure of practical distinction between the two, consistent with our experience.[3]

(1) In the perception 'the jar is white', the whiteness and the jar cannot be regarded as coterminal and coextensive. The jar is something more than its whiteness. When one is asked to fetch a white thing, one does not necessarily fetch a jar. (2) The two terms, the jar and whiteness, are not synonymous in connotation, for there is no contradiction in saying that the jar is not white as there would be in saying that the jar is not a jar. (3) The jar is perceived irrespective of its whiteness as when a blind man feels its presence with his hands, even when he is unable to perceive its whiteness. This shows that the perception of a jar is not the same as the perception of its color. When the whiteness of the object is changed into redness by a coating of paint, we still continue to perceive and recognize the pot as such, though not in its former color. All this points to an undeniable distinction between the ideas of substance and attributes. The attributes not merely subsist, but exist. Their distinction from the substance is not illusory, as there is no correcting judgment to the contrary. At the same time, the attributes have no reality *apart* from the substances and are always presented in all judgments about them as identical with their substances : शुक्लः पटः, नीलो घटः । Apposition of form and content between the subject and the predicate (सामानाधिकरण्यम्) is an accepted proof of identity (अभेदे प्रमाणम्). It is in this crossing or intersection of identity and difference that Madhva finds the clue and justification for his concept of Viśeṣas, to

---

3. दृश्यन्ते च भेदकार्याणि (१) पटशौक्ल्यबुद्ध्योरन्यूनानतिरिक्तविषयत्वाभावः (२) तच्छब्दयोरपर्यायित्वं (३) अपर्यायशब्दस्मारकत्वम् (४) जलाहरणाद्यर्थक्रियाभेदः। (५) पटमानयेत्युक्ते यत्किंचिच्छुक्लानानयनं, (६) अघटः पट इतिवत् अशुक्लः पट इत्यनयोर्विरोधाभावः (७) अन्धस्यापि पटोऽयमितिवत् शुक्लोऽयमिति च प्रतीत्यनुत्पत्तिः शुक्लाप्रतीतिवत् पटाप्रतिपत्त्यभावः (८) महारजनसंपर्केण शुक्लत्ववत् पटस्याप्यावृतत्वाभावः (९) पटवद्वा शौक्ल्यस्याप्यनावृतत्वाभावः **इत्येवमादीनि**। न चैषा प्रतीतिर्भ्रान्तिः। बाधितत्वाभिमानाभावात्। व्यवहाराद्यविसंवादाच्च। तदेतयोरभेदभेदकार्ययोः प्रतीत्योरन्यथानुपपत्त्या निर्भेदेऽपि पटे अस्ति कश्चनातिशयो भेदप्रतिनिधिः यद्वशादिदं सर्वं समंजसं स्यादित्येव कल्पनीयम् स चातिशयोऽभिन्नेऽपि **विशेषकत्वात् विशेष इति गीयते** ॥ (*NS* p. 106 b)

bridge the gulf between substance and attributes and preserve the basic unity of experience without in any manner sacrificing the numerous distinctions demanded and drawn by the necessities, niceties and nuances of scientific usage and practical utility. We can never do without "Viśeṣas", in whatever way we may choose to conceive of substance. Madhva would, therefore, willingly endorse the criticism of D.M. Datta that "the necessity far an interposition of a third entity or relation arises from a narrow and exclusive conception of 'terms'. If we widen our outlook and think of an entity as possessing in addition to its essential, non-relative and intrinsic character, other extrinsic relative characteristics which it might have in the infinite situations in which it may be placed, then we can easily dispense with the existence of a third entity or relation. A thing thus comes to be viewed as an identity of some intrinsic and extrinsic forms or aspects. Different words are then found to denote different forms of the same thing in different aspects" (*Six Ways of Knowing*, p. 115). This criticism will *not apply* to Viśeṣas as conceived by Madhva, which are not extrinsic to or different from the terms. Viśeṣa is neither a "third entity" *nor a relation.* It is part and parcel of the terms and yet capable of distinguishing them where and when necessary. Its help is *indispensable* in any attempt to "widen our outlook and think of an entity as possessed, *in addition to its essential and intrinsic character*, other extrinsic characteristics, which it might have in the infinite situations in which it may be placed" (*ibid.* italics mine). It would be impossible to effect an "identity" between "the intrinsic and the extrinsic forms or aspects" of a thing, without the agency of Viśeṣas. It is the only way out.

Viśeṣa is thus the same as the principle of identity-in-difference. Madhva defines it as "the potency of things in themselves which determines the use of non-synonymous expressions in predicating something of them, provided however that in such cases, there is no absolute difference between the given thing and its predicates":

भेदहीने त्वपर्यायशब्दान्तरनियामकः ।
विशेषो नाम कथितः सोऽस्ति वस्तुष्वशेषतः ।।

(*AV* 1.1.2)

Viśeṣa is thus the peculiar characteristic or potency of things which makes description and talk of difference possible, where as a matter of fact only identity exists. It is a differentiating or pluralising agency which serves at the same time to exhibit the pluralities as flowing centripetally from a given object and which happen to occupy the focus of attention on account of a dominant pragmatic interest at the moment. It renders possible the validity of countless viewpoints while the object itself retains its unity, independence and integrality. Jayatīrtha defines it as

भेदहीनेऽप्यमनुपचरितभेदव्यवहारनिमित्तम् (*NS* p.106)

or the principle of thought whereby, in all cases of identity judgments a real practical distinction of a non-figurative nature, is or has to be drawn and accepted, if the judgments in question are not to be tautologous (*paryāya*), belonging to the pathology of thought as घटो घटः (*the pot is a pot*).

Madhva and his commentator show that such experiences, involving the mediation of Viśeṣas, are to be found everywhere in the Scriptures and in our daily life of lay and scientific commerce :[4]

'सत्यं ज्ञानमनन्तं ब्रह्म', 'आनन्दं ब्रह्मणः', 'पुरुषस्य चैतन्यम्', 'शुक्लवर्णः', 'अहेः कुण्डलम्', 'समवाय एकः', 'सामान्यं सत्' etc.

They introduce order into the world of substances (*padārtha*) and keep intact the unity of substance in and through all its various modes, predicates, aspects, attributes and relations. Madhva indicates in his *BT* about six places where Viśeṣas usually come into play :

1) "अवयव्यवयवानां च 2) गुणानां गुणिनस्तथा ।
3) शक्तिशक्तिमतोश्चापि 4) क्रियायास्तद्वतः तथा ।
5) स्वरूपांशांशिनोश्चैव (नित्याभेदः * * * ॥" (*BT* xi.7.49)

It is this "power of things in themselves" which, through an underlying identity of essence, enables us to distinguish (1) a particular from its universal; (2) a quality from its substance; (3) motion or power or energy from things possessing them;

4. Cf. यथा कालस्य पूर्वेणाभेदेऽपि काल इति विशेष्यो भवति, पूर्वं इति विशेषको विशेषादेव । तथा गुणात्मकस्यापि ब्रह्मणो विशेषादेव 'गुणि ब्रह्म' इति विशेषणविशेष्यभावो युज्यते इति भावः । (*TP III*. 2.30)

(4) the Svarūpa from the Svarūpin and Svarūpatvam. Jayatīrtha points out that in the term "Svarūpatvam", the use of the suffix '*tva*' stands for Viśeṣas and that without acceptance of such a shade of meaning its use would be redundant. Viśeṣa is, therefore, but another name for the potency of the thing in itself whereby it maintains its unity and continuity through all its modes, predications and aspects :

स्वक्रियाभिस्तथैवैक्यं नित्यं स्वावयवैरपि ।
स्वरूपेषु विशेषो यः स्वरूपं तस्य सोऽपि तु ।
विशेषस्य विशेषोऽन्यो न चैवास्ति कदाचन ।
स्वस्यापि तु विशेषश्च स्वयमेव भविष्यति ।
यथा जनेर्जनिर्नान्या तस्या वस्तुजनिर्जनिः ।
स्वरूपेणापि संयोगः स्वरूपस्यैव युज्यते ॥

(Madhva, commentary on *BrhUp* 1.4.9)

A luminous stone is not something totally different from its luminosity. It stands self-related to its lustre :

यथा रत्नस्य संयोगः स्वरूपस्यैव युज्यते ।
यथा रत्नस्य संयोगः तत्प्रकाशेन नित्यदा ।
रत्नस्य च प्रकाशस्य न भेदः कश्चिदिष्यते ॥

(Commentary on *BrhUp* 1.4.9)

The thing itself is so constituted :

द्रव्यमेव ततोऽनन्तविशेषात्मतया सदा ।
नानाव्यवहृतेर्हेतुरनन्तत्वं विशेषतः ॥ (*AV* ii.2.13)

that it can relate itself to and distinguish itself from its modes, predicates or properties, without invoking the aid of any other relation or a "third entity" (as Prof. Datta terms it). It is *Svanirvāhaka*, self-explicable, self-contained and self-related. It is only by the acceptance of such a potency in things that we can "widen our outlook" and conceive of a substance "as an identity of some intrinsic and extrinsic forms or aspects" (Datta, p. 115). This conception of substance as a unity of countless Viśeṣas :

द्रव्यमेव ततोऽनन्तविशेषात्मतया सदा (*AV* ii.2.13)

held by Madhva, resembles the Jaina theory of substance as that which has many qualities forming its essence: अनन्तधर्मात्मकं वस्तु (Haribhadra Sūri). There is however this difference that the Jaina theory of substance as a dynamic reality, an identity that *changes*, would be incomplete, without the acceptance of something like Viśeṣas to round it off. It will be difficult to maintain the basic identity of substance *per se*, without the Viśeṣas.

Viśeṣas should not, therefore, be *mistaken* for *new* or *additional attributes of things*, that mediate among other relations and manage to distinguish them where necessary. Such a view will be not only opposed to the nature and role of Viśeṣas, as conceived by Madhva, but also defeat the very purpose for which they have been conceived. It is such a misunderstanding of the nature of Viśeṣas that is at the back of the criticism that "If Viśeṣa is different from the subject, it breaks its integrity. If it is non-different from it, we *cannot call it Viśeṣa*" (Radhakrishan, *I. Phil.* ii, p. 746) (Italics mine).

The same confusion of thought regarding Viśeṣas in Madhva's system, that it is either an *attribute* of the substance, or *an additional entity*, is to be seen in the writings of even distinguished traditional critics of the system like Madhusūdana Sarasvatī and Brahmānanda. The author of the *Advaitasiddhi* writes :

भेदे ऐकरस्यश्रुतिविरोधवत् अत्रापि (सत्यविशेषेऽपि) तत्तादवस्थ्यात् * * * न । स्वभावविशेषादेव सर्वस्याप्युपपत्तेः । न तर्हि विशेषांगीकारेण मन्मतप्रवेश इति वाच्यम् । **तत्तादसाधारणस्वरूपस्यैव स्वभावविशेषशब्दार्थत्वेन, त्वदुक्तविशेषानुक्तेः ॥** (Nirnayasagar Press edn. p. 807)

This criticism that the acceptance of Viśeṣas in Brahman would destroy its oneness quite as much as the acceptance of an internal difference of substance and attributes therein, betrays a presumption that Viśeṣas must be different from the substance (Viśeṣin) which is categorically denied by Madhva. The criticism also suffers from self-contradiction in that Madhusūdana himself declares that there can be no Viśeṣas other than *the distinctive nature of things*, and nothing more is claimed for the Viśeṣas by Mādhva philosophers also. To say, as does the author of *Advaitasiddhi*, that it is *not* the nature of Viśeṣas in the Dvaita system, simply shows that he has *not* rightly understood their true nature according to the Dvaitins. But strangely enough, he himself goes on to point out that "the Dvaitins unlike the Nyāya-Vaiśeṣikas, *do not* regard their Viśeṣas as *different from* the essence of things:

दृष्टान्त इव दार्ष्टान्तिके स्वरूपातिरेकस्य त्वयैवानङ्गीकारेण वैषम्यात् ।
(p. 807)

The author of *Taraṅgiṇi*, therefore, points out that the talk (of the Advaitin) of *there being no Viśeṣas, other than the "distinctive natures of things"* (तत्तदसाधारणस्वरूप) in itself involves the presumption of Viśeṣas :

विशेषं विना स्वरूपासाधारण्यायुक्तेः । (*Tg* p. 383)

In view of so much confusion even in learned quarters about the true nature and scope of Viśeṣas, it would be better to set forth its authentic nature in the words of the original works clearly and categorically :

द्रव्यमेव ततोऽनन्तविशेषात्मतया सदा ।
नानाव्यवहृतेर्हेतुः * * * ॥ (*AV* ii. 2. 13)

Jayatīrtha defines Viśeṣas in the clearest terms as the "potency of things" :

स्वनिर्वाहको विशेषो नाम, पदार्थशक्तिरभिषिच्यताम् ।
(*Vādāvaḷi*, p. 97 b)

Rāghavendra's commentary on it clinches the matter once for all : **पदार्थशक्तिरिति न वस्त्वन्तरत्वमित्यर्थः ।** Jayatīrtha again writes elsewhere: नन्वयं विशेषो यदि द्रव्यात्मैव, कथं तर्हि द्रव्यस्य विशेषः स्यात्? मैवम् विनापि भेदेन तत्प्रतिनिधिना विशेषेणैव विशेषस्य तदीयत्वोपपत्तेः । The *Vādaratnāvali* (written a century before *Nyāyāmṛta* and *Advaitasiddhi*) expounds the nature of Viśeṣas as "nothing but the potency of things themselves" :

अयं वस्तुशक्ति. विशेषो हि अभिन्नेष्वपि विशेषकत्वात् विशेष इति गीयते । दीपदीप्त्योरिवेत्युदाहरणार्थम् । एकमेव द्रव्यं प्रभाप्रभावद्द्रव्याकारेणावतिष्ठते । तथा शक्तिविशेषोऽस्तीति चेत् हन्त तर्हि स एव विशेषः ।
(*Viśeṣavāda* MS)

There is, thus no point in the criticism that "if it is non-different from substance, we cannot *call it* Viśeṣa". Call it by whatever name you will, Viśeṣa will be there in the nature of things as it is only *another name* for substance, with all its wonderful capacities.

Madhva is thus fully justified in holding that it would be impossible to establish any adequate theory of the relation between substance and attributes without invoking the aid of Viśeṣas, which are also called Svarūpaviśeṣas in order to show that they are not *other than* the Substance. Such Viśeṣas are forced upon us by the very laws of thought as a Sarvatantrasiddhānta, says Madhva :

अखण्डखण्डवादिभ्यां * * * * ।
महादरेण शिरसि विशेषो धार्य एव हि ।
एतादृशे विशेषेऽस्मिन् को द्वेषो वादिनां भवेत् ?

(*AV* ii.2.28)

They lurk everywhere in relations between substance and attributes from whatever angle they may be approached, as the "mysterious Mrs. Harris of metaphysics" as one writer has racily put it. Viśeṣa is just a "peculiarity", an unnameable something recognized by all, tacitly, and Madhva has only tried to give it an apt and special name and a form and has rendered its existence explicit, in the interest of clearness of thought and judgements. *This is no small service to scientific thinking and metaphysics.*

Viśeṣa as a Sarvatantrasiddhānta

Madhva undertakes to convince the open-minded that Viśeṣas must be accepted as a postulate of thought. There are only three possible ways in which the relation of substance and attributes can be conceived, *viz.* (1) that they are entirely *different* from each other (*atyantabhinna*), (2) *absolutely identical with each other* (*abhinna*), or (3) *both identical and different* (*bhinnābhinna*). These three views have been put forward by the Naiyāyikas, the Advaitins and the Bhāṭṭas respectively. Madhva shows by argument that everyone of these views has ultimately to fall back on Viśeṣas. He, therefore, examines and rejects them all, in favour of a fourth view of Saviśeṣābheda (identity based on Viśeṣa) as the only acceptable view, free from the difficulties incidental to the other three.

The theory of absolute difference between substance and attributes is not only full of difficulties but cannot also commend itself to our philosophic imagination. Is the said difference no. 1, different from the terms or identical with them? In the first case, is the difference no. 2, also different from or identical with the terms and so on indefinitely, so that we are left with a regress. If difference no. 1 were *identical* with the terms, it cannot be conceived as the difference of *this* or *that* term, as such descriptions would themselves presuppose a difference. The terms and the differences would all be synonymous. If the said difference were said to be self-supporting, is such self-sufficiency (*svanirvāhakatvam*) different from or identical with the terms and with the act of self-supporting? In the former case, an endless regress is sure to arise. In the latter case, the attributes of 'nirvâhya' and 'nirvâhaka' given to Samavāya would make the subject and the predicate overlap in the same act of self-supportingness. If it be said that the difference between substance and attributes is naturally endowed with such self-supporting and self-linking capacity, it would be but another name for "Viśeṣas" and such potency could as well be claimed for and vested in the substance itself, instead of in "difference"!

If substance and attributes are to be different and externally related by Samavâya, the question arises if the Samavāya relation too, is similarly related to the relata by another Samavāya and so on. If Samavāya is self-linking (*svanirvāhaka*), without the aid of *another* link, such a self-linking capacity may as well be posited of the substance itself, at the very outset, so that the luxury of an additional relation (padârtha) may be dispensed with: धर्मिकल्पनातो धर्मकल्पना वरम् ।

If the difference between substance and attributes were, however, *identical* with the relata, there would be no *difference* left *as such*, but only the two *terms*. In the absence of any difference, we cannot even speak of there being *two terms*, substance and attribute *as such*, as even this idea is born of difference. If the terms and difference are identical, one may contend that difference alone exists as a matter of fact and no terms whatever! Difference then, between substance and attributes must be accepted *not* as being *absolutely identical* with the terms but "identical with a qualification" (*Saviśeṣābheda*), that would preserve all three of them intact and prevent their mutual synonymity. Such distinction of reference may indeed be most profitably attributed to the substances themselves, instead of the relation of difference.

The Bhedābheda view of substance and attributes is in need of Viśeṣas at the very outset. Identity and difference being opposites and therefore mutually exclusive, cannot be brought together and conceived to coexist (*samānādhikaraṇa*) without the aid of a mediating factor. Either of them could, therefore, be invested with the peculiar capacity of putting up with its opposite : भेदसहिष्णुरभेदः or अभेदसहिष्णुर्भेदः. Such a peculiar capacity of making opposites meet will indeed be a "Viśeṣa ".

Even supposing that substance and attributes are connected by a relation of Bhedābheda, what will be the sort of relation between the identity and the difference, mutually and to the terms? If that is also one of *bhedābheda*, there will be a regress. If the *bhedābheda* is to be accepted as *svanirvāhaka* (self-linking), it can only be so with the help of a peculiar potency in it called Viśeṣa, for want of a better name. If *bheda* and *abheda* are different from the terms, there will be a regress. If identical, they *cannot* be represented as "belonging" to them (*tadiya*) without some kind of a peculiarity. Nor can difference and identity between the terms, be again identical with them. If they are, *difference and identity will both become identical in their turn*, which will lead to an absurdity and there will be no possibility of establishing a relation between them.

The doctrine of undifferenced reality (*akhaṇḍatā*) of the Advaita is equally dependent on Viśeṣas. This may be illustrated with reference to the famous definitive text (*lakṣaṇavākya*) सत्यं ज्ञानमनन्तं ब्रह्म which is in the nature of a proposition or judgment on the nature of Brahman and ascribes to it three attributes of reality, consciousness and infinitude. It will be necessary to call to aid Viśeṣas if the unity of the judgment and the oneness of Brahman in and through the three attributes are to be preserved. Are the attributes *satyam*, *jñānam* and *ānantyam* mutually different or not ? If they are, we have to admit an element of plurality in Brahman, which cannot be. If they are all the same, there is no need to predicate *three* of them, as anyone of them would do. They will thus be synonymous in effect (*paryāya*) and hence redundant. It cannot be that there are subtle shades of difference among them; for Brahman is *ex hypothesi* Nirviśeṣa i.e., without any shade of any kind of difference or plurality. Nor can their employment be defended on the assumption of *affirmation through negation of the opposites* (अनृतादिव्यावृत्तिमुखेन). Even there must be recognized some kind of distinction from the opposites negated, as otherwise, the entire negation would be a meaningless proposition.[5] The distinction from unreality must perforce be distinct from distinction from ignorance, limitation etc. The doctrine of Saviśeṣābheda is thus forced upon all as a universal principle (सर्वतन्त्रसिद्धान्त). None who cares for the laws of thought can escape it.

Madhva's Viśeṣa is thus the counterpart of the principle of identity-in-difference recognized by many Western philosophers and that of Samavāya and Svarūpasambandha recognized by the Nyāya-Vaiśeṣikas and the Advaitins respectively. *But it is not just another name for Samavāya*. In fact, it is *not a relation* at all, *in the sense Samavāya is*, though it is *svanirvāhaka* like the latter. It has a clear advantage over Samavāya, in that its self-sufficiency is more directly and easily established than that of Samavāya. The acceptance of Samavāya has to be supplemented by the assumption of its self-sufficiency and ability to render a distinction of reference without a distinction of essence possible (अभिन्ने भेदव्यवहारनियामकम्) which is the hall-mark and *raison d'etre of* Viśeṣas (धर्मिग्राहकप्रमाणसिद्धम्).

Samavāya Too Needs Viśeṣas

Moreover, Samavāya itself has different characteristics such as its own existence, being inherent in the whole and its parts, being nameable, knowable and being in relation. These characteristics cannot be differentiated from the essence of Samavāya. For, if different from Samavāya, these characteristics will have to be brought into relation with it externally. Such a relation cannot be Saṁyoga (contact) which being a 'guṇa' is admissible only in a *dravya* (which Samavāya is *not*). If the characteristics are identical with Samavāya, how are we to

---

5. Cf. व्यावृत्ते निर्विशेषे तु किं व्यावर्त्यबहुत्वतः ? (Madhva, *AV* i. 2.21)
Also व्यावृत्तविशेषश्च व्यावर्तकविशेषनिबन्धनः ।

account for the reference to them in non-synonymous terms, their predicative relation with Samavāya and syntactic reference to its characteristics by the use of the genitive case : *Samavāyasya sattā, jñeyatvam*, etc., and the plurality of its characteristics or the condition of some of its characteristics remaining unknown while Samavāya itself is perceived, unless Samavāya, in its turn, is equipped with the resilient power of Viśeṣa to differentiate itself from its own self, for purposes of such distinction of references without involving distinction of essence? These difficulties cannot be satisfactorily explained, unless it is forced to take the help of "Viśeṣas".

Viśeṣa is not just another name for Samavāya, though, like the latter, it is also self-distinguishing (*svanirvāhaka*). In fact, Viśeṣa is neither a relation nor something different from substance itself, in the sense in which Samavāya is.[6] It is the immanent dynamics of substance itself expressing itself through its essential properties that is distinguished as Viśeṣas of substance and referred to in non-synonymous terms (*aparyāyaśabda*) in apposition (*sāmānādhikaraṇyaprayoga*) as in "Satyam jñānam anantam Brahma."[7]

Substance is not a bare abstraction without facets scintillating from its being. While the self-explicability of Viśeṣas is the self-explicability of substance itself and does not fall outside its scope, the self-linking capacity ascribed to Samavāya in the Vaiśeṣika system comes into play *only when we cross the third stage* from substance itself, viz., its attributes, their difference and the nexus of Samavāya.

Thus, Viśeṣas conceived as substance's own power of self-expression in terms of subject-property relation (*dharmadharmibhāva*) within itself has a *decided advantage* over Samavāya, in that such self-expression is rendered possible by the intrinsic power or nature of the subject itself whereas Samavāya with its power of Svanirvāhakatva, stands a few removes away from the

---

6. समवायः संबन्धात्मकत्वात् स्वनिर्वाहकः, न द्रव्यमिति चेन्न । तदसिद्धौ संबन्धस्याप्यसिद्धेः । (*NS* p. 356 b)

7. गुणादीनां द्रव्यविशेषत्वेन, द्रव्यमेव विशेषशक्त्यैव अपर्यायशब्दवाच्यत्वादिव्यवहारहेतुर्भविष्यति । (*NS* p. 357b)

subject, in the process of integration. There is, therefore, no special advantage in going so far from the subject (*dravya*) to Samavāya and investing it with the power of self-explicability and self-linking. The preference can be given to substance itself at the very outset, in deference to the law of economy : *Dharmikalpanāto dharmakalpanā varam.*

Samavāya has been put up by the Vaiśeṣika school to account for the intimate relation as between cause and effect, part and whole, subject and its attributes, etc., on the ground of inherence of the latter in the former,—expressed in terms of an '*iha pratyaya*' such as 'the cloth in the threads here' (*iha tantuṣu paṭaḥ*) given in an inseparable relation (*ayutasiddha*), as distinguished from absolutely different objects like a horse and a cow.

But a closer examination resolves the inseparability into an identity through Viśeṣas. This can be seen from comparing two such cognitions of '*iha pratyaya*' as 'the threads and the cloth' (*tantu-paṭa*) and 'fruits in the basket' (*iha kuṇḍe badarāṇi*). Though the relation of supporter and supported (*ādhara-ādheya-bhāva*) is common to both these predications, we perceive a difference in their complexion. That difference must lie in the identity of cloth with threads and the difference between fruits and basket. Judgments like '*iha tantuṣu paṭaḥ*' have, therefore, to be treated as judgments of identity as distinguished from '*iha kuṇḍe badarāṇi*'. It cannot be contended that the difference between the two judgments is due (not to the identity or the difference, but) to the inseparability (*ayutasiddhi*) of the relata in the one case and their separability in the other and that 'ayutasiddhi' is evidence of Samavāya. For, at the time of the existence of the *ādhara-ādheyabhāva* between the threads and the cloth and the basket and the fruits, the inseparability of the cloth from the threads and the separability of the fruits from the basket, though true, make no difference to the complexion of the two cognitions *at the time*. It is irrelevant to the point that there may occur the separation of the fruits from the basket later on, while there *may not* be the separation between the threads and the cloth. But as Vyāsatīrtha rightly points out in his *Nym*, the perceptual cognition of 'threads-cloth' (*tantupaṭa*) when it arises, does not take the form "the relation between the cloth and the threads is *not going to be destroyed*" or "*that sepa-*

ration of the threads from the cloth is not going to take place in future". Similarly, the cognition of the fruits in the basket, when it arises, does not take the form "the relation between the basket and the fruits will be snapped or that their separation will take place at some future time". The form of both the cognitions is simply restricted to the existence of the cloth in the threads and of the fruits in the basket. Nor does the cognition of *tantupaṭa* as such cognize the relationship in terms of their Samavāya or inseparability of the relata. For this reason, the cognition of Tantupaṭa should be distinguished from that of kuṇḍabadara only as a cognition of identity of the threads and the cloth and that of the fruits and the basket as one of their difference.[8]

So long as the difference and relationship are both admitted by the Vaśeṣikas, in respect of the threads and the cloth on the one hand and the fruits and the basket on the other and insofar as the subsequent termination of their relation or the future separation of the relata has *no bearing on the perception* of *Tantupaṭa* and *Kuṇḍabadara* respectively, no difference in the nature of the two cognitions can be felt. Since a difference is clearly felt, the differentium of the cognition of *Tantu-paṭa* from that of *Kuṇḍabadara* has necessarily to be admitted to consist in the identity of the threads and the cloth, leading to the acceptance of Viśeṣas to sustain their *dharmadharmibhāva*, *ādhara-ādheya-bhāva*, etc.

The argument for Samavāya from *Ihapratyaya* is *not*, *therefore*, *conclusive*.

The concept of Viśeṣas is thus Madhva's most original and substantial contribution to the problem of substance and attributes in Indian ontology. He is in no way indebted to Samavāya or any other category of the Nyāya-Vaiśeṣika for this. The general impression of many that Mādhva philosophy is based on the doctrine of the Nyāya-Vaiśeṣikas and their categories has already

---

8. आश्रयाश्रयिभावनियमो ह्ययुतसिद्धिः । तत्र तदानींतनाश्रयाश्रयिभावः कुण्डबदरादावपि भवति। नियमस्तु न तन्तुपटादिबुद्धावपि । नहि प्रत्यक्षा तन्तुपटधीः, तन्तुपटनाशो वा, तन्तुपटविभागो वा न भविष्यतीत्याकारा । नापि कुण्डबदरधीः तयोः सम्बन्धनाशो वा, कुण्डबदरादिविभागो वा भविष्यतीत्याकारा । तस्मादभेदविषयत्वेनैव वैलक्षण्यं वाच्यम् । (*Nym* ii. 16)

been shown to rest on ignorance of facts and imperfect understanding of the basic principles of ontology on which the realism of Madhva is constructed. It may perhaps be said with better reason that the 'Viśeṣas' of Madhva *are reared on the ashes of Samavāya.*

Lastly, it has nothing save its name in common with the Vieśeṣas of the (Nyāya-) Vaiśeṣikas. It is easily distinguishable from the Vaiśeṣikas' Viśeṣas which are *ex hypothesi* restricted to eternal entities *alone*: नित्यद्रव्यवृत्तयो विशेषास्त्वनन्ता एव (*Muktāvali*). But Madhva's Viśeṣas are *not* confined to eternal substances. They exist in non-eternals also. The purpose and function of Viśeṣas too are different in the two systems. According to the Vaiśeṣikas these peculiarities are found in eternal things alone like *paramāṇus* and serve to *distinguish* one eternal from another and one eternal of a genus from others of the same class. They are accordingly known as "Vyāvartaka-Viśeṣas" and apply where such differentiation (*vyāvṛtti*) is *not otherwise possible* through class-concept or other means, as between a pot and a cloth. They are not, therefore, recognized by the Naiyāyikas in "Sāvayava" entities, which can be distinguished from one another through distinction of parts.

Function of Viśeṣas

The function of Viśeṣas, in Madhva's philosophy, is *not merely* to distinguish, but *to unify* the part and the whole, and to render a distinction of reference, without one of existence or essence possible, where necesssary or desired, into substance and attribute, part and whole etc., *within inseparable wholes.* The Viśeṣas of the Vaiśeṣikas, on the other hand, operate *only in cases of absolute difference. This fact is of utmost importance.* It suffices to keep the Viśeṣas of the two systems as the poles apart and expose the fallacious assumption of some scholars that the Viśeṣas of Madhva's system are either derived from or inspired by those of the Nyāya-Vaiśeṣikas. It is the failure to grasp the true nature of Viśeṣas taught by Madhva, that is responsible for the wholly misleading estimate of its role in his philosophy that we have in such sweeping assertions as "By means of the category of Viśeṣas, it will be possible for us to account for the world of distinction without assuming them to be ultimate" (Radhakrishnan, *I. Phil.* ii, p. 746); "It is through the functioning of Viśeṣas that we have difference or Bheda" (*ibid* 746). It is, therefore, necessary to point out that Viśeṣas have been admitted by Madhva *only in cases of absence of actual difference*, as between parts and whole, substance and attributes, etc. and where despite such absence of actual difference, a certain measure of internal distinction of parts, qualities or aspects is met with, in lay and scientific parlance and validated by experience. Viśeṣa is, thus, a category of thought or a power of things inherent in them which, by definition, is intended to justify and rationalize this lay and scientific acceptance of "difference in identity". The *Vādaratnāvali* makes this *raison d'etre* of the acceptance of Viśeṣas, clear: न चैवं घटपटादेरपि भेदाभावमङ्गीकृत्य, विशेषबलेनैव भेदव्यवहारसिद्धिः स्यादिति वाच्यम् । तत्र भेदस्य प्रत्यक्षसिद्धत्वात् । यत्र हि भेदाभावे प्रमाणमस्ति, भेदव्यवहारश्च प्रमितः, तत्रैव भेदप्रतिनिधिर्विशेषः प्रमाणद्वयान्यथानुपपत्त्या हि उपपादकतया भेदकार्यकृदित्याकारेणैव कल्प्यते । It can, on no account, be applied or *extended* to cases *where a genuine and absolute difference reigns supreme*, and where there is no room for the slightest trace of factual identity (*svarūpaikya*) or coexistence (*sāmānādhikaraṇya*). It cannot, therefore be universally substituted in all cases of actual difference in the world as between man and a horse and difference *as such* and as a *category of thought*, *banished* from the world of experience, or dismissed as *not being* "*ultimate*". To attempt such a substitution is to confuse the original with the substitute and prevent the function of the latter by extending it beyond its legitimate scope and sphere of application. Difference and Viśeṣa have each its own place in life well-defined and their jurisdiction is fixed beyond possibility of encroachment. It will be illegitimate then, to suggest that difference as such can be replaced by Viśeṣas *everywhere* under all circumstances and that we may account for the world of difference without assuming it to be "ultimate", through the miraculous help of Viśeṣas. It should not be lost sight of that Viśeṣas are strictly limited to cases of proved basic identity, which however admit of an internal distinction of reference, valid in experience : यत्र भेदाभावः प्रमाणावसितो भवेत्, तत्रैव विशेषो व्यवहारनिर्वाहकोऽङ्गीक्रियते । गवादिषु तु भेदस्यैव प्रमाणसिद्धत्वात् न व्यवहारो विशेषनिबन्धन इति ।

(*Jayatīrtha* : *GT-Nyāyadīpikā*, *p*. 182)

The position cannot be made clearer than this. Nor can the operation of Viśeṣas in their own sphere of difference-in-identity in any way lessen the ultimacy of Difference as a category of experience in other spheres. The one does not and cannot annul the other from its legitimate sphere. Both are necessary for an intelligible and satisfactory interpretation of reality. "Bheda" and "Viśeṣa" may, therefore, be described as the two facets of Madhva's ontology.

Madhusūdana Sarasvatī has objected that as both Difference and Viśeṣa fulfil the same function of differentiating, there is no sufficient reason to give the chief place to Difference and make Viśeṣa its substitute only (*pratinidhi*). It may as well be dispensed with. The *Taraṅgiṇi* answers him. The consensus among philosophers is sufficient reason to accord Difference the chief place. There is no such consensus in regard to Viśeṣas. Even the Māyāvādin admits Difference though he regards it as "mithyā", but he will not recognize Viśeṣa even on those terms: ननूभयोरपि भेदकार्यकारित्वान् न मुख्यो भेद इत्यत्र प्रमाणमस्ति। मैवम् सर्वाविवादस्यैव मानत्वात्। नहि विशेषे सर्वाविवादोऽस्ति। सर्वसंकरवादिना भेदवत् मिथ्याभूतस्यापि विशेषस्यानङ्गीकारात् । (*Nym Taraṅgiṇi*, p. 334 b.)

In his *NS* Jayatīrtha has brought out the point that multiplicity is not necessarily concomitant with absolute difference in all cases. In other words, we have to accept two kinds of Vyāpti: (i) where the language of difference (*bhedavyavahāra*) is employed as between two or more absolutely different substances or things and (ii) where a subject-attribute relationship (*dharma-dharmibhāva*) is recognized within a single substance, in regard to its essential attributes which are otherwise established by valid means of proof to be *identical with the substance* itself and spoken of in appropriate language as admitting of a distinction of reference in practical parlance and scientific thought and usage (without implying a distinction of essence).

CHAPTER VIII

MADHVA'S DOCTRINE OF "DIFFERENCE"

MADHVA rejects the universal as a natural corollary of his doctrine of the uniqueness of the particular, be it a person or a thing. This uniqueness is to be understood in terms of difference from all else. Difference is not merely a component part of reality, but constitutes its very essence. So much so, that to know a thing is to know it as distinct from *all others, in a general* way and *from some in a particular way* : प्राय: सर्वतो विलक्षणं हि पदार्थस्वरूपं दृश्यते (*VTN*).

This is because difference constitutes the essence of things (*dharmisvarūpa*) and is not merely an attribute of them, related from outside. A substance, according to Madhva, is not a bare substratum of qualities, or an abstraction, but a synthetic unity, capable of inner distinction of parts and aspects, in speech and thought, according to exigencies under the *aegis* of Viśeṣas. For, difference cannot be taken to be flatly and colorlessly identical with objects (but only colorfully identical or *saviśeṣābhinna*) lest judgments of both identity and difference, that we do have of them, should become unaccountable.

Such, in brief, is Madhva's theory of Difference. It is plainly different from the Nyāya-Vaiśeṣikā and Mīmāṁsā view and this is another striking proof that the logico-philosophical bases of Madhva's system are in no way borrowed from or inspired by these pre-Madhva realisms and that they are the result of independent cogitation on the problems of philosophy.

We have seen that God, matter and souls constitute the three major realities of Madhva's system. The number of souls is unlimited and the modifications of matter are numerous, in various states. These three are conceived as distinct entities. The reality of God is of the independent grade. That of the rest is dependent. Between matter and souls, the former is of a lesser grade of reality. It is only in this sense that we can speak of 'degrees' of reality in this system. The reality of things in space and time involves the differences in name, form, attributes, relations, and tendencies. These manifold differences are generally classified under these heads : (1) Sajātīya or difference of one thing from others of its own kind, (2) Vijātīya or difference from those of another kind, and (3) Svagata or internal distinctions within *an organic whole*. The last one is not admitted by Madhva in its absolute sense. In the sphere of the other two differences he has adumbrated a scheme of "five-fold Difference" (Pañcabheda)[1] :—

```
    Jīva ———————————————— Īśvara ———————————————— Jaḍa
    (                       2                     3 )
1   (                                               )   4
    (                                               )
    Jīva                    5                     Jaḍa
```

This fivefold difference is callectively spoken of by Madhva as "Pra-pañca"—प्रकृष्टः पंचविधो भेदः प्रपंचः (*VTN*). It is real and eternal and admits of no stultification.[2]

Advaitins have sought to deny the reality of this fivefold difference in establishing their thesis of the falsity of *all the three* entities.

स्वाज्ञानकल्पितजगत्परमेश्वरत्व-
जीवत्वभेदकलुषीकृतभूमभावा ।

(*Saṁkṣepaśāriraka*, i. 2)

They have, therefore, subjected the concept of Difference to a searching criticism and sought to discredit the logical realism of the Nyāya-Vaiśeṣika and Mīmāṁsā schools, grounded in the reality of difference. Realistic Vedāntins like Rāmānuja and Madhva have, therefore, been obliged to review these criticisms of the famous dialecticians of the Advaita school and *redefine* their

---

1. Jayatīrtha, in his Commentry on *VTN* shows how this five-fold distinction is clearly presupposed in the very terms of predication made in the *MāndUp* text अनादिमायया (1.16) and अद्वैतः सर्वभावानाम् (i.10) ...

2. Jayatīrtha has explained the derivation of the term on the basis of Pāṇini, V. 1.60:

पंचानां वर्गः पञ्चः । 'पञ्चद्दशतौ वर्गे वा' इति वाशब्देन पञ्चशब्दस्यापि निपातांगीकारात्, प्रकृष्टः पञ्चः प्रपञ्चः । **प्रकृष्टता च, मोक्षांगज्ञानतया भवति ।** (*NS* i. 230 b)

attitude to Difference in such a way as to overcome the difficulties raised by them. We may, therefore, examine Madhva's position with reference to some of these criticisms of the category of "Difference", urged by the Advaitic dialecticians.

There are only two possible ways in which difference could be conceived: (1) as an attribute of things (*dharmabhedavāda*) and (2) as an integral part of the thing itself (*dharmisvarūpa*). Neither can be said to be entirely free from logical difficulties. All attempts at conceiving of difference in a logical manner are eluded by it. Advaitins therefore hold that it cannot be "real" (*prāmāṇika*) and must, therefore, be put down as a product of Avidyā. For the conception of difference is vitiated by many fallacies, such as interdependence and infinite regress, if regarded as an attribute of things. Whether difference is viewed as in its turn 'different' from its relata or as different-cum-identical with them, this relation again will have to be similarly viewed as so related and that again similarly, *ad infinitum*.

The supposition of 'identity' between difference and the object will tend to abolish the reality of difference altogether and leave the object alone to exist, inasmuch as difference cannot claim to have a separate existence of its own, apart from an object: भेदस्य वस्तुनो भेदे, भेदाभेदे च, तस्य तस्य भेदाद्वस्तुनश्च अन्योऽन्यो भेद इति अनवस्थानान्न कश्चित् भेदो वस्तु संस्पृशेत् । अभेदे तु, एकमेव, तच्च वस्त्वेव, न भेद एव । वस्त्वभावे तस्याप्यभावात् । (*Iṣṭasiddhi*, *GOS*, p. 23)

The theory of difference as "Dharmisvarūpa", held by the Prābhākaras, is equally objectionable. For difference, being in the nature of disjunction (*vidāraṇātmā*), the oneness of a thing will be in danger of disruption by the numerous disjunctions (distinctions) which will form part of or constitute its nature and penetrate its very essence and individuality. The oneness or integrality of the object will thus be destroyed and in the absence of oneness, manyness also would cease to be, so that only nullity (*Śūnyatā*) would be left in the end: विदारणात्मनो भेदस्य वस्तुस्वरूपत्वे, न किं चनैकं वस्तु स्यात् * * * * एवं च शून्यतैव तात्त्विकी विश्वस्य आपद्येत । (Ānandabodha, *Nyāyamakaranda*, pp. 45-46)

Thirdly, if difference were included in the essence of a thing, such difference should become fully known, once the object is known, and there will be no more room for doubts of any kind subsequently, so far as that thing and its difference from others are concerned. But such is not the case in experience. This shows that difference cannot be treated as the essence of things, but as something outside their content : यदि च स्वरूपं भेदः, तदा धर्मिणि दृष्टे स्वरूपं दृष्टमिति क्वचिन्न सन्देहः स्यात् ।

(Śrīharṣa, *Khaṇḍanakhaṇḍakhādya*, p. 210)

Lastly, difference is not cognized by itself and independently but only in relation to its terms, either as qualifying them, or as being qualified by them. But in any case, unless the terms themselves are previously cognized, their difference from each other which is either attributive, or bound up with the cognition of the correlate, and counter-correlate, cannot be. But then, the cognition of the terms is dependent on that of the difference already referred to. There is thus an inescapable (mutual) interdependence involved in any attempt to define the nature of difference or conceive of it.[3]

It is evident from the writings of Madhva, that he has carefully examined the problem in the light of these and many other criticisms of the Advaitic dialecticians like Maṇḍana, Vimuktātman, Ānandabodha, Śrīharṣa and Citsukha and has attempted to find a way out. His position may be summed up in a few words: Whatever may be the difficulties in the way of expounding the nature of difference and accounting for its perception, the fact of its experience cannot be denied. If logical difficulties are felt in elucidating the process by which it comes to be apprehended, it is open to us to go beyond the accepted theories on the subject and explore the possibilities of other suitable explanations and adopt newer angles of vision in dealing with the issue, without discrediting the very truth and reality of the experience of difference itself as such. It would be unphilosophical to give up the attempt as beyond solution: नहि प्रक्रियापरिक्षयो वस्तुपरिक्षयात् बलवान्—(Jayatīrtha, *Mith. Kh.*, p. 8)), much more so,

---

3. भेदो हि न स्वतंत्रः प्रतीयेत किंतु, घटपटविशेषणतया, तद्विशेष्यतया वा । तथाच, घटपटाविति वा, घटपटयोरिति वा द्वित्वावच्छिन्नयोर्घटपटयोर्विशेषणविशेष्यतया प्रतीतौ, भेदप्रतीतेः । विशेषणादिप्रतीतेर्विशेष्यादिप्रतीतिकार्यत्वात्, विशेषणविशेष्यभावप्रतीतेश्च भेदप्रतीत्यपेक्षा । तथा चान्योन्याश्रयता । (*VTNt*, p. 48)

to try to esscape the responsibility by condemning the perception of difference as a delusion and giving it a bad name (and hanging it) as the Advaitins have done!

Moreover, granting that all known theories on the nature of difference are untenable, it would still be impossible to prove that the conception of difference is itself a delusion, simply because of our incapacity to make it conform to a definite pattern already familiar to us, or to define it in some particluar way. The Advaitins have *not shown* and could not show that the ways and means of accounting for the perception of difference, which they have attempted to overthrow, are the only ways of defining it or that they could not be bettered or improved by suitable devices : किंच, स्पष्टदृष्टं भेददर्शनं प्रकारान्तरं कल्पयिष्यति, अस्मिन्नेव वा प्रकारे कमप्यवान्तरविशेषं कल्पयति । न तु स्वयं निवर्तते । (*VTNt*, p. 52).

They could not show that the concept itself was fraught with such inherent contradictions that in whatever way it may be defined, one cannot escape them. To show that particular definitions or methods of explanation are wrong, is not to show that the things themselves are indefinable and, therefore, unreal. In order to show *that*, a particular concept has got to be analysed on the basis of its own occurrence and the inconsistencies involved in such an anylysis, shown. The Advaitins could not afford to do this as *they themselves are obliged to accept the category of difference and make use of it*, not in criticizing the doctrines of their rivals, where one could plead the right of परन्यायैस्तु दूषणम्, but in formulating some of their own Siddhāntas on topics like Anirvacanīya and Jīva-Brahmaikya. For example, "*anirvacanīya*" is defined by Advaitins as सदसद्विलक्षणत्वम् or *the nature of being different from Sat and Asat, in essence.* This element of "difference" from Sat and Asat, which is the nature of Mithyātva, must be real and true; in which case it would be impossible to hold *all* differences to be false. It cannot be claimed that the distinction from Sat and Asat, present in the conception of Mithyātva, is a spurious one, while the difference that is sought to be denied by the Advaitin is of the genuine order (पारमार्थिक), and that, therefore, there is no self-contradiction in his theory of difference and its application. In that case, Sad-vailakṣaṇya and Asad-vailakṣaṇya being both of them admittedly false, the universe will have to be regarded as both existent and non-existent (*sadasadātmaka*), rather than as something *different from both*. Such a position will be inconsistent with the Siddhānta of the Advaitins.

Difference is Implicit in Bādhakajñāna

The dismissal of difference as a fiction of thought and its relegation to the category of a delusion as a product of Avidyā, gives rise to a serious difficulty in defining the *nature of tattvajñāna*, in Advaita. This knowledge of ultimate truth is said to be knowledge of non-duality (*abheda-jñāna*) which operates as a 'Bādhaka-jñāna" in stultifying the agelong perception of difference and duality. Such a sublating cognition must naturally involve an element of difference and "opposition" to the past. One is, therefore, entitled to ask if the Bādhaka-jñāna of non-duality embodies some content of difference from the earlier state of knowledge, or it simply takes the 'form' non-difference? In the former case, the reality of difference of some kind will stand conceded and come to stay *even after the birth of Tattvajñāna*, if it is not to relapse into the former state of ignorance ! If, however, the *tattvajñāna* of the Advaitin is simply one of *non-duality*, it will be necessary to *define* the precise significance of the negative element (*a-bheda*) in terms of one or the other of the three well-known meanings of 'otherness", 'negation' or 'opposition'. In any alternative, difference and its reality will be implicated. For the stultifying knowledge which is to take the form of "absence of difference" or *bhedābhava*, must necessarily fix and define its content as something different from its counter-correlate (*bheda*). It must, in other words, be expressed in any of these three forms: 'There is *not*, difference' (now); or 'there is *no* difference (here)' or else 'that something has till now been passing for difference'. Everyone of these forms of the sublating cognition will involve an element of difference and would be powerless to transcend it. In this way, the denial of the reality of difference, by the Advaitin, will involve a self-contradiction, in the last analysis.

Madhva meets the logical objections to the reality of difference, positively also. The so-called difficulties of interdependence etc., are no bar to the *validity of the experience* of difference: अन्योन्याश्रयस्य प्रमात्वाप्रतिबन्धकत्वात् (Jayatīrtha, *VTNt, p.* 52).

It is possible to find other ways of overcoming these and justify the perception of difference and its reality. Otherwise, it would be equally impossible for the Advaition to show that the realization of non-difference is the highest teaching of Vedānta, to be attained by study and meditation; for the conception of Abheda (non-difference) is *as much open to these logical difficulties* as 'Difference' itself.

It should be noted, in this connection, that most of the criticisms of the Advaitic dialecticians of the concept of difference, made *before* the time of Madhva, have reference primarily to the views about difference held by the Nyāya-Vaiśeṣika and Mīmāṁsā realists. The former have treated difference as an attribute of objects. Such a position is hardly tenable, as writers like Vimuktātman and Citsukha have rightly shown. But the other view of difference as "Dharmisvarūpa", or as constituting the essence of objects, does not seem to have been held by any save Mīmāṁsakas of the Prābhākara school. The Advaitic dialecticians have, no doubt, urged objections against this view also, But their criticisms in this respect, *do not affect the new and distinctive theory* of the nature and status of difference formulated by Madhva, and expounded by Jayatīrtha, on the basis of the new principle of "Viśeṣas" and "Saviśeṣābheda", proposed by Madhva, These early Advaitic dialecticians, till the days of Citsukha, *and including him, do not seem to have been aware of the doctrine of Viśeṣas introduced by Madhva for the first time in Indian philosophy*, or its repercussions on the discussion and settlement of the problem of difference. This is conclusive proof of the fact that Madhva's new doctrine of Viśeṣas and its application to the rationalization of the perception of difference, heralds almost a revolution in the history of logic and Vedānta, in the Middle Ages. With its help Madhva gives a new orientation to the doctrine of difference and tides over the difficulties raised by Advaitic dialecticians against the theory of Dharmisvarūpabhedavāda. He straightway agrees with his critics that difference as an attribute of things (*dharmabhedavāda*) is untenable.[4] In

4. This is the reason why Vyāsatīrtha and the other followers of Madhva have not felt called upon to meet the arguments directed against

doing this, he has gone far ahead of the Rāmānuja school which clings to the theory of Dharmabhedavāda. If the new solution of Difference as Saviśeṣābhinna (colorfully identical) with the substratum, does not commend itself to Advaitins who came *after* Madhva, it is not because of any further difficulty in the conception of difference viewed in the light of Viśeṣas, but because of a deep-rooted metaphysical bias in favor of the *unreality* of difference and of the Nirviśeṣatva of reality.

Difference, then, according to Madhva, is not something that falls outside the content of an object or what is generally considered to constitute its essence :

धर्मिप्रतीतिरेव भेदप्रतीतिरिति प्रतीतिद्वयाभावात्[5] (*VTNt*, p. 48)

The 'thing-in-itself' is a metaphysical abstraction. A thing is what it is, *just because of* and not *in spite of* its difference from others. In perception, the essence of a thing is the sum total of its distinction from others : अतो व्यावृत्तिरेव स्वरूपम् (*Taitt Up Bhāṣya*, p. 10). A world of difference lies latent and hidden in the bosom of everything. But these differences are not all of them necessary or presented to cognition in detail, every time an object is perceived. The number of differences that might be perceived and correlated depends on the exigencies of the situation and selective interest. Out of the world of differences with which an object is for the nonce placed in apposition, only such as are relevant to the occasion or interest of the percipient are marked and emphasized and the rest excluded and ignored without any reference to their counter-correlates. It follows then, that in all acts of perception of an object, its difference from others is revealed in the same act, *in a general way* and for the most part : प्रायः सर्वतो विलक्षणं हि पदार्थस्वरूपं दृश्यते (Madhva, *VTN*). Where however doubts arise, they must be put down to

---

the conception of difference as *Pṛthaktva, Vaidharmya* etc. For further remarks on this *see* Dasgupta; *I.Phil.* IV. pp. 179-80; Chandradhar Sharma, *Cri. Sur. I. Phil.* p. 375; Dr. Narain, *Critique of Madhva Refutation of Śaṅkara Vedānta,* p. 195 and my *HDSV* pp. 313-14.

5. "The perception of a given object is the same as the perception of its difference from others. There are no *two perceptions here*—the perception of the thing in itself and of its difference from others. Hence, there is no room for the fallacy of interdependence in perception, as alleged".

the perception of differences from a *few* prominent counter-correlates *only* and missing the differences from others, owing to their bearing a more or less close degree of resemblance to the object in question, aided by other unfavorable conditions like distance, want of sufficient light etc. : कुतश्चित् व्यावृत्तस्य वस्तुनः प्रतीतावपि व्यावृत्तिविशेषाग्रहणादेव संशयोपपत्तेः (*Vādāvali*, p. 83). The sphere of doubt is thus limited to cases of resemblance and other contributory factors. It is by no means *unlimited* as the objectors make out : यदा तु संशीयते, तदापि कुतश्चित् व्यावृत्तमेव दृश्यते । **नहि सर्वमिदं भवति, नवेति कस्यचित् संशयः** (*Taitt Up Bhāṣya ii*) ; ज्ञात्वैव प्रायः सर्वतो वैलक्षण्यं यत्किंचिदेव सदृशे संशयं करोति (*VTN*, p. 5). This disposes of the objection of Śrīharṣa :

यदि स्वरूपं भेदः स्यात्, तदा धर्मिणि दृष्टे, स्वरूपं दृष्टमिति क्वचिन्न संशयः स्यात्
(*Khaṇḍana* ii., p. 210).

Difference being thus *dharmisvarūpa*, the so-called perception of the object is nothing but the perception of its difference—, in other words, the perception of an object is the same as the perception of its difference from all others in a general and from some in a specific way. Inasmuch, then, as there are *no two perceptions here, but only one unitary act of cognition*, and inasmuch as there are no *two things* cognized (viz., the object *and* difference) but *only one*, there is no room for the fallacy of interdependence at all : स च भेदो धर्मिणः स्वरूपमेवेति धर्मिप्रतीतिरेव भेदप्रतीतिरिति प्रतीतिद्वयाभावात् नान्योन्याश्रयता (*VTNt*, p. 48).

This disposes of the objection of interdependence raised by Citsukha and others. Though, difference is admittedly the nature (*svarūpa*) of objects, the acceptance of Viśeṣas in the svarūpa of these objects renders occasional doubts possible : सविशेषत्वेन ज्ञाताज्ञातत्वोपपत्तेः (*NS*, p. 382).

This disposes of the objection of Śrīharṣa that doubts would be unaccountable if difference were regarded as the essential nature of objects, and of Vimuktātman : अभेदे त्वेकमेव तच्च वस्त्वेव, न भेद एव. As Jayatīrtha points out, the mediation of Viśeṣas meets all these difficulties effectively :

विशेषेण अन्यतरमात्रावशेषश्च न भवति—विशेषस्य भेदप्रतिनिधित्वात्
(*VTNt*, p. 52)

Dr. Narain has raised another objection in his *Critique of*

Mādhva Refutation of Śaṅkara Vedānta that if the Mādhva theory of Svarūpabheda and the reality of difference be accepted, then the presence of the pot in the jar (*dharmi*) should be maintained, which is ludicrous (*Op. Cit.* p. 193).

This objection has been met by Jayatīrtha and Vyāsatīrtha in the *NS* (p. 382) and *Nym* (ii. 15) with the answer that the counterpositive in such cases functions merely as an indicating factor (*upalakṣaṇa* or *jñāpaka*) in producing the knowledge of the indicated (*upalakṣya*) while itself remaining (*taṭastha*) outside the *dharmi*.[6]

There is thus no logical impediment, whatever, in regarding Difference as "Dharmisvarūpa" constituting the essence of objects. In the light of Viśeṣas, the category of difference has been fully vindicated by Madhva and shown to be perfectly valid and intelligible.

---

6. Read :—प्रतियोगिघटितस्य भेदस्य धर्मिस्वरूपत्वे प्रतियोगिनोऽपि तत्र निमज्जनं स्यादिति चेत्—किं संभावनयेदमुच्यते, उत व्याप्त्या? नाद्यः, प्रशिथिलमूलत्वात् । नापि द्वितीयः । 'चित्रगुरानीयतां', 'काशीनिवासी समागत' इत्यादौ तदभावात् । * * * व्यावर्तकत्वमात्रेण प्रतियोगिनामुपयोगादिति ब्रूमः (*NS* ii. p. 381)

ननु प्रतियोगिनः उपलक्षणत्वे कदाचित्काकाज्ञानेऽपि गृहज्ञानवत् प्रतियोग्यज्ञानेऽपि भेदज्ञानं स्यादिति चेत्, तर्ह्यज्ञानाद्यज्ञानेऽपि कदाचित्तन्निवृत्त्यादिज्ञानं स्यात् ।

अथोपलक्षणस्यापि प्रतियोग्यादेर्ज्ञानमुपलक्ष्य–अभाव साद्रश्यादिज्ञानकारणं दृष्टमित्यदोषमिति चेत्, समं प्रकृतेऽपि । तस्मात् प्रतियोगिन उपलक्षणत्वान्न धर्मिण्यन्तर्भावः । एवं च—

"पुरुषार्थे दुःखमिव ब्रह्मण्यज्ञानवत्तथा ।
मोक्षे च मोहवत् नान्तर्गतं कुंभादिकं पटे ॥
तटस्थत्वेऽपि कुंभादेरप्रतीतौ न भेदधीः ।
अज्ञानादेरप्रतीतौ तद्धान्याद्यप्रतीतिवत् ॥" (*Nym* ii. 15)

CHAPTER IX

SOME OTHER CATEGORIES : VIŚIṢṬA, AṀŚĪ AND ŚAKTI

WE may now turn to a few other categories of Dvaita ontology which have a bearing on Madhva's theology and cosmology also. These are (1) the group of three represented by Viśeṣaṇa, Viśeṣya and Viśiṣṭa, (2) the pair represented by Aṁśa and Aṁśī, and (3) Śakti.

VIŚIṢṬA

Viśiṣṭa includes the Viśeṣaṇa and Viśeṣya. Viśiṣṭa means the composite whole. Viśeṣaṇa means the component or the qualifying element or adjunct and Viśeṣya or Śuddha the substance to which the qualifying element is attached,—in other words the thing-in-itself.

The conception of Viśiṣṭa varies in the different schools. The conceptual Realists would not look upon it as objectively real:

विशेषणं विशिष्टं च तत्संबन्धफलार्पकम् ।
ज्ञानरूपं स्वसामर्थ्यात् विशिष्टमिति गीयते ॥

The Vaiśeṣikas also do not recognise the Viśiṣṭa to be other than the Viśeṣaṇa, Viśeṣya and their relation. Thus, the Viśiṣṭa is that entity which is the object of the qualified judgments such as *Agnimān parvataḥ, Daṇḍī Devadattaḥ, Īśvaras Sarvajñaḥ.*

It cannot be contended that the qualified justifying 'the Viśiṣṭavyavahāra' is engendered by the Viśeṣya, Viśeṣaṇa and their relation and is, therefore, nothing more. For the judgment is something more than the collective knowledge (*samūhālambanajñāna*). It is a unitary cognition. Moreover, the counter-correlate of Viśiṣṭābhāva cannot be either the bare Viśeṣya or Viśeṣaṇa. We have, therefore, to recognize that Viśiṣṭa is a new entity (*dravyāntara*) produced by Viśeṣaṇa acting as the material cause in contiguity with Viśeṣya—the contiguity acting as the efficient cause of the transformation. Or, Viśeṣya itself may be regarded as the material cause, or both Viśeṣaṇa and Viśeṣya severally—their products being mutually identical. Or, Viśiṣṭa may be regarded as produced conjointly by Viśeṣaṇa and Viśeṣya. In such a case, there is no fear of overlapping of genus (*jātisāṅkarya*) in the effect, as between *dravyatva* and *guṇatva* in the product. For these two being mutually concomitant, there is no room for mutual intersection of natures.

Viśiṣṭākāra is thus neither Viśeṣaṇa nor the relation as such but Viśeṣya. But it is not the mere Viśeṣya. The Mīmāṁsakas believe in the relation of Bhedābheda among the three. The monists hold them to be simply identical.

Madhva holds that every new relation alters or modifies a substance to a greater or less extent. His view of Viśiṣṭa is akin to the conception of whole and part in Hegelian philosophy, according to which the whole is something more than the sum of its parts though dependent on them for their existence in the physical world. The subtraction of any one of the parts, destroys the whole. Only, Madhva would add that a new Viśiṣṭa would step in then :

दण्डादिविशेषणसंबन्धेन देवदत्तो विशिष्टरूपं द्रव्यान्तरमुत्पादयति (*VTNt*)

दण्डकुण्डलसंबन्धात् विशिष्टद्वयस्यैवोत्पत्तेः (Up. Kht)

Madhva distinguishes carefully between relations and qualities which are coeval (*Yāvaddravyabhāvī*) with substance (viśeṣya), as for example, God and His attributes of omniscience and those which are changing and impermament (*ayāvaddravyabhāvi*). In the former case, there is identity always subject to internal distinction of reference through Viśeṣas. Hence such identity is termed Sa-viśeṣābheda. In respect of changing attributes and relations, there is only Bhedābheda or difference-cum-identity, as in वह्निमान् पर्वतः—

अयावद्द्रव्यभाविविशेषणेन, विशिष्टस्य विशेष्येण भेदाभेदाङ्गीकारात्

(*GTt*, *p*. 188 b; *NS* 365)

The same principle applies to Aṁśāṁśis also. The concept of Viśiṣṭa has important bearings on Madhva's theory of causation, as will be shown hereafter.

AṀŚA AND AṀŚĪ

These two terms may be taken roughly to correspond to the idea of fraction and unit understood metaphorically. They are also sometimes used for part and whole respectively. Madhva applies the idea of *aṁśa* and *aṁśi* to sentient beings also. He distinguishes between Svarūpāṁśa and Bhinnāṁśa. The Avatāras of God are His Svarūpāṁśas. The Jīvas are Bhinnāṁśas. The Devas also have their *aṁśas* (cf. Indra and Arjuna). The theory figures in Madhva's theology to a great extent. In respect of ordinary Jīvas also, the operation of *aṁśāṁsibhāva* is considered necessary to account for the harmonious working of the quantitative adjustment of their innate potencies for bliss, volition and activity in regard to requisite ends, through the agency of Viśeṣas (See *BSB* ii.2. adhi. 7).

ŚAKTI

Śakti is supersensuous (*atīndriya*). Sahajaśakti is recognized to exist in God[1] as well as other Cetanas[2], in insentient things and substances like fire and in qualities also. As indicated by their names, 'Sahajaśakti' is intrinsic and 'Ādheyaśakti' is induced by external factors, such as consecration in an image (*pratimā*). The acceptance of '*ādheyaśakti*' is necessary also to account for the sense organs producing invalid knowledge, due to vitiation by defects, the Sākṣī grasping the invalidity of knowledge by instituting tests in the case of discrepancy of knowledge and Saṁskāras giving the visual organ the power of recognition (*pratyabhijñā*). Vyāsatīrtha has adduced syllogisms to establish Sahaja and ādheyaśaktis.[3]

Śakti is accepted by Madhva as *nitya* and *anitya* according to the nature of the substance in which is resides. They are, of course, inseparable from their substances, if they are coeval with them, and *bhinnābhinna*, when impermanent.

---

1. परास्य शक्तिर्विविधैव श्रूयते स्वाभाविकी (*Svet. up.* VI.8.)

2. संसार्यात्मा अदृष्टात्मेतरसकलस्वजन्यानुकूलधर्मवान्, आत्मत्वात्, सत्त्वात्, ज्ञेयत्वाद्वा, ईश्वरवत् (*TT* ii.9)

3. 'व्रीहीन् प्रोक्षति' इत्यत्र प्रोक्षणजन्यस्य व्रीहिनिष्ठस्यातीन्द्रियस्य ईप्सितातिशयस्य अभावेन 'व्रीहीन्' इति ईप्सितकर्मणि द्वितीया **न** स्यात् *TT* ii.10.)

The differentiation of Śakti and Śaktimat, is rendered possible by the agency of Viśeṣas, as in the case of *aṁśa* and *aṁśī*, etc.

The creative energy of Brahman is, for instance, identical with Brahman; but it can be distinguished by the play of Viśeṣas. The Śaktis themselves have two aspects : *Śaktitā* (latent state) and *Vyaktitā* (manifested state), also regulated by the play of Viśeṣas. Hence they do not operate in mutual conflict, at the same time. To illustrate, the creative and destructive energies of Brahman are both eternal and identical with its being[4]. But there is an inner pre-established harmony which regulates their working periodically and without overlapping. At the time of dissolution, the creative energy of Brahman is in dormancy (*śaktirūpa*) and comes into play (*vyakti*) only at the right time. The distinction of Time into 'the time of creation' and 'the time of dissolution' is likewise based on internal Viśeṣas in Time which are also Saviśeṣābhinna from it.[5]

4. शक्तय: सर्वभावानामचिन्त्यज्ञानगोचरा:
यतोऽतो ब्रह्मणस्तु सर्गाद्या भावशक्तय: (*Viṣṇu Purāṇa* i.3.2)
भावशब्द: स्वभावपर:, स्वाभाविक्य: शक्तय इत्यर्थ:
(*Śrutaprakāśa* on *Śrībbāṣya*, i.1.2).

5. शक्तिरूपस्थिता सैव क्रियाशक्तिरितीर्यते ।
सा च व्यक्तिस्तु जनिवत् क्रियाया रूपमेव तु ।
तथापि तु विशेषेण स्वरूपेण विशेषिणी
जनेर्जनिवदेवासौ ज्ञातव्याव्यतिरेकत: ॥ (*Commentary Brh. Up.* i.4.9.)

CHAPTER X

SĀDṚŚYA *VS* THE UNIVERSAL

SĀDṚŚYA (resemblance) is a category that replaces the Universal in Madhva's system. Here, Madhva parts company with the Nyāya-Vaiśeṣikas and Mīmāṁsaka-realists and joins hands with the modern Nominalists and the Jainas.

There are three main theories in Western philosophy about universals. The Nominalists look upon particulars alone as real. There are only individual things in nature and particular ideas in the mind. There is no universal at all. Only the name is common to many. This view approximates to that of Madhva and the Jainas.

The Conceptualists think that though only individual things exist in nature, without any universal class-essence running through them, the human mind has the power of forming abstract and general ideas about them. Universals, then, exist in our minds as concepts. The Realists, on the other hand, maintain that universals exist both in nature and in the mind.

In Indian philosophy, the Buddhists are extreme nominalists, splitting even the so-called individuals into momentary essences (*svalakṣaṇam*). The Nyāya and Mīmāṁsā schools show varying degrees of realistic bias in their conception of the universal. The argument from universals to monism is easy to guess. The Jainas have argued that the nature of universal is not one of class-essence, but of similarity or resemblance. Such resemblance is actually experienced and should be taken as the objective ground of the notion of universals.

The same is the stand taken by Madhva. His rejection of universal (*sāmānya*) is a direct corollary of the pluralistic implications of his Svarūpabhedavāda. He believes in the distinctiveness, nay, uniqueness of each individual and particular[1]. He could ill afford, then, to recognize a single universal class-essence running through a number of particulars, which will surreptitiously open the door to monism in the end. He therefore, sets his face resolutely against the universal and gives it no quarter.

In his discussion of the problem of Sādṛśya vs Universal, Madhva has surprisingly anticipated many of the arguments against the Nominalist view of the real universal advanced by modern thinkers. The Realists' contention is that most of the words we use in common life refer to things, qualities and relations or their actions (dravyaguṇakarmāṇi) which do not exist by themselves. Unless our words express some elements which a number of particular things, qualities or relations have in common, the purpose of language and thought would not be served. To that extent inference based on Vyāpti between *hetu* and *sādhya* would also be impossible, as our words and thoughts could not rise above particulars, and inferences take us from particulars to the general.

It is urged by modern Realists that the Nominalist's attempt to meet these difficulties by substituting 'resemblance' for universal is futile. Resemblance itself, as proposed to be used, would be a true universal in order to apply to different kinds of resemblances. These 'resemblances' would be far too vague, as everything resembles everything else in some respect or other. We should have to admit a different kinds of resemblance for each universal term. It would be simpler and less cumbersome to admit an objective universal characteristic corresponding to each term instead of trying to detect more and more particular forms of resemblance.[2]

Madhva points out in reply that there is a basic difference in the *modus operandi* of resemblances and universals, which the Realist has failed to note in his arguments. It is this. The extension of significance of terms to a number of resembling particulars is achieved by 'Resemblance' not because

---

1. Cf. किंच, **न सत्त्वं नामैकमनुगतं** किंतु प्रतिवस्तु सत्वानि भिद्यन्ते (*NS* i.1.1) 'भिन्नाश्च भिन्नधर्माश्च पदार्था निखिला अपि' (*AV* ii. 2.24).
2. See A.C. Ewing, *Fundamental Questions of Philosophy*, p.213.

it represents the conventional sense (*Śabdaśakti*) of the word for the particular entity or the appellative basis (*pravṛttinimitta*) of the application of the word to that particular, but merely because it operates as a mark of inference, in helping us to know that all the other particulars bearing a strong resemblance of a specific kind and measure to the given one admit of being denoted by the same name or word (*vācakatva śaktiḥ sādṛśyasya vyāpikā atas tām śaktim tattadviṣayatayā sādṛśyam sphuṭaṁ jñāpayati*—*NS*, p. 373). This potentiality for extension of reference to other similar particulars is learnt in the very first act of learning the use of the word and its connotation. The very purpose of learning and teaching the use of words in any language is to be able to secure such extended rapport:

> 'अयं गौः' इत्यस्य अयमेतत्सदृशाश्च सर्वे गोशब्दवाच्या इत्यर्थोऽभिप्रेयते वक्त्रा। द्वयोरपि सार्वत्रिकव्युत्पत्तिकामत्वेन, एकवाक्यस्य एकपिण्डविषयकत्वकल्पनानुपपत्तेः। (*NS*, p. 372)

Though in Madhva's philosophy, resemblance, like *saṁyoga*, *vibhāga* and *bheda* is an asymmetrical relation, still by reason of its being experienced always in relation to a counterpositive relatum it is quite within its competence to extend the sphere of its reference beyond the given particular to many others of like nature according to exigencies. Likewise, the ascertainment of Vyāpti and causal relationships are also within its competence and there is no need to requisition the services of the universal for these purposes.

The Nyāya-Vaiśeṣikas have tried to get over such difficulties by relying on class-essence in some cases, *svarūpasambandha* in some others and 'imposed properties' (*upādhi*) in yet others. Madhva's philosophy offers *a uniform principle of Sādṛśya as the basis of all extension of reference* with *vācyatva* (connotation) and *pravṛttinimitta* (appellative basis) limited *ab initio* to distinct particulars. The extended significance being already understood in the first instance of learning the language, there is no difficulty in limiting or extending the significance to suit the exigencies of a given context. The further objection that "we cannot distinguish a vast number of resemblances, by inspecting the resemblances of each relation", is pointless, says Jayatīrtha, as such partial resemblances could not be eschewed even in respect of universals :

नच वाच्यम्--गोसादृश्यमश्वेऽप्यस्तीति तत्रापि गोशब्दवाच्यतानुमानप्रसंगः । जातिनिमित्तेष्वपि एवं प्रसंगस्य समानत्वात् । (*NS* p. 373)

If the universe of reference is narrowed down to specific forms of the universal and not to too generalized ones, the same thing could be done in the case of 'resemblances' too :

जातिविशेषों निमित्ततयांगीक्रियते, अतो न व्यभिचार इति चेत्, तर्हि, सादृश्यविशेष एव लिंगं यो लक्षणभूत इति वदामः । (*NS*, p. 373)

Madhva also takes the wind out of the sails of the Realist by maintaining the extreme Nominalist position that even resemblance is *not a universal* and that it is *sui generis* in each case. This is consistent with his Svabhāva-bhedavāda according to which no single characteristic can be the essence of more than one entity.[3]

न सर्वधर्म एकोऽस्ति * * * * * ॥
एतादृशं च सादृश्यं पदार्थेपु पृथक् पृथक् ।
नरत्वादिकमप्येवं तत्तद्धर्मतयेष्यते ॥ (*AV* ii.2.13)

Similarity is not a perfectly symmetrical relation. There is some difference between the similarity of A to B and that of B to A, as Viśeṣas are relative to the point of view from which they are examined.

The uniqueness of resemblance does not however prevent its facilitating inferential extension of significance of terms in required cases, as there is sufficient likeness between a group of particulars described as similar to one another, to justify the application of the same name or general term, just as "differing" attributes are apprehended as "different" without requiring the help of another difference to render them intelligible.

Madhva argues that the contention that extension of significance of terms would be impossible without the idea of a universal will be suicidal. For, if that be so, we would have to admit a series of universals one behind the other, in order to justify the title of each universal to be so called and hypothesized. Similarly to know all the particulars by the name 'particular' we will have to admit a 'universal' of 'particulars'.

---

3. सर्वस्य भवतः स्वभावत्वानुपपत्तेः (Udayana : *Kusumāñjali*, i.5)

जातितश्चेत् कथं तासु, तत्र चेदनवस्थितिः ।
तथैव व्यक्तिविज्ञानं व्यक्तित्वाभावदूषितम् ॥ (*AV*, ii.2.13)

We refer collectively to the essentiality (*svarūpa*) of several things. But there cannot be a single essential nature common to many Svarūpas, as "Svarūpa" by definition is strictly particular, belonging to only one thing. If another generality of Svarūpatva is admitted to run through many Svarūpas, that one and the other (remaining) Svarūpas will have to be brought under the purview of another "Svarūpatva" in its turn and so on *ad infinitum*. The difficulty can be avoided only by recognizing with Madhva that the different Svarūpas are referred to by the same term "Svarūpa" to show that each has a Svarūpa of its own *like* any other and that no real thing is without a Svarūpa of its own.

The ontological consequence of Madhva's view that resemblance is *sui generis* in each case, appears to be that the Pratibimbatva of each individual self to God, based on a certain measure of Sādṛśya, is also unique and distinctive in each case and that no two individuals will bear the same resemblance to the Bimba (viz. God), in respect of their spiritual attributes of consciousness and bliss.

CHAPTFR XI

SPACE AND TIME

THE Hindu theory of Mahāpralaya which can be traced to the Ṛg Veda (X. 129) presupposes an absolute theory of time and space according to which they have a being in themselves apart from the things in space and events in time. Space and Time must *ex hypothesi* be infinite. If we deny this, there will be the great logical difficulty of conceiving a boundary to finite space and time. We shall have to recognize more space and more time beyond them and this will lead to a regress.

'अत्र देशो नास्ति', 'इदानीं कालो नास्ति', इत्यस्य व्याहृतत्वात् देशकालयोः परिच्छेदनिरूपणयापि तयोरपरिच्छेदसिद्धिः । देशकालयोः स्वोपाधौ निषेधे विरोधेन, अविरोधाय निषेधोपाधितया देशकालान्तरयोरावश्यकत्वाच्च । (*Nym* 1.5)

No doubt the conception of infinite Space and Time also has its difficulty of involving the contradiction of a completed infinite. But Mādhva thought with its most serviceable concept of Svarūpa-Viśeṣas overcomes this difficulty and makes it possible to hold that space and time have infinite potential divisibility and have existence in themselves through Viśeṣas.[1]

The concept of Space as Avyākṛtākāśa in Madhva's philosophy must be recognized to be a remarkable advance in Vedāntic thought, if we consider Thibaut's comment in Vol. II, p. 3, fn 1 of his translation of Śaṅkara's *BSB* that "the Vedantins *do not* clearly distinguish between empty space and an exceedingly fine matter filling all space, which, however attenuated is yet one of the elements and as such belongs to the same category as air, fire, water and earth" (SBE Vol. XXXVIII, p. 3). Madhva shows himself fully aware of this necessary

---

1. देशः सर्वत्रास्ति, कालः सदास्ति, पूर्वः काल, इत्यबाधितप्रतीत्या, तयोः स्वनिर्वाहकतया, प्रमेयत्वादिवत् स्वसंबन्धसंभवाच्च । (Vyāsatirtha, *Nym*, i.5)

distinction[2] and its scientific significance :

अवकाशमात्रं ह्याकाशः कथमुत्पद्यते ऽन्यथा ? (*AV* ii. 3.1)

He, therefore, holds that Space and Time are distinct entities, intuited by Sākṣī and that they are *not* merely 'forms of intuition' as in Kantian thought. Otherwise, they could *not* be intuited :

गगनं साक्षिगोचरं प्रदेश इति विज्ञेयम् । (*AV* ii.3.1)

The Mādhva conceptions of Space and Time is thus much ahead of that of other Indian schools and looks surprisingly modern in some respects. This is due not a little to their being interpreted in the light of the new doctrine of Sākṣī and Viśeṣas which are Madhva's most striking contributions to philosophic thought. They seem to hold great possibilities for the future of metaphysics. With these two ideas Madhva overcomes the antinomies which beset the conception of Space and Time in other philosophical systems of ancient and modern thought as well.

Space is termed "Avyākṛtākāśa" by Madhva as distinguished from ether (*bhutākāśa*). The former is eternal and uncreated and the latter is a product of matter. This twofold classification of Ākāśa is a special feature of Madhva's philosophy. It is tersely termed as "*Ākāśa-dvaitam*" by Jayatīrtha and Vyāsatīrtha (See my *BSPC* Vol. II p. 126).

The Nyāya-Vaiśeṣikas hold that there is one eternal ubiquitous space (*vibhu*) which is not open to perception, but is only inferred from the spatial characteristics of proximity, remoteness, etc. But spatial properties and relations like distance, size, etc., can be perceived directly through touch, sight, etc. The Mīmāṁsakas hold similar views. The Sāṁkhya and Yoga schools look upon Space and Time as categories of the understanding (*buddhikalpita*). Some Naiyāyikas regard space as perceived by the visual sense. Jayatīrtha dismisses this as impossible on the Nyāya view that space is colorless. Nor can Space be left to be entirely inferred through sound, as even the cogenitally deaf have a perception of space.

---

2. भूतमप्यसितं दिव्यदृष्टिगोचरमेव तु ।
उत्पद्यते, अव्याकृतं हि गगनं साक्षिगोचरम् ।
प्रदेश इति विज्ञेयं नित्यं नोत्पद्यते हि तत् । (*AV* ii.3.1)

Madhva's theory of the intuitive perception of space and time has received assent from many modern European thinkers. The ordinary 'scientific' view of space is what makes movement possible. The idea of possible movement is formed by abstraction from the experience of movement. This is circuitous. Madhva says that we cannot understand movement as such without being already conscious of space. Movement does not explain space. Space explains movement. He, therefore, suggests that space must be accepted as a reality given by direct perception, *not* of the ordinary senses, *but of Sākṣi*, which is specially fitted to sense the supersensuous. No memory of movement is, therefore, necessary to establish space inferentially and mentally, as some of the older Naiyāyikas thought and some modern philosophers do.

Madhva's definition of space as distinguished from ether, is true to its essential nature of providing room for bodies to exist:

अवकाशमात्रं ह्याकाशः (*AV* ii.3.1)

This is explained by Vyāsatīrtha as अवकाशप्रदत्वम्. This is supported by a passage from the *Bhāgavata* (iii.30.43) quoted by Madhva. He holds that space and time are infinitely divisible, into further spaces and further parts of time, each such part being held to be a "natural" part of it and not merely conditioned by Upādhis. For, "Upādhis", according to Madhva, are not so much the causes of distinction (where they do not actually exist) (भेदकारका:) as 'pointers' (ज्ञापकाः) thereof.

He shows that it is logically inconceivable that Space is *created* :

अवकाशमात्रं ह्याकाशः कथमुत्पद्यते ऽन्यथा ।
यद्यनाकाशता पूर्वं किं मूर्तनिबिडं जगत् ? (*AV* ii.3.1)

We cannot conceive of the antecedent non-existence of space anywhere, if space is to be created. Production also needs a material stuff and there is no such stuff out of which space could be created. If Prakṛti is that stuff, the question could be repeated in respect of it, as to why it should alone be uncreated. If the reply is that the production of Prakṛti from another stuff is inconceivable, the same thing could be said of space also. The Buddhists' view of space as मूर्तद्रव्याभाव (absence of tangible reals) would lead to other difficulties such as that such reals existed at a time when space was not yet in existence (or created). This would reverse the ideas of Sṛṣṭi and Pralaya. Madhva, therefore, pleads strongly that space must be accepted as an uncreated and eternal substance—a view which receives striking support from the remarks of Herbert Spencer : "If space is created, it must have been previously non-existent. The non-existence of space cannot, however, be imagined by any mental effort. If the non-existence of space is absolutely inconceivable, then, necessarily, its creation is absolutely inconceivable" (*First Principles*, p. 27).

As a Vedāntin believing in the Brahmakāraṇatvavāda of the entire universe, Madhva seeks to reconcile the essential uncreated nature of space (and other *ex hypothesi* eternal reals) with the Vedāntic axiom : that everything in the universe is, in some sense, created by Brahman (*BS* i. i.2[3]) by interpreting the 'creation' of eternal substances like space, and time in a Pickwickian sense[4] of "Parādhīnaviśeṣāpti" (पराधीनविशेषाप्ति) which will be explained later. This shows that Madhva has been the only commentator, who has had the right insight into the *raison d'etre* and metaphysical significance of the principle of Samanvaya enunciated by the Sūtrakāra. He explains the references to actual creation of Ākāśa, in Upaniṣadic cosmology, as referring only to Bhūtākāśa and this is the reason why he has admitted two kinds of Ākāśa, in his system.

3. 'Creation' includes other cosmic determinations also like 'Sthiti'.

4. "Pickwickian sense" does not stand for 'explaining away'. Nor does it mean 'misleading' or connote insincerity, dishonesty or anything of that kind. It carries a good sense and has been used only in a sense acceptable to serious philosophical writing.

The following reference will make this clear :

(i) Webster's *New International Dictionary of the English Language* (2nd Edn. London, 1953) defines it as :

"A sense that is esoteric, constructive, recondite or the like, a peculiar sense" (p.1857 cols. 1 and 2).

(ii) Prof. A.C. Ewing uses it in his well-known work : *Fundamental Questions of Philosophy* :

"In general, we must be very cautious about transferring direct to Philosophy statements which though useful are only true in a Pickwickian sense i.e. in a sense quite different from the literal one. This almost certainly applies to such assertions as that space is curved...It may be difficult to decide whether one is using some expression in a Pickwickian sense and if so in what sense" (p. 146 *op. cit.*).

TIME

Time, in Dvaita Vedānta, is the essential constituent of all experience :

तेन च कालेन सविशेषणतयानुभूयते इति सर्वाधारतयास्थेयम् (*Vādāvali*, p. 95)

But it is *not*, as in Advaita, apprehended by the ordinary sense of perception.[5] It is held to be perceived by the Sākṣī, on the testimony of 'सौषुप्तिकानुभव'. At the stage of Suṣupti, there is no functioning of the sense organs, including the mind. Hence, there is no scope for Pratyakṣa or Inference. The perception of time in this *dreamless state*, is borne out by the immediate evidence of its intuitive experience, recollected immediately on waking[6] up and expressed in the judgment: एतावन्तं कालं सुखमहमस्वाप्सम् (I have slept in bliss so long). This cannot be disregarded as a mere recollection as there can be no recollection of what has never been experienced by oneself. For the same reason of its immediacy, it cannot be treated as an inference to a condition of complete freedom from any kind of infelicity "at the period of time just elapsed". If such a condition has been *experienced* by the person who draws the present inference, he should have had a direct experience of "that period of time which has just elapsed". There can be no inference of its condition, had it never been experienced by him. There would thus be no explanation of the experience of dreamless sleep (सौषुप्तिकानुभव) unless the perception of time (besides that of Ātman and of bliss i.e. स्वरूपसुखम्) is accepted. For the same weighty reasons, the intuitive perception of time by the Sākṣī, must be admitted :

कालो हि साक्षिप्रत्यक्षः सुषुप्तौ च प्रतीतितः[7] (*AV* i.4.11)

The Naiyāyikas look upon Time as only inferable and not open to direct perception as it is formless. But as Madhva rightly points out, the inference of time would itself presuppose

---

5. नीरूपस्यापि कालस्येन्द्रियवेद्यत्वाभ्युपगमात् । (*Vedānta-Paribhāṣā*, p. 22, Calcutta)
6. औत्तरिकानुस्मृतिसिद्धसौषुप्तिकानुभवसिद्धत्वात् (*TP* i.1.1)
7. अतीतानागतौ कालावपि नः साक्षिगोचरौ ।
पक्षीकर्तुमशक्यत्वात् नानुमा तत्र वर्तते ।
तदेतदिति सर्वत्र दृश्यं वा स्मृतिगोचरम्
साक्षिसिद्धेन कालेन खचितं ह्येव दृश्यते ॥ (*AV* i.4.11)

time as its Pakṣa (minor term) and the ascertainment of Vyāpti in respect of time would be impossible without a prior perception of time. There is, thus, no other Pramāṇa, than the Sākṣī, by which time could be proved. The Nyāya, Sāṁkhya and Yoga philosophers would appear to hold that time is more a category of the understanding (बुद्धिकल्पित)—as a necessary "*form* of intuition" known only through inference as there is no perception of blank time without a sensible content. Madhva shows that this is *not so*. It should be regarded, says he, as a fundamental ontological category that conditions all our being and becoming. No experience is possible without it. It is experienced along with the experience itself :

स्मृत्यनुभवाश्च सर्वाः प्रतीतयः न केवलमर्थमवगाहन्ते, किंतु कालकलितमेव ।

The organ by which the intuiting Self becomes aware of time, is termed the Sākṣī or *Svarūpendriyam* which is no other than the Sākṣī itself turning its own inner searchlight, so to say, upon itself. This answers the difficulty felt by many Western thinkers like William James that we have no sense for bare time, that we cannot intuit a mere duration. The difficulty lies in our taking only the waking experience as the basis for philosophizing. The Vedānta, on the other hand, draws its certified data from the other states also, including Suṣupti, in particular, which is the highest state of ideal experience (of bare ego, bare time and bare felicity, if you please) of which everyone of us has had direct experience, as the coveting of it so conclusively proves. Madhva has thus anticipated Kant's notion of pure intuition of time without any sensible content in his doctrine of the intuitive perception of Time by the Sākṣī. His view has also a remarkable affinity with Alexander's acceptance of the intuition of time and space, prior to sensations and his view that it is through intuition that they are immediately perceived.

Madhva does not hold that time is an undifferenced and indivisible whole (*akhaṇḍa*). It is infinite and infinitely divisible[8]. It is an infinite stream of duration without beginning or end.

8. In his *BT* (iii), Madhva gives an interesting table of the smaller units of time starting from the one occupying a point of three *trasareṇus*. Three *truṭis* make one *vedha*, three *vedhas* *a lava*, three *lavas a nimeṣa*, three *nimeṣas a kṣaṇa* and so on.

Each duration is pervasive. As in the case of Paramāṇus, the shortest conceivable duration is also theoretically divisible still further. Electrons in physics, though physically indivisible are not logically so. Madhva holds that at whatever size they might be said to be "atoms", we can always conceive parts of them smaller than the whole, although it may not be possible for physical reasons to split them : अविभाग : पराणुता (*AV*)[9]. This enables him to hold that the divisions of time are all "natural" parts of it and not merely औपाधिक or superimposed : अस्माभिः काले स्वभावतः एव भेदोंगीक्रियते (*NS* p. 387 b). As in the case of space, so in respect of time, Madhva posits that it is eternal and uncreated in the sense of bare empty time (*anādi*) and non-eternal (divisible). Both are intuited by Sākṣī. This is how he reconciles the Vedic, Upaniṣadic and Purāṇic texts *which speak of time in both the ways* :

नासदासीन्नो सदासीत् **तदानीम्** (*RV* X. 129.1)
द्रव्यं कर्म च **कालश्च** (*Bhag* ii. 10.12)
सर्वे **निमेषा** जज्ञिरे (*TA* X.1.2)
नित्यौ कालश्च सत्तम (*Viṣṇu Purāṇa* quoted by Madhva)

It is also pointed out by Madhva that unless intrinsic parts are accepted in Time, the established order of time in Sṛṣṭi and Pralaya could not be maintained without risk of overlapping and the admission of Upādhis for this purpose would be pointless, unless there were already natural distinctions in time to which these Upādhis could attach themselves apart from the difficulty of interdependence which would also ensue, in the event of Upādhis *de novo*.[10]

---

9. Cf. यस्य भिन्नावयवेषु सत्स्वपि, तेषां विभागो न कदापि भवितुमर्हति, **स परमाणुरिति व्याख्यानात्** (*NS* p. 349 b)

10. कालभेदेन जगत्सृष्टिप्रलयव्यवस्था च परमते न घटते । कालस्य भावात्, ईशस्य नित्येच्छत्वात् । स्वमते तु, कालभेदसद्भावात् सृष्ट्यादिव्यवस्थोपपन्ना (*SNR* p.19)

CHAPTER XII

CAUSATION

THE Mādhva theory of causation cannot be understood without relation to its doctrine of Viśiṣṭa, already referred to. The true bearing of this doctrine on the question of creation of "eternal substances like Prakṛti, Jīvas, Space, Time, etc., would not be missed if the distinction of Yāvaddravyabhāvi and Ayāvaddravyabhāvi relations is clearly borne in mind. Jayatīrtha's statement : विशिष्टाकारश्च वस्तुस्वरूपाभिन्न इति तस्यैवायमुपजनो भवति (*NS* p. 431) if rightly understood, in the light of the important distinction drawn between these two types of relations, would have prevented the utterly baseless though sensational conclusion of the 'essential creation' (स्वरूपसृष्टि) of the Jīvas (as of other eternal substances) according to Madhva's theory of Causation, drawn by Prof. H. N. Raghavendrachar.[1] This has evoked protests from many orthodox quarters, as a misinterpretation of Madhva. The embodiment of selves and such other Viśeṣaṇas of finite reality, being in the nature of the things, *not coeval* with the entities concerned, there is no possibility at all of applying the principle of Saviśeṣābheda between them. The proposition विशिष्टाकारश्च वस्तुस्वरूपाभिन्नः (*NS* p. 431) would *not*, therefore, apply to them.

Madhva's doctrine of Bhedābheda between Viśiṣṭa and Viśeṣya (or Śuddha) in respect of changing attributes and relations of things, leads to the corollary of "Sadasatkāryavāda" of causation, which is his general theory of causation.

---

1. *Dvaita Philosophy, Its Place in the Vedānta*, Mysore University, 1941.

Causation implies a change, a beginning and and end :

सन्निति व्यवह्रियमाणमेव पदार्थस्वरूपं, उत्पत्तेः प्राङ् नाशोत्तरं च नास्तीति सर्वो लोको व्यवहरति——

आद्यन्तयोः सर्वकार्यमसदित्येव निश्चितम् ।
यद्यसन्न विशेषोऽत्र जायते, कोऽत्र जायते[2] ? (*GT* ii. 16)

"Causation", therefore, has reference only to the "Viśeṣa"-aspect of the substance in question. Madhva, therefore, rejects the Satkāryavāda of the Sāṅkhyas and the Asatkārya-vāda of Nyāya philosophy as halftruths. He combines them into a new theory of Sadasatkāryavāda; for change is not merely something *new* appearing, but it presupposes a substratum that changes, in form or state. *Ex nihilo nihil fit*. Causation would be impossible and meaningless, without the assumption of continuity of the cause in and through the changes it has undergone. Hence Jayatīrtha defines causation as follows :

तदेव हि वस्तु अवयवोपचयापचयाभ्या**मन्यथा क्रियते । न पुनरन्यदेव भवति इति हि परिणामवादिनो मन्यन्ते** (*NS* p. 394).

Such a definition is intended to meet the criticism that if cause and effect were different events they would be absolutely separate and there would be no *relation* between them. The gulf between the two will then remain unbridged. The Buddhist doctrine of causation as an ever-changing, constant, ceaseless flux, each moment (kṣaṇa) of existence being but a "specious present" with no duration, is sharply criticized by Madhva and Jayatīrtha. We cannot think of a "change" without a changing thing at the back. There *must be* a "something" that is not contained in the succession which carries on each vanishing point of the succession and *adds* it to the next (*BS* ii. 2.21). Such a link would be missing in the Buddhist doctrine of Kṣaṇikatva, as a *kṣaṇa* is, according to the Buddhist view, indivisible like a mathematical point (and *nirviśeṣa* at that). There would be no split-second interval between any two

2. The existence of things which are referred to as 'existing' is recognised by all persons, as having *no existence before* they came into being and *after they cease to be*. At the beginning and the end all effects are non-existent. If the non-existent factor which subsequently comes into being is *not* a 'Viśeṣa' what else is it that is "born"? (Tr.)

vanishing points of moments at which the cause and effect could have met and "causation" taken place by the transference of "Saṁskāras". For, mere sequence or succession (in time) is *not* causation.

Madhva holds, therefore, that the effect is *partially* non-existent in its definite form and shape, while being existent in the form of the cause:

असद्यत्कार्यरूपेण कारणात्मतयास्ति हि (*AV* ii. 1-19)

तन्तुभ्योऽन्यः पटः साक्षात् कस्य दृष्टिपथं गतः ? (*GT.* ii. 14)

He does not, however, subscribe to the Sāṁkhya view of *absolute identity* of cause and effect, as that will render causal effort superfluous and causation meaningless. Even if that were understood in the sense of "manifestation", the same difficulty would arise in its case :

व्यक्तावपि समं ह्येतन् अनवस्थान्यथा भवेत् । (*GT* ii. 16)

Manifestation and non-manifestation cannot be understood in the sense of the effect being perceived or not perceived (though per-existent in the cause). That will land us in solipsism (दृष्टि सृष्टि) There will be no answer to the question why the effect is *not manifested* if it were really, *absolutely* and without any qualification (Viśeṣa) identical with the cause and so pre-existent in it. The idea of manifestation itself will be similarly open to an antinomy of production or manifestation.

CHAPTER XIII

NEGATION (ABHĀVA)

NEGATION, as a fact of experience, is a Prameya. It is an important ontological category. As a thought-category it lies at the root of many other philosophical conceptions like Bhāvarūpājñāna, Mithyātva, Bheda and Causation. The positive and the negative represent the two aspects of reality. The Mādhva philosophers agree with the Naiyāyikas in accepting the negative as a separate category of experience. The argument by which some philosophers have sought to deny independent status to negation, by equating it with the mere existence of the *locus*, has been rejected by Jayatīrtha in his *TSt.* He points out that the judgment 'there is no jar on the ground' must signify something more than the mere *locus* and that that something must be a negation Without reference to such a negation, it will be impossible to define what is meant by the *locus per se*. Otherwise, it would be open to us to speak of the non-existence of the jar, even when it *is* present on the ground, as the *locus* as such exists even while the jar is there in it.

Madhva defines negation as : प्रथमप्रतिपत्तौ निषेधरूपत्वम् (*AV* ii. 1.8) or what is presented in the primary act of perception as involving the *significant negation* or denial of a "something" or of a relation or property to a given something or in respect of a particular locus : आपातजायां संविदि विशेषत: सप्रतियोगिकप्रतिषेधाकारेण प्रतीयमानत्वम्. In other words, the perception of negation is conditioned by raference to a particular counter-correlate (प्रतियोगी), according to the exigencies of the situation. The doctrine of "Saviśeṣābheda" between substance and attributes enables Madhva to admit the logical possibility of integrating negative aspects with positive entities and *vice versa*, in propositions.[1]

Madhva recognizes three types of Negation : antecedent (*prāgabhāva*), subsequent (*pradhvaṁsābhāva*) and absolute (*sadābhāva*). The first has an upper limit; the second a lower and the last is unlimited. The countercorrelate (*pratiyogī*) in the case of absolute negation is the absolutely non-existent itself, e.g., the square circle, hare's horn, tortoise-hair. Such non-existence is also called *niṣpratiyogika* or *aprāmāṇika-pratiyogika*, a negation whose counter-correlative is a myth.

Jayatīrtha and Vyāsatīrtha argue that there is nothing illogical in an utterly non-existent figuring as Pratiyogī (counter-correlate) in respect of its absolute negation. For, being the counter-correlate (*pratiyogitvam*) is not an attribute which requires or presupposes the actual existence of a referent like other predications of attributes like color. To be the counter-correlate of a negation is merely being the referent of such knowledge as would enable us *to form the idea* (*nirūpaka*) *of a* negation :

अभावज्ञानोपयोगिज्ञानविषयतामात्रस्य प्रतियोगित्वात्[2] (*Tdyt*).

If the physical existence of the Pratiyogī or its factual reality *at the time of the perception of abhāva* is insisted upon, even the perception of the antecedent and subsequent negations would become equally impossible, as there surely is no Pratiyogī in actual existence at the time of the perception of *prāgabhāva* or of *dhvaṁsa*. That a Pratiyogī (like the jar) is *going to come* into existence *later* or *that it did exist earlier* (in the case of *dhvaṁsa*) makes no difference to the point at issue. If then, it is the idea

---

1. Cf अस्मतपक्षे विशेषस्य सर्वत्रांगीकृतत्वतः ।
नास्ति दोषः क्वचित् भावो ह्यभावश्च स एव हि ॥
अभावस्य च धर्माः स्युः भावास्तेषां च तेऽखिलाः ।
प्रत्यक्षमानतः सर्वमेतन्नो वारणक्षमम् ॥ (*AV* ii.2.adhi 6)

घटोऽपि हि प्रथमं विधित्वेन धर्मिरूपेण प्रतीतोऽनन्तरं पटो न भवतीति पटनिषेधात्मकतया प्रतीयते । प्रागभावादिरपि प्रथमं निषेधत्वेन धर्मिस्वरूपेणावगतोऽनन्तरं प्रमेय इति विधितया प्रतीयते । अभेदेऽपि धर्मधर्मिभावो विशेषशक्त्या संगच्छत इत्युक्तमेव । (*NS* p. 286)

2. तस्मादभाव इत्युक्तौ कस्येत्याकांक्षायामस्येत्यधिकरणादिविलक्षणतया अभावनिरूपकत्वेन संबद्धस्य यस्याभावोऽनुयोगित्वेन सम्बध्यते स एवाधिकरणादिविलक्षणो **निरूपकः प्रतियोगी** (Vyāsatirtha in *Tvt Mandāramañjarī*, p.5).

of the Pratiyogi that counts such an idea or notion of it is possible even in regard to mythical things like the hare's horn. The concept of an *Aprāmāṇika-pratiyogika-abhāva* holds the key to Madhva's theory or illusion. The Anyonyābhāva of the Nyāya School is equated by Madhva with "difference" which has already been treated at length as it differs in configuration from pure negation and presupposes a positive content :

'भावाभावस्वरूपत्वान्नान्योन्याभावता पृथक्' इत्युक्तत्वेन, पक्षद्वयेऽपि अन्योन्याभावस्य भावप्रभेदरूपत्वात् (Śrīnivāsa, *TVt Gloss*, p. 11).

III. EPISTEMOLOGY

CHAPTER XIV

THE THEORY OF PRAMĀṆAS

LIFE and human experience being at times vitiated by illusions, it becomes necessary to define truth in experience so as to enable us to distinguish it from the false. The ascertainment of truth being the first and foremost aim of philosophy, it is incumbent on it to define truth and error in clear terms and indicate the instruments or channels of their ascertainment. The value of such preliminary ascertainment of the sources, bounds and limitations of human knowledge cannot be too highly commended. In the words of Max Muller, "Such an examination of the authorities of human knowledge ought, of course, to form the introduction to any system of philosophy. To have clearly seen this is, it seems to me, a very high distinction of Indian philosophy. How much useless controversy would have been avoided, particularly among Jewish, Mohammadan and Christian philosophers, if a proper place had been assigned *in limino* to the question of what constitutes our legitimate and only possible channels of knowledge, whether perception, inference or anything else. Supported by these inquiries into the evidences of truth, the Hindu philosophers have built up their various systems of philosophy or their various conceptions of the world, telling us what they take for granted and then advancing step by step from the foundation to the highest pinnacles of their system".[1]

Man is essentially an epistemological animal. His irrepressible thirst for knowledge is itself a thesis about knowledge. Whatever differences of opinion there may be about the status and validity of particular experiences, there can be no two

---

1. *Six Systems*, 1913, Preface xiii.

opinions that there are and needs must be, certain experiences which are veridical; for, if logical certainty is denied or impugned, logic itself would be without foundation. All our experiences presuppose the existence of certain *a priori* or objective standards by which they are judged. A wholesale denial of such criteria would cut at the very roots of our experience and bring all reasoned activities to a standstill. Any inquiry into the true and specific nature of such standards has meaning only when their existence is admitted in a general manner. Absolute scepticism would be unsustainable, even for a moment. If everything is invalid, the contention of scepticism itself would be invalid. The possibility of doubt is itself a sufficient proof of something that is not open to doubt. The contention of Buddhism and Advaita, that there is nothing in this phenomenal world that is valid or that there is nothing the certainty of which could be accepted, is therefore, inadmissible. It stands to reason then, that there are things of which definite and valid knowledge is possible. That being so, an investigation into the means of such knowledge is naturally in order.

In Indian philosophy, such validity is known as *prāmaṇya.* But the term pramāṇa (from which it is derived) is used in two senses: (1) true knowledge and (2) the means or instruments by which it is engendered, according to the two senses of the suffix "*ana*" (*lyuṭ*)[2]. Madhva has done a distinct service to epistemology in distinguishing these two senses and usages of the term and coining two separate terms "Kevala" and "Anu" pramāṇa, to denote them, without ambiguity. He defines pramāṇa in both the above senses as 'Yathārtham'.

"Pramāṇa" in the first sense (of valid knowledge) refers to the capacity of true knowledge to reveal the nature of an object as it really is : यथावस्थितज्ञेयविषयीकारित्वम्. As applied to Anu-Pramāṇas like Perception, Inference and Śabda, it signifies the means (*sādhana*) by which such correct knowledge of objects is obtained. But there is no difference in the directness of their relation to their objects.[3] The Anupra-

2. भावे ल्युट् and करणे ल्युट् as they are technically known.

3. The term "Yathārtham" is an Avyayībhāva compound, composed of "*yathā*" and "*artham*". The adverb '*yathā*' signifies: पदार्थानतिवृत्तित्वम् or

māṇas function with as much immediacy as the "Kevala". But the instruments produce knowability in the object while Jñāna merely acts as a manifesting condition thereof. Hence the two classifications are based on their respective mode of *relation* to knowability.

This definition is suitably expanded by Jayatīrtha and others so as to bring out the full force and significance of the terms "यथा" and "अर्थम्" as applied to valid knowledge on the one hand and its means on the other. Pramāṇa is defined by Jayatīrtha as the knowledge of a thing as it actually is, with reference to a particular space-time setting: यथावस्थितमेव ज्ञेयं विषयीकरोति, नान्यथा, in other words, as knowledge which "answers" to the nature of the thing. But by correspondence here is meant *not* either spatio-temporal co-existence of Pramāṇa and Prameya or correspondence on all fours extending to one and all of the aspects of a given object. It is no more than यावदावेदितस्य सत्त्वम् or the existence of such aspects as are actually perceived by each person according to the extent of his capacity or understanding and other conditions governing the rapprochement to the object : यत् यद्देशकालयोः यथाप्रतीतं तस्य तद्देशकालयोः तथात्वम् or the actual existence of an object with reference to a spatio-temporal setting in the manner perceived *with reference to that setting*.

The problem of perception looms large in modern philosophy: whether physical objects are directly perceived, and if so, to what extent. The main obstacle to the theory of direct perception of objects as opposed to the theory of perception of the sense-datum is the alleged 'gap between evidence and conclusion'. The Mādhva theory overcomes these difficulties by a frank admission that the way in which things appear to us is causally determined by a number of factors which are extraneous to the thing itself and that there are gradations of knowledge and finally that no knowledge at the human level could lay

---

not going beyond the "artha". "Artha" denotes a knowable object from the root √ṛ to go with the *uṇādi* suffix "*tha*", the root itself being understood in the specialized sense of "knowing" *avagati* :

अर्यतैव ज्ञेयतैवार्थत्वं अर्थशब्दप्रवृत्तिनिमित्तमस्माकं विवक्षितम् । **अर्यंत** इत्यर्थं इति व्युत्पत्त्या तद्वाचितास्त्येव । अर्तेरौणादिकस्य 'थ' प्रत्ययस्य प्रसिद्धत्वात् । गत्यर्थानां च ज्ञानार्थ (क)त्वा-दिति । (*NS*, p. 247b)

claim to complete comprehension of a thing, in all its innumerable aspects and relations: कस्यापि सर्वात्मना विषयीकरणाभावात् (*NS* p. 251). But this limitation of knowledge does not make it 'invalid'. The correspondence to the object (ज्ञेयाव्यभिचारित्वम्) is to be understood naturally with reference to certain definite space-time setting and other properties of objects conditioned by external factors and subject to the 'normal conditions' of perception being fulfilled.[4]

Kevala-Pramāṇa is divided into four types, in the descending order of merit as Īśvara-jñāna, Lakṣmī-jñāna, Yogi-jñāna, and Ayogi-jñāna, on the basis of intrinsic differences in quality, luminosity and range. The first two are in the nature of Svarūpa-jñāna alone while the other two include Vṛtti-jñāna (sensory knowledge) also. The classification though partly theological, is not without mystic, epistemological and psychological significance. Īśvarapratyakṣa is accepted by the Nyāya and Vedānta schools as the necessary presupposition of all human knowledge (as in Berkeley). It is, according to Madhva, all-comprehensive, always veridical, eternal and independent and part of the divine nature itself and extremely luminous,—luminosity being an intrinsic quality of this knowledge itself, unrelated to objects. Lakṣmī-jñāna is next only to God's, in these respects and dependent on God. The ramifications of Yogi-jñāna include those of Ṛju, Tāttvika and Atāttvika souls and of the last into those of Muktiyogas and others. The nature of the constitution of the Svarūpajñāna of these is explained by Jayatīrtha in his *Pramāṇapaddhati*.

Kevala-pramāṇa has two aspects: knowledge consisting of the essence of selfhood and that arising from mental processes. These are graded in regard to validity as regards both, into *uttama*, *madhyama* and *adhama*. Details have been given by Jayatīrtha.

---

4. यद्यथाभूतं प्रतीतं, तस्य तथाभूतस्य सत्त्वम् । देशकालयोरपि विशेषणान्तरवत् यथाभूतमित्यनेनैव गृहीतत्वात् । विशेषानुक्तेरुक्तदोषाप्रसक्तेश्च । (*NS* p.248b)

CHAPTER XV

PERCEPTION, INFERENCE AND VERBAL TESTIMONY

SENSE-PERCEPTION is defined by Madhva as निर्दोषार्थेन्द्रियसन्निकर्षजन्यं ज्ञानम् or knowledge produced by the right type of contact between flawless sense organs and their appropriate objects. Such contact would be in the nature of an Anu-Pramāṇa. The Naiyāyikas accept six different kinds of contact (*sannikarṣa*) including a special one for *abhāvapratyakṣa.* With the rejection of Samavāya of the Nyāya school, all these stand rejected by Madhva. He accepts only one direct type of *sannikarṣa* of the different senses, including the Sākṣī, with their appropriate objects and their negations. The senses (*indriyas*) being the products of *Taijasa-ahaṁkāratattva*, such contacts are presumed to be effected through the medium of "rays". Another view is that in the case of the eyes alone, the contact is through "rays" and in others, directly between the organs and the objects and their *abhāvas.*

The flawlessness of the senses and their contact etc., is to be borne out by the truthfulness of knowledge, within the meaning of "*yathārtha*" already given, which is itself ascertained by the Sākṣī. Hence there is no mutual dependence in the establishment of the flawlessness of the senses etc. Absolute flawlessness of *indriya*[1] is possible only in respect of the knowledge of God, Lakṣmī and the released. The Svarūpa-jñāna of Uttamajīvas is always true while the Vṛtti-jñāna of all the three classes of un-released souls, is subject to error, as the senses in their case are material. These limitations in the nature of Svarūpa-jñāna and Vṛtti-jñāna of the different orders of beings may perhaps explain from the Mādhva point of view the impossibility for ordinary human perceptions

1. Technically, Svarūpajñāna also is engendered by Svarūpendriyas.

to know the "*ding an sich*" as it is. It is another way of explaining that our senses are not constituted in such a way as to enable us to know *all* about given objects of perception but only as much of reality as is adequate to our normal life. This would suffice to answer the argument of sceptics about our right to make a transition from sense experience to physical objects. The contents of individual experiences are proverbially fragmentary. Even of the reality of which I take note, I can never perceive *more* than just those aspects that attract my attention for the time being or have relevance to *my* interests. There is an element of selective attention in individual experiences. Experience is not a mere awareness of a succession of presented objects or relations, undetermined by the controlling interest or purpose of the knower (*pramātā*). We are thus obliged to admit the necessary existence of a superhuman experience to which the whole universe of being is directly presented (God's knowledge being only Pratyakṣātmaka, according to Madhva) as a complete and harmonious system. As reality has been defined as अनारोपितं प्रमितिविषय: it follows that it can have no meaning apart from presentation to a sentient experience. Hence Madhva posits a graded series of more and more harmonious wholes culminating in the perfect and systematic unity of the absolute experience of Brahman, which embraces the totality of all existence, all at once in its sweep (*sarvagatasarvaviṣayam*). The Mādhva theory has thus deep philosophical significance though apparently treated as a purely theological doctrine.

As all reality is Saviśeṣa in essence and in the last analysis, and the 'bare something' being inconceivable, all Pratyakṣa is considered to be fundamentally "Savikalpaka" or determinate in origin and nature, arising from direct contact with both object and its properties. Hence there is no need to make knowledge of adjunct as such (*viśeṣaṇajñāna*) the cause of the knowledge of the qualified entity (*viśiṣṭajñāna*). Therefore, the division of perception into Savikalpaka and Nirvikalpaka (determinate and indeterminate) accepted in the Nyāya and the Advaita systems is rejected by Madhva.[2]

The Sākṣī intuits its own self (Ātman) and its characteristics

2 विशेषणविशेष्योभयसन्निकर्षाभ्यामेव विशिष्टज्ञानोत्पत्तौ, विशेषणज्ञानस्यापि तत्र कारणत्वे मानाभावात् । (Vedeśa : gloss on *PP*)

of bliss, consciousness etc., as well as the mind and its modifications (*vṛtti*), Avidyā, knowledge arising from the external senses, the feelings of pleasure and pain, time, space and God : स्वरूपेन्द्रियं साक्षीत्युच्यते। तस्य विषया आत्मस्वरूपं, तद्धर्मा, अविद्या, मनस्तद्वृत्तयो, बाह्येन्द्रियज्ञानसुखाद्याः, कालोऽव्याकृताकाशश्च इत्याद्याः। (*PP*)

The mind comprehends external reality through the sense organs and acts as the independent instrument of memory, aided by the Saṁskāras providing the contact.

INFERENCE

According to Madhva, inference consists in the knowledge of the mark of inference as pervaded by the Sādhya and invariably connected with it, leading to the ascertainment of the Sādhya (*nirdoṣopapattiḥ*). The Buddhist logicians regard the principles of essential identity (*tādātmya*) and causality (*tadutpatti*) as the specific grounds of determining Vyāpti, while the Vaiśeṣikas enumerate five such specific grounds in the Sūtra : अस्येदं कारणं कार्यं, सम्बन्धि एकार्थसमवायि विरोधि च (*VS*). The Sāṁkhyas enumerate seven such principles on which we may base a universal proposition.[3] Madhva holds that invariable concomitance is the only relation on which all inferences ultimately rest. Even Pakṣadharmatā (the middle term spatially being a coexistent characteristic of the Pakṣa or minor term), is not considered by him to be an essential factor in inference, as even a Vyadhikaraṇahetu (which is not spatially coexistent with the *sādhya*) can lead to valid inference.[4] He also rejects the claim of the Naiyāyikas that presence of similar instance and absence of contrary instance are necessary conditions of inference as these are not obviously to be found in the Kevalānyayī and Kevalavyatirekī types of inference. Madhva dismisses "Vyatirekavyāpti" as providing any independent basis for inference, as it merely corroborates the positive concomitance between Sādhya and Sādhana in cases of doubt. Consistent with this position Madhva repudiates the threefold

---

3. Cf. 'मात्रानिमित्तसंयोगिविरोधिसहचारिभिः ।
स्वस्वामिवध्यघाताद्यैः साङ्ख्यानां सप्तधानुमा ॥'

4. व्याप्तत्वे व्याश्रयत्वं तु कथमेव हि दूषणम् ?
रोहिण्युदय आसन्नः कृत्तिकाभ्युदिता यतः ।
इत्युक्ते साधनं नो किं, न ह्याज्ञैवात्र साधिका ॥ (*AV* iii.2.4).

classification of inference as Kevalānvayī, Kevalavyatirekī and Anvayavyatirekī, based on purely positive, purely negative and combined concomitance respectively and recognizes only one genuine type of inference based on *anvaya-vyāpti*. Jayatīrtha puts down the acceptance of the other types to a love of classification or for the sake of facility of understanding.

The Nyāya school insists on a five-member syllogism in Parārthānumāna. The Buddhist logicians require two and the Mīmāṁsakas three.[5] Madhva is not in favor of any hard and fast rule. The irreducible minimum for him, is the statement of the Vyāpti. The rest would depend on the exigencies of the occasion. Where the subject-matter of dispute is clear to the disputants, the statement of the "Pratijñā" could as well be dispensed with. In any case, if the five-member syllogism serves merely as a reminder to the person addressed, who has already ascertained the invariable concomitance of smoke with fire, he could reach the desired conclusion by just remembering the Vyāpti alone. In that case, the use of the other members would be superfluous. If the five-member syllogism is intended to act as an authoritative pronouncement (*āgama*), it will have no force as the disputants in a Vāda have no faith in each other's trustworthiness. Want of faith would naturally provoke further questions and expectancy which would require the employment of further *avayavas*. If it is taken on trust, it can be done so outright without the paraphernalia of a five-member syllogism. Moreover, if it should act as an Āgamavākya the Kevalavyatirekī type of inference would have no legs to stand upon. If the five-member syllogism is looked upon as a dialectic method, Madhva points out that it would entail the same being pursued till all difference of opinion is finally set at rest and absolute agreement reached between the parties. This would require a series of five-member syllogisms *and not one*.

The errors in reasoning are classified into formal and material. The most important of these are *Virodha* and *Asaṅgati* in which are subsumed all the defects of reasoning including the fallacies and Nigrahasthānas (grounds of defeat) of the Naiyāyikas.

---

5. तत्र पञ्चतयं केचित् द्वयमन्ये वयं त्रयम् ।
उदाहरणपर्यन्तं यद्वोदाहरणादिकम् ॥

VERBAL TESTIMONY

Madhva makes out a strong case for according verbal testimony an independent status as a Pramāṇa. The Vaiśeṣikas regard verbal judgments as inferences (वाक्यं वाक्यार्थेऽनुमानम्). The Prābhākaras while assigning an independent status to Apauruṣeyavākya subsume verbal judgments of human origin under inference. This is invidious as the accessories to verbal judgments (such as समयस्मरण, शाब्दन्यायानुसंधानम्) are the same in both the cases. As verbal judgments do not involve any Vyāptijñāna, they cannot be treated as inferential in character and should be given a separate status.

Śabdapramāṇa is divided into Pauruṣeya and Apauruṣeya. The Vedic literature is regarded as "Apauruṣeya" and the Smṛtis, Purāṇas and other works based on Vedic authority are accepted as Pauruṣeya Āgama. Madhva is the only Vedāntin after the Mīmāṁsakas to have given the question of the infallibility and the Apauruṣeyatva of the Vedas serious attention. He has taken special pains to establish the doctrine with some new and original arguments of his own which go beyond the usual and conventional arguments based on the conception of the eternality of Varṇas and the impossibility of proving that the Scriptures were spoken or uttered by a particular person.

The Vedas are self-valid. Their validity cannot be derived from the authority (*āptatva*) of any author, human or divine. To the modern mind, the ascription of Apauruṣeyatva and Anāditva to the Vedas may seem absurd. But Madhva introduces a new line of argument which is indeed thought-provoking in that it goes to the very crux of the problem—the *raison d'etre* of any Apauruṣeyavākya in the domain of Pramāṇas. Accordingly the ultimate sanction for all religion, ethics and morality and for the acceptance of all supersensuous values like *dharma* and *adharma* will have to be founded on some textual authority which is not the composition of any particular individual and does not derive its authority or validity from being the words of any person regarded as reliable (*āpta*). Unless our ideas of *dharma* and *adharma* are grounded in such impersonal authority, it would be impossible to establish the very existence of values and concepts on any satisfactory basis. A philosopher who will not admit the existence of such supersensuous values as *dharma* and *adharma* would have no scope for his Śāstra, as the object of a Śāstra is to show the ways and means of realizing those truths which cannot be secured by other means, falling within the scope of perception and inference. Nor can such a philosopher claim that his system would, by the *negation of dharma, adharma* and other supersensuous values, confer a real benefit on humanity by ridding society of its superstitious belief in them. Madhva points out that far from benefiting humanity, such teachings undermining the faith of the people in *dharma, adharma,* etc., would let loose violence and disorder everywhere by lending support to the policy of 'might is right'. In the long run, the people will curse the philosopher whose teachings would expose them to such misery. As such teachings will only lead to adverse results and as he has no faith in any other unseen benefits, his Śāstra would be futile, either way.

Insofar then as *dharma* and *adharma* and other supersensuous values will have to be admitted by all rational thinkers and since there is no other ultimate sanction upon which they could be grounded, save the impersonal authority of a Śāstra, one has to accept an Apauruṣeya-Śāstra as furnishing the basis of universal faith in *dharma, adharma,* etc. There is no other way in which their existence could be established. It is hardly possible to determine their nature and existence on the supposed authority of individuals, however great they may be; for, every human being will have the limitations of ignorance and of being liable to deceptiveness. It will not be justifiable to postulate for this purpose the existence of some teacher who will be omniscient. That will be postulating much more than what is warranted in our experience; for omniscience in any individual is not a matter of our ordinary experience. One would have to postulate, moreover, not only omniscience to an individual but also that such an individual is not given to deceiving others and further that he is the author of a particular statement or doctrine or body of texts about the natures of *dharma* etc.

Postulation of the existence of an Apauruṣeya-Śāstra, on the other hand, would be the simplest thing. It would not necessitate any further assumptions. As there is no ascertainable author of the Vedas, their authorlessness would follow automatically. On the contrary, it would be an unwarranted assumption that they have an author, when no such author is ascertained or ascertainable. The analogy of worldly testimony would be powerless here as in respect of worldly testimony there is no conception that it is authorless, as there is, in respect of the Vedas. There is no fear that at this rate any statement from any irresponsible source may be claimed as Apauruṣeya; for established traditions would always be a sufficient check against such wild claims and there are other ways of ascertaining the genuine from the spurious, when such claims are made.

The qualification of *nirdoṣatva* (flawlessness) applies to every Pramāṇa. Verbal testimony, to be valid, must be free from such flaws as want of an objective reference to the words employed, lack of syntactic connection or denotative fitness. There are different theories as to how the verbal judgment is produced by the distinctive elements forming part of a sentence. Madhva holds the Anvitābhidhāna view, according to which the words in a sentence convey their specific senses compositely through requisite syntactic interconnection with the rest. This obviates the necessity for recognizing Sphoṭavāda and other theories. The Prābhākaras also hold the Anvitābhidhānavāda. But while, according to them, every word in a sentence is invested with the capacity to convey the net syntactic relation as a whole and in that process its own specific sense also, Madhva would appear to recognize *two stages* in the process of *anvaya*, each word having at the outset, only a general capacity to convey its definite sense as correlated to *such others* to which it stands immediately related by fitness and *then* by juxtaposition in the sentence taken as a whole, with yet others, an additional capacity to convey a more specialized form of the same *anvaya*, in all its completeness.

Other Pramāṇas like Arthāpatti are not given an independent position by Madhva. Arthāpatti (presumption) shows a way out in cases of *apparent conflict* between two facts. Given that X is alive, if he is not at home, he must be presumed to be out somewhere. This can be easily put in a syllogistic form :

चैत्रो बहिरस्ति, जीवनवत्त्वे सति गृहेऽसत्त्वात् । यो जीवन् यत्र नास्ति स ततोऽन्यत्रास्ति, यथा अहम् (*PP*).

The point here is that both the alternatives, *taken togother*, constitute the mark of inference. There can be no real conflict between the two alternatives of a man being alive and his not being at home. So there *can be no* difficulty in one of the alternatives qualifying the other and collectively leading to the inference. Should the conflict be real, there would be no room for Arthāpatti either; but only a doubt as to what may have happened to X. Similarly, Upamāna also, as a means of establishing similarity between two things, may be brought under inference, perception or verbal testimony, according to the conditions of each case. Anupalabdhi also, in the same way, could be brought under any of the three according to the nature and conditions of the experience. When a jar is suddenly removed from its place, the perception of its non-existence is the result of direct perception by the Sākṣī, the non-perception of the jar being merely the logical consequent of the former. Where one feels the absence of the jar in darkness by judging through groping with his hands, the non-perception serves the purpose not of an instrument of *abhāvapratyakṣa* but as a mark of inference. The necesity of recognizing Anupalabdhi, as a separate Pramāṇa, is thus obviated by the acceptance of a possibility of direct sensory contact with *abhāva* as in the case of *bhāvas*.

The well-known "Tātparya-liṅgas" like "Upakrama", "Upasaṁhāra" and *Śruti, liṅga, vākya, prakaraṇa*, etc. are also similarly to be brought under the purview of inference.

CHAPTER XVI

THE STATUS OF MEMORY

THE contribution of memory to knowledge is quite considerable and important. The question of its status and title to be admitted as a Pramāṇa or source of valid knowledge has engaged the attention of philosophers in the East and in the West. While some modern philosophers have been very critical and sceptical of the claims of memory, others have overweighted it. In Indian philosophy, the prevailing tendency has been to exclude memory from the title of 'Pramāṇa' on the ground of its 'merely' representative character. The Mīmāṁsakas and the Naiyāyikas have deliberately defined Pramāṇa in snch a way as to exclude memory from its scope.[1] The Advaitins generally follow the Mīmāṁsaka view. The followers of Rāmānuja seem to be divided in their opinion. Meghanādāri seems to be definitely *against* the admission of memory to the title of Pramāṇa, as can be seen from his definition of Pramāṇa as : अन्यप्रमाणानपेक्षं अर्थपरिच्छेदकम्[2] while Vedānta Deśika is quite in favor of it :

स्मृतिमात्राप्रमाणत्वं न युक्तमिति वक्ष्यते ।
अबाधितस्मृतेर्लोके प्रमाणत्वपरिग्रहात् ॥ (*Nyāya-Pariśuddhi*)

As a realist Madhva stakes his all on the validity of memory and supports its claim to be admitted as a Pramāṇa or source of valid knowledge :

प्रामाण्यं नानुवादस्य स्मृतेरपि विहीयते ।
याथार्थ्यमेव प्रामाण्यशब्दार्थो यद्विवक्षितः ॥ (*AV* ii.1.4)

He brings Memory under Pratyakṣa and considers it as a direct perception by the mind : प्रत्यक्षं सप्तविधम्, साक्षिषडिन्द्रियभेदेन; मानसप्रत्यक्षजा स्मृतिः (*PL*). Its validity cannot, he says, be treated

---

1. Cf. अनधिगतार्थगन्तृ प्रमाणम् (Mīmāṁsaka definition)
2. *Nayadyumaṇi*, quoted by Dasgupta, *I. Phil.* iii.p.239.

as merely inferential. Otherwise, even the perception of an object can be treated as an inference from a *kārya* to a *kāraṇa* :

साक्षात्कारेण कार्येण कर्मकारकतया घटाद्यनुमानम् । (*NS* p.227)

Apart from that, it cannot be said that we know the past by inference from the retention of the impression of the past experiences or from its revival as an image. Such inferences in their turn would involve memory. Moreover, if memory is invalid as a source of knowledge, then all inferences which are based on the remembrance of Vyāpti between a *hetu* and a *sādhya* would cease to be valid; for no knowledge can be valid when it has its basis in what is invalid. Inference then, would be at a standstill. It can similarly be shown that the other Pramāṇas accepted by the other schools would also involve memory of some kind as one of their basic conditions.

Madhva holds that Saṁskāras (former impressions) provide the necessary contact (*sannikarṣa*) of the mind with the past. The possibility of such a penetration into the past, by the mind, is established, says he, on the evidence of Yogic perception of past and future, and is not, therefore, inconceivable. It is indeed very remarkable that Madhva should have anticipated the views of Western thinkers like Russell, Hobhouse and others in recognizing memory as a primary source of our knowledge concerning the past. He agrees with them that the immediate knowledge by memory is the source of all our knowledge concerning the past by inference. Otherwise we should never know that there was anything past to be inferred at all. If the validity of memory is questioned, there would by no proof of our past experiences having occurred to us :

पूर्वानुभूते किं मानमित्युक्ते स्यात् किमुत्तरम् ? (*AV* ii.1.4).

It is no argument against this point that "the fact that one seems to remember an event is a good reason for believing that it occurred; but it is only because there is independent evidence. If we are all to lose our memory of events, it would be harder for us to reconstruct the past events, but not impossible. The cross-checking of written and other physical records, the utilization of scientific theories which they support, would suffice".[3] This would *not* apply to the question of one's own personal ex-

3. A.J. Ayer *The Problem of Knowledge* (1956), p. 186

perience and *its remembrance*. If I lose *my memory*, I cannot by any written or other records reconstruct *my* past experience *for myself*. Others with their memories intact may be able to do so. But that will hardly help *me* or have any binding force *so far as I am concerned*. If the reconstructor should lose his memory, no interpretation or correlation of evidence would be possible. The part played by memory in human life, is thus considerable and it would be suicidal to question its validity *in toto*. Of course, there are erroneous memories at times. But so are there cases of erroneous perceptions and inference too ! That does not affect the validity of memory *per se*. Madhva's insistence on "*nirdoṣatva*" of the causal conditons would be sufficient to cover such cases.

The general objection to the validity of memory is that it does not fulfil the condition of correspondence (*yāthārthyam*). The state or condition in which an object was first apprehended is no longer present at the time of its subsequent remembrance. Thus memory cannot lay claim to be faithful to the experience and reproduce it exactly. This objection is answered by Madhva, by pointing out that it is not the re-presentation of the experience *in toto* that makes for the validity of memory but faithfulness to its object-content.[4] The existence of an object in the same former condition whenever it is known is not essential for the validity of knowledge. What is required is that the particular state or condition, in which knowledge apprehended a given object with reference to a particular space-time setting, should really belong to it in *that* space-time setting. What memory does is to recall the *fact* that *the particular object was in such and such a condition or state at such and such time* (तदासौ तादृशः). This certainly is *so*. It is irrelevant to the validity of memory that the former condition is *no longer present*. Its existence *now* in the same state or condition, or in a different one, is simply irrelevant to the validity of memory. It is only in this sense that scientific deductions about the past or future conditions of phenomena could be held to be valid. The same applies to memory also :

स्मरणकाले तदवस्थत्वाभावादयाथार्थ्यं स्मृतेरिति चेन्न, अतीतानागतविषयानुमानागम-प्रामाण्यप्रच्युतिः (*NS* p. 251)

---

4. स्यादिदं यद्यनुभवानुसारित्वं याथार्थ्यमिति वदामः, **अर्थानुसारित्वं तु तथेत्युक्तम्** (*NS* p.251)

There is not much force in the objection that it is not the function of a pramāṇa to make known to us an already known object. For, it can never be seriously maintained that no further knowledge can arise in regard to a known object. Neither is knowledge opposed to knowledge in any way, so that subsequent knowledge may be barred. It cannot also be held that want or absence of knowledge is a part of the conditions which produce knowledge. Knowledge is bound to arise if the necessary conditions for its production are there. The objection that a pramāṇa should not be dependent on anything else or any other knowledge would cut at the very root of inference. There is thus no justification of defining "Pramāṇa" in such a way as to exclude memory from its purview.

Memory is generally supposed to be caused by Saṁskāras (impressions) left on the mind by the first experiences. A difficulty arises in this connection. Such impressions, then, could only relate to the actual state of the object as it *was experienced.* But the "experience" did not certainly present its object with the words "I am past" stamped on it, as it were. If, then, Saṁskāras corresponding to the objective content of experience produce memory, how is this discrepancy to be explained[5] ?

This is really a ticklish question. The difficulty seems to have been felt by some modern writers also on the subject. But their explanation is vague and non-committal. The correct answer according to Ayer is that "perhaps, there is no one thing that is present in every such instance of remembering. Sometimes it is the matter of one's having a vivid image; sometimes with or without image, there is a feeling of familiarity; sometimes there is no specific mental occurrence".

This leaves the difficulty unsolved. Madhva overcomes it by boldly formulating a new theory that our memory experiences are not purely and simply the reflections of Saṁskāras, impressions, feelings or beliefs. They are direct apprehensions of the

---

5. ननु, पूर्वानुभवजनितसंस्कारः स्मृतिकारणम् । स चानुभवविषय एव स्मृतिजननस्येष्टे । नचानुभवेन निवृत्तपूर्वावस्थतया अर्थो गृहीतः । तत्कथमनुभवसमानविषयसंस्कारमात्रजन्या स्मृतिरर्थं निवृत्तपूर्वावस्थतया विषयीकुर्यादिति ? (*PP*)

mind penetrating into the past.[6] Only such a theory as this would justify the position taken by modern thinkers like Russell that memory resembles perception in point of its *immediacy* and differes from it in being referred to the past.[7] That the mind has got this power to penetrate into the past and the future is established on the evidence of Yogic perceptions of past and future, which are recognized as direct perceptions (Sākṣātkāra) and not as inference. Such mental perception in the case of memory is, however, limited to the sphere of previously experienced objects or events by the nature of the limitations imposed by the Saṁskāras, which act as the connecting links (*sannikarṣa*) with the past; whereas, in the case of Yogic perceptions of the past and future, such *sannikarṣa* or connecting link is supplied by the power of Yogic merit itself. Hence, Yogic vision is more comprehensive than ordinary mental or memory experiences. This explains why memory is, by its very nature, connected with one's *past* experiences.

The position taken up by Madhva that Memory should be regarded as an immediate perception of the past by the mind is quite unique. It goes very much beyond the views of the Jainas who have valiantly upheld the right of memory to be accepted as a source of valid knowledge, but have classified it as a form of mediate knowledge (*parokṣa*). Madhva's view of memory as a direct perception of the past by the mind is a remarkable anticipation of the views of some modern philosophers like Russell who claims that "we often remember what we have seen or heard or had otherwise presented to our senses and in such cases, *we are still immediately aware of what we remember*, in spite of the fact that it appears as past and not as present" (*Problems of Philosophy*, p. 76).

Another minor objection to the right of memory to be admitted as a "Pramāṇa" is its alleged inability to serve any useful purpose (*niṣphalatvam*), as a source of knowledge. This is pointless, says Madhva. In the first place, validity is a matter of *fact* and hardly one of utility. Apart from that, not all instances of

6. Cf. the view of Samuel Alexander that "the object is compresent with me as past" (*Space, Time and Deity*, i.113, quoted by Ayer).

7. *The Problems of Philosophy*, p.76.

memory can be dismissed as serving no useful purpose. We feel happy to remember pleasant experiences and seek to dwell on them and go from one to another. Exercise of memory increases the potencies of impressions. Feelings of love and hatred are evoked by agreeable or disagreeable memories.

Insofar then as memory is uncontradicted and true, it would be fully entitled to the status of Pramāṇa in the sense of *yathārtha*. It has been argued, however, that there is a peculiarity about memory which deserves notice. "The only claim of memory to the status of knowledge and acceptability rests upon an explicit reference to a past experience, which it professes to *reproduce faithfully*. A remembered fact is believed to be true just because it is regarded as identical with the content of a past experience, which it claims to reproduce.[8] This conformity to a past experience and falling back upon it for its own validity are said to be proof of its "self-abdication" in favor of its archetype. Thus, the question of treating memory as a distinct type of knowledge is "barred by definition". In this view, the Advaitin follows the Bhāṭṭas, who hold that the only kind of knowledge, so called, is knowledge of the already unacquired: *anadhigatārthagantṛ*. Memory, though not, therefore, a distinct source of knowledge, is still a distinct *experience* that has to be distinguished from knowledge and given a separate name. "The experience in which the new emerges is called 'Anubhūti' and reproductive knowledge is called 'Smṛti'" (D.M Datta, *Six Ways of Knowing*, pp. 22-23).

As a Realist, Madhva establishes the right to validity of memory and *anuvāda, both in the enlarged sense of the term "Yathārtham"*, as defined by him *and in the narrow sense of 'anadhigatārthagantṛ' accepted by the Bhāṭṭas and the Advaitins* :

प्रत्यक्षं मानसं चैव स्यादतीतार्थगोचरम् ।
तदा स्मृतिप्रमाणत्वं अतीतत्वविशेषितम् ।
आधिक्यमनुभूतात्तु यदतीतत्वमिष्यते ॥
मानता च कथं न स्यात् स्मृतेर्बाधश्च नात्र हि ।
मानत्वं प्रत्यभिज्ञाया अपि सर्वानुभूतिगम् ।
अतीतवर्तमानत्वधर्मिणी सा च दृश्यते ॥

8. D.M. Datta, *Six Ways of Knowing*, pp. 22-23.

न च सा स्मृतिमात्रार्था तदिदंत्वग्रहैकतः ।
अतो न वर्तमानैकनियमः स्याद् ग्रहेऽक्षजे ॥ (*AV* iii. 2.3)

He argues that we *experience the past* by means of Mānasa-pratyakṣa aided by Saṁskāras. The experience of memory is valid insofar as it is uncontradicted. Thus, it is *not* barred by definition. Apart from that, there *is* an element of "novelty" (*anadhigatārthatā*) in memory. It is not a mere photographic reproduction of a previous experience or wholly "identical with the content of the past experience". For, it comprehends events, or objects *qua past* i.e., as qualified by the special attribute of "being past" : अतीतत्वविशेषितम्; whereas, the first experience of them would, naturally, have conceived of them *qua present* ! Memory, then, involves an element of novelty,—a something more than a mere photographic reproduction of experience. As Hobhouse puts it, "Memory is an assertion of the past *as past*". In the same way, an analysis of Pratyabhijñāna (recognition) shows that it is an indivisible act of cognition, produced by the visual sense aided by Saṁskāras :

अनुभवरूपमेकरूपमेव विज्ञानं संस्कारसचिवेन चक्षुषा जातम् (*NS*, p. 496 b)

and that it is neither a simple perception of a mere "this" nor an act of memory involving a "that"; nor even two separate cognitions consisting of a perception and a memory; nor even a *compound* of "mental chemistry", as the Jainas would have it : तदिदंत्वग्रहैकतः (*AV*).

Jayatīrtha quotes Vācaspati Miśra to show that he too is *not* averse to recognizing the validity of memory in the sense of possessing "yāthārthya" (validity). For, in commenting on the definition of Pramāṇa in the Sūtra : उपलब्धिहेतुः प्रमाणम् Vācaspati first qualifies the term "Upalabdhi" (cognition) by the adjunct of "being correct" (*Yathārtham*) to avoid the overpervasion of the definition in respect of doubts. But, lest the definition as modified, viz. यथार्थोपलब्धिहेतुः प्रमाणम् should embrace "memory" also, he qualifies "Upalabdhi" once again, by saying that यथार्थोपलब्धि does not here include *all correct* knowledge, *as such*, but only immediate experience. This shows that the validity of memory is accepted by him. Otherwise, he would not have raised any further objection to the qualified definition of Pramāṇa as यथार्थोपलब्धिहेतु : which would have sufficed to rule out memory, if it had been intended to be excluded from valid knowledge.

Or, having raised an objection of that kind, he should again have excluded the validity of Smṛti by the selfsame adjunct "yathārtham" instead of restricting the term Upalabdhi to "anubhava" as distinguished from memory. This establishes that in the opinion of Vācaspati, memory is ruled out, not because of its containing any element of invalidity (*ayāthārthyam*), but because of its *not* being in the nature of a direct or a primary experience (*anubhava*). This shows that its validity is irrefutable and *ergo*, a proper definition of "Pramāṇam" must be such as to *include it*. There is no point in giving a partial definition and then exclaiming that memory is "barred by definition!" It is unfair to interpret or define the term "Pramāṇam" in such a way as would fail to achieve such a result or foil it. Hence, the need for redefining "Pramāṇa", so as to bring within its range all types of valid knowledge, without any invidious distinction or preconceived ideas.

Madhva has thus done a great service to the cause of truth in restoring memory to its rightful place as a valid source of knowledge and therefore fully entitled to be accepted as a "Pramāṇa". He has also given a great lead to philosophers in bringing it under "Pratyakṣa" by assigning to it a special place as "Mānasa-pratyakṣa" under his scheme of sevenfold division of Pratyakṣa. It is a tribute to the keenness of his mental powers that his recognition of the immediacy of Memory is receiving assent from several modern thinkers like Ewing who have come to recognize the 'direct view' of memory.

CHAPTER XVII

DOCTRINE OF VALIDITY

PRAMĀṆAS give us valid knowledge of things "as they are in fact". The nature of this validity and correspondence with facts, as understood by Madhva, has already been defined. The problem that remains is that of the criteria of truth by which we convince ourselves of the validity of our experiences and judgments. Modern philosophers have put forward different tests of truth such as correspondence, coherence, pragmatic tests and even intuition. In Indian philosophy also these different criteria figure under different names.

The Sāṁkhyas have held that both validity and invalidity are innate to knowledge. This means that the same factors which *produce* knowledge make for the validity pertaining to it, and similarly in the case of invalidity. The same principle applies to the *apprehension* of that validity or its reverse. The factors which make known the knowledge are alone responsible for the apprehension of its validity or invalidity. This theory seems to rest on a naive commonsense realism that both validity and invalidity are organic to knowledge.

The Sāṁkhya position is clearly self-contradictory. It may, however, be explained by the Sāṁkhyas that as the machinery of the production of knowledge cannot at any time be expected to be absolutely free from *guṇas* or *doṣas* that arrest the capacity to produce invalidity or validity as the case may be, one cannot altogether escape the conclusion that knowledge is bound to be intrinsically true or false, according to the prevailing condition of the *karaṇas* that produce it. The only excuse for such a roundabout explanation will be the acceptance of the principle that knowledge by itself cannot have the contradictory features of validity and invalidity at the same time. The same fear of self-contradiction should have alerted the Sāṁkhyas against attributing two mutually conflicting *capacities* to the *karaṇas* themselves, in their attempt to justify the dual nature of knowledge. Such a view will actually make the auxiliaries responsible for the Karaṇas' acquiring this dual capacity. That will land the Sāṁkhyas in the extrinsic theory (paratastva) of *both validity and invalidity*, instead of their *svatastva*, as they want to maintain.

Reflection shows, then, that truth alone is organic to knowledge and invalidity must be extraneous to it and must not be put down to the same causes as produce knowledge, but to defective adjustment of conditions or environment.

It is clearly illogical to regard both validity and invalidity as innate characteristics of knowledge. One of them must be natural and organic and the other extrinsic. Tests and verifications are needed to make sure of validity only in cases of reasonable doubt, and not as a rule. This confirms the position that validity is intrinsic to knowledge and must be so.

According to the Nyāya school, both the genesis and apprehension of validity and invalidity are extrinsic to knowledge, caused by factors other than those which give rise to or make known the knowledge. This is consistent with the practical realism of Nyāya and its pragmatic theory of truth. Knowledge, according to this school, is generated by well-defined contact of sense organs with objects or by other specific factors (guṇas) (which differ according to the nature of each case, i.e. perceptual, inferential or verbal); while its validity is brought about by certain special virtues in the *indriyas* or other causal conditions according to the type of knowledge. Invalidity, on the other hand, is produced by defects of sensory contact or other pertinent factors. This school also holds that while knowledge *per se* is apprehended by mental perception, *its validity is inferred* from correspondence or other tests. Invalidity, likewise, is inferred from want of correspondence, unworkability, etc.

The weakness of the Nyāya theory lies in its making validity depend upon external tests. This is clearly unsatisfactory. If the tests require further tests to validate them, there will be a regress of them *ad infinitum*. If the first or second test itself is sufficient guarantee of validity without the need for further tests, it would be tantamount to an admission of self-validity of the result of *that test* which is also as much a piece of knowledge as the earlier ones.

The Buddhists, on the other hand, regard validity as extraneous and invalidity intrinsic to knowledge, as all ordinary knowledge according to them is discursive and hence based on mental construction (*kalpanā*) in terms of name, form, etc.

The Bhāṭṭas accept validity to be innate and invalidity to be extrinsic. But then, valid knowledge itself, according to them, is inferred by the peculiar mark of "cognised-ness" (*jñātatā*) which is a property produced in knowledge, while invalidity is inferentially established through want of correspondence, etc. The Prābhākaras regard knowledge as self-luminous and therefore capable of manifesting its own validity in the same act. But they do not accept any invalid knowledge as such,—the so-called "invalid" one, of popular conception, being regarded by them as due merely to a failure to *distinguish properly* between an actual perception of a given something and a memory of something else (resembling it), arising almost in a flash.

Madhva disagrees with all these theories. According to him, the sense organs themselves are capable of producing correct knowledge by proper contact etc. There is no need to assume any special characteristic (*guṇas*) for this purpose. But when vitiated by flaws, the natural capacity of these is arrested or distorted and they give rise to invalid knowledge. As knowledge, by itself, is *jaḍa* (insentient) as a modification of the *antaḥkaraṇa* and therefore incapable of self-revelation, we have to admit some other principle by which the knowledge itself and its validity could be intuited. Such a principle is the Sākṣī or Svarūpendriya of the knowing Self, which being Caitanyarūpa is capable of being both Svaprakāśaka and Paraprakāśaka. Both knowledge and its validity are, thus grasped by the Sākṣī, in the ultimate analysis. But in respect of invalid knowledge the Sākṣī grasps only its bare content or essence (*svarūpam*) while its invalidity, as such, is ascertained by the Sākṣī indirectly through incoherence (*visaṁvāda*) or other tests. In respect of Anupramāṇas, their validity is inferentially grasped from their ability to stand the test of correspondence, etc.

Implications of Madhva's Doctrine of Validity

It will thus be seen that validity, as defined by Madhva, cannot admit of any degrees, such as are recognized in Buddhism and Advaita, in terms of Vyāvahārika and Pāramārthika prāmāṇyam. It is indeed difficult to justify the theory of degrees of validity in the light of Svataḥ-prāmāṇyavāda, ostensibly admitted by the Advaita, just as it is in the other systems of Vedānta. Degrees of reality will be inconsistent with the dictum: *Abādhācca pramāṇatvam vastunyakṣādivat śruteḥ*. On the Advaitic view, it will be more appropriate, logically and terminologically to speak of degrees of invalidity or unreality of experience. Validity, if intrinsic to knowledge, must be *ipso facto* absolute and unlimited and not relative or confined to particular moments or periods of time :

प्रामाण्यस्य च मर्यादा कालतो व्याहता भवेत् (*AV* ii.2.3)

Even supposing that unstultifiability for all the three periods of time (*traikālikābādhyatvam*) is the true test of reality, it will *not* be difficult to secure such *abādhyatvam* (unstultifiability) to our empirical knowledge, which insofar as it is uncontradicted with reference to its own space-time setting, is technically '*Traikālika-abādhyatvagrāhi*'.

स्वकाले ह्यस्तितां गृण्हन् साक्षात्कारस्त्रिकालगाम् ।
...गृह्णात्येवात्यबाध्यताम् ॥ (*Nym* 1.18)

This point has already been made clear in our discussion of the criterion of reality.

If our knowledge is absolutely sure to be disillusioned and be set aside at a subsequent period of noumenal level, it would be tantamount to saying that it *has not been valid* and true to facts *even when it has been appearing* to be so, all along.

कालान्तरेऽप्यमानं चेदिदानीं मानता कुतः ? (*AV* ii.2.3)

In other words, it would mean that we have been subjected to a cruel deception all the time and have been dealing with metaphysical shadows instead of the realities of life. The Advaita philosopher is inconsistent with himself in accepting the doctrine of Svataḥ-prāmāṇya of knowledge and advocating the doctrine of degrees of reality and of validity in the same breath. The Mādhva view of validity as "Yathārthatvam" is free from the defect. On this view, correspondence (*yāthārthyam*) is nothing more than having a real object conceived as it truly is with reference to a given place and time.

तद्विषयत्वमेव तदाकारत्वम् । नहि ज्ञानज्ञेययोरेकाकारता (*Tdy*). It inclines more to the correspondence theory than to pragmatism. Madhva lays stress on the fact that emotional satisfaction does not make a proposition true, nor the fact that a particular belief may induce such a satisfaction. *Phalavattvam na cāsmābhiḥ prāmāṇyam hi vivakṣitam* (*AV*, ii.1.4). This is one of the strong points in favor of realism. Madhva has naturally pressed home this argument (from the self-validity of Pramāṇas to the reality of the world and of its experiences). On the other hand, the Advaitic philosophers, though paying lip service to the Svataḥ-prāmāṇya doctrine of pramāṇas have been at great pains to stigmatize Pratyakṣa as vitiated by flaws (of Avidyā), referring to phenomenal reality (व्यावहारिकभेदपर) being limited to the present (वर्तमानमात्रग्राहि) and so on, and hence incapable of establishing the absolute reality of our experiences. The tendency to pick holes in Pratyakṣa and impugn its validity is found among Idealist thinkers of the West also. Dismissing the belief in the reality of the world as a superficial doctrine of naive realism, the Advaitins have tried to invalidate it both by inference (मिथ्यात्वानुमान): विश्वं मिथ्या दृश्यत्वात्, जडत्वात् etc. and by an appeal to monistic texts like नेह नानास्ति किंचन which are supposed to deny the reality of world experience.

In combating these moves, Madhva has naturally tried to take his stand on the validity of Pratyakṣa in its own right. The theory of Pratyakṣa being vitiated by fontal flaws (*doṣajanyatvaṁ*) cannot be put forward until the *unreality of experience is otherwise established* and that cannot be done until the Doṣajanyatva of Pratyakṣa is proved. There is thus a palpable interdependence in argument. The argument from illusions : विश्वं मिथ्या दृश्यत्वात्... शुक्तिरूप्यवत्, to the unreality of all experience is equally illegitimate. The normal experiences of life are not on a par with passing illusions. They are not contradicted within our own experience, as illusions are. The plea of *future stultifiability of experience* is dubious. Inferences being dependent on sound Pratyakṣa for their *Vyāptiniścaya* cannot possibly go against their very prop and support (*Upajīvya*). Perception may be limited to the present, but with the help of the Sākṣī, it can assure itself of absence of stultifiability, as in the case of the perception of falsity of silver in the shell, *which is vested with absolute certainty by the Advaitin himself.*

Finding these attempts to discredit Pratyakṣa unsuccessful, the Advaitin tries to base his conclusion on the authority of the identity-texts which, by implication and by express reference, are supposed to establish the erroneousness of dualistic experiences.

This he does by turning to his advantage the primacy of the status of Śruti among Pramāṇas, in Vedic tradition, pitting the so-called 'Advaita Śrutis' against the consolidated experience of humanity, of the truthfulness of its worldly experience, its transmigratory career and the limitations of its own finite powers of understanding etc. and depriving them of their reality and meaning on account of their opposition to the truth of the oneness of all existence. The bondage of the souls is thus attributed to beginningless ignorance and the pluralisation of the one impartible pure consciousness into many finite selves through superimposition of difference.

Madhva's position is that the conflict of Pramāṇas must be resolved by resorting to some objective epistemological criterion and not on the basis of purely sentimental respect for *one set of Śrutis as against the other* or on that of personal predilections. The criterion of "Upajīvya-upajīvakatva" between Pramāṇas is an objective one by which he prefers to resolve such conflict of Pramāṇas. The Upajīvya is the logical and ontological ground or starting point of all further predications about a subject. The nature of this ground or starting point as it is *ex hypothesi* determined furnishes the basis of all subsequent thought and predication. Any predication or denial which runs counter to this ground as given by the proof of the existence of the entity (*dharmigrāhakapramāṇa*) has to be rejected as untenable. An Upajivaka must, in all cases, be subservient to the Upajīvya and cannot overrule it. This is the essence of the criterion of *Upajīvyapramāṇaprābalya*. It is clear that in the event of a conflict between the Upajīvya and Upajīvaka, both could not be held to be valid, lest the thing in question should cease to have any character of its own. Now, Sākṣipratyakṣa and the Bheda Śrutis clearly establish the authenticity of human experience. No amount of identity texts can falsify their verdict.

The conflict of Upajīvyapramāṇa will persist even when the existence of Brahman is sought to be established through a causal argument, instead of through Śruti. The inference of a Supreme Creator would involve the assumption of His Omniscience and Almightiness which would mark Him off from the Jīvas. The thesis of identity of Jīva and Brahman and the falsity of world-experience are thus opposed to Upajīvyapramāṇa in the form of (1) Bheda Śrutis and (2) Sākṣipratyakṣa and (3) Causal inference.

Without minimising the importance of Śrutis in principle, as 'Jātyā prabala' among the three Pramāṇas :

'प्राबल्यमागमस्यैव जात्या तेषु त्रिषु स्मृतम्'

Madhva holds that the authority of the Śruti is absolute and unqualified *only in matters which fall exclusively within its province*—such as the nature and attributes of God, His Personality and the esoteric truths of theology:

आगमैकप्रमाणेषु तस्यैव ह्युपजीव्यता (*AV*, ii.1.4-5)

But in matters which fall within the legitimate sphere of valid perception and Sākṣyanubhava, such as the reality of the world and the self's own experiences of the joys and sorrows of life and its own finiteness and limitations, the verdict of such Pratyakṣa and Sākṣyanubhava will hold the field as Upajīvya with reference to such scriptural statements as 'Tat tvam asi' which purport to make the individual self one with the infinite Brahman:

'लौकिके व्यवहारेऽत्र प्रत्यक्षस्योपजीव्यता' (*AV*) **'लौकिके'** प्रत्यक्षादिसिद्धजीवादिविषये, ब्रह्मात्मकत्वादिबोधनरूपे **'व्यवहारे'** तत्त्वमस्याद्यागमेन क्रियमाणे, अत्र (आगमे)—**आगमं प्रति** प्रत्यक्षस्योपजीव्यता (Jayatīrtha, *NS* p.593)

The relation of Bādhyabādhakabhāva (stultified and stultifier) as between Pratyakṣa and Āgama is *not* therefore, *uniform and unqualified everywhere*. It is determined by the criterion of Upajīvyatā. And such Upajīvyatā depends on the merits of the case. In certain cases Āgama is the Upajīvya of Pratyakṣa *while* in some others Sākṣipratyakṣa is the Upajīvya of Āgama.[1]

1. नहि निर्विशेषणयोः प्रत्यक्षागमयोः परस्परं बाध्यबाधकभावः, किंतु, उपजीवकत्वेन बाध्यत्वं, उपजीव्यत्वेन बाधकत्वम् । तच्च **तत्रान्यथा अत्रान्यथा** इति (न विरोधः) (*NS* p.593)

Human perception registering defects in the Avatāra Forms of the Lord are invalidated by the evidence of Śruti which establishes that the Mūla and Avatāra Forms are *equally defectless*. But in respect of facts within the competence of sound Pratyakṣa and Sākṣyanubhava and their legitimate sphere (such as the anthenticity of our worldly experiences), such Pratyakṣa and Sākṣyanubhava are the Upajīvya of scriptural texts purporting to say something to the contrary. The latter are to be put down as Upajīvaka and hence *not competent to contradict or sublate the evidence* of such Pratyakṣa and Sākṣyanubhava.

This well-defined demarcation of the grounds which must govern the operation of Bādhyabādhakabhāva between Pratyakṣa and Sākṣyanubhava on the one hand and the deliverances of Śruti on the other, formulated by Madhva, shows how very much misplaced is the criticism one sometimes hears from 'unattached' modern scholars that "philosophy in India could never free itself from the crushing burden of the Śrutis" (A.M. Ghosh, "Modern Indian Philosophy", *Times Illustrated Weekly*, Bombay, Dec. 20th, 1959).

Madhva has thus shown himself to be a very balanced thinker in fixing the boundaries of the different Pramāṇas. It is not, therefore, correct to say, as does Dr. Narain, that "the Mādhvas in their *fervor of enthroning Pratyakṣa* went to the extent of explaining scriptural testimony in consistency with the results of Perception" (*Critique of Mādhva Refutation of Śaṅkara Vedānta*, p. 27). What Madhva has done is to see that neither Pratyakṣa nor Śruti oversteps its own well-defined spheres. Dr. Narain's statement that "the Advaitins disparage the philosophy of the supremacy of perception by arguing that the theory that *every Perception is absolutely valid* is contradicted by both reason and experience. In several cases, the knowledge acquired through preception is contradicted both by inference and testimony. *If perceptions are always valid, what about illusions and their explanation in a textbook on Philosophy*"? (*op. cit.* p.126). The question would not have troubled Dr. Narain's composure if he had taken care to remember Madhva's definition of perception as flawless contact of flawless organs with flawless objects (*nirdoṣārthendriyasannikarṣaḥ pratyakṣam*).

Dr. Narain goes on to say, "The Mādhva objection that because perception provides the data for inference and scriptural testimony its validity should *not* be questioned is also invalid—because the *mere precedence* of one cognition to another is no argument in favor of the strength of the preceding cognition. Had it been so, the illusory presentation of silver, by virtue of precedence would be more valid than the later cognition that the object in question is conchshell" (*op. cit.*, p. 127). It is not good to indulge in such philosophical *naiveté*, once too often !

A reference to Vyāsatīrtha's *Nym* would make it clear that the actual position of Madhva's philosophy is that it is not mere temporal precedence of one cognition to another that suffices for its upajīvyatva. It is precisely to avoid such a superficial sense that Vyāsatīrtha has taken special care to observe that what makes for *prābalya* or superior strength of the upajīvya is that it has been *well-tested* : न ह्युपजीव्यत्वमेव प्राबल्ये तन्त्रम्; किंतु, परीक्षितत्वविशिष्टम् (*Nym* i.p.108).

The analogy of illusory congnition of shell as *silver is thus out of place in this context.* For the erroneous cognition (*idaṁ rajatam*) is *not* the upajīvya of the sublating cognition (*nedaṁ rajatam*) except to the extent of recapitulating what is to be negated (*niṣedhyasamarpaka* or *dharmyarpaka*). In reality, it is the aspect of "thisness" (*idamaṁśa*) alone that constitutes the true subject, well tested and *not thisness qualified by 'silverness'*. Hence "thisness" is the well-tested Upajīvya in this case. This is at no time contradicted by the subsequent cognition of *nedaṁ rajatam.*

एवं च, यदुपजीव्यं तन्न बाध्यम् । इदमंशस्याबाधात् । **यच्च बाध्यं** रजतत्ववैशिष्ट्यं, **न तदुपजीव्यम् ।** रजतत्वविशिष्ट **स्याधर्मित्वात्** (*Nym* p.593).

Accordingly, texts which tend to dismiss the world as *not* real have to be understood in the sense that it does not exist independently of Brahman. That which has a beginning and an end has no independent existence. This world's "non-existence" means its eternal dependence. But it is not for that reason a myth as it is experience by all. So the right way of understanding its description sometimes as 'not-existing' is that it is always under Brahman's control and hence non-existent *in its own right*. It is just a way of speaking, even as a son who is dependent on his father for all practical purposes is treated as of no account :

अविद्यमानता नाम जगतः परतन्त्रता ।
यथाशक्तस्तु पुत्रादिरसन्नित्युच्यते बुधैः ॥

(Madhva, *BT* XI. 28.26-27)

CHAPTER XVIII

THE DOCTRINE OF SĀKṢĪ

THOUGH Madhva accepts that validity is intrinsic to Pramāṇa, defined as *Yathārtham,* he does not rule out the possibility of error in experience. Under ideal conditions, of course, error will have no chance. But the actual conditions of life being what they are, error cannot altogether be eliminated. This leads us to the question of greater and less chances of error among the different Pramāṇas and to the most important question of epistemology, viz., the quest for an ultimate basis of certainty of all experience and knowledge, without which all our claim to secular and scientific knowledge must remain suspect and for the conditions which exclude not merely the fact but even the possibility of error. *It is only the discovery of such a principle that could be regarded as the true fulfilment of the epistemological quest.* The attempt to put knowledge on a foundation that will be impregnable and will not be open to doubt is historically associated with the philosophy of Descartes in the West. In Indian philosophy, the issue has engaged the attention of the different schools *from much earlier times.* The frequently occurring discussions on "Svatastva" and "Paratastva" of Prāmāṇya are essentially concerned with this moot problem. But unfortunately, most of the schools have touched only the fringe of the problem and have not tackled it in all its bearings and in its proper perspective, as we shall see presently.

We have shown earlier that the right theory of knowledge is that which admits that truth is organic to knowledge:[1]

---

1. Cf. ज्ञानं च भावाभाव लक्षणं स्वविषयं सत्त्वेनैवावगाहते, नासत्त्वेन, नाप्युदासीनेन रूपेण ।
(*NS* p.217b)
प्रमाणं चेन्न अतत्त्वावेदकम् । अतत्त्वावेदकं प्रमाणं चेति व्याघातः । (*Vādāvali*)

प्रामाण्यं हि ज्ञानस्योत्सर्गतः, अपवादादप्रामाण्यमिति विद्वत्सम्मतिः ।

Knowledge carries and *must carry its own proof*. If the truth of a cognition should depend upon its agreement with some other factor, such agreement, again, will have to be similarly demonstrated on the basis of further agreement and so on *ad infinitum*. If the validity of the confirming and corresponding knowledge could be intrinsic, such a distinction could as well be conferred on the first knowledge itself at the first blush. The Mādhva philosophers point out that if the function of 'agreement" (*saṁvādapramāṇa*) were just one of "removing grounds of mistrust" the validity of the knowledge in question would turn out to be intrinsically made out :

अतोऽवबोधकत्वेन दुष्टकारणवर्जनात् ।
अबाधाच्च प्रमाणत्वं वस्तुन्यक्षादिवच्छ्रुतेः ॥
(Sureśvara, quoted by *Nym* 1.17)

If, on the other hand, the *saṁvāda* should establish validity inferentially, the validity of the mark of inference would have to be established first and if that is also to be inferred, there would be a regress of inferences. Nor can the provenness of validity be established by the absence of falsification (*bādhakābhāva*) as the conviction of the fact of there being no falsification is itself a knowledge like the affirmation of validity and it cannot have a greater value attaching to it, than any other earlier knowledge : नहि बाधकस्य शृंगमस्ति. If agreement with *another item of knowledge* is to determine validity, such agreement also, as we have shown, will need further corroboration and ratification.

Jayatīrtha points out in the course of a penetrating analysis of the problem of validity, that there are only six possible ways in which validity can be ascertained : (1) by reason of its being caused by flawless senses; or (2) the certainty of its not being generated by defective sense-organs; or (3) on the basis of practical or pragmatic efficiency; or (4) agreement with another knowledge; or (5) at least absence of disagreement with another; or else (6) lastly, *in its own right*. And in everyone of these cases, the acceptance of the doctrine of "Svataḥprāmāṇya" in *inevitable*. For, in the first case, the flawlessness of the senses will itself be open to question. If that is to be decided in the light of the validity of the knowledge itself, there will be a clear interdependence between the two. The same difficulty will remain in the second case also. The test of practical efficiency will not apply to cases of neutral acts of awareness or passive witnessing (*udāsīnajñāna*). The awareness of pleasure and pain, being unique forms of intuition, standing apart from other ordinary acts of knowledge, will not admit of coherence with others. If agreement of knowledge with one of its own kind is to be the test of validity, even a succession of illusory impressions (*dhārāvāhikabhrama*) will have to be passed as valid knowledge. If the intended coherence is with another unit of *valid knowledge*, the validity of the latter will have to be similarly established and so on *ad infinitum*, Mere absence of contradiction, so far, will not be a sufficient proof of validity as there may conceivably be uncontradicted or perpetual illusions, in experience, like the common belief of the sky being blue. Any attempt to establish the validity of knowledge through external aids is thus foredoomed to failure. *We are thus left with the only other alternative of the inherent validity of knowledge.*

But even this is not altogether free from difficulties. Knowledge, as an activity of the mind, cannot be invested with any kind of self-luminosity :

वृत्तिज्ञानानां स्वप्रकाशत्वमेव तावदसत् । प्रमाणाभावात् (*NS* p. 591)

अचैतन्यज्ञानस्य स्वप्रकाशत्वाभावात् (*NS*, p. 436b).

Judgments like "I know this" point to the existence of a knowing self which alone can be claimed to be self-revelatory. Even assuming that knowledge *as such* is capable of revealing itself, it can only manifest its *content* or form; but *not*, also, its validity: अस्तु वा ज्ञानं स्वप्रकाशम् । तथापि स्वरूपमात्र एव । न तु स्वधर्मे प्रामाण्येऽपि (*NS*, p. 591). If validity is inherently revealed by knowledge, the knowledge arising from Vedic texts must make its validity felt by unbelievers like Buddhists. If they do realize its validity, they could not possibly refute it, as they do. This shows that the validity of knowledge is not revealed by the mere awareness of such knowledge—in other words, that validity is not made known by the knowledge itself, even if it be Svaprakāśa. The power of self-illumination, as has been shown, can at best, help knowledge to manifest its essence, to itself. But it cannot have any power to *endorse the validity of its content*. Such a power can *only belong to a principle of truth-determination which is not materially constituted*, like the mind, and can, therefore, be credited with absolute validity in all judgments. Madhva finds such an ultimate and absolute principle of knowledge and validation in the inner sense-(organ) of the self of man—his "Svarūpendriyam" which he calls the "Sākṣī" and which is "Jñāna-grāhaka" (intuitor of knowledge) and of its validity too (*jñānaprāmāṇya-grāhaka*). It may be identified as the 'Apperceiver' of all our conscious states and their validity where such validity is present and is desired to be grasped. It corresponds to the faculty of *a priori* cognitions and is individual to each person. The *raison d'etre* of attributing to Sākṣipratyakṣa absolute infallibility and self-validation, which is denied in respect of ordinary perceptions of the mind and the senses, is that *the mind is liable to err and is open to doubts*, albeit rarely; *whereas, the judgments of the Sākṣī cannot be doubted and have never been shown to have been in the wrong and invalidated at any time in life* :

मानसे दर्शने दोषाः स्युर्नवै साक्षिदर्शने (*AV*, iii.4.41).

दोषाश्च मानस एव दर्शने भवन्ति । अतः तत् संशयात्मकं जायते । निश्चयतया जातस्य विषये वा आहार्यः संशयो भवति । नतु साक्षिदर्शने दोषसंभवः (*NS* p.591)

The best proof of the unerring precision and infallibility of Sākṣī is furnished, says Madhva, by the most intimate and poignant experiences of life (of pleasure and pain) of which none of us has occasion to entertain the least doubt in his life :

न जातुचिन्मम सुखमस्ति न वेति संशयो, नापि प्रतीयमानमिदं सुखं सत्, असद्वेति संशयः (*NS*, p.591 b).

सुदृढो निर्णयो यत्र ज्ञेयं तत् साक्षिदर्शनम् ।
इच्छा ज्ञानं सुखं दुःखं भयाभयकृपादयः ॥

* * *

साक्षिसिद्धं न कश्चिद्धि तत्र संशयवान् क्वचित् ॥ (*AV*, iii.4·41)

The whole of rational existence in the world would be made impossible, if the verdict of our Sākṣī as the ultimate reference, foundation and criterion of all knowledge and validity is questioned or proved to be in the wrong, *even in one single instance at any time*. The entire basis and superstructure of all religion, philosophy, and science and of every activity of life will be blown up to nothingness, as by an atom bomb, the moment we *dare to question* or doubt the verdict of the Sākṣī :

कोऽपि ह्यर्थो न निश्चेतुं शक्यते भ्रमवादिना ।
भ्रमत्वमभ्रमत्वं च यदैवानुभवोपगम् ।
एकस्य भ्रमता तत्र परस्याभ्रमता कुतः ? (*AV* ii.3.28)

साक्षिणो व्यभिचारश्चेत्, आगमार्थ-अनुमाननिर्दोषत्वाध्यवसाये च भ्रमः । अत ऊर्ध्वदिवसे अभेदवाक्यस्य भेदोऽर्थः स्यात् । निर्दोषानुमायाः सदोषत्वं, सदोषानुमाया निर्दोषत्वमित्यव्यवस्था ।
(Madhva, *Pramāṇalakṣaṇa*)

The case for the acceptance of Sākṣi cannot be put in more moving terms.

It is, thus, incumbent on all thinking persons to accept the primacy of Sākṣī as the ultimate criterion of all knowledge and evaluate experience on its basis. The doctrine of Sākṣī, rightly understood, will be seen to be both the true foundation and the crowning point of a really sound and thoroughgoing theory of knowledge. *No theory of knowledge can really be complete without it. While all other adherents of the Svataḥprāmāṇya view have been content with assuming that knowledge itself carries with it its own validity, Madhva has been the only one among Indian philosophers to insist upon a further analysis and to probe the problem and go a step further and demonstrate that only the verdict of the Sākṣī can be the true terminus of validation.* This marking off of the spheres of Vṛtti-jñāna and Sākṣi-jñāna constitutes a remarkable advance of Madhva in Indian epistemology. It may be seen to bridge a gap in the theory of self-validity and answer conclusively the objection of Udayana: प्रामाण्यं न स्वतो ग्राह्यं, संशयानुपपत्तितः. It is no use to contend, as do most adherents of Svataḥprāmāṇya, that if knowledge had no power by itself to affirm its validity, nothing on earth can give it that power and there will be no way in which such validity can be affirmed. But then, is the Svataḥprāmāṇyavādin aware of any single instance or form of knowledge that is incontrovertible and uncontroverted ? If there is any such knowledge or judgment, it must perforce be the verdict of the Sākṣī and nothing else. It is only at that point that real self-validation and self-luminosity are possible : यदि ग्राहकातिरिक्तस्य यथाकथंचिदपि प्रवेशात्

प्रामाण्यस्य परतस्त्वमिति मतम्; तदा साक्षिण एव स्वतः प्रामाण्यं, अन्यस्य परतः इत्यंगीकारेऽपि न कश्चित् विरोध इति सङ्क्षेपः (*NS* p.218).

The *ordinary* doctrine of Svataḥprāmāṇya explains that doubts do not arise in all cases, but only where there is positive knowledge of conditions which seem to contradict the knowledge we have had; and if arguments are employed to test knowledge, it is not so much for the positive task of establishing its validity, as for the negative one of *eliminating the chances of contradiction and clearing doubts.*[2] The essence of Svatastva is that knowledge carries with it its own validity, which is implicit in it. This is seen from the behavior of persons who act unquestioningly upon their knowledge, as soon as they have it, without waiting for its truth to be tested and ratified by a validating inference. This shows that non-contradiction is the only test of validity and that this guarantee does not forsake knowledge till it is positively disproved or doubted.

It has been objected that this sort of explanation is unsatisfactory as it "confuses logical certainty with mere psychological belief". A belief of validity is no indubitable index of its truth and no substitute for certainty. Prof. D.M. Datta argues that "this distinction though apparently sound, is, in the last analysis, untenable. Certainty is nothing but a quality of knowledge. It would be useful if we could ascertain the degree of strength or amount of reasoning that would be necessary to turn a mere belief into a logical certainty. But this is logically and psychologically impossible, as different persons require different degrees of certification[3] for the validity of their knowledge and because no objective or logical limit can be set to the degree of strength

2. तेन दोषाभावस्याप्रामाण्यनिरासोपक्षयेण, ज्ञानसामग्रीत एव प्रमा जायत इत्युत्सर्गो न भग्नः (Rāghavendra, Commantary on *TT* i.p.206).

औत्सर्गिककार्यपवादनिरासरूपस्यापि दोषाभावस्य हेतुत्वे, इदमौत्सर्गिकं, इदमापवादकमिति व्यवस्थित्ययोगात् (Vyāsathīrtha, *TT* 1.15)

3. Cf. "As to evidence, the kind and amount required to warrant knowledge, in distinction to opinion or belief, varies generally according to the character of the cognizing mind and the kind and amount of knowledge obtainable. The term 'sufficient reason' affords no help here. (G. Trumbull Ladd, *Philosophy of Knowledge*, p.239)

that is required to establish certainty. *There is no way hitherto discovered of wholly eliminating risks of error*" (*Six Ways of Knowing*, p.356).

It is precisely at this point that Madhva interposes his criterion of Sākṣipratyakṣa, backed by Parīkṣā (tests) as the terminus of all tests and processes of reasoning by which "belief could be converted into a logical certainty". The approbation of the Sākṣī is the logical limit of all certainty, clarification and validation, as it is intuitive.

न परीक्षानवस्था स्यात् साक्षिसिद्धे त्वसंशयात् । (*AV* iii.4.41)

He explains all cases of doubtful cognitions as "mental perceptions" *not* reaching down to the rock bottom level of personal and intuitive level of *Sākṣinirdhāraṇa*.

यत्क्वचित् व्यभिचारि स्याद् दर्शनं मानसं तु तत् ।
मानसे दर्शने दोषाः स्युर्न वै साक्षिदर्शने ॥ (*AV* iii.4.41)

As Jayatīrtha explains, "The Sākṣī, is the ultimate criterion of all knowledge and its validation. Being however accustomed to truth and error in respect of sensory, inferential and verbal knowledge, the Sākṣī is not able to come to a decision straightway about the validity of particular items of knowledge placed before it, when faced with doubts or the possibility of invalidity. *However, it is the mind and not the Sākṣī which is open to doubts*:

नाप्रामाण्यशंका साक्षिणः, किंतु मनस एव (*Jayātīrtha*, *VTNt*, p.15).

To this end then, it resorts to the application of tests and experiments till it reaches a certain level where knowledge issues in an *intuitive perception of pleasure, pain, satisfaction, relief or similar intuitive reactions*. Since such intuitive experiences of the Sākṣī have not been known to have miscarried in any instance before, it is not assailed by any further misgivings about their truthfulness and so desists from the application of further tests of truth-determination and rests *satisfied* in the validity of the knowledge and judgment so arrived at". (*NS*, p. 218 b translated).[4]

---

4. *Read* also :

यद् दर्शनं क्वचित् शुक्तिरूप्यादौ विषये व्यभिचारि वाधितं स्यात्, तत् चक्षुरादिकरणकं, मनःपरिणामरूपमेव, न साक्षिरूपम्। कुत एतत् ? मानसदर्शनस्य बाध्यत्वांगीकारेऽनिष्टाभावात् साक्षिणस्तु तथात्वे सर्वव्यवहारविलोपस्योक्तत्वात्। तदिदमुक्तं 'हि'शब्देन। संभवति चास्य मानसत्वमन्यथाख्यातिसमर्थनादिति । (*NS*, p.591 b-591)

Knowledge, then, receives its true and highest validation by the verdict of the Sākṣī and no theory of the self-validity of knowledge will be complete without the acceptance of such a final principle of validation. Such is the position of Madhva's epistemology.

CHAPTER XIX

SĀKṢĪ AS THE ULTIMATE CRITERION OF TRUTH

THE Mādhva theory of knowledge distinguishes between ordinary knowledge through sensory channels termed 'Vṛttijñāna' and intuitive perception by the self called Sākṣijñāna. This distinction helps Madhva to give a consistent account of both valid and erroneous or doubtful cognitions, without impugning the fundamental claims of truth and knowledge to universal acceptance. It is conceded by him that the normal judgments of the mind are generally correct and valid and that certification by tests is *not always necessary*. Tests are, therefore, instituted only when validity is desired to be assured of or argumentatively established or *logically ascertained in case of doubt*. The acceptance of the Sākṣī obviates the necessity to carry on verifications upto "three or four stages" as proposed by Kumārila (*Ślokavārtika,* ii.61). For if truth is to be ascertained and judgments of validity are to be passed at any stage of the process it *cannot be at any level prior to ratification by the Sākṣi.* From the ultimate point of view, even tests of non-contradiction would be helpless as guarantors of validity, *unless the Sākṣi is summoned to vouch for the satisfaction of the condition of there being not only no contradiction but also no possibility thereof.* Non-contradiction, again, may be uncontradictedness so far; or non-liability to contradiction for ever. The latter cannot be asserted on any authority save that of the Sākṣī.

The epistemological necessity for such an ultimate principle of knowledge and its validation is accepted by the Advaitin also.[1]

---

1. Cf. तथाहि--प्रमाता सन्दिहानोऽप्यसंदिग्धः विपर्यस्यन्नप्यविपरीतः (*Bhāmatī* ii.2.28).

मानानां तात्त्विकं किंचिद्वस्त्वनाश्रित्य दुर्भणा ।

But such a principle cannot be a mere registering machine, as in the Advaita. The very purpose of recognising the Sākṣī as a *validating principle* would be lost if, as in Advaita, the great censor of Sākṣī, the Apperceiver, were to be put down as a common and passive witness to true and false knowledge alike.

साक्षिज्ञानस्य भ्रमप्रमासाधारण्येन प्रमाणाबाधकत्वात् (*Advaitasiddhi* i.11). This is why Madhva places the Sākṣī above all doubts and vacillations and makes it an absolute principle of infallibility[2]. It is untouched by any breath of uncertainty. Its credentials are never dubious. The reason for this is precisely the same as is given in Advaita : साक्षिणो बाधे, तस्य साक्षीऽन्यो वाच्यः, तस्याप्यन्य इत्यनवस्था (*Brahmānandīya* i,p.438, Bombay). The same point is thus elucidated by Madhva :

भ्रमत्वमभ्रमत्वं च सर्वं वेद्यं हि साक्षिणा
स चेत्साक्षी क्वचित् दुष्टः कथं निर्णय ईयते ।
तस्मात्सर्वप्रसिद्धस्य व्यवहारस्य सिद्धये ।
साक्षी निर्दोष एवैकः सदांगीकार्य एव नः ॥
शुद्धः साक्षी यदा सिद्धः ... ।
स्वप्रामाण्यं सदा साक्षी पश्यत्येव सुनिश्चयात् ॥ (*AV* ii.3.28)

"Whether a given experience is true or false is to be ascertained by the Sākṣī. If this Sākṣī (the truth-determining principle) should become tainted *even in a single instance*, there can be no certitude at all in epistemology. In order, therefore, to stabilize and guarantee the validity of all the accepted values of life and its transactions, lay and scientific, carried on on their foundations, the Sākṣī will have to be accepted (whether one likes it or not) as the one flawless principle and criterion of validity by all of us. Once the flawlessness of Sākṣī is established, there is no fear of any regress in accepting the Sākṣī as the validating principle; for it is capable of grasping its own validity and the validity of its judgments without appealing to any further authority, outside itself."

The place of Sākṣī in Madhva's philosophy is unique. From what has been said above it should be clear that it will not do to think of the Sākṣī merely as a sense organ or item of

2. Cf. साक्षाद् द्रष्टरि संज्ञायाम् (*Pāṇ.* v.2.11).

Pratyakṣa. Its function certainly does not end merely with apprehending knowledge and its validity if it is valid and such other things. For the Sākṣī is no other than *the self.* It is also its *Caitanya-indriya* (essential sense organ partaking of the nature of consciousness). Its distinction into *self* and *its organ* is one of reference and not of essence. Their relation is one of Saviśeṣābheda in Madhva's terminology. The Sākṣī is certainly the criterion of truth and validity. There is no fear of Madhva's philosophy being reduced to the position of the Cārvāka by giving primary importance to Sākṣipratyakṣa. For the Cārvāka does not go beyond the ordinary (external) sense perception and Sākṣijñāna is *not* the same as ordinary (external) sense-perception. Sākṣipratyakṣa is perception by the Svarūpendriya (inner sense organ) of the Ātman. That is why Madhva draws a special distinction between ordinary Pratyakṣa by the sense-organs (including the mind) and perception by the Sākṣī (See Chap. XVIII), and, speaks of seven types of Pratyakṣa, arising through the five sense-organs, the mind and the Sākṣī: *pratyakṣam saptavidham, Sākṣi-ṣaḍindriyabhedena* (*Madhva's Pramāṇalakṣaṇa*).

The Sākṣī being the fundamental criterion of validity, of truth and error, in the last analysis of experience, even the truth of the unreality of the world or the identity of Jīva and Brahman, which are supposed to be taught in the Scriptures by the Advaitins, have to be brought before the bar of Sākṣī before they can be accepted without question. This is not flouting Scripture and elevating Pratyakṣa to a higher pedestal.

There is one significant point to be noted in determining the scope of Upajīvyatva (foundational support) with reference to truths falling exclusively within the domain of revelation and those which are within the limits of our own consolidated experience. Madhva formulates a guiding principle in the light of which alone this question has to be decided :

प्रत्यक्षमुपजीव्यं स्यात् प्रायो युक्तिरपि क्वचित् ।
आगमैकप्रमाणेषु तस्यैव ह्युपजीव्यता ॥ (*AV* ii.1.4-5)

"Generally speaking, perception is the criterion of truth. In some cases, it is also inference. With regard to things presented only on the evidence of Scripture, the position of being the criterion belongs only to it."

This does not, however, falsify the claim made regarding the primacy of the Sākṣī, as the Upajīvyapramāṇa even as against Śruti. For Madhva himself has clearly given *one more ruling* which is to be read concurrently with the above :

तत्प्रत्यक्षविरुद्धार्थे नागमस्यापि मानता ।
उपजीव्यमक्षजं यत्र, तदन्यत्र विपर्ययः ॥
लौकिके व्यवहारे ऽत्र प्रत्यक्षस्योपजीव्यता ।
अवतारादिदृष्टौ स्यादागमस्योपजीव्यता ॥ (*AV* iii.4.41)

"Therefore Scripture (Āgama) has no overriding validity where it conflicts with the well-tested Pratyakṣa; because, in such cases, the knowledge arising from sense-perception is the basis or fundamental ground (Upajīvya). *In other cases* where Scriptural statements happen to be the sole proof and guarantor of the truths which fall *exclusively within their purview* (and do not fall within the range of ordinary perception including the Sākṣī), the position is reversed. In matters which fall entirely within the scope of worldly experience, it is perception (of the senses as tested by the Sākṣī) that remains the basis and standing-ground (Upajīvya) with reference to Āgama when its teachings conflict with the testimony of *such* Pratyakṣa. As an instance of where Scripture is to be accepted as the sole basis of knowledge (*Upajīvya*) of particular facts or truths, may be cited the way in which ordinary human perception looks upon Avatāras of God as human beings subject to various human frailties and imperfections. In such cases, as the Avatārahood is established solely on the authority of Scripture, and as Scripture posits that God is flawless (*nirdoṣa*) the ordinary human perception which looks upon the bodies of the Avatāras as human and made of flesh and blood like those of ourselves and being subject to various imperfections, *has to be rejected as unauthoritative*".

Jayatīrtha, explaining Madhva's position as set forth above, sums up the whole discussion (in his *NS*) in the clearest terms which leave no room for doubt that when texts like "Tat tvam asi" and "Neha nānāsti" *appear* to teach the identity of Jīva and Brahman and the unreality of the world, such a teaching (or interpretation of those texts) has to be *unhesitatingly rejected as invalid because it goes against the Upajīvyapramāṇā which, in the present case, is the tested Sākṣi-anubhava* of the difference between the individual self and Brahman and of the reality of the world of experience:

'लौकिके' **प्रत्यक्षसिद्धजीवादिविषये ब्रह्मात्मकत्वादिबोधनरूपे** 'व्यवहारे' तत्त्वमस्यादि–आगमेन क्रियमाणे, 'अत्र' आगमं प्रति, प्रत्यक्षस्योपजीव्यता । (*NS* iii.4.p.593)

Madhva has thus gone far ahead of his contemporaries and compeers in having postulated a new principle of truth-determination in epistemology in the form Sākṣī, as the ultimate criterion of truth which is infallible and intrinsically valid. Its *raison d'etre* are (1) that it alone can be the ultimate guarantor of the validity of all other Pramāṇas, (2) that it is the logical fulfilment and culmination of any really self-complete theory of knowledge, and (3) that it is the only means of intuitive perception of certain supersensuous categories like Time, Space, the nature of the self and its attributes, the mind and its modes, all knowledge of pleasure and pain, etc.[3] These experiences are regarded by Madhva as immediate experiences (*sākṣātkāra*) and not as inferences, as in other systems. Take for instance the category of time as revealed in dreamless sleep, embodied in the recollection of the happy repose of sleep, expressed in the judgment "I have slept soundly and blissfully all this time". This direct experience of time and bliss in Suṣupti cannot obviously be put down to the activity of *the mind, which is admittedly at rest then*. We have, therefore, to attribute them to the instrumentality of *a special sense organ, which is active even during dreamless sleep*, when the mind itself is at rest, and coordinates the inmost experiences of the self. It is this spiritual sense organ of the Self that is designated as the Sākṣī, very appropriately :

सुखादिविषयं स्वरूपभूतं चैतन्येन्द्रियं हि साक्षीत्युच्यते (*NS*, p.258).

Once the existence of such an instrument of intuitive perception is recognized, it would be easy to bring other intuitive perceptions of life, under its scope. The Sākṣī, as an instrument of knowledge and validation is not something extraneous to the knowing self or Pramātā as such : साक्षिणश्च आत्मत्वात् (*PLt.* p.30). The distinction of Sākṣī into *Svarūpa* and *Indriya* (self and organ) is only one of reference and not of essence. Such a distinction is rationalized by the play of "Viśeṣas" (already dealt with).

3. तस्य विषयाः, आत्मस्वरूपं, तद्धर्मा, अविद्या, मनः, तद्वृत्तयो, बाह्येन्द्रियज्ञानसुखाद्याः कालोऽव्याकृताकाशश्च, इत्याद्याः । (*PP*)

We cannot go beyond the verdict of the Sākṣī. It is the last word on validation, not only of ordinary experiences, sense-perception and inference, *but even of the teachings of Scripture.* Even the identity-texts of the Advaitins, to be valid, must concede the infallibility of the identity-judgments based on the verdict of the Sākṣī ratifying their expressed sense or experience as understood by them.

It is easy to see that the validity established by Sākṣī must *ex hypothesi* be absolute and true for all time (*ātyantika*) or त्रैकालिक सत्तायुक्त and not merely provisional or Vyāvahārika. If it were not so, even the personal conviction of oneness said to be produced by the identity texts will have merely a provisional and limited validity and would not hold good for all time, so much so that it might be liable to be set aside by some other doctrine of the Buddhist or other philosophers :

तात्कालिकं प्रमाणत्वमक्षजस्य यदा भवेत् ।
ऐक्यागमस्य किं न स्यात् ? तदप्येतादृशं यदि ॥
ऐक्यप्रामाण्यमिथ्यात्वं यदा विश्वस्य सत्यता ॥ (*AV*, iii.2.3)

The verdict of Sākṣī must, willy-nilly, then, be credited with absolute validity for all time, *by every philosopher, be he a Dualist or a Monist, a Realist or an Idealist.* It is the basis, prop and support of all theory of knowledge :

साक्षिप्रत्यक्षतो त्वेवं मानानां मानतेयते ।
ऊरीकृत्य च तान् सर्वान् व्यवहारः प्रवर्तते ॥ (*AV* ii.3.28)

Madhva deserves the highest recognition for having discovered and formulated such an *a priori* criterion of epistemological reference and certitude and built up his system of metaphysics, on its solid foundations : विश्वसत्यतामपि तेनैव साधयाम इत्यपि **हृदयम्** ।
(*NS*, p.210)

अस्माभिरपि दुःखादिबन्धस्य सत्यतायां साक्षिप्रत्यक्षमेव उपन्यस्तमिति हृदयम् ।
(*NS*, p.30 b)

Dr. Narain's criticism in his *Critique of Madhva Refutation of Śaṅkara Vedānta* that "The Mādhva philosophers exhibit their weakness in their zealous advocacy of *perception* and overemphasize the capacity of perception when not assailed by defects and being overpowered or invalidated by inference or tests, *because for ascertainment of defects one has to resort to critical examination and thereby depend on reasoning*" (p.128) is thus *off the track.* For such ascertainment according to Madhva is made at *the Sākṣi-level and not merely through inference.* As for Dr. Narain's self-assurance that *in spite of all this "the inference of the falsity of the world is more valid than the perceptual experience* and it has *such solid foundations* that it can stand the vehemence of the assault of Mādhva criticism" (p.128) we can only say: *Viduṣām nottaram vācyam* or *Cakṣuṣī nimīlya tat tatheti vadataḥ kaḥ pratimallaḥ* ?

Dr. Krishnakant Chaturvedi (*Dvait Vedant kā Tāttvik Anuśīlan* p.210) holds that Madhva's position that the Abheda Śrutis cannot, on account of their opposition to their Upajīvyapramāṇa be accepted in their literal sense but must be suitably modified in other ways short of Svarūpaikya "restricts the power of the Śrutis to convey their meaning and devitalizes them—which does not do credit to the prestige of the founder of a school of *Indian* Philosophy" ! (*Op. Cit.* p.210).

We have seen that the principle of Upajīvya-pramāṇaprābalya is universal in its application to epistemological and textual exegesis. There will be no *raison d'etre* for Pūrva and Uttara Mīmāṁsā if the literal sense of Śrutis is to prevail everywhere without question in *vidhis, arthavādas* or statement of facts and philosophical pronouncements. The resort to Gauṇārtha in cases of Upajīvyavirodha is an exegetical principle accepted in Mīmāṁsā, while the criterion of Akhaṇḍārtha and two-level theory of truth as Pāramārthika and Vyāvahārika is only the brain-child of Śaṁkara Vedānta. The former is an objective standard while the latter is purely subjective, drawn as a corollary from Brahmājñanvāda, which depends on other gratuitous assumptions of a Nirviśeṣa-Brahman being obscured in part by Ajñāna (*Ajñānāsambhavād evà mithyābhedo nirākṛtaḥ*).

Dr. Krishnakant Chaturvedi's inability to correctly appraise the merits of Madhva's way of harmonizing the Dvaita and Advaita Śrutis, in their right perspective, is shown by the manner in which he has completely ignored the *grammar of Samanvaya of the whole of Upaniṣadic philosophy* in a nutshell in the light of the metaphysical ideology of one Svatantra-Advitīya Brahman so impressively spelt out by Jayatīrtha in one of the most important and moving passages of his *Nyāyasudhā* (beginning with the words : *Sarvāṇyapi hi Vedāntavākyāni*.........quoted in Chap. III). One looks in vain for this famous passage from Jayatīrtha's NS in Dr. Krishnakant Chaturvedi's own study of Dvaita Vedānta running to 231 pages. His criticism of the adequacy of Sākṣī as

Upajīvyapramāṇa in resolving the conflict of Bheda and Abheda Śrutis in Madhva's philosophy suffers from putting the Sākṣī on a par with sense-perception in principle and substance, which defeats the very purpose for which Sākṣī has been recognised by Madhva as the seventh cognitive sense constituted entirely of the stuff of Caitanya and enjoying absolute certainty (*niyatayāthārthya*) and the instrument of both knowledge and its validity by its intrinsic power (*sahajaśakti*) and in cases of *mānasadarśana* taking the help of Parīkṣā or critical examination only to eliminate doubts *but not to establish validity*.

CHAPTER XX

THEORIES OF ERROR IN INDIAN THOUGHT

ERROR is the reverse of valid knowledge. It is an experience where an object is cognized as something else or as having certain characteristics that really fall outside of its being. The cognition of a shell as silver, of a rope as a snake, and so on are instances in point. The explanation of errors of perception has been a live issue in philosophy. Is error due entirely to the object or solely to the subject or equally to both ? Quite a number of interesting theories have been propunded by Indian philosophers as to how error arises and what should be the status assignable to the object presented therein. Five main theories of error are generally referred to in Indian philosophical literature :

आत्मख्यातिरसत्ख्यातिरख्यातिः ख्यातिरन्यथा ।
तथानिर्वचनख्यातिरित्येतत् ख्यातिपञ्चकम् ॥

These are held by the schools of Buddhist idealism, nihilism, the Mīmāṁsakas, the Naiyāyikas and the Advaita-Vedāntins respectively. To these must be added the Rāmānuja theory of error known as "Akhyātisaṁvalita-Yathārthakhyāti" and the Mādhva theory of "Abhinava-Anyathākhyāti". The Mādhva theory is the outcome of an implicit criticism of the other theories. Madhva, in his *AV* has briefly reviewed the Advaita theory of error, while formulating his own definition of what constitutes "Bādha" (sublation) :

विज्ञातस्यान्यथा सम्यग्विज्ञानं ह्येव तन्मतम् (*AV* i.1.1).

Jayatīrtha takes advantages of this opportunity, while commenting on the above passage, to initiate a fullfledged discussion of all the leading theories of Error held by the different schools and reviews them critically in the light of Madhva's own theory, which he shows to be the most satisfactory one, in the end.

In his review of the various "Khyātivādas", Jayatīrtha raises many subtle questions about the problem. His arguments touching the details of the controversies regarding the Khyātivādas are sure to provoke thought on fresh lines among modern scholars and students of Indian philosophy. It seems worthwhile, for this reason, to give a resumé of his examination of the different Khyātivādas, before we come to his exposition of Madhva's own theory of error.

(1) The Prābhākara View

Error, according to the Prābhākara school of Mīmāṁsā, is made up of a fusion of two different cognitions. They may both be presentations or representations or one may be a percept and the other a memory image. In any case, error is only a partial truth. It is only imperfect knowledge. It is an omission rather than a commission. In the 'illusory experience' of shell as silver, which takes the from "*Idaṁ rajatam*" (this is silver), the "this" refers to the perception of the given object. Owing to abnormal conditions of defects, it is perceived as just a shining, white something. There is no perception of the specific class-essence of nacreness (शुक्तित्वसामान्यविशेष). This partial perception produces a memory image of silver by reviving the impressions of it, owing to the similarity subsisting between the whiteness and brightness of the present object and the brightness, etc. of silver recalled by the memory image. Though memory, as a rule, is representative in character, yet, on account of abnormal conditions of defect, it functions here in a purely presentative capacity, by losing its representative aspect of "thatness".[1] Thus, for want of discrimination between the essential features and content of these two different cognitions, they get fused into one and give rise to an identity judgment, in respect of their relation, owing to the similarity of the

1. This is called 'प्रमुष्टतत्ताकस्मरणम्' ।

forms of the cognition and this is expressed in a judgment of their identity as "Idaṁ rajatam", and the person acts on it.

Jayatīrtha rejoins that the illusory cognition is felt to be a single determinate cognition of a given object (as in ordinary perception) : विशिष्टविषयकमेकं विज्ञानम्. It is *not* felt to be a composite cognition or a cross or amalgam of two different psychoses—a percept and a memory. There will be no responsive activity on the part of the percepient, if there is no positive determinate cognition of the given thing. In the last analysis, the Prābhākara must admit that this dual-cognition appears as what it is *not*, viz., a single determinate cagnition. That would be a tacit admission of error as a misapprehension (*viparyaya*), which he is fighting shy of. His attempt to take shelter under alleged non-discrimination between the true nature of the two cognitions, to account for the ready responsive activity, is futile. For, non-discrimination, as mere confusion of knowledge, cannot be the basis of such sure activity as follows the cognition. Moreover, the Prābhākara will have to face a serious difficulty in defining the precise nature of the difference between the two cognitions which, according to him, is missed in the illusory experience. This *difference* between the two cognitions cannot be put down as the essence (*svarūpa*) of the cognitions themselves; or as their severality (*pṛthaktva*), or contrariety (*vaidharmya*). As knowledge, according to the Prābhākaras, is self-luminous in respect of itself and its content *and as no erroneous knowledge as such is recognized in the system*, how could the difference between the two cognitions, which is, in reality, part and parcel of the content of a self-luminous cognition, be missed and remain unrevealed ? Nor can the said difference be a severality (*pṛthaktva*); for cognition which is an attribute of the self cannot have another quality residing in it. If the difference in question were to be viewed as Vaidharmya (contrariness), one will have to define the nature of such *vaidharmya*. Is it of the nature of a mutual difference (*anyonyābhāva*) ? Even then, is it the mutual difference between "this" and "silverness" that is *not revealed* in the experience; or the reciprocal negation between "this" and "silver"? It will not be possible to hold, that where distinctive terms like "idam" and "rajatam" are used in the proposition, in non-synonymous notation, the difference between "this" and "the class-essence of silverness" remains unrecognized. For, *Vaidharmya*, in the sense of reciprocal negation of identity, is to the Prābhākara absolutely identical with its substratum (अधिकरण-स्वरूप). It is, therefore, impossible for the Prābhākara to contend that even though there are two different cognitions here, in the illusory experience, the mutual difference between them as a percept (*idam*) and a memory image (*rajatatvam*), is *not* realized. For the same reason, the difference between the cognition of "this" and "silver", also, cannot remain uncognized. Similarly, the contrariness between "thisness" and "silverness" must also be admitted to be cognized by the very terms of the judgment—"Idam rajatam", where the attribute of "thisness" (*idantva*) which is incompatible with the silver is cognized in the object presented to vision and the attribute of "silverness" (*rajatatva*), which is incompatible with the object presented to the eye, is also grasped in the silver. The explanation that what is missed in the illusion is the *absence of association* between "this" and "silverness" (इदंरजतत्वयोरसंसर्ग-ग्रहः) and *not the presence of their difference*, would also be futile. For, 'absence of association' (असंसर्ग) is the same as negation of such association (संसर्गाभाव) and such negation, according to Prabhākara, is absolutely identical with its correlative locus (अधिकरणात्मक). Hence, neither difference between the cognitions in question nor absence of association can remain uncognized, on the Prābhākara view. Jayatīrtha is quick to point out that no such difficulty will be there on the Mādhva theory of Anyathākhyāti, wherein also the given entity is mistaken for something else, by missing the difference between the presented and the actual objects; for to Madhva, 'difference' or Anyonyābhāva is not *absolutely* identical with the correlatives, but something that is only colorfully identical with it (सविशेषाभिन्न). The Prābhākara cannot also explain the responsive activity to secure the silver, in the illusory experience, on the ground that there is the non-comprehension of the specific attribute of the given object viz., shellness which would distinguish it from silver and of the specific attribute of silverness as being present somewhere else which would distinguish it from the given object. Jayatīrtha says that the two non-comprehensions together will prevent all activity. They will hardly explain the person greedy of silver stretching out his hand to the object before him unless he is under the strong (mis-) conception that what lies before him is the silver (that his memory image has brought up before him, as the Prābhākara would have it). Such activity, then, is a clear proof of the perceiver laboring under a misapprehension. The Prābhākara attempt to evade the fact of misapprehension in illusory experience and explain it away as a case of non-discrimination between two separate cognitions is epistemologically unsound.

(2) Rāmānuja's View

Rāmānuja propounds the Yathārtha-Khyāti view which he inherits from the precursors of his school, though he expresses approval of the *Anyathākhyāti* view also. However, it is the Yathārthakhyāti view that has come to be prominently associated with his school, as its official view. Accordingly, Jayatīrtha also takes special notice of it and ignores the other view in dealing with Rāmānuja's theory.

According to Rāmānuja, the object represented in error is always real and there is, strictly speaking, no invalid cognition at all. His theory is influenced by the Prābhākara view. The cognition of silver in the shell is relatively true and not absolutely false. The perception of silver in the shell is true enough, with reference to the element of silver present in the shell. For, says Rāmānuja, every object in the world has some elements of the other objects in its constitution in varying proportions. He finds support for this idea in the doctrine of triplication (त्रिवृत्करण) and of quintuplication (पंचीकरण) of elements (out of *tejas*, *ap* and *anna*) taught in the Upaniṣads and Purāṇas. He also argues that Vedic texts which permit the substitution of Pūtika for Soma and of Nīvāra for Vrīhi (in the case of non-availability of the original), clearly presuppose that the substitutes have in their make-up some elements of their originals. Perception also establishes so many resemblances among things. Such resemblances must necessarily be on account of their possessing common elements. Hence, the experience of silver in shell is to be treated as a valid experience to the extent that it is a perception of the actual silver elements in it. The reason why it is regarded by ordinary people as *invalid* is because it has no practical utility. The question of designation and acceptance of validity of a particular experience is governed, in normal life, by the fact of given objects possessing a preponderance of the distinctive elements that constitute their being. The cognition of silver in the shell is, no doubt, a correct one in the sense already explained Only, it is a partial experience of silver in the shell. But owing to certain defects in the sense organ, there is a distortion of the shell element and the small portions of silver which constitute the shell get undue attention for the nonce and we have a perception of the silver in what is really shell-silver. This perception is wrong, not because it is a cognition of the unreal or what is not in fact there, but because, it is a partial view or an imperfect cognition of the real. Thus, error, according to Rāmānuja, is not so much a misapprehension of one real as another, but a blundering into a subtle truth about things, unawares, which, under normal conditions, is generally missed or ignored.

Jayatīrtha rejects this theory as a picturesque fancy. The doctrine of Trivṛtkaraṇa (triplication of elements) on which Rāmānuja takes his stand to support this novel theory of illusions, has reference primarily to the combination of the primal elements of *tejobanna* in primordial creation. It would be extremely far-fetched to attempt to legitimize our perceptual error on its basis. If remote causal relation is to be relied upon to validate the mis-perception of silver in shell, on the basis of Trivṛtkaraṇa, it should be possible to have the illusory perception of ever so many other things also in shell. It cannot be argued that owing to the perceiver's Adṛṣṭa (unseen merit) and other special factors, only silver comes to be perceived in shell. Such an explanation would be in order only *after* it is conclusively established that silver is actually present in shell.

The presumptive reasoning based on the examples of Pūtika and Soma, etc., is equally unsustainable. For then, the question would arise : Are we to ascribe to Pūtika a preponderance of Soma elements; or an equal measure of them; or only a very small number of Soma parts? In the first case, Pūtika would be indistinguishable from Soma and could not be treated as a mere substitute for it. Indeed, even Soma, according to this theory of Rāmānuja, is not *pure and simple Soma* but something else besides and called Soma by virtue of preponderance of Soma-parts in its composition. If, then, the Pūtika also should have a preponderance of Soma-parts, there is hardly any reason why it should not be regarded as Soma itself instead of as a substitute for it. If the Pūtika should contain Soma and Pūtika parts in equal measure, it will lead to the perception of both, in the object. If Pūtika should contain a small number of Soma parts it could nor carry out the function of Soma. Otherwise, even the shell could be used for silver in normal life. If the authority of the Śruti confers such right on Pūtika, one could as well bow to the Śruti and dispense with the luxury of ascribing to Pūtika parts more or less similar to Soma on the basis of some farfetched theory of things possessing all sorts of undetected elements of all other things.

The question of responsive activity, in such cases of illusory experience, would pose a serious difficulty to Rāmānuja. What on Rāmānuja's view is it that makes one who desires silver, as in the case of Śuktirajatabhrama, stoop to pick up the shell? It can hardly be the non-perception of the preponderant elements of shell in the given object. For non-perception cannot lead to such activity and if it does, even a man in his sleep may be expected to act that way. It cannot also be the perception of the limited number of silver-elements in the shell. In that case, it should be clarified by Rāmānuja if it is the perception of the *small number* of silver-elements *as such* that inspires the activity or their perception *as preponderant*, or their merest perception (ज्ञानमात्रम्). On the first view, the shell will never be perceived as silver and there will be no responsive activity to pick it up. The second view would open the door to Anyathākhyātivāda or the theory of misapprehension, which Rāmānuja seeks to avoid. On the last alternative every other object in the world bearing similarity with silver elements may come to be picked up and the activity may not be confined to the shell.

Again, why should the perception of the small number of silver elements in the shell be normally regarded as an 'erroneous experience'? If it is only because it is an experience of a partial truth and not a complete truth comprehending the fulness of the attributes of the given object, then, the Viśiṣṭādvaitin will have to accept that knowledge of the Supreme

Brahman attained even by the very best among gods and men will have to remain the biggest error.[2]

(3) Buddhist Views

The idealistic school of Buddhism looks upon the silver represented in the illusion as real but not external as in the Nyāya school. This silver, if actually non-existent, can neither be presented in the illusion nor sublated. There is no proof of its existing elsewhere, outside, as an extra-mental reality. Error consists in projecting subjective ideas as objective extra-mental facts. The silver represented in illusion is thus merely "ideal" and, therefore, "internal" (*jñānarūpam*) and its immediate apprehension without actual sensory contact also proves its internal existence. The sublating cognition also merely corrects the misinterpretation.

Jayatīrtha shows that this (Yogācāra) view of error is not supported by the sublating cognition, which clearly establishes the truth that the silver represented in the illusion is totally non-existent (सत्त्वे, असदेव रजतमित्यसत्त्वावेदकप्रत्ययविरोधस्योक्तत्वात्). We have no right to twist its verdict and confer upon the silver represented in the illusion any reality of its own either internal or external. The Buddhist idealist himself has to admit that the totally non-existent can be represented in illusions, when he opines that what is internal appears as external. Does this not amount to an acceptance of the position that illusion is the presentation of a given something as something that it is not or as involving a non-existent association ? The quality of externalness (*bāhyatā*) that is presented here, on the Yogācāra view, is certainly not something that pertains to the silver, which is claimed to be a purely internal reality. The contention of the Yogācāra that there is immediacy in the presentation of silver, without sensory contact, is untenable as there is *actual sensory contact with the shell*, which is responsible for the misrepresentation. The theory of internal reality of objects represented in illusion would lead to absurd results. There would be an actual burning sensation

---

2. कथं चास्य ज्ञानस्य भ्रान्तित्वम् ? अल्पांशग्रहणादिति चेत्; नूनं ब्रह्मज्ञानमपि महाभ्रान्तिरापन्ना । (*NS*, p.53b)

inside the body when there is an erroneous superimposition of fire on a heap of Guñjā weights. The Yogācāra view seems to be more interested in finding ontological support for its doctrine of Vijñāna as the sole internal reality than in giving a straightforward explanation of illusions. The Asat-Khyāti of the Mādhyamika school of Buddhism holds that error lies in the manifestation of *the non-existent as existent.* But it fails to recognize that this illusion is due to the contact of the sense-organ with the shell as the *adhiṣṭhāna,* and under certain conditions. This point is brought out by Madhva in his theory of Neo-Anyathākhyāti.

(4) Nyāya View

The Nyāya theory of Error is "Anyathā-Khyāti". It explains error as the misapprehension of *one real object as another real object existing elsewhere.* What happens, according to the Naiyāyika, in an erroneous perception of silver in shell is simply this. The visual perception of shell as "this", takes place in the ordinary normal way. The attribute of "silverness" which belongs to the real silver existing elsewhere, is presented in this cognition as an attribute of shell, which is before the eye, in a general way. Neither the real silver which is present elsewhere nor its characteristic of silverness could, however, be connected with the visual organ through ordinary sense-contact. But as no perception of silverness as synthetically connected with the substratum can arise without such sensory contact, the Nyāya philosophers have thought it fit to invest a special type of extra-ordinary sense-relation connecting the real silver and silverness with the visual sense. This contact is the contact through cognition (ज्ञानलक्षणा प्रत्यासत्तिः).Thus, in the present case three things are presented : a "this" (*idamākāra* or *adhiṣṭhāna*), the silver (*āropyam*) and their identity (*tādātmya*); or a "this" (*idam*), silverness (*rajatatvam*) and their synthesis (*saṁsarga*). The Naiyāyikas argue that as silver, silverness (and the substratum) remain uncontradicted (even after the sublating cognition arises)—as existing elsewhere in actual life—and as only the identity of "*idam*" and "*rajatam*" or the association (*saṁsarga*) between "*idam*" and "*rajatatvam*" stands contradicted, the sublating cognition must be understood to negative only the aspect of this identity or association and not the very reality of the silver. The "Bādhakajñāna", in other words, should not be taken to establish that the "silver" represented in the illusion is non-existent (*asat*). *It does exist elsewhere.* If the silver which was represented in the illusion was non-existent, it could never have been presented directly to our perception. We are thus justified in assuming that *the silver* represented *has an existence elsewhere*, and that the sense-organ vitiated by defects, though in contact with the shell, causes it to be perceived as identical with the silver existing elsewhere.

Jayatīrtha opens his criticism of the above theory by pointing out that it is opposed to the verdict of the sublating cognition which roundly and categorically asserts that there was no silver anywhere in the place occupied by the given substratum and that what appeared was totally non-existent : सत्त्वे सति, रजतस्य 'असदेव रजतं प्रत्यभात्' इत्यनुभवविरोधात् (*NS*, p.54b).

The point is this. There is no evidence in the Bādhakajñāna that the *very silver* that was represented in the illusion has an actual existence of its own elsewhere. The existence of real silver (elsewhere) in a real world is one thing and the claim that *that selfsame silver* was represented here is another thing. The question is not whether silver really exists in the world! The question is of the *status* of the *superimposed silver* (*āropitarajata*) *and not of the unsuperimposed real silver* (*anāropitarajata*). Madhva readily grants that the knowledge of the "*āropita*" presupposes the knowledge of the "*anāropita*" and that no superimposition is possible without the reality of the substratum, and the prototype (*pradhāna*) of the superimposed object.[3] But all that does not mean that we should give more than what is due to the superimposed object and regard it as having an existence of its own *per se* elsewhere. That, says Madhva, is going beyond the verdict of Bādhakajñana. The Naiyāyika realist seems to be in the grip of a mortal dread of admitting 'non-existence' (*asat*) coming anywhere within the range of any of

3. अधिष्ठानं च सदृशं सत्यवस्तुद्वयं विना ।
न भ्रान्तिर्भवति क्वापि . . . . ॥ (*VTN*)

our psychological experiences, for fear that it may undermine the foundations of his realism. But this is sheer nervousness. *If the unreal and the non-existent cannot intrude upon our consciousness even in our illusions, where else can they intrude* ? Not certainly in our valid experiences. If our faith in realism is strong enough, it can resist the siren song of *Viśvam mithyā dṛśyatvāt......śukti-rūpyavat*. But more of this later.

Jayatīrtha rightly points out that it cannot be seriously contended that the illusory experience itself is an evidence of the actual existence of *the silver figuring in the illusion* elsewhere. For, this illusory experience is in itself an invalid one. What probative value can it have, then ? If it has such value, why should we not give the go by to the Bādhakajñāna and accept that the silver is actually there in the substratum where it is experienced at the time of the illusion ? Nor can the sublating cognition itself be cited as evidence for the actual existence of the *superimposed silver, elsewhere*. Its function is simply to deny the presence or existence of the silver actually *in the locus where it was apprehended*. It is neutral to the question of its existence or non-existence *elsewhere*. There is not much substance in the contention that an illusion cannot be satisfactorily explained without assuming the actual existence of the 'represented object' (as such) elsewhere. As the illusion cannot be accounted for without the reality of the substratum, sensory and environmental defects, etc., only those factors can be taken to be established by implication. The question : how silver can be perceived *if it is not existent*, can be met by another : how can the silver existing *elsewhere* be perceived *here* ? The existence of an object elsewhere is not an indispensable contributory factor for or a necessary antecedent to its subsequent projection in another place. The insistence on its existence elsewhere may be deemed necessary either to account for the sensory contact with it or for the purpose of providing the requisite mental impressions for the revival of a memory image. In the present case, sensory contact with silver (existing far away) is clearly out of the question and there is actual sensory contact with the substratum, which will do to revive the Saṁskāras of formerly experienced silver and thus account for the appearance of the illusion without obliging us to invest the very silver (अत्र प्रतीतस्यैव रजतस्य) that is superimposed, with a factual existence elsewhere. One can understand the point that Saṁskāras of silver presuppose a prior experience of silver. And that experience, if valid, would, in its turn, presuppose the real existence of that silver somewhere within the range of our own experience. But all this has nothing to do with the *āropita-rajata* with which we are here and now concerned in error.

The Naiyāyika seems to be obsessed by his over-zealous attitude in favour of realism, and so he tries to confer a sort of vicarious reality upon the superimposed object. But forgetful of his own epistemological dictum that the non-existent cannot be presented, he is prepared to admit that the identity of the given (shell) with the other real (presented) or the association (*saṁsarga*) between "idam" and "rajatatva" that is presented is non-existent (*asat*) and that they *are somehow presented.*

Madhva's question is : why should we draw the line at 'identity' or 'saṁsarga' and not extend it to the *āropya* as such ? Take again the case of jar which has been destroyed or one which is to be produced. Suppose it is mistaken for some other jar. Some of us at anyrate, fall into the former type of error. How will the Naiyāyika explain such cases ? Will he maintain that the jar that is no longer in existence or is yet to come into being has even now a physical existence of its own, elsewhere and figures in the misapprehension ? That the jar in question did once exist or may come into existence at a future time, may be true enough. But the point is that such existence at other times has no *direct bearing* on the appearance of the illusory experience of it now. The existence of the object is useful only in producing the necessary impressions of it, which may, under certain conditions, engender a misapprehension. The Naiyāyika is fighting a ghost of his own imagination if he is presuming that theoretically it is possible for any philosopher to explain a perceptual illusion without recognizing the reality of both the *adhiṣṭhāna* and the pradhāna (prototype) of the superimposed object (*āropya*). Perhaps the position taken up by the Buddhist Mādhyamika or the Māyāvādin made him think of such a possibility and safeguard the interest of realism by insisting on the reality of the superimposed object elsewhere with a vengeance. But the Mādhva philosophers, by insisting on the equal necessity of accepting the reality of both the prototype (*pradhāna*) and the substratum (*adhiṣṭhāna*) in accounting for illusions, have taken the wind out of the sails of the Nyāya realist.

(5) Advaitic View

The Advaitic theory of error is known as Anirvacanīya-khyāti. It prefers to treat the object presented in illusions as "neither real and existent' (as in the Nyāya and Mīmāṁsā schools) nor as unreal and non-existent as in Buddhistic nihilism; nor even as 'internal' as in Yogācāra. Starting to explain illusion as an epistemological problem, it ends by metamorphosing it into a metaphysical problem. It introduces certain complicated and cumbersome technicalities (Prakriyā) in explaining the genesis of error. By clever dialectical quibbling it invents the conecept and category of an 'indescribable and undefinable' *tertium quid* between the poles of Sat and Asat and introduces it deftly into the realm of erroneous experiences in the first instance and ultimately seeks, by more ingenious dialectics, to extend it to the whole gamut of human experience (including the so-called "Vyāvahārika") and sweep it off from the sphere of reality and liquidate it in the bosom of the great Anirvacanīya. The Anirvacanīya-khyāti is, therefore, to say the least, metaphysically-motivated. It regards the cognition of silver in shell as a dual-cognition. It also holds that after the contact of the defective sense-organ with the shining shell there is a mental modification in the form of 'this object' (*idamākāra-vṛtti*). Then, through the operation of Avidyā, supported by the former impressions of silver revived by the similarity of characteristics of the given object, there is the *actual production* of 'indescribable silver' (अनिर्वचनीयरजत). This indescribable silver lasts as long as the illusion itself lasts (*dhīkāla*). But then, its status is only "Prātibhāsika" (apparent). It is neither real (existent) nor unreal (non-existent) nor both (*sadasat*). Its special status as defying characterisation in terms of Sat and Asat (and both together) is established by the famous Arthāpatti argument adumbrated by Śaṁkara : सच्चेन्न बाध्येत, असच्चेन्न प्रतीयेत. The concepts of Sat and Asat being mutually exclusive, their coexistence also is ruled out.

This theory has its own defects. In the first place, the view that the illusory silver is *produced* by nescience and is destroyed by the true knowledge of the substratum, will be inconsistent with the terms of the sublating cognition which denies the existence of the silver *per se* with reference to all the three periods of time : तथात्वे, त्रैकालिकनिषेधायोगात्। रूप्यं नासीदस्ति भविष्यति इति स्वरूपेणैव निषेधात् (*Nym*).

The illusory silver being a transformation of Avidyā, which has the Ātman for its locus, cannot be presented as an external reality. The externalisation of this illusory silver cannot be explained on the ground that as the Ātman is pervasive, it pervades the shell also and that in this way the silver which is a transformation of Avidyā having its locus in the Ātman delimited by the shell, comes to be cognized externally as associated with the shell.

Assuming that this is so, this silver should be open to perception by other persons also who may be looking at the shell at the time. Anyway, granting that this silver is actually produced, *we may ask how it is actually apprehended.* Is it by sensory contact or through Saṁskāras (impressions) or by Sākṣī ? In this case, there is no silver prior to the contact. It is said to be produced at the very time of its apprehension. There is a stalemate here. As the illusory silver has had no prior existence, its apprehension by Saṁskāras is out of the question. Nor can the cognition of the silver be ascribed to the witness-consciousness as in the case of the inner perception of bliss. For this cognition is invariably concomitant with sensory activity and cannot therefore be put on a par with the perception of bliss etc. by the Sākṣī. It cannot be said that as the sensory activity terminates with the awareness of the substratum there is need for the witness-self to cognize the silver produced by Avidyā. For, as the knowledge of the substratum does not seem to have any direct hearing on the perception of the silver, on the Advaitic theory, its indispensability would seem to suggest strongly that far from being due to a transformation of Avidyā and all that, the apprehension of the silver in the shell is the outcome of a mental distortion of the given datum caused by the sense organ being vitiated by certain defects and abnormal conditions and that it is a case of Anyathākhyāti and nothing more.

By implicating the Sākṣī in the error the theory takes away the right of the Sākṣī to pronounce judgment upon it through the Bādhakajñāna. *For it cannot both be the accused and the judge.* The Mādhva theory, as will be seen, shows a correct appreciation of the position and the role of the Sākṣī in the sphere of epistemology. However, even supposing that sensory contact with the substratum is in some way contributory to the apprehension of the illusory silver by the Sākṣī, in the Advaitic theory, it will entail a compromise with the Akhyāti theory, inasmuch as the cognition of the Prātibhāsika silver is thus a compound of two cognitions, one of the substratum by the sense-organ and the other of the Āvidyakarajata by the Sākṣī. Such dual cognition will bar activity. Even if the Sākṣī is made to apprehend the identity of silver with the shell and make activity possible, still the fact that there are two cognitions here will militate against the fact of the present cognition of silver being felt to be a single determinate cognition. The attempt to establish a unitary cognition on the basis of the simultaneous reflection of the witness-self in both the mental states of *idamākāra-antaḥkaraṇa-vṛtti* and *rūpyākārāvidyāvṛtti* presupposes the acceptance of a pet theory of the Advaita school.

The concept of "Anirvacanīya" itself rests on the presumption that the object presented in illusions cannot be a non-existent thing as the non-existent cannot be directly presented *as existent* in experience. This assumption itself is not well-founded. In fact, the Advaitin himself cannot explain the illusion without accepting the fact that the non-existent *does appear* and *is presented as existent* directly, *in our illusions*. For the anirvacanīya-silver *must appear as existent* in order that there may be the practical activity on the part of the perceiver. If the anirvacanīya is *presented as anirvacanīya* there will be *no illusion* to speak of, or, if it should appear as non-existent (*asat*). The error can arise only when and where it is presented as existent (*sat*). How then can the Advaitin assert : *Asac cen na pratīyeta* and conclude that *ergo* the object presented *in the illusion* cannot be *asat*? Advaitic dialecticians have indulged in a lot of dialectical verbiage and quibbling to cloud the issue. Jayatīrtha has fully brought out their untenability.

The practical activity inspired by the illusion cannot be explained on the assumption that there is merely a presentation of silver without its presentation "as existing" (*sat*). There can be no direct knowledge which is not expressed without a specific determination either positively or negatively. Hence, the question has got to be answered as to what is meant by the contention that the Vyāvahārikasattvam" of the shell which comes to be superimposed on the silver (which is apprehended) is *also* 'anirvacanīya'. For, as 'anirvacanīya' it must partake of the nature of either the Vyāvahārika or the Prātibhāsika. If it partakes of the nature of the Vyāvahārika, the silver would also be Vyāvahārika, in its turn, instead of being purely Prātibhāsika as it is deemed to be. In the other alternative, the question will be as to how it *actually comes to be apprehended*,—whether as Prātibhāsika (as it actually is in point of fact) or as Vyāvahārika. If the Pratibhāsika appears as Prātibhāsika, there will be no effort on the part of the perceiver to pick it up as he knows that a Prātibhāsika can serve no practical purpose. In order to account for purposeful activity, it has to be admitted that the Prātibhāsika silver comes to be presented in the immediate cognition as Vyāvahārika. The question will now arise, if such Vyāvahārikatva as is presented is really existing in the superimposed silver or not existing there. If it exists there, it cannot be regarded as Prātibhāsika any longer. If it does *not* exist there and is still presented to cognition *as existing* there, we have a clear case of a non-existent something presenting itself to our immediate perception in such illusory cognitions *as existing*. We are thus face to face with *Asatas sattvena aparokṣatayā pratītiḥ*, in erroneous knowledge (*bhrama*) which the Advaitic dialecticians have been trying their best to avoid and deny.

If it is *still* contended that even such Vyāvahārikatva is actually 'anirvacanīya' and is superimposed,[4] the whole series of alternatives will have to be raised again in regard to the *manner*

4. अनिर्वचनीयपरमार्थत्वस्यासत एव दृष्टचंगीकारात् । (Madhva, *VTN*)

This criticism of Madhva is directed against Citsukha's exposition. Jayatīrtha has quoted passages from Citsukha while explaining the relevance of the above criticism.

of appearance or presentation of the second, third and subsequent "anirvacanīyas" that the Advaitin may try to take shelter in, until the regression terminates somewhere. Where it does so, the difficulty in regard to the practical activity in the absence of the direct perception of something non-existent *as existing* will rear its head again.

Thus, the concept of 'Anirvacanīya" as applied to the object 'presented in our erroneous perceptions (such as of silver in the shell or its relation) makes the problem of error in Advaita philosophy more confused and complicated than in any of the other schools.

CHAPTER XXI

MADHVA'S THEORY OF ERROR: ABHINAVĀNYATHĀKHYĀTI

A realistic theory of knowledge has no reason to fight shy of errors and illusions in human life. Illusions do not upset the normal foundations of life and knowledge. On the contrary, they serve as foils to valid experience and give it its significance and value. The Mādhva theory of knowledge is, as we have seen, wide enough to provide a place for dreams, errors and illusions in life. The Mīmāṁsakas and Rāmānuja, however, fight shy of errors and seek to explain them away. Madhva feels that there is hardly any justification for doing so. Life is wide enough to hold both truth and error. Human nature and conditions of life being what they are, it is not possible to eliminate errors or expect our experiences and knowledge to be always veridical. This is proof of the limitations of the individual. A sound theory of knowledge, therefore, must take note of the limitations of life and human understanding and reckon with occasional jolts, disappointments and illusions in life and be able to explain their true nature and conditions, so as to arm us against them.

It is idle to shut one's eyes to errors and refuse to recognize them as such or call them by different names as "Vivekāgraha", "Pramuṣṭatattākasmaraṇa" and so forth. The senses deceive us at times. But that is only rarely and in exceptional cases and under definite conditions. Madhva feels, therefore, that there is hardly any justification for either extreme of banishing errors altogether from life and transforming them into truths and half-truths by verbal juggleries and theological quibbles[1]

1. यथार्थं सर्वविज्ञानमिति वेदविदां मतम् ।
अतो यथार्थं रूप्यादिविज्ञानं शुक्तिकादिषु ॥ (*Śrībhāṣya*, i.1.1)

or dismissing *all experience*,—errors as well as certainties as the merest illusions *a la* accepted ones, as in the case of the Buddhist nihilism and Advaita:

यथा माया यथा स्वप्नो गन्धर्वनगरं यथा ।
तथोत्पत्तिस्तथा स्थानं तथा भंग उदाहृतः ॥ (*Mādhyamika Kārikā*)
स्तंभादिप्रत्ययो मिथ्या प्रत्ययत्वात्तथापि हि ।
प्रत्ययः स मृषा दृष्टः स्वप्नादिप्रत्ययो यथा ॥
(Kumārila : *Ślokavārtika*, Sūtra, 5, verses 2-3)

The Mādhva theory of truth and error is expressed in the following formula :

औत्सर्गिकं ज्ञानानां प्रामाण्यं, अपवादाद्विपर्ययः । साक्षी खलु निश्चितयाथार्थ्यः कदाचिदपि संशयानास्कन्दितः, अन्तःकरणवृत्तीनां याथार्थ्यं स्वयमेव गृह्णाति । परीक्षासहकृतस्तु अयाथार्थ्यमिति **बादरायणीयं** मतम् ॥ (*NS*, p. 48 b)

"Knowledge has validity as a rule. Errors are the exceptions. Sākṣī the Apperceiver is always assured and certain of the validity of his judgments and grasps directly the modifications of the mind without being assailed by doubts. When the mind is assailed by doubts, the Sākṣī assures himself of the invalidity of the knowledge with the help of tests. Such is the position of the adherents of Bādarāyaṇa".

असतः सत्त्वप्रतीतिः, सतोऽसत्त्वप्रतीतिरित्यन्यथाप्रतीतेरेव भ्रान्तित्वात्
(Madhva in *VTN*)

"Illusion consists in an unreal or non-existent object or relation being presented in immediate perception as real and existing and of a really existing object or relation as not-existing".

This appears to be the most rational attitude to take to the problem of truth and error and stands for a dispassionate assesment of experience.[2] Madhva is no sophisticated realist to deny that there can be illusions of any kind in our cognitions or to dispute the central assumption of logic and philosophy that things are *not always* what they seem. The occurrence of illusions,

2. Cf. Rāmānuja's admission :

ख्यात्यन्तरवादिनामपि सुदूरमपि गत्वा, अन्यथावभासोऽवश्याश्रयणीयः । असत्ख्यातिपक्षे सदात्मना, आत्मख्यातिपक्षे अर्थात्मना, अख्यातिपक्षे अन्यविशेषणमन्यविशेषणत्वेन ज्ञानद्वयमेकत्वेन च, विषयासद्भावपक्षेऽपि विद्यमानत्वेन * * * (Śrībhāṣya i. 1.1)

at times, only confirms the normality of true experiences at other times.

The Mādhva theory of perceptual illusions is a bold and dexterous combination of the salient features of the Asat-khyāti and the Anyathā-khyāti views. Madhva defines illusion as the appearance of a thing as different from what it really is, i.e. of an unreal or non-existent object or relation *as real or existent and vice versa* :

असतः सत्त्वप्रतीतिः सतोऽसत्त्वप्रतीतिरिन्यथाप्रतीतिरेव भ्रान्तिः (*GT* ii. 26).

It is easy to see that such must be the nature of an illusion, if reality is defined as "*Anāropitam*" and "Pramāṇa" as यथार्थम् or यथावस्थितज्ञेयविषयीकारित्वम्. The root of this theory is the presentation of some non-existent entity, fact or relation *as existent* and real *in a given substratum,* with which the sense organ is in contact and when other conditions propitious to the erroneous cognition are also there :

अत्यन्तासतो रजतत्वस्य शुक्तिकायां, अत्यन्तासन्नेव संसर्गो वा, रजतस्यैव तादात्म्यं वा भ्रांतिविषयः । (*VTNT* p. 55 b)

वक्ष्यति चासतो रजततादात्म्ययोः ज्ञानविषयतामाचार्यः । (*NS* p. 47)

This element of false presentation is the mark of illusions :

अन्यथात्वमसत् तस्माद् भ्रान्तावेव प्रतीयते (*AV* i. 1.28).

It would be futile to deny it :

Cf. तस्माद्यदन्यथासन्तमन्यथा प्रतिपद्यते ।
तन्निरालम्बनं ज्ञानमसदालम्बनं हि तत् ॥[3]

(Kumārila : *Ślokavārtika.* p. 245)

The Asatkhyātivādin is, therefore, right in holding that the object of illusions is utterly unreal. But he is *not* justified in denying any kind of reality to *any of the constituents of that experience*, including *the adhiṣṭhāna*, etc. and dismissing the entire fabric of that experience as a baseless fancy (*nirālambanam*):

निरधिष्ठानभ्रान्तेरयोगात् ।

If nothing in the constituents of an illusion is real, there will be no possibility of sense-contact, without which there will be no perceptual knowledge, true or false. Jayatīrtha clarifies another important point in Madhva's theory of illusions, which is that

3. The Mādhva view agrees only with the first half and disagrees with the second half.

the superimposed object and its iden tity with the substratum are both non-existent when the former is far away from the latter as in the illusion of the snake in the rope. But when, as in seeing a mango tree and a jack tree standing close to each other from a distance, one misses their distinction and errs in thinking that there is only one of them, only the identity is non-existent.[4] Madhva, therefore, holds that notwithstanding the unreality of "the silver in the shell", it is through contact with the real piece of shell that the sense-organ, vitiated by defects, gets a distorted apprehension of it as a piece of silver. It is subsequently realized that this silver is absolutely non-existent within *that* spatio-temporal setting. Jayatīrtha gives classical expression to this view :

शुक्तिकासंनिकृष्टं दुष्टमिन्द्रियं तामेवात्यन्तासद्रजतात्मना अवगाहमानं ज्ञानं जायते, स भ्रम इत्यंगीकारात् । (*NS* p. 48 b)

He also indicates clearly the parting of the ways between the Mādhva doctrine and the Buddhistic view of Asat-Khyāti in this respect :

न वयं शून्यवादिन इव रजतज्ञानं **निरालम्बनं** ब्रूमः । शुक्तिविषयतांगीकारात् ।
(*Tdyt* p. 11 b)

अत एव नासत्ख्यातिप्रसंगः । यावत् खलु विगीते प्रत्यये भासते तस्य सर्वस्य असत्त्वे खलु असत्ख्यातिः स्यात् । न चैवमित्युक्तम् ।[5] (*NS* p. 48b)

It is, thus, needless and impossible to confound the Mādhva theory with "Asat-khyāti", in the accepted sense of the term.

Since the acid test of an illusion is in the sublating cognition (बाधकज्ञानम्), its true nature should be fixed in the light of the Bādhakajñāna. Now, the stultifying cognition takes the form : "There is no silver here; only the non-existent silver had

---

4. तर्त्कि सर्वत्रारोप्यमाणमत्यन्तासदेव ? उच्यते—यत्रारोप्यमधिष्ठानसन्निहितं तत्र **तत्तादात्म्यमात्रमसत्** । यत्र पुनः असन्निहितमारोप्यं तत्र तत्, तत्तादात्म्यं चोभयमप्यसत् ।
(*NS* p. 54)

5. "We do not, like the Śūnyavādins, regard the cognition of silver as 'baseless' (i.e. without a real substratum). We accept that this cognition has the shell for its object though it does not cognize it truly *as shell*. For the same reason, there is no question of our view being the same as 'Asatkhyāti'. There will be 'Asatkhyāti' only when it is held that whatever is presented in erroneous perception (including the substratum) is all non-existent. Such is not our view. (How then can our view be mistaken for Asatkhyāti ?)"
(*NS* p. 54)

appeared to exist".[6] Madhva takes his firm stand on the express authority of this Bādhakajñāna, in adjudging the status of the object of illusion as an utter unreality (*atyantāsat*).

The Anyathākhyātivādin merely intoxicates himself with an inferential unction that the superimposed object must have a reality of its own elsewhere, which is hardly relevant to the form or content of the sublating knowledge. This is precisely the point of departure between the Nyāya and Mādhva view of Anyathākhyāti. It is to bring out this distinction of Madhva's theory that Jayatīrtha christens it as "Abhinavānyathākhyāti" (neo-Anyathākhyāti) and contrasts it with the Nyāya theory. He points out that the scope of the Bādhakajñāna is strictly limited to *denying* the presence of silver in the given substratum and its identity with it, and that it is quite indifferent to the question of the existence of the silver *elsewhere*. The difficulty of establishing a sensory contact with an object existing elsewhere (*anyatra sat*) would also be insurmountable. It is unnecessary to assume the *reality* of superimposed objects elsewhere, when illusions could be satisfactorily explained without such an assumption, by certain defects in the nature of the sensory contact. Even the Anyathākhyātivādin must admit that, in point of fact, sensory contact has been only with the actual substratum before the perceiver, viz., the nacre. If then, sensory contact with the shell should, as has been the case here, actually produce the misapprehension of silver, for the nonce, it is surely a piece of misplaced ingenuity to propound a very elaborate theory that the *selfsame silver* must be having an actual existence somewhere else (*anyatra sat*). That is imagination running riot. What has actually happened in this case is simply that sensory contact with nacre has *somehow* led to its erroneous perception as identical with silver that is *not there*, i.e. to say, purely non-existent. The existence of *real silver* similar to the one perceived in the illusion, elsewhere, in the shop, is one thing and to claim that *that very thing* has come over here or that that very thing is there, is quite another. Real silver may be remotely responsible for furnishing the background to the present illusion. Madhva does not deny *that*. What he denies and what the Naiyāyika asserts is

6. 'नात्र रजतं, असदेव रजतं प्रत्यभात्' ।

that the selfsame silver (that was superimposed) *is* existing elsewhere (and could not otherwise have appeared). The Naiyāyika unhappily is mixing up the issues. The first proposition is entirely true and unexceptionable,—that there is a real silver outside the present illusion. It is not only conceded by Madhva but is laid down by him as the necessary precondition and invariable concomitant in all illusions :

अधिष्ठानं च सदृशं सत्यवस्तुद्वयं विना ।
न भ्रान्तिर्भवति क्वापि स्वप्नमायादिकेष्वपि ॥ (*VTN*)

Without two real entities, viz., a substratum and a prototype of the superimposed object being given outside the illusion, no illusory experince can be explained even in dreams or magical creations. But, there is no justification, says he, for the dogma of the Nyāya Realists that the superimposed object must *always, as such and in its own self,* have an actual existence elsewhere :

अत्र प्रतीतस्यैवान्यत्र सत्त्वे मानाभावात्। असत्त्वे कथं प्रतीतिरिति चेत्? **अन्यत्र सत्त्वेऽपि कथम्? न ह्यन्यत्र सत्त्वं अत्र प्रतीतेरुपकारि!** (*NS* p.54).

In the light of this clear and unmistakable criticism of the Nyāya view one cannot but express astonishment at P. Nagarajarao's remark about Madhva's doctrine that "the radical Realist that he is, Madhva wants to give a complete *objective basis to the content of error after the model of the Nyāya school*" (P. Nagarajarao, "Error, Doubt and Dream in Dvaita Vedānta," *Journal of Oriental Research*, Madras, xi, pt. 4, p.295). If anything, Madhva *denies* that the content of error (*bhramaviṣaya*) has an objective basis : **को हि ब्रूते रजतं सदिति?** (*NS* p.46)

The existence of an object of illusion elsewhere may be deemed necessary either for securing sensory contact with it in order to render the perception of silver (or the like) possible, or for awakening the impressions of silver in the mind (*rajatasaṁskārodbodha*). Neither ground is admissible. There is no possibility of sensory contact with an object existing somewhere else and if such existence is required merely to furnish the necessary mental impression of the object, such a result could be explained by the past experience of it, without making the selfsame object come down and present itself in the illusion.[7] It is for

7. इन्द्रियार्थसन्निकर्षार्थं वा तदास्थेयं, संस्कार-सिद्धयर्थं वा ? नाद्यः । संस्कारश्च रजतान्तरानुभवमात्रेण भवतीति व्यर्था तस्यैवान्यत्रसत्त्वकल्पना । (*NS* p. 54b)

this reason that Madhva insists on the reality of a "Sadṛśa" (prototype) in addition to that of an *adhiṣṭhāna* (substratum) as the *sine qua non* of all illusions. But there is no reason to assign an intrinsic reality of its own to the *superimposed object per se.* One should not miss this subtle distinction between the Nyāya and the Mādhva views of the status of the *āropya* and confound the two.

A careful examination of the various theories of error held by different schools of Indian philosophy shows that the ideas of "*asat-khyāti*" and "*anyathākyhyāti* constitute their greatest common measure of agreement. Madhva's theory of "Abhinavānyathākyāti"[8] combines these two common elements of the theories of illusion in right proportions and formulates a balanced theory of error. Its most important finding is, of course, the fact of the presentation of the non-existent in illusions (असतः सत्त्वेन प्रतीत्युपपत्तिः). The whole theory of Madhva turns on this hypothesis. This is itself derived from the nature of the Bādhakajñāna (असदेव रजतं प्रत्यभात्). The question of the presentability of "Asat" (the non-existent) in erroneous knowledge (असतः सत्त्वेनापरोक्षतया भ्रमे प्रतीत्युपपत्तिः, as it is technically known) has been ably argued and established at length by Jayatīrtha[9] and Vyāsatīrtha following Madhva. As a matter of fact, the category of Anirvacanīya itself, by definition, is made to rest on the presumption of the non-presentability of 'Asat'. But the assumption itself is gratuitous and inconsistent with the conviction of difference from *asat* (*asad-vailakṣaṇya*), which the monistic philosopher has, in respect of the world :

असद्विलक्षणज्ञप्त्यै ज्ञातव्यमसदेव हि ।
तस्मादसत्प्रतीतिश्च कथं तेन निवार्यते ॥ (*AV* i.1.1)

One of Dr. K. Narain's criticisms against Madhva's doctrine of illusion is that "*it violates the basic principle of epistemology that the object of immediacy is identical with the object of cognition*" (*Op. cit.* p. 152).

This objection has been met by Vyāsatīrtha who makes it clear that the principle referred to is *true only of Aparokṣapramā* (immediate valid knowledge) and *not* of Bhrama (misapprehen-

8. वक्ष्यामो ह्यभिनवान्यथाख्यातिम् (*NS* p. 46b)
9. For details see my *HDSV*, pp. 262-64 and pp. 350-51.

sion). *Otherwise,* the Advaitin too would be hard put to it to explain sensory contact with '*anirvacanīya*' silver which, according to his theory, is produced at the very moment of its apprehension : The object in order to come to be perceived by sense-contact with the eye must exist prior to the moment of its coming to be perceived. But this is hardly possible in *āvidyakarajata* which is said to be generated at the moment of its apprehension.

नहि धीमात्रशरीरं रूप्यं स्वज्ञानात् प्रागस्ति । अतः प्रतीतिसमय एव रजतजन्मांगी-कारे रजतस्येन्द्रियसन्निकर्षादुपलब्धिः कथं तव मते ? (*Nym*, p. 420)

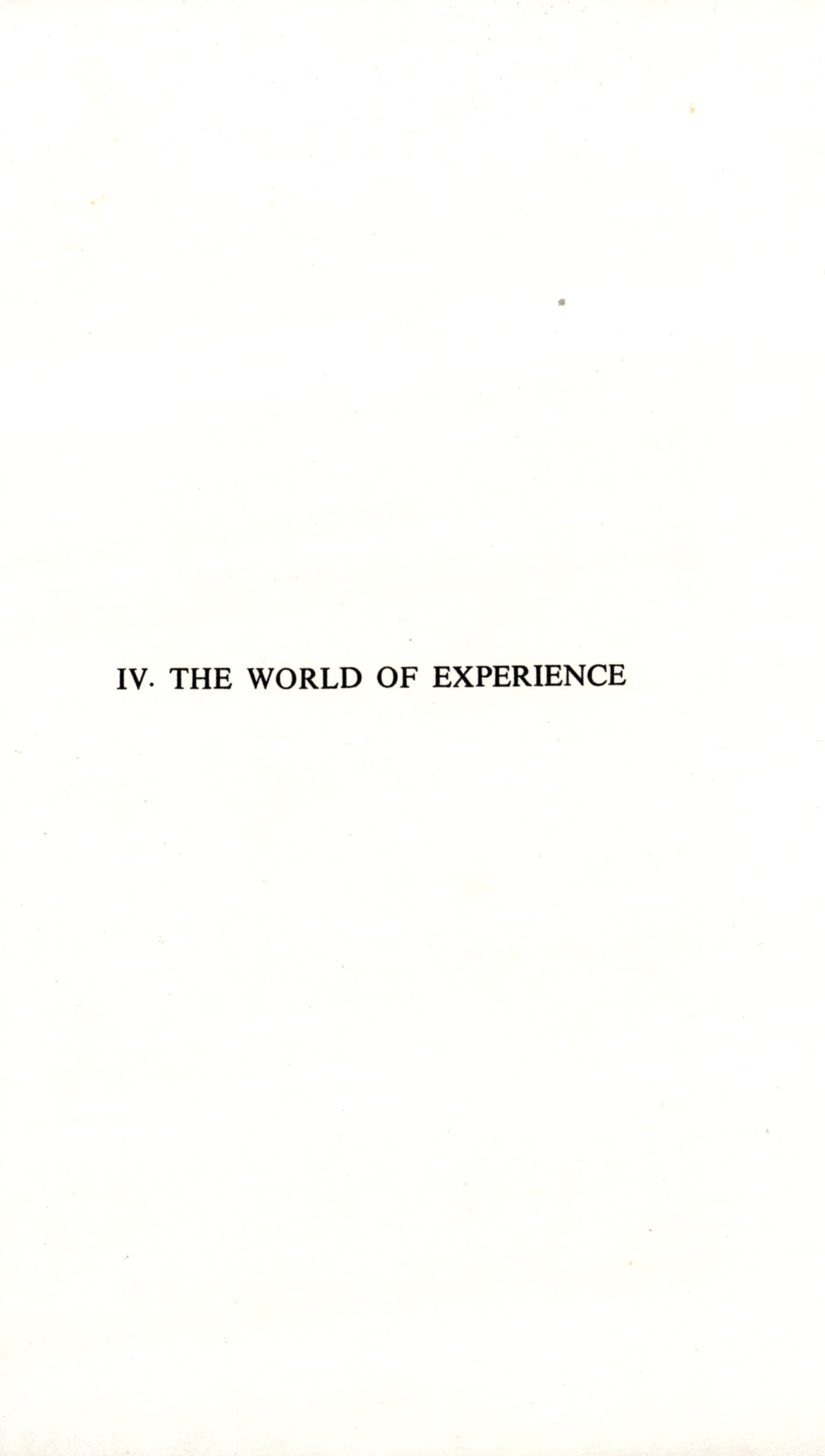

IV. THE WORLD OF EXPERIENCE

CHAPTER XXII

REALITY OF WORLD EXPERIENCE

BELIEF in the reality of the world and its values is, naturally, one of the fundamental tenets of theism. It is a metaphysical doctrine and not a mere theological dogma. We may, therefore, turn to the grounds on which it is based. These may be brought under the three heads of perceptual, rational and scriptural grounds admitted in the system of Madhva.

We have seen that Madhva recognizes an additional sense or instrument of knowledge, —the Sākṣī (besides the other six). The reality of world-experience follows as a consequence of the acceptance of the doctrine of Sākṣī and the implications of the doctrine of Pramāṇa (applied to the other instruments of knowledge). The knowledge produced by the senses is normally valid and true, under requisite conditions of knowledge and proper types of contact of the sensory apparatus and this knowledge is not ordinarily contradicted. It is accepted in all schools of Vedānta that knowledge carries with it its own validity which is intrinsic to it. The Dvaita, Advaita and Viśiṣṭādvaita are pledged to this view. Validity implies the factual reality of the object of knowledge with reference to a given spatio-temporal setting : नहि विषयाबाधमनन्तर्भाव्य प्रामाण्यग्रहणं नाम (*Nym* i.18). The reality of the world would thus follow from the doctrine of self-validity of knowledge:

यदि स्वतस्त्वं प्रामाण्ये विश्वसत्ता कथं न ते ? (*AV* iii.2.3)

The Advaitin, doubtless, pleads that perception cognizes only the provisional reality (vyāvahārika-satyam) of objects; while inference of unreality and texts to that effect disprove the absolute or noumenal reality thereof and that, therefore, there is no conflict of Pramāṇas :

पारमार्थिकमद्वैतं प्रविश्य शरणं श्रुतिः ।
विरोधादुपजीव्येन न बिभेति मनागपि ॥ (*Khaṇḍana* 1.23)

But this is counting the eggs before they are hatched, inasmuch as the threefold classification of reality into Pāramārthika, Vyāvahārika and Prātibhāsika, upon which the theory of provisional validity of Pramāṇas is based, is still an unproved assumption. The very idea of provisional validity (which ceases to be valid after some time) is meaningless and repugnant to the basic idea of Prāmāṇya :

प्रामाण्यस्य च मर्यादा कालतो व्याहता भवेत् ।
कालान्तरेऽप्यमानं चेदिदानीं मानता कुतः ॥ (*AV* iii.2.3)

Vyāvahārika-prāmāṇya is, therefore, a myth. It is invalidity writ euphemistically large. If the principle of self-validity of knowledge is to have any meaning, there can be no denying or escaping from the conclusion of the reality of world-experience :

प्रमाणानि हि स्वगोचरे प्रवर्तमानानि तत्त्वमिदमित्येव प्रवर्तन्ते; न पुनः सांव्यवहारिकं नः प्रामाण्यं, न पुनस्तात्त्विकमित्येव प्रवर्तन्ते ! (*Bhāmatī* ii.2.32)

There is, thus, no need to go in search of subtle and elaborate reasonings in support of the validity of Pratyakṣa. As Madhva says elsewhere, reason may have to be summoned, if at all, only to prove the falsity of particular experiences in case of serious doubts, but hardly to demonstrate validity of normal experiences : दृष्टवस्तुनो मिथ्यात्वांगीकारे च युक्त्यपेक्षा, न पुनः सत्यत्वे ! Such validity is furnished by the perception itself where it is normally constituted, as we have seen under the theory of Pramāṇas. Nor are we without sufficient means of testing the soundness of the conditions of knowledge. It is open to us to institute the necessary tests (*parīkṣā*) and make sure of the reality of normal experience. Madhva contends that all our normal experience and perceptions are capable of bearing such scrutiny and have been so tested and found to be true and valid. It would be preposterous to say that we could never trust our senses and that our perceptions are proverbially and inherently misleading and that we could never know the truth of things or that perception is capable of revealing only the present and that we could never be sure of what the future may hold and so on. Such wild and irresponsible objections would be suicidal to the monist himself. If the verdict of normal perception is to be disbelieved in every case, there will be no distinction between truth and falsity in experience. There will be nothing to distinguish illusions from valid experience. All experience will be suspect and no logical or scientific advance will be possible. If the perception of silver in the nacre and the stultifying cognition "this is *not* silver" were both of them on the same par of incredibility, all distinction between truth and falsehood would have to be given up. As Vyāsatīrtha says in a humorous vein, the monist will stand to lose his principal in trying for the interest.[1] If he does not concede the validity of the stultifying cognition, "this is not silver", he can never establish his pet theory of the unreality of the universe, which rests upon the analogy of the illusion of silver in nacre.

Sense-perception cannot, therefore, be deprived of its validity, *except by a more valid perception* : दृष्टवस्तुनो बलवद्दृष्टिं विना नान्यद् बाधकम् (*VTN*). It cannot be set aside by any amount of specious reasoning or bald texts, unless the latter could be shown to be more valid than the perception in question. The attempt to upset perception by inference or authoritative texts would thus involve a fallacy of interdependence, inasmuch as the inference or the verbal testimony cannot be invested with greater validity unless perception is shown to be invalid, and that cannot be unless the inference or the verbal testimony is proved to be more authoritative, for whatever reasons. The validity of perception, on the other hand, is self-evident and does not need any ratification from outside. The superiority of perception to inference and *āptavākya*, is also self-evident in that it is able to grasp even the minutest features of objects which are beyond the ken of inference and correct confusion of quarters which the pious words of an Āpta (authority) are powerless to do. The perceptual judgment 'Fire is hot' is intrinsically superior to any inference of its being cold. The reality of experience derives support from the combined evidence of a number of facts like perception of difference, reasoning in support of such perception, the cosmogonic texts, texts prescribing 'Saguṇopāsanā' and the drift of the

1. नेदं रूप्यमिति प्रत्यक्षप्रामाण्यमावश्यकम् । अन्यथा 'इदं रूप्य'मित्यस्याप्रामाण्यं न स्यादिति, वृद्धिमिच्छतो मूलहान्यापत्तेः । (*Nym*, i.17)

entire Karmakāṇḍa. Albert Schweitzer rightly emphasizes this point when he says, "The ethics of action is hard hit by the assertion that the world has no meaning. Man cannot engage in ethical action in a world with no meaning. His ethical life in such a world must be limited to keeping himself pure from it. But if, further, the reality of the world is denied, then, ethics altogether ceases to have any importance." (*Indian Thought and Its Development*, p. 60)

From another point of view also perception where tested and found correct, has to be recognized as the basic ground or Upajīvya of any inference or texts in a contrary direction. Such a basic ground cannot be repudiated by any amount of wild reasoning or bald assertions of texts. This is known as the principle of "Upajīvyapramāṇavirodha" or conflict with the basic ground. The experience of the world rests on such Upajīvya-pratyakṣa. It is not the superficial one (of the Śukti-rajata-type) which is liable to be mistaken but one which has passed the test of personal endorsement by the Sākṣī after due examination. It is what Madhva calls "*dṛḍhadṛṣṭa*" or *suparīkṣita*, which is indubitable and is the last word on tests, having reached down to the innermost intuitive level of certification by the Sākṣī, which (as has been established) is the terminus of all Parīkṣā and converts belief into certainty. Madhva contends that the finite experiences of pleasure and pain in life belong to this category of Pratyakṣa certified by Sākṣī and must, therefore, be accepted as impregnable. So too the consolidated experience of humanity of the reality of an objective universe and of its values, not to mention the realization of human limitations and the consciousness of a Power transcending human conception. *It is on this rock of Sākṣipratyakṣa that Madhva has built his edifice of Dvaita-Vedānta.*

He points out that such universal experience of joys and sorrows of life with a deep sense of their reality is not of the hollow variety of the silver in the shell, inasmuch as it stands the test of practical utility and response-satisfaction. The objection of Vācaspati, therefore, that if the verdict of identity (of human souls and Brahman) and the consequent unreality of the experience of duality, is disputed on the ground of conflict with the basic Pratyakṣa (Upajīvya pratyakṣa), even the subsequent perception "this is *not* silver", would have to be dismissed as invalid, because it is opposed to the original (basic) perception 'this is silver' is disingenuous.[2] It purposely confuses the issue. The present is a question of strength between perception and inference or authoritative texts, and the instance cited is one of conflict between two perceptions, which is irrelevant to Madhva's position that no perception can be invalidated save by a more powerful perception. In other words, perception cannot be negatived by mere reasonings not based on some other and more powerful perception. Moreover, the basic nature of reality claimed for perception in this case is not based on considerations of its temporal priority or logical dependence for purposes of negation only (निषेध्यसमर्पकत्वेन) but upon an intrinsic dependence established by rigid tests. The capacity to stand such a practical test is lacking in the illusory cognition of 'silver in the nacre'. But in respect of our normal experience of the world all practical conditions of validity are fulfilled. They cannot, therefore, be regarded as illusory with any justification.

As for Śruti texts, which may appear to teach the identity of Brahman and Ātman not only will they be patently in conflict with numerous others which do teach their difference, but also with the personal experience (of its own limitations and difference from Brahman) of the Sākṣī. If personal experiences of the Sākṣī are to be set aside by other Pramāṇas, however powerful, the foundations of philosophy will collapse; for, then, there would be no surety left *anywhere*, in perception, reasoning or revelation. Even the conviction of identity reached by the monist *qua* personal and reached at the Śakṣī level, will be in the grip of doubt and stultification by some other conceivable form of knowledge such as all is void so that nihilism would be the end of philosophical quest. Madhva, therefore, insists that the verdict of the Sākṣī must be accepted as the basis of logical and philosophical certitude. It must be accepted as the ultimate criterion of all validity in experience,

2. That does not prevent Dr. K. Narain from repeating the same argument in slightly different garb : "If perceptions are always valid what about illusions and their explanations in a text-book on philosophy?" (*Critique of Madhva Refutation of Śaṅkara Vedānta*, p.126)

including the validity of Scriptural knowledge. Unless this is done, there can be no Philosophy worth the name and there will be nothing but a reign of universal doubt and illusions *galore.* It would be simply suicidal, then, to dare to question the verdict of the Sākṣī or attribute the slightest touch of fallibility or doubt to its findings. This point has already been conclusively established earlier in Chapters XVIII and XIX.

If Sākṣipratyakṣa cannot reach beyond the present as contended by Madhusūdana Sarasvatī, how can its final perception of Advaitic truth sublate the world and negate its reality *with reference to all the three periods of time*, with absolute certainty and assurance of subsequent uncontradictability ? Even in the interests of his own position, the Advaitin will have to accept the power of Sākṣī to intuit all the three periods of time and absence of contradiction therein for its final judgment of the *mithyātva* of the world !

The primacy of Sākṣī having been firmly established, the question of giving suitable and reasonable explanations to some identity texts which appear to support the identity of the human souls with Brahman and by implication or otherwise deny the reality of the world, against the firm conviction of the Sākṣī, will not be such a difficult thing after all, having regard to their mystic, figurative and analogical methods of philosophic discourse in the Śrutis and approved canons of interpretation of texts, accepted by all.

Madhva cites, for example, the Vedic text ""यजमानः प्रस्तरः" ('the handful of grass is the Sacrificer'). Here the literal sense of the text cannot be accepted. We have the authority and sanction of the *Pūrva-Mīmāṁsā* to reinterpret such seemingly absurd or inconsistent declarations as figurative statements based on functional, genetic, etymological, mystic and other grounds: तत्सिद्धिः जातिः सारुप्यप्रशंसभूम लिङ्गसमवायात् (*PMS* i. 4 23-28). Madhva claims the same right in interpreting the monistically worded texts, *in conformity with Sākṣipratyakṣa and the numerous other texts which teach the reality of the world* and the difference between the human souls and Brahman. He has, accordingly indicated some fresh points of view from which these "monistic texts" can be more properly explained :

यजमानप्रस्तरत्वं यथा नार्थः श्रुतेर्भवेत् ।
ब्रह्मत्वमपि जीवस्य प्रत्यक्षस्याविशेषतः ॥
स्वातंत्र्ये च विशिष्टत्वे स्थानमत्यैक्ययोरपि ।
सादृश्ये चैक्यवाक् सम्यक् सावकाशा यथेष्टतः[3] ॥ (*AV* i. 1.1)

Even the most warmly cherished "Mahāvākyas" of the Advaitins will have to stand on the ground of the Sākṣi for their ratification, in the same way as any intimate personal experience of the joys and sorrows of life. There is not the least difference in the status of these two *experiences of the Śāksi* and one cannot be partial to the one at the expense of the other. The highest deference and most fitting homage that we can pay to the Scriptures will be by trying to find their true import in conformity with the logic of Sākṣyanubhava—instead of being swept off one's feet by the literal sense of such quasi-mystic statements of identity and acosmism :

न ब्रूमो वयम्—नास्तीदं वाक्यमिति, नाप्येषां पदानामत्र शक्तिर्नास्तीति । किंतु, अस्य वाक्यस्य प्रपंचमिथ्यात्वे तात्पर्यं नास्तीति । उपपत्तिविरोधाभावो हि प्रतीतार्थे तात्पर्यस्य ज्ञापकः । अत्र चास्ति उपपत्तिविरोध इति ।[4] (*NS.* p. 601)

It is too well known that the literal sense of a proposition is, more often than not, found modified by so many exigencies of practical and theoretical considerations, syntactic and other difficulties or philosophical necessities. Literalism will scotch philosophy as nothing else will.

---

3. Even though there is the Śruti text which says "the bundle of sacred grass is the sacrificer" it is not admitted in its literal sense. In the same way, Brahmanhood of Jivātman supposedly proclaimed in the Śruti. Descriptions of identity with one Supreme Brahman admit of several other meanings from the point of view of the independence of the One, its being the highest reality that exists and from the point of view of identity of place, harmony in thought, similarity, etc." (See my *BSPC* II, p. 217-20)

4. "We do not deny that such a text exists; or that the words do not possess the meanings assigned to them. What we deny is that the *purport* of such passages is the unreality of the world. For, absence of conflict with sound reasoning is the main criterion in taking the apparent meaning of a passage to be its intended import also. But in the present case we have shown that there is serious conflict with sound reasoning in accepting the apparent sense of the passage as its real and true import".

CHAPTER XXIII

SOME OBJECTIONS TO THE REALITY OF THE WORLD ANSWERED

THE Advaitin's attempts to challenge the reality of the world on the doubtful analogy of dreams and illusions is like the proverbial drowning man catching at a straw to save himself. If our experience of the reality of the world can be negated by the knowledge that Ātman alone is real and that all else is false, on the ground that *perception is strictly limited to the present* (even though the conviction of its reality may have been implanted in us from time immemorial and have stood the test of time), the position of the negating knowledge which is also claimed to be a perception (though not by the eyes) would be much worse, inasmuch as it has admittedly a distinct beginning and is practically an unknown quantity till now. If we could persuade ourselves that what is known and held to have been true and valid from time immemorial by the universal consent of human beings all the world over, is sure to be superseded by some unknown fact of knowledge to come, what is there to prevent our supposing that the same fate may overtake that new knowledge also ? If the known is false and the unknown alone true, one may seriously contend that cows and bulls are really without horns, even though they appear to have them and that hares *have* horns even though they are not visible to any of us. The same kind of *reductio ad absurdum* would hold good in respect of any inference about the unreality of the universe. If this inference also is untrue in its turn, the reality of world-experience will remain unscathed. If it is real, the ground of generalization (*dṛśyatvahetu*) being obviously fallacious in this case, may be equally so in other cases. The vague possibility of a future contradiction cannot be seriously entertained to the extent of repudiating the consolidated experience of all humanity. Belief in the reality of the universe within the meaning of uncontradictability in the three periods of time is held by Madhva and his followers to be established *not* by sense-perception but by *the intuitive perception of the Sākṣi*. This is where Mādhva philosophy is on the vantage ground as compared with the Nyāya school of realism in meeting the challenge of Advaitins. Most of the dialectics of the school centres naturally on this aspect of the question and refutes the plea of the Advaita that perception is incapable of establishing the truth of things beyond the present. Jayatīrtha says that the perception of uncontradictedness for the present involves the perception of uncontradictability for the future also. This does not mean that it is or must be so in all cases; or that there is no possibility of illusions in experience. It is, therefore, necessary to explain the Mādhva point of view a little more clearly. So long as all Vedāntins are agreed that the validity of knowledge is intrinsically made out and that invalidity alone is dependent on contradiction, the normal and healthy perceptions of life cannot be dismissed as illusory. Even the most ruthless tests fail to prove the contrary, so that the uncontradictability of normal experiences can not be doubted by any reasonable creature. It will be absurd to presume contradictability of experience on mere inferential considerations or as a bare hypothetical possibility. The inference itself will have to depend upon another valid perception for the ascertainment of a sound relation of concomitance and cannot, therefore, afford to destroy its own standing ground (Upajīvya) by casting a universal doubt on all perceptions as such. Even the perception of the blueness of the sky is a defect of distance and is not seen to arise in proximity or in case of verifiable scientific explanations. If perception *as such* is to be suspected of invalidity, there is nothing to forbid a similar fate overtaking the identity texts on the analogy of "the text referring to the old ox singing foolish songs fit for the Madrakas" : जरद्गवो गायति मद्रकाणि.

The reality of experience should thus be admitted as fully borne out by practical and theoretical considerations alike. The test of practical efficiency (*arthakriyākāritvam*) is a potent one in respect of reality. It is in this connection that Madhva raises the question of the reality of certain aspects of dream phenomena. Dreams are not absolutely unreal phenomena occurring without assignable cause. The element of unreality lies in the identification of the experiences therein with those of the waking state, i.e., in taking them, *at the time*, to be objects of waking experience.[1] But, the passions, feelings, etc., stirred up in the course of the dream and the experiences as such are uncontradicted and are even remembered with feelings of pleasure or aversion as the case may be and are often accompanied by incontrovertible proofs of their factual occurrence, as in erotic dreams (*Svāpnakāminisambhoga*). Gauḍapāda (*Kārikā* ii.1-7) and Śaṅkara (*BSB* iii.2. 2) have adduced some arguments for the unreality of dreams. These have been refuted by Jayatīrtha in his *NS* and *TP*. Śaṅkara (following Gauḍapāda) argues that dreams lack spatio-temporal conformity to facts. There is no material stuff out of which objects could be produced in dreams. They cannot be regarded as different from the dreamer or identical with him. In the former case, they should be perceivable by others too and in the latter case, they would be unreal as it is obviously impossible for the perceiving self to metamorphose itself into so many objects that appear in the dream.

The objections are irrelevant to the Mādhva view that dreams are the experiences created by God for the benefit of the Jivas and are destroyed by Him immediately. The dream-creations are made of the stuff of Vāsanās (agelong potencies) embedded in the minds of Jīvas. As these Vāsanās are subtle and supersensuous by nature, their objectifications also are so and can be accommodated within the dream-centres of the mind (or the brain), so much so that there is no necessity for the dreamer to go out of his physical body to experience those phenomena, or any other difficulty regarding spatio-temporal conformity etc.,[2] as dreams have their own subtle space-time setting constructed

1. यदन्यथात्वं जाग्रत्त्वं सा भ्रान्तिः । (Madhva, *BSB* iii.2.3)

2. यदि बाह्यकारणकाः स्वप्नविषयाः तदा सम्यगभिव्यंज्येरन् । न चैवम् । अतः संस्कारोपादानका एवेति भावः । एतेनोक्तकण्ठकोलाहलाः प्रत्युक्ताः । वासनामयानां मेरुमन्दवसन्तादीनां शरीरादनिर्गत्यैव मनसा दर्शनसंभवात् । बाह्यकारणाभावात् मृत्पिण्डादिप्रतीतेरप्रसंगात् । (*TP* iii.24)

by Vāsanās :

वासनाः सर्ववस्तूनामनाद्यनुभवागताः ।
सन्त्येवाशेषजीवानामनादिमनसि स्थिताः ॥
त्रिगुणात्मकं मनोऽस्त्येव यावन्मुक्ति सदातनम् ।
तत्रैवाशेषसंस्काराः संचीयन्ते सदैव च ।
संस्कारैर्भगवानेव सृष्ट्वा नानाविधं जगत् ।
स्वप्नकाले दर्शयति **भ्रान्तिर्जाग्रत्त्वमेव हि** ॥ (*AV* iii. 2.3)

Śaṅkara himself endorses the position that dreams are the products of Vāsanās;[3] but he seems to limit them to the Vāsanās of the waking state of the present life, which is hardly justifiable in the light of the Hindu belief in the influence of past lives and past Karma and their Vāsaṇās on our present lives. The acceptance of Vāsanās as the Upādāna (material) out of which dream objects are created and projected will answer most of the objections raised against the reality of dreams. Śaṅkara himself admits that in dreams it is the objective element that is contradicted by waking experience and not the experience as such[4]. Madhva goes a step further and claims a special status for dream-creations as products of these beginningless Vāsanās embedded in the minds of Jīvas and, therefore, entitled to a reality of their own (of a subtler order).[5] They are, not made of external ingredients (*bāhyakāraṇaka*) like objects of waking experience. That is why they are of such subtle nature as to be constructed by the mind and experienced internally. Madhva, therefore, interprets the term "*māyāmātram*" in the Sūtra (*BS* iii. 2.3) (1) as 'created by Vāsanās' (as material cause) and (2) by the will of God (as their efficient cause—*nimittakāraṇa*).[6]

3. जाग्रत्प्रभववासनानिर्मितत्वात्तु स्वप्नस्य । (*BSB* iii.2.6)

4. यद्यपि स्वप्नदर्शनावस्थस्य सर्पदर्शनोदकस्नानादिकार्यजातमनृतं तथापि तदवगतिः सत्यमेव । (*Ibid.*, ii.1.14)

5. भावनापरनामकाः संस्काराः । अनाद्यनुभवप्रवाहोत्पन्नाः । संस्कारैरित्युपादानकीर्तनम् । न च तेषां गुणत्वेनोपादानत्वानुपपत्तिः । मनोवृत्तित्वेन द्रव्यत्वात् । संस्काराणां चातीन्द्रियत्वेन त्र्यणुकजन्मविनाशयोरिव प्रागूर्ध्वं चानुपलम्भो न दोषाय । (*NS* p.460)

6. 'माया वयुनमभिख्या' इति प्रज्ञानामसु पाठात् । प्रज्ञाशब्दस्य वासनोपलक्षणत्वात् । न केवलं जैवी प्रज्ञा माया, किन्तु ऐश्वरी च । यदि च 'वासनामात्रं' इति मुख्य एव प्रयोगः क्रियेत, तदा ईश्वरप्रज्ञा न संगृहीता स्यात्, पृथगभयग्रहणे गौरवं स्यात् । अतो मुख्यामुख्यविवक्षयोभयग्रहणाय 'मायामात्रम' इत्युक्तम । (*NS*)

These dream objects, because they are the products of Vāsanās, are different from physical objects of our waking experience. It is for this reason that they do not exhibit the properties of grossness or serve one's external needs.[7]

But that does not make them any the less real. The element of falsity in dreams lies not in the constitution of dream-objects but in their being (mis-) taken for waking realities *during the dream* :

प्रतीतं स्वप्नविषयाणां जाग्रत्पदार्थत्वमेव बाध्यते (*TP*).

Rāmānuja also agrees with Madhva's view that dreams are real creations of God. According to Vādirāja when sentient creatures are presented in dreams, their bodies are made of Vāsanās of the dreamer and they are temporarily made to be tenanted by some souls at the will of God.

Like dreams, illusions of snake in the rope etc., inspire fear and other reactions by virtue of the indisputable reality of such forms of consciousness underlying those experiences :

सर्पभ्रमादावपि हि ज्ञानमस्त्येव तादृशम् ।
तदेवार्थक्रियाकारि, तत्सदेवार्थकारकम् ॥ (*AV* i. 4.11)

The hypothetical assumption of the unreality of world-experience, on the analogy of illusions will end in making out a case for the reality of *some other world* very much like ours, as the prototype of the one superimposed for the nonce. In trying to damn the reality of *this* world, as we know it and stigmatize it as an illusion, the Advaitin is in danger of catching a Tartar and accepting the reality of two worlds and thus make the remedy worse than the disease :

भ्रान्तिकल्पितत्वे च जगतः, सत्यं जगद्द्वयमपेक्षितम् । यदि जगत् भ्रान्तिकल्पितं स्यात् तर्हि कल्प्यमानजगत्सदृशस्याधिष्ठानप्रधानपूर्वकत्वमंगीकर्त्तव्यं प्रसज्येत ।

As between the known world and its prototype to be, it will be simpler, says Jayatīrtha, to admit and be satisfied with the known :

सत्यजगद्द्वयांगीकारात् अस्यैव जगतः सत्यत्वांगीकारस्य लघुत्वात् ।
(*Vādāvali*, p. 53)

---

7. यस्मात् स्वप्नषिया मनोजन्या वासनाविकारा अत एव ते बाह्यवत् स्थूलाः संवृतदेशेऽवकाशानर्हा न भवन्ति । तेषां तथा बाह्यवत् क्वचित् स्पष्टता बाह्यार्थक्रियाकारिता नास्ति ।
(*NS* 499b)

There is one more obstacle to the reality of the world, raised by Advaitins, viz., the impossibility of establishing any logically satisfactory relation between consciousness and the objects of consciousness in the world[8] (दृग्दृश्यसंबन्धानुपपत्ति) within the framework of accepted relations like Saṁyoga, Samavāya, etc. It is, therefore, urged by them that a "real world" cannot shine forth (*na prakāśeta*) in our consciousness. The objection is as old as the *Iṣṭasiddhi*. Jayatīrtha silences it by pointing out that the question "of the how" of the revelation of the objective world to consciousness is an illegitimate one : विचारागोचरत्वात् । वृत्तिविषयत्वेनैव व्यवहारोपपत्तेः । (*Vādāvali* p. 61-2)

There is no logical difficulty in assuming that objects are revealed to knowledge through a process of "mental chemistry" called Vṛtti facilitated by the senseorgans or by the intuitive self itself, immediacy being as much a characteristic of both, even as knowledge is a common characteristic of mediate and immediate knowledge. He concludes the argument by saying that the difficulty of establishing a nexus between consciousness and objects within the framework of accepted logic or its devices, is no reason to doubt the existence or reality of such relations between them. The paucity of our vocabulary and logical devices to correctly define the relation between the two in precise terms is no proof of there being no such relation in fact or that such relationship is unreal and superimposed by us. It only means that we have to revise and reorientate our thought-moulds about which there is no sacrosanctity :

अन्य एव कश्चित् वास्तवः सम्बन्धः किं न कल्पनीयः ? नहि वस्तुपरिक्षयात् प्रक्रियापरिक्षयो गरीयान् ! (Jayatīrtha, *Mith. Kh. ṭ.* p. 8b)

The difficulties raised are proofs, if at all, of nothing more than the defect in our technique. It is time we sharpen our wits and try to understand the true mechanism of knowledge; but inability to do so and penetrate further into it than we have done, is no proof of the unreality of the relation of the knowledge itself !

The incapacity to define a thing, in some particular way, cannot mean that the thing itself is false. Jayatīrtha winds up

8. Cf. Similar objections in modern philosophy, based on the 'dualism of mind and matter' and of the difficulty of bridging the gulf between them.

the argument with a pertinent question : How is the position bettered by agreeing to treat the world as lacking in reality ? मिथ्यात्वेऽपि दृश्यत्वं कथम् ? (*Mith. Kh.t.* p. 8b)
How is the nexus between consciousness and its objects rendered easier or more intelligible on the assumption of the unreality of the latter ? If the objects are superimposed on consciousness and have no real existence of their own, everyone should be able to see and know everything or none anything at all. How, then, is the individualization of consciousness and the fixity of objects to be explained on the theory of the falsity (*mithyātva*) of all Dṛśya (objects) ? If the individualization etc., are to be accounted for by reference to contacts etc., why make a fetish of the superimposition of objects ? Why not allow them to be real too ?

CHAPTER XXIV

TEXTUAL EVIDENCE IN SUPPORT OF THE REALITY OF THE WORLD

IN view of what has already been said about the primacy of Sākṣī as the criterion of all validity and of the doctrine of intrinsic validity of knowledge, it will be superfluous to cite a large number of texts from Śrutis and Sūtras in support of the reality of the world of experience. As Dasgupta observes : "There are so many passages in the Upaniṣads that are clearly Theistic and Dualistic in purport that no amount of linguistic trickery could convincingly show that they yield a meaning that would support Śaṅkara's position that Brahman alone is the ultimate reality and all else is false" (*I Phil*, ii, p. 2). Śaṅkara introduces an interpretational *tour de force* by distinguishing between an ordinary commonsense view of things and a philosophical view and explains the Upaniṣads in the light of this twofold assumption that while there are some passages which describe things from a purely philosophical point of view as the one reality without a second, there are others—naturally more numerous—which teach the commonsense view of "a real world, real souls and a real God as their Creator". This method is applied to the Sūtras also. But such a bifurcation of standpoints would seem to be hardly consistent with the fundamental presupposition of all Vedānta philosophers that there is only one uniform system of thought in the Upaniṣads and Sūtras. That apart, such a distinction of standpoints into philosophical and commonsense turns upon a distinction of (two) degrees of validity as absolute and provisional, which has been shown to be unsustainable. The argument for the reality of the world has thus been concluded by Vyāsatīrtha[1] :

किंच, यदि जगत् कल्पितं स्यात्, तदा त्वन्मतेऽपि—

(१) 'जन्माद्यस्य यत' इति सूत्रे 'यतो वा' इत्यादौ च जन्माद्युक्तिः

(२) 'ईक्षतेर्नाशब्दम्' इति सूत्रे 'तदैक्षत' इतीश्वरस्येक्षापूर्वककर्तृत्वोक्तिः

(३) 'लोकवत्तु' इति सूत्रे आप्तकामस्य च प्रयोजनाभावेऽपि लीलया सृष्टयाद्युक्तिः

(४) 'वैषम्यनैर्घृण्ये न' इति सूत्रे कर्मसापेक्षत्वेनावैषम्योक्ति;

(५) तेज आदेर्वाय्वादिजन्मोक्तिः

(६) पृथिव्यादिलयोक्तिः इत्याद्ययुक्तं स्यात् । नहि कल्पितस्य जन्मादिकमीक्षापूर्वकं स्रष्टृत्वं वा, तद्भ्रान्तेः प्रयोजनापेक्षा वा । (*Nym*, i.25).

The Mādhva philosophers, on the other hand, seek to reconcile the monistic descriptions in the Śrutis with the realistic texts, from the standpoint of One Independent Transcendent-cum-Immanent Reference viz., Brahman, as explained earlier. In doing so, they have not been obliged to do any violence to the reality of world-experience. According to the Advaita thinkers, the Scriptures would appear to be speaking with a double voice and deceiving us all along, with realistic descriptions of the world and its creation, which is manifestly untrue :

अपि च, नेयं पारमार्थिकी सृष्टिश्रुतिः, येनानुयुज्येत प्रयोजनम् । (*Bhāmati*, ii.1.33)

Such a position is hardly complimentary to the Scriptures or compatible with their high position of validity as *Āptavākya*. It has already been stated that texts supporting the reality of creation and of "a real world, real souls and real God" are to be met with everywhere in the Upaniṣads and Sūtras and in the

1. If the world were imaginary the preoccupation of the Śrutis and Sūtras with the genesis of the world, purpose behind creation, order of evolution and involution of elements, the Lord's impartiality in ordering the world taking diversity of individual Karma into account would all be inexplicable and uncalled for.

earlier and later literature also[2] and it is hardly necessary to quote them here, *in extenso*.

2. Significant passages are *RV* ii. 15. 1; 24, 6: vii. 88. 6-7; x. 55. 6; 173. 4.

BrhUp; iii. i. 13-24; *SvetUp* V. 5.; 1. 9.

MundUp. iii.1.12. *Kaṭha Up*. ii.2.12; *IsaUp* 3, etc. and many others cited in my *HDSV*, p. 17.

CHAPTER XXV

THE MEANING AND NATURE OF CREATION

THE material universe, according to Madhva, is neither a transformation (*pariṇāma*) of Brahman nor a production *de novo*. It is merely an actualization of what is in the womb of matter and souls by the action of Brahman. This creation is a reminder, however inadequate, of the Majesty of God.[1] However vivid and profound a man's religious consciousness may be he can only be conscious of God through His manifestations and working in the universe. Creation, thus, gives us a glimpse into the majesty of God : भीषास्माद् वातः पवते भीषोदेति सूर्यः (*TaittUp*, ii. 8). Reason bids us assume a first cause for the universe. The first cause is advisedly one. Creative activity presupposes a complete foreknowledge of the effects, accessories, degree of effort and consequences of the act and a conscious effort directed towards its achievement. To say, then, that God is all-creator means that He is omniscient (Sarvajña), all-powerful and Satyakāma (Jayatīrtha, *KNt*, p. 4 b).

Madhva is aware that creation as an event occurring at a specific date in the past, at the fiat of the Deity, is open to serious difficulties and inconsistencies. The awkward question

---

1. बहुचित्रजगद्बहुधाकरणात् परशक्तिरनन्तगुणः परमः (*Dvādaśa-Stotra* iv.3). Cf. also सृष्टिश्च प्राधान्यार्थमत्रोच्यते (Madhva, Commentary on *ChanUp* vi. 1). Contrast in this connection, Śaṅkara's remarks on *BS*, i. 4. 14 and Jayatīrthat's spirited rejoinder to it : अपुरुषार्थत्वान्न प्रपंचसत्यतायां तात्पर्यमिति चेन्न। सत्यजगन्निर्मातृत्वादि परमेश्वर महामहिमज्ञापनस्यैव पुरुषार्थहेतुत्वात् । (*NS*, i. 4, p. 200)

arises at once,—as to what induced the Deity, which had obviously kept in its shell, all the time, to suddenly take it into its head to come out and call a Universe into being.[2] The objections apply, in the first place, to creation *ex nihilo*. But no Vedāntin subscribes to such a view. The hypothesis of creation *in time* and the argument to the existence of God from the supposed necessity of a prius to the temporal series are definitely abandoned by Madhva. Creation, to him, is no doubt a real process. But it is a continuous creation,—a *constant dependence* of the world on the Supreme for *all its determinations*: कालकर्मस्वभावादि नित्यमेवेश्वरेच्छया (*BT* ii. 5.21). Insofar as it is only the starting point in the process of eightfold determinations, Madhva would, in a sense, endorse the view of Ulirici, that "God is *not first* God and *then* the Creator". This would not amount to tying down the Deity, as the various attributes are part of His nature (*svarūpalakṣaṇa*) and there can be no limitation of His Self, and this creative energy of God has a dual aspect of *śakti* and *vyakti* (latency and patency) to be exercised as occasion demands :

अनित्यत्वात् क्रियाणां तु कुत एव स्वरूपता ।
इति चेत् स विशेषोऽपि क्रियाशक्त्यात्मना स्थितः ॥
शक्तिता व्यक्तिता चेति विशेषोऽपि विशेषवान् ॥ (*AV*, i.2.9)

The acceptance of intrinsic Viśeṣas in God's eternal activity as in His other attributes of knowledge and power, as identical with His essence enables Madhva to account for the well-established periodicity of cosmic creation and dissolution without any hitch, by the exercise of His eternal will. Their periodicity cannot be smoothly explained (in other systems) without admitting *natural distinctions in time*, based purely on Upādhis in terms of time of creation and time of dissolution as suggested by the Vaiśeṣikas. Their explanation involves interdependence, as the Upādhis cannot operate unless there is a prior time of creation or dissolution, independent of them. The Upādhis cannot operate on the distinctions *which they themselves have brought into being*. This difficulty does not exist for Madhva who accepts natural distinctions (*svābhāvikaviśeṣas*) in time through Viśeṣas, to regulate periodicity of cosmic

2. Pringle Pattison, *Idea of God*, p. 303.

creation and dissolution at the will of God. The eternality of God's creative energy (*kriyāśakti*) too expresses itself through its own internal Viśeṣas as latent (*śakta*) or patent (*vyakta*) according to exigencies at His will, which explains the smooth periodicity of creation and dissolution :

* * * अस्मन्मते हरेः ।
विशेषकाल एवैतत् सृष्ट्यादीच्छा सदातनी ।
विशेषाश्चैव कालस्य हरेरिच्छावशाः सदा ।
तत्कालसृष्टिमेवातो वाञ्छतीशः सदैव हि ।
स्यात् कालः स तदैवेति कालस्य स्वगतत्वतः ॥ (*AV*, ii.2 *adh*.6)

अस्माभिः काले स्वभावत एव भेदोऽभ्युपगम्यते । तथा च, कालविशेषस्यैव सृष्टिं संहारं च प्रति कारणत्वात् तद्भावाभावाभ्यां सत्स्वपीतरकारणेषु सृष्ट्यादिसमयनियमो युज्यत इति भावः। (*NS* p.387 b)

Madhva uses the term "cause" in the sense that a world of imperfect beings and of ceaseless change is explicable only as being maintained by and dependent on a Supreme Being, who is Himself unchanging and perfect in every way and whose constant presence *in them*, educes the series of forms latent in matter and brings the souls nearer to their self-development at every step and so brings them into full play and actual manifestation[3] :

बलमानन्द ओजश्च सहो ज्ञानमनाकुलम् ।
स्वरूपाण्येव जीवस्य व्यज्यन्ते परमाद्विभोः । (*BSB*, ii.3.31)

प्रकृतावनुप्रविश्य, तां परिणाम्य तत्परिणामनियामकतया **तत्र स्थित्वा** आत्मनो बहुधाकरणात् । (*BSB*, i.4.27)

The universe thus depends on God as its ground and *ratio essendi*, but not as its cause in the narrow sense of the term :

अधिष्ठानमिति प्राहुर्मूलाधारं विचक्षणाः ।
यत्स्थितं दृश्यते वस्तु संस्थानं तदुदीरितम् ।
उभयं हरिरेवास्य जगतो मुनिपुंगव ॥
(*Vāmana Purāṇa, quoted in BT*, ii.5.2)

As this will inevitably lead to the assumption of the co-existence of matter and souls with God, like Aristotle and the

3. Cf. पाच्यांश्च सर्वान् **परिणामयेद्यः** । (*SvetUp*, v.5)

Greek philosophers, Madhva looks upon the orderly realm of natural process as having neither a beginning nor an end (*pravāhato anādi*). The cosmos is as everlasting as the God on whom it depends. The changing no less than the Unchangeable is an ultimate component of reality as a whole :

स्वतन्त्रं परतन्त्रं च द्विविधं तत्त्वमिष्यते । (*TS*)

द्विविधं हि प्रमेयं स्वतंत्रं परतन्त्रं च । (*NS*, 286 b)

CHAPTER XXVI

DOCTRINE OF "ETERNAL CREATION" THROUGH "PARĀDHĪNA-VIŚEṢĀPTI"

THE belief in the metaphysical dependence of all finite reality upon Brahman obliges Madhva to hold that all finite existence is in some measure created, preserved, destroyed or otherwise determined in numerous ways by the Supreme Being. He has enumerated twelve such determinations. These are the *expression* of this metaphysical dependence of the world of matter and souls (including the Cetana-Prakṛti) on the One Source of all existence, activity and consciousness. The Śruti texts which declare Brahman to be the ultimate source and *Creator of everything* : स इदं सर्वमसृजत and others like यतो वा इमानि भूतानि जायन्ते (*Taitt Up*), should therefore be understood to imply different forms of *metaphysical dependence* of countless substances, qualities and forces that constitute the world from the highest order of being to the lowest.

Of the twelve determinations, creation or coming into existence is ontologically the most important one. It is understood by the Nyāya-Vaiśeṣikas in the gross and literal sense of the term as a creation *de novo* and *ex nihilo* : असतः सत्तासमवायो जनिः । Madhva does not, as a Pariṇāmavādin, recognize अभूत्वा भवनम् or "Asat-kāryavāda" in any instance of causation, whatsoever. But this does not mean that all things in the world are eternal and uncreated, *in every respect*, or abolish "*Abhūtvā bhavanan*" *in any form or aspect altogether*. Madhva has shown, on grounds of logic, elsewhere, that the beginningless and eternal existence of certain fundametal substances or categories like space and time, must be accepted by every scientific-minded philosopher, as an unquestionable axiom. It has already been sho..n that the creation of time and space is an impossible hypothesis.[1]

1. See Chapter XI, on Space and Time.

The question then arises : How is the existence of uncreated substances like space and time and souls to be metaphysically reconciled with the fundamental presupposition of Vedānta and its ideal that all finite reality is explicable only as *derived from One Supreme Source of all. This problem has not occurred to and has not been raised by any other Indian philosopher or commentator of the Upaniṣads and the Vedānta Sūtras.* This shows how far in advance of his times Madhva's philosophic perceptions were, over those of his compeers. Madhva's answer to the question rests on an analysis of the concept of causation wherein he shows that it is capable of being distinguished into two kinds: (1) production of a substance *de novo* in the commonsense view of the term and (2) production in the sense of acquisition of a change of state or peculiarity that *depends on the will of another*, i.e. God (*Parādhīnaviśeṣāpti*). This distinction places the entire question of creation of eternal substances in an altogether new perspective and breathes a new meaning into the entire doctrine of creation and marks a striking advance of thought in Indian philosophy, where the idea is quite novel. In the light of this new theory of creation, it cannot be said that Madhva "finds it impossible to reconcile the traditional Hindu doctrine of the eternity of the world and souls, with their creation" or that "it is a pity that the teaching of St. Thomas on the possibility of Eternal Creation, never reached his ears".[2]

A correct understanding of Madhva's view of the creation of eternal substances through "Parādhīna-viśeṣāpati", to be explained presently, will show that it is the same as St. Thomas's 'Eternal Creation' in the sense of positing an eternal and *constant dependence* of all finite reality in each and every one of its states of being and becoming (*ṣaḍbhāvavikāras*) and the eight-fold cosmic determinations (*Sṛṣṭyādyaṣṭakam*), upon the One Infinite and Independent Principle viz., God or Brahman.

This is the utmost limit to which any philosophical theory of creation can go, short of assuming creation *in time* of even eternal

2. Cf. Remarks in a review of my work "Svatantrādvaita or Madhva's Theistic Realism" in the *Light of the East*, Calcutta, Feb. 1943, p. 31. (Ed. Fr. Dundoy S.J.). It is interesting to note that St. Thomas Aquinas and Madhva were close contemporaries.

substances, in some remote undiscoverable past, *ex nihilo*, which is fraught with logical contradictions. Such a doctrine of creation in time has been abandoned by speculative thinkers both before and after St. Augustine and Madhva's position that creation should be regarded as an eternal act coeval with the Divine nature and existence, is in perfect agreement with that of many early Christian Fathers particularly Origen. Only, we should understand by "creation", according to Madhva, not only the manifestation of being which is the starting point in the series of eightfold determinations, but one and all of the rest according to the nature and fitness of each case. On this view, it will be impossible to conceive of anything at any time that could fall outside the jurisdiction of one or the other of the eightfold determinations or predications of finite existence: viz.,

सृष्टिः स्थितिः संहृतिश्च नियमोऽज्ञानबन्धने ।
बन्धो मोक्षः सुखं दुःखमावृतिर्ज्योतिरेव च
विष्णुनास्य समस्तस्य समासव्यासयोगतः ।[3] (*TS*, 11)

---

3. "Creation, maintenance, dissolution, impulsion, knowledge, bondage, liberation, happiness, sorrow, obscuration and enlightenment all these determinations abridged or extended, as the case may be, originate from the Supreme Being alone in respect of *all the finite reals*".

"The words 'for all these finite reals' is to be supplied. One may object that this is contradictory to what has been said before. It would cancel the eternality of certain reals if everything should have a birth and destruction. It is also self-contradictory to speak of the conferment of knowledge on the insentient. These objections are met by the words "by abridgment or expansion". The meaning is—of the various determinations mentioned, only as many as are compatible with each particular case should be taken as intended. Where, in respect of a particular category of being, only a few of the above-mentioned determinations are applicable, only those few should be taken into account and *not all*. Where more are applicable, that much must be taken into account, as coming under the sway of the Lord with reference to that particular being or category. In any case, the essence and nature of one and all are to be understood as being absolutely under the control of God. Maintenance and impulsion are applicable to all; birth and destruction to the eternal-cum-non-eternal and to the non-eternal".

It should be noted here that Jayatīrtha's reference to *anitya* and "*nityānitya*" substances alone does not rule out the "Nityapadārthas" (eternals) from the purview of creation etc., as the term *Nityānitya* itself, includes the *Nitya* in their subtle aspects, as explained by him, in his own commentary on *TV* (p. 3-4) and as elucidated by Vyāsatīrtha in his gloss on the same (p. 7 b).

The position is clearly explained by Jayatīrtha, in commenting on the concluding passage of the *TS* :

अस्य समस्तस्यास्वतंत्रस्य । नन्वेतत् पूर्वमेवोक्तम् । समस्तस्य सृष्टिसंहारोक्तौ नित्यत्वोक्ति-विरोधः । अचेतनस्य बोधविरोधश्चेति । तत्रोक्तम्—'समासत' इति ।

उक्तधर्मेषु यत्र तत्त्वे अल्पीयांसः संभवन्ति तत्र तावन्तो विष्ण्वधीना ज्ञातव्याः । यत्र तु बहवः, तत्र तावन्तः । सर्वथा स्वरूपस्वभावौ अस्य तदधीनाविति ।

तत्र स्थितिनियमौ सर्वस्य । सृष्टिसंहृती नित्यानित्यस्यानित्यस्य च । (*Tst*)

The eternal and absolute dependence of all eternal substances upon the Deity is not logically inconceivable. If there is nothing illogical in holding that impermanent things are so, not of their own accord, or for no imaginable *reason* (*akasmāt*), the same would apply to eternal substances also. Else, the impermanent objects may be expected to be destroyed the very moment after their coming into being. This does not happen, because there is something by which its impermanence is *determined*. The eternal substances, also, could, in the same way, and for a similar reason, of "eternal dependence" on an eternal reason, be regarded as *dependent*. Simply because the non-eternality (*anityatva*) of the non-eternals is *limited*, we don't find it terminating and making the non-eternals eternal ! Even so, there is no possibility of eternal substances becoming non-eternal just because their eternality is said to be 'determined' or 'dependent' on something else like the Will of God. *Dependence is thus a relation which could be true of both eternals and non-eternals.* It is something in the nature of things. So long then, as Creation is not defined in the narrow sense of *Abhūtvā bhavanam* and *prāgasatas samutpattiḥ* as in the Nyāya, the acceptance of the creation of eternal substances also in the sense of subjection or liability to new phases of being or becoming at the will of some other agency (viz. God), cannot be said to involve any logical incompatibility.[4]

---

4. नन्वेत दयुक्तम्—नित्यस्य पराधीनतासंभवादित्यत आह—**'नित्यमिति'** । यथा अनित्यं घटादिकमनित्यतया नियम्यते, तथा नित्यमपि नित्यात्मना नित्यं सर्वदैवेश्वरो नियामयति-यथा हि घटादयोऽनित्यस्वभावा अपि नाकस्मादनित्या भवन्ति । तथात्वे चोत्पत्युत्तरक्षण एव विनाशसंभवात् । एवं नित्यस्यापि नित्यता यदि पराधीना तदा को दोषः ? नचानित्यता पराधीनेति कदाचिन्नित्यता घटादेः प्राप्ता ! विनाशकारणोपनिपातश्च व्यात् । तथा नित्यस्य नित्यतायाः पराधीनत्वेऽपि, न जात्वनित्यताप्राप्तिः । तन्नियमननियमादिति । (*NS*, p. 330)

Though in one sense all material transformation presupposes a basic continuity of essence of the cause, even after the change of name, form, properties and utility have taken place, there are cases in which the original substance remains intact without surrendering any of its fundamental qualities, temporarily or absolutely. There are also yet other instances of change where the nature of the substance is changed to such an extent or in essential particulars and qualities, so as to be no longer recognizable or nameable by the same term, as the basis of its modified state. We are thus obliged to recognize two kinds of change (1) one in which the substratum and most of its essential features are intact धर्मिणः तादवस्थ्ये सति धर्ममात्रपरिवृत्तिः though certain additional traits may have crept in in the process of change; and (2) another, in which as a result of the complete change effected in the substance, in the course of the causal process we are faced with a total change in the constitution of the substance itself so as to make it almost a new and a different one for all practical purposes धर्मिस्वरूपस्यैव परिणामः Madhva designates the former kind of change as *Parādhīnaviśeṣāpti* and the latter as "*Abhūtvā bhavanam*".

Applying these types of change to objects of experience or to ontological entities, whose existence we are appraised of by scripture or reasoning, we find that most of them come under the second type of change and are, therefore, to be regarded as "anitya" and *ipso facto* created at a particular time and place and *have a beginning and an end.* In regard to some others, however, experience and reason and the authority of Scripture oblige us to put them in the former group. They are, therefore, regarded as Nitya or uncreated in essence, though still open to certain new influences. It is useless to deny that the Hindu Scriptures do teach the existence of at least a few of such "eternal" entities called Nityapadārthas or Anādinitya, which are conceived as existing from eternity without a beginning or an end, such as Time, Space, Matter, Souls and the Vedas. The question is, therefore, how to reconcile such eternality of theirs with the axiom of the absolute all-creatorship of Brahman, which is not only one of the prominent attributes of Godhead, conceivable by man, but is also the philosophical justification for a Deity. Is it possible to hold that *even* eternal things are *created* in some sense?

If so, *in what sense* should such creation of eternals be understood ? This question is of the utmost importance, though it does not seem to have been appreciated in its true bearings by any Indian philosopher before or other than Madhva. It is in connection with this momentous issue that he introduces his new theory of 'Eternal Creation' or Creation of Eternal entities, through Parādhīnaviśeṣāpti. *This is his most significant contribution to Indian philosophy.*

"Parādhīnaviśeṣāpti" means the acquiring of a new trait or complexion that depends on (the will of) an "Other" (God). These new traits would differ according to the nature of the substance concerned. Some of these have been enumerated and explained by Jayatīrtha :

Nityapadārtha	*Nature of Parādhīnaviśeṣāpti.*
1. Cetana Prakṛti सिसृक्षुत्वव्यक्तिविशेषः	The manifesting of the particular desire to set creation in motion.[5]
2. Avyākṛtākāśa मूर्तसम्बन्धः (Space)	Coming into contact with tangible entities.
3. Prakṛti महदादिरूपेण विकृतिः	Modification in the form of Mahat and other tattvas.
4. Kāla प्रवाहिजन्म	Birth of time-instants in the series.
5. Mahadādi उपचयापचयावाप्तिः	Going through states of contraction and expansion of parts.
6. Jīvas देहोत्पत्तिः	Acquisition of body, senses, etc.
7. Vedas नियतविशिष्टानुपूर्वकित्वेनार्थबोधकशक्त्याविर्भावः	Manifestation of the power to connote the sense of words having an unalterable and definite order of arrangement

5. स एव भूयो निजवीर्यचोदितां स्वजीवमायां प्रकृतिं सिसृक्षतीम् ।
अनामरूपात्मनि रूपनामनी विधित्समानोऽनुशशास शास्तिकृत् ॥
(*Bhāg*, i.10.22)

The most important point to note in connection with the doctrine of Parādhīnaviśeṣāpti is that the special kind of change or creation applies to the aspect of the *Viśeṣas* (*traits*) *only* that have been assumed by the substance in question *and not to its basic essence or Dharmisvarūpa*. Were it not so, the entire change would have been more directly termed as "Parādhīna-*svarūpāntarāpatti*". The specification of the change as (Parādhīna-) *Viśeṣāpti* instead, is, therefore, *significant*. The point is that it is not the Viśeṣyākāra (substratum) that is produced by the acquisition of the new traits (*apūrvaviśeṣa*), but only the "whole" (*Viśiṣṭākāra*). The new traits, moreover, cannot, in the nature of things, be coeval (*yāvaddravyabhāvi*) with the substance, in regard to the Jīvas, Prakṛti, Space, Time, etc. In such cases, the *Viśeṣyarūpa* and the *Viśiṣṭa* cannot be said to be absolutely identical with each other, but only "*bhinnābhinna*" as stated by Jayatīrtha (vide *TVt*, p. 5, line 5 and Vyāsatīrtha's gloss on it : *Mandāramanjarī*, p. 8, line 16)[6]. We cannot, therefore, ignore this important point of distinction and treat the birth of the new trait as equivalent to the birth of the "Whole", taking Jayatīrtha's remark—

अपूर्वविशेषोपजनने **हि विशिष्टाकारोपजनोऽवश्यंभावी।** विशिष्टाकारश्च वस्तुस्वरूपाभिन्न इति तस्यैवायमुपजनो भवति । (*NS* p. 431)

as an unqualified dictum. This statement of Jayatīrtha must be read along with the important distinction of attributes in question, as "Yāvad-dravyabhāvi" and "Ayāvad-dravyabhāvi" drawn by Madhva and accepted by Jayatīrtha himself in his *TVt* and elsewhere. *It is the failure to take note of this crucial point that has led to disastrous results in H. N. Raghavendrachar's claiming* in his *Dvaita Philososhy, Its Place in Vedanta* (Mysore Uni. 1941), *that in Madhva's philosophy, there cannat be any "eternal" or "uncreated" entities, in any sense of the term, and that all Substances, including Space, Time, Souls and Matter undergo "Svarūpa-Sṛṣṭi" in the full sense of the term, inclusive of the very core of their being. This is a most unfortunate perversion of Madhva's teaching.*[7]

---

6. अयावद्द्रव्यभाविगुणगुण्यादौ भेदाभेदौ ।
   यावद्द्रव्यभाविगुणगुण्यादौ सविशेषाभेदः ।

7. H. N. Raghavendrachar's contention of Svarūpa-Sṛṣṭi of Jīvas in Madhva's philosophy was repudiated by orthodox spokesmen like Pandit

H. N. Raghavendrachar's therory of 'Svarūpasṛṣṭi' of eternal substances like Jīvas, Prakrti, Space and Time would be repugnant to the very acceptance of eternal substances as such in Madhva's philosophy. *There will be no need for going in for a new concept of creation in terms of Parādhīnaviśeṣāpti if 'Svarūpasṛṣṭi' is to be accepted in its absolute sense.* The concept of Parādhīnaviśeṣāpti has been specially introduced by Madhva to reconcile the eternality of these Nityapadārthas with the other fact of the all-creatorship of Brahman (*Sa idam sarvam asṛjata*) in a special 'Pickwickian' sense of the term.

This special sense is that of Parādhīnaviśeṣāpti whose meaning has already been explained. Since the association of the Jīvas with any kind of embodiment (in *Liṅgaśarīra* or gross body) has necessarily to be an impermanent and non-eternal association, if release from bondage is to have any meaning, such an association of the Jīva with an appendage like the Liṅgaśarīra or the gross body in the form of an 'Apūrvaviśeṣopajana' (birth of a new trait) cannot, in the nature of things, be deemed to be coeternal (*yāvaddravyabhāvi*) with the Jīvasvarūpa itself. For this reason, the passage in Jayatīrtha's *NS*, "*Apūrva Viśeṣo*pajane hi......" (p. 431) has to be read along with its clarification given by himself with reference to 'Yāvad-dravyabhāvi' attributes and should *not* be interpreted without reference to the clarification given by him again in his *GTt* :

अयावद्द्रव्यभाविविशेषणेन विशिष्टस्य विशेष्येण भेदाभेदांगीकारात् (p. 187 b).

This distinction is further clarified by the following authoritative pronouncement by Vyāsatīrtha in his *Mandāramañjarī* on Jayatirtha' *TVt* : "In respect of impermanent attributes, the relation between substance and attributes is one of both difference and identity. In respect of permanent attributes, lasting as long as the substance itself, the relation is one of "Saviśeṣābheda" or "colorful identity" :

अयावद्द्रव्यभाविगुणगुण्यादौ भेदाभेदौ ।
यावद्द्रव्यभाविगुणगुण्यादौ सविशेषाभेदः ।
(*TV Mandārmañjarī*, p. 8, line 16)

D. Vasudevachar in his Kannada work *Dvaitapradīpa* and others. But it appears that H. N. Raghavendrachar still feels convinced of the correctness of his own view. See his later Kannada woık: *Dvaitavedānta*.

It does not require any argument to see that the Jīva's association with bodies is *not a permanent* one which will last forever as long as the Jīvasvarūpa itself. In such cases, the relation of the Jīvasvarūpa to the subtle or gross bodies has necessarily to be conceived as "bhedābheda" and *not* as "Saviśeṣābheda". For, in such cases the new trait acquired is not absolutely identical with the "Viśeṣya". Nor are the Viśeṣya and the Viśiṣṭa (the thing in itself and the qualified entity) "Saviśeṣābhinna" in such cases. Without such colorful identity between them, there is no basis for the contention that the 'Viśiṣṭākāra' and the 'Vastusvarūpa' (i.e. the Viśeṣya) are one and the same and that therefore there is "Svarūpasṛṣṭi" of eternal verities like the Jīvas in Madhva's system, as contended by Raghavendrachar.

What Jayatīrtha has said about 'kriyā' (activity) arising in a sentient being in his *GTt* xi.15, p. 184, quoted earlier (See Chapter VII) does *not* upset the above finding. For a 'kriyā' in a sentient being can be in its latent form (*śaktirūpa*) or in its patent form (*vyaktarūpa*). For this reason 'activity' of a Cetana can be regarded as 'Yāvad-dravyabhāvi' and hence accepted as Saviśeṣābhinna or colorfully identical with it. But association with a physical body (gross or subtle) which is termed "birth" or creation is always a patent state. Hence the relation of 'Saviśeṣābheda' *cannot be thought of in that connection.*

Jayatīrtha makes it clear that creation in the ordinary sense of 'abhūtvā bhavanam' (*de novo*) applies in the full sense of the term *only to the Viśeṣas,* which is, therefore, fittingly termed "*apūrvaviśeṣopajana* or birth of a new trait that was not there before. The substratum (*viśeṣya*) could not, however, be said to be produced.[8] This implies that the change or "creation" is only with reference to the Viśeṣa in respect of eternal substance and it is through and because of this acquiring of new traits that the "Viśiṣṭa" (e.g. Jīva) comes to be designated as "created". There is no point in describing the "Viśeṣyākāra" as अवस्थितस्वरूप "if the Svarūpasṛṣṭi" of the Viśeṣya is possible. Madhva and his commentator would not have labored so much to distinguish four

8. Cf. अस्माकं तु, अवस्थितमेव द्रव्यमवयवोपचयापचयाभ्यां तत्तपरिणामात्मकतया विक्रियत इति दर्शनम् । (*NS* p. 399 b)

kinds of change and draw a distinction between *Abhūtvābhavanam* (creation *de novo*) and creation in a restricted sense of *Parādhīnaviśeṣāpti* by virtue of the viśeṣya acquiring some new trait, applicable to certain 'eternal entities' only, like Space, Time, Matter and Souls. These could never have any other kind of creation; whereas objects like jars could be created in the ordinary sense of *abhūtvābhavanam*.

"Parādhīnaviśeṣāpti" is the only kind ot creation that is possible in respect of Nityapadārthas. An objection may, however, be raised in this connection. From the point of view of Pariṇāmavāda or evolution theory accepted by Madhva the production of a jar or a piece of cloth is hardly other than a case of Parādhīnaviśeṣāpti, defined in terms of अवस्थितस्वरूपस्यैव वस्तुनो विशेषाप्तिमात्रेण जन्मव्यवहारः, so that, strictly speaking, there can be no other kind of creation maintainable in the system for any material object. This being so the restricted application of creation through Parādhīnaviṣesāpti to 'eternal entities' alone is pointless. Jayatīrtha meets this objection in this way. The crux of creation through Parādhīnaviśeṣāpti is the fulfilment of the condition : अवस्थितस्वरूपस्यैव वस्तुन अपूर्वविशेषाप्तिः. The creation of a jar, out of clay, is *not* a case of this kind, i.e., धर्मिणस्तादवस्थ्ये सति धर्ममात्रपरिवृत्तिः even though the material stuff of clay may continue still to underlie the jar. The fact is that there have taken place, in the course of the change of clay into pot, some *far-reaching changes*; so much so, we have no longer the clay intact, nor can we *designate it as clay now*, nor recognize its original shape or arrangement (*saṁsthāna*). We have a "new entity", jar, i e. धर्मिस्वरूपस्यैव परिणामः Hence we say: मृत् घटो जातः, क्षीरं दधि जातम् and so forth :

* * * जन्मनः स्थूलताभवः ।
पूर्वशब्दविलोपश्च यदि जन्मेति कीर्त्यते ।
रमाया नैव जन्माप्तिः चेतनस्यापि केवलम् ।
प्रधानस्य च वेदस्य * * * ॥ (*AV* ii.3.8)

But no such essential transformation could be detected in the case of the eternal substances named. Hence, these are best put down in a separate category of creation by themselves, namely, Parādhīnaviśeṣāpti.

This new doctrine of creation is intended by Madhva to reconcile and rationalize the existence of certain Nityapadārthas, with the all-creatorship of God[9].

9. Śaṅkara gives greater importance to the statement of the Śruti that Brahman has created everything and interprets texts like आकाशवत् सर्वगतश्च नित्यः as gauṇa. He does not concede the existence of uncreated eternals and is not aware of *Parādhīnaviśeṣāpti*.

CHAPTER XXVII

MADHVA'S THEORY OF THE EVOLUTION OF THE WORLD

MADHVA'S theory of the constitution of matter and the evolution of the world is based on the 'Sāṁkhya' metaphysics of *Upaniṣads*, the *Epics* and *Purāṇas*. He quotes profusely from the *Mahābhārata*, the *Bhāgavata*, and other Purāṇas and from the vast literature of the *Pañcarātras*, which still await exploration at the hands of modern scholars. Even a cursory view of the quotations made by Madhva from the literature of the Pañcarātras bears witness to the strong and persistent theistic tradition of Upaniṣadic thought embodied in them and which Madhva inherited from them[1] and upon which he indented so largely, in the reinterpretation of the Upaniṣads and the Sūtras and in the exposition of his own system. The school of Rāmānuja, though ostensibly connected with the *Pañcarātras*, has not, in its *interpretation of the Vedānta*, touched anything more than the fringe of that literature. A reference to the numerous quotations from a large number of forgotten Saṁhitās of the *Pañcarātra*, occurring in the works of Madhva,[2] dealing with various problems of logic and philosophy would make this clear.

As a follower of the Epic Sāṁkhya, Madhva has naturally accepted the doctrine of evolution of matter (Prakṛti) as against the theory of Ārambhavāda or 'atomic genesis' of the Nyāya-Vaiśeṣikas. The latter, as explained by Jayatīrtha, is fraught with hourly danger to the stability (*sthiratva*) of the world of objects. According to the Pīlupākavāda of the Vaiśeṣikas, even the slighest displacement of a single atom in a jar would entail

1. *MV* viii. 4.
2. See my *HDSV*, Appendix I.

the ultimate destruction of it. Hence, Madhva would have none of it.[3]

He, therefore, accepts the theory of the evolution of matter from a subtle to a gross state. This has the advantage of guaranteeing the basic identity and stability of the material stuff in and through the various changes it undergoes in its process of development from a subtle to a gross state. Only Pariṇāmavāda will be consistent with Madhva's theory of causation and our faith in the stability of material objects.[4] He, therefore, accepts a primordial material stuff called Prakṛti which undergoes various modifications and develops by a process of evolution and involution of effects. The existence of Prakṛti is not logically established by Madhva. He takes it over bodily from the Upaniṣadic, Epic and Purāṇic Sāṁkhya cosmology. It is an eternal insentient stuff of the most subtle kind :

अनादेरुपादानस्य भूतसूक्ष्मशब्दाभिधेयस्य प्रधानत्वात् । (*NS*)

Madhva has stoutly opposed the attempts of other commentators on the Vedānta who have denied a place to Prakṛti as the material stuff out of which the universe is evolved by Brahman in the philosophy of the Vedānta. He establishes on sound textual authority, the Śāstric character (*Śābdatvam*) of Prakṛti as an insentient, dependent material principle which is the material cause (*Upādāna-kāraṇa*) of the world, and repudiates the theory of Abhinna-nimittopādānatva of Brahman adopted by other Bhāṣyakāras of the Vedānta.[5] Madhva thus champions the cause of the Sāṁkhya against the Advaitin and fights successfully for a place for Prakṛti in Vedāntic cosmology. Rāmānuja also, has perforce to recognize a material principle as defined in the metrical Upaniṣads, the Epics and the Purāṇas. Neither of them, however, could recognize, with the Sāṁkhya, the independence of that principle. Madhva's point is that *the status* of

---

3. Cf. यदा हि घटादिषु सूच्यग्रादिना एकोऽपि परमाणुरपैति तदा नष्टव्यमेव तदारब्धेन द्व्यणुकेन, विभागेनासमवायिकारणस्य संयोगस्य नष्टत्वात् । द्व्यणुकनाशे, समवायिकारणनाशात् त्र्यणुकनाश इत्यनेन क्रमेण घटनाशोऽप्यवश्यंभावी । (*NS*, p. 394 b)

4. **तदेव हि वस्तु** अवयवोपचयापचयाभ्यामन्यथा **विक्रियते**, न पुनरन्यदेव भवतीति **परिणामवादिनो** मन्यन्ते। अतः प्रत्यक्षयोग्येषु सर्ववस्तुषु प्रत्यभिज्ञया स्थिरत्वग्रहणं युक्तमेवेति। (*NS*, p. 394)

5. The point has been fully discussed in my *HDSV* pp. 101-105.

Prakṛti, as claimed by the Sāṁkhyas, has nothing to do with its being recognized by Vedāntins as the material stuff out of which the universe is to be evolved. It is accepted as a principle dependent on Brahman (Paratantra) by Madhva and *Rāmānuja*, according to the Upaniṣads.

Prakṛti is both directly and indirectly the material cause of the world. It is the direct material cause of time and the three qualities of *sattva*, *rajas* and *tamas* and indirectly of Mahat, Ahaṁkāra, etc. It is both eternal and pervasive; but not unlimited.[6] The three guṇas are supposed to be differentiated at the beginning of creation, in the ratio of 4 : 2 : 1 (*BT*, iii.11.14). The evolution of other forms of matter takes place on account of the disturbance in their equipoise which gives rise to the twentyfour principles commonly recognized, viz. Mahat, Ahaṁkāra, Buddhi, Manas, ten sensory organs, five sense-objects and the five great elements. Mahat is the first and finest evolute of matter and energy. Ahaṁkāra is the principle of individuation, Buddhi that of discrimination, and Manas of thought. The principle of Ahaṁkāra is divided into three classes of Vaikārīka, Taijasa and Tāmasa. From Taijasa the ten sense organs are produced, and the five sense objects (*viṣayas*) and the elements are the products of Tāmasa-Ahaṁkāra. The *tanmātras* stand for qualitatively distinct and irreducible sense-qualities with a definite leaning towards their appropriate objects. These twentyfour evolutes of Prakṛti are the constituents of the microcosm and the macrocosm of the entire Brahmāṇḍa. Madhva gives a proper reorientation to this theory of material evolution by *linking it up with a systematic hierarchy of presiding deities from top to bottom*. It is under the constant supervision and guidance of these Abhimāni-devatās (or Tattvābhimānins) that all material transformations and psychophysical functions are carried on. The Supreme Brahman itself is ultimately behind all these activities and of each and every one of them :

तत्र तत्र स्थितो विष्णुस्तत्तच्छक्तीः प्रबोधयन् ।
एक एव महाशक्तिः कुरुते सर्वमञ्जसा ॥ (*BSB* ii. 3.11)

The three forms of matter, viz., Sattva, Rajas and and Tamas, are specially controlled by the three aspects of Cetana-

6. न च परिमितस्यापि मूलप्रकृतित्वे बाधकम् । (*NS*, 326 b)

Prakṛti, viz. Śrī, Bhū and Durgā : शक्यत्वात् शक्तयो भार्याः शक्तिः सामर्थ्यमुच्यते. (*BT* x. 94.15)

The period of creation is said to be one-eighth of the period of involution :

लयस्य त्वष्टमो भागः सृष्टिकाल उदाहृतः ।
तत्रैव वेदसंचारोऽन्यदा स्तुतिमात्रकाः ॥ (*BT* p. 71b)

Involution takes place by the merger of the effects in their causes in the reverse order of evolution. This applies to the Tattvābhimāni-Devas also, both in Saṁsāra and in release. For details see my *BSPC* vol. II Chapters 18-20; Vol. III adhy. 4, pāda 2.

CHAPTER XXVIII

CRITIQUE OF BRAHMA-PARIṆĀMA AND VIVARTA

MADHVA'S conception of the material world and its rela tion to Brahman is free from the difficulties that beset the Pariṇāma and Vivarta theories. Pantheism pulls down the Deity. It is worse than irreligion[1]. It utterly negates the independence of God. For, all material modifications are dependent originations (Parādhīnaviśeṣa). They fall under two main heads of change : change of substance (धर्मिपरिवर्त) and change of aspect or attributes (धर्मपरिवर्त). Each of these may again be distinguished into reversible and irreversible modifications. All these four kinds of change are dependent upon external agencies[2]. It would be impossible to recognize any such external cause of change in respect of Brahman, as that would immediately reduce it to a position of dependence. Pariṇāmavāda, moreover, stands committed to the view that Brahman alone existed in the beginning and that there was no other substance in existence then. It does not believe in any other eternal existent, uncreated by Brahman or co-existent with it (as those who believe in creation through Parādhīnaviśeṣāpti do). No modification of Brahman is thus conceivable or possible in such circumstances, as the urge or direction for such modification must come from an outside agency.

It will be inconsistent with Divine perfection to assume that Brahman itself out of its own free will chooses to transmute

1. Rāmānuja calls it a more heinous view than Śaṅkara's Brahmājñānavāda : ब्रह्माज्ञानपक्षादपि पापीयानयं भेदाभेदपक्षः (*Vedārthasaṅgraha* p. 14, Rāmānuja Granthamālā, 1956, Kancipuram).

2. See *NS* 1. 4. p. 195-96.

itself into the world of beings and objects,—a world which is a state of sin, evil and misery. *We cannot say that the Brahman does not recognize the misery and imperfections of the world as it is.* For it is *ex hypothesi* Sarvajña. If Brahman does not experience the suffering in the world, who does ? Not the Jīva : for he, too, is a modification of Brahman and/or is essentially the same as Brahman. Even supposing that the Jīva is only partially identical with Brahman it would not wholly exempt Brahman from a share in the misery of the world. Even the most subtle modifications in the development of sentient creatures are subject to external forces. Sentients are never known to undergo change of state or condition of being at their own free will. It is useless so argue that Brahman being Almighty can change itself at Its own Will, without reference to any external stimulation or provocation or direction. For, the *change* from a state of blessedness and perfection to one of obvious misery and limitation can hardly be a token of Almightiness. It would be sheer dogmatism to say that we should not raise logical objections in a case that transcends all reason. In that case, all philosophy should have to be given up as a wild goose chase. The plea of 'transcending logic' or even 'transcendental logic' can be urged with propriety only in cases where the authorities are *unanimous.* In this case, however, it is *not* so, as there are many texts which clearly *deny* to Brahman any kind of physical or material modification (निर्विकारोऽक्षरः शुद्धः) so that the employment of reason becomes imperative in coming to a definite conclusion on the vexed question.

It is equally unavailing to put in that the change of state undergone by Brahman is a special kind of modification that does not affect its "deeper nature". For the fact remains that the change of state attributed to Brahman by the Pariṇāmavādin is precisely and unfortunately of this very kind that plunges it into the abyss of misery and imperfection of the world from a state of bliss and self-sufficiency. How can we pretend that this does not affect its "deeper nature ? That being so, and so long as it is conceded that Brahman does not undergo any change of state that is determined or controlled by external agencies, any state of *becoming* in which we might find It, will be as natural to It as any other ! Since it is admitted (by the Pariṇāmavādin) that Brahman is with and without the forms of grossness at different times, it will be impossible to define which of them is Its "natural" state and which is adventitious; so that both the states would be quite natural to its being. Granting for argument's sake that a transformation of Brahman with a complete loss of original nature is possible, the question will still remain if such a transformation will be partial or complete. As Brahman is partless and indivisible, the former alternative could not be true. In the latter case, Brahman having been spent or "exhausted" in the transformation, there would be none left (*as Brahman*) during the lifetime of the world, with the result that all talk of acquiring knowledge of Brahman, with a view to attaining the bliss of Mokṣa, will have to cease.

Madhva, therefore, rejects the view of Bhāskara and many others that Brahman is in itself the stuff of which the universe is made. So far as all our received knowledge and the testimony of the Scriptures go, there would appear to be an unbridgeable gulf between Spirit and matter : Cit and Jaḍa :

न चेतनविकारः स्याद्यत्र क्वापि ह्यचेतनम् ।
नाचेतनविकारोऽपि चेतनः स्यात् कदाचन ॥ (*AV* i. 4.11)

Brahman is essentially Saccidānanda. How, then, can such a perfect being of pure intelligence and bliss evolve, out of itself an effect that is inert and wholly lacking in intelligence and is, in addition, the abode of so much misery and subject to ceaseless change ? There is no use in taking shelter behind alleged statements in the Śruti to the effect that Brahman is immediately and in its own person the material cause of the world. For not even the vociferation of a hundred texts can make the crow white ! Reason may test even where it cannot build. Where conflicting authorities claim to interpret the Śruti each to suit his own metaphysics, the employment of reason becomes more important than the bare text itself.

Not even the Scripture says *directly* that the intelligent becomes the unintelligent. In that case, Brahman could as well become the individual souls, and simplify matters for all philosophers. Moreover, the Śruti says emphatically that Brahman is immutable and unchanging : निर्विकारोऽक्षरः शुद्धः. Since no causation is possible without *some change* or modification in the cause, we must naturally look for the material cause of the universe, elsewhere than in Brahman[3].

A strict adherence to the logic of facts and the spirit of the Śrutis compels Madhva to reject the profanity of Brahmapariṇāmavāda in any garb. Even the oft-paraded promissory statement about the knowledge of the One leading to the knowledge of the many (on which Śaṅkara himself tries to base the case for Brahmapariṇāma) does not necessarily warrant the conclusion that Brahman is the *material cause* of the universe. *Madhva has been the first critical commentator on the Chāndogya Upniṣad to draw attention to the difficulties in the wording and form of the propositions, as they stand worded which definitely militate against any facile conclusion of material causality* (ब्रह्मोपादानत्वम्) *being drawn from that text. No other commentator, ancient or modern, seems to have realized this crucial point.* The difficulty pointed out by Madhva is a real and serious one and cannot be lightly passed over. The examples of *mṛtpiṇḍa, lohamaṇi and nakhanikṛntana in the form in which they appear in the text of ChanUp* vi. 1. 4-6 are virtually incapable of establishing anything more than a general resemblance or point of contact between Brahman and the world. The terms "*eka*" (used thrice), *piṇḍa*, *maṇi* and *nakhanikṛntana*, prevent the establishment of an intimate causal relation (उपादानोपादेयभाव) among the pairs named in the text : अन्यथा, एकशब्दः पिण्डशब्दश्च व्यर्थः स्यात् । 'मृदा विज्ञातया' इत्येतावता पूर्णत्वात् । न ह्येकमृत्पिण्डात्मकानि अन्यमृण्मयानि । सादृश्यमेव हि तेषाम् । न ह्येकमण्यात्मकमन्यत् लोहमयम् । न चैकनखनिकृन्तनात्मकं सर्वं कार्ष्णायसम्[4] ! (Madhva, *VTN*, p. 25b)

जगतो ब्रह्मविकारत्वेन तदारोपत्वेन वा एकविज्ञानेन सर्वविज्ञाने, **'मृदा विज्ञातया मृण्मयं विज्ञातं स्यात्'**, 'लोहेन विज्ञातेन लोहमयं विज्ञातं स्यात्', 'कार्ष्णायसा विज्ञातेन कार्ष्णायसं

3. The supposed reference to Brahmapariṇāmavāda, in the teaching of the *Brahmasūtras* (i. 4. 24) has been convincingly shown by Madhva to have no relevance to *that problem* at all. For a full discussion of the issue and refutation of the remarks of V. S. Ghate and Bhandarkar on this point, see my *HDSV* (pp. 105-108) and my *BSPC*. Vol. I. pp. 307-313.

4. "Otherwise, the words "one" and "lump" would be meaningless. It would have sufficed to say "by knowing clay...". Surely, all that is made of clay is *not* the effect of *one* clod of clay ! There can only be a resemblance among them. All that is of the nature of metals in the world is *not* the effect of *one* nugget of gold or some such metal and not all that is made of lead the *effect of one single nail-cutter*!"

विज्ञातं स्यात्' **इत्येतावतैव पूर्णत्वात्** त्रयाणामेकशब्दानां, पिण्डमणिनखनिकृन्तनशब्दानां, 'सर्वं' शब्दानां च विगतार्थत्वं स्यात्। सर्वमृण्मयादीनामेकमृत्पिण्डादिविकारत्वाभावात्। विरुद्धार्थता च स्यात्।[5] (*NS*, i. 4. p. 226)

There is no use pleading that we should not take the text literally but look to the spirit; for the spirit itself has got to be deduced from the wording. However that may be, the third and the last illustration of nail-scissor has *not even the semblance of a causal argument. It gives the whole case away.* For, the *nakhanikṛntana* is itself *an effect* and *not the cause of anything else* and cannot, in the nature of things, be the "cause" of "*all that is made of kārṣṇāyasa*". It should be clear then, that the argument for the material causality of Brahman *breaks down completely* and at the very first touch of criticism in *this* instance. *The position is hardly better in the other two cases.*

Madhva, therefore, prefers to take the teaching of Uddālaka in terms of the primacy of the knowledge of Brahman over all other forms or kinds of knowledge. To know Brahman is to know at one sweep *all that is worth knowing* about the world that is so utterly *dependent* on It : यज्ज्ञात्वा नेह भूयोऽन्यज्ज्ञातव्यमवशिष्यते (*Gītā*, vii. 2). The knowledge of Brahman is the end and aim of all secular learning and the culmination of all Scriptural knowledge. Sage Uddālaka is naturally at pains to impress this great truth on his son who is conceited enough (cf. स्तब्ध एयायं *ChanUp*) to gloat over his learning divorced from Brahman-knowledge.

There is much truth in Madhva's contention, therefore, that a relation of material cause and effect could *not* be easily established among the pairs named in the text, consistently with its actual wording. The utmost point of contact between

---

5. When the knowledge of the many by the knowledge of the one is posited, whether on the view of the world being a transformation of Brahman or a superimposition on it, the words "*eka*" (one) (used thrice), "*piṇḍa*" (lump), "*maṇi*" (chief) and "*nakhanikṛntana*" (nail-cutter) and "*sarvam*" (all) would not only be meaningless—as the sense can be conveyed even by saying "by knowing clay all that is made of 'clay' is known, by knowing gold all that is made of gold is known and by knowing lead all that is of the nature of lead is known; *but the statement worded as it stands* would be positively misleading". A little reflection will show the truth of the criticism.

the example (*dṛṣṭānta*) and that which is the subject of the example (*dārṣṭāntika*) that these examples could establish is one of *resemblance* of some kind : सत्यमस्ति सादृश्यं, किंतु, सत्त्वादिनैव (*NS*, p. 451). The point is conceded by the *Bhāmatī* also in the *pūrvapakṣa* :

'यथैकेन मृत्पिण्डेन' इत्यादिदृष्टान्तः परमात्मनः प्राधान्यं सूचयति । यथा सोमशर्मणा एकेन ज्ञातेन सर्वे कठा ज्ञाता भवन्तीति ।

The other familiar examples of (1) scorpions being produced from cowdung; (2) hair and nail growing from the human body; and (3) the growth of man from childhood to youth and old age, quoted to establish the material causality of Brahman, are equally unavailing. The point at issue is the possibility of an unintelligent (*jaḍa*) effect being produced *solely* from a sentient being. The analogy of scorpions etc. is, therefore, doubly irrelevant as the scorpion is a living creature and the cowdung insentient. Even if such production were biologically true, it admits of other explanations insofar as the scorpion has a material body which might be derived from the dung. But the soul of the scorpion (insofar as it may have one) cannot be a product of dung! Śaṅkara's explanation (*BSB* ii. 1. 6) that Brahman has *sattā* in common with its effects like Ākāśa, overlooks the fact that this *sattā* is not, like the body of man, distinguishable from Brahman. The growth of hair and nails from the human body is possible only so long as it is tenanted and sustained by a soul and not at other times. But the Pariṇāmavādin has necessarily to conceive of a state when Brahman alone existed in an incorporeal or pre-corporeal state and later produced a world out of itself. But a non-embodied Brahman cannot, on the very same analogy of men, produce anything. It would, in any case, be impossible to show that nails and hair are directly produced from the soul! The example of the development of man from childhood to old age pertains, in the opinion of all Śāstrakāras, only to the body (*śarīradharma*) of man and not to his soul. The ripening of wisdom with the advance of years and the appearance of virility in youth, are possible only in the event of a body sustained by the presence of a soul. None of the developments instanced can or is known to take place *in the soul as such.* And in all these cases, the purely physical developments are traceable to the physical part in the causal complement.[6] Consistently then with the implications of these analogies, the Pariṇāmavādin must admit that the purely material part of Brahman—if it can be credited with any—is the material cause of the world and that soul or spiritual element in its make-up is the operative cause. This would be tantamount to a restatement of Madhva's position, in less accurate terminology. In such a contingency, the material part will have to be regarded as not-Brahman as there cannot obviously be anything material about Brahman ! This could give us but a Kevala-nimittakāraṇavāda, in the end :

भागेन परिणामश्चेद् भागयोर्भेद एव हि ।
यो भागो न विकारी स्यात् स एवास्माकमीश्वरः ॥

(*AV*, i. 4.11)

Insofar as most Pariṇāmavādins like Bhāskara and Yādavaprakāśa do *not* admit the co-existence of a purely material principle (Prakṛti) which can figuratively be styled the 'body' of Brahman, the illustration of scorpions etc. cannot, with propriety, be cited by them. Bhāskara is the only Vedāntin who holds fearlessly to actual Brahmapariṇāma and regards not merely the material world but the souls also as products of Brahman. This lands him in further difficulties of having to *visit* the miseries and imperfections of the finite selves also, on Brahman, against repeated assertions in the texts to the contrary : अनश्नन्नन्योऽभिचाकशीति (*MundUp* iii. 1) ; संभोगप्राप्तिरिति चेन्न वैशेष्यात् (*BS* i.2.8).

Rāmānuja is generally regarded as a believer in Abhinnanimittopādānatva of Brahman. *This gives him an apparent advantage over Madhva. But this is altogether deceptive.* Rāmānuja *cannot afford* to go to the same length as Bhāskara and *deny* the co-existence of a purely material principle called Prakṛti, though it may be subject to Brahman and act as its 'body' (यस्याव्यक्तं शरीरम्). Rāmānuja frankly admits the existence of Prakṛti :

न वयमव्यक्तं तत्परिणामविशेषांश्च स्वरूपतो **नाभ्युपगच्छामः** । अपि तु, परमपुरुषशरीरतया तदात्मकत्वविरहेण । तथानभ्युपगमादेव तन्त्रसिद्धप्रक्रियानिराकरणम् ।

(*Śrībhāṣya*, i. 4.3)

---

6. पित्रादिदृष्टान्तानामयं खलु निष्कृष्टोऽर्थः—यत्पित्राद्युपभुक्तमन्नं तच्छरीरभूतं पुत्रादिगताचेतनांशोपादानं भवतीति । पक्षान्तरस्यासंभवात् । (*NS*, p. 197)

The so-called Brahmopādānatva, on his view, is really on a par with the procreation of a son (i.e. his body) by his father or the emergence of nails and hair from the body nourished by the soul :

अपादानत्वमेवास्य यद्युपादानता भवेत् ।
अंगीकृतं तत्पितृवन्नैव विश्वात्मना भवः ॥ (*AV* i.4.11)

The position of Rāmānuja uttimately boils down to Kevalanimittakāraṇavāda of Brahman, so far as the Brahma-caitanya is concerned and all talk of Abhinnanimittopādāna, indulged in by him and his school, turns out to be *a mere terminological exaggeration* and flourish. The point is fully brought out by Jayatīrtha in a searching analysis and criticism of Rāmānuja's position :

अत्र कश्चित् 'प्रकृतिश्चे' त्यादीनि सूत्राणि ब्रह्मणो जगदुपादानतया व्याख्याय सूत्रतात्पर्यमेवमाह—परमसूक्ष्माचित्प्रधानशरीरं ब्रह्म 'योऽव्यक्ते तिष्ठन्' 'यस्याव्यक्तं शरीर' मित्यादिश्रुतिप्रसिद्धम् । तथा च, **ब्रह्माधिष्ठितं ब्रह्मात्मकं प्रधानं जगदुपादानमिति ब्रह्मैव जगदुपादानतयाङ्गीक्रियत इति** । तं प्रत्याह—**अपादानत्वमेवेति** ।

एवं हि वदता, पितुरिव पुत्रजन्मनि, जगदुत्पत्तौ ब्रह्मणोऽप्यपायावधित्वलक्षणमेवोपादानत्वमिष्टं स्यात् । सर्वंथा निर्विकारस्य ब्रह्मणो विकारिप्रधानशरीरकस्य तदधिष्ठातृत्वेनोपादानतया उदितत्वात् । **एवंभूतं चोपादानत्वं ब्रह्मणोऽस्माभिरप्यंगीकृतमेवेति नात्रास्माकं प्रद्वेषः ।**

नन्वंगीकृतं चेदुपादानत्वं ब्रह्मणः कथं तर्हि तन्निराकरणमित्यत आह—नत्विति । शुद्धचैतन्यस्यैव ब्रह्मणो विश्वात्मना भवो **भास्करा**द्यंगीकृतो नास्माभिरंगीक्रियते अतस्तन्निराकरणमुपपन्नमेवेति ।

अत्रायमभिसंधिः—यद्यपि परव्युत्पादितं ब्रह्मणो जगदुपादानत्वं **नास्माकमर्थतो विरोधि, तथापि नैतेषां सूत्राणामर्थः** । तथाहि—किमत्रास्य व्युत्पादनस्य कृत्यम्? न तावद्भास्करस्येव निमित्तोपादानभेदनिराकरणम्; **प्रधानस्योपादानतयाङ्गीकृतत्वात्**। विकारिवस्त्वधिष्ठातृत्वमेव मुख्यमुपादानत्वमिति चेन्न । लोकविरोधात् । लोकव्यवहारानुसारेणैव हि परीक्षकैर्लक्षणं कार्यम् । न स्वाभिप्रायेण लोकव्यवहारो नियन्तव्यः ॥ (*NS*, i.4.p. 197 b)[7]

---

7. "Here, Rāmānuja having interpreted the Sūtras "Prakṛtiśca...... (*BS* i. 4. 23) in terms of Brahman's material causality of the universe, has explained the import of the Sūtras as follows : Brahman has for its body the most subtle insentient matter. This is supported by the Śrutis "He who remaining in unmanifested Matter" Whose body is insentient unmanifested matter" etc. Thus, insofar as Pradhāna (Matter) which is ensouled by Brahman and is controlled by Brahman happens to be the material cause of the universe, it is accepted by us that Brahman itself is the material Cause. This view is rebutted (by Madhva) with the words—"If by material cause..." (as above).

The position of Śrīkaṇṭha and other (Brahma) Śaktipariṇāmavādins like Nimbārka, Vallabha and others, is hardly better. Insofar as this (Sat)-Śakti of Brahman, which according to these writers, is the immediate stuff of the Pariṇāma is distinguished from the soul-part of Brahman conceived as Cidānandātmaka, the latter ceases to be the real substratum of the change. It is the Sacchakti, Śakti or energy (or 'body' as Rāmānuja would call it) that turns out to be the *real* and immediate *material cause* of the world. Even this is a far cry from actual and immediate cent-per-cent Upādānatva or Pāriṇāmitva of Brahman. Thus, in most cases, the so-called Upādānatva of Brahman through Sakti or Sat-śakti, as the case may be, turns out to be nothing more than an "Apādānatva" i.e. अपायावधित्वलक्षणम् 'acceptance of Brahman as the residual spirit' that remains unaffected and untransforming in any given instance of change taking place in its tenement. This point also is convincingly established by Jayatīrtha :

By saying so, the nature of the material causality of Brahman in the birth of the world would be nothing more than its being the residual limit of separation or evolution of matter from God, as that of a father in the birth of his son. For it is accepted by Rāmānuja that the material causality of Brahman which is absolutely without personal modification and which has the transforming Prakṛti as its body, eonsists in it being merely the superintending principle of the transformation of Prakṛti. Such a kind of material causality is readily accepted by us also. We have no quarrel with it.

If that be so, why do you criticize it ? We answer—We do not accept the transformation of Brahman (*as such*) which is pure consciousness, into the form of the world, as accepted by Bhāskara and others. Hence its refutation is appropriate.

The point is this : Even though the material causality of Brahman with regard to the world, *as made out by Rāmānuja, is not in substance opposed to our position, still it cannot be accepted as the purport of these Sūtras in question.* For, let us ask, what is the point in elucidating this view here under these Sūtras ? It cannot be, as in the case of Bhāskara, the repudiation of the distinction between an efficient and a material cause, so far as Brahman is concerned. For, Rāmānuja accepts Prakṛti as the *material cause.* (Otherwise, there is no reason for him to admit the existence of Prakṛti *as such.*) If it is said on his behalf that 'material cause' primarily means that which controls and superintends the transforming stuff, we have to point out that such a definition of a material cause cannot be accepted as it is opposed to accepted usage of the term. Philosophers should propound their definitions in accordance with recognized usages of the world. They should not restrain the accepted usages according to their own will and pleasure or fancy" (Tr.).

अथ मतम्—द्विरूपं हि ब्रह्माभ्युपगम्यते, अनन्तानन्दचिदात्मकं सदात्मकं चेति। तत्राद्येन रूपेण निमित्तं द्वितीयेनोपादानम् । अतो न कश्चिद्दोषः। निर्विकारित्वं चिच्छक्तिविषयत्वाददूषणम् । तेन सच्छक्तिकं ब्रह्म परिणामीत्यंगीकारे न युक्तिविरोधोऽपि ० ० ० ।

यदि ब्रह्मणः सद्‌भागेन परिणामश्चिद्‌भागेन निर्विकारित्वमंगीक्रियते, तदा वक्तव्यम् । तयोर्भागयोरभेदो, भेदाभेदो वा ? न तावदभेदः । द्वयोरपि परिणामित्वापत्त्या भागद्वयकल्पनावैयर्थ्यात् । नापि भेदाभेदौ । अभेदेन संकरप्रसंगात् । भेदोऽभेदकार्यं निरुणद्धीति चेत्किं तर्ह्यभेदेनाप्रयोजकेन ? तस्माद्‌भागयोरत्यन्तभेद एवांगीकार्यः । ततः किमित्यत आह—'यो भाग' इति ।

परस्परमत्यन्तभिन्ने द्वे वस्तुनी । तत्रैकं निर्विकारं जगन्निमित्तमेव । अपरं परिणामि जगदुपादानमेवेत्यंगीकारे, नेश्वरस्य केवलानिमित्तत्ववादिनामस्माकं कश्चिद्विरोधः । निर्विकारस्य जगन्निमित्ततयास्माभिरीश्वरत्वेन, परिणामिनो जगदुपादानस्य प्रधानत्वेन चांगीकृतत्वात् ॥ अत्र 'यो भाग' इति पराभ्युपगमेनोक्तम् । स्वमतेन तु 'यद्वस्तु' इति ज्ञातव्यम् ।[8]

(*NS*, p. 200)

This criticism covers every shade of Brahmapariṇāmavāda, through aspects, modes or powers cansidered as essential organic parts of Brahman.

Review of Vivartavāda

As for Vivartavāda, it is, strictly speaking, no theory of causation at all, as it does not accept any true effect that has got to be accounted for,

8. If you hold—"There are two aspects of Brahman,—one that is essentially blissful and of the nature of consciousness, the other of the nature of existence (*sat*). It is efficient cause in its first aspect and material cause in its second aspect. The immutability of Brahman is thus to be understood with reference to its first aspect. There is no clash with logic in thus holding that Brahman in its aspect of Sat transforms itself into the material world..."

The advocates of such a position will have to say if these two aspects are identical with each other or are partly different and partly identical. They cannot be identical, as both will have to transform. Nor can they be different and identical. For at least in respect of identity there will be the same nemesis. If it is argued that the difference would prevent the identity from bringing about the said nemesis, why not dispense with the identity that is *so palpably powerless against the difference* ?

Therefore, it must be conceded that the two aspects are entirely different. It comes to this that there are two different entities, one of which is essentially immutable and acting as the operative cause alone of the universe. The other one is liable to transformation and acts as the material cause of the world. If this be so, we, who are advocates of the view that 'God is the operative cause only of the universe' have no reason to quarrel with you. For according to us God is that which is immutable and is the efficient cause of the world. What actually transforms and acts as the material cause of the world is designated by us as 'Pradhāna' (matter). In the above discussion, the term "part" or "aspect" should be understood to have been used from the point of view of the other party. From the Siddhāntin's point of view the proper term would be 'entity'.

but only an appearance. Quite apart from this, there is the difficulty of *accounting for* the obscuration of Brahman by Ajñāna, which is the root-cause of the appearance of the world. There is again greater diffiulty than even in the Pariṇāmavāda interpretation, in reconciling the promissory statement of एकविज्ञानेन सर्वविज्ञानम् with the illustration of clay etc. and the requirements of *real* Vivartavāda :

आरोपितत्वं तु एकस्यापि मृण्मयस्यैकस्मिन् मृत्पिण्डे नास्ति, किमुत सर्वस्य ? युक्त्या समर्थ्यत इति चेत्; तर्हि विवादास्पदत्वेन दृष्टान्तानुपपत्तेः । 'लौकिकपरीक्षकाणां यस्मिन्नर्थे बुद्धिसाम्यं स दृष्टान्त' इति हि न्यायविदः[9] । *NS*, i. 4.5. p. 226)

It would be truer to say from the Vivarta standpoint that the knowledge of the One *sublates* or *puts an end* to the knowledge of the many, rather than that it *produces* or gives rise to any such knowledge (Cf. the wording: अश्रुतं श्रुतं **भवति** । अमतं मतं **भवति**). There is not merely terminological inexactitude. The expressions used by Uddālaka are capable of suggesting a different and more sensible interpretation. There is nothing to show that Uddālaka was trying to equate the *many* with the *unreal.* The unreal is something which has been mistaken for another : अध्यासो नामातस्मिंस्तद्बुद्धिः (Śaṅkara, *BSB*, i.1. 1). But the "many" in the promissory statement includes also things which have not at all been brought within the scope of Śvetaketu's understanding or *misunderstanding* : **अश्रुतं** श्रुतं **भवति** In any case, the illustrations of clay etc., would appear to assume the reality of effects,—the connecting link between the One and the many being nothing more than a resemblance; as actual cause-and-effect relation is *unsustainable, for reasons already explained.* Clay is never the Vivartopādāna of pots. Since no causal relation could be made out among the pairs named in the text without distorting the actual purport of the terms of the text, or glossing over or ignoring some of them like *eka*, *maṇi*, *piṇḍa*, and also asserting a

9. "There is no question of superimposition even in the case of a single pot upon a single lump of clay. *Where then is the quastion* of regarding all the objects made of clay being superimpositions on *one* lump of clay? The Vivartavāda interpretation of this illustration is, therefore, untenable. If the Advaitin should say *that he is going to establish such a position by reasoning*, our reply is that in that case, it cannot with propriety be cited as an *illustration*; *as it is still a disputed point.* For as the Logicians point out, an example in a syllogistic reasoning is that about which there is consensus among laymen and philosophers. (In the present case, it does not seem to be so.)"

palpable travesty of a causal *argument in the last instance of the nail-scissors, the interpretations* of Śaṅkara and Rāmānuja are misplaced.

The Advaitic theory of Abhinnanimittopādānatva of Brahman has been discussed by Vyāsatītha in his *Nym* in the light of the exposition by Prakāśātman in his *Vivaraṇa.* According to the *Vivaraṇa,* there are *three ways* in which the position that Brahman is the material cause of the universe may be explained : (1) that Brahman conjointly with Māyā is the material cause (*upādāna*) of the world, like the two strands of a thread which go to make the string. (2-3) Māyā which may be viewed as a power of Brahman or as dependent on Brahman is the material cause and Brahman through its association or connection with it, is also, in a way, the upādāna *through such Māyā.* Prakāśātman further explains that on the first view, inasmuch as Brahman *and* Māyā would both conjointly constitute the material cause of the world, there would be no violation of the Nirvikāra Śruti which should be understood with reference to Brahman in its state of isolation (i.e. when *not* in conjunction with Māyā). In the other two cases, also, the Nirvikāra Śruti is to be understood to refer to Brahman when it is *not* colored by Māyā or is *not* acting through Māyā.

Vyāsatīrtha criticises all these explanations. He points out that in the first case, like the two threads conjointly going to make the string, Brahman also would be *as much an upādāna or transforming cause as māyā* and there would be no point in claiming Brahman alone to be "Nirvikāra" in the process. Moreover, as both Brahman and Māyā are the material causes of the world, we should expect to find the essential characteristics of Brahman, viz., Pāramārthika reality, consciousness and bliss in the effect, viz. the world : It cannot be said that only a superposition of the essential character of the upādāna is expected in the effect and not the actual presence of those characteristics. In that case, how is the Advaitin justified in claiming that the world actually *possesses* the character of *anirvacanīyatvam* as a product of Māyā or Avidyā ? If he should say that the world does not possess the character of Pāramārthika reality because it is not solely the product of Brahman (*sanmātropādānakam*), then by the same token, he should refuse to call the world *anirvacanīya* because it is *not solely produced by Anirvacanīya Māyā* ! Again, if Brahman associated with Māyā is regarded as changing and Brahman unqualified is to be accepted as unchanging (*nirvikāra*), the question will be 'Is the qualified entity (*viśiṣṭa*) to be designated as Brahman or not ? If the qualified entity *is* Brahman, it could hardly be unchanging ! If it is not to be regarded as Brahman, the question of regarding Brahman as Upādāna would simply *not* arise. Further, if the transformation of the Viśiṣṭa is admitted then such transformation would be of the same order of reality as the substratum, which sould go against the requirements of the Vivarta theory, in which the product of Vivarta has a lesser reality than its substratum. It cannot also be held that real transformation takes place in the Viśiṣṭa while only an illusory transformation takes place in the Viśeṣya (the substratum). For, in order to speak of a Vivarta at all, there should be some illusory transformation in the Śuddha also. Hence it would be difficult to say that the Śuddha is absolutely Nirvikāra. If it is said that there is no *real* Vikāra in the Śuddha, then, it would be equally wrong to speak of any actual transformation in the Viśiṣṭa too, since it is primarily in the Viśeṣaṇa (Māyā) that any real transformation is taking place. As for the third view that Brahman is to be regarded as Upādāna through Māyā and *not directly*, like the constituent parts (*aṁśa*) of threads forming the cloth, Vyāsatīrtha shows that the analogy is misplaced. The constituent parts (*aṁśa*) of the thread are really the material cause of the cloth. But Brahman is not the constituent cause of Māyā. How then could Brahman be regarded as the constituent cause of the world through Māyā ?

It would be equally unavailing to define 'Upādānatvam' as being the substratum of an illusory change. The term "Upādānā" is nowhere used in philosophical writings in this sense. No one would designate "clay", which is the material cause of pot, as the substratum of the illusory appearance of the pot ! Nor is the shell, the substratum of an illusory appearance of silver spoken of as the 'material cause' of silver, If the Advaitin proposes to define Upādānatvam in a novel way which has no relation to the connotation of the term as other philosophers understand it, he may please himself with such a diversion. But it will not make Brahman the material cause of the world in the accepted sense of the term ! Finally, Vyāsatīrtha points out that the Advaitic position that Īśvara is efficient cause (*nimitta*) of the world, Māyā the material cause (*upādāna*) and Śuddha-Brahman the substratum of the illusory appearance of the world makes the thesis of "Abhinnanimittopādānatva" of 'Brahman' so eagerly sought to be read into the Prakṛtyadhikaraṇa of the *Brahmasūtras*, by Śaṅkara, pointless.

Madhva thus establishes his point that Brahmopādānatva theory is logically and textually unsustainable, and philosophically unsound. We have to stick to Kevala-nimittakāraṇatva only. This will not land us is a plurality of causes. The clear fact that Prakṛti is a metaphysically dependent principle like Space and Time (though eternal), will effectively bar the possibility of plurality of causes. This point has been established by Madhva under BS ii.1.15 *et. seq.*

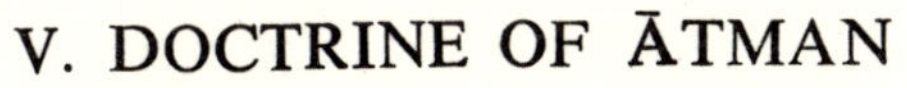

V. DOCTRINE OF ĀTMAN

CHAPTER XXIX

ESSENCE OF SELFHOOD

SOULS are conceived in Madhva's system as finite centres of conscious experience, each with a unique essence of its own. The essence of individuality is that one finite centre of experience cannot possess, *as its own immediate* experience, the experience of another. It is this non-transferable immediacy of experience that distinguishes one self from another, in spite of their possessing certain similar characteristics:

चैतन्यावच्छिन्नमैक्यं अनुसन्धानैकप्रमाणकम् । अनुसंधानं नाम भोगसमाख्यातः स्वीयतया दुःखादिसाक्षात्कारोऽभिमतः । (*NS*, p. 507)

Each has a specific content of consciousness, reality and bliss and constitutes a focalization which is nowhere exactly repeated in nature. Their very *raison d'etre* is to be distinct personalities or exclusive focalizations of a common universe. The best definition of self is that given by Jayatīrtha: कर्तृत्वभोक्तृत्वशक्त्युपेतं साकारं देहादिव्यतिरिक्तं रूपमहमिति साक्षिसिद्धम् (*NS*, p. 633). This refers to a dynamic personality endowed with the triple properties of will, cognition and activity. The basis of individuality is to be found in the uniqueness of 'personality', which is a blending of consciousness, experience and works, in proportion to its intrinsic stature (*yogyatā*). It is the core of all hedonistic, ethical and spiritual activities of man :

अहमित्येव यो वेद्यः स जीव इति कीर्तितः ।
स दुःखी स सुखी चैव स पात्रं बन्धमोक्षयोः ॥[1]

The nature of the souls, at its best, is said to be one of unalloyed bliss and pure intelligence. It is essentially free from

1. "He who enjoys the happiness and suffers the ills of life, who is subject to bondage and release is the Jiva. He is indeed in a position to know himself in all his states as 'I am'".

any kind of misery or pain; स्वतश्चिदानन्दात्मकस्य जीवस्य (*UKt*), though subject to a natural gradation of intelligence and bliss in a cosmic hierarchy of selves and subject always to the Supreme, in bondage *and in release*. The sense of misery, which is bondage, is external to their essence and is brought about by a *real* though *misplaced sense of independence of initiative and conduct* :

तस्य **अपरायत्तत्वावभासो**ऽविद्यानिमित्तको भ्रमः[2] । (*NS*, p. 26)

जीवस्य सुखरूपस्य न दुःखं किंचिदिष्यते ।
अतो मनोऽभिमानेन दुःखीभवति नान्यथा ॥
(*BT* XI. 23. 54)

The question has been raised : "If each individual possesses in finite and material outlines, the perfection of consciousness, it seems to become a mere point of existence when it casts off the body and enters release. Will there not be overlapping of souls there ? If not, what is it that distinguishes one from the other ?" (Radhakrishnan, *I. Phil.* II. p. 719). In other words, what is it that constitutes the essence of selfhood, if we are to subtract from it, as we should, in the state of release, all the content and vestures that enfilm its essence and are obviously incidental and non-fundamental to its being or makeup in each case ? "We seem to be reduced to an abstraction of pure being or intelligence,—a monadism. It is merely then an *assumption* to hold that the single colorless unit, called 'self', is *different* in each individual".

It is easy to ask such a question or pass such *ex cathedra* judgments. But it is not easy to give a thoroughly convincing answer to it, here and now *sub-specie alterni*. Indeed, we should be in possession of the highest form of self-realization, which is the goal of religion and philosophy, if we should be able, *here and now*, to place our finger on what constitutes individuality and define it in precise terms. That will be unravelling the greatest of all mysteries, that has remained inscrutable for ages. We should cease to be embodied, if we *catch* our *selves* in their pristine essence of selfhood unconditioned by the floating perceptions

---

2. Dasgupta (*His. of I. Phil. iv.* p. 113) unhappily has misread and *misinterpreted this passage from the NS*. Krishnakant Chaturvedi (*Dvait Siddhānt Kā Tāttvik Anuśīlan*, p. 175) misreads "*Aparāyattatvāvabhāsaḥ*" as "Parāyattatvāvabhāsaḥ" which makes no sense.

of heat and cold, light and shade, pleasures and pain. If the Advaitin can silence the objection to Avidyā with the lofty remark that "if we can understand the relation of Ātman to Avidyā, we must be beyond the two"[3], the Dvaitin could as well plead with equal propriety that it would not be possible to deny the doctrine of intrinsic plurality of selves and their natural gradation, so long as we have no means of realizing the true essence of selfhood here and no means of proving that there is no basis of distinction in release. Madhva does not, after all, lay stress merely on sensations, feeling and bondage, in support of his doctrine of plurality of selves, as if these were the only movements of the real. It does not require much argument to show that the real nature of the souls and their true essence of individuality are now hidden from us by some mysterious veil of ignorance called Avidyā[4] (Svaguṇācchādikā). Thanks to the light of Scripture and the exercise of reason and introspection, we may however expect to lift the veil ever so little and to take a peep into the truth of things and the vision might be enlarged as we go up in the scale of discipline and Aparokṣa. We can arrive at some kind of working solution of the problem now by examining the evidences of Scripture and advancing logically from the known to the unknown. This is the utmost that the best of us can do and we need not despair or despise this method, so long as we have no other means of approach open to us. This individuality of experience and the impossibility of our entering into others' experiences with the same fourth dimensional inwardness, *as our own* are sufficient proofs of the basic distinction of Selves :

एवं व्यवस्थया नानात्मानः सिद्धाः। न ह्यस्माभिः धर्मभेदो वा भिन्नाश्रयधर्मभेदो वा व्यवस्थेत्यंगीक्रियते । अपितु, सुखदुःखानुसन्धानभावाभावरूपव्यवस्थाया अंगीकृतत्वात् । अनुसंधानं नाम अनेन सुखेनाहं सुखी इत्यनुभवः । (*Vādaratnāvali* ii)

The Nyāya-Vaiśeṣikas grounded their doctrine of multiplicity of selves in the observed fact of the divergence of individual

3. Radhakrishnan, *I. Phil.* ii, p. 577.

4. उपपादयिष्यते हि ज्ञानानन्दादिरूपोऽयं जीव इति 'पुंस्त्वादिवत्' इत्यादिना । तद्भावानुपलब्धिश्च अनुभवसिद्धा । तेनावगम्यतेऽस्ति किमप्यावरकं, येनावृतः स्वप्रकाशचैतन्यरूपोऽपि नात्मनः तत्त्वं वेद । (*NS* i. 1.1)

experience of happiness and suffering in life : *Vyavasthāto nānā*. Citsukha criticized their concept of 'Vyavasthā' on the ground that it is inconclusive. If 'Vyavasthā' stands for variability in the experience of pleasure and pain among different persons, such variability is equally to be seen in one and the same person, sametimes. Happiness and misery are also experienced by the some person at the same time in different parts of his own person. Mutual opposition or conflict (*vadhyaghātakabhāva*) between, the experiences of pleasure and pain, to be effective, must be present in a common theatre of operation which cannot be thought of in respect of individuals having different bodies. For these reasons, the Logicians' argument in support of plurality of selves on the basis of 'Sukhaduḥkhavyavasthā' is inconclusive. Madhva breaks through this counter-argument of Citsukha by defining 'Vyavasthā' in a more inward sense of 'Anusandhāna' or the identifying experientiality in respect of one's own experience of happiness and suffering in life, which every individual in the world is normally in a position to have and is capable of having, as his distinctive feature. चैतन्यैक्येऽनुसन्धानं प्रमाणं नैव चापरम् ।

(*AV* iii. 2. 18)

This criterion of 'Anusandhāna' is the *sine qua non* of identity of being (*svarūpaikya*) in a sentient person :

चैतन्यावच्छिन्नं ऐक्यं अनुसन्धानैकप्रमाणकम् । (*NS*, p. 507)

It is this identifying experientiality in respect of one's innermost experiences of happiness and suffering that determines identity of consciousness or personal identity and no other factor. Where such identifying experientiality is *not* present, the so-called oneness of our selves that one sometimes speaks of in some expansive mood has to be put down as mere rhetorical flourish (*nāmamātram*).

Jayatīrtha points out that the absence of such 'Anusandhāna' in respect of one's past lives does not nullify the truth of this criterion.[5] For, it is not claimed that all sentient beings at all times have this identifying experientiality, even with respect to their own earlier experiences in the same life, let alone those of previous lives. The example of 'Jātismaras' recognized in the Yoga Śāstra is a strong proof that such *anusandhāna* is not a

5. न च प्राग्भवीयदुःखाद्यनुसन्धानमिदानीं नास्ति, अस्ति चैक्यमिति व्यभिचारः शंकनीयः । न हि वयं सदानुसंधानं ब्रूमः । (*NS* p. 507)

myth. Due allowance has to be made for the human frailty of forgetfulness and loss of memory. However, what is contended and affirmed, as Jayatīrtha says, in respect of 'anusandhāna' is that a sentient being who sometimes experiences an identifying experientiality with a being is identical with it and one who never at any time in his life does so is not identical with that being. Since identifying experientiality is the sole criterion of self-identity, it goes without saying that where it is absent self-identity too must necessarily be non-existent.

यश्चेतनो यत्स्वरूपं कदाचिदनुसन्धत्ते, स तेन अभिन्नः, यो नानुसन्धत्ते स तेन नाभिन्नः इति तदेकप्रमाणकस्य तन्निवृत्तौ निवृत्तिरेव । न च चेतनत्वं शक्यनिवर्तनम् । उभयवादिसिद्धत्वात् । **तस्मादेकतैव निवर्तते ।** (*NS*, p. 507)

The criterion of 'Anusandhāna' in respect of Caitanyaikya or oneness of being between sentients is also sufficient to rule out identity of Jīva and Brahman in Mokṣa. So far as the Jīva is concerned, it is accepted by all that he is not, here and now, in a position to experience such 'anusandhāna' in respect of his identity with the 'Nityaśuddhabuddhamuktasvabhāvam Brahma'. If that Brahman too, in its turn, is *not* experiencing its oneness with the Jīva, *it is as good as a non-existent identity.* It cannot be argued that the absence of 'anusandhāna' of his identity with Brahman by the Jīva here and now in the state of bondage is merely due to the impediment of Avidyā and is *not* due to the fact of its *not* being true. One would like to know how the Monist is so sure of this. The Dualist philosopher, on the other hand, is persuaded that the identity is not a fact because there is no identifying experientiality of it. It will be conceded that whatever may be the impediments in the way of the Jīva experiencing such identity, now, Brahman which is all-knowing is under no such predicament or impediment. It should, therefore, be experiencing such identity. *But it is clear from the Lord's pronouncement in Gītā* XV. 18 *that the Supreme Brahman is fully conscious of its difference and distinction from the individual self.*[6] It is no answer to this objection that Kṛṣṇa of the Gītā is only 'Īśvara' (God). For, we have no evidence of a Being higher than Kṛṣṇa to be called 'Brahman'. For Kṛṣṇa Himself assures us in the same context that He is the highest Puruṣa known as

6. See बहूनि मे व्यतीतानि जन्मानि तव चार्जुन ।
तान्यहं वेद सर्वाणि न त्वं वेत्थ परंतप ॥ (*Gītā*, IV. 5)

'Paramātmā' (XV.18). Even in Śaṅkara's philosophy, Īśvara is deemed to be *omniscient*. An identity which is neither felt nor experienced by an omniscient being can hardly be a fact. Madhva has not left us in any doubt as to the true nature of state of the souls in Mokṣa. They are not formless beings or colorless points but atomic individuals with their own specific forms and lineaments. They have spiritual bodies of their own with appropriate organs (See *BS* iv. 4. 10, 16 and *BSPC*. Vol. III, pp. 790-94) and have names and forms which are beyond the knowledge of those still in bondage.[7]

7. मुक्तानां संज्ञापि नान्यैर्ज्ञायते शास्त्रं विना ।
(Madhva's Commentry on *BrhUp* iv. 4)
अज्ञैरनवगतान्यपि विष्णौ स्थितानां मुक्तानां भिन्नान्येव नामरूपाणि सन्त्येव ।
(Madhva's commentary on *Praśna Up*. vi)

CHAPTER XXX

METAPHYSICAL DEPENDENCE OF SOULS

IN SPITE of their intrinsic nature of consciousness and bliss, the souls, as finite beings, are in a state of absolute dependence and limitation at all times, *in bondage and release*. Release is only from the fetters which prevent the realisation of their true natures and their metaphysical dependence on Brahman. *Dependence is not a passing chapter in their lives*. The eightfold determinations of the cosmos are simply the *expression* of such dependence. Such dependence is most vividly felt in the prenatal and post-mortem conditions of life,

यस्माद् गर्भस्थस्य जीवस्येश्वरत्वं नास्ति, अतो निधनानन्तरं नरकादिगमनान्न विद्यते ।

(*BT*, x.37.23)

as well as in Pralaya, dreams, deep sleep and swoons. It is only in the *Waking* state of *sthiti* that man is found to arrogate independence to himself. He lies helpless and weak at other times, both before and after. It may, therefore, be concluded that even this temporary assumption of independence is misplaced.

विष्णोरधीनं प्राक् सृष्टेः तथैव च लयादनु ।
अस्य सत्त्वप्रवृत्त्यादि विशेषेणाधिगम्यते ॥
स्वातंत्र्यं स्थितिकाले तु कथंचित् बुद्धिमोहतः ।
प्रतीयमानमपि तु तस्मान्नैवेति गम्यते ॥ (*BT*, ii.9.33)

तन्वा स्वस्वामिसंबन्धः प्रपंचोऽस्य शरीरिणः ।
वस्तुतोऽसौ न चैवास्ति परमात्मवशे यतः
तन्वादिकः तथाप्येष ह्यभिमानात् प्रदृश्यते ॥

(Commentary on *MandUp*)

The description of impending death in *ChanUp* vi.15, where all psychophysical powers are merged in their causes one after the other is another graphic example of the soul's absolute dependence. The very fact of its achieving freedom from the shackles of Prakṛti by the grace of God is an unmistakable proof of its continued dependence on Him, *even in release.* It would be preposterous to expect the essential metaphysical dependence of finite beings on the Independent to be cut off at any time. It cannot be destroyed without destroying the very constitution of the self as a Pratibimba of the Infinite. The relationship of Bimbapratibimba between Brahman and Jīvas, being the result of Avidyā, in Advaita, is taken to be destroyed in release along with the extinction of individuality as such. But the same relation being Svābhāvika and *not due to Upādhis,* in Madhva's view, is not, therefore, liable to destruction in Mokṣa. Hence its persistence in release also along with the persistence of individuality, shorn of all obscuring elements. Madhva, therefore, holds that even in the state of Mokṣa the realization of personal bliss, to the full, is dependent on the will of the Supreme :

अज्ञानां ज्ञानदो विष्णुर्ज्ञानिनां मोक्षदश्च सः ।
आनन्ददश्च मुक्तानां स एवैको जनार्दनः ॥ (*AV*, i.1.1)

The limitations of the soul are, therefore, partly intrinsic and partly extrinsic—

पराधीनश्च बद्धश्च स्वल्पज्ञानसुखेहितः ।
अल्पशक्तिः सदोषश्च जीवात्मा * * * (*BT*, i.2.22)

The extrinsic ones are terminable. The intrinsic remain with the self. The limitations of the self are, in general expressed in and through the eightfold determinations of cosmic life, which includes life in Mokṣa also, to which they are subject. Though essentially uncreated, they are, nevertheless, associated from eternity with a series of material coils known as Āvaraṇas. They are : (1) Liṅga-śarīra or the subtle body or psycho-physical mechanism of sixteen elements. This carries the causal potentialities that lead to a number of future lives, in the fulness of time; (2) Prārabdhakarma or Karma which has begun to bear fruit; (3) Kāma or desire which is the seed of activity; and (4) positive ignorance (भावरूपाज्ञान) or Avidyā which is both *real* and destructible. This is *not* simply a negative element

(ज्ञानाभाव)[1]. It must be recognized as a positive force in view of its being a product of Tamoguṇa encircling the soul and getting destroyed by Aparokṣajñāna. The essence of this Ignorance is the assumption of independence and initiative and looking upon the accessories given to the self as *his own*, in his own right :

तस्यापरायत्तत्वावभासोऽविद्यानिमित्तको भ्रमः । (*NS*, p. 26)

The locus of this Ignorance is the self. Such ignorance is not incompatible with the self-luminous character of the self, inasmuch as the Supreme Being which is Independent and All-powerful (अघटितघटनापटीयान्) obscures a part of the self's nature by means of Prakṛti. This positive nescience has two aspects—Jīvācchādikā and Paramācchādikā. The former conceals the true nature of the self (*qua* Pratibimba and metaphysically dependent on Brahman) from itself (*Svaguṇācchādikā*) whereby man comes to assume independence of initiative and believes himself and the world around to be self-subsisting :

द्वितीया प्रकृतिः प्रोक्ता तद्रूपा हि गुणास्त्रयः ।
तेषां संपातजो भावो ममाहमिति या मतिः ॥ (*BT* ii.9.2)

Indeed, it is the assumption of this independence that is the root-cause of bondage : प्रमादात्मकत्वात् बन्धस्य (*BSB*). The marvellous hold of this ignorance on people which makes them oblivious of their own weaknesses, while being alive to the shortcomings of others, is effectively portrayed in the *Viṣṇurahasya* :

परेषां रोगहर्तारः स्वरोगं न विजानते ।
एतन्मायाबलं विष्णोर्महाशक्तेर्महात्मनः ॥

It would, thus, be seen that dependence is the distinctive mark of the finite *at all times*. It may find expression in one or more of the eightfold determinations of cosmic development. It is for this reason that Madhva brings the eternal substances

1. Dasgupta (*I. Phil.* iv, p. 159) is not correct in stating that ignorance (*avidyā*) in Madhva's system "is a *negative substance* which, by God's will veils the natural intelligence of all". He has misread and misinterpreted the passage from the *NS* relating to this topic. Dr. K. Narain (*Critique of Mādhva Refutation of Śaṅkara Vedānta* (p. 158) also repeats the *same mistake.*

Read: अतःकामकर्माद्यतिरिक्तं मायाविद्याप्रकृतिरित्यादिशब्दाभिधेयं अनाद्येव किमपि द्रव्यमंगीकर्तव्यम् । (*NS*)

also under the causal scheme of Brahman, by means of the doctrine of Parādhīnaviśeṣāpati.[2]

The second type of Ignorance prevents the souls from realizing the true nature of their dependence on God and their intrinsic resemblance to Him. Such ignorance is beginningless but has an end. There is no logical impropriety in conceiving of an end to what may be beginningless and conversely of an endless continuity to what may have a beginning,—e.g. Mokṣa. These are facts accepted by reason and supported by Śrutis :

अनादिमायया सुप्तो यदा जीवः प्रबुध्यते (*MandUp* ii.7)

The source of bondage is also in the same way to be put down ultimately to the will of God. There is no other explanation of the beginningless association of ignorance obscuring the selves except the mysterious will of Brahman :

अतो बन्धोऽपि तत एवेत्यर्थः—

सतां विमुक्तिदाद्विष्णोर्मुक्तिर्यद्यभ्युपेयते ।
बन्धोऽपि तत एव स्यात् यस्मादेकः तयोः प्रभुः ॥
(*BT*, X.94.16)

बन्धको भवपाशेन भवपाशाच्च मोचकः ।
कैवल्यदः परं ब्रह्म विष्णुरेव सनातनः ॥[3]
(*Skānda* quoted by Śrīdhara)

It is the will of the Lord that the souls shall know Him and realize their respective selfhood only by cleansing themselves of the impurities of Prakṛti and the distractions of Avidyā, after a long arduous process of physical, intellectual and moral effort and spiritual discipline. The seed must be planted in the earth before it could sprout and develop into a fruit-tree. The accessories af Liṅgadeha, Prārabdha-Karma, etc. are just the material environment provided by God to help the Jīvas to

---

2. The dependence of eternal substances on God, is accepted by Vedānta Deśika also : नित्यानां स्वरूपस्थित्योः परमात्मसंकल्पानुविधायित्वं नाम तन्नित्येच्छासिद्धत्वम् ।

He defines such dependence as the possibility of reversal when it no longer pleases God to let them be : तच्च अनिच्छासंभवे निवर्तयितुं शक्यत्वमात्रम् । (Commentary on *RGB* p. 9. Ananda Press Edn., Madras).

3. "If it is accepted that release is conferred on good souls by the giver of Mokṣa, it must be admitted that bondage also is due to Him as the Lord of both is the same."

"Viṣṇu is the eternal Brahman, the giver of Mokṣa. He is the one who binds the souls with the bonds of rebirth and frees them".

unfold themselves. This is indeed the *raison d'etre* of creation according to the *Viṣṇurahasya* :

अनादिकर्मणा बद्धा जीवा नित्यं ह्यनन्तशः ।
लिंगदेहयुवाः सर्वे पतिता मूर्च्छिता इव ॥
यदि ते स्थूलदेहेन युता न स्युरिमेऽखिलाः
कथं कर्माणि कुर्वीरन् विष्णुभक्तिपराङ्मुखाः
अपूर्णभक्तयस्ते वा कथं मोक्षमवाप्नुयुः ॥[4] (*Chap.* V)

There is, thus, no problem at all of the first Fall of Man, in Madhva's philosophy. *The question is only of the Ascent of Man by degrees*, after he has qualified himself steadily through sincere effort to realize the full force and content of his personality. Not having possessed the freedom and purity of the Supreme at any time in their lives, or having been "in any way sharers in the Divine nature", the question does not also arise for Madhva, of how the souls come to "lose these and transfer themselves to the rule of Karma" (Radhakrishnan, *I. Phil.* ii, p. 695). "Rāmānuja holds that neither reason nor Scripture can tell us how Karma got the souls into its power, because, the Cosmic process is beginningless" (*ibid.* 695-696). It is true enough that the cosmic process is beginningless; but, it is the souls that forge their own chains due to the basic nature of their Svarūpa.

4. "Countless are the souls bound by beginningless karma. They lie in the womb of Prakṛti, wrapped in their Liṅgaśarīra as in a swoon. If they are not pulled out of their sleep and provided with gross bodies, sense organs, etc., how can they perform Karmas devoted to the Lord; and unless their devotion expresses itself in concrete forms and reaches fulfilment, how can they attain Mokṣa ?"

CHAPTER XXXI

SELF-LUMINOSITY OF SOULS

THE individual soul, as a sentient being, is admitted by Madhva to be self-luminous (*svaprakāśa*). It is *not merely* of the form of knowledge (*jñānasvarūpa*) but is a knower (*jñātṛ*). The conception of the self as a conscious personality is the same as it is in respect of God :

स्ववेत्ता वेदनं च स्वं स्वेन वेद्यः स केशवः ।
परस्य वेत्ता वित्तिश्च वेद्यश्चापि परैः * * * ॥ (*GT* xiii.13)

except for the fact that *even the self-luminosity of the Jīva is dependent on the Supreme*, which makes bondage possible :

जीवानां स्वप्रकाशत्वं तत्प्रसादात् स्ववेदनम् । (*GT* xiii.13)

Self-luminosity, in the Advaita, is a state of pure consciousness, without a subject-object relation : अवेद्यत्वे सति, अपरोक्षव्यवहारयोग्यत्वम् (Citsukha). But this is self-contradictory. The Ātman must be both a knowing subject (*jñātṛ*) *and the object of his own knowledge*. He should know *himself and others* and be known by them also. Jayatīrtha, therefore, rejects the Prābhākara view of the self as essentially *jaḍa*, in that it is non-intelligent, being only the *substratum of qualities like consciousness*, action, enjoyment and suffering[1]. The Bhāṭṭas, though conceding the Ātman to be both conscious and the substratum of consciousness, hold that he is not self-conscious (*sva-jñātṛ*), but is only inferred through *aham-pratyaya* (ego-consciousness). This is also rejected by Madhva, who holds that the Ātman must be self-intuiting.[2] The epistemological dogma

---

1. स च ज्ञानस्वरूपेण भिन्नत्वाज्जडः, जानामीति ज्ञानाश्रयत्वेनैव भाति, न तु ज्ञानरूपत्वेन । (*Nyāyaratnāvali*)

2. न चात्मनः स्वप्रकाशत्वे विवदितव्यम् । अहमित्यनुभवात् । न चायं मानसोऽनुभवः । तस्यापि ज्ञायमानत्वेनानुभवान्तरान्वेषणेऽनवस्थानात् । कस्यचिदनुभवस्य स्वप्रकाशत्वे, स्वात्मन

of Advaita that the subject of all knowledge cannot itself be an object of knowledge, for fear of offending the dictum of the impossibility of the subject operating on itself (*kartṛkarmabhāva-virodha*) is rejected by Madhva as unwarranted by Scripture and experience.[3] The acceptance of "Viśeṣas" in the self, enables Madhva to get over the difficulty of partial obscuration of the self's nature, in bondage, without denying the law of identity. Viśeṣa is the agency by which Madhva is able to divide consciousness from itself.

Such an explanation *will not be available to the Advaitin,* to whom Ātman is essentially colorless and aspectless (*nirviśeṣa*) so that there is bound to be great difficulty in accounting for the *temporary and partial obscuration* of ātma-svarūpa by Avidyā or Ajñāna :

एव तत् । जिज्ञासायामेवानुभवोऽनुभूयत इति न वाच्यम् । अनुभवविरोधात् । न ह्यज्ञायमानज्ञान-सद्भावे किंचिन्मानम् । न च स्वप्रकाशसंविदाश्रयतया आत्मा अवभासत इति युक्तम् । औत्तरिकानुस्मृतिसिद्धसौषुप्तिकानुभवाभावप्रसंगात् । न हि सुषुप्तावात्मातिरिक्ता संविदस्तीति संभवति । संविदात्मकत्वाच्चात्मनो न संविद इव संविदाश्रयतया प्रतीतिः । (अतः स्वप्रकाश आत्मा)

TP. i. 1. 1.

"The self-luminosity of Jīva cannot be disputed as there is the indubitable experience of the Self as 'I am'. This cannot be explained away as an experience by the mind, as the Logicians do. For, as the mental perception is also the objective content of consciousness, it would lead to a regress if we admit another consciousness of which it would be the objective content and that again of another and so on. If there is, however, some experience in the chain which is self-revealing the distinction may as well be given to the primary experience of 'I am'. It is far-fetched to argue that knowledge is revealed only when there is a desire to know that it has arisen. Such a position is unfaithful to everybody's experience. The Prābhākara view is that the self is established only as the substratum of consciousness which alone is self-evident (in respect of knowledge, knower and known). In that case one will have to forswear one's experience of one's own self in the state of dreamless sleep, given by the recollection of it immediately after one wakes up from it. There is no evidence that there is any consciousness other than the Ātman in dreamless sleep. As this Ātman is itself of the nature and essence of consciousness, there is no need for it to be presented as the *substratum of another consciousness,* even as the Saṁvid (consciousness) of the Prābhākara philosophy is not presented as the substratum of *another Saṁvid.* Thus the Svaprakāśatva (self-revealed nature) of Jīvātman is established without difficulty."

3. न च कर्तृकर्मविरोधो नामास्ति इत्यत्र किंचित् मानम्; श्रुत्यनुभवसिद्धत्वाच्च स्वदर्शनादेः । (Madhva's Commentary on *AA* II. 2. 3)

निर्विशेषे स्वयंभाते किमज्ञानावृतं भवेत् ? (*AV* i.1.1.)

निर्विशेषत्वादात्मनो नानधिगतो विशेषः। सिद्धत्वात् स्वरूपस्य, विशेषाभावाच्च नाज्ञानं कस्यचिदावरकम् । (Madhva, *Māyāvāda Khaṇḍana*)

The Śrutis also establish Ātman to be an active knower, employing terms like *Vijñātṛ* with the suffix (*tṛ*) in the active sense, which Śaṅkara is at pains to explain away as a reference to a *philosophical looking back upon the world that was* (भूतपूर्वगत्या निर्देशः). But this explanation breaks down, elsewhere, in *BṛhUp* i.4.10, where the Supreme Being is said to have known itself as "I am Brahman", when it existed all alone prior to creation in a state of blessedness. The knowability of the self must be recognized, if the pursuit of *Brahmavicāra* is to have any meaning. The plea of *kartṛkarmabhāvavirodha* is unsustainable here. We can not surrender facts to a mere dogma : नहि वस्तुपरिक्षयात् प्रक्रियापरिक्षयो बलवान्. Jayatīrtha says that the opposition of subject-object in a proposition like 'I know myself', if due merely to the way of defining objectivity in the manner of the grammarians as *Parasamavetakriyāphalaśālitvam* (or "reaping the fruit accruing from an act, inhering in another), can be overcome by redefining subject and object in such a way as to avoid the overlapping: क्रियाश्रयः कर्ता, क्रियाविषयः कर्म. The Advaitic Ātman could not be invested with any kind of self-luminosity. The idea would presuppose some objective content. Such a content may be either one's own self or an "Other". The Advaitin is prepared to concede neither. The self cannot be the object of such a luminosity. The reality of *another self* is not admitted. The only sense then in which we are entitled to speak of the Ātman as Svaprakāśa in Advaita will be that it has *no luminosity* with reference to either (*Tdyt*, p. 18b). In the absence of any objective or subject reference of luminosity, it would be just non-luminous : विषयवर्जितः प्रकाश एव न भवति (*Tdy*), which is elucidated by Jayatīrtha: आत्मा न प्रकाशः, प्रकाश्यशून्यत्वात्, घटवत्. There is no reason to make an exception in the case of the Ātman alone and claim luminosity for him even in the absence of an objective reference or content—स्यादप्येवं यद्येवं प्रमाणं स्यात्, नैतदस्ति (*Tdyt*, p. 19b).

Nothing beyond the pale of Pramāṇas could be described as real : प्रमाणाभावे सत्यत्वं न स्यादित्यस्य, प्रमाणेन विना सिद्ध्यतीत्यस्य अनुत्तरत्वात्; सिद्ध्युपायान्तरस्यानुपन्यस्तत्वात् । (*VTNt*, p. 96b)

CHAPTER XXXII

MADHVA'S THEORY OF BONDAGE : SVABHĀVĀJÑĀNAVĀDA

ACCORDING to Madhva, souls exist from eternity in the choas of a material *milieu* under the ken of God. At the conclusion of each Mahāpralaya, He brings them to the forefront of creation.[1] He has no purpose in doing so, save that of helping the souls[2] to exhaust through enjoyment (*bhoga*) the heavy load of Karma and Vāsanās lying to their credit from time immemorial and thus work out their destinies.[3] Creation is, thus, an indispensable requisite for the ripening of individual Karma and the full development of each soul. This self-development, when complete, leads the soul to its deserts. Madhva thus guarantees both the integrality of the souls, insofar as they exist from eternity as finite beings and the independence of God as their Ruler. This enables him to meet and satisfy the demands of both the moral and the religious consciousness of man.

The bonds and impurities of the souls are not, however, their essential nature (*svarūpa*), at any rate, of those of the highest order.[3a] The good among the uncreated souls lying in

---

1. *MbhTN*- I. 1-3.
2. भूत्यै निजाश्रितजनस्य हि **सृज्यसृष्टावीक्षा** बभूव । (*ibid*)
3. आत्मप्रयोजनाय स्पृहां श्रुतिरवारयत् ।
   'न प्रयोजनवत्वेने' त्यत आह जगद्गुरुः ॥ (*AV* ii. 1. 33)

अतो 'न प्रयोजनवत्त्वात्' इति हेतुं ब्रुवाणः सूत्रकारः आत्मप्रयोजनोद्देशमेव निवारितवान्, न परप्रयोजनोद्देशमपीति । श्रुतिरपि 'आप्तकामस्य का स्पृहा' इति हेतुगर्भविशेषणं प्रयुञ्जाना आत्मप्रयोजनस्पृहामेवाक्षिपति, परप्रयोजनस्पृहामभ्युपैतीति ज्ञायते । (*NS*)

Cf. 'यत्र त्रिसर्गो मृषा'—यत्रेति विशेषणान्नान्यत्र । तद्विषय एव मृषा । (*BT* i. I. 1)

3a. बलमानन्द ओजश्च सहोज्ञानमनाकुलम् ।
    स्वरूपाण्येव जीवस्य * * * ॥ (*BSB*, II.3.31)
    एतच्च सज्जीवविषयम् । (*TP*)

the Womb of Prakṛti from the beginningless past are like impure gold which has to be dug out of the rocks and mines and duly processed before it could be converted into jwellery. They are like the veins of gold and nuggets imbedded in the rocks. They can be reclaimed only after they have been crushed, washed, sifted and melted down in the crucible. The same principle applies to the other categories of souls also, all of whom are to be brought to the surface of life from the depths of Prākṛtic stupor in which they have lain all along. God in His mercy provides them with the conditions suitable to their gradual evolution, at the right time, at the end of each Mahāpralaya. This is known as '*sṛjyasṛṣṭi*'.

Creation is beginningless in time, but is all the same subject to the Lord's pleasure. He is the ultimate cause (metaphysically) of their bondage,—not in the sense that He threw them into it at a certain point of time in history, but that its continuous association with them is, in every way, subject to Him and its riddance will depend on His grace and cooperation.[4] Its onset is rendered possible by the power of concealment or obscuration of the true nature of souls, which is vested in the Lord[5] and which corresponds to the "Tirodhāna-Śakti" recognized by Śrīkaṇṭha and in Tamil Śaivism, as one of the five characteristics of Parameśvara.

The bondage of souls is due to a deep-rooted and beginningless involvement (*abhimāna*) with the modifications of the mind stuff after being brought to the surface of creation. This involvement finds expression in a superimposed identifying experientiality towards them as *belonging to their own selves, independently of any higher dispensing Power*. As such an identifying experientiality responsible for the happiness and miseries of life is an incontestable fact of our lives as we know it from our own personal experience of Sākṣī; it cannot be dismissed as unreal or imaginary. The involvement no doubt presupposes an element of superimposition but it is *superimposition of what is real*

4. पराभिध्यानात्तु तिरोहितं ततो ह्यस्य बन्धविपर्ययौ । (BS iii.2.5)
5. मत्तः स्मृतिर्ज्ञानमपोहनं च । (*Gītā* XV. 15; Cf. *SvetUp* VI. 16)

in itself on account of inextricable personal association.[6] The termination of this entanglement with Prākṛtic meshes can only be achieved by God's grace earned through Sādhanas. Such is the essence of Madhva's view of the reality and terminability of bondage.

It may, no doubt, appear to be a despotic thing for God to envelop the souls in beginningless Māyā;[7] but as already pointed out, it is a necessary evil in the scheme of the universe. The association with Prākṛtic bonds is a necessary step in the spiritual evolution of souls and is, therefore, permitted by God. It is an ordeal through which everyone of them has to pass before attaining his or her full stature,—whatever that might be. It is the desire of the Almighty that the *souls shall fulfil themselves only in this way and in no other.* And there is no questioning His Will, as He is Satyasaṁkalpa.

The phenomenon of beginningless bondage may be looked at from another angle also. It is generally referred to as an "obscuration" or concealment of the nature of Souls, a 'Tirodhāna' as the author of the *BS* calls it (iii.2.5). This is more in the nature of a benevolent act of prevention of their premature manifestation which would be harmful to them. The Sūtrakāra has given us a significant analogy : *Puṁstvādivat* (*BS*, ii.3.31). Manifestation of sexual power *in children* is rightly prevented by God's law of nature, till adolescence sets in when all the other parts of the body and the mind are duly developed and prepared to contribute to its successful implementation and enjoyment.

---

6. *Read* : दुःखादीनां चान्तःकरणपरिणामत्वेन **परमार्थत्वात्** तदनुसन्धातृत्वस्य दुःखित्वस्य जीवे **परमार्थत्वात् न कस्यापि मिथ्यात्वमित्यर्थः ।** (UpKh. *Mandāramañjarī*)

Read : न चान्तःकरणशरीरेन्द्रियविषयाणां तद्धर्माणां दुःखादीनां च **मिथ्यात्वम्** । स्वरूपसतामपि तादात्म्यतत्संबन्धित्वाभ्यामारोपेणैव व्यवहारोपपत्तेः । न च आरोपितत्वमात्रेण मिथ्यात्वम् । आत्मनोऽपि अन्तःकरणादिष्वारोपितत्वेन मिथ्यात्वप्रसंगात् । अंगीकृतं च परेण अन्तःकरणादिष्वात्माध्यासः, **यथोक्तम्**—"तं प्रत्यगात्मानं सर्वसाक्षिणं तद्विपर्ययेणान्तःकरणादिष्वध्यस्यति" इति ॥ (*NS*)

7. 'Māyā' is understood in Madhva's philosophy as the mysterious will of the Lord (Madhva, *BSB* 1.4.25). A similar power is ascribed to Ajñāna itself in Advaita अज्ञानमावरणविभ्रमशक्तियोगात् (*Saṁkṣepaśārīraka*, i. 20). It is not inconceivable that a *Svatantra-Cetana* should have such a power.

Instead of questioning the wisdom of this 'obscuration' it would be wiser for us to know that in our present imperfect state, bondage and obscuration induced in us by the Will of the Lord *are verily blessings in disguise*. Our life would be intolerable to us if through the power of Bhāvarūpājñāna we are *not* bound by attachment and affection to our near and dear ones and the responsibilities of our life and *not* kept mercifully ignorant of what goes on in other's minds and their and our past and future misdeeds !

The bonds of souls are thus *real* in that they are *not imaginary*. They have no beginning in time though depending always on His will. The essence of this bondage is ignorance and misunderstanding of the true nature of God and of one's own self :

तस्य **स्वप्रकाशस्यापि जीवस्य परमेश्वरेच्छया** परमेश्वरे स्वधर्मेषु **चाज्ञानं संभवत्येव । अज्ञानमपि सत्यमेव न अज्ञानकल्पितम् ।**[8] (*NS, p.* 54)

That is precisely what the Brahmājñānavāda of Śaṅkara denies. According to it, it is Brahman that is really obscured by ignorance and appears as the individual.[9] Madhva's view has certainly one advantage over it, in that one can understand a finite being suffering from ignorance; but not an Infinite Independent Brahman. The greatest stumbling block to the Advaitic view is that Ignorance can *never* invade Brahman which is both independent and of the nature of self-luminosity and absolute consciousness (Svaprakāśajñānasvarūpam). Madhva rightly points out the weakness and untenability of its theory of bondage.[10]

अज्ञताखिलसंवेत्तुर्घटते न कुतश्चन ।
उपाधिभेदात् घटत इति चेत्स स्वभावतः ।
अज्ञानतो वा ? द्वैतस्य सत्यता स्वत एव चेत् ॥ (*UpKh*)

---

8. "Even though the Jīva is self-luminous, it is possible that by the will of God he remains in ignorance of some aspects of his own self and of the Supreme Being. There is nothing impossible in this, because the Jīva (as conceived in Madhva-philosophy) is a Sa-viśeṣa personality. Such ignorance is also real and *not* an unreal something brought about by Mūlāvidyā (as the Advaita would have it.)."

9. ब्रह्मैवाविद्यया संसरति मुच्यते च । (*Bhāmatī*)

10. Cf. नहि कश्चिदपरतंत्रः बन्धनागारमात्मनः कृत्वानुप्रविशति ।
(Śaṅkara, *BSS* ii. 1.21)

If Brahman is the only real that exists, where and whence can ignorance come in ? If it is rendered possible by the intervention of "Upādhi", the question would arise about the Upādhi itself, viz., whether it is a real and an essential feature of Brahman or is itself due to an earlier layer of Ignorance. A real Upādhi would annul Advaita. To rely on a previous ignorance to create a subsequent Upādhi would give rise to a double fallacy of a *regressus ad infinitum* and a mutual interdependence between Upādhis and ignorance-layers. It is thus impossible to make out any logically intelligible relation between Upādhi and Brahman. It is passing strange that so insuperable a difficulty should have been represented as a point of honor to the Advaita :

दुर्घटत्वमविद्याया भूषणं न तु दूषणम् । (*Iṣṭasiddhi* i. 40)

Commenting on Deussen's remark that "On this question of how ignorance could possibly affect Brahman, the authors of the Upaniṣads give us no information", Radhakrishnan writes : "They give no information because *no information is possible*. It is true no explanation is possible of the rise of bewildering force of Avidyā, creator of false values, which has *somehow* come into being, in spite of the eternal and inalienable purity of the original self-existent Brahman" (*I. Phil.* ii, p. 578). "How Avidyā and Brahman can co-exist, is just the problem *for which we don't have any solution*" (p. 577). Such is the solution of the problem of the origin of bondage in the system of Śaṅkara which is said to be "*unmatched for its metaphysical depth and logical power, where thought follows thought naturally, until Advaitism is seen to complete and crown the edifice.*[11] (*Op. cit.* ii, 657). The worst that could be said of Madhva's view of the origin of bondage is that it involves God in a benevolent despotism. But Śaṅkara's reduces Brahman to a position of helpless submission to its own ignorance. Certainly, there is much to choose between the two. It is necessary to note in this connection that while the power of Paramācchādikā of the Lord's Prakṛti interposed between Him and the creature does not compromise *Him* in any manner, the play of Avidyā on Brahman in Advaita makes for His appearance as many. The

11. Italics mine.

two principles of Avidyā and Paramācchādikā are not, therefore, on a par in their relationship to Brahman or how they affect Him.

According to Madhva, though bondage is *real*, it does not follow that it is eternal and indestructible. The possibility of its termination does not make it any the less real as a fact so long as it lasts. This follows from his definition of real as what is प्रमितिविषयः There is no difficulty either in conceiving of the final disruption of ignorance and bondage as a result of the prolonged effort of the Jīvas and the grace of God :

तथाविधस्यापि बन्धस्य निवृत्तिं वक्ष्यामः । (*NS*, p. 64)

The objection of the Advaita that if bondage were *real* it could not be destroyed, suffers from a confusion of ideas; for reality is not always the same as eternal existence. If the Lord wills it, even beginningless (real) ignorance can be terminated : अघटितघटनानन्तैश्वर्यगुणवान् (*NS*). The Monist could not appeal to any such mysterious power of God, *as self-delusion, through Ajñāna, is hardly a sign of independence and sovereignty of Brahman* !

Madhva's theory is realistic. It is not obliged to dismiss any stage of bondage as unreal. It accepts the *kartṛtva* (doership) and *bhoktṛtva* (enjoyership) of Jīvas as actually existing in them, though dependent on God (*BS* ii. 3. 33). But instead of realizing that these capacities of Jīvas are derived from the Supreme Being, the Jīvas, in their ignorance, look upon them as self-derived. *This is Avidyā.* Such Avidyā is real, both in itself and as pertaining to the self. Similar is the case with *buddhi*, the senses, bodies and their objects of enjoyments. These are also as much real as anything else; but God-given. We, however, in our ignorance, look upon them as entirely under *our* control and as *our* 'possessions'. The fact, however, is that *they are 'our possessions', subject to the Lord's wish* : बुद्धीन्द्रियशरीरविषयाः स्वरूपसन्त एव ईश्वरवशा अपि अविद्यावशात् आत्मीयतया अध्यस्यन्ते (*NS*, p. 26). These various 'possessions', though different from the essence of self-hood, are not apprehended by the selves as clearly and vividly distinguished from 'self' on account of intimate permeation of the self in the body and on account of deep attachment to these. Hence on account of their inextricable association, the self comes to regard them as its very own and under the influence of this identification it has a feeling of being fortunate or unfortunate and of elation or shrinking of its personality as a result. This leads to love and aversion and similar pairs of opposite feelings in successive efforts to seek what is agreeable and avoid what is disagreeable in the embodied state. Every successive step is thus directed by this misplaced sense of values. This is the essence of what is known as Saṁsāra, leading to countless births and deaths in the cycle of life. It is only true knowledge of the soul's relation to God that can redeem it from this bondage. The true and final explanation of bondage is, thus, the will of the Lord and not merely, Karma, Ajñāna, Kāla, Guṇas, etc.[12]

Dr. Chandradhar Sharma raises the following objection in his *Critical Survey of Indian Philosophy* (p. 371) against Rāmānuja's theory of bondage : "If the soul is essentially pure and changeless and self-conscious subject, why should it get associated with Karma and be bound ? If the soul is tinged with Karma, it is already bound. Rāmānuja explains this difficulty by the conception of a beginningless Saṁsāra. But if you have to fall back on something beginningless why not admit the beginningless Avidyā ?" This however, cannot apply to Madhva. For Madhva has gone beyond Rāmānuja in tracing the origin of bondage, ultimately to Divine Will.

The acceptance of Viśeṣas in the nature of the Jīvas, by Madhva, explains the difficulty raised against the "pure, changeless self-conscious subject becoming associated with Karma and becoming bound" by the Divine Will. Dr. Chandradhar Sharma is very much mistaken if he thinks that falling back on beginningless Avidyā will be a panacea which will cure all the ills. For both Karma and Avidyā are equally insentient principles and cannot imprison or obscure the self *on their own initiative.* It is conceivable that the finite and ever-dependent souls can be subjected to temporary and partial obscuration of their full nature by Divine Will. But the other (Advaitic) theory that

12. तांश्चात्मनो विविक्तानपि विस्पष्टतयानुपलभमानः तद्धर्मान् दुःखादीन् सत्यानेवात्मीयत्वेन पश्यन्, तत्कृते नीचोच्चलक्षणे विकृती सत्ये एव प्रतिपद्यते । ततो रागद्वेषाभ्यां प्रयुक्तः तन्निवृत्तये यत्करोति तदप्येतादृशमेव इत्यनेकयोनिषु बंभ्रमीति । न क्वाप्यात्यन्तिकं तदुपशमं लभते, विना परमपुरुषाराधनादिति । (*NS*, p. 26)

the Infinite and Independent Brahman itself deludes Itself by throwing the veil of concealment over its own being :

स्वाज्ञानकल्पितजगत्परमेश्वरत्वजीवत्वभेदकलुषीकृतभूमभावा ।
स्वाभाविकस्वमहिमस्थितिरस्तमोहा **प्रत्यक्चिति**विजयते भुवनैकयोनिः ॥

(*Saṁkṣepaśāriraka*, i. 2)

and becomes the empirical ego, to which Chandradhar Sharma evidently subscribes, is surely not more convincing logically ! For, he himself agrees that "the why and the how regarding Avidyā are illegitimate questions and, therefore, an insoluble mystery" (*Op. cit.* p. 281).

Of the three important views regarding the origin of bondage of souls in Hindu philosophy which is committed to the acceptance of souls as *anādi* and *nitya*, Śaṅkara's theory traces it to the play of beginningless Avidyā (ignorance) on the One Cit, *somehow*, and giving rise to the *appearance* of many transmigrating selves, suffering the delusion of happiness and misery, doership and enjoyership. Rāmānuja traces the souls' bondage to their beginningless karma. The inadequacy of these two explanations is that Avidyā and Karma are both insentient principles and it would be highly illogical to let Caitanya Svarūpa as such, which is *a much higher principle than they*, to be obscured and overpowered by them to any extent—*unless they are empowered to do so by the Will of a Being superior to all of them*,—souls, Avidyā and Karma. For, as insentient principles neither Avidyā nor Karma can have any independent initiative *to do anything*. Madhva lays the finger on the precise weak point of these explanations when he points out their inadequacy for this reason :

न च कर्मविमामलकालगुणप्रभृतीशमचित्तनु तद्धि यतः ।

(*Dvādaśa Stotra* iii. 6)

He takes a more serious look at the problem. His position that the bondage of souls must, in the last analysis, be traced to God's Will is *logically unexceptionable* as an over-all view of the problem.

While most of the commonly accepted theories about the origin of the bondage of Souls in Hindu philosophy seek to explain "the how" of it, very few have to say anything of significance as to "the why of it", beyond the usual one that it is all an expression of Divine *sport*. Madhva understands "Divine sport" involved in creation in terms of effortless ease. It is highly significant that among all the Vedāntins Madhva is the only one to admit a benevolent purpose in creation while wholeheartedly agreeing that Brahman is indeed *Āptakāma*. He sees no contradiction between Āptakāmatva so far as the Lord's own wants are concerned and His being moved to creation for the benefit of the souls. His words :

भूत्यै निजाश्रितजनस्य हि सृज्यसृष्टावीक्षा बभूव परनामनिमेषकान्ते ।

(*MbhTN* i. 3)

offer us a more purposeful explanation of the rationale behind God's putting thc souls through the necessary process of transmigration.

Madhva calls his theory of the origin of bondage "Svabhāvājñānavāda"[13] or the theory of the souls' ignorance of their own true nature and of their dependence on the Supreme Brahman.

स्वस्य भावो धर्मः पारतंत्र्यादिः, तद्विषयकमज्ञानं **जीवस्य** इति वादः **स्वभावाज्ञानवादः।**

(*NS*, p. 64)

The term "Svabhāva" here has been explained by Jayatīrtha in *five different ways*. The first explanation is as given above. The second takes "Svabhāva" to mean *what is a fact* and what is not imagined by ignorance. On this view, Ajñāna which is the cause of the Soul's bondage exists in reality and is not merely something that is imagined to exist or is neither real nor unreal nor both together but other than all these predications viz. *anirvacaniya*. Thirdly, "Svabhāva" signifies "Independent Being" or God; fourthly the Jīva's own nature of metaphysical dependence. Thus "Ajñāna" of the true nature of God and one's own dependence on Brahman is "Svabhāvājñāna". It is also explained as "Ajñāna" that is teleologically willed in the Jīva by the Independent Being viz. God.[14]

---

13. **स्वभावाज्ञानवादस्य** निर्दोषत्वान्न तद्भवेत् । (*AV*, 1.1.1)

14. (i) तथा स्वयमेव भवत्यस्तीति स्वभावो, नाज्ञानकल्पित इति यावत्; (ii) स्वश्चासौ भावश्चेति **स्वभावो जीवः**, तदाश्रितं तदावरणं वाज्ञानमिति वादः **स्वभावाज्ञानवादः**, (iii) स्वः स्वतन्त्रो भावः परमात्मा, स्वस्य भावो धर्मः पारतंत्र्यादिर्वा स्वभावः, तद्विषयकमज्ञानं **जीवस्य** इति वादः **स्वभावाज्ञानवादः**; (iv) स्वभावभूतमेवाज्ञानं, **न मिथ्या** इति वादः; (v) तथा स्वभावेन स्वतंत्रेण परमेश्वरेण अज्ञानं जीवस्य इति वादः । (N*S*, p. 64)

Madhva contends that even though the Jīva is a self-luminous being, still it is *not inconceivable* that he should become subject to ignorance of his own true nature and the nature of God and of his own true relation to Him, as he is a dependent and finite being. The difficulty of the incompatibility of ignorance obscuring aspects of a self-luminous being which is bound to arise in Brahmājñānavāda will *not arise* in Madhva's theory; for, the Jīvas are here, by definition, "dependent" and also endowed with aspects (*sa-viśeṣa*) and are *not nirviśeṣa or aspectless*, like the Advaitic Ātman. It is with the help of these Svarūpa-Viśeṣas that while *some aspects* of the self (such as his existence) are *not obscured* yet others like the manifestation or experience of its Svarūpānanda (essential bliss) *remain obscured* in Saṁsāra. This is *where Madhva's theory has its advantage over the Advaitic theory of the nirviśeṣatva* of Ātman. On the 'Nirviśeṣatva' viewof Ātman (or Brahman) the obscuration would be simply inexplicable and inconceivable (*durghaṭam*):

निर्विशेषत्वादात्मनो नानधिगतो विशेषः ।

(Madhva, *Māyāvāda Khaṇḍana*)

The difference between the Dvaita and Advaita points of view here lies in the fact that an explanation of the Souls' bondage is *possible in the Dvaita theory, whereas it is only plausible* in the Advaita theory. In the first place, as Jayatīrtha puts it: Even though the Jīva is self-luminous (*svaprakāśa*) in the Dvaita view, it is possible to conceive of his being placed in a state of obscuration of his own knowledge about *some aspects* of his own nature and of the Supreme Being too, by the Will of God Himself:

स्वप्रकाशस्यापि जीवस्य परमेश्वरेच्छया परमेश्वरे, स्वधर्मेषु च अज्ञानं संभवत्येव ।

(*NS*, p. 64)

The difficulty of the Advaita theory is that it makes its Brahman itself become obscured by Ignorance and appear as the individual self (*Svājñānakalpitajagatparameśvaratva-jīvatvabheda-kaluṣīkṛtabhūmabhavā—Saṁkṣepaśārīraka*). One can understand, says Madhva, a finite being being put into a state of temporary obscuration and suffering by the will of a Superior Power; but it is not so easy to understand how an Infinite Being, such as Brahman, can ever submit to ignorance or throw around itself voluntarily a veil of ignorance and become finitised or appear to be so. The other fact of the Jīva-Caitanya being a Saviśeṣa personality (in Madhva's philosophy) admits of the self-luminous Jīva failing to realize *a part of his own full nature.*

The same thing cannot be said of the Nirviśeṣa-Caitanya (bare consciousness without any Viśeṣas or aspects) of the Advaita theory. Being an indivisible, undifferenced and aspectless whole (akhaṇda-nirviśeṣa) and, therefore, *not a unity in diversity*, ignorance cannot invade *a part* of the pure being of Brahman (or the self) leaving another part or aspect of it untouched and self-shining. The worst that could be said of Madhva's view of the origin of bondage is that it involves God or Brahman in a benevolent despotism. But Śaṅkara's position reduces Brahman to a helpless submission to Ignorance which is yet supposed to be *foreign* to its nature ! The difference between these two views is both *significant and considerable.*

Even the power of "Paramācchādikā" of God referred to by Madhva whereby the Supreme Being comes to be obscured from the knowledge of the finite selves affects, it should be carefully noted, *not* Brahman at all but the Jīva; whereas in the Advaita theory, there being no two beings in reality the Śuddhacaitanya itself has to be taken to become obscured by ignorance, while being the seat or locus of this very ignorance :

आश्रयत्वविषयत्वभागिनी निर्विशेषचितिरेव केवला । (*Saṅkṣepaśārīraka*)

The objection brought up by Madhva against this Advaitic theory of boundage does not thus recoil on his own theory. There may be other objections against it such as 'cruelty' which it may have to answer. That is quite a different matter for which suitable explanations can be thought of (*See* Chap. XLIV).

Dr. Chandradhar Sharma dismisses the arguments by which the Sāṁkhyas and Rāmānuja have tried to establish the quantitative pluralism of the spirit as "flimsy" (*Op.cit.* p.168) and reaching not beyond the empirical egos "whose individuality nobody denies" (p. 369). It is true that a quantitative pluralism of transcendental subjects cannot be derived as a logical conclusion from the concept of Puruṣas in the Sāṁkhya system as stereotyped, indifferent and inactive beings, who take no real part in the cosmic drama. But this cannot be said of Rāmānuja's theory of selves, in which the Puruṣas are active self-conscious individuals participating whole-heartedly in the struggle of life for their deliverance from bondage. No doubt, Monistic idealism thinks that there will be inconsistency in holding one and the same individual to be subject to actual bondage and suffering in the beginning and achieving freedom from suffering later on in the state of Mokṣa. But as these two states of bondage and blessedness are not coexistent or simultaneous, there is no inconsistency or violation of the principle of non-contradiction, in *both being real states of the individual*. The contradiction is purely imaginary. There is only a temporary obstruction of the capacities of the individual in bondage and this obscuration is a reality and a fact and is caused by the Divine will and its removal too is as much due to the same Divine will. This is obviously the opinion of the Sūtrakāra :

पराभिध्यानात्तु तिरोहितं ततो ह्यस्य बन्धविपर्ययौ[15] । (*BS* iii.2.5)

The Idealist, on the other hand, is only trying to run away from the problem by dismissing the very problem as an illusion. It is difficult to see how Svājñānavāda of Ātman or Brahman allowing itself to be deluded by Avidyā and getting finitized into empirical egos and fighting mock battles to regain their forgotten status is a better hypothesis than that of Realistic Pluralism. There is, however one weak point in Rāmānuja's theory of selves that they are only numerically different, but otherwise absolutely and essentially alike. Difference and distinction constitute individuality. If the selves are essentially the same in every respect, there is no meaning in their quantitative plurality. A difference is no difference unless *it makes a difference*[16]. Madhva, therefore, removes this anomaly by laying equal emphasis on quantitative and qualitative distinctions among them. The doctrine may be "peculiar" to Madhva; but it is nevertheless quite essential for a reasoned theory of pluralistic realism and it is the failure to accept it that consti-

15. For criticism of Śaṅkara's devious explanation of this Sūtra see my *BSPC* Vol. III.

16. The admission of a special class of souls known as "Nitya Sūris" placed above the "Baddha" souls in Rāmānuja's siddhānta gives unequivocal support to Madhva's acceptance of Tāratamya among souls in release also. *See* Chapter LVII.

tutes the logical inconsistency in the case of the Jainas, the Sāṅkhyas and Rāmānuja. Even the most merciless critic of Madhva must admit that he is *utterly consistent* in accepting the quantitative and qualitative pluralism of souls. We fail to understand why critics who have been quick to point out the inconsistency in the position of the Sāṅkhyas and Rāmānuja should *not* have expressly noted the *improvement* made by Madhva in this respect.

CHAPTER XXXIII

PLURALITY OF SELVES AND THEIR SVARŪPA-BHEDA

THE glaring inequalities of equipment, endowments and rewards of life have rightly been made the starting point of the presumption of the plurality of selves by the Sāṅkhyas :

जननमरणकरणानां प्रतिनियमादयुगपत्प्रवृत्तेश्च ।
पुरुषबहुत्वं सिद्धं त्रैगुण्यविपर्ययाच्चैव ॥

(*Sāṁkhya Kārikā*, 18)

This stock argument emphasized by the Sāṁkhyas and Rāmānuja has been sought to be dismissed as proving nothing more than the plurality of the empirical egos "whose individuality nobody denies". Madhva shows the fallacy of this argument by showing that we have to arrive inductively at some fundamental bases of distinctions among souls taking empirical facts into consideration. Empirical facts and empirical egos cannot be laughed out of existence. They have to be reckoned with. Philosophy is concerned as much with the problem of our genesis as with that of our future and destiny. We have to see if empirical facts can or do throw any light on the 'how' of Saṁsāra. How have empirical differences arisen ? By themselves or by earlier empirical ones and they by yet others *ad infinitum* ? Do they presuppose or go back upon something that is fundamental ? Can *all* the complex variations and differences in the psycho-physical, mental and spiritual lives of beings be explained without going back upon intrinsic and fundamental differences in the essence of beings, with the help of the Law of Karma *alone* or of the theory of the beginninglessness (*anāditva*) of Saṁsāra ? That the theory of Avidyā is an illegitimate intrusion into Hindu religion and metaphysics is clear from the fact that even in the Sūtras of Bādarāyaṇa only the two theories of Karma and Anāditva of Saṁsāra have been mooted as legitimate explanations of the divergences in life. *These two theories of Karma and Anāditva of Saṁsāra presuppose the reality of existing differences among selves and try to explain them on some real and more fundamental basis*. But neither the law of Karma nor the Anāditva of *Saṁsāra will be consistent with a repudiation of the present differences as really superimposed ones*. The impression that the law of Karma and the Anāditva of Saṁsāra are merely empirical explanations is due to an incapacity to understand their real and true significance in throwing light on empirical differences. This point comes out clearly in Madhva's interpretation of the law of Karma as applied to the explanation of empirical differences. The inexorable law of Karma is commonly taken to be the final explanation of these inequalities in the lives of beings. But, it will break down as an ultimate explanation of cosmic differences, unless it is admitted that these differences themselves are, in principle, rooted ultimately in the nature of beings. *This is the decisive contribution which Madhva has made to the interpretation of the problem of life and its diversities. He has thus gone beyond the principle of Karma, unerringly, to the "Svabhāvabheda" (intrinsic or essential differences in the nature of beings). Herein lies the boldness, originality and thoroughness of Madhva's approach to philosophical problems*. He does not stop at any half-way house on the philosophical road to Truth.

It is interesting to note that starting from another angle Dr. Albert Schweitzer also comes to the same conclusion as Madhva, in his interesting work : *Indian Thought and Its Development* : "How do individual souls come into existence from the Universal Soul and how are they reabsorbed into it....The doctrine of reincarnation in no way requires the assumption that the individual souls have issued from the Universal Soul and will return to it again. Indeed, it can do nothing with it. For this doctrine, the most natural thing is simply to start from the fact *that in a way, which cannot be further explained, all through eternity there have been an endless number of eternal individual souls (which constitute the spiritual elements in the Universe), for which is prescribed the passing of a constantly renewed existence in the world of senses*[1], *until finally they succeed in winning freedom from it.* And what need is there to regard liberation from the cycle of rebirth and return of the soul into the Universal Soul as equivalent ? The doctrine of reincarnation has no interest whatsoever in asserting such an inexplicable thing as that the individual soul, in the end *loses its individuality*[2]. It is sufficient for it to establish the fact that as a result of the freedom attained, the Soul is in a state of perfect bliss" (*Op.cit.* p. 61). (Italics mine)

Karma implies *freedom of choice* to do right or wrong, good or bad. *The exercise of this freedom itself has naturally to be viewed as an expression of the basic nature of the person who makes the choice.* We are thus thrown back on the hypothesis of the presence of innate distinctions of nature among selves—their *Svarūpabheda*, in the ultimate analysis of the problem. All other explanations break down in the end. The inequalities of Karma do not carry us very far. It is, therefore, only a half-truth to say that it is because of different Karmas that men are not alike. It simply begs the question and lands us in a prior distinction of natures, aptitudes and outlook. However beginningless the chain of karma may be, it is still incapable of explaining why a particular course of action has been pursued in preference to another, without reference to an ultimate difference in the nature and make-up each moral agent. Even a beginningless chain of Karma *could not fully explain* why all souls are not equally good or bad, when all of them are equally beginningless and eternal and their karmas too equally beginningless and *their start also simultaneous* ! Karma has *no self-contained answer* to give to this question. Karma is itself the effect of something else—or the expression of something else. Desire is the seed of action. This desire or inclination must then be admitted to differ in each case to such an inscrutable extent as to render diversity of natures and activities intelligible. If all souls are constituted *absolutely alike*, it would be impossible to account for the different courses of action pursued by them, as a result

---

1. With this compare Madhva's Ṣvabhāvājñānavāda.
2. Cf. बन्धमिथ्यात्वं नैव मुक्तिरपेक्षते । (Madhva, *AV* i.1.1)

of which, they accumulate a heavy load of *different* Karma through ages. If the inequalities of endowments and opportunities and rewards are to be made consistent with freedom and free will of souls, they must be attributed to an essential or intrinsic distinction in their very nature and constitution. The *plurality of souls cannot, therefore, be explained with reference to the material plane alone* as it will *not* explain the difficulties involved in the theory of *anādi-karma* unless these distinctions are proposed to be dismissed as *not ultimate*. But that is running away from the problem and not solving it. As Jayatīrtha points out, the Sāṅkhya doctrine of plurality of selves really suffers from this basic defect :

यत्पुरुषबहुत्वं सांख्येनांगीकृतं, तदपि मायावादिभिरभ्युपगतमेव, **न तु स्वरूपे कश्चिदस्ति परस्परतो विशेषः।** (*NS*, p. 328)

If plurality is to be ultimate, it must be grounded in something more than Prākṛtic vestures and influences, *including karma*. No doctrine of plurality of selves that shies at this logical decision to ground it in a principle of intrinsic distinction of nature among selves and invariable concomitance of natural selection of good or bad which that would lead to can ever hope to give a solution that would be consistent with pure reason. The same is the weakness of Rāmānuja's position. According to him, there is *no basic distinction of Svarūpaviśeṣas* among souls, in the sense of a qualitative gradation or distinction of properties of *jñāna*, *ānanda*, moral character and inclination. All are equally endowed in every respect. There is no distinction of measure. Madhva objects to this on the ground that multiplicity without distinction (of essence or nature) would be inconceivable *particularly among Cetanas*. Sameness or equality of essence does not rule out individual variations (in an infinite scale) which may be too subtle to be obvious. But such underlying variations of degrees *must be recognised* if plurality of selves is to have any real meaning or justification. However much they may be alike there can be no absolute likeness in all respects between any two sentient beings in creation. If there is, they would all be identical and not *merely similar* to one another. Difference in essence is thus bound up with the idea of *fundamental peculiarity*. In the case of physical or material objects, it is possible to distinguish between likes on the basis of difference in organization of parts or atoms. But in regard to spiritual entities like souls which are impartible wholes there is no way to account for multiplicity except through an essential though mysterious distinction of natures (*Svarūpabheda*) or Svarūpa-viśeṣas which are not the same in any two individuals. We have to extend the same principle to the Kingdom of Heaven too, on the analogy of Arnold's famous lament on the death of his little daschhund :

"And not in the course
Of all centuries yet to come,
And not the infinite resource
Of Nature with her countless sum
Can ever quite repeat the past
Or just thy little self restore[3]"

To the ordinay passer-by, the sheep may all be just so many *numerable units*; but to the shepherd who lives with them all through their lives and in daily contact, they are *real individuals* each with very different features and characteristics. Even so, to Madhva, the Divine Shepherd who knows all about the constitution of the souls, knows how to distinguish one soul from another, on the basis of essential peculiarities embedded in their natures !

The wide range, then, of deep-rooted inequalities in the lives of the living beings, extending over the human, animal, plant, aquatic and other species of life, cannot be satisfactorily explained except on the hypothesis of *intrinsic differences of nature*, expressing themselves in potentialities for good or bad. It is no use, says Madhva, to take refuge against this inescapable fact in so-called disparities of past Karmas shaping the lives of beings. These Karmas are, in fact, conditioned by some subconscious influences of past deeds and unseen merit accruing therefrom (*adṛṣṭa*); which, again, presupposes an earlier merit (*adṛṣṭa*) and that another and so on endlessly. We are, thus, ultimately left with a practically beginningless gradation of fitness and potentialities for good or for bad, termed अनादिस्वरूप-योग्यता or natural fitness or 'Haṭha' by Madhva (See Chapter XLIII).

3. Quoted from Pringle Pattison, *Idea of God*, p. 222. (2nd Edn. Academic Publishers, Calcutta, 1967).

If this unseen merit which determines the disparities of karma is inexplicable and devoid of a reason at any particular stage in the history of a soul, the same reason could be trotted out at the outset, so that the very need for a previous birth and belief in metempsychosis can be dispensed with. If this unseen merit recedes in an interminable recession, we have really a beginningless distinction of essential natures and potentialities accepted in a different manner. If such unseen merit is *not* produced by a previous merit and that by another, but is taken to find its *raison d'etre* in the intrinsic nature and worth of each soul, we accept the principle of intrinsic difference among souls (*anādisvarūpayogyatābheda*) without further ado :

यद्यनादिर्विशेषो न साम्प्रतं कथमिष्यते ?
अदृष्टादेव चादृष्टं स्वीकृतं सर्ववादिभिः ।
आकस्मिको विशेषश्चेत् अदृष्टे क्वचिदिष्यते ।
सर्वत्राकस्मिकत्वं स्यात्, नादृष्टापेक्षिता क्वचित् ।
अदृष्टाच्चेत् विशेषोऽयमनादित्वं कुतो न तत् ?[4] (*AV* iii.4.41)

The uniqueness of individual experience (*Vyavasthā*) and the inequalities of equipment etc. among souls point ultimately to the existence of *inalienable, incommunicable essence of personality* which underlies all states of experience and coordinates them into a meaningful whole, which is never seen to be repeated or to overlap in any two instances. It cannot be seriously contended that there is actual overlapping of consciousness in release where all material conditions fall off. Such overlapping would be *inconceivable without identity of essence here and now also* and identity of consciousness would render the present multiplicity of personalities purposeless. If it should be true then, that there is really one individual throughout the universe, that one being must be in a position to coordinate to itself the experience of

4. "Unseen merit, which accounts for similar merit in the present life, should presuppose and go back upon a previous merit. This series should regress *ad infinitum*. If it breaks down in any particular instance, the principle of unseen merit can as well be dispensed with. If it holds good in all cases without exception, as far back as human thought and logic could reach, it will be a clear admission, in an indirect way, of the fact that such unseen merit is *ingrained in the nature of the individuals themselves from time immemorial*". There is no disputing the inexorable logic behind this argument.

all other apparently different centres, which is *not the case*, so far as we are aware. Moreover, all selves struggling for freedom should get automatically released the moment a single centre gets switched off from the main. *The very existence of both freed and bound souls at the same time, is a proof of their distinction and plurality*[5]: संसारिमुक्तव्यवस्थया च भेदः सिद्धः । **न च कोऽपि मुक्तो नास्तीति प्रलापो युक्तः** (*Vādaratnāvali*, ii).

The theory of Svarūpabheda of souls elaborated by Madhva is, thus, the only solution of the age-long problem of plurality of selves, their freedom and free will. Questions like the following have been asked by thinkers, all the world over : "The Jīva was not created of a void, at a particular time. But he is, nevertheless, an expression of the nature of God. How then does he happen to be so imperfect while his archetype is also the type of perfection ?" St. Augustine's agony of soul was still more poignant: "Who made me ? Did not God who is not only good but goodness itself ? Whence then, came I to will evil and nill good, so that I am thus justly punished ? Who set this in me and ingrafted in me this plant of bitterness, seeing that I was made, wholly of my most sweet God" (*Confess*. Bk. VII, 4; 5) The question is answered by Madhva, under *BS* ii. 3.51 :

प्रतिबिम्बानां मिथो वैचित्र्ये कारणमाह—'अदृष्टानियमात्' इति । अनादिविद्याकर्मवैचित्र्यात् वैचित्र्यम् ।

—on the basis of a fundamental difference in beginningless Karma, Vidyā, etc., which rest ultimately upon an intrinsic difference in *nature*. This interpretation is clearly endorsed by Rāghavendra Tīrtha :

स्वरूपोपाधिवैचित्र्यस्यैव 'अदृष्टानियम' पदेनाभिप्रेतत्वात् । विवृतमेतत् चन्द्रिकायाम् । (*Bhāvadīpa*, p. 224b)

This is an original and suggestive interpretation of the *Brahmasūtra* in question by the Mādhva school. It goes beyond the commonly accepted theory of Karma for an ultimate solution of the problem of distinction and inequality among souls. And the solution given is much more definite and precise than the vague one of 'original sin', which would not be adequate as an explanation of inequality of nature of souls.

---

5. Madhva opens his *Tattvodyota* with precisely the same argument : विमतो भिन्नः, **मुक्तत्वात्,** यदित्थं तत्तथा यथा सम्प्रतिपन्नम् ।

It is, thus in the nature of some souls to will evil and nill good and of others to will good and nill evil. Yet others there may be of mixed nature and these, in the language of Hume, will be "neither good enough for a supper, nor bad enough for a drubbing". These will correspond to the "Nitya-saṁsārins" of Madhva. It is thus only a half-truth to say that "freedom is the cause of our doing evil" (Augustine). The question must inevitably arise as to *why*, when one is "free" to will good and nill evil, one does *the contrary* ? Not because one has *free* will ! For, the same will might have suggested to him the other course ! That it has *not done so must depend on something more fundamental and foundational to the nature of the individual. That something*, says Madhva, is the *core* of the individual—*his svarūpa.* It will be difficult to dispute the ruthless logic of this position, however distasteful to someone's *amour propre* the conclusion may be. The tripartite classification of souls put forward by Madhva is only a comprehensive theory embodying the same idea of 'Svarūpabheda' of souls and giving it a definite shape in the form of *a broad generalization.* It will be dealt with in the next chapter.

CHAPTER XXXIV

RATIONAL BASIS OF INTRINSIC GRADATION AMONG SOULS AND THEIR TRIPARTITE CLASSIFICATION

MADHVA'S doctrine of the Soul insists not only upon the distinctiveness of each soul but also upon an intrinsic gradation among them based on varying degrees of knowledge, power and bliss. This is known as Tāratamya or Svarūpatāratamya, which comes out all the more clearly in the released state, where the souls realize their true status. *This position is peculiar to Madhva and is not found in any other school of Indian philosophy*. Together with the allied doctrine of Jīva-traividhya or tripartite classification of Souls into (1) Muktiyogya (salvable) (2) Nityasaṁsārin (ever-transmigrating) and (3) Tamoyogya (damnable), it has come in for a good deal of adverse criticism at the hands of modern scholars.

These criticisms suffer mostly from sentimental bias against Tāratamya and appear to confuse the Mādhva doctrine of Svarūpatraividhya, with the Calvinistic theory of Election, without examining the ethico-philosophical grounds on which the twin theories of Traividhya and Tāratamya are based by Madhva. The theory of Election rests upon a dogmatic exercise of Divine prerogative without reference to the worth or eligibility of the souls chosen for deliverance or damnation. In fact, there is no room for any question of fitness or eligibility of the souls, in the view of Augustine, Aquinas and Calvin, that "each soul is specially created and made to vitalize the embryo at the moment of conception".[1] The Mādhva doctrine, on the

1. James Ward : *Pluralism and Theism*, p. 453

other hand, is a philosophical theory intended to justify and reconcile the presence of evil with divine perfection, in the only rational way in which it could be done,—*by fixing the responsibility for goodness or evil upon the moral freedom born of diversity of nature of the souls who are themselves eternal and uncreated in time.*

This question has been discussed at length by Alexander Campbell Fraser, in his *Philosophy of Theism* (Gifford Lectures, 1894-6). His conclusion affords a striking parallel to the position of Madhva; and it is not unlikely that he would have expressed himself more decidedly in favor of the position taken by Madhva, had it been known to him. Fraser's analysis of the problem is, therefore, of great interest to us in this connection. Says he :

"The mixture of good and evil in the universe is a sure enigma to Theism and a challenge to it. To believe in perfect goodness is to believe that all is as it ought to be and this is destroyed if anything is found existing that ought not to exist, however insignificant the place in which it is found or however rare the occurrence. Pain, error, sin and death are the chief evils in our world. Sin is absolutely evil. Pain is the correlative of pity and sympathy. It is natural and, therefore, a divine means of education of spiritual life. *But the continued presence of what is unconditionally bad cannot be disposed of in this way. How to relieve the mystery of moral evil, including what seems an unfair distribution of pleasure and pain* and an *unequal adjustment of opportunities* for moral growth, has been a human perplexity from the beginning. (Italics mine) It finds expression in the Hebrew poets like Job and in the Greek dramatists like Aeschylus. How can it be reconciled with the goodness of God ?"

Discussing the merits of three possible solutions of the problem in terms of (1) a Manichaean Dualism or (2) an Imperfect Deity; or (3) an Indifferent Power of the Monist, he continues : "that this world of good and evil must be the issue of a constant struggle between two rival and eternal powers, the one benevolent and the other malevolent is an explanation of these strange appearances. This is symbolized in Zoroastrian anthropomorphism of Ormuzd and Ahriman. Its implied subversion of the primary ethical postulate must alone discredit this dualistic hypothesis. A similar difficulty attends Monism which concludes either that the Universal Power is itself a mixture of good and evil[2] or that both are unreal. Manichaean Dualism in the form of two eternal powers or Monism of a single eternal power partly good and partly evil or else indifferent to good and evil are both inconsistent with the indispensable moral hope and faith.

"Can moral evil be a necessity of finite personality or of the intractableness of matter or a mere negation? Several attempts have been made to explain the fact of evil in a morally governed universe. Some are conjectures formed at the expense of moral perfection of the Universal Power. Others explain away moral evil as an unconditional necessity of finite existence or treat it as an unreal negation or hide the difficulty by referring to a Tempter".

Then comes the Professor's own view :—

"The question why God admits into His Universe what is bad seems to involve an unproved assumption. *What ought not to exist*, it is assumed, *cannot coexist with God*. But this dogma has never been proved. *As moral agents, persons must be free to originate voluntary acts that are bad or undivine as well as those which are in harmony with the Divine order*. To say if God is perfect, free agents cannot produce volitions which they ought *not to* is *not* to vindicate Divine perfection but to destroy it. Omnipotence cannot be power to realize contradictions. God cannot make two and two five, cannot make a square circle. Inability in morally responsible persons to make themselves bad is *as much a contradiction*, though less obvious. If free to act, one must be able to originate evil acts as well. Offences must needs be, if persons exist. It does not appear that even Omnipotence can exclude what ought not to exist while there are beings whose essential character is that they are able to bring this into existence."

"Is the existence of persons who can make and keep themselves bad *only a transitory episode in the history of the Universe or must there be ever bad persons* increasing in number and *increasingly bad*? *The question is incapable of settlement*. That the moral agency of persons, their personal power to depart from their moral

2. As it would be in the Pantheism of Bhāskara and others.

ideal, deepened and confirmed by habit *may become an absolute final 'election' to evil by themselves*, which even Omnipotent God cannot overcome, consistent with the free personality of those who *persist in keeping themselves undivine is one conjecture*[3]. It involves the mystery of existence, in the Divine Universe, of innumerable persons increasing in number and becoming worse[4]. Another possible view is that such persons and their acts are capable of extinction by God and only morality progresses, so that only the good are allowed to survive,—those who persist in ungodliness being reduced to unconsciousness[5] Perhaps, man's present moral education requires that this mystery should remain unsolved as a teleologically needed mystery" (p. 320-21). (Italics mine)

Judged in the light of these weighty remarks of the Professor, it will be seen that the doctrine of innate distinctions of nature among souls, propounded by Madhva, will have to be recognized as the most necessary presupposition of the Hindu law of Karma which would become a Vagarious principle, in the absence of such a basis of distinction of the character and behavior of souls. Sir P. S. Sivaswami Ayyar in his *Kamala Lectures* (1935, p. 143) comes very near to conceding as much when he admits frankly that "though the doctrine of Karma professes to explain the origin of evil and suffering, *it does not really do so*, inasmuch as it involves an infinite regression as expressed in the doctrine that Karma is *anādi*". As for Traividhya (threefold classification) of souls, it is only a comprehensive hypothesis based on the same premises. It may not be flattering to human complacency, as the doctrine of Sarvamukti may be; but no spurious or irrelevant considerations should be allowed to interfere with reasoned metaphysical investigations, which should be carried on in an atmosphere free from all passion and prejudice and from personal and sentimental predilections. "We want hard and straight thinking and not soft or emotional

3. This answers to Madhva's view.
4. Cf. वैगुण्यमेव पश्यन्ति न गुणान् विनियुञ्जते ।
   तेषां तमःशरीराणां तम एव परायणम् ॥ (Mbh, XII. 261. 50)
5. 'Tamoyogyas'?

or sentimental thinking. Philosophy should say what is true. *It does not matter whether it pleases or irritates.* It must prove logically derived conclusions and not defend at all costs pious wishes and pleasing imaginings. It would be unphilosophical to endeavour the refutation of any hypothesis by a pretence of its dangerous consequences to religion and morality[6]." If there is a possibility of moral and social paragons, it is equally possible to hold that there may be persons who act on the motto 'Evil, be thou my good' and such Satanic conduct could only merit eternal misery.

The doctrine of intrinsic gradation among souls would follow as a matter of course, once the principle of their plurality is admitted, as in the system of Rāmānuja. Much more so when the prerogatives of God are not claimed for the released souls and certain irrevocable limitations are set to their sovereignty in release and so long as God is put down as the inner guide (Antaryāmī and Śeṣī) of the souls, who are subject to His control (*niyāmya*). If the souls attain to a position of absolute equality with the Supreme in release, it would be difficult to find a rational basis for the stupendous difference between them and God, when they, the souls, had still been in bondage, suffering the worst miseries, while the Supreme remains untouched by evil and suffering. The Rāmānujīyas who posit reciprocal dependence between souls and God and claim that the joy of Brahman is enhanced every time a new soul attains release and comes to it[7], can hardly deny that the bliss of Brahman and of all the released souls at any given time will be several times more than that of any of the souls still weltering in Saṁsāra. But what should be there to justify such a vast difference between them, if their original and basic natures are the same ? Why should some souls alone get released *ages before the others* and enjoy communion with Brahman for a considerably longer period than the rest ? Why should the others lag behind or be denied the opportunities and advantages for *so long* ? If the fault be that of the later arrivals in Mokṣa, why

6. Radhakrishnan, *Reign of Religion in Contemporary Philosophy*, 1920, pp. 13-14.

7. Vide the passage from *Nītimālā* quoted *ante* Chapter III.

should they have been delayed for so long ? All explanations of such difficulties based on Karma would be unavailing in the absence of an ultimate appeal to the diversity and gradation of natures. Why should God alone be independent and the souls dependent *for ever* on Him according to Rāmānuja ? Why should Brahman be for ever exempt from the ills of saṁsāra and the Jīvas alone consigned to suffering at least for the time being ? Why again should Brahman alone be unlimited in space (*aparicchinna Vibhu*) and the Jīvas put down (in Rāmānuja's view) as essentially atomic in size (*aṇu*) ? These and other essential distinctions between Jīva and Brahman naturally imply some kind of an intrinsic superiority of the One over the others—i.e. to say, *Svarūpa-Tāratamya*[8]. It would be preposterous to say that the Jīvas who realise their essence by the grace of God, manage somehow to shoot up to a position of absolute equality with the Universal King, overnight. Such a position would not only be blasphemous but would offend all logic and commonsense. It will also be a betrayal of the spirit of religion inculcated by the scriptures :

न ते विष्णो जायमानो न जातो
देव महिम्नः परमन्तमाप ॥ (*RV*, VII.99.2)
न त्वत्समोऽभ्यधिकः कुतोऽन्यः (*Gitā*, XI.43)
न तत्समश्चाभ्यधिकश्च दृश्यते (*SvetUp*, VI.8)

These texts bespeak the intrinsic difference that exists between the Supreme Lord and the other beings and thereby the Tāratamya that exists between them. Texts referring to the intrinsic

---

8. It is suggested by some that free will can explain all such difficulties. But free will merely recognizes that as persons are free to act one way or the other, they choose one way instead of the other. But the difficulty remains as to why all those free-willed persons *do not choose the right way only*. That some among the free-willed choose the right way and some others the wrong way when both the ways are equally open to them, shows that their free will is guided by their own intrinsic nature. In other words, it shows that free will does not necessarily choose rightly or wisely. What makes it choose rightly or wisely in some cases and unwisely in other cases must be their own basic nature (*svabhāva*). This is the conclusion to which Madhva is led by the behavior of free will as such in different individuals. The conclusion may be unpalatable to our *amour propre* but it is an inescapable fact. We have to leave it at that.

differences and Tāratamya among souls themselves will be found cited in their proper place.

The recognition of special class of souls called "Nityasūris" who are *ex hypothesi* exempt from Saṁsāra for ever like God Himself in the system of Rāmānuja,[9] not to speak of the recognition of a class of "Nityasaṁsārins" also, by a section of the followers of Rāmānuja, will be similarly inexplicable without the acceptance of an intrinsic gradation of souls into ordinary and "elect" and so on. The higher position of Śeṣitva assigned to Śrī in respect of the Nityasūris also points to a natural gradation among souls.

The classification of souls into human and divine (*deva*) in Hindu religious literature is no passing show based on Karmic disparities only. The *Brahma-sūtras* recognize the gods as a class of specialized beings and discuss the question of their privileges. One Śruti text refers to the presence in the state of release of "earlier batches of Sādhyas (*muktas* ?) who are Devas"[10]. As already mentioned, the Viśiṣṭādvaitins recognize the existence of Nityamuktas like Viṣvaksena, Garuḍa, Ananta etc. who always remain free from Saṁsāra which entangles other souls. The Vedic and Purāṇic literature assign to the four-faced Brahmā a very high place among the gods, not only as the Creator of all but as the first-born son of the Supreme Being and as the Saviour of mankind :

यो ब्रह्माणं विदधाति पूर्वं यो वै वेदांश्च प्रहिणोति तस्मै (*SvetUp*, vi. 18)
स एतस्माज्जीवघनात् परात्परं पुरुषमीक्षते (*Praśna Up*. v.2)
स एनान् ब्रह्म गमयति (*ChanUp*, iv.15.6)
स वै शरीरी प्रथमः स वै पुरुष उच्यते ।
आदिकर्ता स भूतानां ब्रह्माग्रे समवर्तत ॥
(quoted by Śaṅkara)

In the *TaittUp* (ii.1) the released souls are said to realize all their desires "in company with the wise Brahmā". This is supported by a Purāṇic text quoted by many commentators on *BS*, iv.3.11 :

---

9. Cf. इह सयूथ्याः, परे च केचिदाहुः इतः पूर्वमिव पश्चादपि केचित् न मोक्ष्यन्ते । 'एकं पादं नोद्धरति' 'क्षिपाम्यजस्रमशुभान्' 'मामप्राप्यैव' इत्यादिभिरेतत् सिद्धम् । (*Tattvamutākalāpa* of Vedāntadeśika, Medical Hall Press, Banaras, p. 138)

10. 'यत्र पूर्वे साध्याः सन्ति देवाः'

ब्रह्मणा सह ते सर्वे संप्राप्ते प्रतिसंचरे ।
परस्यान्ते कृतात्मानः प्रविशन्ति परं पदम् ॥

(*Kūrma Purāṇa*, 1. 12.269)

In this and in another text : *Sa enān brahma gamayati* (*ChanUp*, v.2) the four-faced Brahmā is given a premier position as the Great Usher of the released souls into the presence of the Supreme as their Saviour and Guide. In fact, all other souls who have attained enlightenment in the course of a particular Brahmakalpa are believed to bide their time and wait for the fourfaced Brahmā to be released and to conduct them to the kingdom of God. This role of Brahmā is a striking proof of his spiritual excellence and superiority over other souls. Such a distinction in rank must necessarily confer on him some kind of extraordinary merit not found in or attainable by others. This preeminent position of Brahmā as the presiding deity of *Mahattattva* or the first evolute of Matter, is indisputable. We are told that such special merit of his lies in his being "intrinsically" endowed with four great excellences :—

ज्ञानमप्रतिघं यस्य वैराग्यं च जगत्पतेः ।
ऐश्वर्यं चैव धर्मश्च **सहसिद्धं चतुष्टयम्** ॥

(Madhva in *BrhUp bhāṣya* 1.4)

Similar excellences possessed by other Devas of the Hindu pantheon and references to the marvels of spiritual discipline attained by them, obliges Madhva to formulate a comprehensive theory of intrinsic gradation in the entire Cosmos,[11] upon which the whole of reality is grounded in a scheme of grades and graduted order. The cosmic scheme of gradation is omnipenetrative, says Madhva, running up and down the scale—from the highest of the gods to the vilest of fiends :

अनादियोग्यतां चैव कलिवाणीश्वरावधिम् ।
को निवारयितुं शक्तो युक्त्यागमबलोद्धताम् ? (*AV* iii.4.41)

Gods and men are not equal in their basic nature and powers, or in the innate tendencies for good or bad, which determine their future development.[12] The doctrine of intrinsic gradation

---

11. इन्द्रियेभ्यः परा ह्यर्था अर्थेभ्यश्च परं मनः । (*Katha Up*, i.3.10)
12. न ह वै देवान् पापं स्पृशति । (*Brh Up*. i.5.20)

of souls is thus a reasoned and reasonable hypothesis of human nature and destiny, suggested by the moral law and supported by reason, revelation and experience.

"*Evolution is not only a movement forward.* In many cases, we observe a marking of time and still more often, a deviation or turning back. It must be so".[13] Individual development, according to Madhva, is only an unfolding or an unwrapping. The progressive differentiation of selves into one or the other of the three classes is contained in the germ and embedded in the being of each. This reminds us of the Leibnizian theory of pre-established harmony. Taking a comprehensive view of human nature in all its aspects, we find that some men are intrinsically good and some are intrinsically bad and the rest—perhaps the vast majority of us—are midway between the two; though it would be impossible to assign any individual to a particular class without superhuman insight into his fundamental nature. We could, however, draw a generalization on the basis of the consolidated experience of humanity that all men are not alike and there are many orders of goodness, intelligence and ability among them, as also of evil, ignorance and weakness. We can't gather grapes of thorns, or figs of thistles. Even so, every good tree brings forth good fruit and every corrupt tree brings forth evil fruit. Adam and Eve succumbed to the temptation of Satan; but Christ thrice said "no" to his Tempter. The stories and the national Epics of every land are replete with the records of the highest acts of purity, benevolence and self-sacrifice, or ordinary kindness and diabolical cruelty and fiendishness. We must, therefore, take a full view of human nature at its best and at its worst and adjudge its nature and destiny, uninfluenced by sentimental considerations. Taking, then, the immense and irreducible diversities of life into consideration, Madhva holds that we could not satisfactorily account for the presence and continuation of evil in a world created and ruled by a most perfect Being unless it is taken to be natural to some as goodness is to others. Without such a fundamental division of human nature, the disparities of life reflected in the seemingly unfair distribution of pleasure and pain and opportunities for moral growth are not satisfac-

13. Bergson, *Creative Evolution*, p. 100.

torily explained. X is a millionaire's son who rides a Rolls Royce merrily, while Y the pauper scowls jealously at him as he flies past and grinds his teeth at the injustice of Fate. The light of law and religion have not yet penetrated many dark corners of the world, inhabited by barbarous tribes while they shine brightly on more fortunate beings elsewhere. Why? The law of Karma cannot carry us very far in the quest for an ultimate explanation of such bewildering inexplicabilities. It cannot explain why given two alternatives of good or evil, certain persons show a marked preference or tendency towards the one and others to the opposite. Moral worth, knowledge, works, experience, heredity, opportunities, culture—*none of these* explanations of diversity *solves the riddle pushed to its starting point.* The final solution can only be found in the inherent nature of beings. It is the magnetic needle which attracts and deflects the Karmas of souls according to its own currents and gives the first move to their career.

न कर्तृत्वं न कर्माणि लोकस्य सृजति प्रभुः ।
न कर्मफलसंयोगं स्वभावस्तु प्रवर्तते ॥ (*Gītā* V.14)

It would, therefore, be illogical to dismiss the theories of Svarūpabheda and Tāratamya of Jīvas on extra-philosophical and emotional grounds. Criticisms such as that on this view of Predestination, "the moral character of God is much compromised and the qualities of divine justice and divine love are emptied of all meaning and value" and that "unless we are in a position to believe in the spiritual possibilities of everyone who bears the human form divine, we cannot have a really useful ethics" (Radhakrishnan, *I. Phil.* ii.p.751), not only betray the very weakness to indulge in "soft emotional thinking" and to attempt to refute a hypothesis "by a pretence of its dangerous consequences to religion and morality"[14] but also an incorrect understanding of the true nature and bearing of the doctrine of Traividhya of Jīvas propounded by Madhva and *the premises on which it rests*. After all, philosophy has to find out what is true. It does not matter whether it pleases or irritates. The doctrine of Traividhya is no doubt an unpleasant truth, uncomfortable to some. That cannot be helped. As Prof. Thilly says : "The

14. Against which the Professor himself has spoken in his *Reign of Religion in Contemporary Philosophy*, quoted *ante*.

mere fact that a theory leaves no room for free will, immortality or God does not make it false, even though belief in such ideas should happen to help us over the dismal places in life"[15]. A gloomy truth is a better companion through life than a cheerful falsehood (such as *Sarvamukti*?). It would be irrational to discredit the intellect because its conclusions are not flattering to the future of *homo sapiens*, in all cases or because it does "not give us the world we want, or the heaven we want or the God we want." "The diremost need" as Prof. Thilly puts it, "cannot make black white, though it may persuade us to paint it white".

15. Quoted in Radhakrishnan's *The Reign of Religion in Contemporary Philosophy*, p. 14.

CHAPTER XXXV

TEXTUAL EVIDENCE OF INTRINSIC GRADATION AMONG SOULS

MADHVA and his commentators have cited many texts from the Vedic and post-Vedic literature, in support of the acceptance of the Traividhya among Jīvas. It will be enaugh to indicate only the most obvious and prominent of these, in which the doctrine is clearly discernible or has been expressly taught. The passages point clearly to the prevalence of a religious tradition in which the doctrine was accepted and handed down and which other currents of thoughts were unable to expurgate altogether.

Texts from Vedic Literature

1. खले न पर्षान् प्रतिहन्मि भूरि
   किं मां निन्दन्ति शत्रवोऽनिन्द्राः ।(*RV* X. 48.7)
2. श्रृण्वे वीर उग्रमुग्रं दमायन्
   अन्यमन्यमति नेनीयमानः ।
   एधमानद्विळुभयस्य राजा
   चोष्कूयते विश इन्द्रो मनुष्यान् ॥ (*RV* vi. 47.16)
3. परा पूर्वेषां सख्या वृणक्ति
   वितर्तुराणोऽपरेभिरेति ।
   अनानुभूतीरव धून्वानः
   पूर्वीरिन्द्र शरदः तर्तरीति ॥ (*RV* vi. 47.17)
4. दिवे दिवे सदृशीरन्यमर्धम् । (*RV* vi. 47.21)
5. **अनारंभणे तमसि** प्रविध्यतम् । (*RV* i. 182.6)
6. इन्द्रासोमा तपतं रक्ष उब्जतं
   न्यर्पयतं वृषणा तमोवृधः ।
   पराश्रृणीतमचितो न्योषतं
   हतं नुदेथां निशिसीतमत्रिणः ॥ (*RV* vii. 104.1)

7. इन्द्रासोमा वर्तयतं दिवस्परि
अग्नितप्तेभिः युवमश्महन्मभिः ।

* * * * *

तपुर्वधेभिरजरेभिरत्रिणः (*RV* vii. 104.5)

8. असुर्या नाम ते लोका अन्धेन तमसा वृताः (*IsaUp* 3)

9. सैषा आनन्दस्य मीमांसा भवति, ते ये शतं मानुषा आनन्दाः स· एको ब्रह्मण आनन्दः श्रोत्रियस्य चाकामहतस्य (*TaittUp* ii.8)

10. एकं पादं नोद्धरति (Śruti quoted by Deśika)

Post-Vedic Literature

11. दैवी संपद्विमोक्षाय निबन्धायासुरी मता (*Gītā* xvi.5)

12. द्वौ भूतसर्गौ लोकेऽस्मिन् दैव आसुर एव च (xvi.6)

13. **मामप्राप्यैव** कौन्तेय ततो यान्त्यधमां गतिम् (xvi.20)

14. ऊर्ध्वं गच्छन्ति सत्त्वस्था मध्ये तिष्ठन्ति राजसाः
जघन्यगुणवृत्तिस्था अधो गच्छन्ति तामसाः ॥ (*Gītā* xvi.18)

15. त्रिविधा भवति श्रद्धा देहिनां सा **स्वभावजा**.
सात्त्विकी राजसी चैव तामसी चेति (*Gītā* Viii.2)

16. * * *यो यच्छ्रद्धः स एव सः (*Gītā* xvi.3.)

17. मुक्तानामपि सिद्धानां नारायणपरायणः ।
सुदुर्लभः प्रशान्तात्मा कोटिष्वपि महामुने॥ (*Bhag* vi.14.5)

18. दुर्ज्ञेयं घोररूपस्य त्रैलोक्यध्वंसिनः प्रभोः ।
दैवतैर्मुनिभिःसिद्धैः * * * * ॥ (quoted in *AV* iii.4, adh.4)

19. ऐकात्म्यं नाम यदिदं केचित् ब्रूयुरनैपुणाः ।
शास्त्रतत्त्वमविज्ञाय शास्त्राणां शास्त्रदस्यवः ॥
तेषां तमःशरीराणां तम एव परायणम् ॥ (*Mbh* XII. 261. 47-50)

20. नित्यदुःखं सुसंपूर्णं निरस्तानन्दमव्ययम् ।
तमो यान्त्यन्यथाज्ञानात् द्वेषाद्वा हरिसंश्रयात् ॥
(*Paramasaṁhitā* quoted in *BT* x.94. 24)

21. नारायणप्रसादेन समिद्धज्ञानचक्षुषा ।
अत्यन्तदुःखसंलीनान् निःशेषसुखवर्जितान् ।
नित्यमेव तथाभूतान् विमिश्रांश्च गणान् बहून् ॥
निरस्ताशेषदुःखांश्च नित्यानन्दैकभोगिनः ।
अपश्यत् त्रिविधान् ब्रह्मा साक्षादेव चतुर्मुखः ॥
(*Pādma* quoted by Madhva in *BSB* iii.i.21)

22. जीवास्तु त्रिविधा राजन् नानाकाराः स्वभावतः ।
सात्त्विका मुक्तिभाजः स्युः तामसास्तु तमोऽनुगाः ।
मध्यमाः संसृतौ नित्यं ऊर्ध्वाधःपरिवर्तिनः ॥
(*Viṣṇu Rahasya* XXXIII)

23. एवं सात्त्विकमध्यस्थतामसान् त्रिविधानपि ।
सृजत्यवति हन्तीशो लीलया भक्तवत्सलः ॥ (*Viṣṇu Rahasya* Ch.V)

The question is likely to be raised : Do any of there texts teach *unalterable threefold nature* ? Can they not be understood as referring to selves as they *are or have been* and not as barring all possible improvement even in the distant future lives ? Some may even feel that eternal damnation is so alien to Indian thought that Christian influence is not unlikely.

The theory of tripartite classification of souls as proposed by Madhva has to be judged on its own merits and evidences, *as a broad hypothesis of human nature and destiny*. No useful purpose will be served by importing unnecessary sentiment into the discussion of the problem. Madhva and his commentators have put forward what they consider to be adequate grounds and textual authority in support of the theory. Kali and Vāṇīśvara (i.e. Brahmadeva) as Madhva says, represent the two poles of evil and goodness. They must have their reward. The doctrine of Traividhya is thus a corollary of Anādiyogyatā (beginningless fitness) which seems to be the ultimate explanation of diversity of natures, propensities and opportunities, going beyond all other explanations offered by the hypothesis of Karmabheda (differentiation by Karma) and every other explanation including free will.[1] In matters like this no one can speak with prevision of the future. We can only argue from the known to the unknown. What is true and has been true may also hold good in the future. The assessment of the problem as given by a thinker of Alexander Fraser's standing cannot be dismissed as utterly irrational. All that we can say is that there is as much to be said in support of the theory of "Jīva-traivi-

1. सिद्धौ हि कर्मभेदस्य स्यादुपाधिविभिन्नता ।
तत्सिद्धौ चैव तत्सिद्धिः इत्यन्योन्यव्यपाश्रयः ।
आत्मस्वरूपभेदस्य विदोषत्वेन चाखिलः ॥ (*UpKh*)

dhya", objectively speaking, as perhaps *against* it. An intrinsic divergence of nature and faith into *sāttvika, rājasa* and *tāmasa* which is rooted in the core of individual nature (*dehinām svabhāvajā*) as stated in the *Gītā*, is the ultimate basis of this theory according to Madhva. What is thus ultimately traced to the essential nature (*svabhāva*) of the selves must indeed be unalterable. One may of course, prefer to understand "*mām aprāpyaiva*" (without attaining Me *at all*) and similar references, liberally rather than strictly literally. *But those who insist on understanding the words literally are not debarred from doing so by the rules of grammar and language.* Text No. 21 refers to the vision experienced by Brahmā *after* enlightenment in the state of Mahāpralaya. This cannot be regarded as a description of anything but the great cosmic destiny of souls, when the whole universe lies submerged according to the Purāṇas. Words like "*nityam eva tathābhūtān*" 'He saw those that had been steeped in darkness like that *for all time*', do not admit of any other explanation.

To attribute Christian influence to Madhva in formulating the theory of Jīva-traividhya and threefold destiny of souls is too far-fetched. The theory is not incapable of being derived and developed from within the framework of Indian thought and facts and ideas recorded and established in Indian religious tradition and Scriptures and the presuppositions of the law of Karma itself, apart from an adequate measure of recorded evidence suggestive of a belief in such a general theory of human nature and destiny. It is perfectly capable of being explained by the immanent dynamic of Svarūpabhedavāda.

Madhva's theory is more a theory of natural selection *from within*, in the spiritual field rather than a theory of predestination arbitrarily imposed on the souls *from without*. It will not do to ignore this difference in comparing the Tamoyogyas of Madhva's theory with those consigned to eternal damnation in the Christian theory, more or less arbitrarily, by Divine fiat.

Lastly, there is no class of souls corresponding to Nityasaṁsārins in the Christian theory. This shows that Madhva's theory is developed from the doctrine of Trividhā-Śraddhā in the *Gītā* and its 'Sāṅkhyan' counterpart to be traced, *ultimately*, to its proper source in the nature of the Jīvas themselves.

The existence of a class of 'Nityasaṁsārins' as already mentioned has been accepted in the Viśiṣṭādvaitic tradition[2] also and by some early Naiyāyikas too, as indicated by Jayatīrtha in his *NS* :

नित्यसंसारिणां केषांचित् सत्त्वस्य तैरप्यंगीकृतत्वात् समर्थयिष्यमाणत्वाच्च ।

(*NS* iii. 3, p. 547)

जीवात्मपक्षीकारे संसार्येकस्वभावानां जीवानां स्वयमेवोररीकृतत्वेन तत्र बाधात् ।

(*NS*, p.548 b)

The references, according to the commentators, are to the view of Udayanācārya : संसार्येकस्वभावा: केचिदात्मान: । We also have it on the authority of Citsukha that certain Vaiśeṣika thinkers like Kandalīkāra (i.e. Śrīdhara)[3] and Līlāvatīkāra held the view of *nityasaṁsāra* for some souls :

कन्दलीकारादिभिः कैश्चित् वैशेषिकविशेषैः सर्वमुक्तेरनङ्गीकारात् ।

(*Citsukhī*, p. 357)

The doctrine of Traividhya is *not thus an invention of Madhva.* It has the support of Vedic and post-Vedic tradition and is the natural corollary of the doctrine of Svarūpabheda of souls without which the Hindu doctrine of Karma would have no force or meaning. It is *not* simply an extension of the Sāṁkhya theory of Traiguṇya or based upon it, as is sometimes *superficially assumed.*[4] The three guṇas of Sāṁkhya metaphysics are but the modes of Prakṛti; whereas the terms Sāttvika, Rājasa and Tāmasa applied to the Jīvas in their tripartite classification, according to Madhva, have reference to their basic nature of

---

2. In the background of the Viśiṣṭādvaitic acceptance of Nityasūris and of Nityasaṁsārins by one section, the addition of one more category of Nitya-tamoyogyas cannot possibly be ruled out as farfetched. (See Chapter XXXIV fn. 9). The "Sayūthyas" are most probably the Tengalai-Vaiṣṇavas. There is no reference in the writings of *modern scholars on Indian Philosophy,* to the acceptance of this peculiar position regarding the classification of Souls in the ancient tradition of the Viśiṣṭādvaita school itself. Dr. Chandradhar Sharma's *A Critical Survey of I. Phil.* (London 1960) is no exception to this.

3. Prof. Jadunath Sinha gives Śrīdhara's date as 1000 A.D. He was thus at least three centuries earlier than Madhva.

4. See R. Nagaraja Sarma, *Reign of Realism in I. Phil.* pp. 174, 653 and 664. Cf.

पुरुषबहुत्वं सिद्धं त्रैगुण्यविपर्ययाच्चैव

(*Sāṁkhya Kārikā*, 18)

Caitanya going beyond the play of Prakṛti and its guṇas : यो यच्छ्रद्धः स एव सः (*Gitā*, xvii. 3). This is clear from Madhva's comment on the above verse, where he interprets the term सत्त्वानुरूपा (सर्वस्य श्रद्धा) as चित्तानुरूपा which is further more explicitly rendered by Jayatīrtha as **चित्तं चैतन्यं जीव इति यावत्** (*GB*, *Prameyadipikā*, xvii. 3).

CHAPTER XXXVI

THE SOULS' RELATION TO BRAHMAN

SEVERAL figures of speech and symbolic expressions have been used in the Śāstras to make clear the relation of metaphysical dependence of the Jīvas on Brahman. Commentators have also added some more of their own choice, in interpreting those ideas. Terms like "Rūpa-Pratirūpa", "Aṁśa-Aṁśī", "Chāyā-Puruṣa", "Śarīra-Śarīrin", "Ābhāsa", "Agnivisphuliṅga" occur in the original texts. The Advaita philosophy looks upon this relation as one of 'Adhiṣṭhāna-āropyabhāva' (the substratum and the superimposed appearance) or "(Bimba)-Pratibimbabhāva". Rāmānuja prefers to call it "Śarīra-Śarīribhāva" or "Śeṣa-Śeṣibhāva". For reasons already set forth, Madhva does not subscribe to any of the ideas underlying these terms *as understood by* Advaitins, Bhedābhedavādins and Viśiṣṭādvaitins. He has, therefore, thought it fit to give a new and deeper significance to the term "Bimba-Pratibimbahhāva", met with in the texts and use it in the symbolic sense of metaphysical dependence of Jīva on Brahman. Along with it, he has also used the other terms used by the Sūtrakāra viz., "Aṁśāṁsi", "Ābhāsa-ābhāsaka," which he interprets in the same sense. We may now discuss the question fully.

The term "Bimba-Pratibimbahāva" is derived by Madhva from the significant passage in *RV* VII. 47.18:

रूपं रूपं प्रतिरूपो बभूव
तदस्य रूपं प्रतिचक्षणाय ।[1]

It is confirmed by Madhva on the basis of the coeternality of the Jīvas with Brahman, taught in Gītā ii, 12 read together

1. "With reference to each form of Jiva, He (the Lord) becomes the original Form. His Form is for this one (the Jīva) to perceive".

with the repeated emphasis laid on the Jīva's dependence on Brahman for his existence, consciousness and activity, for all time.

The underlying idea behind all these descriptions is the same, viz. that Brahman is the One Independent Source of all reality, consciousness and activity found in the individual selves and which cannot, therefore, be explained without reference to their dependence on Brahman for their being. As no creation of Jīvas *de novo* is admitted in Vedānta, the figure of Pratibimba should *not be* construed literally in the sense of the Jīvas being the actual reflections projected by Brahman like that of a concrete object in a mirror. Madhva warns his readers against taking the scriptural description of Jīva as a Pratibimba of Brahman in its gross physical sense of *an actual reflection*. That is why he is so careful and particular to insist that there is *no external medium* (*bāhya upādhi*) of reflection *in this case*. This would at once bring out the difference between Madhva's and Śaṅkara's conception of Jīva as a Pratibimba of Brahman. According to Śaṅkara, the Jīva is a *false appearance* or projection of Brahman on the screen of Avidyā. This relation, therefore, can be transcended.

जीवत्वं च मृषा ज्ञेयं रज्ज्वां सर्पग्रहो यथा ।

(Śaṅkara : *Aparokṣānubhūti*, 43)

But to Madhva, the relation of Bimbapratibimbabhāva between God and Soul is a *sacred and inviolable relation*, which is true for all time and goes to the very core of the Jīva and constitutes his very essence and could never be annulled or transcended. Its full significance, missed in Saṁsāra, is realized in Mokṣa. Mokṣa in fact is the complete realization of this intrinsic relationship of metaphysical dependence on and similarity (in some respects) to the Supreme. "Pratibimbatva" according to Madhva is *not a false relation which the Jīvas are to be ashamed of and should try to shake off*, as in Advaita. It is the truest, and the most beautiful permanent bond with the Supreme Being and the purpose of Philosophy is its progressive realization by the Jīva. The two doctrines are thus diametrically opposed !

Madhva brings out the idea of metaphysical dependence contained in the various other expressions, by a proper interpretation of them. There is, first of all, the idea of *a man and his shadow*, in one of the Upaniṣads :

यथैषा पुरुषे छाया एतस्मिन्नेतदाततम् । (*PraśnaUp.* iii.3)

The point of this analogy is dependence and similarity:

छाया यथा पुंसदृशी पुमधीना च दृश्यते ।[2] (*AV* ii.2.18)

The two outstanding features of a shadow are its resemblance to the original object and its dependence upon it for its existence and for its being perceived. The Jīvas also to some extent resemble Brahman (*BS*, iii.3.29) and are metaphysically dependent on It. Hence the figure. The term "Aṁśa-aṁśi" also conveys the same truth:

जीवस्य परमेश्वरांशत्वं तु, तत्सादृश्यं, तदधीनसत्तादिमत्त्वं चेत्यर्थः ।

(*NS* ii, p.453)

Madhva develops this idea at some length in his *Gītā Bhāṣya* and shows the inapplicability of the relation of part and whole in this case:

न चांशत्वविरोधः । तस्यैव (प्रतिबिम्बत्वस्यैब) अंश (शब्दप्रवृत्तिनिमित्त)त्वात् । (II.24)

The analogy of Chāyā-Puruṣa also conveys the idea that God is immeasurably more than and superior to the Souls as the substance is greater than its shadow. The shadow is there because of the substance. It is bound to the object which casts the shadow but not *vice versa*. The dependence is thus unilateral and not reciprocal. The shadow is outwardly similar to the object in form. The souls have the same form and content of reality, consciousness and bliss, *resembling* Brahman's.[3] It should always be remembered that analogies should not be stretched indefinitely. The point of the analogy is strictly confined to the ideas of dependence and similarity and nothing more. Satyanātha Tīrtha, in his *Abhinavacandrikā*, therefore, rightly reminds us that the figure of Pratibimbatva of the Jīva is merely a technical figure (Pāribhāṣika) and has nothing to do with the conventional sense of the term. Madhva also gives a similar warning : नातिसाम्यं निदर्शने (*AV*), that we should not

---

2. क्वचित् चेतनेऽपि छायाशब्दप्रयोगः प्रतिबिम्बत्वसाम्याद्भवति ।

(*MS* p. 68)

3. The description of Jīvas as '*Vipluḍānandabhāginaḥ*' by Madhva explains the significance of the comparison.

stretch the analogy to the point of *the lifelessness of the Pratibimba*: जडत्वादिभिरपि नेत्यर्थः (*NS* p. 505). It is the association of the ideas of physical reflection and the presence of an Upādhi, in the conventional usage of the term (as current in the Advaita) that cause an initial confusion in understanding clearly the nature and implications of the doctrine of Bimbapratibimbabhāva, according to Madhva. This should, therefore, be strictly guarded against. That is why Madhva draws special attention to the fact that the analogy of reflection (*pratibimba*) should not be taken to presuppose the existence of any external reflecting medium between Jīva and Brahman. The reason is that such a medium would immediately render the reflection transient (*anitya*), impermanent and non-eternal. That would snap the relation of coeternality between the two (द्वा सुपर्णा सयुजा सखाया). Commenting on *BS* iii. 2.18, Madhva shows the significance of the emphatic particles अत एव च in drawing equal attention to the points of comparison *and contrast* in the employment of the simile : *Sūryakādivat*. The points of contact are the possession, by the Jīva, of certain characteristics of reality, consciousness and bliss *similar to those of Brahman* and depending upon it for them. The points of contrast from an ordinary reflection are: (1) *not being conditioned by an external medium* (*Upādhi*); (2) *not being liable to destruction by virtue of the destruction of such Upādhi*; and (3) *not being an insentient* (*lifeless*) *effect*. The fulll significance of the Sūtra, according to Madhva, lies in pointing out in what sense the Jīva is to be understood as a reflection of Brahman and *in what sense he is not to be understood as a reflection*. The emphasis laid by the Sūtrakāra on the two expressions 'अत एव' points unmistakably to the reasons *already stated by him*, on which the Pratibimbatva of the Jīvas rests. These have been rightly identified by Madhva as difference, dependence and similarity (भिन्नत्व, तदधीनत्व and तत्सादृश्य) taught in the *preceding sūtras* ii. 3. 28; iii. 1.1; ii. 3. 29. It also *implies a point of contrast* which is again well brought out by Madhva by adding a rider : न तूपाध्यायतत्त्वादिना. If no point of contrast is intended by the Sūtrakāra, the suffix वत् in सूर्यकादिवत् (iii.2.18) would be pointless and redundant as pointed out by Jayatīrtha and the Sūtra could as well have been worded अत एव सूर्यकादिः उपमा.

What is, therefore, sought to be emphasized by the figure of

Bimbapratibimbahhāva is nothing more than an essential eternal metaphysical dependence of the Jīvas on Brahman. This relation is natural and intrinsic to them and is not conditioned by anything other than the nature of the Pratibimbas, such as Avidyā in Advaita. This is achieved by making such Pratibimbatva an essential characteristic (*svalakṣaṇa*) of the Jīvas, resting on an intrinsic relation (*nirupādhikasambandha*). Were it not so, the relation itself would be snapped, the moment the Upādhis or conditioning factors that have caused and sustainned the relation cease to exist. *The Jīva would then be no more* ! But since the Jīvas and Brahman are *both ex hypothesi* eternal to the Vedānta[4] their mutual relation, too, must be equally so. So, Bimbapratibimbabhāva must be eternal : यावदात्मभावी. It is easy to see that any relation that is *not grounded in the nature of Brahman and the Jīvas* themselves could *not* be eternal. *Obviously, Avidyā is not, and cannot be, such a relation* ! Hence, Madhva is justified in thinking of a fresh and more lasting relationship between the Jīvas and Brahman, which would be true of them in bondage and in release. He finds such a relation in the symbolism of "Bimbapratibimbabhāva" which is actually foreshadowed in the Ṛg Vedic passage रूपं रूपं प्रतिरूपो बभूव which he quotes in his Bhāṣya. There is evidently a deep scientific idea behind this symbolism. The objection that all ordinary reflections are brought about by conditioning factors is met by pointing out that *here we have a symbolism and not a prosaic analogy*. Even otherwise, the point of the illustration could be understood in a deeper metaphysical sense (*alaukika*) than in a conventional sense (*laukika*).

If, however, in deference to the letter of the Sūtra and the technical requirement of Pratibimbatva one *must* insist on having some sort of a medium in the case of the Bimbapratibimbabhāva relation between Jīva and Brahman *also*, Madhva has suggested that the Jīva-svarūpa itself can be treated as the 'Upādhi'. This is called "Svarūpopādhi". This is a complicated

---

4. Cf. नित्यो नित्यानाम् (Kaṭha Up. iii. 2.13)
नित्यः सर्वगतः स्थाणुः (*Gītā* ii. 24)
नत्वेवाहं . . . (*Gītā* ii 2)

idea. On this view, the Jīva would constitute both the medium and the reflection *by the force of his internal Viśeṣas.* This point will be explained later. The introduction of the idea of "Svarūpa-Upādhi" is for the purpose of denying the presence of any *external* upādhi in the relation of the Jīva to Brahman (as there is in Advaita : ब्रह्मैवाविद्यया संसरति).

The same is the case with other expression "Ābhāsa" used by the Śūtrakāra (*BS* ii.3.50). This term also signifies, according to Madhva, the ideas of dependence and similarity.

ब्रह्माभासत्वादिति हेतोः ब्रह्माधीनत्वात् तत्सादृशत्वाच्चेत्यर्थः, न तु सूर्यकादिवत् प्रतिबिम्बत्वादिति। (*NS* p. 505)

It is needless to say that in dealing with such profound themes, we should not vulgarise thought by the admixture of popular fancies and superficial association of ideas. Madhva goes into the esoteric etymology of the word "Ābhāsa" in which the Sūtrakāra has chosen to describe the Jīva's relationship to Brahman.

तत आभासते नित्यं तद्वद् आभासतेऽपि च ।
भानमस्तित्वमपि चैवासमन्ताद्यतस्ततः ।
जीव आभास उद्दिष्टो सदैव परमात्मनः । (*AV* iii.2.50)

Jayatīrtha, explaining the point writes that the Jīva is termed Ābhāsa for two reasons : (1) that his consciousness of himself and others is essentially dependent on Brahman and (2) that he is luminous like Brahman.[5] The etymological details of this explanation are thus set forth by him :

भानं ज्ञानं, अस्तित्वं सत्त्वम् । भा च सा च भासे । आ सर्वकालवर्तिन्यौ भासे आभासे, परमात्माधीने आभासे यस्यासौ जीवः परमात्माभासः । (*NS*, p. 503)

Consistent with this inerpretation of 'Ābhāsa' Jayatīrtha has also given us a new interpretation of "Tat tvam asi" text in terms of Bimbapratibimbabhāva relation between Brahman and Jīvas in his commentary on Madhva's *Tdy*.

Elsewhere, in his bhāṣya on the *BS* Madhva has given us another illustration of a puppet in emphasizing the conative dependence of Jīvas on God.

यथा दारुमयीं योषां नरः स्थिरसमाहितः ।
इङ्गयत्यङ्गमङ्गानि तथा राजन्निमाः प्रजाः ॥ (*BSB* ii.1.24)

5. तेन परमात्मना निमित्तेन आभासते प्रतीतो भवतीति प्रतीतौ तदधीनत्वमुच्यते। तद्वत ब्रह्मवत् आभासत इति तत्सदृशत्वम् । (*NS* p. 505)

It may be noted in this connection that the Sūtrākāra ascribes the creative activity of Jīvas to the Supreme (ii.3.41). This is merely to emphasize their dependence. It is not as if human beings are like puppets without life or initiative. It is only that the Pratibimba has no *independent* activity: नहि प्रतिबिंबस्य क्रिया । स हि बिम्बक्रिययैव क्रियावान् (Madhva, *GB*), which should be carefully interpreted to signify बिम्बाधीनक्रिययैव क्रियावान् as pointed out by Jayatīrtha (*GBt* p. 83).

In his Bhāṣya on *BS* ii.3.50, Madhva brings out the implication of the figure of "Bimbapratibimbabhāva" between Jīva and Brahman by drawing a clear distinction between ordinary reflections which are dependent on external media (*sopādhipratibimba*) and those which are not so dependent and in that sense mediumless (*nirupādhipratibimba*) :

सोपाधिरनुपाधिश्च प्रतिबिम्बो द्विधेयते ।
जीव ईशस्यानुपाधिः, इन्द्रचापो यथा रवेः ॥

(Madhva in *BSB* ii.3.50)

The image of a face reflected in a mirror is entirely dependent on the external medium of the mirror and it is liable to disappear as soon as the mirror is removed from the range of the *bimba* or is destroyed. But as there is no destruction of the Jīva at any time[6] the mutual relation between Brahman and Jīvas cannot be attributed to the action of any external Upādhis. Madhva cites the phenomenon of rainbow as an instance of a Nirupādhi-pratibimba of the Sun's rays to elucidate his conception of Jīva as a Nirupādhipratibimba of Paramātman. As this is an unusual illustration, with a deep philosophical significance, which is not obvious on the surface of it, it requires further clarification to show in what sense the phenomenon of rainbow is to be understood as a Pratibimba without an external medium. As everyone knows, rainbow is caused by the Sun's rays falling on drops of rain-water. The rays enter the drops and are refracted and again reflected and then broken into the components of the "Vibgyor" as they emerge out of the rain drops, in resplendent colors as the 'rainbow' manifested by the rays

6. Cf. अविनाशी वा अरेऽयमात्मा अनुच्छित्तिधर्मा । (*BrhUp* iv. 5.14)
सर्गेऽपि नोपजायन्ते प्रलये न व्यथन्ति च । (*Gītā* xiv. 2)
जीवो नित्यो धातुरस्य त्वनित्यः । (*Mbh* xviii.5.50)

themselves. As such the rainbow is an image of the Sun's rays acting as their own medium. We have similarly to conceive of the Jīva as the image and the medium by the power of Viśeṣa, at the same time.[7] The mirror merely throws back the light falling upon it. The rain-drops, however, receive the light and they let it traverse through them and emerge out of them again and in this process exhibit the glory of sunlight. The rain-drops must be deemed to be active, unlike the mirror which is merely passive.

The simile of the Sun and the rainbow given by Madhva brings out the significance of the relationship between Brahman and the Jīva in a very impressive manner. The Jīva is the agent, the vehicle for the manifestation of the Divine light falling upon himself. What we know now of God, of His love and goodness, His compassion and other auspicious attributes is from our association with godly men and women, His devotees, who in their lives manifest these virtues. They are the raindrops, that reveal the majesty and the glory that lie concealed in the white rays of the Sun. By this analogy Madhva wants to convey that everyone of us is a tiny raindrop whichstill has the potency, the capacity to receive and manifest the Divine light and transmit it. The figure of Bimbapratibimba thus gives

---

7. That the rainbow is also popularly regarded as a 'Sopādhika-Pratibimba' will be clear from the *Bhāṣyadīpikā* (p. 634) which dismisses such an interpretation of the passage quoted by Madhva, as untenable.

अत्र दृष्टान्ते बिम्बातिरिक्तोपाध्यभावो दार्ष्टान्तिके तु प्रतिबिम्बातिरिक्तोपाध्यभावः। अतिरिक्तोपाध्यभावस्तु उभयत्र सम इति द्रष्टव्यम्।

केचित्तु—सोपाधिप्रतिबिबस्य इन्द्रचाप उदाहरणम्। तस्य सूर्यमण्डलं वा, सूर्यतेजो वोपाधिः। उपादानं च तदेव। निरुपाधिप्रतिबिम्बस्यतु जीव उदाहरणम् इति यथाशब्दावृत्त्या वाक्यद्वयमपि दृष्टान्तपरतया योजयन्ति। तत्तु चन्द्रिकाननुगुणत्वात्, मूलाभावाच्चोपेक्ष्यम्।

The rainbow is a 'nirupādhipratibimba' of the colours of the Sun's rays in the sense of having no *upādhi* other than and external to them, to manifest the colors (*Bimbātiriktopādhyabhāva*). As for the 'dārṣṭāntika' (viz. the Jīva) he needs no other medium than his own pristine essence (*pratibimbātirikta-upādhyabhāva*) to be able to intuit, capture and realize his intimacy of nature as "Tadguṇasāra" with the Lord. M. A. Krishnaswani Rao, Retired Professor of Physics has explained the symbolic bases of Madhva's description of the rainbow as a *nirupādhipratibimba* of the Sun's rays, in an article published in the *Dharma Prakash* Journal of the ABMM Madras (Vol. VI. No. 3, 1976). See also Vol. VII No. 4 of the same Journal.

meaning, expresses a great religio-philosophical truth and value and establishes an intimacy of relationship between Man and God, which is the noblest truth of philosophy and religion, to be attained by us. The reader can see in this and in Madhva's equally suggestive interpretation of the Sūtra : *Ambuvad agrahaṇāt tu na tathātvam* (*BS* iii.2.19), the poetic quality and the mystic inwardness of his conception of the eternal and intimate relation that binds Jīva to Brahman[8].

The conception of "Svarūpopādhi" may now be examined. Madhva clarifies his position in his *BT* IV.22.26 :

जीवोपाधिर्द्विधा प्रोक्तः स्वरूपं बाह्यमेव च ।
बाह्योपाधिर्लयं याति, मुक्तावन्यस्य तु स्थितिः ॥
सर्वोपाधिविनाशे हि प्रतिबिम्बं कथं भवेत् ?
कथं चात्मविनाशाय प्रयत्नः सेत्स्यति क्वचित् ?
अपुमर्थता च मुक्तेः स्यादभावात् पुंस एव तु ॥[9]

The "internal medium" is nothing more than the constituent elements of selfhood, operating as "Upādhis" as it were, by the power of "Viśeṣas" which are self-linking:

उपाध्युपाधिमद्भावो विशेषबलेन इति भावः ।

(Jayatīrtha : *GBt.* ii.18)

There is no difficulty, says Madhva, in the Jīvasvarūpa operating as its own medium as it is essentially self-luminous:

स्वयमेवात्र प्रदर्शकः चित्त्वात् ।

(*GB* ii.18) (See Chapter XXXI)

It may be objected that all this is somewhat mystifying. Would not the Jīvasvarūpa itself operating as its own medium of reflection be premature, insofar as the Jīvasvarūpa itself would be inconceivable without a Jīva already being there? And if he should already be there, where is the need to reflect?

---

8. See my *BSPC* Vol. III, pp. 106-07.

9. The Upādhis (manifesting conditions) of Jivas are twofold, intrinsic and extrinsic. The extrinsic Upādhis are liquidated in Mokṣa. The other one continues to be(in Mokṣa). If all Upādhis are destroyed, how can Jīva continue to be a Pratibimba of the Supreme Being in Mokṣa ? If Mokṣa were the liquidation of Ātman himself who will strive for it ? If Mokṣa means the extinction of the self it will cease to be a Puruṣārtha (aim of the Puruṣa to achieve). *He* himself *will not be there to attain it.*'

Again whom is he to reflect? Or whose reflection is he? Not God or God's nor even of himself as there is no point in it.

The correct answer to these and other difficulties is on these lines. We must first of all understand the true significance of the expression Svarūpopādhi and its function. The Upādhis of Jīvas are of two kinds—external and internal. The external Upādhis are the body, mind and its modifications. The internal Upādhis are the elements which constitute the Jīvacaitanya—viz. its finitude, its eternal dependence on God for its existence and functioning and for its possessing the attributes of jñāna, ānanda, etc., similar to those of Brahman to a limited extent. The external Upādhis give rise to a distorted image of the Jīva in Saṁsāra, inducing in him a mistaken notion of his identification with his bodily possessions, on account of long intimate association with them from the beginning of creation. They make him react to their influences, as if they are part of his own essence and belonging to him in his own right independently of God's Will. The analogy of a cracked dust-stained mirror which gives a distorted picture of face will help to understand the part played by the Jīva's external Upādhis in life. On the other hand the Svarūpopādhis being no other than the essential constituents of Jīvahood are competent to reflect and manifest to the Jīva himself his true nature and attributes and his relation to the Lord, when they come into full play in the released state:

द्विविधो हि जीवोपाधिः आभ्यन्तरो बाह्यश्च । तत्र **स्वरूपप्रतिभासहेतुराभ्यन्तरः । स्वरूपविपरीतावभासहेतुः अन्तःकरणादिः बाह्यः ।** (*NS* p. 506)

The description of Jiva as a "Nirupādhipratibimba" (image without a medium) is used to convey the fact that the core of Jīva is not determined by any of his external Upādhis:

निरुपाधिप्रतिबिम्बवाचोयुक्तिरपि बाह्योपाध्यधीनत्वाभावाभिप्रायेण नेतव्या ।
(*NS* p. 506 b)

As Bhakti grows in depth, intensity and maturity, Jīva realizes more and more his metaphysical dependence, difference and similarity to the Supreme. And in Mokṣa also, where these conditions of dependence, difference and likeness to Brahman, which constitute the essence of Jīvas, persist they continue to be the Pratibimbas of Brahman, with the fullest realization of that fact, unlike in Saṁsāra, where this truth of their real nature and relationship to Brahman is hidden by Ajñāna and other factors, by the will of God. True devotion and loving attachment to God are, however, capable of moving the Supreme to grace and realization of the true nature of one's own svarūpa by Jīva (and of the nature of God) then becomes easy and possible. Such in fact is the place, function and role of Svarūpopādhis, in the system of Madhva.

The relation of "Aṁśāṁśibhāva' ' also stands for the same idea of dependence and similarity:

प्रतिबिम्बत्वस्यैव अंशशब्दप्रवृत्तिनिमित्तत्वात् (Jayatīrtha : *GB* ii.24)

Jīva is an *Aṁśa* (fraction) of Brahman. This is a purely symbolic idea. He is the ectype of God endowed with a smaller measure of resembling attributes of reality, consciousness and bliss. The figure has no doubt some association with 'part and whole' and may imply some kind of identity-cum-difference as between the cloth and its threads, as understood by Bhāskara and others. But Madhva rejects the relation of "bhedābheda" between Jīva and Brahman and accepts fundamental difference between them. He, therefore, substitutes '*aṁśatva*' for 'identity' (*abheda*), "aṁśatva" being understood as equivalent to Pratibimbatva. In his commentary on *BS* ii. 3.43, where the term *aṁśa* is used by the Sūtrakāra to define Jīvātman's relation to Brahman, Madhva *cautions* us against understanding the term as equivatent to *bhedābheda*—i.e. an affirmation of both difference and identity of natures as *equally true* and primary:

अतश्चांशत्वमुद्दिष्टं **भेदाभेदौ न मुख्यतः** ।[10]

He distinguishes two kinds of "aṁśas", viz. 'Svarūpa-aṁśa' and 'bhinnāṁśa'.[11] The manifestations of the Lord as Matsya, Kūrma and other Avatāras are His Svāṁśas or Svarūpa-aṁśas, identical with Him and possessing the same degree and extent of all powers. Jīvas are Bhinnāṁśas (ectypes) with relatively

10. This passage does *not* mean "*separateness and non-separateness ought not to be understood literally*" as misconstrued by J.E. Carpenter (*Theism in Mediaeval India*, 1921, p. 411). We need not, therefore, deplore with him that "Unhappily Madhva did not adhere to this suggestion". See my *HDSV* p. 120. H.N. Raghavendrachar too has similarly misunderstood and misrepresented the meaning of this text in his Kannaḍa work : *Dvaita Vedānta*.

11. स्वांशश्चाथ विभिन्नांश इति द्वेधांश इष्यते । (Madhva : *BSB* ii. 3.47)

lesser order of powers. The difference is one of both degree and order. It is innate and cannot be transcended:

विभिन्नांशोऽल्पशक्तिः स्यात् किंचित्सादृश्यमात्रयुक् । (*AV* ii. 3.48)

This relation of aṁśa is also used by Madhva to reconcile the conflict of Bheda and Abheda Śrutis. He accepts difference between God and Soul as real and true and uses the concept of *aṁśatva* to convey the sense of "belonging to": तत्सम्बन्धित्वमेवतदंशत्वमिति वक्ष्यामः (*TP* ii.3.43). For purposes of reconciling the "Bheda" and "Abheda" Śrutis, Madhva holds that "Abheda" or identity should be understood not in the sense of identity of essence but of *aṁśatvam* (belonging to):

श्रुतिद्वयान्यथानुपपत्त्या भेदमंगीकृत्य, **अभेदस्थाने अंशत्वं** वक्तव्यमिति भावः ।
(*TP* ii. 3.43)

The point is this. As difference and identity cannot both be accepted in their primary sense at the same time as between Jīva and Brahman and as difference persists even on the other side of Mokṣa, it is best to construe "identity" in the sense of *aṁsatvam*, as defined, in order to avoid the self-contradiction in accepting *bheda* and *abheda* as equally true:

अतश्चांशत्वमुद्दिष्टं **भेदाभेदौ न मुख्यतः ।**
(Madhva : *BSB* ii. 3.43)

The term '*bhedāhedau*' is a *dvandva* compound and means difference *and* identity. What Madhva means by the above statement is that as difference and identity understood in their primary senses (*mukhyataḥ*) will be self-contradictory, both of them cannot be accepted on an equal footing. As applied to the relationship between Jīva and Īśvara, one of them has to be understood in a figurative or secondary sense. Which of the two is to be accepted in its primary sense and which in a figurative sense is clarified by Madhva when he says: Without prejudice to the Bheda Śrutis which are the Upajīvya, the Abheda Śrutis are to be understood in the sense of *aṁsatva* standing for resemblance, and possession of reality dependent on Brahman. Here *aṁśa* does not mean any physical identity of part and whole which is *one* of its accepted meanings. Its use here is purely figurative as applied to the Jīvas who are Bhinnāṁśas of the Lord:

मुख्यांशसादृश्यं तत्सत्तयैव सत्तावत्त्वलक्षणमेव जीवस्यांशत्वम् । गौणोऽयमंशशब्द इति यावत् ।
(*NS* p. 453)

Śaṅkara also interprets the term Aṁśa in the Sūtra ii.3.43, as "a part *as it were*" (अंश इवांशः). Aṁśa is thus a figurative expression for dependence and presupposes difference as admitted by Śaṅkara himself. The latter half of the Sūtra refers to some kind of identity that would be compatible with Svarūpabheda, already accepted. Such an identity, then, could only be grounded in similarity and dependence.

Madhva concedes freely that there are points of contact between Jīva and Brahman. Their distinction, however great and ineradicable, is one of order and degree and not of kind. The soul of man at its best possesses the characteristics of reality, consciousness and bliss similar to those of Brahman. It is in virtue of this that any relation with Brahman is possible, and Jīva is sometimes identified with Brahman— तद्गुणसारत्वात्तु तद्व्यपदेशः (ii. 3.29). The freed soul has a nature akin to God which enables it to be in harmony with the divine in Mokṣa :

मुक्तानां सत्यकामत्वं सामर्थ्यं च परस्य तु ।
कामानुकूलकामत्वं नान्यत्तेषां विधीयते । (*BSB* iv. 2.18)

It should be obvious then that Madhva is not for any irreconcilable *opposition* between the two. He allows even the most exaggerated and high-flown description of the affinity between the two in mystic or philosophical parlance, provided the modicum of difference between them, borne out by the authorities, is not tampered with. Absolute *exclusiveness* of Jīva and Brahman is *not* thus a characteristic of Madhva's position. Brahman is the Antaryāmi of Ātman and as such could never be *excluded from him*. Some community of nature is certainly there and even with that it is possible to keep the position distinct from the complete merger of the Advaita. The intrinsic natures of the two are such that no merger is possible :

अल्पशक्तिरसार्वज्ञं पारतंत्र्यमपूर्णता ।
उपजीवकत्वं जीवत्वमीशत्वं तद्विपर्ययः ॥

(*Mahāviṣṇupurāṇa* quoted by *Vādaratnāvali*)

The Mukta, too, does not bloom into a sovereign lord, overnight or at any time. The released are under an irrevocable limitation with regard to the exercise of cosmic functions of the Supreme, according to *BS* iv. 4.17. These differences which persist in Mokṣa, too, should thus be intrinsic (*svābhāvika*) and not brought about by Avidyā, or association with bodies. It is on these grounds that Madhva refuses to merge and absorb souls in God.

At the same time, God and Soul are not as irreconcilably *opposed* to each other as light and darkness. We have seen that Madhva recognizes that some of Jīvātman's essential properties like *Jñāna* and *ānanda* are akin to those of Brahman. On that basis he is sometimes spoken of as identical with Brahman. *Tadguṇasāratvāt tu tadvyapadeśaḥ* (*BS* ii.3.29). Excluding Svarūpaikya there are other acceptable standpoints from which such figurative '*aikya*' can be accommodated :

सादृश्याच्च प्रधानत्वात् स्वातंत्र्यादपि वाभिदाम् ।
आहुरीशेन जीवस्य न स्वरूपाभिदां क्वचित् ॥[12] (*AV* ii.3.29)

12. "The Śrutis speak of the oneness of Jīva and Brahman on the basis of the former's bearing some measure of similarity to Brahman and the primacy of and independence of Brahman. They do *not* speak anywhere of their identity of essence." For further details vide my *BSPC* ii. pp. 217-20.

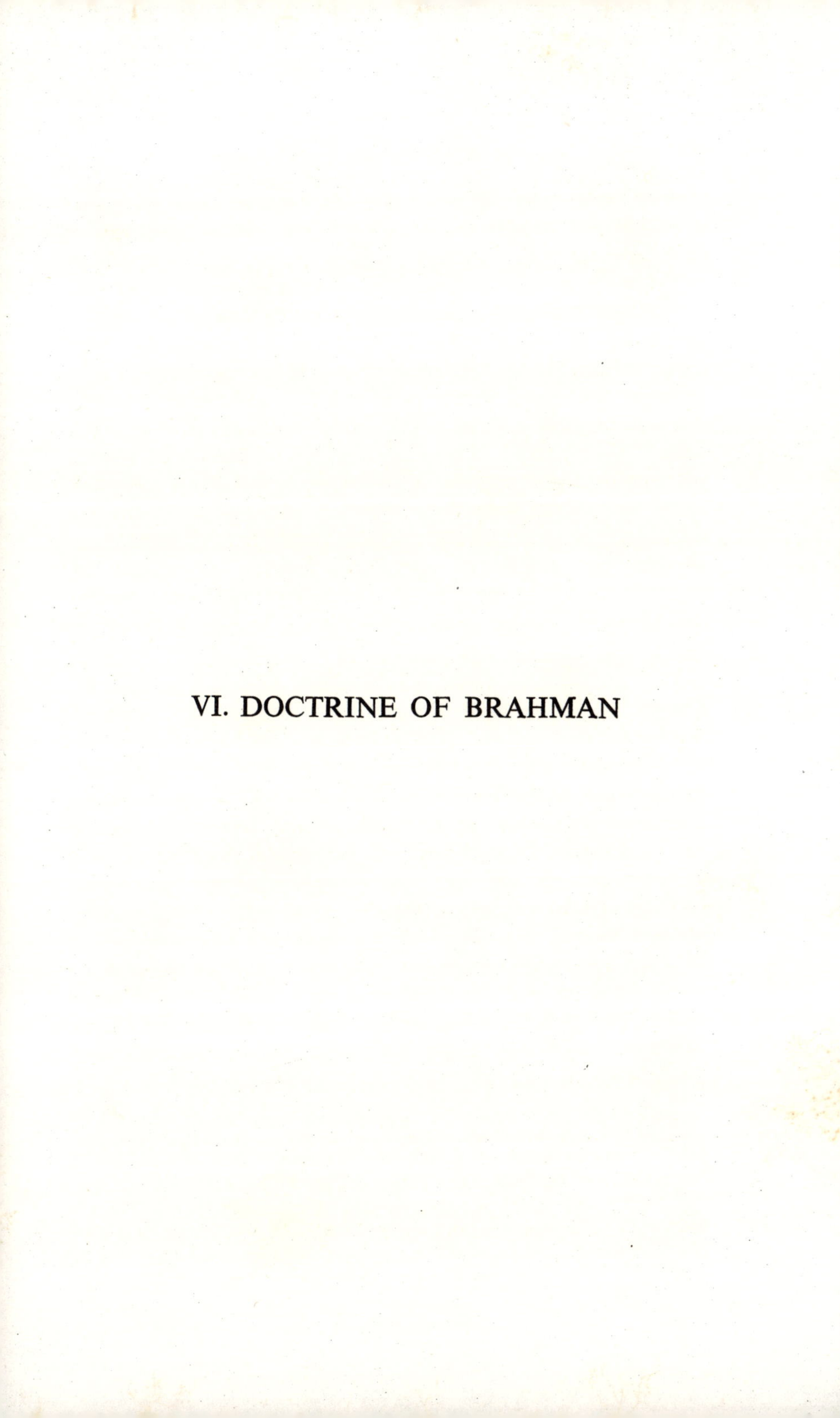

VI. DOCTRINE OF BRAHMAN

CHAPTER XXXVII

INDEPENDENCE OF BRAHMAN

THE independence of Brahman is the most vital point in Madhva's conception of God. The twin principles of "Svatantra" and "Paratantra" constitute the pith of his philosophy. It is to this central ontological concept of his philosophy that the traditional name "Dvaita" given to his system has reference. It has been shown that Madhva has gone beyond all other Indian thinkers in emphasizing the absolute independence and unutterable majecty of Brahman. His conception of Svatantra rises above the Dualism of Prakṛti and Puruṣas by denying them any kind of independent existence, (consciousness) or activity. We have seen how even the eternal entities have been brought by Madhva under the sway of Brahman by means of the doctrine of creation through "Parādhīnaviśeṣāpti". How keen and lively was Madhva's insight into the importance of this concept of the metaphysical independence of Brahman is shown by his unerring reference to the famous text of the *Ṛg Veda* x. 81.2 in interpreting the term "*ārambhaṇa*" embodied in the crucial Sūtra of Bādarāyaṇa ii.1.14 which has become 'the bone of contention' of commentators on the Sūtra, ancient and modern.[1]

1. Most of our modern writers on the *BS* have been content with accepting Śaṅkara's view that the keyword "*ārambhaṇa*" in this Sūtra refers to *ChanUp* vi.1.4 and interpreting the Sūtra on that assumption, in a manner that exposes their interpretation to *excessive redundancy*. J.A.B. van Buitenen is the first modern scholar to have made a commendable departure from this beaten track. He proclaims boldly in his Introduction to his critical edn. and translation of Rāmānuja's *Vedārthasaṁgraha* (Deccan College Monograph Ser. no. 16, Poona, 1956), that "there can be little doubt that the term *ārambhaṇam* in *BS* ii.1. 14 is taken from or inspired by Ṛg Veda x.81.2" and that "with this connection in mind, Rāmānuja tries to show that the

The majesty of Brahman is only imperfectly revealed by the eightfold cosmic determinations: निःसीमाः शक्तयोऽस्य हि (*AV* i.1.12). This universe is just one among the myriads pulsating in the pores of the Supreme Being : रोमकूपेष्वनन्तानि ब्रह्माण्डानि भवन्ति ते ।

Madhva is not very much enamoured of the teleological argument and knew its limitations long before Hume and other modern philosophers. It is only good enough so far as it goes. It cannot go the whole way, and yield complete knowledge of the Deity. It is all very well to argue that the entire universe is a huge machine divided into infinite number of parts, these parts again, being sub-divided to a degree beyond human comprehension and that all these are mutually adjusted with such consummate accuracy and provision as to wrest our admiration and worship of the Supreme Mind (Cf. बहुचित्रजगद्बहुधा करणात्परशक्तिरनन्तगुणः परमः—Madhva : *Dvādaśa-Stotra*, iv. 3) that should have designed and executed so stupendous a thing. But then, this sort of teleological argument could yield us nothing more than an "architect" of the universe, a sort of Demiurge and not a Creator on whom all things will be metaphysically dependent.

Madhva raises another vital question : Does God have to work under a limitation ? Is he obliged to accept and adapt Himself to *conditions independent of His will* and attain His ends only by such arrangements as these will admit of? His answer to this question has already been set forth in the chapter on Creation. It is obvious, from what has been stated there, that God is not merely an artificer of the universe, a mere "Brahmāṇḍakulāla", but the very source of its being and becoming : प्रकृत्यादिसत्ताप्रदत्वं चांगीकृतमीश्वरस्य (*BSB* ii.2.5). This is sufficient to

---

Sadvidyā by '*advitīya*' denies a separate adhiṣṭhātṛ" (*op. cit.* p. 11). He is also the first modern writer to approve of Madhva's "even more explicitly" referring to this Ṛg Vedic verse as Viṣayavākya of this Sūtra and disagree with V. S. Ghate's curt dismissal of Madhva's interpretation on the ground that "the topic is irrelevant". The relevance and the importance of the topic discussed by Madhva under this Sūtra have been conclusively established by me in my reply to V. S. Ghate's review of Madhva's Sūtra Bhāṣya (See my *History of Dvaita School of Vedānta and Its Lit.* pp. 114-117). The interested reader should note the slight misquotation from Madhva which has crept into the text cited by van Buitenen.

show how particular Madhva is in maintaining the metaphysical independence of God. Save for the difference in terminology, his position is the nearest Hindu approach to the Christian standpoint. Of the two, however, Madhva's is much more philosophical, as creation *in time has its insurmountable difficulties.* The only sense in which the world can be said to be a creation of God is that of *an eternal dependence of one beginningless real on another and a more powerful one.* Madhva makes a concession *in theory* to Christian Theism by conceding that *hypothetically* God *can* reverse His present method or create from nothing. But for His own reasons, He has chosen to evolve a world from coexistent matter and souls, which coexistence too, is as much at His will and pleasure (*Bhag* ii.10.12). The Vedāntin, if he can admit eternal and uncreated souls (See Śaṅkara on *BS* ii.2.42), need not *shy* at the acceptance of equally *uncreated matter.* No Indian philosopher has been able or temerarious enough to *derive* matter from God. It exists on the Advaitic view also as a *force latent in Brahman.*[2] Madhva, therefore, adopts the only sensible and straightforward course by which the sovereignty of God can be made consistent with the existence of *such* Matter and *such* Souls, viz., by making them *ex hypothesi* dependent on God for their very being, and becoming. This is substantially the view of the Viśiṣṭādvaitins also.[3] It will also be seen that Madhva has done the right thing *in raising* this important issue of Theism in general and Vedāntic Theism in particular in an appropriate context in the Brahmasūtras (ii. 1. 15).[4]

The conception of omnipotence has been much misunderstood and abused by theological controversialists. Can God achieve contradictions? is a dilemma to Theism. Mere power is the earliest and crudest perfection of Divinity. Pri-

2. परमात्मन्योतप्रोतभावेन समाश्रितं वटकणिकायामिव वटबीजशक्तिः

(Śaṅkara: Commentary an *Katha Up.* 1.3.11)

Cf. "Māyā exists even in Pralaya, depending on the Lord" (Radhakrishnan, *I. Phil.* II, p. 573).

3. See Deśika : *Tattvamuktākalāpa*, p. 255.

4. See Chap. xxvi. fn. 4. For details of Madhva's interpretation of this Sūtra and examination of Śaṅkara's and Rāmānuja's see my *BSPC* i, pp. 266-79.

mitive man, inured to the arbitrary despotism of a chief who uses power and glory for his own ends and uses the subjects as feeders of his own pomp and glory, is most easily impressed by the idea of physical power and gigantic strength. In most religions the attitude of the proverbial "Oriental Ruler" is transferred unconsciously to the idea of God. Madhva, therefore, raises this familiar problem of Theism whether God or Brahman can do *anything whatever*; or whether there are things He cannot do and whether all existent reality other than He has been created by Him or whether there are other beings, personal and impersonal, whose existence is as ultimate and uncaused as His own. If there are things whose existence is as ultimate, He could not have prevented their existence and to that extent His power over them is limited. An omnipotent God could get the ends without the means, if He chooses to do so. *Ergo*, it must be inconsistent with His wisdom to use them since they are of no value to Him except to serve a purpose which He could as well have achieved without them, *as with them.*[5] While conceding theoretically that God can do, undo and reverse His ways, Madhva and his commentators remind us that *He has not chosen to do otherwise than what the established facts show*. Vijayīndra Tīrtha writes that even the omnipotence of God cannot achieve logical contradictions and absurdities : भगवदैश्वर्यमपि लोकमर्यादानुरोधीत्यंगीकारात् । नहीश्वरोऽपि स्वस्यैश्वर्यविरोधिभूतमर्थं संकल्प्य करोति । (*Madhvādhvakaṇṭakoddhāra*, p. 58) Cf. Descarte's views : *Encyclopedia of Philosophy*.

As for the contention that it would have been better for God to have done without the accessories, as *with them*,[5] Jayatīrtha observes that it enhances the greatness of God to make Him act utilizing the accessories that are metaphysically dependent on Him : निरपेक्षतया कर्तृत्वस्योभयपक्षसाम्येन महिमोत्कर्षसाम्येऽपि, साधनसत्ताभ्युपगमेन एकाकिनः सकाशात् सोपस्करस्याधिक्योत्कर्षलाभात् । (*TP* ii. 1. 19)

This partiality of the Vedāntin for recognizing accessories in creation is not a sentimental one. It is, as explained by Madhva, due to the necessity of abiding by the facts vouched for by ex-

5. तर्हि, उभययापि महिमोत्कर्षसिद्धेः किं साधनापेक्षाग्रहेणेति (*TP* ii. 1. 19)

perience and scripture.[6]

It is difficult for any Theist to assert that all logical contradictions may be consistent with Divine nature ! It has been asked, from the point of view of ethical Theism, if the moral law is so fundamental that it is meaningless to speak of a Being who is not bound by it. According to some, the reply is not that an omnipotent God is bound by it, but that God is *not* omnipotent. Madhva resolves the antinomy on the basis of self-limitation by God. The supreme criterion in all such cases, he says, lies in consistency with the majesty of God:

नायुक्तमीशितुः किंचिदीशत्वस्याविरोधि यत् ।
ईशत्वस्याविरोधेन योजयित्वाखिलाः प्रमाः ॥ (*AV* iii.2.18)

Nothing can be accepted that will lower or abrogate the sovereignty of the Lord.

यत्किंचित् विरुद्धमिव प्रतीयमानमपि ईश्वरे तदिरत्र वा प्रमाणसिद्धं, **ईश्वरैश्वर्यंविरोधि च न भवति** यथाणुत्वमहत्त्वयौगपद्यादि, तत्सर्वं ईश्वरैश्वर्यबलेन घटत **इत्यंगीकार्यम्** । ननु निराकार्यम् । **यत्पुनरप्रमितं** तदीश्वरैश्वर्याविरुद्धमपि न कल्पनीयम् । शशविषाणादिकल्पनापत्तेः । यच्च प्रमितमपि ईश्वरैश्वर्यविरोधि, तन्न कल्पनीयमेव । कल्पकविघातकत्वात् । किंतु, तस्य प्रमाणस्य यथायोगमाभासत्वं वर्णनीयम् ।[7] (*NS* p. 511)

In the present case, God's ultilization of accessories in creation that depend on Him does not constitute any loss or abrogation of His majesty :

---

6. Cf. आम्नातस्यार्थं प्रतिपत्तुं प्रभवामो, नाम्नातं पर्यनुयोक्तुम् ।
(Śaṅkara, *BSB* i. 4.3)

7. "Whatever is *not incompatible* with the Lord's sovereignty *is not inconsistent* or untenable. All means of proof must be applied so as to be in keeping with the Lord's sovereignty.

Whatever *appear to be contradictory* in the Lord or elsewhere, but is otherwise borne out by Pramāṇas and is *not* opposed to Divine majesty, such as the coexistence of extreme minuteness and immeasurable infinitude in the Lord, such things must be accepted as compatible with Divine majesty. They should not be rejected as illogical. What is not established by Pramāṇas ought not to be assumed, even though it may not be incompatible with Divine majesty. Otherwise, it may lead to the contingency of having to accept the existence of the hare's horn. What goes against Divine majesty ought not to be accepted even if it *seems to be backed by some sort of Pramāṇa.* In such cases, that Pramāṇa should be shown to be a travesty".

सहकारिभिरारंभे न स्वातंत्र्यं विहन्यते ।
तत्सद्भावप्रवृत्त्योश्च स्वाधीनत्वव्यवस्थितेः[8] ॥
(Vedānta Deśika, *Tattvamuktākalāpa*, p. 255)

8. "God's sovereignty is not compromised by His making use of accessories in creation, as the very existence and functioning of those accessories are completely dependent on Him". Here, Deśika talks the language of Madhva.

CHAPTER XXXVIII

ATTRIBUTES OF BRAHMAN

MADHVA'S conception of God emphasizes two aspects of Divinity—the perfection of being (*sarvaguṇapūrṇatvam*) and freedom from all limitations (*sarvadoṣagandhavidhuratvam*). These two aspects cover and exhaust all that is great and good in the idea of God. We have an 'epistemological argument' for the perfection of God:

अतोऽशेषगुणोन्नद्धं निर्दोषं यावदेव हि तावदेवेश्वरो नाम.... (*AV.* iii. 2. 18).

that God is the highest form of perfection conceivable by human intelligence. He is the *id quo maius cogitari non potest*:

इत इदमधिकं इतोपीदमिति सर्वाधिकत्वेन ततोऽधिकाभावेनावशेषितत्वेन (*BT* X. 94. 16).

The ideas of transcendence and infinite bliss of God are similarly brought out by Madhva in his interpretation of the Sūtra : भूमा संप्रसादादध्युपदेशात् (i.3.8). This perfection of the Divine is to be understood in terms of an unlimited pervasion in time, space and fulness of attributes :

देशतः कालतश्चैव गुणतश्च त्रिधा ततिः सा समस्ता हरेरेव.... (Madhva's *GT* ii. 17).

According to Madhva, this threefold perfection is possessed by the Supreme alone. The whole of finite creation is limited in one way or another. The Goddess Lakṣmī, for instance, presiding over Prakṛti, though unlimited by time and space, is limited in attributes (*guṇair apūrṇā*) and, therefore, dependent on Brahman. The souls are limited both by space and in attributes and possess only temporal pervasion (*kālato vyāpti*) in the sense of existing at all times.[1]

The limitations of finite existence are the following :

1. Rāghavendra, *Gītāvivṛti*, ii. 18.

अज्ञत्वं पारवश्यत्वं वेधभेदादिकं तथा ।
तथा प्राकृतदेहत्वं देहत्यागादिकं तथा ।
अनीशत्वं च दुःखित्वं साम्यमन्यैश्च हीनताम् ॥

"Ignorance, dependence, liability to misery, material defilement and equality with or inferiority to others".

.... पारतंत्र्यं जनिर्मृतिः ।
पराधीनपदप्राप्तिरज्ञत्वं प्रलयेऽभवः ॥ (*AV* ii.2. 37)

The Supreme Lord is absolutely free from all the above. His superconsciousness remains undimmed by Time and Space and in all states of His being.

देशतः कालतो योऽसाववस्थातः स्वतोऽन्यतः ।
अविलुप्तावबोधात्मा . . . . ॥ (*Bhag* iii. 7.5.)

The term 'Ātman' itself, as applied to the Supreme in its highest sense signifies that which is all-pervasive (*ā-tata*) and all-perceiving (*mātṛ*):

आततत्वाच्च मातृत्वादात्मा हि परमो हरिः
(*Tantra* quoted by Śrīdhara Svāmin)

The above texts emphasize the infinitude of God and His immutability. His nature remains the same at all times and places (*BS* iii. 2.11). He is above all change and limitation, loss or obscuration of His powers, at all times: "*Avikāras sadā śuddhaḥ*". He is not subject to any variation of degrees of power or potency. Such limitations as are caused by external factors are powerless to affect His nature which is absolutely self-contained, uniform and self-sufficient. He transcends all, having neither peer nor superior. He is not a Person in the sense of being just one among many or possessing any material form or measurable lineaments. His Form consists of reality, absolute consciousness and bliss unlimited. We have an impressive enunciation of this in the following passages of Madhva's *Mahābhārata Tātparya Nirṇaya*:

एकः समोऽप्यखिलदोषसमुज्झितोऽपि सर्वत्र पूर्णगुणकोऽपि बहूपमोऽभूत् ।
निर्दोषपूर्णगुणविग्रह आत्मतंत्रो निश्चेतनात्मकशरीरगुणैश्च हीनः ॥
आनन्दमात्रकरपादमुखोदरादिः सर्वत्र च स्वगतभेदविवर्जितात्मा ।
कालाच्च देशगुणतोऽस्य न चादिरन्तो वृद्धिक्षयौ न तु परस्य सदातनस्य ।
नैतादृशः क्व च बभूव न चैव भाव्यो नास्त्युत्तमः किमु परात्परमस्य विष्णोः ।
सर्वत्र ईश्वरतमः स च सर्वशक्तिः पूर्णाव्ययात्मबलचित्सुखवीर्यसारः ॥
(*MbhTN* 1.10-12)

It is this uncompromising faith in the spotless purity and perfection of God that is responsible for Madhva's determined resistance to Pantheism and Illusionism :

कथं मायाव्यवच्छिन्नः पूर्णो मुख्यतया भवेत् ? (*AV* 1.1.9)

It is for the same reason that he refuses to invest even the Avatāras of popular theology with any material vesture. For, once the Monotheist grants the possibility of the unlimited becoming limited, it becomes immaterial if such a limitation takes place in *one* particular instance or more. That is why Madhva stands valiantly for the monotheistic unity of Godhood and its absolute freedom from material defilement and makes use of Purāṇic fictions and theodicies to justify the seemingly ungodly acts and career of the Avatāras on earth.

पूर्णमदः पूर्णमिदं पूर्णात्पूर्णमुदच्यते ।
पूर्णस्य पूर्णमादाय पूर्णमेवावशिष्यते ॥ (*BrhUp* v. 1)
न च गर्भेऽवसद्देवो न चापि वसुदेवतः ।
न चापि राघवाज्जातो न चापि जमदग्नितः ॥
न वै स आत्मात्मवतामधीश्वरो
भुङ्क्ते हि दुःखं भगवान् वासुदेवः ।
स ब्रह्मवन्द्यचरणो जनमोहनाय
स्त्रीसंगिनामिति रतिं प्रथयंश्चार ॥ (*Bhag* v. 19.6)
तथाप्यसुरमोहाय परेषां च क्वचित् क्वचित् ।
दुःखाज्ञानश्रमादींश्च दर्शयेन्नटवद्धरिः ॥

The perfections of God are *ex hypothesi* infinite :

मय्यनन्तगुणेऽनन्ते गुणतोऽनन्तविग्रहे ।[2] (*Bhag* vi. 4.48)

They are natural to His being and are *not*, as in Advaita, brought about by contact with Avidyā. This is supported by the clear statement of the *SvetUp* (vi.8.) :

परास्य शक्तिर्विविधैव श्रूयते स्वाभाविकी ज्ञानबलक्रिया च ।

In the light of such a large number of clearly worded statements, we cannot deny all attributes to the Supreme on the strength of a solitary Nirguṇa text. Besides, as pointed out by Madhva, the Nirguṇa text itself (केवलो निर्गुणश्च) posits a number of attributes

2. According to Jayatīrtha "*Guṇato anantaḥ*" means these countless attributes *severally* have countless aspects and viśeṣas in their turn (*NS* p. 383).

such as oneness, divinity, transcendence, immanence and omniscience,[3] so that the solitary term "Nirguṇa" occurring by the side of such an array of positive predications could only be taken in some restricted sense. The description of Brahman in several Upaniṣadic passages as 'unsullied by sin' (अपहतपाप्मा) and 'spotless' (निरवद्य) gives us the proper clue to a consistent interpretation of the Nirguṇa texts in the sense of denying Prākṛtic or empirical attributes like grossness to Brahman. Such an interpretation has the support of the Purāṇic tradition also :

सत्त्वादयो न सन्तीशे न सन्ति प्राकृता गुणाः ।
(*Viṣṇu Purāṇa* i. 9.43)

ज्ञानशक्तिबलैश्वर्यवीर्यतेजांस्यशेषतः ।
भगवच्छब्दवाच्यानि **विना हेयैर्गुणादिभिः ।**
(*op. cit.* vi. 5.79)

त्रैगुण्यवर्जितमजं विभुमाद्यमीशम् । (*Mbh.* i. 1.1)

The plea that "when the Absolute is said to be Nirguṇa it only means that it is trans-empirical, as guṇas are products of Prakṛti and the Absolute is superior to it" (Radhakrishnan, *I. Phil.* ii. p. 536) is quite acceptable to Madhva. In his latest work on the *Brahma-Sūtras* (1960) Dr. Radhakrishnan comes out with a pronouncement : "The creative thought 'Let me be many' *belongs to* Brahman. It is not simply imagined in Him. The *energy* that manifests itself in Brahman is *one with and different from Brahman*:

भेदाभेदात्मिका शक्तिः ब्रह्मनिष्ठा सनातनी ।

The world should become an ordered beauty. If we do not accept such a subtle power, abiding in God, God cannot be a creator. He cannot move towards creation" (p. 142). [Italics mine] All this, however, is inconsistent with Śaṅkara's conception of Brahman as "Nirviśeṣa",—as a Being that is essentially and fundamentally devoid of any attribute whatever, whether such attributes *qualify* it or *are separate from* it, as in the Nyāya philosophy; or are non-material and part and parcel of it, as in Madhva's view. Otherwise, Śaṅkara could not have so vehe-

---

3. एको देवः सर्वभूतेषु गूढः सर्वव्यापी सर्वभूतान्तरात्मा ।
कर्माध्यक्षः सर्वभूताधिवासः साक्षी चेता केवलो निर्गुणश्च ॥ (*SvetUp* vi. 11)

mently *denied and criticised the doctrine* that "*Brahman has in it elements of manifoldness*" *and that* "*unity and manifoldness are both true*", *as he has done in his commentary on BS* ii. 1.14. The statement that "Brahman and Īśvara are not distinct entities but *different aspects* of the same Reality" and that "it is wrong to imagine that the Absolutistic doctrine is for the philosophically initiated and the Theistic for others" and that "the view that the representation of Brahman as Īśvara (i.e. Saguṇa) is a concession to the weakness of the human mind, as some Advaitins hold, is *not* supported by the Brahmasūtras" (*op. cit.* pp. 126-127), show a sense of *intellectual dissatisfaction with* "*Nirviśeṣa-Advaita*" as propounded by Śaṅkara in his accredited works[4] and a reluctance to accept it as the true interpretation of the philosophy of the Upaniṣads. Madhva's opposition to the concept of Nirguṇa Brahman is also based on precisely the same dissatisfaction with Nirviśeṣādvaita.

The question of Saguṇa *vs* Nirguṇa Brahman has been fully discussed by Viṣṇudāsācārya in his *Vādaratnāvali* (Pariccheda iv) and by Vyāsatīrtha in his *Nym* (ii. 4). There is much confusion of thought in the popular mind over the terms 'Saguṇa' and 'Nirguṇa'. Unfortunately, such *loose ideas* have sometimes a tendency to rear their heads even in the writings of (supposed) *experts* on Indian philosophy ! "When the Absolute becomes embodied as a personal God we have the 'Saguṇa'" is *not* a proper definition of 'Saguṇa', as understood and debated in the original texts of the Vedāntic schools. The 'Saguṇa' of the Upaniṣads is certainly *not* what is endowed with empirical attributes. For the Śrutis clearly refer to Brahman endowed with attributes like *Satyakāmatva* as the transcendent Being (*ādityavarṇam tamasaḥ parastāt*). The Chāndogya and other texts also refer to the act of seeing (*īkṣaṇa*) on the part of Brahman, *prior to the emergence of antaḥkaraṇa* and other upādhis of the empirical creation.[5] It can-

---

4. Cf. also निर्विशेषं परं ब्रह्म साक्षात्कर्तुमनीश्वराः
ये मन्दास्तेऽनुकम्प्यन्ते सविशेषनिरूपणैः ।
(*Kalpataru* on *BS* 1.1.20)

5. Cf. "The creative thought 'Let Me be many' *belongs* to Brahman. It is *not simply imagined* in Him". (Radhakrishnan, *Brahmasūtra*, 1960, p. 142) (Italics mine)

not also be argued that the texts like "*Satyakāmaḥ satyasaṁkalpaḥ*" which speak of the various attributes of Brahman are merely intended for the purpose of meditation (*upāsanā*) *without any implication af their being actually present in the Supreme Brahman.* In the first place, there is no reference to Upāsanā in texts like "*Yas Sarvajñaḥ sarvavid*" (*SvetUp*) and secondly there are texts like "*Ātmetyevopāsita*" etc. which refer to meditation on the attribute of identity, which is not an unreal one but is actually present (according to the Advaitin, in the self). Further, Śaṅkara himself in his Bhāṣya (on *BS* iii. 3.11, 37) admits frankly that the qualities of "*ānanda*" etc., and the mutual identity of ātman and Īśvara should be *meditated upon*. This shows that the fact of *being prescribed for meditation* docs not take away the ultimacy of the attributes in question. Nor can the Saguṇa texts be explained away as mere re-statements (of facts already known or established) to be set aside by the Nirguṇa texts. For, the very conception of Brahman as "Sa-guṇa" is derived (from the Śrutis themselves) by Dharmigrāhakapramāṇa. The Nirguṇa texts cannot, therefore, falsify these very attributes which the Śrutis themselves have, on their own authority, given to Brahman.[6] It is thus impossible to resolve the apparent conflict between Saguṇa and Nirguṇa texts of the Śruti on the basis of such fanciful and subjective criteria as the standpoint of Upāsanā and Anuvāda put forward by Advaitins. The right way of resolving the conflict will be to apply to their harmonization such recognized principles of Mīmāṁsā exegesis as (i) the Upakrama-nyāya; (ii) Śrutiliṅga-nyāya; (iii) Viśeṣa-sāmānya-nyāya; (iv) Niravakāśa (sāvakāśa)-nyāya; (v) Bāhulya-nyāya (vi) Upajīvyopajīvaka-nyāya; (vii) Saviśeṣa-nyāya and others, some of which have admittedly been followed by the author of the *Brahma-Sūtras*, himself, even according to Śaṅkara's showing.

The following is a brief elucidation of the application of some of these principles of interpretation, to the present question, based on the *Vādaratnāvali* of Viṣṇudāsācārya : (i) The Saguṇa texts should have precedence over the Nirguṇa as they are pres-

6. तस्मात् सगुणत्वनिर्गुणत्वयोः विरोधेन समुच्चयायोगात्, अनुष्ठान इव च वस्तुनि विकल्पासंभवात् एकेनान्यस्य प्रतीतार्थत्यागरूपे बाधे वक्तव्ये, निर्गुणवाक्यस्यैव स युक्तः नतु प्रबलस्य सगुणवाक्यस्य । (*Nym* ii.4)

criptive in form and content, whereas the Nirguṇa texts are *proscriptive;* and in cases of a conflict between the initial and final statements (*upakrama* and *upasaṁhāra*) as in एको देवः सर्वभूतेषु गूढः सर्वव्यापी सर्वभूतान्तरात्मा * * *निर्गुणश्च (*SvetUp* iii. 11) the decision has been taken in the Vedopakramādhikaraṇa of the Pūrva-Mīmāṁsā that the first part shall prevail over the last and determine the scope and meaning of the other. (ii) Texts which predicate certain auspicious attributes of Brahman cannot put up with any but their literal sense (*niravakāśa*); whereas the Nirguṇa texts can easily be accommodated in the sense of denying material or empirical attributes and so find their fulfilment of purpose. It will not be possible to establish an absolute negation of attributes as the very same text: एको देवः सर्वभूतेषु गूढः lays down certain attributes like oneness (एकत्व), divinity (देवत्व), etc., in Brahman, in the first half (or major part of the text) and uses the term "Nirguṇa" at the tail end. It is, therefore, necessary to *restrict the scope of this negation* conveyed by the expression निर्गुणश्च to material attributes alone (त्रैगुण्यनिषेध) just as the prohibition of killing in the Vedic text: न हिंस्यात् सर्वा भूतानि is restricted by the Mīmāṁsakas to cases other than those statutorily recognized as in अग्नीषोमीयं पशुमालभेत. If it is contended that the prohibition न हिंस्यात् refers only to injuries provoked by human passions (रागतः प्राप्त) and not to those enjoined by Vedic injunctions (वैध), it may be answered back that in the present case also the text "*Nirguṇaśca*" does not negative the attributes duly predicated by Śrutis like यः सर्वज्ञः सर्वविद् तस्य नाम महद्यशः etc. but only such attributes as are conceived or advanced by the empirical intellect or imperfect logic. Absolute and unqualified negation of attributes cannot, therefore, be accepted in any case, since both the predication of attributes and their denial have equal statutory recognition. It thus becomes necessary to interpret the denial in a way which will *not* annul the attributes solemnly predicated. If even statutory prescriptions can be totally set aside, there will no need for recognizing Vikalpa (alternative or optional rule) provided in the Mīmāṁsā Śāstra, in such cases as उदिते जुहोति, अनुदिते जुहोति. The very conception of a Vikalpa (optional rule) is based on the presumption that what is laid down by law cannot be totally repudiated. (iii) The Nirguṇa texts are *general in scope* and cannot negative special attributes of Brahman expressly mentioned by the Śruti texts. But *specific* negations like '*Asthūlam anaṇu*' can always be taken at their face value and made to deny material attributes like grossness that may come to be suggested by spurious reasoning. After all, grossness and other attributes are *not laid down* in regard to Brahman, in any Vedic text. Nor are they inherently auspicious attributes though their opposites may be so. (iv) The Saguṇa texts are logically self-consistent; while the Nirguṇa texts bristle with contradictions.[7] If the Nirguṇa Brahman is *endowed* with the necessary characteristics which justify its being characterised as "Nirguṇa", it will not be really and *wholly* Nirguṇa—or attributeless. If there is no such appellative basis in the Nirguṇa Brahman, it cannot be regarded as Nirguṇa in the true sense of the term. (v) The Saguṇa texts should be regarded as "sustainers" (*upajīvya*) of the Nirguṇa texts. The sustainer being independent of the sustained (*upajīvaka*) will obviously be *more powerful* than the sustained, in the event of a conflict of interest or meaning between them. The latter then will have necessarily to submit to the former. This may be illustrated by the inference of fire being cold, which has absolutely no chance of survival against the evidence of tactile perception of its heat. It cannot be argued that the Saguṇa texts are sustainers of the Nirguṇa texts *only to the extent of providing a subject for negation* (*niṣedhyasamarpakatvena upajīvyatvam*) by the Nirguṇa texts. For there are no texts, so far as we can see, which say Brahman is *not-Saguṇa, not-sarvaśaktimat* and so on. The omniscience of Brahman is thus gathered only on the evidence of Śruti. Such an august truth cannot therefore, be simply set aside. There is no force in the contention that the Nirguṇa texts depend on the Saguṇa texts and require their help only to the extent of requiring a "bare existence" (*svarūpamātram*) of the thing to be divested of attributes and nothing more. Such a "bare existence" can be found in many other things also besides the present subject (Brahman) so that the denial of attributes, in the circumstances will *not* necessarily affect "Brahman" and deprive it of its attributes ! It will be futile to argue further that the attributes

---

7. Cf. निर्विशेषविषयकज्ञानस्य निष्प्रकारत्वे निर्विशेषत्वासिद्ध्या तत्सिद्ध्यर्थमेव विशेषाभावरूपविशेषविषयकत्वस्य आवश्यकत्वाच्च । (*Nym* ii. 5)

of the subject of a proposition (*uddeśya*) have generally no syntactic value as in '*Graham sammārṣṭi*' and that, therefore, the omniscience of the subject of the proposition (*uddeśya*) in the present case, viz. Brahman, is not taken into syntactic account. The Mīmāṁsā interpretation of '*Yasyobhayam havirārtim ārcchat*' does not support this interpretation. Even in the Sammārgādhikaraṇa, it is seen that the specific attribute of 'grahatvam' plays a decisive role in restricting the cleaning (*sammārjana*) to the Grahas (*cups*) as against other vessels like the "Camasas", by virtue of the distinctive attribute of 'Grahatvam' which is intended to be taken into full syntactic account. It is only the *singular number* of "Graha" in *Graham sammārṣṭi* which is *not* taken into account, by reason of there being *not one* but many vessels (*grahāḥ*) to be cleaned with a piece of cloth :

दशापवित्रेण ग्रहं सम्मार्ष्टि ।

But so far as the distinctive attribute of "Grahatva" itself is concerned, it *is certainly* taken into syntactic account, lest the injunction *Graham sammārṣṭi* should apply to some other vessels also, used in that sacrifice. That is why Bhavanātha says : Else, we could not establish the distinctive essence of the *uddeśya* :

नो चेदुद्देश्यस्वरूपालाभात् । उद्देश्यस्वरूपे लब्धे, यदधिकं तद्विशेषणं न विवक्षितम् ।

Once this has been achieved, other additional attributes of the *uddeśya* are superfluous and need not be taken into syntactic account for purposes of the Vidhi. Applying the same principle of interpretation to the present case, we have to accept that Brahman being inconceivable without the attribute of its omniscience, it can become the subject of a proposition, affirmative or negative only as characterised by the attribute of omniscience. In the circumstances, a conflict with the basic evidence of the subject (*dharmigrāhakapramāṇa*) is *bound to arise*, if the Nirguṇa texts are taken to deny attributes to Brahman *absolutely*.

It will be proper to hold that texts like "*Satyaṁ jñānam anantaṁ Brahma*" which posit certain attributes of Brahman should be taken in their *expressed sense* which is also their *primary sense*. Resort to any *laboured* explanation of such texts, in terms of the *elimination of the opposites of the qualities named*[8] (*tadvirodhyarthasa-*

8. Technically known in Advaitic works as *atadvyāvṛtti*. Read :
अनृतजडविरोधिरूपमन्तत्रयमलबन्धनदुःखताविरुद्धम् । (*Saṅkṣepaśārīraka*)

ṁtyāgaḥ) made by the Advaitins will naturally entail an abandonment of the primary sense of the text. The text on such a view, will *not* teach that Brahman is possessed of the characteristics of reality, consciousness etc., but that it is merely devoid of *unreality*, *ignorance*, *limitation*, etc. The Advaitin is thus fighting shy of the positive construction and running away from the express and primary sense of the terms "Satyam jñānam" and running after roundabout meanings and *distant echoes* of the primary senses. But such roundabout explanations cannot be accepted as the *proper, legitimate or straightforward* meaning of the propositions. Such far-fetched meanings *extracted* laboriously from the first sense of the words cannot be accepted as the import of Vedic propositions, as pointed out by the Mīmāṁsakas :

यश्चार्थादर्थो न स चोदनार्थः ।

(Śabara on *PMS* XI. 3.6.14)

Sureśvara himself has admitted that the roundabout explanation of "*satyam jñānam,...*" adopted by the Advaitin, in terms of the elimination of the opposite sense of the terms employed, is *not* derived from the actual expressions used, but from their 'potential fitness': तद्विरोध्यर्थसंत्यागः सामर्थ्यान्नतु शब्दतः. It is thus clear that the primary sense of the texts "Satyaṁ jñānam anantaṁ Brahma" is maintainable only on the Saguṇa view.

(vi) The Saguṇa texts, being *specific enunciations* (विशेषविधायक) are more powerful *in their own right* than the Nirguṇa texts which only function in a *general way* and tell us that Brahman is निर्गुण 'attributeless'. They do not tell us what particular attributes it lacks. It is, therefore, open to us to interpret this *general statement* without prejudice to the specific enunciation of attributes like "Sarvajñatvam" and hold that the denial of attributes has reference to attributes *other than those specifically predicated.* That will be the right attitude to take. As the *Mahābhāṣya* of Patañjali points out, *exceptions only restrict the scope of the general principles*: अपवादैरुत्सर्गा बाध्यन्ते. The Nirguṇa texts are *general statements* and the Saguṇa texts are exceptions. The latter have, therefore, the right of *overriding* the former and laying down the law as to the sense in which they can and should be *restrictively interpreted*. This is based on the well-known principle of interpretation : सामान्यविहितस्य निषेधस्य विशेषविधानेन बाधो युक्तः—that a negative proposition in general terms should be modified and interpreted in the light of other categorical and affirmative statements about the same subject-matter embodying specific predications. The difficulty of how a prior fact or enunciation can override a subsequent one is easily met. We have in Pāṇinian grammar a prior enunciation मृडमृधगुध (i.2.7.) overriding the subsequent prohibition न क्त्वा सेट् (i.2.18). It is clear then that mere posteriority or negativeness of content of one statement as against another, is not sufficient ground to override the positive. We have, therefore, no reason to set aside the conception of Brahman as endowed with numerous transempirical attributes taught by the Śrutis.

CHAPTER XXXIX

KNOWABILITY OF BRAHMAN

THERE is difference of opinion between the views of Dvaitins and Advaitins about the knowability of Brahman. While both look upon Brahman as self-luminous, Advaitic dialecticians have denied the knowability of Brahman by defining self-luminosity in a manner that precludes its accessibility to knowledge even of its own self or being :

अवेद्यत्वे सति अपरोक्षव्यवहारयोग्यत्वम्। (Citsukha)

Madhva, on the other hand, emphasizes the knowability of Brahman, though not to its fullest extent and in all its glory and completeness. However imperfect our knowledge of Brahman may be, it is still knowledge so far as it goes. Each one of us can know God and realize His majesty so far as lies in his power to do so :

पश्यन्तोऽपि न पश्यन्ति मेरो रूपं विपश्चितः। (*BSB* i. 1.5)

Here again, the difference between the two schools is one of substance and *not of mere words*. They are as sharply divided as the views of Christian Mystics and Theists are from those of Spencerian Agnosticism. Pringle Pattison hits off this difference so well that it is worthwhile quoting him : "Can'st thou find out the Almighty unto Perfection? If He is as high as Heaven, what can'st thou do? Deeper than hell, what can'st thou know? If to comprehend means to grasp as it were with one hand, to understand thoroughly, see all round an object, then unquestionably the infinite must *ever remain* incompassable by the finite. So far as Agnosticism simply emphasizes the unfathomability of the Absolute by any human sounding-line and *opposes the little we know to the vast unknown,* it is a praise-worthy lesson in humility. Curiously, neither Hamilton nor Spencer seems to realize the fundamental difference between the two conceptions—

that of the inherently unknowable and that of the unknown, the not-yet-known and doubtless *never-by-us-to-be-fully-known*, but still, the ever-to-be-better known" (*Idea of God*, p. 165).

The Śaṅkara-Advaitin seems to be in the same boat; for these remarks apply *mutatis mutandis* to the views of Advaitic dialecticians as against that of Madhva, that God or the Absolute is neither absolutely unknowable nor fully knowable :

नातिवेद्यो न चावेद्यः, तस्मात् स परमेश्वरः ।

(Madhva, Commentary on *Kena Up.*)

Madhva says that partial knowability establishes at least partial characteristability : *īkṣaṇīyatvād vācyam eva* (*BSB* 1.1.5). The very possibility of Ignorance concealing particular aspects of Brahman, while disclosing it in its *general aspect* of pure consciousness (as admitted by Śaṅkara) is sufficient to prove that Brahman is *not* altogether unaspected (*nirviśeṣa*) or devoid of characteristics.[1] It is philosophically impossible to speak of an absolutely featureless reality being obscured by partial ignorance, even for the nonce:

निर्विशेषे स्वयं भाते, किमज्ञानावृतं भवेत् ? (*AV* i.1.1.)

Ignorance cannot spread over a blank and conceal it from anything. There can be no total eclipse of Brahman's reality and consciousness as it is admitted that the pure consciousness of its being is manifested in the consiousness of the ego. An absolutely uncharacterizable entity is, therefore, a myth. It would be inaccessible to proofs and, therefore, beyond the jurisdiction of logical and metaphysical thinking. It is always possible and easy enough to seek refuge in the 'Unknowable'. But such refuge is not a place of superior enlightenment.

Madhva's stand on the knowability of Brahman though not in its entirety but commensurate with our limited powers of understanding according to the Svarūpayogyatā of Adhikārins of various orders receives striking assent from the weighty observations on this question made by the great 17th century

1. Read Śaṅkara's comment on 1.1.1 beginning with तत्पुनर्ब्रह्म प्रसिद्धमप्रसिद्धं वा and the reply to it तस्मात् सामान्यतः प्रसिद्धे धर्मिणि विशेषतो विप्रतिपत्तौ युक्तः तद्विशेषेषु जिज्ञासा in the *Bhāmatī* and Vyāsatīrtha's rejoinder:

ज्ञातं सामान्यतोऽज्ञातं विशेषेण विचार्यते ।
ज्ञाताज्ञातविभागस्तु निर्विशेषमते कथम् ? (*TC* 1.1.1)

Platonist Ralph Cudworth: "It doth not at all follow that because God is incomprehensible to our finite and narrow understanding, He is utterly inconceivable by it, so that we can't form any idea of Him at all. For, it is certain that we have not such an adequate and comprehensive knowledge of the essence of any substantial thing, so that we can perfectly master and conquer it. Truth is bigger than our minds and we are not the same with it but have a lower participation only of the intellectual nature and are *rather apprehenders than comprehenders* thereof. This is indeed one badge of our creaturely state. * * * Yet many rational souls frame certain ideas and conceptions of whatever is in the orb of being, *proportionate to their own nature* and *sufficient for their purpose*. Though we can't fully comprehend the Deity, nor exhaust the infiniteness of its perfections, yet may we have an idea of a Being absolutely perfect, such a one as is agreeable and proportionate to our measure and scantling *nostro modulo conformis* as we may approach near to a *mountain* and touch it with our hands, though we cannot encompass it with our arms." (quoted in Chamber's *Encyclopaedia of English Literature*, Vol.i, 1894, p. 373). The sentiments expressed by Cudworth have been fully anticipated and shared by Madhva who has, surprisingly enough, given the very same analogy of a Mountain in his *BSB* 1.1.5. (*See* p. 340 *ante*)

CHAPTER XL

BRAHMAN IS A SA-VIŚEṢA PERSONALITY

A Brahman which is by hypothesis Nirviśeṣa cannot be the object of any superimposition also :

सर्वधर्मविहीनस्य धर्मारोपः क्व दृश्यते ? (*AV* iii.2.3)

The assumption of a characterless entity (Nirviśeṣa) on the ground of alleged absence of all terms or bases of reference is refuted by Trivikrama Paṇḍita who points out *inter alia* that it would be equally impossible, in that case, to connote such a reality even through secondary signification (*lakṣaṇāvṛtti*) as proposed by Advaita. Immesurable as are the attributes of divinity, the unity of God in and through all of them, is secured by Madhva through the mediation of Viśeṣas. It is also possible to bring the numerous attributes under four leading ones (for meditation) as Sat, Cit, Ānanda and Ātmā.[1] 'Sat signifies absolute perfection and freedom from all defects and limitations (*nirdoṣa*). The term "*ātmā*" is explained as possessing pervasion and overlordship : आततत्वात्, मातृत्वात् आत्मा. From another point of view, the conception of God as "Svatantra", in the sense of the definition of the term already indicated, will comprehend *all the other attributes*.[2]

The Supreme Brahman is thus a Person in that He has a character of His own. The term personality as applied to Godhead denotes, according to Madhva, not merely the existence of self-consciousness so conceived, but also that the entire universe is to be thought of as an experience and not as an abstract content,—not limited to the intermittent and fragmentary glimpses

1. सर्वगुणानामपि गुणचतुष्टयविशेषत्वस्य वक्तुं शक्यत्वात् । (*TP* iii. 3. 13)

2. *BS* III. 3.18

of this or that finite consciousness, but as embracing the whole life of the world in a way that is necessarily incomprehensible save by an absolute knowledge. The Divine personality constitutes such a centrality of reference, endowed with the faculties of cognition, conation and activity, as part of its being—a being whose *esse* is to be conscious, to experience, to think, will, love and control the universe through rational purpose.

अजडं स्वात्मसंबोधि नित्यं सर्वावगाहनम् ।
ज्ञानं नाम गुणं प्राहुः प्रथमं गुणचिन्तकाः ।
स्वरूपं ब्रह्मणस्तच्च गुणश्च परिगीयते ।
(*Ahirbudhnya* III. 2.53)

इच्छाशक्तिर्ज्ञानशक्ति : क्रियाशक्तिरिति त्रिधा ।
शक्तिशक्तिमतोश्चापि न भेदः कश्चनेष्यते ॥ (*BT* i. 1.18)

The term 'Person', as applied to Brahman, should, therefore, be distinguished carefully from the circumscribed connotation of the term as a spiritual being embodied in a psycho-physical tenement. Limitation *is no essential constituent of personality.* It all depends. We may understand God to be a great centre of consciousness, will, force and action,—as a unit whose strength and capacities are beyond measurement or conception: अतिपरिपूर्णतमज्ञानैश्वर्यानिन्दयशःश्रीशक्त्यादिमांश्च भगवान् (Madhva, *GB* ii. 72); परो मात्रया तन्वा वृधान (*RV* viii. 99. 1) इति देशतः कालतो गुणतश्चापरिछिन्नत्वमुक्तम् (*NS* p. 421). If the Supreme Reality is not to be a mere indeterminate mass of non-willing, non-thinking and non-acting being, described as Saccidānanda, *just for courtesy's sake*, we must recognize, with Madhva, that it *is both knowledge and knower, bliss and the blissful*. There is nothing anthropomorphic about Madhva's conception of God as a Person, everything about whom is non-material. He has, by definition, no form of gross or subtle matter :

न तस्य प्राकृता मूर्तिर्मांसमेदोऽस्थिसंभवा ।
(*Varāha* xxxiv. 40)

स्त्रीपुंलिङ्गाभियोगात्मा देहो विष्णोर्न जायते ।
किंतु निर्दोषचैतन्यसुखां नित्यां स्वकां तनुम् ॥
* ** (*VTN* iii)

Madhva brings together a number of texts from the Upaniṣads and Purāṇas, in support of such a dynamic conception of the Divine personality: तस्यापि शरीरश्रवणात् 'आनन्दरूपममृतम्' (*MundUp* ii.2.7);

'सुवर्णज्योतिः' (*TaittUp*) ; दहरोऽस्मिन्नन्तराकाशः (*ChanUp* viii. 1.1.) इत्यादिषु । यदि रूपं न स्यात्, आनन्दमित्येव स्यात्, नत्वानन्द'रूप' मिति । कथं सुवर्णरूपत्वं स्यादरूपस्य ? 'सहस्रशीर्षा पुरुषः' 'रुक्मवर्णं कर्तारम्' 'आदित्यवर्णं तमसः परस्तात्' 'विश्वतश्चक्षुरुत विश्वतोमुखः' इत्यादिवचनात्, विश्वरूपाध्यायोक्तेश्च रूपवानवसीयते । 'परास्य शक्तिर्विविधैव श्रूयते स्वाभाविकी ज्ञानबलक्रिया च', 'यः सर्वज्ञः सर्वविद्', 'आनन्दं ब्रह्मणः'; 'मय्यनन्तगुणेऽनन्ते गुणतोऽनन्तविग्रहे, (*Bhag* vi. 4.48); 'विज्ञानशक्तिरहमासमनन्तशक्तेः' (*Bhag* iii. 44.24). But then, these attributes are not separate from the essence of God. God is not a "bare something" qualified or clothed with a number of attributes from without. We have seen that Madhva's conception of substance as an identity in difference, maintained by the self-differentiating capacity of intrinsic Viśeṣas enables him smoothly to preserve the integrality of being of the Supreme Person, in and through His numerous attributes which are an expression of *His Being* and not so many external trappings attached to Him. Madhva's view of the attributes of God is the same as that of his close western contemporary, the great Christian thinker St. Thomas Aquinas that "in God the distinction between existence and essence must fall away. God can have no nature or essence distinguishable from His actual existence. Here (*and here only*)[3] the distinction between existence and essence would have no meaning and *consequently the distinction between an attribute and that which is subject of the attributes would be* meaningless also. Of the Divine Being we can say (as of no other) that it is its own goodness. Its goodness is *not adjectival* to it because, in it, it is all one—*to be and to be good*" (quoted from Dawes Hicks : *Philosophical Bases of Theism*, 1937).

All this does not mean that there are no attributes of goodness, beauty, omniscience, sovereignty, bliss, etc., as a matter of *fact* in the Supreme Lord. It is only a *significant negation* of the otherness (*pṛthaktva*) of the attributes from the Lord. It does not, therefore, reduce Brahman to 'Nirviśeṣa' as in Advaita.

According to Madhva God has His own body and limbs : बुद्धिमनोऽङ्गप्रत्यंगवत्तां भगवतो लक्षयामहे बुद्धिमान् मनोवानङ्गवानिति ।[4]

This means that He has a spiritual Form with its own instru-

3. The reader knows that Madhva extends the principle of Guṇaguṇyabheda to all *Yāvaddravyabhāvi* attributes of all substances.

4. This is from the Ekāyana Śruti of the Pañcarātra tradition. After Madhva, it has been quoted by Vedānta Deśika.

ments of knowledge and activity which is all one of knowledge and bliss.

यदात्मको भगवान् तदात्मिका व्यक्तिः । किमात्मको भगवान् ? ज्ञानात्मक ऐश्वर्यात्मकः शक्त्यात्मक इति । (*Ekāyana Śruti*)

सद्देहः सुखगन्धश्च ज्ञानभाः सत्पराक्रमः ।
ज्ञानज्ञानः सुखसुखः स विष्णुः परमो मतः ।। (*Paiṅgi Śruti*)

Insofar then as the several attributes partake of the nature of Brahman they are also inseparable from Him and from one another:

तानि सर्वाण्यन्योऽन्यानन्यरूपाणि । (Madhva, *GB* ii. 22)

So far as it is necessary to concede that the supreme Reality has a *profound* character of its own and is by no means an utter blank, it would be unphilosophical to limit the attributes to six or to eight, as the Naiyāyikas have done. Madhva quotes the *Śvetāśvatara* text, परास्य शक्तिः विविधैव श्रूयते (vi. 8) and that of *Bhāgavata*, मय्यमन्तगुणेऽनन्ते... (vi. 4.48) to refute such a narrow view. Jayatīrtha points out that the six qualities commonly associated with the epithet "Bhagavān", are capable of subsuming the countless other attributes : षाड्गुण्यमित्युपलक्षणम् । षाड्गुण्ये सर्वगुणान्तर्भावो वा ।
(*GBt* ii. 72)

The term "*guṇa*" is understood in the sense of an attribute (*dharma*), and the qualities of knowledge, power and activity spoken of in the *Śvetāśvatara* and other texts would naturally be seen to posit a variety of them (*vividha*). In the light of the clear statement of *SvetUp* vi. 8, that the attributes are "intrinsic" (*svābhāvikī*), the plea of Ānandabodha and others that even the omniscience of Brahman actually *presupposes, rather than opposes, the presence of ignorance in Brahman* : सर्वज्ञत्वमप्यविद्यावत्त्वमाक्षिपति, नतु प्रतिक्षिपति, can only be characterized as *audacious*.

According to the Nyāya-Vaiśeṣikas, the knowledge, activity and other attributes of God are abstract, objectless wholes (*akhaṇḍa*). Such a position would render the conception of omniscience etc. meaningless. Omniscience is knowledge of all that exists. Creative and other powers also would similarly have reference to relevant objects. No knowledge or activity can thus be conceived as objectless. The eternality or non-eternality of objects has nothing to do with the question.

In the absence of something like an internal Viśeṣa to demarcate the distinctive terms of reference, it would be rationally impossible to define the limits of the creative and destructtive activities and powers in God and explain the orderly arrangement of the evolution and involution of the world and the succession of events. In other words, God must be accepted as "Saviśeṣa". Though Madhva admits with the Naiyāyikas that divine knowledge is eternal and all-embracing, it is not, on that account, undiversified. It is multi-colored *anantaviśeṣātmakam* and adjusted to the different exigencies of creation, dissolution etc., by the agency of Viśeṣas. There are two aspects of the Divine Will, the latent (*śakti*) and the patent (*vyakti*) which operate in preestablished harmony, preventing overlapping and encroachment (See Chapter XXV).

The Divine nature is not only all-knowing but is also self-luminous. God not only knows everything but *knows also that His knowledge is all-embracing.*

In this connection, Madhva refutes the view of a section of the Vaiśeṣikas to whom God's knowledge is *not self-luminous* and of some others that God's knowledge is *not unitary* but is twofold, —one knowing all else *excluding itself* and *another which includes it.* But then if God is not aware that He has two such knowledges, He cannot be all-knowing. If He is aware of the fact that He has *two such knowledges*, the question is how—whether by one of those two or by a *third one.* In the former case, one of the two would have been admitted to be self-luminous. If it is by a third one, the original position that God has only *two kinds of knowledge is forfeited.* Apart from it, the question would remain if God knows that He has a threefold knowledge or not. If He does not, He will cease to be all-knowing. If He does, the question will be repeated whether it is by the same (third one) or by a fourth. If by the former, we can as well regard one of the two earlier ones itself all-knowing and dispense with the luxury of the third one. If it is by a fourth one, the same question will get repeated endlessly :

स्वप्रकाशत्वमपि तु यैर्ज्ञानस्य निवार्यते ।
कथं सर्वज्ञता तस्य स्वज्ञानाधिगमं विना ?
ज्ञानं विश्वाधिकं त्वेकं तज्ज्ञानविषयं परम् ।
इति ज्ञानद्वयेनैव सर्ववित् परमेश्वरः ॥
इति चेदेष एवार्थः तज्ज्ञानावसितो यदि ।

स्वप्रकाशत्वमेव स्यात् ज्ञानं ह्येतद्विशेषणम् ।
ज्ञानान्तरेण चेदत्र भवेदेवानवस्थितिः ।
स्वप्रकाशत्वमेतस्मात् दुर्निवारं समापतेत् ॥

(*AV* II.2, adh. 6)

The question of Divine omniscience in respect of human illusions has been raised by some writers. Does God know our illusions also? If not, He is *not* omniscient. If He does, He would be as much subject to them as we are. Jayatīrtha disposes of this dilemma by pointing out that God only perceives everything *as it is in reality*. When we perceive silver in shell God sees that we have fallen into a delusion :

न चेश्वरप्रमा शुक्तिरजतादिविधिरूपा, किंतु भ्रान्तोऽयं शुक्तिकाशकलं कलधौततया कलयतीत्यनुवादरूपैव[5]। (*TVt* p. I)

Madhva also takes special pains to point out that though the attributes of God are *transcendental and trans-empirical*, they are, nevertheless, designated by the same terms as are applied to corresponding empirical qualities. This is merely symbolic and intended to give us some *idea* of them, however limited and inadequate (*BSB* iii.2. 32-34). The transcendental cannot be fully made known or represented by empirical categories and epithets.

"अलौकिकोऽपि ज्ञानादिः तच्छब्दैरेव भण्यते ।
ज्ञापनार्थाय लोकस्य यथा राजेव देवराट्" । इति पाद्मे ।

लौकिकविलक्षणेऽप्यानन्दादौ तत्पदप्रयोगो युज्यते । तस्यानुकूलवेद्यत्वादिज्ञापनार्थत्वात् । ज्ञाततावन्मात्रस्य श्रुत्यन्तरबलेन अलौकिकत्वबुद्धिश्च भवतीति । (*TP* iii. 2.34)

This has a remarkable parallel and contemporary affirmation from across the seas in St. Thomas Aquinas's famous doctrine of "analogical senses" underlying all human concepts of God.[6]

---

5. Cf. तथापीश्वरज्ञानं न प्रमा, विपर्यस्तत्वात् । यदा खल्वेतदस्मदादिविभ्रमानालंबते, तदा एतस्य विषयमस्पृशतो न ज्ञानावगाहनसंभव इति तदर्थोऽप्यालंबनमभ्युपेयम् । तथाच तदपि विपर्ययः . . . . . न । विभ्रमस्याप्रामाण्येऽपि तत्त्वमुल्लिखतोऽभ्रान्तत्वात् । एतदालंबनस्य च एवमुल्लिखतः सर्वत्र यथार्थत्वात् । नहि न तद्रजतं, नापि तत्रासत्, नापि नावगतमिति ।

(Udayana, *Kusumāñjali* iv)

6. See my *BSPC* Vol. III, p. 176.

CHAPTER XLI

COSMIC ACTIVITIES OF BRAHMAN

THE cosmic powers of the Supreme are eight in number : creation, preservation, dissolution, control, enlightenment, obscuration, bondage and release.[1] It is the sole and ultimate source of everyone of these determinations. The accounts in the Epics and Purāṇas dividing these activities among the members of the popular Hindu Trinity are taken by Madhva in a deeper monotheistic sense. He holds that the Supreme Being itself (identified with Viṣṇu) acts through the instrumentality of the other gods :

निमित्तमात्रमीशस्य विश्वसर्गनिरोधयोः ।
हिरण्यगर्भः शर्वश्च कालाख्यारूपिणस्तव ॥ (*Bhag* x.71.8)
तत्र तत्र स्थितो विष्णुः तत्तच्छक्तीः प्रबोधयन् ।
एक एव महाशक्तिः कुरुते सर्वमञ्जसा ॥
(Quoted *BSB* ii.3.11)

This applies to the processes of nature also :

मत्तः स्मृतिर्ज्ञानमपोहनं च । (*Gītā* X.8)

तापिनी पाचिनी चैव शोषिणी च प्रकाशिनी ।
नैव राजन् रवेः शक्तिः, **शक्तिर्नारायणस्य सा ॥**
(*Pādma* quoted in *TC* p. 645)

This is how Madhva reconciles the apparent polytheism of the Vedic and post-Vedic sources with the monotheistic idea of the

---

1. Cf. "Madhva believes that the characteristics mentioned *belong to the nature of Brahman*. Creative activity is an essential defining quality of Brahman'! (Radhakrishnan, *Brahma Sūtra*, p. 237) and his own remark (in regard to Śaṅkara) : "If we do not accept such a subtle power *abiding in God, God cannot be a creator*. He cannot move towards creation" (Op. cit. p. 142). [Italics mine]

One Supreme : एकः शास्ता न द्वितीयोऽस्ति शास्ता (*Mbh*). But he finds for the popular gods (Devas) of Hinduism a place in his theosophy and regards their limited jurisdiction over particular aspects of cosmic determination as a delegation of powers or as an *imperium in imperia*.[2] This overcomes the limitations of a plurality of causes by making the Supreme Brahman *alone* the ultimate and independent source in every act of emergent evolution. This point has been explained by Madhva in his comments on *BS* i.4.15 and ii.3.11. In this sense, God is called 'Kāraṇa-kāraṇa'[3] (cause of all causes) working in and through each of them :

ब्रह्मविष्ण्वीशरूपाणि त्रीणि विष्णोर्महात्मनः ।
ब्रह्मणि ब्रह्मरूपोऽसौ शिवरूपी शिवे स्थितः ॥
पृथगेव स्थितो देवो विष्णुरूपी जनार्दनः ॥ (*BT* 1.2.24)

It is the same Brahman that sustains the selves in and through everyone of their five states in life : Jāgrat, Svapna, Suṣupti, Mūrchā and Maraṇam. So too in the other states of dissolution and release. The dependence of souls on God in the state of dissolution is obvious enough. Dependence in release too is clearly taught in the scripture : उतामृतत्वस्येशानः (*RV* X.90.2); मुक्तानां परमा गतिः (*Mbh* XII.254.17); मुक्तोपसृप्यव्यपदेशात् (*BS* 1.3.2); जगद्व्यापारवर्जम् (*BS* IV.1.17).

The *Viṣṇu Rahasya* puts the idea tellingly :

सर्ववस्तुषु या शक्तिः सा मदीयैव नान्यथा ।
मयैव दत्तं स्वातंत्र्यं केवलेष्वपि वस्तुषु ।
तावन्मात्रेण मोमुग्धा स्वातंत्र्यं मन्वते निजम् ।
स्वातंत्र्येऽपहृते पश्चाज्जानन्ति परतंत्रताम् ॥ (XII.22-23)

The *BT* states that both intrinsic and empirical forms of knowledge of selves are dependent on God.

---

2. खण्डाधीशाः सार्वभौमस्य यद्वत्
ब्रह्मेशाद्याः कुर्वते तेऽनुशास्तिम् । (*BT* X.94.169)

3. कारणकारण पूर्णवरेण्य (*Dvādaśa Stotra*, v. 3)
अवान्तरं कारणं च (*Aṇubhāṣya*)

स्वरूपभूतं ज्ञानं तु सदा जीवस्य विष्णुना ।
नियतं, प्राकृतं ज्ञानं भक्त्या तेनैव दीयते ॥ (XI.22.11)

The Supreme is thus the ultimate source of every one of the sixfold determinations of organized matter and the eightfold determinations of the lives of thinking beings. Of these, release from bondage is the most cherished ambition of man. No conception of God can, therefore, be complete without making room for its fulfilment by the Supreme. God, then, is the ultimate source of redemption of the world : संसारमोक्षस्थितिबन्धहेतुः (*SvetUp* vi.16); and no definition of Brahman that does not embody this idea will be complete or proper. That is why Madhva goes beyond every other commentator on *BS* i.1.2, and interprets "*ādi*" there to include a pointed reference to the redemptive function and some others also. The very need for an inquiry into Brahman arises because of the desire for redemption, which cannot be achieved without the grace of God; which is facilitated by knowledge :

यतो नारायणप्रसादमृते न मोक्षः, न च ज्ञानं विना अत्यर्थप्रसादः, अतो ब्रह्मजिज्ञासा कर्तव्या ।
(*BSB* i.1.1).

Philosophical reason bids us assume that God should be the ultimate 'cause' of bondage, if He is to be the source of our redemption. There is no escaping this. Madhva accepts this position, with the Sūtrakāra (*BS* iii.2.5). The logic of this is confirmed by the following texts :

सतां विमुक्तिदाद्विष्णोर्मुक्तिर्यद्यभ्युपगम्यते ।
बन्धोऽपि तत एव स्याद्यस्मादेकस्तयोः प्रभुः ॥ (*BT* X.94.16)
बन्धको भवपाशेन भवपाशाच्च मोचकः ।
कैवल्यदः परं ब्रह्म विष्णुरेव सनातनः ॥
(*Skānda* quoted by Śrīdhara Svāmin)

Madhva carries the point further and shows how even *in* release the full manifestation of intrinsic bliss of the selves is brought about by the grace of God Himself, thus making the soul's dependence on God complete and true in every respect :

अज्ञानां ज्ञानदो विष्णुर्ज्ञानिनां मोक्षदश्च सः ।
आनन्ददश्च मुक्तानां स एवैको जनार्दनः ॥ (*AV* 1.1.1)

The giver of Mokṣa should *ex hypothesi* be independent and self-determined (Svatantra) and Pūrṇa. God then as the Redeemer of our selves stands out as the one independent transcendent Being of metaphysics :

मोक्षदो हि स्वतंत्रः स्यात् परतंत्रः स्वयं सृतौ ।
वर्तमानः कथं शक्तः परमोक्षाय केवलम् ? (*AV* iii.3.1)

CHAPTER XLII

MANIFESTATIONS OF BRAHMAN

THE Supreme Lord of all creation remains wrapped up in His glory and bliss at a time when the entire Universe is in a state of nebulous chaos (*RV* x.129.2-3). Later, He puts on a multiplicity of forms to evolve the universe through different stages. These forms, though innumerable, are nevertheless identical with one another, save for their numerical distinction. The first in the order of Divine manifestations is the quaternion of Vāsudeva, Pradyumna, Aniruddha and Saṅkarṣaṇa, popularly known as the (Catur-)Vyūha, credited with redemptive, creative, sustaining and destructive functions. The Supreme further differentiates itself into ten (familiar Avatāras) or twelve, hundred, thousand and so on (*GT* ix; *MbhTN* i.10). These personal manifestations of the Lord are spoken of as Śuddha-Sṛṣṭi, in *Pañcarātra* terminology. They are also designated as Vyūhas (groups) in a general sense. The Rāmānuja school recognizes five kinds of manifestation of God : (1) Images (2) Avatāras (3) Vyūhas (4) the Transcendent and (5) the Immanent.[1] Madhva accepts all *but the first one*, though he does not use this nomenclature. But there is one important difference that in Madhva's view, these various manifestations are absolutely on a par with one another. There is no gradation among them in respect of powers or potentialities. Madhva is vehemently opposed to the idea of making any invidious distinctions among these manifestations of God or putting some on a higher pedestal than others. *There is no room for Svagatabheda in the Supreme* (*neha nānāsti kiñcana*). It is the same Infinite in every manifestation. This vigorous note of monotheistic puritanism is *absent in Rāmānuja's system*, wherein the Para-Vāsudeva or the Transcendental Brah-

1. Cf. स्वलीलावशात् अर्चाविभवव्यूहपरान्तर्यामिभेदेन **पञ्चधावतिष्ठते ।**

man and the Vyūha-Vāsudeva alone are credited with *all the six qualities* of godliness, while the other members of the Vyūha, Saṅkarṣaṇa, Pradyumna and Aniruddha, are assigned two attributes each.[2] The "Bimbarūpa" of Madhva may be taken to correspond with the "Antaryāmi" of Rāmānuja. The Bimbarūpas have a special place in Madhva's system in that they constitute the archetype of each soul a vision of which is the *sine qua non* of liberation (*BS* iii.3.53).[3] The Avatāras are on a different footing and are concerned with specific functions like *Balakārya*, *Jñānakārya* etc. Their number exceeds ten as commonly recognized. There are other Avatāras like Haṁsa, Datta and Hari, not included in the popular list of ten. Neither Śaṅkara nor Rāmānuja seems to have been inclined to treat Kṛṣṇa-dvaipāyana-Vyāsa as a full-fledged Avatāra of the Supreme, though the latter's commentator Sudarśana Sūri is prepared to follow Madhva's lead that Vyāsa is a real full-fledged Avatāra of Viṣṇu. But his younger contemporary, Vedānta Deśika, thinks otherwise and treats Vyāsa as subject to the influence of Prārabdha-karma, as an ordinary human soul (Rāmānuja, *GBt* iv.9). This will be nothing short of a sacrilege, according to Madhva. To him, all Avatāras are of equal merit and status. There is no question of degrees of fulness among them, no "partial" and "complete Avatāras"[4]. He takes his uncompromising stand on the authority of the Upaniṣadic and Pañcarātric texts and rejects the commonly accepted interpretation of the *Bhāgavata* text : * * * कृष्णस्तु भगवान् स्वयम् (i.3.28) as inappropriate on philosophical and syntactic grounds (See Madhva, *GB* X.41). He has thus no partiality or preference for any particular

---

2. *Jñāna* and *Bala* are manifested in Saṅkarṣaṇa, *aiśvarya* and *vīrya* in Pradyumna and *śakti* and *tejas* in Aniruddha.

3. हृदिस्था या हरेर्मूर्तिः जीवो यत्प्रतिबिम्बकः ।
यद्वशे वर्तते जीवः सा तु जीवकला स्मृता ।
See my *BSPC* iii, pp. 433-438.

4. See : पूर्णमदः पूर्णमिदं पूर्णात् पूर्णमुदच्यते ।
पूर्णस्य पूर्णमादाय पूर्णमेवावशिष्यते ॥ (*BrhUp* V.1.); उदरमन्तरं कुरुते (*TaittUp* ii. 7) ; **वासुदेवा एवैते सर्वे** (Śaṅkara's *BSB*. ii. 2.44).

Avatāra of God and treats *all of them as equal in rank, attributes and powers.*

Śaṅkara holds the bodies of Avatāras to be Māyic and material in stuff. The Rāmānuja school regards them as essentially non-material (दिव्यमप्राकृतम्—Rāmānuja, *GB* iv.9) and formed out of the transcendental form of the Lord residing in the highest Heaven : अवतारविग्रहस्यापि अप्राकृतपरमपदनिलयविग्रहांशविशेषणत्वम् (Vedānta Deśika on Rāmānuja's *GB*, Ananda Press Edn., p. 13). Deśika quotes the *same authority* as Madhva :

न तस्य प्राकृता मूर्तिर्मांसमेदोऽस्थिसंभवा ।

(*Varāha Purāṇa*, XXXIV. 40)

But the Rāmānujīyas seem to regard the Avatāras as *non-eternal*. This is not acceptable to Madhva:

सर्वे नित्याः शाश्वताश्च देहास्तस्य । (*BT* i.3.1)

VII. SĀDHANA-VICĀRA

CHAPTER XLIII

FREEDOM AND FREEWILL IN MADHVA'S PHILOSOPHY

THE question of human freedom and Divine control assumes great importance in philosophy and ethics. Madhva emphasizes both and maintains that they are mutually consistent. In the first place, it is man himself and not God who is responsible for the evil and suffering in the world. This is the corollary of the Svarūpabhedavāda of Madhva. In the Advaita school of Śaṅkara, which regards the Ātman as essentially *nirviśeṣa*, the self is not really an agent. All activity is due to the play of Avidyā or ignorance and is essentially the result of a superimposition on the Ātman. Since Mokṣa, in this school, is understood in terms of identity with Brahman, it is not something to be achieved afresh, but is the essence of the Ātman itself, though seemingly obscured and hidden. Hence, on this view, even the spiritual effort cannot be regarded as a true purposive activity of the self in all seriousness. Madhva is unable to accept such a position which reduces all activity on the part of the self, whether hedonistic, or ethical, secular or spiritual to a mere make-believe. It is, therefore, necessary to ascribe *real activity* to the self. If, as is contended by the Advaita school, the *kartṛtva* of the Ātman is merely due to a superimposition of the *kartṛtva* that really belongs to the mind, just as the redness of the japā flower is superimposed on the crystal that is placed by its side, then just as one has both the kinds of experience in a case of Sopādhikabhrama viz., that (i) the crystal is red and at other times (outside the *bhrama*) that (ii) the japā flower is red, even so, one should have the distinctive experiences : that 'the Ātman is the doer', 'the mind is the doer'. Since the mind is also open to the perception of the Sākṣī, the doership that is said to belong in reality to the mind (or *buddhi*) cannot possibly fall outside the perception of the Sākṣī.

Following the Sūtrakāra (कर्ता शास्त्रार्थवत्त्वात् ii.3.33) and consistent with his ethical realism, Madhva maintains that the human soul is a real agent in all its actions. If we do not admit this, the Śāstra which lays down injunctions and prohibitions with reference to the obtainment of specific results and the moral law in which these are ultimately grounded will lose all significance and lapse into a cry in the wilderness. The Śāstra cannot be addressed to the insentient or to God. The Jaḍa is incapable of responding to any mandatc[1] and God is above the purview of commandments. They cannot, therefore, have reference to any but the souls.

The means of realisation of Brahman such as *Śravaṇa*, *manana* and *nididhyāsana*, prescribed in the Śāstras clearly imply that they are to be carried out by a real agent. If the activities in respect of these are only a matter of superimposed assumption, there is no possibility of the fruits of such Sādhanas practised being realized by the aspirants. The Advaitin is hardly justified in denying doership (*kartṛtva*) to the Ātman and relegating it to Buddhi inasmuch as Śaṅkara himself in his bhāṣya on *BS* ii.3.36, has categorically rejected the view of the Sāṅkhya that Kartṛtva pertains to buddhi and has upheld the position that it belongs really to the Jīva, as the Siddhānta view. The absence of discrimination (*vivekāgraha*) between *buddhi* and Ātman has been alleged by the Sāṅkhyas also. Hence the position of the Advaitin would hardly be different from the Sāṅkhya view, if he were to reject the position that kartṛtva does really belong to the Ātman. Moreover, if bondage in the form of doership and enjoyment viewed as an undesirable state (*anartha*) were to be regarded as belonging only to the *buddhi*, then deliverance from such bondage should also logically be for the benefit of *buddhi* alone and not for the benefit of the Jīva. Even Ajñāna which is regarded by the Advaitin as pertaining to the Jīva is a

1. जडं हि परकृतेन नोदनादिना क्रियावत् भवति, न त्वागन्तुककारणमन्तरेण स्वेच्छया। जीवस्तु. . . . (Jayatīrtha, *GBt* XVIII. 18)

source of misery to the Jīva, by giving rise to the feelings of enjoyment and suffering. So then, unless such *kartṛtva* and *bhoktṛtva* brought about by Ajñāna are really accepted in the Jīvas, they need on no account bother about deliverance from them.[2]

Whatever may be the aim of spiritual effort—whether to achieve something new or to discover a forgotten state, the *effort* in that direction must be a very real serious effort on the part of a true and real agent. It is for this reason that Albert Schweitzer argues that the doctrine of reincarnation cannot accept the hypothesis that the Soul's contact with the bodily experiences is *not real*. His contention is the same as Madhva's that "if moral conduct is to play any part in the liberation of the Soul from the cycle of rebirth, the soul must, in some way, participate in the corporeal and be affected by the human experience and action, so the doctrine of reincarnation can in no sense agree to the assertion that the Universe is not real but must hold fast to its reality" (*Op. cit.* p. 62).

The acceptance of real agency (*kartṛtva*) to the soul does not, however, make the Jīva an *absolutely independent agent*. He is still circumscribed by factors like the physical body, the sensory apparatus etc., which are the "gifts" of God. As Rāmānuja points out, under *Gītā* XVIII.16, where the activity of the soul is said to be *not* independent, but dependent on the five determining factors of the body, an agent, organisation, bodily functions and the direction of the Lord (परमात्मदत्तैः तदाधारैश्च करणकलेवरादिभिः तदाहितशक्तिभिः स्वयं च जीवात्मा तदाधारः तदाहितशक्तिमान् * * *) the ultimate power of direction is vested in the Lord. The Jīva pursues of his free will a course of action which is determined mostly by his own deep-rooted nature, inclinations and past karma. But even this is possible because God has given him the power to do things in conformity with his own innate goodness or its opposite. He is not, therefore, a mere puppet in the hands of God. The right to choose between right and wrong is his own, made on his own responsibility and at his own risk (*yathecchasi tathā kuru*). This explains why some are

2. See ft. note no. 1.

Muktiyogyas, some remain in bondage and others qualify for Tamas.

It may, therefore, be said that the Jīva is both a doer and a non-doer from different points of view like a carpenter in the service of a building architect. He works with his own hands and tools but looks up to the architect for directions. The skill of the carpenter is *his own*. He does not owe it to his master. But not so in the case of the Jīva. He has derived even his ability to do things, metaphysically, from the Creator (*BS* ii.3.41). But for God, he cannot move an inch (*RV* x.112.9). This does not, however, involve God in the meshes of action and make Him responsible ultimately for the behaviour of souls. For, God merely *enables* the Jīva to pursue a course of action, not arbitrarily, but in relation to his former life and deserts (कृतप्रयत्नापेक्ष: *BS* ii.3.42).[3] He does not *interfere* with the Jīva's decision in any way. He susstains put never constrains (*Gītā* xviii.63). The Jīva chooses out of his freewill a particular line of action for good or for bad with sufficient foreknowledge of its moral worth and has himself to thank for the consequences. He cannot, therefore, blame anyone, least of all God, for the unpleasant consequences of his acts, should he have chosen wrongly. He has freedom of choice within the realm of works.[4] God does not throw the creatures blindfolded into an unknown region or set them adrift chartless on the high seas. Each is provided with a chart, a book of instructions of where lies the haven and how to reach it. This book is the Śāstra (*vidhiniṣedhātmakam*).

Another overriding consideration why the individual should be regarded as a dependent agent is set out, according to Madhva, in *BS* ii.1.26 : कृत्स्नप्रसक्तिर्निरवयवत्त्वशब्दकोपो वा. For, any theory that makes the Jīva the sole initiator of his actions, will have to face a dilemma sooner or later. The creative energy of the Jīva (*sāmarthya* or *prayatna*) is not something that can be treated as different from his essence.[5] That being so, everytime

---

3. तदन्तरवस्थितः परमात्मा स्वानुमतिदानेन तं प्रवर्तयति इति जीवस्य स्वबुद्ध्यैव प्रवृत्तिहेतुत्वम् । (Madhva *GB* xviii. 15)

4. स्यादिदं प्रवृत्तिविधिवैयर्थ्यं यदि जीवस्य क्रियास्वातंत्र्यलक्षणं कर्तृत्वं सर्वथा न । (*NS* p. 327)

5. We are not talking here of muscular or any such other energy.

any task is to be accomplished, the individual would have to throw in the optimum of his creative energy into it, irrespective of the magnitude of the task. That will hardly be wise or fair. Nor can we create internal parts into the Jīva's personality to get over this difficulty. That will destroy the unity of his being, by introducing an element of multiplicity. We cannot take the help of Viśeṣas also at this stage, as they are not known to possess anything more than a capacity to render internal distinctions possible in an identity of essence. But what we require here is something more than that—a power to *regulate* the proportion of effort to the given task, which is *not* a normal power of Viśeṣas, such as we find in other places, say in an insentient object. Someone is, therefore, required to put such a power *into* the Viśeṣas. It is not in the competence of the Jīva itself to confer such a new power on the Viśeṣas, which is not found elsewhere. The only *deus ex machina* who can do this would be God. By His mysterious power of accomplishing the seemingly impossible (अघटितघटनापटीयसी शक्तिः), He could very well do what the Jīva cannot do and set the Viśeṣas in motion investing them with the capacity to secure proportional adjustment of effort and creative energy of the Jīva to carry out different tasks.[6] In this way, the Jīva cannot do without the regulating control of God in his actions. *This is, indeed, a very remarkable point made by Madhva in support of the Jīva's dependence on God in putting his creative energy to use.*

There is still another difficulty. If God's inexorable impartiality is secured by the doctrine that He renders unto every man according to his work, the other view in the *Kauṣītakī Upaniṣad* (iii.8) that He himself is the one who causes man to do right and wrong, according to His pleasure (*BS* iii.2.41) remains unexplained. "If God pulls the strings for every kind of action, He is the agent as well as the patient. Here, the Śūtrakāra

---

6. अनंशस्यापि जीवस्य क्रियासामर्थ्ययोजनात् ।
कार्येषु यः करोत्यद्धा नमस्तस्मै स्वयंभुवे ।
यदि भागेन कार्येषु जीवशक्तिं न योजयेत् ।
हरिस्तदा हि सर्वत्र कृत्स्नयत्नोंऽशितापि वा ॥ (*AV* II. 1. 27)

resorts to Śruti ; but he does not attempt to remove the contradiction" (Radhakrishnaṇ, *I.Phil.*ii,p.441). The contradiction can only be removed by accepting Madhva's interpretation of the Śūtra :

उपपद्यते चाप्युपलभ्यते च। (ii. 2.37)
वैषम्यं निर्घृणत्वं च वेदाप्रामाण्यकारकम् ।
नाङ्गीकार्यमतोऽन्यत्तु न वैषम्यादिनामकम् ॥ (*AV* ii.1.35)

"A partiality which interferes with right and wrong is a blemish. Hence it has been rejected in the Śūtras. The proper control of right and wrong by meting out rewards and punishments in accordance with them, is not a fault. It is an asset. Hence it is acceptable to the Sūtrakāra." As Jayatīrtha explains: "There are two kinds of partiality and pitilessness. One results from disregard of individual karma and deserts. The other lies in *depending* on them and taking them into account insofar as they are themselves subject to God. Of these, the first one must be rejected as it impairs the validity of the Vedas. For the Vedas prescribe right as the means of achieving happiness and warns us against unrighteousness as it brings on misery. Such being the case, if God should act in a partial and pitiless way in utter disregard of individual karma and deserts, it would mean that the law of right and wrong taught is the Vedas will be rendered meaningless. They would then lose their validity. Therefore the Sūtrakāra, while admitting the view of God's acting in accordance with karma has set at rest the possibility of partiality and pitilessness in Divine dispensation. The sort of partiality and pitilessness in meting out punishment and rewards in accordance with one's deserts is not, strictly speaking, a foible. It does not amount to a defect."[7]

The solution of the conflict between the seemingly fatalistic determinism of the *Kauṣītakī Upaniṣad* (iii.8) and the rationalism of the karma theory lies, as propounded by Madhva, in

7. द्विविधं खल्विदं वैषम्यं निर्घृणत्वं च । एकं कर्माद्यनपेक्षताप्रयुक्तम् । तत्राद्यं वेदाप्रामाण्यकारकत्वेन दूषणत्वान्नांगीकर्तुमुचितम् । वेदो हि धर्मं सुखसाधनमधर्मं दुःखसाधनमाह । तत्र. यदीश्वरो धर्माधर्मावनपेक्ष्य विषमो निर्घृणश्च स्यात्, तदा वेदोदितधर्माधर्मयोः सुखदुःखकारणत्वमसत् स्यात् । तथाच, कथं तस्य प्रामाण्यं स्यात् ? अतः सूत्रकारेण कर्मादिसापेक्षतापक्षमुररीकृत्य तत् परिहृतम् । अतोऽन्यत्तु द्वितीयं वैषम्यं नैर्घृण्यं च न वैषम्यादिनामकम् । दोषरूपं न भवतीति यावत् । (*NS*, p. 312 b)

the doctrine of Svarūpabheda of souls. Most Indian commentators would take shelter under the inexorable law of Karma to reconcile the presence of evil and inequalities in this world with the goodness of God. Madhva has been *the only one to push the question to its logical end. Karma implies freedom and freedom implies a choice. But it does not explain why a particular choice is made unless the freedom itself is an expression of the innate nature of each soul.* Even a chain of beginningless Karma could not explain why all souls are not equally good or bad, as all of them are equally eternal and their karmas too were equally beginningless and the start simultaneous. The only possible explanation is that offered by Madhva viz., that the Karma itself is the result of the distinctive nature of each soul (हठ) which is intrinsic to it (*Svarūpa-yogyatā*). This point is elaborated by Madhva in his *MbhTN* (xxii.84-88) :

स्वभावाख्या योग्यता या **हठाख्या** ।
या अनादिसिद्धा सर्वजीवेषु नित्या ।
सा कारणं प्रथमं तु, द्वितीय—
मनादिकर्मैव, तथा तृतीयः ॥
जीवप्रयत्नः पौरुषाख्यस्तदेतत् ।
त्रयं विष्णोर्वशगं सर्वदैव ।
हठाच्च कर्माणि भवन्ति कर्मजो
यत्नो यतो हठकर्मप्रयोक्ता ॥
विना न यत्नं न हठो नापि कर्म
फलप्रदो वासुदेवोऽखिलस्य ॥
स्वातंत्र्यशक्तेर्विनियामको हि
तथाप्येतान् सोऽप्यपेक्ष्यैव युञ्जेत्
एतानपेक्ष्यैव फलं ददानी—
त्यस्यैव संकल्प इति **स्वतन्त्रता** ।[8]

8. The innate fitness of Jīvas for good or evil, which makes them Sāttvika, Rājasa or Tāmasa, as the case may be, is called 'haṭha'. It clings to them with the persistency of the green moss-like substance to the surface of water. This 'Haṭha' is the innate disposition which finds divergent expression in internal and external behavior through intensive effort. All these three factors depend on God's will for their existence and functioning, like everything else in finite life. 'Haṭha' or Svarūpayogyatā and recognizable Karma which is its outcome can hardly operate and bear fruit without 'Prayatna' or intensive conscious effort. It will thus be clear that while 'Svarūpayogyatā' is the basic determinant of human destiny, it lies more or less dormant until

Madhva's doctrine of *Anādisvarūpayogyatā* takes us one step *definitely beyond* the stage of *anādikarma* of Jīvas and traces it to the intrinsic nature (*anādi-svabhāva*) or fitness (*svarūpa-yogyatā*) of individual selves. He gives it the name of "Haṭha". From this "Haṭha", Karma flows as its outward expression in terms of good or bad actions, through volitional activity (*Puruṣaprayatna*) without which the Svabhāva cannot be developed to its full stature : स्वभावस्य बाह्यप्रयत्नसचिवस्यैव कार्यकारित्वात् (*NS* p. 316). All these factors are however *ex hypothesi* dependent on the will of God, for their *sattā* (existence) and *pravṛtti* (functioning). In allowing this basic nature of the souls to develop without detriment to the moral law, God is not open to any charges of partiality or cruelty; for there is no violation or flouting of the moral law, which is God's own law. He allows it to have its course. He does not interfere in its working and change the nature of beings. *Theoretically, He may have* the power to do whatever He pleases; but the fact remains that *He does not choose to upset the moral law* or change the nature of beings.

And facts matter more than vague musings and conjectures of what may be possible for God. The evidence of Scripture and level-headed reason uphold the supremacy of the moral law as an expression of the Divine will itself.[9] "The ghost of Darius moralises on the Persian downfall: 'When, of our own free will, we rush into sin, God Himself becomes our ally'" (Radhakrishnan, *I. Phil.* ii, p. 419 f.n.). The nature of the soul is allowed to have its course, whatever it may be. There is no fear of the sovereignty of God being compromized on this view. The moral character of God is not also challenged on this view. For, one can accuse God of partiality and cruelty only when He changes

---

it is awakened and transmuted into Karma through intensive effort. Human effort or endeavour is thus made to play the key role in making man the architect of his own future in keeping with his own basic nature. Madhva makes Bhīmasena the ideal exemplar of Śuddha-Bhāgavata Dharma and champion of Haṭha, in the *Mahābhārata* story (see Vanaparva) and the chief spokesman of this realistic theory of Jīvakartṛtva in God's government of the universe.

9. Cf. न च प्रकृतेः संसाराभावादिना ईश्वरेणाप्यन्यथाकर्तुमशक्यत्वेन सुदृढत्वात् सर्वसाम्यमेवेश्वरेणेति युक्तम्; ईश्वरस्य महामहिमत्वात्, नित्यमसंसारित्वस्य नित्यं तदनुग्रहेणैवोपपत्तेः ।
(*Nyāya Vivaraṇa*, iv. 2. 6)

the nature of some in preference to others. Moreover, to change the Svarūpa of the Jīvas would be to destroy, to annihilate, the Jīvas; for, the "Svarūpa" is the essence of Jīvahood and any change of "Svarūpa" would be tantamount to a destruction of individuality.

The theory of Svarūpabheda and Svarūpayogyatā elaborated by Madhva is thus the most *far-reaching* and at the same time highly *suggestive solution* of the problem of plurality of selves and their freedom and freewill and of the presence of evil and suffering in a moral universe under the government of a moral and merciful God. Questions like the following have been asked all the world over : The Jīva was not created out of a void at a particular time. But he is, none the less, an expression of the nature of God. How then does he happen to be so imperfect, while his archetype is also the type of perfection? St. Augustine's agony of soul was still more poignant. "Who made me? Did not God who is not only good, but goodness itself? Whence, then, came I to will evil and nill good so that I am thus justly punished? Who set this in me and ingrafted in me this plant of bitterness, seeing that I was wholly formed of most sweet God?" (*Confessions*, *Bk*. VII, 4-5). The answer to these questions is found by Madhva in *BS* ii. 3.51 (अदृष्टानियमात्) in the intrinsic diversity of human nature (*adṛṣṭāniyama*). It has been shown earlier that this "*adṛṣṭa*" is another name for the "*anādi-svarūpa-yogyatā*" of the individual souls. Rāghavendra Tīrtha brings out this point, very clearly, in his gloss *Bhāvadīpa* on Jayatīrtha's *TP* :

स्वरूपोपाधिवैचित्र्यस्यैव अदृष्टानियमपदेन अभिप्रेतत्वात् । विवृतमेतत् चन्द्रिकायाम् । (*Bhāvadīpa*, ii. 3. 53)

Trivikramn Paṇḍita makes a clear and *very important statement* that while Anādisvarūpayogyatā is the potential factor in attaining Aparokṣa in the end, it is possible only by zealous and intensive effort in the direction (*mahotsāha*) as exemplified in the case of Indra, in the story from the *Chāndogya Up*. :

योग्यतैव ज्ञानहेतुरिति न ब्रूमः, येनोत्साहवैयर्थ्यम् । **योग्यस्य महोत्साह इत्येव ब्रूमः ।**
(*TD* ii. 41.34)

In view of this plain speaking, Dr. Radhakrishnan's criticism against Madhva's position that "*individual effort loses its point*, since whether one believes himself to be the elect or not-elect, one is bound to lapse into indifference and apathy" (*I. Phil.* p. 751), is misplaced.

Evil has also a cathartic part to play in the moral economy of our world. It has teleological purpose. Evil in good souls is foreign matter. It needs must be thrown out. Struggle against evil helps its ejection. In Madhva's theology, good souls are helped by the Tattvābhimānidevatās who preside over our mind and other organs, in exercise of their appointed cosmic functions. Their grace and guidance are necessary to rid ourselves of evil. One has to guard against temptations placed by evil beings (*Asuras*) who seek to establish their sway over us, obstructing the Tattvābhimānidevatās in their benevolent work by leading us astray. (See the parable in the *Chāndogya Up.* about the attacks of the Asuras on the other *Indriyābhimānidevatās* and their unsuccessful bid to overpower Prāṇa.) Those who come out of this perpetual struggle between the forces of good and evil and succeed in throwing out evil from their persons with the support of the Tattvābhimānidevatās attain the grace of God and liberation from Prākṛtic bonds. This accounts for the importance of "tattvanyāsa" in Madhva's code of daily worship.

In keeping with His teleological purpose, God allows the souls the fullest scope of the complete expression of their individual natures for good and evil. Though omnipotent, He does not wish to stifle evil souls. He allows them freedom of activity. Their activity is in a way beneficial to good souls. For resistance to evil releases the latent energies of good souls, helps them realize the good in their essential nature. For all categories of souls in Saṁsāra have an admixture of both good and evil in greater or less proportions in the constitution of their Liṅgaśarīra and other appurtenances, composed of the three strands of *sattva*, *rajas* and *tamaṣ*. When evil souls are pitted against good ones they react in keeping with their evil nature by hating and traducing them. By the law of spiritual osmosis they shed the little good in themselves and absorb the evil that is in the others.[10] As the Divine law operates, the evil

10. दुःखे च सुखमानिनः (*BT*)

souls sink under the accumulated weight of their own evil into Tamas, while the good souls thus relieved of their evil, rise to higher planes of spiritual development. So goes on the drama of "self-election" of souls to their respective destinies.

अन्धे तमसि मग्नस्य चेतनेन्द्रियसंतता ।
सुखानुभवशक्तिर्या सा विनश्यति सर्वथा ॥ (*BT* xi. 12. 19)

CHAPTER XLIV

PROBLEM OF EVIL IN RELATION TO ETHICAL ADVANCEMENT

THE problem of Evil and suffering in the world is the most difficult one in Theism. We have explained Madhva's attitude to the allied problem of freedom and freewill on the basis of the doctrine of natural selection (*anādisvarūpayogyatā*) of good or bad and of the tripartite classification of souls. It is not, therefore, necessary for Madhva to answer the question of the compatibility of evil with Divine goodness. This question has also been touched upon in the Vaiṣamyanairghṛṇyādhikaraṇa of the *BS*. It is possible to hold, on the *Traividhya* view also, that the presence of evil is an incentive to the better class of souls, to keep off from its temptation :

....ततोऽन्यान् जीवान् मध्यमतामसान् ।
सृजत्यवति हन्तीशो भक्तानां भक्तिवृद्धये ॥

(*Viṣṇurahasya* V.12)

There are many worshippers of Satan and his ways and they have no moral code or spiritual values. They are unmitigatedly anti-social in their outlook. Their type is outlined in the Scriptures.[1]

Any thoroughgoing theory of man's spiritual destiny must, therefore, take note of the irreducible distinctions of human nature and formulate a theory that would cover the diverse aspects of its character as a whole. If reason and experience

---

1. Cf. *Gītā*, xvi. 16-20; निरामिणो रिपवो येऽन्मेषु जागृधुः (*RV* ii. 23. 16) and **अथ ज्ञानोपसर्गा**—ये चान्ये मिथ्यावादैः कुहकेन्द्रजालैर्वैदिकेषु परिस्थातुमिच्छन्ति, तै सह न संवसेत् । (*Maitrī Up*. vii. 8).

are any guide in such matters, Sarvamukti or universal salvation would appear to be a day-dream. Bondage is not only real, but it may be absolutely irremediable for some. It all depends on the basic nature of free beings. It is futile to throw up our hands and exclaim that we cannot have a really useful ethics unless we believe in the spiritual possibility of everyone "who bears the human form divine". Why forget the animal and other forms divine? Ethical systems all over the world have been devised only for the benefit of those who may care to profit by them. The ethicization of the entire cosmos is no practical politics. The utmost that any useful system of ethics can do is to show the ways and means of advance. Whether particular ethical doctrines will be accepted by all sections of humanity, and acted up to, is more than any ethical system can predict or guarantee. Believers in I.C.B.M. as a means of banishing capitalistic ideology from the world as well as those who believe in peaceful co-existence of nations with different ideologies will always be there. With due deference to those "who bear the human form divine", Madhva maintains that their future is unpredictable. The diversity of human nature is such that we cannot shut our eyes to it, or squeeze everyone into the same mould. An ethical system would be of no use if people are indifferent to it or are not prepared to abide by it : नहि सर्वाधिकारिकं शास्त्रम्. Some are bound to look askance at the most perfect system of ethics or scoff at it. The existence of professional liars does not invalidate the noble commandment of Christ and the Upaniṣads to speak the truth. It is hardly necessary, then, to shed sentimental tears over the doom of Satan, Beelzebub, Balial, Kali or Kālanemi. They have their reward, each according to his own deserts. As men and women are not machine-made, they will and must differ from one another in most minute respects. Difference of character and temperament is the law of the universe :

अनादियोग्यतां चैव कलिवाणीश्वरावधिम् ।
को निवारयितुं शक्तो युक्त्यागमबलोद्धताम् ॥? (*AV* iii. 4.41)

Experience shows that all men are not moved by the same considerations or values of ethical conduct. Some are frank hedonists to the core, who not only take delight in their hedonism, but are proud of it. Philosophy or no philosophy, they won't care. You may call them "philosophical swines", but they will treat your condemnations as those of babes and imbeciles who run away from the charms and pleasures of life unfit constitutionally to enjoy the gifts of nature. Cf.

यथा यूनः परमरमणीयापि रमणी
कुमाराणामन्तःकरणहरणं नैव कुरुते ।
(*Naiṣadha, Epil.* 1)

It is quite possible that, say what you will, this type of men and women who may presumably form the majority of the race, may go on content with this philosophical hedonism. The Omar Khayyam type is by no means a hypothetical monstrosity. Below this self-complacent, pleasure-loving type in creation, is the wicked and unmoral type of the most devilish propensities for destruction, vice and moral degradation. Such a type is typified by the demons and Asuras of the Purāṇas and its counterpart is not difficult to recognize in our own times of atomic and ballistic warfare. It is unphilosophical to close our eyes to the darker sides of life and dismiss them as mere illusions or passing shadows. We must find a place for the best and the worst of natures in our philosophy of life. Madhva has had the boldness to look at it from the practical point of view. There is no need for the philosopher to be a moral alchemist and seek to convert base metals into gold. As a practical philosopher, Madhva refuses to subscribe *to the idea of Sarvamukti*. Man will be served according to his deserts,—neither more nor less. Mukti is not a prize for good conduct to be conferred from without. It is nothing but the realization of our being by each one of us :

मुक्तिर्हित्वान्यथारूपं स्वरूपेण व्यवस्थितिः । (*Bhag* ii. 10.6)

Nature will find its expression in anyone of the three patterns indicated already. We need not fight shy of nature's laws.

The question why there is evil and suffering in this world is no doubt legitimate. It is there and cannot be driven out of existence on any ground of alleged incompatibility with the moral perfection of God and His government. We have to reckon with it and fight against it if we can; or else go down under its weight. Such has been the history of man all through. And philosophy proposes to show us how to rise above the influence of evil and attain goodness. And it stands to reason that while many may falter on the way and fail to reach the goal, others may struggle on and on till they reach the summit—while some others may not even care to think of the goal.[2]

Attention to the baneful effects of evil helps to cleanse the personality of all dross. It hastens Vairāgya which strengthens devotion to a life of purity and godliness : साधनेषु वैराग्यमादावपेक्षितम् । तदर्थं गत्यागतिस्वर्गनरकगर्भवासादिस्वरूपं निरूप्यते गत्यादेः खलु दुःखरूपतां श्रुत्वा भावयतोऽधिकारिणः स्वर्गादिष्वपि रागो विच्छिद्यते (*TP* iii. 1.1).

It is to draw attention to the miseries of Saṁsāra that the Śāstras describe at some length the souls' sojourn through heaven and hell and their sufferings in the womb (*BS* iii.1,29). The desire for release is in proportion to the intensity of suffering and the keenness of its realization.

2. Whether these three classes of souls are a passing phase in the history of the universe or represent a broadly continuing pattern is a matter to be decided on objective grounds and the pronouncements of the Śāstras on the subject. It cannot be decided on subjective likes or dislikes.

CHAPTER XLV

CLASSIFICATION OF ADHIKĀRĪS

THE scheme of Sādhanas embraces the entire field of man's spiritual uplift comprising the physical, moral and spiritual perfection of the individual. The paths of Karma, Bhakti and Jñāna of the Śāstras pertain roughly to the physical, emotional and intellectual aspects of Sādhana. The scheme of Sādhanas is set out by Madhva with reference to different orders of aspirants (Adhikārīs) based partly on generic distinctions (to be acquired). The former class of Adhikārīs is distinguished into (1) the higher, (2) middling and (3) lower type of souls, comprising respectively the gods, Ṛṣi-Gandharvas and the best among men (*manuṣyottama*). It is pointed out that the human souls can only realize the Supreme from without (*bahiḥprakāśa*), the Ṛṣis inwardly (*antaḥprakāśa*) and that the gods can intuit Brahman as omnipresent (सर्वंप्रकाशाः) (Madhva, *BSB* iv.3.16).

A different classification of souls is made in an ascending order of spiritual merit into (1) devoted, (2) purified and (3) enlightened. Such of the human beings as are fit for nothing more than a ceaseless cycle of transmigration and those who are 'damnable' are ranked below the "best of men". The term "Manuṣyottama" does not, however, involve any distinction of caste or sex, though each group of Adhikārīs may have its own distinctive way of approach to spiritual progress. As faithful followers of the Sūtrakāra and believers in the Smārta code, all commentators on the Vedānta have, however, maintained that the attainment of philosophical wisdom through Śāstric investigation is open only to the Traivarṇikas, qualified for Vedic study, (*BS* i.3.36-38) while women and Śūdras are given access to the saving knowledge only through the literature of the Epics and Purāṇas and Pañcarātra. A faithful adherence to the duties of Varṇāśrama is naturally insisted upon. But Madhva does not make a fetish of entering the fourth order of life as an external condition precedent to the attainment of wisdom (as in the Advaita)[1]. At the same time, he concedes the obvious advantages of the Sannyāsa order over other *āśramas* on account of the increased opportunities therein for one-pointed devotion and purity.[2] He is *the only Bhāṣyakāra* who has recognized the existence of women of the highest spiritual attainments, eligible for Brahmavicāra through the Vedānta.[3]

---

1. Cf. the practice of 'Āpatsannyāsa' current in this school (*SGB* II. 72)
2. यत्याश्रमस्तु प्रायत्यार्थो भगवत्तोषणार्थश्च ।
   अप्रायत्यमेव हि प्रायो गृहस्थादीनाम् । (Madhva, *GB* iii. 4)
3. आहुरप्युत्तमस्त्रीणामधिकारं तु वैदिके । (*BSB* 1.1.1)

CHAPTER XLVI

GENERAL SCHEME OF SĀDHANAS

THE aim of metaphysical inquiry is the attainment of release through Divine grace. One has naturally to think of the means of earning it. The Śāstras describe them as leading to one another, in the following order : freedom from worldly attachment (Vairāgya), devotion to God (Bhakti), Śravaṇa (study), Manana (reflection), Nididhyāsana (meditation) and Sākṣātkāra (direct realization) :

सद्भिर्वैराग्यभक्तिश्रुतिमतिनियतध्यानजज्ञानयोगात् गम्यम् ।
(*TP*, introductory verse)

तस्मान्मोक्षाय श्रवणादिसाध्यनिदिध्यासनजन्यसाक्षात्कारेण ईश्वरः प्रसन्नीकरणीयः।
(*Nym* iii.9)

Dispassion or Vairāgya is the first step and primary requisite of a true aspirant. The spirit of detachment and freedom from passions is indeed the most valuable discipline and preparation for a life of genuine godliness and spirituality. It constitutes the essence of spiritual life :

नाविरतो दुश्चरितान्नाशान्तो नासमाहितः ।
नाशान्तमानसो वापि प्रज्ञानेनैनमाप्नुयात् ॥
(*Kaṭha Up*. i.2.24)

शान्तो दान्त उपरतस्तितिक्षुः समाहितो भूत्वा * * * परीक्ष्य लोकान् कर्मचितान् ब्राह्मणो निर्वेदमायात् । (*MundUp* i.2.13)

Attachment to sensuous life is the greatest impediment to devotion to God. One cannot serve two masters. One must choose sooner or later between the two. Attachment to the flesh includes the misplaced notion of possession and independence :

ते वै विदन्त्यतितरन्ति च देवमायां
नैषां ममाहमिति धीः श्वश्रृगालभक्ष्ये । (*Bhag* II.7.42)

Steadiness of attention and exclusive contemplation of the Supreme can only be achieved through deep-rooted love of God. The intimate relation of Bimbapratibimbabhāva, subsisting between God and souls, gives such devotion an element of naturalness and spontaneity that is needed to make it an ideal one. The worship of the Supreme under such favorable conditions earns the grace of God who is pleased to reveal Himself to the seeker. This conviction of the comparative evanescence of worldly goods and the perishability of all material attractions, so necessary for the birth of Vairāgya, is to be acquired by Karma, patient study and reflection.

The knowledge thus acquired is seen to bear fruit in respect of persons who have done good deeds in former lives and who, as a result, are placed in this life in an atmosphere congenial to spiritual advancement and whose temperaments are properly attuned to spirituality. Śravaṇa supplies the basic materials for philosophical thought and Manana (reflection) is needed to give it definiteness of content and freedom from doubts.[1] They are both preliminaries to contemplation which leads to direct vision :—

श्रवणस्याज्ञाननिवृत्तिद्वारा, मननस्य तु संशयविपर्ययनिवृत्तिद्वारा परोक्षतत्त्वनिश्चयसाध्ये साक्षात्कारफलके निदिध्यासने अङ्गता सिद्धा ।

श्रवणं शब्दजं ज्ञानमुपपत्त्यनुचिन्तनम् ।
मतिः, निरन्तरा चिन्ता निदिध्यासनमुच्यते ॥ (*Nym* iii.7)

Śravaṇa is defined as the acquisition of the sense of the sacred texts under the instruction of competent teachers. It dispels ignorance about the subject-matter (अज्ञाननिवृत्ति); Manana is the systematic employment of the canons of textual interpretation and logical examination with a view to arriving at a firm conviction that the final interpretation of the Śāstras thus arrived at is alone the correct and unimpeachable one. Manana removes doubts (*saṁśaya*) and misapprehension (*viparyaya*) and confirms the true import of the Śāstras (*parokṣatattvaniścaya*). Then comes *nididhyāsana* or *dhyāna* (continuous meditation). Dhyāna leads to direct realization (*darśana*). *Śravaṇa* and *manana* are thus subsidiary (*aṅgabhūta*) to *nididhyāsana*, which is

1. मननं च वेदार्थनिर्णयं कुर्वंत् संशयविपर्ययौ निवारयति । (*TP* iii. 3.43)

the chief means (*aṅgi*) of Sākṣātkāra. The Vivaraṇa school of Advaita, on the other hand, gives the place of honor among Sādhanas to Śravaṇa (fixation of the import of the Śāstras) and relegates *manana* and *nididhyāsana* to a secondary position as contributory factors[2] (फलोपकार्यङ्गम्) As against this, Madhva and his commentators accept all the statements : श्रोतव्यो, मन्तव्यो, निदिध्यासितव्यः as primary injunctions (*apūrvavidhi*). These three, according to Madhva, represent the authoritarian, critical and contemplative approach to philosophical truth.

Rāmānuja dismisses श्रोतव्यः and मन्तव्यः in the text : आत्मा वा अरे द्रष्टव्यः श्रोतव्यो मन्तव्यो*** as mere restatements (अनुवाद) and accepts only Nididhyāsana as being actually enjoined by the Śruti. As for direct vision of Brahman (*darśana*) enjoined in "द्रष्टव्यः", he is not prepared to give it any independent position over and above Dhyāna or meditation (*nididhyāsana*) which he regards as the ultimate means of Brahmic realization. He holds that intensified meditation practised without interruption attains the character of a direct perception : सा च स्मृतिर्दर्शनसमानाकारा. But then, Rāmānuja admits also that from the time a seeker comes to accept Brahman as the sole means (*upāya*) of deliverance, his knowledge of Brahman becomes transfigured into a deep attachment for Brahman. In these circumstances, just as one may naturally be expected to go on thinking constantly of a person to whom one has become deeply attached, without the necessity for any special injunction to do so, similarly one can dispense with the necessity for any injunction with regard to Nididhyāsana also. If the injunction is felt to be necessary in the interest of laying down a constant and uninterrupted flow of it, similar injunctions with regard to Śravaṇa to be practised under a proper Guru may also be considered necessary.

In his commentary on *BS* iii.3.44-46 Madhva discusses the place and importance of the ideal Guru and the importance of his grace in the final flowering of the spiritual personality of

---

2. अमृतत्वसाधनमात्मदर्शनं 'द्रष्टव्य' इत्यनूद्य तादर्थ्येन मननिदिध्यासनाभ्यां फलोपकार्यङ्गाभ्यां सह श्रवणं नामाङ्गि विचार्यते ।

(*Vivaraṇa*, *GOS*, Madras, 1968, Part II, pp. 29-20)

the aspirant (*Sādhaka*)[3]. He emphasizes the point that instruction and guidance of a competent Guru and his grace (*prasāda*) are absolutely necessary for Śravaṇa and Manana to bear fruit : आचार्यवान् पुरुषो वेद (*ChanUp* vi, 14.2). This is in keeping with the esoteric traditions of the Upaniṣads, so well exemplified in the story of Satyakāma in the *ChanUp* iv. 9, where the young Brahmacārin, Satyakāma, after receiving instruction from the Devatās still begs to be initiated and instructed finally by his own Guru. Madhva says that the grace of the Guru is part of the *modus operandi* (इतिकर्तव्यता) of the means of jñāna viz., Śravaṇa, Manana etc. It is, therefore, a necessary complement of Jñānasādhana. He further says that of the two viz., individual effort and the grace of the Guru, the latter is to be deemed the more powerful factor and therefore indispensable for one's spiritual realization. *The importance of Guru-Bhakti has not been so well brought out as an integral part of the Theism of the Brahma Sūtras by any other Bhāṣyakāra than Madhva.* The emphasis on Guruprasāda does not mean that individual effort and the deserts of the aspirant do not count. They are the foundations of one's spiritual progress; but Guruprasāda is the crowning point of this development. *There is, undoubtedly, an element of deep religious mysticism in the special significance which Madhva attaches to the role of Guru and his grace in regard to the subject of Sādhanas and their fulfilment.* It is to be noted that this represents a completely new and different interpretation of *BS* iii.3.44-46 as compared with those of Śaṅkara, Rāmānuja and others. It is an interpretation which has the most vital and intimate bearing on the question of spiritual Sādhanas and therefore quite a relevant topic to be considered in the Sādhanādhyāya and one which has the full support of the Upaniṣadic traditions and teaching :

यस्य देवे पराभक्तिर्यथा देवे तथा गुरौ ।
तस्यैते कथिता ह्यर्थाः प्रकाशन्ते महात्मनः ॥ (*SvetUp* vi.23)

A seeker is allowed to change his Guru if he secures another

3. Similar emphasis is laid in the Haridāsa literature (*Kannaḍa*) of the Mādhva tradition : गुरुविन गुलामनागो तनक दोरेयदण्ण मुकुति ।
'Not until one becomes the slave of his Guru, dear brother, can Mokṣa be attained.' See also referenec to such Grace extended by Madhva to his brother Viṣṇu Tīrtha (*M. Vij.* xv. 113.).

with a superior spiritual illumination, provided the latter is able and inclined to impart the full measure of grace and illumination that may be required for the self-realization of the disciple. Where both the Gurus happen to be of equal merit and disposition to grant the full measure of their grace, qualifying for illumination to the aspirant, the permission of the earlier Guru shall have to be obtained before receiving instruction from the other one.[4]

Madhva has given a higher place to Nididhyāsana or Dhyāna than to Śravaṇa and Manana, which are put down by him as aṅgas to Dhyāna.[5] This is because his conception of Dhyāna or Upāsanā is radically different from that of Śaṅkara to whom *all Upāsanā as such is based on superimposition*, as will be made clear. He does not agree to the doctrine of Śabdāparokṣa of Maṇḍana and other Advaitic writers, according to which Śravaṇa alone is the true and ultimate source of illumination in respect of Brahman, Manana and Nididhyāsana acting merely as accessories to it by removing obstacles to steadiness, such as mistrust and misunderstanding. But to Madhva, they are both subsidiary to Nididhyāsana. They merely help to establish the nature of the philosophical truth (*tattvanirṇaya*). Then comes prolonged meditation of particular attributes of Divinity, which is known as Upāsanā.

There is an intimate and balanced relation between Sādhana and Sādhya on Madhva's view. He maintains the position that there should be a gradation of spiritual joy in Mokṣa, commensurate with the amount, quality and intensity of Sādhanas or spiritual effort of different levels and orders of Adhikārins :

"दशकल्पं तपश्चीर्णं रुद्रेण लवणार्णवे ।
त्वक्त्वा सुखानि सर्वाणि क्लिष्टेन लवणाम्भसा ॥
शक्रेण वर्षकोटीश्च धूमः पीतो ऽतिदुःखतः ।
वर्षायुतं तु सूर्येण तपोऽर्वाक्शिरसा कृतम् ॥
सुदुःखेन सुखं त्यक्त्वा धर्मेणाकाशशायिना ।
पीता मरीचयो वर्षसहस्रमतिसादरम् ॥

---

4. See my *BSPC* Vol. III. pp. 405-417.

5. समस्तगुणपरिपूर्णो नारायण इत्ययमेव वेदार्थः इति ज्ञानं वेदार्थनिर्णयः । उपपन्न एवंभाव इत्यधिगमः तत्त्वनिश्चयः । तौ ब्रह्मदृष्टेः पृथगेव । तत्साधनोपासनापूर्वभाविनौ । (*TD* on *BS* iii. 3.43)

अतिकृच्छ्रेण कुर्वन्ति यत्नं ब्रह्मविदोऽपि च ।"
इत्येतदखिलं मोक्षे विशेषाभावतः कथम् ?
युक्तं च साधनाधिक्यात् साध्याधिक्यं सुरादिषु ।
नाधिक्यं यदि साध्ये स्यात्, प्रयत्नः साधने कुतः[6] ?
(*AV* iii.4.16)

A omprehensive scheme of spiritual discipline is thus the very foundation of all spiritual progress. The importance of ethics in philosophy has been accepted by all philosophers, who look upon it as a system of Sādhanas for the achievement of the highest good (*niḥśreyasa*). A complete theory of the universe must necessarily include ethical judgments on the value or worthlessness of objects and thereby secure an influence over our conduct. Since philosophy in India owes its inspiration to the deep yearning for the realization of the religious purpose of life rather than the satisfaction of the speculative instinct, it is natural to expect a remarkable affinity amongst the various systems of Indian philosophy in the postulates and conditions of such a realization. They are agreed on certain general principles of ethical conduct and Sādhanas though there are many differences of emphasis, divergence of detail or technical terminology and the relative position and value of certain forms and items of the discipline. The goal of life, the attitude to the world and, above all, the means of attaining the goal, though broadly the same, are still marked by certain fundamental differences in philosophic theory. The special features of Madhva's scheme of ethics relate to the following points: the place of (1) Vicāra or reasoned thought and philosphic inquiry in the scheme

6. "Rudra performed severe penance in the salty sea for ten eons, abandoning all pleasures and putting himself to great hardship. Indra inhaled smoke for a crore of years with great difficulty. The Sun-god performed penance with his head downward for ten thousand years. Yama lying in the open air exposed himself to the heat of the Sun's rays for a thousand years. Even the knowers of Brahman thus put forth further effort (sādhanas)". How could these and other statements be reconciled, if there were no gradation in Mokṣa? It is proper that there should be results in proportion to efforts. If there be no proportionate increase in results, why should the above persons (and others) be eager to work more and more and put forth more Sādhanas and more intensive ones than others?

of Sādhanas ; (2) of Karma in the triple scheme of Karma, Bhakti and Jñāna Mārgas ; (3) the nature and importance of Bhakti and Upāsanā and (4) the importance of Aparokṣajñāna as the final means of deliverance and (5) the ethical responsibilities of the Aparokṣajñānin.

CHAPTER XLVII

KARMA-YOGA AND JÑĀNA-YOGA

THE most prominent forms of spiritual discipline are those going by the names of Karmamārga, Jñānamārga and Bhaktimārga. Of these, Karmayoga or the path of works is generally believed to constitute the first rung of the ladder. The term Karmayoga is, however, understood in most schools of Vedānta in the narrow sense of *Pravṛtti-Mārga*, as defined by the Mīmāṁsakas, consisting in a faithful performance of the round of Vedic sacrifices and ritualistic rites prescribed by the Śrutis and Smṛtis with the expectation of their rewards in this or in the next world and the adherence to the duties of varṇa and āśrama. Throughout his commentary on the *Gītā*, Śaṅkara denounces the possibility of effecting any synthesis (*samuccaya*) between Karma and Jñāna, all the while defining the Karma in question, to himself, as Kāmyakarma. But he hardly ever envisages the possibility of a *true Samuccaya between "niṣkāma karma and ātma-jñāna"*. Indeed, he seems to deny even the name Karma to be given to the works performed by the enlightened soul as Lokasaṁgraha or the work of Kṛṣṇa himself as a Kṣatriya in upholding Dharma. But the whole emphasis of the Karma-Yoga of the *Gītā* is on recognizing the need for giving a reorientation to the concept of "Karma" and redeeming it from the spell of rewards and fruits, and making it possible for *blending such exalted form of Karma with Jñāna*. Śaṅkara is hardly fair to the spirit of the *Gītā* in denying the possibility of the synthesis of even such exalted form of "Niṣkāmakarma" with "Ātmajñāna",[1] of which Kṛṣṇa himself and persons like Janaka

---

1. साङ्ख्यानां पृथक्करणात् **अज्ञानामेव हि कर्मयोगः** न ज्ञानिनाम् । **ज्ञानिनां तु,** गुणैरचाल्यमानानां स्वतः चलनाभावात् **कर्मयोगो नोपपद्यते।** (Śaṅkara, *GB* iii. 5)

and Priyavrata were standing examples. Madhva's point in not accepting Jñānakarmasamuccaya is not due to any under-estimation of Niṣkāma-Karma as such; but to the unique place which Aparokṣa-Jñāna or direct vision of God occupies in his philosophy. The case is different with Rāmānuja to whom Dhyāna marks the highest stage of Sādhana which is but a mere approximation to direct vision; but is *not* actually a direct vision of the Lord. It is obviously for this reason that Rāmānuja pleads for a Samuccaya of Jñāna and Karma as Mokṣasādhana. Among older Vedāntins, Bhāskara and Brahmadatta too are known to have supported the Jñānakarmasamuccayavāda.

Madhva resolves this apparent conflict between the so-called Karma and Jñāna Mārgas by enlarging the scope of Karma-Yoga as understood by Śaṅkara and raising it to the level of a way of enlightened action (*niṣkāmaṁ jñānapūrvaṁ karma*). He makes a vigorous plea[2] for enlightened spiritual activity *by all*, which cannot be binding in its consequences. There can be no true wisdom without such activity, at least for all of us, mortals, and no true Karma without enlightenment and devotion to God :

तत्कर्म हरितोषं यत् । (*Bhag* iv 29 49).

यज्ञार्थात्कर्मणोऽन्यत्र लोकोऽयं कर्मबन्धनः । (*Gītā* iii.9)

Madhva interprets the statement of the *Gītā* iii.3, that there are *two different groups of Adhikāris* in the world, called Sāṁkhyas and Yogas, to mean that there are two *orders of beings* among *the wise and eligible souls* (i) the select 'few' (Jñānaniṣṭhāḥ) like Sanaka and other born Yogins who pursue the path of knowledge to the exclusion of all Karma (in its external form): गृहस्थादिकर्मत्यागेन ज्ञाननिष्ठाः सनकादिवत् (*GB*) and (ii) all *other enlightened beings*, including some of the divinely appointed leaders of society like King Janaka, Priyavrata and others, who though highly enlightened, have been "commissioned by the Divine will to follow the path of *active* Karma[3] and serve as an

---

2. For an exposition of this topic, according to Madhva, see my *HDSV* 44-46; 92-93.

3. King Priyavrata, the God-intoxicated King, had made up his mind to retire to the forest. Brahmadeva himself comes down to persuade the King to give up his resolution to renounce the world. He is charged by Brahmadeva to stick to his duties and responsibilities as a King, even though

example of disinterested action in their fellowmen and guide them (*lokasaṁgraha*)".[4] The average run of humanity has, therefore, necessarily to work through Karma : कर्मणा ज्ञानमातनोति, ज्ञानेनामृतीभवति ।

But this Karma is *not* to be viewed in the narrow hedonistic or ritualistic sense of the Mīmāṁsakas. Madhva overcomes the difficulty here, by distinguishing the Karma-Yoga of the *Gītā* from what the other philosophers call the Pravṛttimārga of the Vedas. He points out, on sound textual authority,[5] that the latter is deservedly censured in the *Gītā* and other Śāstras and that true Nivṛtti-Mārga is *not* what the other commentators think it to be, viz., the abandonment of all Karma, but *its active performance* in a spirit of devotion and dispassion :

"निष्कामं ज्ञानपूर्वं तु निवृत्तमिह चोच्यते" । (*Vyāsa-smṛti*).

This is indeed the true spirit of "Sannyāsa" and Naiṣkarmya, inculcated in the *Gītā*. Hence it is that Madhva propounds a new theory of typical Vedic injunctions which are almost invariably followed by goodly promise of attractive rewards to come : ज्योतिष्टोमेन स्वर्गकामो यजेत । He suggests that the purpose of these prescriptions is, paradoxically enough, to wean us away from the attractions of perishable rewards and pull us up gradually to a life of disinterested action (Niṣkāma Karma), even as a child is induced by its mother to take a medicinal dose of castor oil, by the tempting offer of sweets in reward.[6]

---

he is a highly enlightened Jñānin. The story of Priyavrata is given in the *Bhāgavata Purāṇa*, Sk. V.1. The relevant passage from the *Bhag* has been cited by Madhva, in his *GB* iii.4.

4. **गृहस्थादिधर्मस्था एव ज्ञाननिष्ठाश्च** । जनकादिवत् ज्ञाननिष्ठा अपि आधिकारिकत्वादीश्वरेच्छया लोकसंग्रहार्थत्वाच्च ये कर्मयोगा भवन्ति, तेऽपि योगिनः । त्वं तु, जनकादिवत् सकर्मैव ज्ञानयोग्यः न तु तत्त्यागेनेत्यर्थः। **सन्ति हीश्वरेच्छया कर्मकृतः प्रियव्रतादयोऽपि ज्ञानिनः ।** तथा ह्युक्तम्—"**ईश्वरेच्छया विनिवेशितकर्माधिकारः**" (*Bhag* v. 1 23) इति ॥ (*Madhva*, *GB* iii. 4)

5. Cf. the passage "**निष्कामं ज्ञानपूर्वं तु** निवृत्तमिह चोच्यते ।' from *Vyāsa Smṛti* cited by Madhva. The same passage occurs in the *Manu Smṛti* also. The *Kūrma Purāṇa* (i. 2. 64) also defines Nivṛtta Karma in the same terms and Rāmānuja in his *Śrībhāṣya* has cited a similar passage from a Pañcarātra text:

तस्मात् सम्यक् परं ब्रह्म वासुदेवाख्यमव्ययम् ।
अस्मादवाप्यते शास्त्रात् **ज्ञानपूर्वेण कर्मणा** ॥ (ii. 2.41)

6. रोचनार्था फलश्रुतिः । (*Bhag* xi. 3.43)

Jayatīrtha puts the case admirably :

अनादिविषयवासनावासितान्तःकरणा न सहसा ज्ञानसाधने कर्मणि प्रवर्तयितुं शक्यन्ते । अतः तेषां कर्मण्यभिरुचिजननार्थं 'स्वर्गकामः' इत्यादिश्रुतिः प्रवृत्ता । कर्मणि प्रवृत्तांस्तु शनैः कामं त्याजयामीत्यभिप्रायवती (*GBt.* ii.47).

Madhva thus makes out that Scripture only *enjoins acts* but *not* also the pursuit of their rewards :

अत एव कामी यजेतेत्यर्थः । **नतु कामी भूत्वेत्यर्थः**। (*GB* ii.47)

Jayatīrtha brings out the technical point of the argument that it is only a *viśeṣyavidhi* and not a *Viśiṣṭavidhi*. The mandate is only with reference to the performance of the act but *not* also with reference to desire for the fruit thereof. The latter is mentioned in the Vidhi only by way of *anuvāda* or an allusion to what is even otherwise established and is not therefore intended to be specially enjoined : कामानुवादेन यजनं विधीयत इति यावत् । कामविशिष्टयजनविधानं तु नेत्यर्थः । We have bare injunctions in Scripture without any reference to the usual statement of rewards, as in वसन्ते वसन्ते ज्योतिषा यजेत, विश्वजिता यजेत, which show that Scripture is not necessarily interested in the pursuit of rewards as the invariable objective of the performance of sacrifices enjoined by it. This line of interpretation (adopted by Madhva) has the support of the Advaitic commentator Śrīdhara Svāmin himself,[7] who is much influenced by Madhva's views in this and in some other respects.

Even this Niṣkāma Karma which is, strictly speaking, the only kind of Karma that is philosophically admissible or effective is not to be admitted as anything more than an accessory to spiritual realization. It is to be pursued for the purpose of acquiring the necessary mental purification : अकामकर्मणामन्तःकरणशुद्धया ज्ञानान्मोक्षो भवति (*GB* iii.4). The reason why Karma cannot be treated as an independent means of release is that it is by nature, irrepressibly found to be inexhaustible by the enjoyment of fruits. It breeds like bacteria. It is estimated that on an average, it takes at least ten future births for an individual to work out the amount of Karma accumulated by him from the fourteenth years of his life, in one birth :

आ चतुर्दशमाद्वर्षात् पुरुषो नियमेन तु
दशावराणां देहानां कारणानि करोत्ययम् ।

7. See his commentary on *Bhag* xi. 3. 45.

स्त्रीवाप्यनूनदशकं देहं मानुषमार्जयेत्
अतः कर्मक्षयान्मुक्तिः कुत एव भविष्यति ? (*BSB* iii.1.8)

It would be a vain hope, then, to expect to work it out by enjoyment. The help of Jñāna is, therefore, indispensable to destroy or neutralize the latent effects of past Karma.[8] Such a power of destroying the accumulated load of past Karma, or rendering it nugatory is ascribed to the actual vision (*aparokṣajñāna*) of God, through meditation (*dhyāna*). Madhva, therefore, regards enlightened activity (Niṣkāmakarma) merely as contributing to such knowledge through Vairāgya,

अकामकर्मणामन्तःकरणशुद्धिद्वारा ज्ञानान्मोक्षो जायते (*GBt* ii.4); (कर्म) योगस्तु अदृष्टद्वारा सत्त्वशुद्धिमुत्पाद्य श्रवणादीनामुपकरोति (*GBt* ii. 52)

Karmayoga, then, is not at all a stumbling block to spiritual progress. It is not, by itself, binding in its effects as it depends on the motive behind it and the end in view with which it is performed. That is why Madhva maintains that *every approved activity after the dawn of Aparokṣa has its reward in the form of a welling up of spiritual bliss* (*ānandodreka*) and never goes in vain[9] :

न हास्य कर्म क्षीयते (*Brh Up* i.4.15)

इति **ज्ञानोत्तरमनुष्ठितेन निवृत्तकर्मणा** प्रसन्नः परमात्मा मुक्तौ **ज्ञानानभिव्यक्तमपि सुखं** व्यक्तीकरोति (*GBt* ii.50)

Madhva is, thus, quite clear that disinterested activity carried on in a spirit of devotion to God is a powerful incentive to the acquisition of knowledge which alone is the highest means of release. Karma and Dhyāna and others are just accessories to it :

अतो, अपरोक्षज्ञानादेव मोक्षः, कर्म तु तत्साधनमेव (*GB* iii.20); सर्वं निवृत्तादिकमन्तरा मध्ये ज्ञानमाधाय मुक्तेः साधनं भवति (*GBt* iii.31).

There is no place, then, for the theory of Jñānakarmasamuccaya:

अत एव समुच्चयनियमो निराकृतः (*GB* iii.32)

Madhva has blazed a new trail in interpreting the message of Karmayoga of *ĪśaUp* 2 and *Gītā* iii.20 by bringing "**Jñānottarakarma**" back to its rightful place in the spiritual life of man at

8. ज्ञानाग्निः सर्वकर्माणि भस्मसात् कुरुते (iv.37). This applies only to such Karma as has not *begun to bear fruit* (*aprārabdha*).

9. * * * **ज्ञानोत्तरकर्मणाम् ।**

मुक्तावनुप्रवेशः स्यादन्यथा तत्कृतिर्न हि (*AV* iii.4. *adhi.* 7)

its highest stage of realization. *He is the first Indian philosopher to use the significant expression "Jñānottarakarma"*. He is also the first to unequivocally and wholeheartedly give the clarion call of service to fellowmen as the greatest moral responsibility of the Jñānī.

नानाजनस्य शुश्रूषा कर्माख्या करवन्मितेः (*GT* vi.3)

He insists that such service to one's fellowmen is a moral obligation, a categorical imperative, laid upon all right-thinking persons like the obligation to pay taxes to one's legally established Government. Social and moral philosophy can hardly claim to have attained to a more salutary conception of service to one's fellowmen. Commentator Jayatīrtha explains that "Nānā-jana" includes all categories of fellowmen—*uttama*, *madhyama* and *adhama*, the nature and complexion of service to each differing accordingly.

CHAPTER XLVIII

CONCEPTION OF BHAKTI, ITS ORDERS AND KINDS

MADHVA has given a uniqve place to Divine grace in his system, in making it the ultimate cause of self-realization and God-realization. But, then, the Deity has got to be *moved* to graciousness (*savyāpārī-karaṇīyaḥ*). This can only be done by Bhakti as the deepest attachment to the Lord, deep-rooted and based on a clear understanding of His greatness and majesty. Jayatīrtha has given us the most comprehensive definition of Bhakti, based on the above, in which the *religious, philosophical and emotional aspects of devotion are beautifully integrated* :

परमेश्वरभक्तिर्नाम निरवधिकानन्तानवद्यकल्याणगुणत्वज्ञानपूर्वकः स्वात्मात्मीयसमस्त-वस्तुभ्योऽप्यनन्तगुणाधिकोऽन्तरायसहस्रेणाप्यप्रतिबद्धः **निरन्तरप्रेमप्रवाहः**[1] (*N*S p.17).

Bhakti is, thus, the steady and continuous flow of deep attachment to God, imprgenable by any amount of impediments and transcending the love of our own selves, our kith and kin, cherished belongings,[2] etc. and fortified by a firm conviction of the transcendent majesty and greatness of God as the abode of all perfections and free from all blemish and by an unshakable conviction of the complete metaphysical dependence of everything else upon Him. *This definition can be accepted as a classical definition of Bhakti.*

When one is flooded by such an intensive and all-absorbing love he gets completely immersed in blissful contemplation

---

1. माहात्म्यज्ञानपूर्वस्तु सुदृढः सर्वतोऽधिकः ।
   स्नेही भक्तिरिति प्रोक्तः, तथा मुक्तिर्न चान्यथा ॥ (*Mbh TN* i.86)

2. प्राणबुद्धिमनःस्वात्मदेहापत्यधनादयः ।
   यत्संपर्कात् प्रिया आसंस्ततःकोन्वपरः प्रियः ? (*Bhag* x. 23.27)

of Him and is lost to all his surroundings. It is this condition of ecstatic communion that has been described in *Gītā* (II. 69) and in *ChanUp* (vii. 24.1) as "where one does not see, hear or understand anything else, that is the infinite", as pointed out by Jayatīrtha.

Such Bhakti is necessary to manifest the natural and intrinsic relationship of Pratibimbatva of the souls to God, which lies dormant in the state of bondage. *Madhva has been the only Bhāṣyakara on the Vedānta Sūtras, who has thought it fit to give Bhakti a locus standi in the Sūtras.* This is as it should be, if the *Brahmasūtras* are to be a complete and self-contained exposition of Bādarāyaṇa's philosophical system, *embodying all the principal aspects of his thought*, derived from the Upaniṣadic and other sources. In view of the clear aud significant contribution that the early metrical Upaniṣads like the *Kaṭha* and *Śvetāśvatara* had made to the doctrine of Bhakti in the Upaniṣads, it would be impossible to brush aside the concept of Bhakti as something either unknown to the Sūtrakāra or as a topic that he did not consider to be an important Sādhana of Mokṣa, in his *philosophy of Theism*. The only rightful place for dealing with the topic will be in the third or *Sādhana-Adhyāya*. *That earlier commentators on the Sūtras like Śaṅkara and Rāmānuja have not been able to find a place for Bhakti within the body of the Sūtras shows nothing more than a defect in their inherited traditions of interpretation or in their way of approach to the Sūtraṣ.*[3]

3. The argument that, as Bhakti has been fully elucidated in the *Gītā*, it need not be dealt with in the Sūtras would be of no avail, when it is remembered that the Sūtras are anterior to the *Gītā* (xiii. 4). As for the Pañcarātras, one would expect the Sūtrakāra, who feels called upon to discuss its Vyūha doctrine in the Sūtras (according to Śaṅkara and Rāmānuja) to be equally solicitous of the claims of Bhakti vs. Jñāna. It would be very strange, indeed, if the Sūtras should leave out "Bhakti" while discussing so many sundry and comparatively less important topics of Sādhana and Upāṣanā, besides many topics dealt with, threadbare, in the Upaniṣads and the *Gītā* itself—each as the way of exit. Nothing but a sort of prejudice against Madhva can be responsible for the general reluctance of many scholars still, to give proper credit to Madhva where his interpretations are decidedly better than those of his predecessors. (See for example some remarks of Svami Adidevananda on this point in his review of my *HDSV* first ed. Vol. I in *Prabuddha Bharata*, May 1964. See also my *RSPC* iii, p. 1-2.)

There is bound to be general agreement that Bādarāyaṇa is presenting a philosophy of Theism in his Sūtras. It will be a *strange type of Indian Theism,* indeed, that he will have expounded in his work on the basis of the *Hindu* Scriptures, if he had decided to *ignore the doctrine of Bhakti altogether in his chapter on Sādhanas, in his great work* ! Even the Saguṇa-Brahmavāda, accommodated by Śaṅkara in his interpretation of the Sūtras cannot afford to *ignore the doctrine of Bhakti as a major Sādhana. Thus looked at from any point of view, the failure of the Pre-Madhva commentators to find a right and rightful place for introducing the topic of Bhakti within the Sādhanādhyāya must be accepted as a serious omission and Madhva must be given special credit for having made good this omission and filled this gap in the Theistic philosophy of the Sūtras.*

The point in Madhva's insistence on Māhātmyajñāna as one of the constituents of Bhakti is that a blind and ignorant devotion is of no philosophical worth. Since the function of Bhakti is to manifest the true relation of Jīva to Brahman, it must naturally be properly informed about that true relation, which presupposes a right knowlede of the majesty and greatness of God as the one Svatantra. Hence, Bhakti has to be enriched by study, reflection and concentration :

पानेन ते देव कथासुधायाः प्रवृद्धभक्त्या विशदाशया ये ।
वैराग्यसारं प्रतिलभ्य बोधं यथांजसा त्वापुरकुण्ठधिष्ण्यम् ॥ (*Bhag* iii. 5.45)

We must, therefore, first of all, enlarge the horizon of our knowledge of God through a wide range of study[4] (*śravaṇa*): शुद्धभावं गतो भक्त्या शास्त्राद् वेद्मि जनार्दनम् (*Mbh* iv). Bhakti is, thus, not a mere wave of sentimentalism or emotionalism, to Madhva. It is the outcome of patient study and deep reflection: ज्ञानधारानुगृहीतम् as Rāmānuja (*GB* ix. p. 65) puts it. It presupposes a certain amount of knowledge in the same way as the pursuit of knowledge needs the urge of devotion : विना ज्ञानं कुतो भक्तिः कुतो भक्ति विना च तत् ? (Madhva *GB* ix. 31). Madhva also demands a high degree of moral perfection from the true devotee of God. He affirms that there can be no true devotion to God without a real sense of moral purity, sincerity of purpose and detachment to worldly pleasures. One cannot serve two masters. True devotion to God would be impossible without the cultivation of a

4. नावेदविन्मनुते तं बृहन्तम् (*TB* iii. 12.9.7) ; औपनिषदः पुरुषः (*BrhUp* iii. 9.26)

natural distaste for the pleasures of the world. It is one of the constitutive elements of true devotion :

भक्तिः परे स्वेऽनुभवो विरक्तिरन्यत्र **चैष त्रिक एककालः** (*Bhag* xi. 2. 42)

स शठमतिरुपयाति योऽर्थतृष्णां तमधमचेष्टमवेहि नास्य भक्तम् ।
(*Viṣṇu Purāṇa* iii. 7. 30)

सा श्रद्धधानस्य विवर्धमाना विरक्तिमन्यत्र करोति पुंसः (*Bhag* iii. 5.13)

Ācāra or purity of life, in all respects, is thus the *sine qua non* of true devotion and knowledge. Devotion without such purity will be a travesty :

अतोऽन्यः कश्चित् भवति चेत् दाम्भिकत्वेन सोऽनुमेयः (Madhva, *GB* ix. 31)

Complete control of the passions of the flesh, calmness of mind, impartiality of conduct and love of God are emphasized by Madhva as the prerequisites of devotion and knowledge :

गुप्तानि चत्वारि यथागमं मे शत्रौ च मित्रे च समोऽस्मि नित्यम् ।
तं चापि देवं शरणं प्रपन्न एकान्तभावेन भजाम्यजस्रम् ।।
एतैर्विशेषैः परिशुद्धसत्त्वः कस्मान्न पश्येयमनन्तमेनम् ?
(*Mbh* XII. 343, *Kumb. Edn.* quoted by Madhva, *GB* ix. 31)

Madhva emphasizes two aspects of devotion, the positive and the negative. The positive has been dealt with by Jayatīrtha in the definition of Bhakti quoted before. It is worthy of note that the theory and practice of Bhakti as taught by Madhva and his followers are free from all traces of erotic manifestations, which dominate or at least color the conception of Bhakti in certain forms of North Indian Vaiṣṇavism like those of Jayadeva, Caitanya and Vallabha. The sensuous and passionate side of it is first to be met with in the writings of the Tamil Vaiṣṇavas (Ālvārs) who preceded Rāmānuja in the South wherein the love of God (Kṛṣṇa) is placed on terms of the tender quality softening down to the rapturous emotion of conjugal love and wherein we come across most of those pathological symptoms of amorous longings which have been systematically reviewed and vividly portrayed in the works of Bengal Vaiṣṇavism. But Madhva's conception of Bhakti avoids these emotional excesses and remains at its exalted intellectual and spiritual level of firm philosophic devotion to the Supreme Lord of the universe who is to be worshipped with loving attachment as the Bimba of all

Pratibimbas (Jīvas). But it is not on that account lacking in intensity of fervour and feeling. For Madhva has recognized in the clearest terms that Bhakti is in essence an ineffable blending of the emotion and the intellect. He gives expression to the intensity of his love of God in its sublime and rapturous aspects in the opening and concluding stanzas of his works. This abiding aspect of his teaching found fuller expression in the writings of the great Mystics of the Haridāsa Kūṭa such as Śrīpādarāja, Vyāsa-Tīrtha, Purandara Dāsa, Vijayadāsa and others. The following verse from the *Harikathāmṛtasāra* of Jagannātha Dāsa furnishes a fine example of how readily God responds to the call of the yearning heart :

मलगि परमादरदि पाडलु
कुळितु केळ्व, कुळितु पाडलु
निलुव, निन्तरे नलिव, नलिदरे ओलिवे निमगेम्ब ।
सुलभनो हरि तन्नवरनरे-
घळिगे बिट्टगलनु रमाधवन
ओलिसलरियदे पामररु बळलुवरु भवदोळगे ॥ (*Kannaḍa*)

"God listens seated, to the Bhakta
Who sings to Him in ecstasy, lying down.
He stands and listens to the one
Who sings to Him—seated comfortably.
He comes dancing unto him that sings standing.
To him that dances and sings,
God says 'I'll show Myself to him'.
Verily, Hari is most accessible to his own.
Never for a moment does He stay away from them.
But fools caught in Saṁsāra
Know not how to make Him their Own".

(*Harikathāmṛtasāra*, ii.5)

But the possibilities of erotic devotion, as a means of contacting the Divine, are not unknown to him. Madhva's distinctive doctrine of intrinsic gradation of fitness among various orders of souls enables him to correlate the different forms of devotion to different orders of selves. In his view, Kāma-Bhakti or erotic devotion is the special privilege of Apsarases *and ought not to be practised by others*. He indicates a variety of standpoints of devotion with reference to different orders of Jīvas and harmonizes the various accounts on the basis of *adhikāras* :

(1) स्नेहभक्ताः सदा देवाः कामित्वेनाप्सरःस्त्रियः ।
काश्चित्काश्चिन्न कामेन भक्त्या केवलयैव तु ।
मोक्षमायान्ति नान्येन भक्तिं **योग्यां** विना क्वचित् ।। (*Pādma*)

(2) भक्त्या वा **कामभक्त्या वा** मोक्षो नान्येन केनचित् ।
कामभक्त्याप्सरःस्त्रीणामन्येषां नैव कामतः ।
उपास्यः श्वसुरत्वेन देवस्त्रीणां जनार्दनः ।
जारत्वेनाप्सरःस्त्रीणां कासांचिदिति योग्यता ।
योग्योपासां विना नैव मोक्षः कस्यापि सेत्स्यति ।
अयोग्योपासनाकर्तुर्निरयश्च भविष्यति ।
तस्मात्तु योग्यतां ज्ञात्वा हरेःकार्यमुपासनम् ।। (*Bhadrikā*)

(3) पतित्वेन श्रियोपास्यो ब्रह्मणा मे पितेति च ।
पितामहतयान्येषां त्रिदशानां जनार्दनः ।
प्रपितामहो मे भगवानिति सर्वजनस्य तु ।
गुरुः श्रीर्ब्रह्मणो विष्णुः सुराणां च गुरोर्गुरुः ।
मूलभूतो गुरुः सर्वजनानां पुरुषोत्तमः ।
गुरुर्ब्रह्मास्य जगतो दैवं विष्णुः सनातनः ।
इत्येवोपासनं कार्यं नान्यथा तु कथंचन ।। (*Vārāha*)

(Madhva, *BT* X.27.15)

Devotion being a state of loving attachment:माहात्म्यज्ञानस्नेहसमुदायो हि भक्तिरित्युक्तम् (*NS*), born of knowledge and regard for the object of devotion,[5] it will be obvious that no contrary emotion of positive dislike or hatred of God could be taken to help in the attainmint of Mokṣa, notwithstanding the presence of certain stray passages in the *Purāṇas* stating that certain persons had reached God even through aversion and hate:

गोप्यः कामाद् भयात्कंसः द्वेषाच्चैद्यादयो नृपाः ।
सम्बन्धाद् वृष्णयः संख्याद्यूयं, भक्त्या वयं विभोः ।।

(*Bhag* VII 1, 30)

---

5. Cf. स्नेहपूर्वमनुध्यानं भक्तिरित्यधिधीयते । महनीयविषये हि भक्तिरिति भावः । अन्यथा स्नेहपूर्वप्रियतमानुध्यानस्यापि भक्तित्वप्रसंगात् (*Rāmānuja*, *GBt* vii.1)

वैरेण यं नृपतयः शिशुपालपौण्ड्र-
साल्वादयो गतिविलासविलोकनाद्यैः ।
ध्यायन्त आकृतधियः शयनासनादौ
तत्साम्यमीयुरनुरक्तधियः पुनः किम्? (*Bhag* xi.5.48)

कामाद् द्वेषाद्भयात्स्नेहाद्यथा भक्त्येश्वरे मनः ।
आविश्य तदघं हित्वा बहवस्तद्गतिं गताः ॥
(*Bhag* vii.1.29)

कामं क्रोधं भयं स्नेहं मैत्रीं सौहृदमेव च ।
नित्यं हरौ विदधते यान्ति तन्मयतां हि ते ॥ (*Bhag*. x. 29.15)

Such passages ought to be treated as *arthavāda*, says Madhva :
द्वेषाद्यन्मुक्तिकथनं श्रुतिवाक्यविरोधि तत् (*AV*)
They are meant to emphasize that God should somehow be kept in mind, always. 'द्वेषाच्चैद्यादयो नृपाः' * * * इति भक्तप्रियत्वज्ञानार्थं नित्यध्यानस्तुत्यर्थं च स्वभक्तस्य कदाचिच्छाप बलाद्द्वेषिणोऽपि भक्तिफलमेव भगवान् ददातीति । भक्ता एव हि ते पूर्वं शिशुपालादयः शापबलाद् द्वेषिणः* * * । (Madhva's *GB* ix.12). The acceptance of "Dveṣa Bhakti" (hatred of God) as a possible means of salvation[6] will be quite inconsistent with the prevailing spirit of the Śāstras, which is to bring out the majesty of God. If the Scriptures meant to teach that God can be reached by cultivating hatred against Him they should have expatiated upon His demerits and imperfections instead of on His great and infinite perfections, as they do. Madhva, therefore, strongly disapproves of "द्वेष भक्ति". The *NS* and the *Sannyāyaratnāvali* undertake to show that none of the contexts and instances cited above is able to contradict the fundamental position of the Vedas that *Mokṣa could not be obtained save by loving devotion.*

Devotion, then, to be meaningful and justifiable must be founded upon a firm and adequate knowledge of the merits of the object of such devotion :

6. *Contrast* : तैसा चि गोपीसीं सकामें । तेया कंसा भयसंभ्रमें ।
एरा घातकें मनोधर्में शिशुपालां ॥
आगा भी एकु लाणिचें खागें । मज एऊये भलेतेणें मार्गे ।
भक्ती कां विषयवैरागें । अथवा वैरें ॥
म्हणौनि पाई । प्रवेशावेया माझां टांइं ।
उपायांची नाहिं । केणि एथें ॥ (*Jñāneśvarī* ix, 465-67)
—(the Marāṭhi *anuvāda* of Jñānadeva in the 13th century).

ज्ञानपूर्वः परः स्नेहो नित्यो भक्तिरितीर्यते । (*MbhTN* i.107)

Madhva speaks of three different types of devotees: (1) Uttama-Bhaktas (2) Madhyama and (3) Adhama, according to the nature and intensity of devotion characteristic of them (*BT* XI.2.42-45). He insists further that devotion, to be impregnable, must be guarded against the insidious influences of various forms of anti-Theistic tendencies :

जीवाभेदो निर्गुणत्वं अपूर्णगुणता तथा
साम्याधिक्ये तदन्येषां भेदस्तद्गत एव च ।
प्रादुर्भावविपर्यासः तद्भक्तद्वेष एव च
तत्प्रमाणस्य निन्दा च द्वेषा एतेऽखिला मताः ।
एतैर्विहीना या भक्तिः सा भक्तिरिति निश्चिता ॥

(*MbhTN* i. 113-15)

Bhakti, then, is the outcome of a profound admiration for Divine majesty coupled with a spontaneous love and regard for the Supreme. It cannot be dissociated from knowledge. *But this knowledge of God is not the cold intellectual apprehension of Reality.* It is a vivid perception of the Supreme Reality as the pivot of one's own reality, consciousness and bliss (सत्ताप्रतीतिप्रवृत्तिनिमित्तं) *with the utmost warmth of love and attraction for one's own Bimba that the soul is capable of.*

Bhakti of the right kind is thus a *blend* of both knowledge and love :

ज्ञानस्य भक्तिभागत्वात् भक्तिर्ज्ञानमितीर्यते ।
ज्ञानस्यैव विशेषो यत् भक्तिरित्यभिधीयते ॥
परोक्षत्वापरोक्षत्वे विशेषौ ज्ञानगौ यथा ॥

(*AV* iii.4.41)

Jñāna is a constituent of Bhakti. For this reason, the latter is very often referred to as "Jñāna" itself in the Śāstras. Where, however, the distinctive aspect of attachment is sought to be emphasized, their fusion is designated by the term "Bhakti"; but they are basically aspects of the same thing, even as mediacy and immediacy are but the integral aspects of knowledge. Texts in Scripture which refer to Jñāna as the means of release have, therefore, to be interpreted as inclusive of the aspect of love also. If this basic affinity between the two is properly understood and kept in mind, much of the controversy regarding the claims of Bhakti and Jñāna to be regarded as the immediate means of release would vanish. Madhva has shown ably that they are but the different facets of the same approach with more or less an interpenetrative content.

He insists further that due regard must be paid to the principle of Tāratamya (gradation) in respect of the nature and extent of devotion to be practised towards the hierarchy of devotees of the Supreme among the gods and men :

तारतम्येन तद्भक्तेष्वपि भक्तिविनिश्चयात् ।
कर्तव्यैषापि तद्भक्तिर्लोकवेदानुसारतः ॥
तस्मात्पूज्याश्च वन्द्याश्च ध्येयाश्च परितो हरिम् ॥ (*AV* iii.4.4)

अतो विष्णौ परा भक्तिः तद्भक्तेषु रमादिषु
तारतम्येन कर्तव्या पुरुषार्थमभीप्सता ।
समेषु स्वात्मवत् स्नेहः सत्स्वन्यत्र ततो दया ।
कार्यैवमापरोक्ष्येण दृश्यते क्षिप्रमीश्वरः ॥ (*AV* iii.3.31)

TĀRATAMYA

Tāratamya or gradational approach in the practice of Bhakti is a necessary element of the doctrine of Bhakti as propounded by Madhva. The devotional homage to the gods and the sages in the spiritual hierarchy is not a matter of courtesy. It is a *must.* The Devas occupy a special position in the government of God's universe as 'Tattvābhimānīs' with special cosmic jurisdiction delegated to them. Copious details regarding the nature of this hierarchy, their distinctive spheres of control and 'abhimāna' over psycho-physical principles of the microcosm and the macrocosm, the bearing of the role of members of this hierarchy on the implementation of the Sādhanas by human beings have all been brought into relief in Madhva's commentaries on the Upaniṣads and other works with appropriate authorities from a wide range materials collected from many ancient forgotten and fading sources of the Pañcarātra and other literature, for the first time. These introduce us to an entirely new and fascinating domain of thought regarding the *interrelation between the world of men and world of the gods.* It is a subject which no other commentator on the Prasthānatraya has worked out so thoroughly and exhaustively as Madhva. On the basis of these materials, he holds that devotion to God depends crucially on the grace of the Devas who are His greatest devotees (*Deva vāva sarvaprakāśāḥ*). They are the highest order of Jñānayogīs and our direct superiors, protectors, guides and Gurus. We cannot even think of God without their grace. It is they who inspire our minds along right lines and turn them Godward and enable us to know and worship Him by their presiding activity over the sense organs, mind, buddhi etc. and bring our Sādhanas to fruition. They are the immediate Bimbas (transmitters of Divine light) of aspiring souls in their hierarchic order ending with Mukhya-Prāṇa who in his turn is the highest 'Adhikārī' of Upāsanā,[7] among the gods. The members of the hierarchy ending with Mukhya-Prāṇa have a direct role to play in the spiritual field. While helping and guiding humanity in its Sādhanamārga, they put forth their own intensive Sādhanas in and through it. Theirs is naturally the highest order of Sādhanas extending over many Kalpas. (For details see my *BSPC* Vol. III. pp. 547-49.) Any scheme of Bhakti which does not include in its scope the gods, ṛṣis and other superior beings, according to Tāratamya, is bound to be futile.

He has thus brought about a remarkable integration between the supposedly endless Polytheism of the Hindu scriptures (from the Vedas down to the Purāṇas) with the fundamental Monotheism of rational philosophy with the help of the concept of *Tāratamya* in which each of the Devatās has his meed of honor without being mistaken for the one superior to him or displacing him.

Madhva distinguishes three stages of Bhakti : (1) that which *precedes* Parokṣajñāna (mediate knowledge of the Deity), (2) one that *follows* it, and (3) a third that comes *after direct realisation* (*Aparokṣajnāna*) and wins the absolute grace (*atyartha-prasāda*) of the Lord. It is this final stage of Bhakti that fully mainfests, by the grace of God, the true relationship that exists between the Jīva and Brahman and completes the fulfilment of realization viz. the full manifestation and enjoyment of the

---

7. आभासकोऽस्य पवनः पवनस्य रुद्रः शेषात्मको गरुड एव च शक्रकामौ ।
बीन्द्रेशयोस्तदपरे त्वनयोश्च तेषामृष्यादयः क्रमश ऊनगुणाः शतांशात् ॥
(*MbhTN* 1.14)

intrinsic bliss of one's own self and the Majesty of the Lord. These three stages of Bhakti have been designated by Jayatīrtha as Pakvabhakti, Paripakvabhakti and Ati-Paripakvabhakti. The last one is an end in itself (*NS*, p.605). These have been most impressively described by Madhva himself as rising to a crescendo of ineffable joy.

भक्त्या ज्ञानं ततो भक्तिः ततो दृष्टिस्ततश्च सा ।
ततो मुक्तिस्ततो भक्तिः सैव स्यात् सुखरूपिणी ।।

(*AV* iii.4. *adhi*.5-6)

Here is a very striking and an almost unique feature of Madhva's philosophy of Bhakti, whose inspiration may be traced in the writings of the Mystics of Maharashtra and the Gosvāmīs of the Caitanya school. It views sublime Bhakti, *not* as a means to an end, but *as an end in itself.* The light of Bhakti shines brightly, not only on this side of release but on the other shore of Mokṣa as well. *For the relation between the individual soul and the Supreme Being is not something that is snapped in release.* For, this relation is not something that is extrinsic to the nature of the soul and imposed from outside by Upādhis, as in the Advaita system. It is to Madhva, a sacred relation that holds good for all time ; something that is rooted in the very nature and being (*svarūpa*) of the soul. Its destruction would mean the destruction of the Jīva. It is a unique relation, a spiritual bond which is indestructible. It is the relation which the great Tamil poetsaint Tāyumānavar so well puts as : *Enṛu nān anṛu nī; un aḍimai allavo*[8] Mukti is merely the shaking off of what is extrinsic to one's nature and reposing in one's own intrinsic nature. The intrinsic spiritual relation between the human spirit and God is so dynamic in its magnetism that the attraction of the latter becomes more fully manifested in release than in Saṁsāra. Indeed, it breaks through and finds expression there in a thousand ways which are beyond our

8. "I and Thou are coeval
But then am I not your slave all the while ?"

Cf. नित्यो नित्यानां चेतनश्चेतनानामेको बहूनां यो विदधाति कामान् ।
तमात्मस्थं येऽनुपश्यन्ति धीरास्तेषां सुखं शाश्वतं नेतरेषाम् ।।

(*Kaṭha Up.* ii. 2.13)

understanding and analysis from 'here'. Surely, it is not open to us, in Saṁsāra, to peep into the released state and try to describe in detail the behavior of the blessed ones in release, towards the Lord or towards one another. That state of blessedness is obviously something beyond our comprehension in its richness and glory. (See my *BSPC*, III, p. 357).

It is what the *Bhāgavata Purāṇa* refers to as the intrinsic devotion of God-intoxicated souls like Sanaka, who feel a natural bond of attraction to the Lord and go on practising Bhakti *even after Siddhi* (Mokṣa) :

आत्मारामाश्च मुनयो निर्ग्रन्था अप्युरुक्रमे ।
कुर्वन्त्यहैतुकीं भक्तिं, **इत्थंभूतगुणो हरिः** ॥ (i.7.10)

and who decline even the special status of Sāyujya and other forms of Mukti and are quite content with their joy of devotional surrender (*ātmanivedana*).

नैकात्म्यतां मे स्पृहयन्ति केचित् (*Bhag* iii.25.34)
* * * एकत्वमाप्युत ।
दीयमानं न गृह्णन्ति * * * (*Op. cit.* iii.29.13)

Madhva himself in the supreme mood of his ecstatic devotion of this kind gives expression to this same exalted feeling at the conclusion of his *Mahābhārata Tātparya Nirṇaya*, thereby giving us a glimpse of the ripe maturity of his true devotion to the Lord :

यः सर्वगुणसम्पूर्णः सर्वदोषविवर्जितः ।
प्रीयतां प्रीत एवालं विष्णुर्मे परमः सुहृत् ॥

Discussing the position and status of Bhakti as the means to liberation in Madhva's philosophy, Dr. K. Narain has held that "the description of Bhakti as available in Madhva literature makes it clear that in this system *it does not acquire that supreme status which is expected from a doyen of the Bhakti movement*" (*Critique of Mādhva Refutation of Śaṅkara Vedānta*, p. 335). He admits that "Śaṅkara's contribution to Bhakti as a means to knowledge is not so great, because of the inferior position that Bhakti occupies in his philosophy, as according to Śaṅkara, it is possible only in the Vyāvahārika plane and is conceivable only as preparatory to the acquisition of knowledge and not as a final instrument in the attainment of liberation".

"Though slightly superior and a little higher in step to the place accorded to it in Śaṅkara's scheme, Bhakti *remains inferior to Knowledge* which is recognized as the final means of evoking the benediction of the Lord. The occasional references to knowledge as a means of liberation in the works of Madhva and his followers create a feeling that the Mādhva philosophers were over-conscious of not degrading the position of knowledge, probably due to the fear of indirectly establishing the futility of philosophical investigation. Both Madhva and Jayatīrtha mention several times that knowledge is the only instrument of evoking God's grace. The utility of Bhakti only consists in its being causative in the production of knowledge through Upāsanā consisting of śravaṇa, manana and dhyāna of the real nature and qualities of Īśvara. Thus, *Bhakti is a second step in the ladder* that leads to Mokṣa, where the *fourth step is knowledge*" (pp. 334-36).

This is a very superficial estimate of the place of Bhakti in Madhva Siddhānta and it is *not* based on a close first-hand knowledge of all that Madhva and his commentator have said in their works on the subject of Bhakti. Dr. Narain's reference to Bhakti in Madhva's system as the "second step in the ladder" of spiritual Sādhana *confirms this*.[9] He seems to be totally unaware of the fact that there are two distinct phases of Bhakti in Madhva's system, one operating at the Sādhana or *preparatory level* and the other at the Sādhya or the fulfilment-level of Mokṣa itself :

हरेरुपासना चात्र सदैव सुखरूपिणी ।
न तु साधनभूता सा सिद्धिरेवात्र सा यतः ।।

(Madhva, *BSB* iv.4.21)

In fact, no other Vedāntin than Madhva has given expression to his firm faith in the indispensability of Bhakti not only in achieving liberation from bondage but in its continuation in the lives of the Muktas as an expression of the blissful fruition of their earlier stages of Sādhana Bhakti:

भक्त्या प्रसन्नः परमो दद्यादज्ञानमनाकुलम् ।
भक्तिं च भूयसीं ताभ्यां प्रसन्नो दर्शनं व्रजेत् ।।

9. 'Bhakti' mentioned in the second phase as an introductory verse in Jayatīrtha's TP on which Dr. Narain evidently relies, is only the preparatory Bhakti. See p. 376 *ante*.

ततोऽपि भूयसीं भक्तिं दद्यात्ताभ्यां विमोचयेत् ।
मुक्तोऽपि तद्वशे **नित्यं भूयोभक्तिसमन्वितः ॥**

(*GT*, Introduction)

"Pleased with the initial Bhakti of the Jīvas, the Lord bestows on them firm knowledge of His nature and attributes. He then reveals Himself. Thereafter He inspires them with still more intensive devotion and after showing Himself to the Bhaktas He cuts the knot of their Prākṛtic bondage. In the released state also, the Jīvas remain under the Lord's control imbued with unalloyed devotion to Him".

It may be pointed out here that Madhva is the only Vaiṣṇava philosopher who has categorically held that the goddess Śrī who holds the unique position of being Nityamuktā and Samanā (having semi-parity with the Lord) in his system, remains the most ardent devotee of the Lord from eternity. He also refers in his *GB* to the existence of "Ekāntabhaktas" who prefer to be Bhaktas instead of Sāyujya-Muktas. The existence of such altruistic devotees has been adduced by Madhva as evidence of Svarūpatāratamya in the state of Mokṣa as well.[10]

Dr. Narain's inference that the occasional references to Knowledge as a means of liberation in the works of Madhva and his followers was probably due to the fear of denigrating philosophical investigation is also off the mark. It will be seen from the passages quoted by Madhva in his *GT* and elsewhere that philosophical investigation (*jijñāsā*) consisting of śravaṇa, manana etc., has not been denied its place of importance and value as Aṅga of Dhyāna.

The purpose of philosophical investigation or Jijñāsā according to Madhva is to remove the obstacles to Aparokṣajñāna, such as ignorance of the subject and doubts and misconceptions regarding the truth and the import of Śāstras. Śravaṇa gives rise to correct knowledge of Para and Aparatattvas and reflec-

---

10. *Read:* यदि तारतम्यं न स्यात् 'नात्यन्तिकं विगणयन्त्यपि ते प्रसादम् (*Bhāg* III.15.48)
नैकात्म्यतां मे स्पृहयन्ति केचित् (III. 25. 24)
एकत्वमप्युत । दीयमानं न गृह्णन्ति (III. 29.13)
इति मुक्तिमप्यनिच्छतामपि मोक्ष एव फलं तमिच्छतामपि स भवति सुप्रतीकादीनामिति कथमनिच्छतां स्तुतिरुपपन्ना स्यात् ? (Madhva *GB* II. 52)

tion helps to fix the import of Śrutis beyond doubt and vacillation :

श्रवणादिफलं चाज्ञानविपर्ययादिदर्शनप्रतिबन्धनिवृत्तिः (Madhva, *BSB* III.3.42)

As an exponent of Bhakti-Siddhānta, Madhva is quite firm in his position that not even the power of Jñāna can, by itself and independently of the grace of God, confer liberation[11] while such grace is itself not arbitrary, but takes into account the deserts of the seeker :

***इत्यादेर्न हरिं विना ज्ञानस्वभावतोऽपि स्यान्मुक्तिः कस्यापि हि क्वचित् । (*AV* i.1.1)

यतो नारायणप्रसादमृते न मोक्षः, न च ज्ञानं विना अत्यर्थप्रसादः अतो ब्रह्मजिज्ञासा कर्त्तव्या । (*BSB* i.1.1)

जिज्ञासोत्थज्ञानजात्तत्प्रसादादेव मुच्यते । (*AV* i.1.1)

Raising the question of what purpose can possibly be served by the continuation of Bhakti even *after Mokṣa has been attained,* Madhva answers that such continuation of Bhakti in the life of the released souls is not at all to be looked upon as a means to some other end. *It is an end in itself.*

साध्यानन्दस्वरूपैव भक्तिर्नैवात्र साधनम् । (*GT* II, *Introduction*)

It is the welling up of the supreme felicity of self-realization and God-realization. As we have already seen, Jayatīrtha refers to three stages of Bhakti in the ascending order. Of these, Pakvabhakti (ripe devotion) is the means of acquiring knowledge of God. The other disciplines of Śravaṇa and Manana just pave the way for it. Similarly, Paripakva-Bhakti (riper devotion) is the means of direct vision of the Lord and not Dhyāna, as such, which is only the means to achieve such a state of Paripakvabhakti. Lastly, Ati-Paripakva-bhakti (mellowed devotion) consists in the welling up of the spiritual joy of communion with the Lord. The visioning of the Lord as one's Bimbarūpa paves the way for this final beatitude of Sādhyānandaphalānubhava, through Paripakvabhakti. (Jayatīrtha, *GT Nyāyadīpikā*).

One wonders what more Dr. Narain would require to be said to satisfy *his* expectations, by any doyen of the Bhakti

---

11. तस्मात् श्रवणादिसाध्यनिदिध्यासनजन्यसाक्षात्कारेण ईश्वरः प्रसन्नीकरणीयः । (*Nym* iii. 9.)

movement, on the supreme place of Bhakti throughout the Sādhana *and the Sādhya levels of* Bhakti-Siddhānta.

Only the Lord's grace has the power to rend the veil of Bhāvarūpājñāna which stands between the Jīva and the Lord concealing His face from the devotee and prevents the full manifestation of the bliss of Mokṣa :

अथान्ये प्रकृती दुष्टे नृषु प्रातिस्विकं स्थिते ।
स्वगुणाच्छादिका त्वेका परमाच्छादिका परा ॥
स्वगुणाच्छादिकां हृत्वा परमाच्छादिकां परः ।
व्याघुट्य मोक्षपदवीं ददाति पुरुषोत्तमः ॥ (*BT* X.94.1-15)

Madhva has done some hard thinking on the interrelation between Jñāna and Bhakti. He does not make them watertight compartments or mutually exclusive Sādhanas. His special contribution lies in integrating them into a single mould of love of God founded on an adequate understanding of His majesty. His definition of Bhakti as :

माहात्म्यज्ञानपूर्वस्तु सुदृढः सर्वतोऽधिकः स्नेहो भक्तिरिति प्रोक्तः * * * (Mbh. T.N.)

makes a beautiful synthesis of the two major ingredients of Bhakti viz., a profound awareness of the Lord's majesty coupled with a deep sense of one's eternal gratitude for His benificence, and an inborn magnetic attraction to Him (*sneha*). 'Māhātmyajñāna' and 'sneha' are integral aspects of it :

ज्ञानस्यैव विशेषो यद्भक्तिरित्यभिधीयते ।
ज्ञानस्य भक्तिभागत्वात् भक्तिर्ज्ञानमितीर्यते ॥ (*AV*. III.4 adhi. 6)

In view of their inseparable union in Bhakti, the Śrutis and Smṛtis sometimes refer to either of them as the means of liberation by way of partial indication of the other constituent by the given one through Ekadeśena ekadeśilakṣaṇā.[12]

12. *Read* : अस्मिन् शास्त्रे यत्र यत्र ज्ञानस्य मोक्षसाधनत्वमुच्यते, तत्र तत्र, ज्ञानमिति पदेन भक्तिरीर्यते, **लक्ष्यते** । कुतः ? सम्बन्धात् । ज्ञानस्य भक्तिभागत्वात् । माहात्म्यज्ञानस्नेह-समुदायो हि भक्तिरित्युक्तम् । ततो ज्ञानं भक्तेर्भाग एकदेशः। तथा चैकदेशैकदेशित्वलक्षणसंबन्धादित्युक्तं भवति ।

प्रकारान्तरं चाह—'ज्ञानस्यैवेति, स यद् यदा ज्ञानस्यैव विशेषः स्नेहादिसाहित्यलक्षणो धर्मो भवति, तदा स पिण्डो भक्तिरित्यभिधीयते । ज्ञानं स्नेहश्च भक्तेरंशौ । तत्र एकेनांशेन अंशान्तरस्योपलक्षणम् । तथाच, अजहल्लक्षणया भक्तिरेव सिद्ध्यति ।

यत्र भक्तिज्ञाने सहोच्येते तदा भक्तिपदं स्वार्थैकदेशत्यागेन स्नेहांशस्य लक्षकं **ज्ञापकं** । अनुपपत्त्यभावात् मुख्यार्थमेव, नतु लक्षकम् । (*NS*, p. 604. 605)

This should dispose of Dr. Narain's supposition that Madhva was held back by the statutory recognition accorded to Jñāna in the Upaniṣadas as the sole means of liberation from giving that place of honor to Bhakti, as behoved a doyen of the Bhakti movement. What Madhva has done in reality is not to fight shy of Jñāna or minimize its importance but to disabuse the notion of apparent rivalry between the two and fuse them together into a single mould.

Śaṅkara as a "Jñānān-mokṣa-vādi" introduced his Brahmājñānavāda and the sublation of bondage by jñāna under cover of '*ataḥ*' in the first Sūtra. Rāmānuja's interpretation of '*ataḥ*' did not dislodge it by giving a distinct meaning to it independently of "*atha*" and justifying the need for inquiry into Brahman.

It was Madhva who replaced Śaṅkara's theory that liberation is to be attained by jñāna *alone* with its natural corollary, in Śaṅkara's sense, of the unreality of bondage and enthroned in its place the doctrine of the reality of bondage and its removal, in the last analysis, by the grace of God alone,—in the consummation of which, knowledge of the majesty of God plays a vital part as a constitutive element of Bhakti and is, therefore, quite necessary and important but never by dispensing with Bhakti :

FN. Contd. from p. 404.

"In this Śāstra, wherever it is stated that Jñāna is the means of Mokṣa, it must be understood that Bhakti is also conveyed by it through secondary significatory power of the word. This is because of the intimate relationship which exists between them, insofar as Jñāna is a constituent factor of Bhakti which has been defined as a blend of knowledge of the Lord's majesty coupled with an absorbing love (*sneha*) for Him. This part and whole relationship between them explains the implicit reference by one constituent factor to the other by way of "*Ekadeśa-ekadeśilakṣaṇasambandha*.

Secondly, this association of sublime love of God forms a specific aspect of Jñāna. Hence this blending of the two as a whole is designated as "Bhakti" by way of '*Ajahallakṣaṇā*' (part put for the whole). Accordingly, the terms Jñāna and Bhakti do duty for each other also—when only one of them is spoken of as the means of Mokṣa.

When both Jñāna and Bhakti are together mentioned as means of Mokṣa, the latter is to be construed primarily as love of God (*sneha*) by surrendering a part of its composite sense." (Tr).

अतो यथार्थबन्धस्य विना विष्णुप्रसादतः[13]
अनिवृत्तेस्तदर्थं हि जिज्ञासात्र विधीयते ॥ (*AV* i.1.1)

By doing equitable Justice to jñāna and Bhakti, Madhva has completely fulfilled the highest expectations of a Theistic interpreter of Vedânta, in restoring the doctrine of Bhakti and Divine grace to their rightful place and proper perspective in the texts and traditions of Prasthānatraya.

In fairness to the wide coverage given by Madhva to all the relevant aspects of the question and his forthright stand "*Yato Nārāyaṇaprasādam ṛte na mokṣaḥ* and "*Na Harim vinā jñānasvabhāvato 'pi syān muktiḥ kasyāpi hi kvacit*" one expects all those who may desire to evaluate his contribution to the doctrine of Bhakti in the Vedânta as the highest means of liberation to take all the facts on which he has taken his stand and arrived at his conclusion into their most careful consideration before pronouncing their opinion—which Dr. Narain has failed to do.

13. मोक्षसाधनं हि साक्षाद् भगवानेव । 'बन्धको भवपाशेन भवपाशाच्च मोचकः' इत्यादि वचनात् । साधनं तु द्विविधम्—सिद्धमसिद्धं च । **सिद्धं च साधनं भगवानेव इति मुमुक्षुणा सव्यापारीकरणीयः व्यापारश्च प्रसन्नता । मोचकेश्वरप्रसादः तद्भक्त्यैकसाध्यः ।** प्रसादो नाम इच्छा-विशेषः (Jayatirtha, *NS* p. 17).On this topic see my forthcoming work "Readings from the Nyāyasudhā of Śrī Jayatirtha."

CHAPTER XLIX

DHYĀNA AND ITS PLACE

MADHVA accepts the position of many Scriptural texts that *direct perception* of God (Aparokṣadarśana) *alone* is the proximate cause of release from Saṁsāra : Cf. : 'दृष्ट्वैव तं मुच्यते'; 'यदा पश्यः पश्यते रुक्मवर्णम्'; 'भक्त्या त्वनन्यया शक्य अहमेवंविधो * * द्रष्टुं च तत्त्वेन' * * * But inasmuch as God is essentially incomprehensible (*avyakta*) in the fulness of His majesty, He cannot be visualized save by His favor (*BS* iii.2.23-27). Once favorably inclined, He reveals Himself (*vivṛṇute tanūm svām*) in any subtle form. The grace of God, which is the ultimate means of realizing Him, can only be obtained by prolonged contemplation (*nididhyāsana*) of His perfections with steadiness and devotion to the best of one's capacity. Such contemplation of the Divine presupposes a preliminary study of the Scriptures (*śravaṇa*), which has then to be supplemented by deep thinking or reflection (*manana*) in order to clear the mind of all uncertainty and misconceptions that may be lurking there from time immemorial and whose presence will retard the constancy and flow of devotion. Hence the need for systematic philosophic inquiry and logical ascertainment of truth (*jijñāsā* or *vicāra*). The special attention given by Mādhva philosophers to dialectic establishment of their Siddhānta and the refutation of rival theories has, thus, to be understood in the light of an indispensable necessity imposed by the very conditions of philosophic inquiry. It is not inspired by a love of controversy as such or a desire to find fault with others.

The knowledge acquired by study and stabilized by *manana* is then made the basis of steady contemplation :

श्रुत्वा मत्वा तथा ध्यात्वा तदज्ञानविपर्ययौ ।
संशयं च पराणुद्य लभते ब्रह्मदर्शनम् ॥ (Madhva, *BSB* iii.3.43)

This combination of śravaṇa, manana and nididhyāsana is termed "Jijñāsā". The last stage of the inquiry may take the form of Dhyāna or contemplation : अविच्छिन्नपरोक्षज्ञानसन्ततिः (*TP* iii.3.52), of certain chosen attributes of God or a profound rumination over the truths of Śāstras (Śāstrābhyāsa) whose import has been definitely settled : निर्णीतस्य श्रवणादिकं समाचरेत्—*NS* 536b. The contemplation of Śāstrārtha is thus treated by Madhva as an independent form of Upāsanā,[1] taught by the Upaniṣads : स्वाध्यायप्रवचने एवेति नाको मौद्गल्यः तद्धि तपः (*TaittUp* i.9).

It is pointed out that such study and reflection should be continued till all doubts are set at rest. The chosen Guru alone would be competent to fix the time-limit up to which they should be carried on (*NS* p. 585). Where such a perfect Guru is not available, one may study the original Śāstras whose import has been fixed by authentic persons.

The study of Śāstras is partly also an aid to contemplation. The other forms of spiritual discipline are *yama*, *niyama*, *āsana*, *prāṇāyāma*, *pratyāhāra* and *dhāraṇā* taught by the Yoga Śāstra. These are to be treated as accessories to Dhyāna.

Dhyāna, defined as अविच्छिन्नपरोक्षजानसन्ततिः is virtually the same as the state of Samādhi or introspection taught by the Yoga system. These three stages of spiritual advance of *śravaṇa*, *manana* and *dhyāna* correspond to the stages of learning (*pāṇḍitya*), reflection (*mauna*) and introspection (*brāhmaṇya*) referred to in the famous Upaniṣadic text :

तस्मात् ब्राह्मणः पाण्डित्यं **निर्विद्य** बाल्येन तिष्ठासेत् । बाल्यं च पाण्डित्यं च **निर्विद्याथ** मुनिरमौनं च मौनं च **निर्विद्याथ**[2] ब्राह्मणः (*Brh Up* iii.5.1).

---

1. On this point See *BSPC* III, pp. 204-206.

2. Madhva has pointedly rejected the view accepted by most of the modern scholars and translators of the Upaniṣad that "a Brahmin should become disgusted with learning" (Hume *Thirteen Principal Upaniṣads*, p. 112). He points out (*GB* ii. 52) that if a turning away in mental aversion (*vairāgya*) from पाण्डित्य, बाल्य and मौन had been intended to be conveyed by the text, it would have used the proper grammatical case : पाण्डित्यात् निर्विद्य (*Pan* ii. 3.28). That apart, it is absurd to suggest that true Jñānins would ever get tired of or fed up with hearing, knowing and reflecting more and more about God :

नहि तत्रैव वैराग्यमुपपद्यते। न च ज्ञानिनां भगवन्महिमादिश्रवणे विरक्तिर्भवति अनुष्ठानाच्च शुकादीनाम्। न च तेषां तत्फलं सुखं नास्ति, **तस्यैव महत्सुखत्वात्।**

It is interesting to note that Śaṅkara also in his *GB* (ii. 11) has cited the *BṛhUp* text in a sense which is fully in agreement with Madhva's. See Śaṅkara *BSB* iii. 4. 47. (Cf. also : पाण्डित्यं पण्डितभावमात्मज्ञानं निर्विद्य **निश्चयेन लब्ध्वा।** (Ānandagiri on above). *But* see S. GB. II. 52.

CHAPTER L

PRATĪKOPĀSANĀ

THERE are numerous texts in the *Āraṇyakas* and *Upaniṣads* which prescribe the meditation of any physical, *adhidaiva* or other principles as *Brahman* :

'नाम ब्रह्मेत्युपासीत', 'उदरं ब्रह्मेत्युपासते शार्कराक्ष्याः', 'आदित्यो ब्रह्मेत्यादेशः'; 'अधिदैवतं आकाशो ब्रह्मेति'; 'ओमित्येतदक्षरमुद्गीथमुपासीत', 'मनो ब्रह्मेत्युपासीत'; 'अन्नं ब्रह्मेति व्यजानात्'. These numerous identifications of the *ādhibhautika*, *adhyātma* and other principles with Brahman through *vibhaktisāmānādhikaraṇya* (case-apposition) very naturally raise the question whether they are meant to be taken as a meditation of their identity (*abhedopāsanā*). The usual answer given to this question is that such texts are to be taken as prescribing "Pratīkopāsanā" or symbolic meditation. For the sake of efficacy of meditation, these various objects of meditation are to be 'treated' as Brahman, for the nonce. In other words, the idea of Brahman is to be mentally *superinduced* on them, so that they can be viewed and meditated upon in an enhanced status. This is Śaṅkara's explanation of what constitutes Pratīkopāsanā : ईदृशं चात्र ब्रह्मण उपास्यत्वं, यत्प्रतीकेषु तद्दृष्टच्यध्यारोपणम् । Rāmānuja also agrees with Śaṅkara's interpretation of Pratīkopāsanās that in respect of such Upāsanās as मनो ब्रह्मेत्युपासीत it is not Brahman that is the true object of meditation, but only the mind and other objects and that as it is conducive to prosperity to look upon and treat the inferior as superior, as in looking upon the King's servant as the King, even so, for purpose of meditation, the mind and other objects are to be meditated upon as Brahman.[1]

---

1. ब्रह्मदृष्टया मन आदिरुपास्यः । अपकृष्टे उत्कृष्टदृष्टिरभ्युदयाय भवति, यथा भृत्यादौ राजदृष्टि; (*Vedāntadīpa* i.) v. 1. 5

Madhva's views are quite different here. He refuses to countenance the idea of any superinduction of *Brahma-dṛṣṭi* on any Pratīka, however sacred or exalted it may be: न प्रतीके न हि सः । नाम ब्रह्मेत्युपासीत' इत्यादिना शब्दभ्रान्त्या न प्रतीके ब्रह्मदृष्टिः कार्या । (*BSB* iv.1.4) The proper way of Upāsanā of any Pratīka is to meditate on Brahman as being *present in it* : किंतु, तत्स्थत्वेनैवोपासनं कार्यम् (*BSB* iv.1.4). It is but natural to expect the Mystic way of speaking in regard to so profound a subject-matter as God-realization and the means thereof, in the *Āraṇyakas* and the *Upaniṣads* which are noted for their love of secrecy and esotericism :

परोक्षप्रिया इव हि देवाः प्रत्यक्षद्विषः (*AĀ* ii.4.3)

Even in the writings of modern Mystics, the tendency to resort to Mystic modes of expression is not rare. Madhva derives the key to the proper interpretation of the subject of Pratīkopāsanā in Vedānta from the famous passage of the *Aitareya Āraṇyaka* (iii. 2. 3) which he quotes in his works:[2]

एतं ह्येव बह्वृचा महत्युक्थे **मीमांसन्ते** एतमग्नौ अध्वर्यवः, एतं महाव्रते छन्दोगाः, एतमस्यामेतं दिवि, एतमाकाशे, एतमप्सु, एतमोषधीषु, सर्वेषु भूतेष्वेतमेव ब्रह्मेत्याचक्षते ।

It is interesting to note that the expression मीमांसन्ते occurring in the above passage has been explained by Śaṅkara also in his commentary on *BS* i. 1. 25 as "Upāsanā". This shows that *Madhva represents correctly and faithfully the genuine tradition of the Vedic and Upaniṣadic Seers in regard to the principles and technique of Brahmopāsanā.*

While repudiating the view that the Pratīka should be meditated upon as "Ātman" Śaṅkara and Rāmānuja are ready not only to condone but to approve of a conscious super-induction of the idea of the Upāsya (Brahman) on the object chosen for meditation on the ground that it would serve to enhance the status of the Pratīka. But while such meditation may enhance the status of the Pratīka, it would almost certainly lower the status of Brahman; for in allowing ourselves to think of and meditate on a limited object or symbol *as* God, there is a great danger of *spiritual fall*. There will be no escaping the fact that

2. 'It is this Paramātman indeed that the votaries of Ṛg Veda meditate upon *in* the great Uktha, the Adhvaryus *in* the fire, the Chandogas *in* the Mahāvrata; Him *in* Heaven, *in* the Ākāśa, *in* the waters; *in* the oṣadhīs and *in* all beings'.

when one meditates upon one thing as another, the identity will apply both ways. It is, therefore, flimsy to talk of meditating upon any Pratīka whatsoever as Brahman :

ध्याते त्वेकस्य तद्भावे, तद्भावोऽन्यस्य किं न तत् ?
तस्मादपेशलं सर्वमन्यस्य ब्रह्मतावचः ॥ (*AV* iv.1.4)

As a true Theist, Madhva feels that he cannot be a party to any interpretation of the Sūtra 'ब्रह्मदृष्टिरुत्कर्षात्' (iv. 1.5) which will either condone or approve of any conscious superinduction of the idea of Brahman on any symbol or Pratīka used in meditation. That will, he feels, be a virtual sanction of idolatry :

तस्मात् वस्तु यथारूपं ज्ञेयं ध्येयं च सर्वदा।
तस्मादतत्त्वं नोपास्यम् इति वेदविदां मतम् ॥ (*AV* iv.1.3)

No Christian missionary could have been more critical of the profanity of idol worship than Madhva has been here. For these and other reasons, Madhva discards the interpretation given by Śaṅkara and Rāmānuja for this Sūtra (iv.1.5) and finds a better interpretation for it by treating it as constituting a new *adhikaraṇa*. According to his interpretation, the Supreme Being should always be meditated upon as Brahman i.e. as a *being endowed with infinite attributes and as transcending all.*

In meditating on Brahman the devotee may concentrate on one or more attributes of Divinity according to his capacity. The highest number of attributes open to human comprehension is four,[3] though the Scriptures posit an infinite number of attributes of the Supreme Being. (Human) souls that cannot concentrate on more than one attribute are termed "Tṛṇa-Jīvas" by Madhva. The range of attributes upon which super-

---

3. Cf. "There are only two attributes of God of which we, humans, have any knowledge at all. The being of God is *not* however confined within the limits of human experience. Our knowledge of God is real so far as it goes. But reality is beyond us. There are an infinite number of other aspects of the Deity along which we cannot travel, since we are restricted to two lines of approach only, viz., mind and matter." (W.G. Bond, *Three Things That Matter—Religion, Philosophy and Science*, p. 73, Watts, London.)

human souls like the gods[4] and the Ṛṣis can meditate is much wider and only the fourfaced Brahmā can meditate on most of them :

सच्चिदानन्द आत्मेति मानुषैस्तु, सुरेश्वरैः ।
यथाक्रमं बहुगुणैः, ब्रह्मणा त्वखिलैर्गुणैः ।
उपास्यः * * * (*Aṇu-Bhāṣya*, iii. 4)

This sort of contemplative correlation and sublimation of both positive and negative attributes of the Divine Being is known as "Guṇopasaṁhāra". It is the subject matter of *BS* iii. pāda 3.

एवं गुणान् सर्वदोषाभावांश्च यत्नतः ।
योजयित्वैव भगवानुपास्यः * * * (Madhva, *BSB* iii. 3.6)

Madhva says further that among all the attributes of Brahman to be meditated upon the attribute of "Bhūmatva", infinitude, is the chief one which is to be meditated upon in unison with the other attributes like *ānanda*. In other words, each one of the attributes of Brahman chosen for meditation is to be viewed as *infinite* in range and content. The Upaniṣads represent Brahman as Bhūmā and Pūrṇa in every respect and emphasize the contemplation of this distinctive aspect as the source of the highest spiritual realization : यो वै भूमा तत्सुखं नाल्पे सुखमस्ति, भूमैव सुखम् (*ChānUp* vii 23).

Human intelligence may be unable to form a precise idea of the infiniteness of any attribute of God. The conception of such infinitude may also differ according to different levels of comprehension. There is however nothing to feel absolutely sceptic about forming some idea of what it would be like within the limits of our own understanding. Jayatīrtha gives us an example. Though infinite is the number of years and the number of months

4. According to Madhva, the *Brahmasūtras* as "Parā-Vidyā" are meant for the benefit of the *gods also*. Hence, the details therein, of Guṇopasaṁhāra by them also. Reference to the mode of Laya of the gods preparatory to their release (*BS* iv. 2. 1-16) as interpreted by Madhva, which V.S. Ghate finds unaccountable, is also to be similarly accounted for. As the *BS* discuss the fitness and the right of the "gods" to Brahmavidyā (i. 3. 33) these other questions concerning their Sādhana and goal, raised by Madhva, should cause no surprise !

that must have gone by since the world began, we are still able to conceive of some difference in the infinitude of these two ideas of infinitude. The same is the case with the different conceptions of the infinite attributes of God which different Adhikārins are able to form. (See my BSPC III. pp. 471-73.)

CHAPTER LI

BIMBOPĀSANĀ

AS already pointed out, the eternal and intimate relation in which individual souls stand to the Paramātman is conceived by Madhva as a distinctive metaphysical relation of constant dependence of the Jīvas on Brahman, not merely in respect of their external outfit of body and senses etc., but even in regard to their very being and becoming. This relation, it has been stated already, is something that is intrinsic to the very nature of the souls and has nothing physical about it. It is diffcult to express it in terms of any other relation within our empirical grasp. The term "Bimbapratibimbabhāva" (Original and Reflection) which has been suggested for it by Madhva, is to be taken as the nearest parallel to it in our experience. *It is not, however, to be taken literally as depending on any external factor or condition* (*Upādhi*), *as in the Advaita school,* which would at once render it a conditioned relation and, therefore, terminable. It is to Madhva an indissoluble and perpetual relation (*svarūpasambandha*). It is a relation of intrinsic dependence of the Jīva and its essential characteristics of reality, consciousness and bliss. It is coeval with the Jīva (यावदात्मभावी)[1] *and becomes fully manifested in release.* The bondage of Saṁsāra is itself due to this relation being missed by the Jīva and his becoming obscured by a false sense of independence in respect of his *Sattā, pratīti* and *pravṛtti.* No wonder that among the various forms of Upāsanā, the meditation on the Bimba-Form of the Lord has been stressed by Madhva as the *sine qua non* of Aparokṣa :

सम्तोऽपि भगवान् स्वबिम्बदर्शन एवैनं मोचयति (*NV* iii. 3)

1. This expression is actually used in *BS* ii. 3. 30. On the various interpretations of this Sūtra according to Śaṅkara and Madhva see my *BSPC* ii. 3. pp. 232-233.

Madhva's commentator gives an example. Mokṣa is attainable only after 'death'. But that does not meān that one gets Mokṣa at the time of *any death at random* from among the innumerable ones through which one has to pass in the course of one's transmigratory career. The same is the case with Bimbopāsanā as the requisite of Mokṣa. The conception of Bimbopāsanā and Bimbāparokṣa may well be considered to fall under the domain of *Mystic communion* between God and soul in Madhva's religious philosophy. By its very name, it is a consummation which is beyond discursive thought, for elucidation. The "Bimba" form is defined as that form of the Lord in the heart of which the Jīva is the pratibimba:

हृदिस्था या हरेर्मूर्तिः जीवो यत्प्रतिबिम्बकः ।
यद्वशे वर्तते जीवः सा तु जीवकला स्मृता ॥ (*BT* xi. 27.2)

CHAPTER LII

PLACE OF GRACE IN REDEMPTION

ACCORDING to Madhva, this knowledge of God is not a mere intellectual realization of the Deity. It is more a feeling of deep attraction and attachment arising from the knowledge of Bimbapratibimbabhāva between God and soul and sustained by a sense of spontaneous attraction and affection flowing from it. Hence, in Bhakti, there is the element of knowledge and attachment combined. In the last analysis, then, it is not pure knowledge that puts an end to the bondage of souls, but the grace of God in gracious acceptance of the souls's *surrender*. *It is Divine grace that plays the most decisive role in the final deliverance af the souls, according to Madhva*. On this point he differs considerable from *other* Vedāntins, particularly Absolutists to whom it is knowledge *per se* that constitutes the highest means of release. Madhva derives his idea from the Śrutis, which emphasize, in addition to knowledge, the importance of "vision" and "grace of God falling on the individual" :

यमेवैष वृणुते **तेन लभ्यः** तस्यैष आत्मा **विवृणुते तनूं स्वाम्** (*KaṭhaUp*. i. 2.23)

The difference is due to the difference in the conception of the origin of bondage. The Advaitic conception of bondage as the outcome of a mysterious ignorance concealing the nature of *Ātman*, which is automatically destroyed by the dawn of knowledge of the Ātman and its essential identity with Brahman : ज्ञानमज्ञानस्य निवर्तकम्, leaves no room for any kind of personal intervention of a Deity or His grace, in the termination of this ignorance. It is within the power and competence of knowledge (alone) to destory ignorance, just as it is within the competence of light to destroy darkness. Once this ignorance is destroyed, the spirit of man shines forth in its pristine form, as a matter of course : आत्मैवाज्ञानहानिः (Śrīharṣa) ; निवृत्तिरात्मा मोहस्य ज्ञातत्वेनोपलक्षितः

(Citsukha, *Tattva-pradīpikā*, p. 390). There is, thus, no scope for the intervention of Divine grace in the accomplishment of Avidyānivṛtti, as such :

तथा च, ज्ञानस्वभावलभ्यायां मुक्तौ किमीश्वरप्रसादेन ? न खल्वन्धकारनिबन्धनदुःखनिवृत्तये प्रदीपमुपाददानाः कस्य चित् प्रभोः प्रसादमपेक्षन्ते । स्वभावो हि प्रदीपस्यायमन्धकार-निवर्तकत्वम् । (*NS*, p.18)

This is the strict metaphysical position of the Advaita accepted by the older writers. But later writers have been obliged to relax its uncompromising rigidity and make a compromise with Theistic tendencies by conceding some sort of a remote connection of knowledge with grace. Accordingly, grace is required to create a "taste for Advaita" :

ईश्वरानुग्रहादेव पुंसामद्वैतवासना । (*Khaṇḍana*, i. p.214)

This is a very unsatisfactory position. As a Theist, Madhva naturally opposes such devious pleas. The theory of Brahmājñānavāda has got to be abandoned as metaphysically untenable. And with it goes the dogma ज्ञानमज्ञानस्य निवर्तकम्. We come back to the position that the vision of God and His grace are both necessary : 'दृष्ट्वैवतं मुच्यते' । 'जुष्टस्ततः तेनामृतत्वमेति' । A proper harmonization of these Śrutis will lead to the acceptance of grace as the most potent factor in achieving deliverance. Taking his stand on both the groups of texts, Madhva argues a strong case for the necessity of Divine grace. No man, says he, can be saved by the sheer power of his own knowledge:

* * * इत्यादेर्न हरिं विना।
ज्ञानस्वभावतोऽपि स्यान्मुक्तिः कस्यापि हि क्वचित् (*AV* i.1.1)

Jayatīrtha throws great light on this point :

नास्माभिः केवलविद्यया मोक्ष उच्यते, येन ध्यानाभाव आपद्येत । किंतु, भगवत्साक्षात्कारादपि (*TP* iii.3.49):

जिज्ञासा तावन्न साक्षान्मोक्षसाधनत्वेनास्माकमभिमता किन्तु, प्रसन्नो भगवानेव । (*NS* 527)

All this is because the Divine will itself and *not merely* a beginningless ignorance or even *Bhāvarūpājñāna* is or can be the ultimate explanation of bondage, as has already been explained. This idea finds expression in Śaiva philosophy also and is supported by the *BS* iii.2.5 and *SvetUp* vi. 16. Rāmānuja under *BS* iii.2.4, comes to *very near the same position as Madhva*[1] on the

1. पराभिध्यानात् परमपुरुषसंकल्पात् अस्य जीवस्य स्वाभाविकं रूपं तिरोहितम्। (*Śrībhāṣya*)

question of what causes the bondage of souls. But his theory does not take us beyond the stage of "*anādikarmaparamparā*"[2] which we shall see, will not be a final explanation of God's concealing or obscuring the self-luminosity of the Jīvas. The striking syntactic juxtaposition of the words : *Parābhidhyānāttu tirohitam* in *BS* (iii.2.5) clinches the issue that way.

According to Madhva, the Sūtra : अम्बुवदग्रहणात्तु न तथात्वम् (iii.2.19), emphasizes the role of Bhakti in finally manifesting to the Jīva his natural and innate affinity with Brahman as Its Pratibimba. Such knowledge of his true relation to Brahman lies hidden from the understanding of the Jīva, by the will of God Himself, (*BS* iii.2.5) in the state of bondage when it is encrusted by Avidyā, Kāma, Karma, etc. It is by the quality of Bhakti (devotion) that the Jīva can rise above these impediments and obscurations of its real personality and realize its true relationship to God. Madhva understands the simile of water (*ambuvat*) employed by the Sūtrakāra here as an allusion to *the quality of clinging consistency of devotion* (like that of water), which alone will enable the soul to know, realize and *adhere* closely and intimately to God forever in the final realization of its intimate and inseparable relation of Bimbapratibimbabhāva to Him. Bearing in mind the keynote of the *Sādhanādhyāya in which this Sūtra is placed* every thoughtful student of the Sūtras will be impressed by this original and felicitous interpretation of the keywords of the Sūtra : *ambuvat* and *grahaṇam. It is also the best Mystic interpretation of this remarkable Sūtra.* If, as Radhakrishnan says, "all signs indicate that it (Mysticism) is likely to be the religion of the future"[3] *the world's unborn soul also will find in Madhva's interpretation of the Sūtra* : अम्बुवदग्रहणात्तु न तथात्वम् the very core of Mysticism. However, one can hardly expect a dry critic like V.S. Ghate, who seems to have started with a preconceived notion against Madhva that "*the very fantastic and forced way in which Madhva interprets many of the Sūtras leaves no doubt that he would even have set aside the Sūtras themselves ; but that their uncontested authoritativeness prevented him from doing so*"

2. अनादिकर्मपरंपरया कृतापराधस्य ह्यस्य स्वाभाविकं कल्याणरूपं परमपुरुषः तिरोधापयति । (Rāmānuja, *BSB* iii. 2.4)

3. *Eastern Religions and Western Thought*, Preface, ix.

to understand and appreciate the great poetic beauty and deep philosophical suggestiveness of this interpretation concerning so refined and deep-seated a spiritual emotion of the human breast as Bhakti or to pronounce any other judgment upon it than that it is a "very fantastic" one.[4] In the light of what has been stated above, it will be seen that it is not merely a bold and original interpretation, but contextually the most appropriate one. The topic of Bhakti is quite in order, here, in Pāda ii after the discourse on "Vairāgya" in the previous pāda.[5] Even according to Śaṅkara, the topic here relates to the Bimbapratibimbabhāva between Brahman and Jīvas.[6] But insofar as such a relation is a purely fictitious one according to Śaṅkara,[7] its relevance to Sādhanādhyāya would be open to question, as such knowledge (of their Bimbapratibimbabhāva, brought about by Upādhis, as between the Sun and its reflection, supposed to be established here as a Siddhānta view) would be a hindrance to Bhakti, rather than a help, inasmuch as true realization, according to Śaṅkara, would consist in *shaking off the idea of Bimbapratibimbabhāva caused by Upādhis.* The use of the *double negative construction* in Sūtra iii.2.19 is also a strong indication that *it is a Siddhānta-Sūtra* as taken by Madhva.

Vādirāja, in his gloss on the *TP* of Jayatīrtha, *has done a great service to Madhva's philosophy by bringing out the true beauty and depth of thought and feeling that are hidden behind Madhva's original*

---

4. For a refutation of V. S. Ghate's criticisms of Madhva's interpretation of the *Brahmasūtra* see my *HDSV*, pp. 99-122.

5. Cf. तत्र प्रथमे पादे संसारगतिप्रभेदः प्रदर्श्यंते वैराग्याय

(Śaṅkara, *BS* iii. 1. 1)

6. Rāmānuja's interpretation of this *adhikaraṇa* as intended to show that Brahman is not vitiated by the imperfections of the world, though immanent in it is, besides being unconnected with the subject of Sādhanavicāra, not entirely free from redundancy (See his commentary on *BS* i. 2. 8).

7. Whereas to Madhva the Jīva's relation of 'Pratibimbatva' to Brahman is a true, real and permanent relation based on dependence and similarity and uncaused by *upādhis*, the *description* as a Pratibimba is not understood in the conventional sense of a lifeless projection, impermanent and caused by a temporary medium. The *description* is "Gauṇa" (*metaphorical*). The difference between the two views of relationship is the difference between *the real and the fictitious.*

interpretation of the Sūtra in question. It is worthwhile quoting his explanation :

अल्पाक्षरत्वलाभाय 'भक्त्यभावात्' इति वक्तव्ये, यत् 'अम्बुवदग्रहणात्.* * *इति सूत्रं, तत् **भक्तेः स्वरूपनिरूपणार्थमिति** भावेनोक्तम्—"अम्बुवत् स्नेहेन, ग्रहणं ज्ञानम्" इति। माहात्म्यज्ञानपूर्वकः स्नेहो हि भक्तिः। तर्हि, 'स्नेहेनाज्ञानात्' इति कुतो नोक्तमित्ति चेत्; सत्यम्। अम्बुनि चिक्कणताख्यः स्नेहो यथा आजानजत्वात् **अतिसुदृढः**, तथा अतिसुदृढत्वलाभाय 'अम्बुवत्' इत्युक्तम्। **अतः प्रौढशिरोमणिः सूत्रकार इति ज्ञेयम्** ॥

(*TP*, *Gurvarthadipikā*, Uḍipi, 1954 p. 139)

(Even though for brevity's sake, the Sūtrakāra should have used the expression "on account of lack of Bhakti (the real nature of the soul's relation to God is not revealed to him)", yet, it should be borne in mind that he has chosen to use the words "ambuvat" ("*like water*") in order to embody a succinct definition of Bhakti at the same time. Keeping this intention of the Sūtrakāra in mind, the commentator, Madhva, has accordingly rendered the word "*ambuvat*" by the word "*snehena*" (with loving attachment) and the word "Grahaṇa" by the word "Jñāna" (understanding or grasping). For, Bhakti is the same as love of God lighted up by a full knowledge of His Majesty. It is true the Sūtrakāra could have written स्नेहाभावात् (because He is not known through love) to convey his meaning, explicitly. But there is a special purpose in introducing a metaphor here. It is well known that viscosity is an inborn and deep-rooted quality of water. Man's love of God (Bhakti) should have this quality of clinging firmly to God at all costs. It is only such a love that is capable of revealing to the soul his true relation to God, as His Pratibimba. It is to convey so much deep meaning that the Sūtrakāra, who is a master of language and thought, has used a telling metaphor here to emphasize the greatness of the quality of Bhakti and its place among Sādhanas.)

Jayatīrtha brings out the *rationale* of Madhva's position with his characteristic brilliance and clarity of thought. We cannot attribute the condition of bondage, ultimately, to any of the familiar causes of Kāma, Karma, etc., each of which has a beginning. Even supposing that each previous stage of Kāma, Karma, etc., begets the next one and so on, it should be open to the soul to get back its original and essential characteristic of self-luminosity, in the states of deep sleep and universal dissolution, when there is no play of any kind of desire or activity. But this is *not* found to be the case. *Hence, there must be something above and beyond our actions and desires* (*however beginningless*), which must be regarded as having cast a veil of ignorance on our essential self-luminosity from time immemorial. This original substance may, therefore, be identified with what the Śāstras speak of under different names as "Māyā", "Avidyā" and "Prakṛti", obscuring the self-luminous soul (which is finite). For, it is in the nature of "Māyā" or "Prakṛti" to act as an obscuring agency. But then, as this "Māyā" or "Prakṛti" is only an insentient principle, *it cannot be said to function independently and of its own free will.* In this way, we are led to accept the position that *ultimately it is God Himself that obscures part of the Svarūpa-Caitanya of the Jīvas* by means of (1) the above-mentioned principle of Prakṛti endowed with the three Guṇas (of *sattva, rajas, and tamas*) and which in the Śāstras is also known as "Avidyā" because it acts as an obstacle to the soul's attaining its self-luminosity and knowledge of its true nature; *and* (2) by His own wonderful and inscrutable power (*acintyādbhuta-śakti*)[8]

---

8. न चाज्ञानमात्रनिबन्धनोऽयं बन्धो जीवस्य। श्रुतिस्मृतीतिहासपुराणादिषु परमेश्वरेच्छानिमित्तत्वावगमात्। ज्ञानानन्दस्वरूपो ह्ययं जीवः। तद्भावानुपलब्धिश्चानुभवसिद्धा। तेनावगम्यते—अस्ति किमप्यावरकं, येनावृतः स्वप्रकाशचैतन्यरूपो ऽपि नात्मनस्तत्त्वं वेद। न च, कामकर्मादिकमेव तथा भवितुमर्हति। तस्यापि सादिनः कारणापेक्षत्वात्। न च पूर्वपूर्वस्मादुत्तरोत्तरमिति युक्तम्। सुप्तिप्रलययोः तद्वृत्त्यभावेन, निष्कलंकचैतन्यवलात् स्वरूपावभासप्रसक्तेः। अतः, कामकर्माद्यतिरिक्तं मायाविद्याप्रकृत्यादिशब्दाभिधेयं अनाद्येव किमपि द्रव्यं (आवरकं) अंगीकार्यम्। न च, मायापि कथं स्वप्रकाशमावृणोतीति युक्तम्। आवरकतयैव तस्याः प्रसिद्धत्वात्। वक्ष्यते चात्रोपपत्तिः। न च, जडस्य स्वतः किंचिदावरकत्वं युक्तम्। **अतः परमेश्वर एव स्वाधीनया प्रकृत्या सत्त्वादिगुणमय्या विद्याविरोधित्वेनाविद्यया, अचिन्त्यद्भुतया स्वशक्त्या च, जीवस्य स्वप्रकाशमपि स्वरूपचैतन्यमाच्छादयतीति युक्तम्॥** (*NS*, p. 19b)

Dasgupta (*I. Phil.*, iv, p. 159, fn.3) has unhappily *misquoted* the last sentence in the above passage from the *NS* and misinterpreted it as a consequence. He has also on this account drawn the erroneous conclusion that "Ignorance" in Madhva's philosophy is a "*negative substance*". The fact is that it is a positive substance (भावरूप) in Madhva's system. Cf. न वयं भावरूपाज्ञानपरिपन्थिनः। किं नाम, परपक्षे तन्न संभवतीति ब्रूमः (*NS*, p. 64 b)

Dr. K. Narain (*Critique of Madhva Refutation of Śaṅkara Vedānta*) also ***repeats*** the same mistake when he says : "Ajñāna is positive; but the

As the ultimate cause of the bondage of the souls, in this sense, God is also the source of their release :

बन्धको भवपाशेन भवपाशाच्च मोचकः ।
कैवल्यदः परं ब्रह्म विष्णुरेव सनातनः ॥

(*Skānda* quoted by Śrīdhara)

This mysterious power or will of God is *also* known by the names of "Prakṛti", "Māyā". These two different senses in which the terms are used in the Śāstras should be carefully noted to avoid confusion.[9]

महामायेत्यविद्येति नियतिर्मोहिनीति च ।
प्रकृतिर्वासनेत्येवं तवेच्छा अनन्त कथ्यते ॥

(Madhva, *BSB* 1.4.25)

This "Māyā" or Prakṛti also has two aspects, one that obscures the soul from comprehending its own essence in full and another which prevents the Jīva from having the vision of the Lord.

अथान्ये प्रकृती दुष्टे नृषु प्रातिस्विकं स्थिते ।
स्वगुणाच्छादिका त्वेका परमाच्छादिका तथा ।
स्वगुणाच्छादिकां हृत्वा परमाच्छादिकां परः ।
व्याघुट्य मोक्षपदवीं ददाति पुरुषोत्तमः ॥

(*BT* X.94.13-15)

It is only the grace of God that can raise these last veils of bondage and uncover the true nature of the self to itself and reveal the true nature of the Lord to it :

हिरण्मयेन पात्रेण सत्यस्यापिहितं मुखम् ।
तत् त्वं पूषन् अपावृणु सत्यधर्माय दृष्टये ॥ (*IśaUp* 15)

The power of God which conceals from the individual his true nature is known as 'Svaguṇācchādikā' (in respect of the Jīva). This has a resemblance to the veiling power of Ajñāna called 'ācchādakaśakti' in Advaita. But there is this difference bet-

---

Mādhva philosopher *is satisfied* with his theory that it is *the negation* of knowledge and its rxistence *quite negative*" (*op. cit* p. 5) What is more astounding is that after repeating the same on p.158 he should have ventured to quote as authority Jayatīrtha's words: *Na vayam Bhāvarūpājñānasya Paripanthinaḥ*, in the *Notes* (p. 359)!

9. Rāghavendra Tīrtha in his *Parimala* on *NS* cautions the reader accordingly to interpret the two instrumentals in the possage from the *NS*, correctly : प्रकृत्येति, स्वशक्त्येति व्यधिकरणे तृतीया ।

ween them that while according to Madhva God is all-powerful and *can* cast His veil or concealing power over *finite selves* who are under His control, it is not so easy to understand how the all-knowing Brahman can throw a veil of ignorance round its own being as the Advaita theory has it.

Not all our Karma, or Jñāna or even Bhakti can remove it without the grace of the Lord withdrawing His obscuration of the Jīva :

'भक्तिरेवैनं नयति, भक्तिरेवैनं दर्शयति, ...' इति भक्तेरेव पृथङ्मोचकत्वान्नेश्वरस्य कृत्यमिति मन्तव्यम्—

अनादितो गुणाः सन्तो भक्त्याद्या न ह्यमूमुचन् ।
जीवं तद्गुणसुव्यक्तिं कृत्वैनं मोचयेद्धरिः ।
कांश्चिन्न मोक्षयेद्वासौ स्वातंत्र्यं तेन तस्य हि ॥

इत्यनादिगुणविस्तरे सत्यपि, अव्यक्त्यादिना तदिच्छां विना मोक्षाप्राप्तेः

(Madhva, *NV* iii.3.33)

Such is the *raison d'etre* of Divine grace, according to Madhva.

CHAPTER LIII

APAROKṢA-JÑĀNA OR GOD-REALIZATION

MADHVA distinguishes carefully and sharply between Dhyāna and Aparokṣa. This is clear from his definition of the former as continuous flow of mediate knowledge (अविच्छिन्नपरोक्षज्ञानसन्ततिः); while the latter is, as its names Aparokṣa and Sākṣātkāra show, *a direct vision* of the Supreme Being, in its "Bimba-form". The form revealed in Dhyāna is, therefore, regarded as just a mental picture of the Yogin's own construction, while the one visualized in Aparokṣa is the *actual* revelation of God in His Bimba-form, as He is :

रूपं रूपं प्रतिरूपो बभूव
तदस्य रूपं प्रतिचक्षणाय । (*RV* vi. 47.18)

जीवसमुदायः परमेश्वरस्य रूपं रूपं प्रतिरूपो भूत्वा वर्तते । **तत् बिम्बरूपं अस्य मुक्त्यर्थं साक्षात्कारविषयो भवति।** (*TP* ii.3.50) (Tr. in Chap. XXXVI, fn. 1)
What is presented in Dhyāna is thus only an image constructed by the impressions of the mind. It is just a substitute and not the original form of God :

तथान्यत् प्रतिषेधात् (*BS* iii.2.37); यथा जीवानन्दादेरन्यत् ब्रह्म, तथोपासाकृतादपि । नेदं यदिदमुपासते (*KenaUp* i.5); इति प्रतिषेधात् (*BSB*)

This is still more clearly explained by Trivikrama Paṇḍitācārya:

उपास्तिस्फुरिततदाकारादन्यत् ब्रह्म । अन्तःकरणप्रविष्टपदार्थाकारस्फुरणं हि स्मृतिः । न च तत्र पदार्थो दृश्यते । तदाकारस्फुरणमेव तत्स्मृतिरित्युच्यते, यथा प्रतिमायाम् ।
(*Tattvapradīpa*)

The highest stage is, therefore, one in which the Yogī or Sādhaka is *face to face with* the object of his meditation and intuits the Divine Form, which is his archetype (Bimba). This is technically termed Bimbāparokṣa, which is the highest form of spiritual perception, without which no one can hope to be released (*BS* iii.3.53) : न च परमात्मनः सर्वत्र गुणसाम्यात् यस्य कस्यापि रूपस्य दर्शनात् सर्वेषां मुक्तिः। समोऽपि भगवान् स्वबिम्बदर्शन एवैनं मोचयति।

(*Nyāya-Vivaraṇa*)

This vivid flash-like intuitive perception of one's own Bimba marks the journey's end. It is the fulfilment and culmination of all Sādhanas. It is what is known as Aparokṣajñāna, which is the penultimate state of final release.

Its intensity and vividness vary according to the innate capacity of the selves. In the case of human beings it is said to be like a lightning-flash; in respect to Devas like the blaze of the Sun. The gods Garuḍa and Rudra visualize it like a reflection of their own faces in a mirror and the four-faced Brahmā sees it in clear outlines (*TaittUp Bhāṣya*).

Though the Supreme Being is *ex hypothesi* unmanifest (*avyakta*) it is possible, says Madhva, to visualize it through grace :

नित्याव्यक्तोऽपि भगवानीक्ष्यते निजशक्तितः।
तमृते परमात्मानं कः पश्येतामितं प्रभुम्। ?

(*Nārāyaṇādhyātma*, quoted in *BSB* iii.2.27)

The Supreme is pleased to reveal itself to the devotees through sheer grace :

यमेवैष वृणुते तेन लभ्यः
तस्यैष आत्मा विवृणुते तनूं स्वाम्। (*Kaṭha Up* i.2.23)

But for this condescension on the part of Brahman, it can never be visualised by any finite being, however much one may try :

परमात्मापरोक्ष्यं तत्प्रसादादेव। न जीवशक्त्या।

(*BSB* iii.2.23)

Brahman is essentially unmanifest. Unlike the elements of fire, etc., which are insensible in their subtle (*tanmātra*) form, but visible and manifest in their gross form, Brahman has no such diversity of aspects as gross and subtle. Hence, it is always and essentially *avyakta* (unmanifest). But though it is essentially *avyakta*, it reveals itself to the Upāsaka, by its own grace and inscrutable power. Without Brahman's choosing to reveal itself, in this way, no one can ever visualize the limitless one.

Aparokṣajñāna, then, is something which by its very nature defies any more explicit description. It is to be experienced and felt. Words are hardly adequate to describe it. It is a flash-like revelation of the Supreme, at the fruition of a long and arduous process of *śravaṇa*, *manana* and *nididhyāsana* in the fulness of absolute self-surrendering devotion to God as our Bimba. Ultimately, it is He that must choose to reveal Himself, pleased by the hungering love of the soul. The Pratibimba (soul) must turn in and seek and *see his Bimba in himself*. That is Aparokṣa-jñāna : आत्मन्येवात्मानं पश्येत् । (*BrhUp* iv.4.23)

Such direct perception of God is attainable only when the mind is specially attuned to the Supreme by full discipline of *śravaṇa*, *manana* and *dhyāna*. Such a perception is immediate and achieved through the mind specially perfected for the task : मनसैवेदमाप्तव्यम् (*Kaṭha Up*. ii.1.11); निदिध्यासनसंस्कृतमनसा अपरोक्षधीसंभवात् (*Nym* iii.9) Vyāsatīrtha explains further that texts like यन्मनसा नमनुते which deny the power of the mind to reveal Brahman have reference to minds not properly trained, because there are other texts which establish the capacity of the 'ripe and disciplined mind' to do so. Texts like यन्मनसा न मनुते do not however conflict with the ability of the mind to reveal Brahman. Such texts merely show that the mind should be perfected and disciplined by *śravaṇa*, *manana* and *dhyāna* before it can be made to visualize Brahman when such direct revelation is given to it by the grace of God Himself. Aparokṣajñāna is believed to confer marvellous powers of eightfold Siddhis, etc.

The Rāmānuja school does not recognize Aparokṣajñāna as constituting a distinctive stage in spiritual realization. According to this school, the highest stage of spiritual attainment open to the Sādhaka is that of *nididhyāsana* itself and the personal impression of the Supreme Being that one can have in this world does not rise above one's own mental image of the Supreme formed through constant flow of thought and meditation :

(i) उपासनं च स्मृतिसंतानरूपं **दर्शनसमानाकारं** ध्यानोपासनाशब्दवाच्यम् ।
(*RGB* vii.1)

(ii) ध्यानं च तैलधारावदविच्छिन्नस्मृतिसन्तानरूपम् । सा च **स्मृतिः दर्शनसमानाकारा** 'भिद्यते हृदयग्रन्थिः छिद्यन्ते सर्वसंशयाः। क्षीयन्ते चास्य कर्माणि तस्मिन्‌दृष्टेपरावरे' इत्यनेनैकार्थ्यात् । एवं च सति, निदिध्यासनस्य **दर्शनरूपता** विधीयते । **भवति च स्मृतेर्भावना-**

प्रकर्षाद् दर्शनरूपता । वाक्यकारेणैतत्सर्वं प्रपञ्चितम्. *** 'उपासनं स्यात् ध्रुवानुस्मृतिः, दर्शनान्निर्वचनाच्च,' इति । तस्यैव वेदनस्य उपासनारूपस्यासकृदावृत्तस्य ध्रुवानुस्मृतित्वमुपवर्णितम् । सेयं स्मृतिः **दर्शनरूपता** प्रतिपादिता । **दर्शनरूपा** च । **प्रत्यक्षतापन्नां** अपवर्गसाधनभूतां स्मृतिं विशिनष्टि । (Rāmānuja, *Śrībhāṣya* i.1.1)

This means that there is no room in the Rāmānuja school for a distinctive state of Brahmāparokṣa or direct vision or immediate intuitive perception of God *in this life* other than the mental image built up by the devotee through constant flow of meditative recollection : ध्यानं च तैलधारावदविच्छिन्नस्मृतिसन्ततिरूपम् (Vedānta Deśika on *RGB* vii.1). This means that the highest kind of direct experience of God open to man as a seeker is but *mediate* (Parokṣavṛtti). Such an experience will be no better than a mental construct and, therefore, in the final analysis not the same as a direct immediate perception of the Lord. Rāmānuja says that the experience of Dhyāna, *though mediate, can be so clear and vivid as to be almost immediate* (दर्शनसमानाकारा) which is thus explained by Deśika: स्मृतेश्च दर्शनसमानाकारत्वं नाम विशदात्मतया दर्शनसमानाकारत्वमेव, i.e. the mental impression of the Lord achieves a vividness that is almost *equal to a direct presentation.* Deśika proceeds further to illustrate his point by the examples of the extravagant fancies of a person deeply in love with a woman and the obsessions of those seized by a sense of fear and so on :

भवति च स्मृतेर्भावनाप्रकर्षवशात् दर्शनसमानाकारता भीरुकामुकादीनाम् । यथा ।—

'लीनेव प्रतिबिम्बितेव लिखितेवोत्कीर्णरूपेव च
प्रत्युप्तेव च वज्रलेपघटितेवान्तर्निखातेव च ।
सा नश्चेतसि कीलितेव विशिखैश्चेतोभुवः पञ्चभि–
श्चिन्तासन्ततितन्तुजालनिबिडस्यूतेव लग्ना प्रिया ।। इति ।

(Bhavabhūti, *Mālatīmādhava*, v.10)

—Quoted by Vedānta Deśika on *RGB* p. 415, Ānanda Press Edn. Madras.

Such a view is not acceptable to Madhva, as it reduces Aparokṣajñāna to the level of a mental picture. That will be hardly in keeping with the profound reality, dignity and supreme significance attached to Brahmasākṣātkāra in Indian philosophical tradition as the highest and the most desirable state which is the consummation of man's philosophical quest:

दृश्यते त्वग्र्यया बुद्धया सूक्ष्मया सूक्ष्मदर्शिभिः (*Kaṭha Up*, i.3.12)

हृदा मनीषा मनसाभिक्लृप्तो य एनं विदुरमृतास्ते भवन्ति (*Op. cit.* ii.3.9)
दिव्यं ददामि ते चक्षुः पश्य मे योगमैश्वरम् । (*Gitā*, ix.8)
* * * बुद्धिग्राह्यमतीन्द्रियम् । (vi.2)
यदा पश्यः पश्यते रुक्मवर्णम् (*Mund Up* iii.1.3)
आत्मन्येवात्मानं पश्येत् (*BrhUp* iv.4.23)
एषोऽणुरात्मा चेतसा वेदितव्यः (*Mund Up* iii.1.9)
परात्परं पुरुषमीक्षते (*Praśna Up.* 5)

The difference between the two views of Rāmānuja and Madhva lies in this that Rāmānuja invariably uses expressions like "*darśana-rūpā*" (resembling direct vision), *pratyakṣatāpannā* (which has attained the *form* of a direct vision), '*darśanasamānākārā*' (having a form *equal* to a direct vision). The comparison instituted by his commentator with the lover's constantly picturing to mind the thoughts of his beloved go to show that Rāmānuja for some reason is not prepared to admit a stage beyond Dhyāna culminating in direct vision (Sākṣātkāra) or Aparokṣa of God. There seems to be this vital distinction between the view of these two philosophers. As Vyāsatīrtha points out in his *Nyāyāmṛta*, Rāmānuja's view reduces the texts which refer to the direct visualization of the Lord by the great seers and Mystics as the highest means of deliverance to a figurative level. Apart from that, it is difficult to see how a meditative cognition can be said to attain a vividness of presentation (विशदात्मना अवभासः) *equal* to that of an actual immediate presentation (दर्शनसमानाकार). It cannot be in the sense of its acquiring a deeper content and a wider range of details than a mere remembrance-series. For, a recollective experience cannot possess a wider range or deeper content than the original experience from which it is derived or the memory image from which it flows. As for actual identity with immediate perception, it is out of the question. It is, no doubt, possible to *imagine* that there is an immediacy of experience in such cases by autosuggestion or under abnormal paychological conditions. But that will not alter the hard facts of reality and, in any case, it will be too much to expect deliverance by such means.[1]

1. ज्ञानस्य विशदतरावभासत्वं न तावदधिकविषयत्वम् । स्मरणस्य स्वजनकानुभवात् तज्जन्यस्मरणाच्चाधिकविषयत्वायोगात् । नापि साक्षात्त्वम्, स्मृतौ तदसंभवात् । पुत्रादिध्यानस्येव साक्षात्त्वस्य भ्रान्तिमात्रत्वे मोक्षहेतुत्वायोगात् । दर्शनश्रुतीनामुपचरितार्थत्वापत्तेश्च ।
(*Nym*, iii. 4)

It is not a pertinent objection to this criticism of the Rāmānuja position that even according to Madhva, Smṛti (memory) is a direct mental perception of the past. For the content of a Smṛti cognition according to Madhva rests on a primary perception now long past. The difficulty in Dhyāna viewed as "Smṛtisantāna" assuming or acquiring a form equivalent to direct perception (*darśana-samāna-ākāra*) as Rāmānuja would have it, lies in this that unlike in the case of Memory (Smṛti) there is no room in Rāmānuja's position for *an earlier direct vision as such* of Brahman, which may possibly come to be ruminated upon in Dhyāna. Hence, the argument based on Madhva's view of Smṛti as a form of Pratyakṣa is untenable.

It may with profit be recalled in this connection that in Madhva's view such mental perception is limited to the sphere of the previously experienced objects and events in view of the limitations imposed by the Saṁskāras which act as connecting link (*sannikarṣa*) with the past. The utmost that can be claimed for Dhyāna is that it will give us a steady mental picture of the object of meditation which may *approximate to a direct vision* but which would *still be far from being an actual direct perception.* Hence Jayatīrtha's criticism: ये तु ध्यानमेव परमपाटवापन्नं अपरोक्षाकारमिति मन्यन्ते, तेषां दर्शनश्रुतय उपचरितार्थाः प्रसज्येरन्। (*NS* p. 18 b)

VIII. DOCTRINE OF MUKTI

CHAPTER LIV

NATURE OF THE RELEASED STATE AND ITS STAGES

IN each system of thought the doctrine of salvation is determined by its conception of the nature of souls and God. The Buddhists believe in Nirvāṇa or utter annihilation of personality as the highest end and aim of life. The reason is simple. They don't recognize even in Saṁsāra, a permanent self other than the five Skandhas, as a transmigrating spirit. Hence, the question of the survival of any such non-material principle after the achievement of release does not arise. Some modern apologists of Buddhism who try to argue that Nirvāṇa is not extinction of self-consciousness or of the Ātman, know not what they are talking about. Buddhism is a frank and fearless Nairātmyavāda and that is that. The monists hold the absorption of the individual self in Brahman to be the highest form of realization, as individuality is merely the result of a pluralization by Avidyā and is not an intrinsic fact. Madhva's conception of the metaphysical dependence of souls on God as His Pratibimbas, not in the sense of a false reflection but as coeval and co-eternal but dependent and finite beings controlled by God as their *Antaryāmī* and his acceptance of intrinsic difference and gradation of fitness (*yogyatā*) among them as individuals, lead naturally to the persistence of an irreducible distinction among these and from God in respect not only of the quality and degree of intrinsic bliss enjoyed by them but also in their capacities for such enjoyment. The final state, according to Madhva, is marked by a complete absence of all traces of pain, evil and suffering, coupled with a positive enjoyment of inherent spiritual *ānanda*. This bliss has nothing material about it and is not conditioned by the possession or enjoyment of material objects. *Ergo*, there is no fear of its being ever diminished or tainted by evil or otherwise becoming tiresome :

विरजी ब्रह्मलोको **न येषु जिह्मं अनृतं न माया चेति ।** (*Praśna Up* i.16)

The criticism that in such a description of the released state we are only transferring the distinctions and values of this life to a world beyond loses its point when it is remembered that the bliss in question is not at all dependent on the presence of external material objects and that it is something welling up from the nature of the selves themselves. Else, any dynamic conception of release would be liable to the facile criticism that it involves a transference of values of this life to the beyond. Is release a state of blissful existence ? If so, we are hankering after a certain value of life and seeking it there ! Is it a state of absolute freedom from all pain and shortcomings ? Even so, we are simply transferring what we regard as valuable here, to a life beyond ! The charge of transference of values is thus a game at which two can play. Madhva maintains that the realization of truth does not mean the abolition of the plurality of life or the personality of selves, but only the removal of the false sense of separateness and independence which is at the root of Saṁsāra. There is no question of transference of values, when it is stated that the bliss of release is not an external posssesion of souls but an essential characteristic of their being that manifests itself completely there. That these released souls do not get themselves dissolved in the Absolute is clear from texts like : आणिं न रथ्यममृताधितस्थुः (*RV* I. 35.6) ; उतामृतत्वस्येशानः (*RV* X 90.2) ; मुक्तानां परमागतिः (*Mbh*) which attribute to the Supreme Being the same kind of sovereignty over the world of the released as in respect of this one. The text : न प्रेत्य संज्ञास्ति (*BrhUp* iv.5.13) has reference only to the termination of empirical consciousness, even as interpreted by Śaṅkara: न च तत्र प्रेत्य **विशेष-संज्ञास्ति** कार्यकारणसंघातेभ्यो विमुक्तस्य. It cannot, therefore, be cited as evidence against the persistence of Svarūpajñāna of souls claimed by Dvaitins. Passages like अविनाशी वा अरेऽयमात्मा अनुच्छित्तिधर्मा (*BrhUp* iv.5.14) have been cited by Madhva, in support of the persistence of personality in release in its refined state. This text of the *BrhUp* makes two significant statements (1) that the

Ātman is indestructible (*avināśi*) and (2) that its *attributes also are inviolable* (*anucchitti-dharmā*). The former carries an implied refutation of Buddhist Nairātmyavāda and the latter of the Nirviśeṣa-Cinmātravāda of Advaita by insisting on the indestructibility of both the Ātman *and its attributes*. This means that the self is not conceived, even in the highest state of Mokṣa as a mere abstraction or a yawning void. It is to be noted that Śaṅkara and his commentators here have tried to escape the implications of the term *anucchittidharmā* by treating it as a paraphrase of the first predication itself viz. "*avināśi*" which makes it redundant.[1] Jayatīrtha points out in his commentary on Madhva's *VTN* that the difficulty felt by Maitreyī was not at all in respect of any supposed contradiction between the earlier and later declarations of her husband :
(1) विज्ञानघन एवैतेभ्यो भूतेभ्यः समुत्थाय तान्येवानुविनश्यति and (2) न प्रेत्य संज्ञास्ति, which may be looked upon as having been set at rest by his explaining the difference between "the human and the Ātmic levels of experience."[2] Jayatīrtha rightly points out that Maitreyī's difficulty was in accepting her husband's statement that there was no consciousness after death (न प्रेत्य संज्ञास्ति) as that would make the goal of Mokṣa unfit to be sought as a Puruṣārtha : मोक्षस्य अपुरुषार्थत्वप्रसंगो हि मैत्रेयीवाक्यार्थः। यदि चोत्तरवाक्ये मुक्तस्य ज्ञानाभाव एव सिद्धान्तः स्यात्, तदा मैत्रेय्युक्तप्रसंगस्योत्तरं वक्तव्यम् । न चोक्तम् । तेन ज्ञायते—मुक्तस्य ज्ञानाभावो नोत्तरवाक्येऽभिप्रेत इति । For, as Rāmānuja rightly points out, in his *Śrībhāṣya*, unless the survival of human personality in Mokṣa is accepted, the whole spiritual programme calculated to help the individual self to get rid of its bondage (whether actually existing or merely taken to be real *due to Avidyā*) and attain to a state of unalloyed bliss for ever afterwards would cease to have any meaning. If all that Vedānta has to tell the earnest seeker is that he himself will *cease to be* at the end of all his efforts, he would bid an

---

1. Cf. ननु, उच्छित्तिर्धर्मो यस्यासावुच्छित्तिधर्मा नोच्छित्तिधर्मा अनुच्छित्तिधर्मा इति स्वरूपाविनाश एवोच्यते, न तु धर्मानुच्छित्तिरिति चेत्; न। स्वरूपाविनाशस्य अविनाशीत्यनेनैवोक्तत्वात् । निर्विकारत्वं तेनोक्तमिति चेत्; तथापि अनुच्छित्तिरिति बहुव्रीहिणैव पूर्णत्वात् धर्मपदवैयर्थ्यम् ॥ (*VTNt*)

2. See Prof. Ranade's 'Yājñavalkyan Fiction' (*Easays*, Jamakhandi, 56) and my criticism of it in *Tattvavāda*, Bangalore, 1956.

eternal goodbye to Vedānta. Surely, it would be no consolation to him to be told that even though he himself as a self-conscious personality may cease to be, some *bare* or rarefied consciousness will survive. For no reasonable person would take the trouble of undergoing all the rigour of spiritual discipline with the fond hope that even when he is lost, there will be left *some pure consciousness of no particular identity or content.* Apart from that, Jayatīrtha points out that if Maitreyī's difficulty was in understanding how Ātman, who was earlier described as a mass of consciousness (*Vijñānaghana*) could subsequently be said to lose all consciousness after 'death' as contended by Śaṅkara, and if the said difficulty was resolved by pointing out to her the difference between the empirical and the trans-empirical levels of consciousness, we should expect to find Maitreyī referring to *the two specific statements of her husband and mention their mutual contradiction*, as it appeared to her. *But, she does nothing of the kind.* She merely refers to *only one text* न प्रेत्य संज्ञास्ति, and says to her husband: **अत्रैव** मा भगवान् मोहान्तमापिपत्—**'न प्रेत्य संज्ञास्ति' इति** that she could not understand how there is no consciousness after 'death'[3] for the individual. This conclusively establishes the point that Maitreyī's difficulty had nothing whatever to do with "the human and the Ātmic levels of experience" as Prof. R. D. Ranade has tried to explain it in defence of Śaṅkara's interpretation of the text. It painly shows that her difficulty was concerned *only* with the denial of the survival of consciousness in the released state which was apparently what Yājñavalkya's words *seemed* to suggest :

ननु, 'अत्रैव मा भगवान्' इति न मोक्षस्य अपुरुषार्थत्वं प्रसंगाभिप्रायः किंतु, 'विज्ञानघन' इत्युक्त्वा, पुनः 'न प्रेत्य संज्ञास्ति' इत्युक्ते, व्याहृत्यभिप्रायेण अत्रैवेत्युक्तम् । तत्र संसारे विज्ञानघनो मोक्षे तु, केन कं पश्येत् इति परिहारः संगत एवेति : ।। मैवम् । तथा सति, अत्रैव मा भगवान् मोहान्तमापिपत् यत् विज्ञानघन इति, न प्रेत्य संज्ञास्तीति च, **इति वाक्यद्वयोपादानप्रसंगात्; व्याघातस्य उभयाश्रितत्वात् । एकस्यैव तु वाक्यस्योपादानात् तद्विषयमेव दोषोद्भावनमिति ज्ञायते ।।** (*VTNt*)

This crucial point, raised by Jayatīrtha, is of the utmost importance in assessing the relative merits of the different interpretations put upon the famous Yājñavalkyan dictum. No modern scholar of Advaita seems to

---

3. 'Death' (*pretya*) here according to all the commentators and the context *refers* to the state of Mukti or cessation of transmigration.

have given serious thought to this point so far. It shows the complete inconsistency of Śaṅkara's interpretation about the nature of Ātman *with the context.* It would follow from this that we cannot take the statements made by Yājñavalkya in reply to his wife's objection beginning with the words : यत्र तु सर्वमात्मैवाभूत् तत्केन कं पश्येत्... as a statement of facts (वस्तुस्थितिकथनम्) but as a vigorous plea for the survival of self-consciousness in Mokṣa, by means of a *reductio ad absurdum.* Such is precisely the stand taken by Madhva.[4] It may be noted that such an interpretation is clearly supported by the two categorical assertions of Yājña-valkya in his clarification that both the Ātman *and its attributes are equally indestructible* : अविनाशी वा अरेऽयमात्मा, अनुच्छित्तधर्मा, which establishes beyond doubt Yājñavalkya's anxiety to emphasize *not merely* the survival of Ātman in Mokṣa, but also *the survival of its attributes of consciousness, bliss, etc.*

The distinction drawn by the Advaitin between the Ātman as the 'pure self' and our 'egopersonality' (*aham-artha*) is un-sustainable. For, even the deepest experiences of the self in our dreamless sleep (which according to Śaṅkara himself reveals the Ātman in its pure state) (See *BSB* iv.4.16) establishes the identity of the 'ego-self' (*ahamartha*) with the witness-self of dreamless sleep. The evidence of this identity is furnished by the reference to the experience of the happy repose of dreamless sleep made by us in recalling the experience immediately on waking up : एतावन्तं कालं सुखमहमस्वाप्सम् । If the ego-self who re-collects himself after waking from that Suṣupti state is not the true inner reality (*pratyagartha*) that stands distinguished from all external reality (*parāg-artha*), one should expect the ego-self, sometimes on waking up from his deep sleep to entertain a doubt whether it was his own self or someone else's that had under-gone the happy repose of sleep ! Here is sufficient evidence that it is the inner self (*pratyagātmā*) itself that is the subject

4. In his *VTN* Madhva has convincingly demonstrated the untenability of Śaṅkara's interpretation of the passage from the *BrhUP* embodying Yāj-ñavalkya's harangue to his wife. Jayatīrtha in his Commantary on the *VTN* has gone into the details of the interpretation of Madhva and Śaṅkara and shown that the latter's interpretation cannot be sustained.

of the recollection of happy repose of sleep and that it is the same *pratyagātman* that is referred to by the term "Aham" when one recalls one's own earlier experience. It is no use to contend against this that though it is only the pure self that is really the subject of the recollective judgment, still, as there is no activity of the *antaḥkaraṇa* (mind) in Suṣupti, the Ātman that is revealed in Suṣupti gets itself fused with *antaḥkaraṇa* on waking up from the Suṣupti state and in virtue of this contact with the mind gets the"ego-feeling" and that this accounts for the configuration of the recollective judgment (*parāmarśa*) in the words : I slept (अहमस्वाप्सम्). The explanation, no doubt is, ingenuity itself. But it creates a more serious difficulty for the Advaitin. For, it is admitted in Advaita that Avidyā or Bhavarūpājñāna is present is Suṣupti and is there intuited by the pure self. Now, according, again, to the Advaita, *ahaṁkāra* is completely merged in Suṣupti and only pure *ātman* is left there. In these circumstances the *intuition* of *avidyā* in Suṣupti by the pure self cannot be recollected by the ego-self (*ahamartha*) later on through a recollective judgment (*sauṣuptikānubhavaparāmarśa*) as *its own former personal intuition* : न किंचिदहमवेदिषम्. In other words, as the ego-self (*ahamartha*) was *not* the actual witness of Ajñāna in dreamless sleep (according to Advaita), it could not give expression to any recollection about it as its own. *This is sufficient to establish that the ego-self and the witness self of Ajñāna in dreamless sleep are one the same being, and that the attempt to distinguish them is a failure.*

The *Chāndogya* text, जक्षत्क्रीडन् रममाण: refers clearly and admittedly to the sportive activities of *Muktas* (Cf. *BS* iv.4.2). There is no mistaking the context here, which is one of final release as can be seen from the opening words of the section :

परं ज्योतिरुपसंपद्य स्वेन रूपेणाभिनिष्पद्यते ।

The *Vedānta Sūtra* sets an insurmountable barrier between Brahman and the released souls by prescribing a limit to the sovereignty of the latter by excluding cosmic responsibilities (जगद्व्यापारवर्जम् iv.4.17) from their province.[5] This sūtra is the

5. P. M. Modi in his '*A critique of the Brahmasūtras*' p. 448, tries to give a new explanation of "jagadvyāpāra", which is redundant in the light of the last sūtra and is at variance with the sense of 'vyāpāra' used in an earlier sūtra (iii. 1.16).

rock on which Vedāntic monism has been shipwrecked every time its ships have attempted to cross over to a haven of safety. Its remarkable significance to a Dualistic interpretation of the Sūtras has been brought out by Thibaut and it is not possible to add anything to his weighty remarks on the point.

Without such persistence of personality, Mokṣa will not be worthy of pursuit. The ideal of Mokṣa will not be worthy of pursuit without the guaranteed persistence and survival of the self that can be assured of its deep sense of repose and happiness earned after so much effort and suffering:

मग्नस्य हि परेऽज्ञाने किं न दुःखतरं भवेत् (*Mbh* xii. 307.83)

संज्ञानाशो यदि भवेत् किं मुक्त्या नः प्रयोजनम् (*GT* ii.18)

अहमर्थविनाशश्चेन्मोक्ष इत्यध्यवस्यति ।
अपसर्पेदसौ मोक्षकथाप्रस्तावमात्रतः ॥ (*Śrībhāṣya*, i.1.1)

That is why Madhva holds that the released retain their individual consciousness *as released* and rest in the full knowledge of their deliverance from all misery :

आजन्ममरणं स्मृत्वा मुक्ता हर्षमवाप्नुयुः (*MS*)

According to Madhva, Aparokṣajñāna or direct vision of God in His aspect of one's Bimba, opens the door to spiritual redemption. It is the dawn of Mukti and carries with it all the promise and potency of the ineffable and endless bliss of complete self-realization and God-realization, to come. It is the foretaste of the bliss of Mokṣa :

शान्ति निर्वाणपरमां मत्संस्थामधिगच्छति (*Gitā* vi.15)

सुखमात्यन्तिकं यत्तत् बुद्धिग्राह्यमतीन्द्रियम् (*Gitā* vi.21)

It is natural that close on the heels of Brahmāparokṣa, the shackles of material bondage should begin to fall off, one by one, and that Aparokṣa should usher in a state of increased blessedness at everyone of its successive stages. Madhva distinguishes four stages of the fruits of Aparokṣa : (1) Karmanāśa, (2) Utkrānti or Laya, (3) Mārga, and (4) Bhoga. Laya has reference to the gods,[6] who have no "utkrānti" as such :

6. V.S. Ghate (*The Vedānta*) has confused these two aspects of Utkrānti and Laya and speaks of the *utkrānti* of the gods (misunderstanding the opening sentence in Madhva's bhāṣya : देवानां मोक्ष उत्क्रान्तिश्च अस्मिन् पाद उच्यते

देवानां स्वोत्तमप्रवेशेन तत्र देहलयः । अन्येषां तु ब्रह्मनाड्या देहोत्क्रान्तिः । (*TP*)

Of the three kinds of Karma that clog the way and dog the steps of the Jīva from time immemorial Sañcita or the accumulated load is consumed by the fire of Aparokṣajñāna :

यस्य पापस्य कार्यं दुःखं भोक्तुमारब्धं तस्यैव ज्ञानेन नाशः । यस्य पुण्यस्य कार्यं सुखं भोक्तुं नारब्धं तस्मैव नाशः (*TP* iv.1.15)

Madhva distinguishes between two kinds of *anārabdha-Karma* (Karma that has *not* begun to bear fruit) viz., इष्ट and अनिष्ट (the agreeable and the disagreeable). The latter is destroyed and the former is "credited" to the account of the relcased in Mokṣa. *The 'Prārabdha' alone remains to be worked out.* This is a fixed quantity, the sources of fresh accumulation having been cut off. Even in regard to Prārabdha Karma, reductions and concessions are possible (*BS* iii.4.16). The Karmas performed by Aparokṣa-Jñānins *after* the dawn of Aparokṣa have the effect of enriching the spiritual bliss in Mokṣa. Knowledge by itself confers release from pain and misery of Saṁsāra; but the welling up of the intrinsic spiritual bliss is possible only by good Karma, Jñāna, Upāsanā or Bhakti :

सर्वदुःखनिवृत्तिश्च ज्ञानिनो निश्चितैव हि ।
उपास्यया कर्मभिश्च भक्त्या चानन्दचित्रता ॥ (*BSB* iii.4.33)

The Aparokṣajñānin is also known as Jīvanmukta.[7] He continues in his physical frame as long as the arrears of *prārabdha* continue to exact their debt :

अपरोक्षज्ञानिनोऽपि स्वयोग्यपरमानन्दहेतुपरमकाष्ठापन्नभक्त्यभावे तत्साध्यस्य मोचकस्येश्वरप्रसादस्याभावेन प्रारब्धकर्मणा संसारानुवृत्त्या जीवन्मुक्तिः (*Nym* iv.4)

(iv. 2). He is also puzzled why the gods should at all be introduced in this context. Well, the gods are recognized as adhikārins for Brahmavidyā both n the *Upaniṣads* and in the *BS*. The question of their release would not, therefore, be irrelevant in the Sūtras. Hence, Madhva allots some space to them (iv. 2, 1-16). In Muṇḍaka iii. 2. 7 we actually read of the entry of the gods in their archetypes and 'merging' into them—a clear case of Laya preparatory to Mokṣa.

7. The term is used by Vyāsatīrtha in his *Nym* (iv. 4). There is a mistaken belief among mony modern scholars that 'Jīvanmukti' is exclusive to Advaita thought and is unknown to Dvaita philosophy and *has no place in it*. This misconception is similar to the one about Bhāvarūpa-ajñāna or positive ignorance in Dvaita philosophy, already referred to.

The destruction of his Liṅga-śarīra takes place along with the four-faced Brahman's :

ब्रह्मणा सह ते सर्वे संप्राप्ते प्रतिसंचरे ।
परस्यान्ते कृतात्मानः प्रविशन्ति परं पदम्[8] ॥(*Kūrma* i.12.269)

It should be noted that there are two distinctive aspects of realization according to Madhva, the negative and the positive phases of the attainment of freedom. The negative aspect consists in riddance of all obscurations of personality by the crust and consequences of past Karma etc. and the destruction of all suffering and the Liṅgaśarīra. दुःखाभाव and लिङ्गभेद as they are briefly referred to, constitute the negative side. The positive aspect is the enjoyment of intrinsic bliss of selfhood. Jayatīrtha accordingly defines Mokṣa in its dual aspect (*dvidalātmaka*) :

आत्यन्तिकदुःखनिवृत्ति and परमानन्दावाप्ति (*VTNt* p. 117)

The system of Madhva accepts also the fourfold distinction of Mokṣa into Sālokya, Sāmīpya, Sārūpya and Sāyujya, (See Madhva *BSB* iv.4.19) taught in the *Bhāgavata Purāṇa*.[9] Vyāsatīrtha in his *Nyāyāmṛta*, mentions that these represent *an ascending order of blessedness*. The nature of Bhoga in release will be dealt with in Chapter LVI.

---

8. Cited by Śaṅkara in his *BSB* iv. 3. 11

9. M. Nandi, in his doctoral thesis at the Bombay University on "The Philosophy of Baladeva" (1955), is quite mistaken in assuming that Madhva does *not* recognize these *four kinds of Mukti* and making it an argument for his supposition that Baladeva, who recognizes them, could *not* have been a follower of Madhva out and out (*Op. cit.* p. 453). These and other contentions of M. Nandi have been refuted in my HDSV pp. 529-31.

CHAPTER LV

CRITIQUE OF THE CONCEPTION OF MOKṢA IN OTHER SYSTEMS

MADHVA and his commentators have briefly reviewed the conception of release according to the other systems in order to bring out the distinctive features of their own conception of it and its superiority.

The Jaina theory of Mokṣa as a ceaseless upward flight in Alokākāśa has nothing spiritual or divine about it, says Madhva, to kindle the heart of the seeker and make it glow.

Entry into Mahāśūnya, advocated by the Buddhist, is equally forbidding in its prospect. The Buddhists are frank Nairātmya-vādins. There is no Ātman or Self, in their view which can be said to coordinate the fleeting experiences of moments into a meaningful whole. Reduction to nullity may thus be said to be achieved every moment of time. From this point of view, there will be nothing to distinguish the reduction of a pot or something else to such a state of disintegration to the limit of Śūnyatā, from the *other* Śūnyatā arising from the annihilation of *a so-called* "individual". The Void being absolutely characterless, there is nothing to mark off one phase or aspect of Śūnyatā from another.

The Advaitic view of absorption into Brahman is hardly different from the Buddhist ideal, save for the difference in terminology : ब्रह्मभावश्च न शून्यभावात् भिद्यत इत्युपपादितम् (*NS* p. 633). The spiritual volatalization of the human personality into the colorless and featureless Absolute is quite as bleak and dreary a prospect as its nullification. It could never touch the heart and make it glow to be told that some spiritual spark will continue to be, even after we ourselves or what we hold dearest viz., our self is destroyed in the process of realization :

मोक्षे अहमर्थाभावे, आत्मनाशो मोक्ष इति बाह्यमतापत्तिः । प्रेमास्पदस्याहमर्थस्य च त्वन्मतेऽपि नाशात् तदन्यस्य शून्यादेः तन्मतेऽप्यनाशात् । 'अहं सुखी स्याम्' इतीच्छावत् 'चिन्मात्रं मुक्तं स्यात्' इतीच्छायाः क्वाप्यदर्शनेन मुक्तेरनिष्टत्वापाताच्च : 'यः कश्चिदात्मा मुक्तः स्या' दितीच्छया च न मुमुक्षुप्रवृत्तिः । 'ममात्मा मुक्तः स्या'दितीच्छा तु अहमर्थस्यैव मुक्तीच्छा

(*Nym* i.56)[1]

It cannot be argued that the aim of life is not so much to 'be happy' as 'to become happiness itself'. Philosophers have to respect the law of life. They cannot change the aim of life to their whims and dictates. Otherwise, the Buddhists and the Nyāya philosopher may as well get away with their dogma that the extinction of the Ātman or the extinction of all happiness is the aim of life.

In the absence of the survival of personality and full scope for the enjoyment of the innate bliss of selfhood, it would be a misuse of language to call the condition of Mokṣa promised by Advaita a state of bliss : आनन्दरूपता च वाङ्मात्रमित्युक्तमेव (*NS* p.584)

The Nyāya-Vaiśeṣika and Sāṁkhya accounts of Mokṣa are purely negative. Pleasure unmixed with pain or unattended by it, they argue, is unknown in the world. If, then, one should be so sentimental as to insist upon the enjoyment of happiness in release, one should by the force of the same logic admit the possibility of some measure of pain and suffering also therein. But that would be ridiculous. It would make release as good or as bad as Saṁsāra. The only rational course would therefore be to accept Mokṣa as a state of complete absence of any kind of pain coupled with the absence of any kind of pleasure or 'joy' so called. Madhva contends that such a purely negative ideal of Mokṣa could not supply the necessary dynamism and motive force for any fruitful spiritual effort to achieve release on the part of the aspirant.[2] Jayatīrtha points out that a positive

---

1. Cf. मयि नष्टेऽपि मत्तोऽन्या काचिज्ज्ञप्तिरवस्थिता ।
इति तत्प्राप्तये यत्नः कस्यापि न भविष्यति ॥ (*Śrībhāṣya* i. 1.1)

2. Cf. "A tendency to escape from oneself into God may have been the central motive of some seers of the Upaniṣads, the Orphic brotherhood in ancient Greece, and some Christian and Sufi Mystics. But there is no evidence that any Mystic achieved such a goal. In the nature of things, evidence of such absorption is impossible. He who has become God cannot return to tell us of his experience; he who narrates his story has not become God" (Radhakrishnan, *I. Phil.* ii. pp 711-12)

hankering after happiness could be seen to lie at the back of attempts of persons suffering from incurable maladies to put an end to their lives by suicide : रोगादिपीडिता उद्बन्धनादिनात्मनाशं कुर्वन्तोऽपि दृश्यन्त इति चेन्न । रोगाद्यायतनदेहपरित्यागेन आत्मानं निर्दुःखीकर्तुमेव तेषां प्रवृत्तिः निर्दुःखी भूयासं इति हि सर्वस्याशीः, न तु भूयासम् इति (*NS* pp. 632-33).

The doctrine of absorption in Advaita cuts at the very root of the idea of self. The self, as we all understand it, is the deepest spring of personality. It is what is revealed and implicated in all our experience as "Aham" ("I"). It is the basic principle of life, the *elan vital*, which possesses an inalienable and incommunicable individuality of its own, which furnishes the basis of the self-conscious psycho-physical mechanism of life carried on through a series of transmigrations. It is this underlying principle that is the most cherished possession of man; तदेतत् प्रेयः पुत्रात् प्रेयो वित्तात् प्रेयः सर्वस्मादन्तरतरं यदयमात्मा (*BrhUp* i.4.8). There is no place in the consolidated experience of humanity for a deeper or a more fundamental essence of the self of man, the one to which he clings with desperate tenacity throughout life and into which we enter in the inmost experiences of our lives. This self must therefore survive in the released state, if that state should have any meaning and reality for us. A self devoid of such a living content and a link with what it was in the state of bondage would be but an empty abstraction and a spectre of the Absolutist fancy. Even supposing that such an abstraction is possible, we cannot be persuaded to love and cherish it above all things in life and hold fast to it, as we love the self we know in the purest moments of our bliss, or go through a lot of trouble to keep some 'pure consciousness' that will rise on the ashes of our own self to manifest itself; न ह्येत-स्माद्रूपाद्विविक्तं किमपि निराकारं रूपमनुसन्धाय, मा न भूवम्, भूयासं इति लोक आशास्ते । **चक्षुषी निमील्य तत् तथेति वदतस्तु कः प्रतिमल्लः** ? (*NS* p. 633).

In any case, it would be little more than a verbal jugglery to say that the Absolutist goal is essentially 'blissful'. It is the capacity to feel and enjoy the bliss and the presence of one who enjoys, that makes happiness meaningful and worth striving for and not the bare presence of happiness much less our 'identification' with it :[3] तत्र, न तावत् सुखात्मता पुरुषार्थः । 'सुखी स्यां' इतीच्छावत् 'सुखं स्याम्' इतीच्छाया

---

3. Cf. The following line from *Dṛṣṭāntapāṭha*, 114, a famous Marāṭhi

अदर्शनात् (*Nym* iv. 3). On the Absolutist view, however, there can be no question of enjoying the bliss of selfhood, in view of the avowed difficulty of 'Kartṛkarmabhāva'. Moreover, one may ask the Advaitin : how is Ātman to be conceived in Mokṣa? If simply as *a bare consciousness*, then, there will be no room left for any realization of bliss (in the Ātman). If it is to be conceived as the essence of bliss *alone*, there will be no *consciousness* or *realization* of *that bliss* ! If it is to be conceived as both of the nature of *bliss and consciousness*, the thesis of Ātman as a *differenceless oneness* is shattered. Without the acceptance of an internal Viśeṣa in the Ātman it will be impossible to have the "aspects" of bliss and its consciousness (or revelation) *integrated* in the being of Ātman : **अपि च, आत्मनः सुखमात्रत्वे, प्रकाशमात्रत्वे च सुखप्रकाशाभावेन अपुमर्थत्वम् । उभयात्मकत्वे च अखण्डत्वहानिः ।** (*Nym* iv. 3)

Apart from this, the bliss of Ātman, being always self-subsistent, will always be there and it cannot therefore be made an object of spiritual pursuit. It is no use contending that this bliss has been obscured by nescience in the state of Saṁsāra (bondage) and comes to be realized only after the obscuration has been removed. For, according to the Advaitin, this bliss is *ex hypothesi* self-luminous and indistinguishable from the self and identical with it. It should, therefore, be capable of being fully revealed *along with* the revelation of the self all along. It cannot be held to be *vaguely or partly and imperfectly revealed* or felt *in the state of bondage and fully manifested in release*. For, such ideas of partial and full manifestations, clarity and obscurity of revelations, etc., imply and presuppose the presence of aspects or Viśeṣas or a diversity of features in the subject or a principle of identity-in-difference in the essence of the Śuddhacaitanya by which the hidden shades come to be progressively realized. But all this is impossible in a theory of Nirviśeṣādvaita or Nirviśeṣa-cinmātravāda or Akhaṇḍa-Caitanyavāda such as has been sponsored by Śaṅkara and his followers. There can be no talk of Sāmānya and Viśeṣa, general and

---

work of the Mahānubhāva Pantha :

साकर होइजे तें नीके कीं साकर अनुभवविजे तें नीके ।

"It is better to be an ant and taste the sweetness of sugar than *become* the sugar".

particular, in the "Nirviśeṣa". There is no place for any such inner shades of being or diversity of content or aspects or by whatever name one may choose to call it, in the conception of Ātman as a *bare consciousness*, without aspects (*nirastasamastaviśeṣam*) adumbrated by Śaṅkara. There can be no new or fuller stages of bliss of being *yet to be intuited* or rediscovered in a pure being that is *ex hypothesi* colorless, shadeless and aspectless :

निर्विशेषत्वादात्मनो नानधिगतो विशेषः

(Madhva, *Māyāvāda khaṇḍana*)

This criticism is not only hard to rebut, but has not been rebutted convincingly.[4]

---

4. **प्रकाशमानोऽप्यानन्दो न विशदः प्रकाशत इति चेन्न। निर्विशेषत्वात्।** वैशद्यावैशद्ययोश्च विशेषनिबन्धनत्वात्। यद्धि सह विशेषैः प्रकाशते तद्विशदमुच्यते। यत्तु साधारणधर्मैः सह, तदविशदमिति ॥ अविद्यावरणापगमे प्रकाशत इति च कोऽर्थः ? किं प्रतीयत इति; उत प्रत्येतीति ? नोभावपि; अनङ्गीकारात् ॥ प्रदीपः प्रकाशत इति कोऽर्थ इति चेत्। भास्वररूपवान् वर्तत इति न किंचिदेतत् ॥ (*NS* p. 634b)

CHAPTER LVI

MADHVA'S VIEW OF MUKTI

MADHVA, therefore, lays, great stress on the survival of every individual personality, as such, in release. This is the corollary of his belief in the distinctiveness of the Svarūpa of each Jīva. As release is the realization of the intrinsic bliss of selfhood by each one of us, it must be a positive experience, to be felt and be realized by each and at the same time incommunicable to others. We cannot, obviously, press the point further and ask *how* the blissful experience of one self differs from that of another. It is purely a matter of intuitive experience of each individual and we have to leave it at that. As Rāmānuja says :

जीवात्मस्वरूपं * * * ज्ञानानन्दैकगुणकम् । **तस्यैतस्य स्वरूपभेदो वाचामगोचरः स्वसंवेद्यः** ज्ञानस्वरूपमित्येतावदेव निर्देश्यम् । (*Vedārtha-Saṁgraha*)

Hence, it will be presumptuous on the part of anyone to attempt to define in clear and precise terms what exactly the released state would be like, *from this side of release* ! Nevertheless, man is irrepressibly curious and inquisitive about what lies in store for him in the great beyond. People expect the philosopher to throw some light on these questions. As an interpreter and an expositor of the traditions of the Vedaśāstra on this point, Madhva bases his account of the released state on a coordinated interpretation of the Scriptural facts and evidences. He also adduces the *reasons* in support of these interpretations. He gives a thoroughly consistent picture of the released state, harmonizing the *realistic and idealistic* accounts of Mokṣa found in the Vedic, Upaniṣadic and post-Upaniṣadic sources. It must be said that *his is a distinctive view of Mokṣa rich in its details, uncompromising in principles, trenchant in its logic and full of Mystic inwardness in some respects.*

The first and foremost fact about Mokṣa emphasized by Madhva is its *positive aspect*. He opposes the purely negative view of Mokṣa, held by the Sāṁkhyas and the Naiyāyikas. To be a "Puruṣārtha" and the highest one at that, it must be a state of supreme bliss. This bliss must be fully manifested, i.e., capable of being actually *felt and enjoyed with a full consciousness that it is being enjoyed*. This would naturally presuppose the survival of the one who is to enjoy the experiences of this blessed state. In this connection, Madhva discusses the famous text of the *Chāndogya* : अशरीरं वाव सन्तं प्रियाप्रिये न स्पृशतः and shows that the juxtaposition of the words : न ह वै सशरीरस्य सतः प्रियाप्रिययोरुपहतिः establishes clearly that it is only the material joys and pleasures that are regarded as disagreeable to the Mukta and therefore ruled out, while the intrinsic bliss of selfhood and its enjoyment are accepted without reserve. Similarly, another Śruti which speaks of the destruction of all desires of the heart (सदा सर्वे प्रमुच्यन्ते कामा येऽस्य हृदि श्रिताः *Kaṭha* ii.3.14) has reference only to the material longings of the *antaḥkaraṇa* : सर्वथापि कामाभावपरेति व्याख्याने, 'हृदि' श्रिता इति कामानां विशेषणं व्यर्थम् । व्यावर्त्याभावात् । अन्तःकरणपरिणतीनां कामानामेव मुक्तावभावः, न तु स्वरूपभूतानाम् । (*NS* p. 573), because other Śruti texts connected with the Mukti state do speak of the fulfilment of every spiritual desire in Mokṣa—भवेदेतत्—यदीदं विशेषणं स्यात् । न चैवं व्यावर्त्याभावात् । सर्वेषामपि कामानां मनःपरि- णामक्त्वमेव न त्वात्मधर्मः कामोऽस्तीत्याशंक्य निषेधति — 'मुक्तानां कामितामाह पृथक् शाखासु च श्रुतिः' । कामश्रुतिस्तावन्निरवकाशा । तदभावश्रुतिस्तु सावकाशा । 'एतत्सर्वं मन एव' इत्यपि सावकाशश्रुतिरिति सांख्याधिकरणेऽभिहितम् । कामश्रुतिस्तु सर्वास्वपि शाखास्वस्ति । तदभाव-श्रुतिस्तु क्वचिदेवेति कथं न बाध्यबाध्यकभावः ? (*NS* p. 573). The *Vedānta Sūtras* specially discuss the question of how the released spirits enjoy themselves at all, as they have transcended the material plane and have no physical bodies or sense organs and answer the question (iv.4.10-16) from different standpoints consistent with the trans-empirical character of the released state. The Sūtrakāra says, for instance, that the released souls can fashion at their will (which is also *satyasaṁkalpa* in conformity with God's will) suitable bodies out of Śuddhasattva or enjoy themselves with their own spiritual bodies composed of *cit*, *ānanda*, etc. These answers are intended to show that we cannot judge the state of Mokṣa from our own limited range and angle and conclude that no kind of enjoyment of bliss is possible for these Muktas, because they have no material bodies like ours and that, therefore, the state of Mukti should be one of utter inactivity and inertia for the souls. This is an unfair view to take of a state of supreme felicity according to all accounts. There is nothing to prevent the Muktas from enjoying themselves in their state of blessedness in ways which human imagination can hardly comprehend. Man has hardly yet fathomed the mysteries of nature. He has just begun to explore outer space. We wish him Godspeed; but it will do him good to remember that there are still many things which are beyond his understanding and are bound to remain so :

अचिन्त्याः खलु ये भावा न तांस्तर्केण योजयेत् ।
प्रकृतिभ्यः परं यच्च तदचिन्त्यस्य वैभवम् ॥
(*Mbh* quoted by Śaṅkara in *BSB* ii.1.6)

अनिन्द्रिया अनाहारा अनिष्पन्दाः सुगन्धिनः ।
(*Mbh* xii.337.29)

देहेन्द्रियादिहीनानां वैकुण्ठपुरवासिनाम् ।
(*Bhāg* vii.1.34)

Realization, then, makes it possible for souls to have a sense of realization of something and rest on their oars and taste the unalloyed bliss of their pure being, which has so long been obscured by the encrustation of Avidyā, Kāma, Karma, etc. There is no difficulty of manifestation of the full-fledged personality of the self in all its richness and entirety of aspects in the state of release on the Dvaita view, as the self there is admitted to be a unity-in-diversity (Saviśeṣa-svarūpa and not Nir-viśeṣa, as in Advaita), some of whose aspects have been obscured by the will of God and the influence of Prākṛtic bonds. There is no impediment therefore to these essential aspects becoming *fully manifested* and realized in Mokṣa, when the Lord is pleased to lift the veil of His 'Māyā' and manifest the true and essential nature of the soul to it in full. The so-called Kartṛ-karmavirodha is therefore an untenable objection since it will be the very negation of the idea of self to deny self-consciousness to it.[1]

Madhva, therefore, regards Mukti as a complete self-expres-

1. तदात्मानमेवावेदहं ब्रह्मास्मीति । आत्मन्येवात्मानं पश्येत् । (*BrhUp*)

sion, self-manifestation and self-realization, in short, a complete unfolding of the self in all its promise and potency :

परं ज्योतिरुपसंपद्य स्वेन रूपेणाभिनिष्पद्यते (*ChānUp* viii.12.3)

मुक्तिर्हित्वान्यथारूपं स्वरूपेण व्यवस्थितिः (*Bhāg* ii.10.6).

Realization of truth does not mean abolition of the plurality of the world but only a removal of the false sense of separateness and independence.[2] It is a new insight that changes the face of the world and makes all things new. The Mukta sees everything through the eyes of God[3] as dependent on God in its proper perspective which he had failed to do in Saṁsāra.

The pleasures of the highest state described in some of the Vedic and Upaniṣadic passages are not the last word on the subject. They are only broad indications of what the supreme state of felicity may be like :

प्रपंचार्थं च मोक्षस्य सिद्धयः संप्रकीर्तिताः।

(*Sāttvata* quoted by Deśika, *BGt* xviii.32)

Consequently, then, we need neither take them *too literally*, nor dismiss them as garish *fancies*. Madhva has left us in no doubt as to the manner of life led by the freed souls in release. Like the Lord, they are for ever *contented*. They don't have to *seek* satisfaction; for theirs is the kingdom of Heaven. Wisdom and enjoyment of perfect bliss are their *own nature*. With all that, there is no *fear* that their condition would be one of stagnation all round. *A Theistic account of Mokṣa cannot, any day, make conditions there more stagnant than an Advaitic view of it* ! Madhva is satisfied that there is scope for activity and full play of capacities for everyone of us there according to his or her abilities. The released may rest in the contemplation of their own blessedness, like the Advaitic Brahman. They may contrast their present with their past and feel thankful for their deliverance. They may adore the majesty of God and sing His praises or worship Him in a thousand ways :

---

2. यो हि ब्रह्मक्षत्रादिकं जगदात्मनोऽन्यत्र **स्वातंत्र्येण लब्धसद्भावं** पश्यति तं मिथ्यादर्शिनं जगत् पराकरोति । (Śaṅkara, *BSB I.* 4.19)

3. स ब्रह्मणा पश्यति, ब्रह्मणा शृणोति ब्रह्मणैवेदं सर्वमनुभवति ।

(Śruti, Madhva, *BSB* iv. 4.5)

ज्ञात्वापि मम माहात्म्यं तत्रोत्सुकतया पुनः ।
विशेषाच्च विशेषेण ज्ञात्वा मामश्नुतेऽधिकम् ॥
(*Vijñāna*, quoted in *BT* xi.11.33)

They may offer sacrifices, if they wish to—the only difference being that *nothing is obligatory there*.

There is no *prescribed round of activities* or code of conduct in Mokṣa, which means there is unlimited scope for spontaneous, creative work of every kind—Karma,[4] Jñāna and Bhakti.[5] There is no call for activity in that there is no one to *call upon you* to do this or that. The urge is from within entirely :

कदाचित् कर्म कुर्वन्ति कदाचिन्नैव कुर्वते ।
नित्यज्ञानस्वरूपत्वात् नित्यं ध्यायन्ति केशवम् ॥
(*BSB* iii.3.30)

The worship and activity in Mokṣa, such as they are, are *an end in themselves*. They are *not means to an end* :

साध्यानन्दस्वरूपैव भक्तिर्नैवात्र साधनम् । (*GT* ii)
हरेरुपासना चात्र सदैव सुखरूपिणी ।
न तु साधनभूता सा सिद्धिरेवात्र सा यतः ॥ (*BSB* iv.4.21)

The assumption of activities cannot reduce the released state to the level of this world as these are no longer determined by injunctions and prohibitions or attended by unpleasant consequences in the event of non-performance. It is this freedom from all conditions that distinguishes the life in Mokṣa from ordinary life. Madhva's point : बन्धप्रत्यवायाभावे हि मोक्षस्य अर्थवत्त्वम्, अन्यथा मोक्षत्वमेव न स्यात् (*BSB* iii.3.3). is really unexceptionable. Unless some kind of activity is recognized, it will be difficult to differentiate the liberated souls from stones and sticks, despite the reputed possession by them of "consciousness". Such service as the freed render to God is purely voluntary and an end in itself :

भक्तिर्ज्ञानं तथा ध्यानं मुक्तानामपि सर्वशः ।
साधनानि तु सर्वाणि भक्तिज्ञानप्रवृद्धये ।
नैवान्यसाधनं भक्तिः फलरूपा हि सा यतः ॥
(Madhva, Commentary on *BrhUp* i.4)

---

4. कृष्णो मुक्तैरिज्यते वीतमोहैः (*Mbh* xiii 18.64)
5. आत्मारामाश्च मुनयो निर्ग्रन्था अप्युरुक्रमे ।
कुर्वन्त्यहैतुकीं भक्तिमित्थंभूतगुणो हरिः ॥ (*Bhāg* i. 7. 10)

There is no relevance in comparing this picture with Śaṅkara's view of the Jñānī's continuing to perform Karma even after attainment of enlightenment in the spirit of 'Lokasaṅgraha' (*Gītā* iii. 20-25). In the first place, the theatre of action is the world of Mokṣa where according to Śaṅkara there is no duality and there is a complete liquidation of all *kriyā*, *kāraka* and *phala*. Secondly, even the concept of 'Lokasaṅgraha' as interpreted by Śaṅkara and Ānandagiri reduces itself to 'a semblance of activity' (*karmābhāsa*)—a sort of reflex action (*involuntary*) of Prārabdha-karma, with no heart, soul or sincerity of purpose in it.

'प्रवृत्तिरूप'मिति रूपग्रहणं आभासत्वप्रदर्शनार्थम् (iii)
कर्मणैव हि (iii.20) इत्यादौ बाधितानुवृत्त्या प्रवृत्त्याभासो गृह्यते
(Ānandagiri ii.11)

Madhva has brought together certain texts bearing upon the nature of life in the released state. The most important of these are :

1. सर्वे नन्दन्ति यशसागतेन सभासाहेन सख्या सखायः (*RV* X.71.10)
अक्षण्वन्तः कर्णवन्तः सखायो मनोजवेष्वसमा बभूवुः (*RV* X.71.7)
2. एतत्साम गायन्नास्ते हाबु हाबु (*TaittUp* iii.10.5)
3. तस्य मध्ये वेतसः पुण्यगन्धो सहस्रशाखो विमलो विभाति ।
तस्य मूलात्सरितः प्रस्रवन्ति मधूकप्रस्रवणा रमण्यः ॥
(quoted in *SNR* from *Mbh* III)

"आचक्ष्व मे परं मोक्षं धीरा यं प्रवदन्ति तम् ।
इत्युक्त आह वाग्देवी परं मोक्षं प्रजापतेः ।
शाखां शाखां महानद्यः संयान्ति परितःस्रवाः ।
धानापूपा मांसकामाः सदा पायसकर्दमाः ।
यस्मिन्नग्निमुखा देवाः सेन्द्राः सह मरुद्गणाः ।
ईजिरे क्रतुभिः श्रेष्ठैः तदक्षरमुपासते ।
प्रविशन्ति परं देवं मुक्ताः तत्रैव भोगिनः ।
निर्गच्छन्ति यथाकामं परेशेनैव चोदिताः ॥

(*Mbh* III.184. 21-25 quoted by Madhva in *AV* ii.3.28)

[Madhva's readings based on a southern recension show important variations here from those given in the critical edn. of Mbh published by the BORI, Pune.]

4. यत्रानन्दाश्च मोदाश्च मुदः प्रमुद आसते ।
दैवैः सुकृतकर्मभिः तत्र माममृतं कृधि ॥ (*RV* IX.113.1)

These texts have been further elucidated by the author of the *Madhvasiddhāntasāra*:

1. केचित् स्त्रीभोगं कुर्वन्ति (Cf. *ChanUp* viii.12.2)
2. केचित्तु रथतुरगादीन् धावयन्ति (*ibid*)
3. केचिदृगादिवेदोच्चारणेन भगवन्तं स्तुवन्ति (Cf. *RV* X.72.11)
4. केचन सुखोद्रेकेण 'हावु हावु' इत्यादि शब्दानुच्चारयन्ति (*TaittUp* iii.10.5)
5. केचन पूर्वाभ्यासेन यज्ञादिकं कुर्वन्ति (Cf. *Mbh* xiii.18.6)
6. केचनाजन्ममरणं स्मृत्वा मुक्ता हर्षमवाप्नुयुः ॥
7. केचनेच्छामात्रेण पित्रादिदर्शनवन्तो भवन्ति ।
(*ChanUp* viii.2.1-10 and Śaṅkara *BSB* iv.4.8)
8. केचन सर्वलोकचारिणः (*ChanUp* viii.25.2)
9. केचम शुद्धसत्त्वनिर्मितलीलाशरीराण्यादाय क्रीडन्ते
(*BS* iv.4.12, and Śaṅkara's commentary thereon).
10. केचन नृत्यन्ति
11. केचन वाद्यानि वादयन्ति

As individuality persists in Mokṣa,[6] there must be some outlet for the energies of the freed. Scripture does not deny desires to the released. It is the desires of a worldly nature and *born of the mind* that are denied :

* * * कामा येऽस्य हृदि श्रिताः[7] ।
इत्यन्तःकरणस्थानां कामानां मोक्षमेव हि ।
प्राह श्रुतिः हृदीत्येव **न चेत् व्यर्थविशेषणम्** ॥ (*AV* iii.4.16)

6. Cf. अविनाशी वायमात्मानुच्छित्तिधर्मा (*BrhUp* iv. 5. 14)

7. Madhva points out that the term "Hṛdi" in the Upaniṣadic text shows that only the desires arising in the mind are intended.

CHAPTER LVII

RATIONALE OF ĀNANDA-TĀRATAMYA IN MOKṢA

ALL Theists recognize the persistence of personality in release. Since the souls are many, their plurality must survive there. But as multiplicity without intrinsic distinctions and gradations is inconceivable among thinking selves as we know them, Madhva finds it necessary to maintain that there are distinctions in the quality, intensity, range, etc. of the Svarūpānanda enjoyed by them in the released state according to their capacities and intrinsic fitness (*svarūpayogyatā*). Rāmānuja in his theory of selves is inclined to put down the difference among the different classes of souls such as gods and human beings as the outcome of Karma and other Prākṛtic accretions and therefore not touching their essence, which he regards as equal in all, though there is numerical distinction. This is not acceptable to Madhva who finds sufficient evidence in the Śāstras to accept the differences between gods and the other classes of souls as inherent distinctions among different orders of beings *not* traceable to Karmic or other causes. As a matter of fact, *Rāmānuja is not quite consistent in not accepting intrinsic gradation among the souls* in his general theory; though the tradition of Vaiṣṇava theology which he inherits from the Ālvārs is committed to the existence of a special class of Nityasūris among the (released) souls as distinguished from the ordinary Muktas who have attained release *after bondage*. This inner inconsistency in the Viśiṣṭādvaitic position has been taken note of by Vyāsatīrtha in his *Nyāyāmṛta* in support of Madhva's theory of Ānandatāratamya in Mokṣa, as against the Sāmya theory of Rāmānuja, as will be shown presently.

Madhva's theory of Ānanda-tāratamya in Mokṣa, is a logical conclusion from the hypothesis of Svarūpabheda and Tāratamya (gradation) among souls. It is one of the main points of disagreement between the schools of Madhva and Rāmānuja; though both are schools of staunch and uncompromising Vaiṣṇava Theism and show many other points of mutual agreement in doctrine and theology. Much controversy has raged between these two schools over this issue from the days of Vyāsatīrtha and some controversial works written on the subject by champions of the respective schools are actually in existence.[1]

It should be borne in mind that a theory of possible difference and gradation in the qualitative enjoyment of Svarūpānanda in Mokṣa has meaning only in a system of thought in which difference among souls is accepted *as a fact*. It has no place in a Monistic system like Śaṅkara's, where all difference among souls (*ātmabheda*) even in Saṁsāra is merely due to false Upādhis and is utterly wiped out in release. It has significance and bearing only in Theistic systems like those of Rāmānuja and Madhva, wherein the plurality of souls is admitted as an ultimate fact. Of course, as against Śaṅkara and his school, Madhva and his commentators have, as we have seen, tried to establish the thesis of plurality of Ātmans as a fundamental fact on strong grounds including textual evidences. Acceptance of the doctrine of plurality of Ātmans is the same as accepting "Svarūpabheda" among Ātmans and rejecting the view of "Ekātmavāda" that there is in reality *only one Ātman* who *appears* as many on account of Upādhis. Once "Svarūpabhedavāda" among Ātmans is accepted as a philosophical fact, it will be easy enough to establish "Svarūpa-Tāratamya" also among such Ātmans, which will logically lead up to Svarūpānanda-tāratamya among them in Mokṣa. The latter is the inevitable logical corollary of the former. Madhva and his commentators feel strongly that the Rāmānuja school is *not* justified in accepting Svarūpabheda of Ātmans warmly but in refusing to subscribe to the doctrine of Ānanda-Tāratamya among them in Mokṣa, which will be the most natural deduc-

1. For details see my *HDSV* p. 406.

tion from it. As for the main arguments in favor of Madhva's theory, they will be dealt with presently.

Since Mokṣa is only the discovery and enjoyment of one's own selfhood, in its pristine purity and bliss, there is no possibility of exchanging one's experiences of bliss with another's, or of its transference to another, whether wholly or in part. Each soul rests fully satisfied and immersed in the enjoyment of its "Svarūpānanda" *to saturation point, so to say.* Many weighty arguments have been urged by Madhva, Jayatīrtha and Vyāsatīrtha in their works, in support of this important doctrine of Theism. As the subject of Mokṣānanda and Svarūpānanda pertains largely to the domain of Mysticism, students and critics of Madhva's doctrine of Svarūpānanda-Tāratamya of souls in Mokṣa should *not fail to take due note of the mystic inwardness of this doctrine*, however strange and unfamiliar it may seem to them, at first sight. Viewed in the light of an expression and an interpretation of the Mystic joy of self-realization in Mokṣa *its contribution to the philosophy of Mysticism itself will be seen to be quite remarkable.*

All souls could not have put forth the same quality or quantity of effort of the same intensity or duration. It thus stands to reason that there must be a proportionate difference in the nature of the reward reaped by them. This is one other ground of Tāratamya (gradation) of *ānanda* (bliss) in Mokṣa. There are highly evolved souls like Brahmā and the other gods whose spiritual perfection *must* certainly be greater than that of us mortals. And it cannot go in vain. The evidence of Scripture tells us of super-human Sādhanas practised by some of the gods and the wide difference in their quality, quantity, duration etc., which are beyond human conception. These could not all be treated on the same par :

'दशकल्पं तपश्चीर्णं रुद्रेण लवणार्णवे ।
त्यक्त्वा सुखानि सर्वाणि क्लिष्टेन लवणांभसा ।
शक्रेण वर्षकोटीश्च धूमः पीतोऽतिदुःखतः ।
वर्षायुतं तु सूर्येण तपोऽर्वाक्शिरसा कृतम् ।
सुदुःखेन सुखं त्यक्त्वा धर्मेणाकाशाशायिना ।
पीता मरीचयो वर्षसहस्रमतिसादरम् ।

अतिकृच्छ्रेण कुर्वन्ति यत्नं ब्रह्मविदोऽपि च ।'
इत्येतदखिलं मोक्षे विशेषाभावतः कथम् ?
युक्तं च साधनाधिक्यात् साध्याधिक्यं सुरादिषु ।
नाधिक्यं यदि साध्ये स्यात् प्रयत्नः साधने कुतः ?[2]
(*AV* iii.4.16)

It is to be noted in this connection that while Mokṣānanda is purely the manifestation of the distinctive innate bliss of souls, Sādhanas in life are absolutely necessary for its manifestation and consummation in Mokṣa with the grace of the Lord. The operation of the principle of parity of Sādhana and Sādhya is also naturally coordinated with each one's *Svarūpayogyatā*.

The Śāstras tell us that there are persons who work deliberately for their salvation as well as great souls like Sanaka (Ekāntabhaktas) who love God for His own sake (and not for their salvation) and even decline the prospect of communion with Him. Surely, any theory of Mokṣa, if it is to be balanced, must take note of these intrinsic differences and give a proper place for Ekāntabhaktas and others, according to their worth. Madhva bases one of his arguments for accepting Tāratamya in Mokṣa on this point also :

नात्यन्तिकं विगणयन्त्यपि ते प्रसादम् (*Bhāg* iii.15.48)
नैकात्मतां मे स्पृहन्ति केचित् (iii.25.34)
* * * एकत्वमप्युत ।
दीयमानं न गृह्णन्ति * * * (iii.29.13)

इति मुक्तिमनिच्छतामपि मोक्ष एव फलं, तमिच्छतामपि सुप्रतीकादीनामिति कथमनिच्छतां स्तुतिरुपपन्ना स्यात् ? (*GB* ii.52)

Vyāsatīrtha in his *Nyāyāmṛta* has given us the best critical exposition of Madhva's doctrine of Ānandatāratamya in its logical and textual aspects. Some of his arguments have been specially directed against the school of Rāmānuja. This school accepts Svarūpabheda between God and the souls and among the Mukta-Jīvas themselves. But it is *not prepared to go further* and accept with Madhva any *Svarūpa-vaicitrya* (distinguishing characteristics) among the souls or any gradation in their Svarūpānanda in Mokṣa. Vyāsatīrtha shows how it has accepted

2. For the English Translation of these verses see Chapter XLVI.

Svarūpatāratamya *in principle not only between Brahman and the Mukta-Jīvas but among the Mukta-Jīvas as well*, at least *in a few cases*. If Svarūpatāratamya can be accepted among Jīvas *in principle*, there is no reason to shy at the acceptance of Svarūpānanda-Tāratamya *also*. For, in the last analysis, Svarūpānanda of each individual and of Brahman is nothing but *the expression of their own nature*. Madhva and his commentators do not also accept the position of Rāmānuja that the differences between the Devas (including Brahmā, Rudra, Indra and the goddesses) and other souls referred to in the Śāstras are not Svābhāvika but are the result of bodily and other Karmic Upādhis *alone*. Madhva is not prepared to endorse such an extreme view, which, he feels, will be *out of tune with the spiritual traditions of the Śāstras*.

Anyway, the principle of Svarūpatāratamya is accepted by the Viśiṣṭādvaitin in respect of the Jīvas and Brahman. Brahman here is conceived as Vibhu, Śeṣi and Svatantra, while the Jīvas are all Aṇu, Śeṣa and Paratantra. In this circumstance complete equality between such widely differing natures is out of the question. It will lead to multiplicity of Īśvaras, if pressed further.

The Sūtra : जगद्व्यापारवर्जम् (iv.4.17) denies cosmic functions to the released souls. Such cosmic activities of Brahman are obviously and admittedly an expression of His own inner joy (Cf. को ह्येवान्यात् कः प्राण्याद्यदेष आकाश आनंदो न स्यात् (*TaittUp*). Rāmānuja himself admits that the Muktas owe the very manifestation of their Svarūpa-ānanda to the eternal will (*saṁkalpa*) of Brahman:

मुक्तस्य सत्यसंकल्पत्वादिपूर्वकस्याप्यानंदस्य परमपुरुष एव हेतुरिति श्रुतिस्मृती दर्शयतः 'एष ह्येवानन्दयाति' इति । (Rāmānuja, *BSB* iv.4.20)

Thus, he accepts the relation of Niyamya-niyāmakabhāva (controller and controlled) between them to be intrinsic to their natures. This should lead to the legitimate conclusion that the bliss of the Niyāmaka (controller) must be greater, wider and more intense than that of the controlled :

ईश्वरानन्दः जीवानन्दादुत्कृष्टः, तदवश्यतन्नियामकानन्दत्वात् । यदेवं तदेवं, यथा सेवकानन्दात् सेव्यानन्दः । (*Nym*). Since Brahman is *capable of enjoying an order of bliss superior to that of the Jivas under its control*, in release, there is no reason why it should *not* do so.

The Sūtra भोगमात्रसाम्यलिङ्गाच्च (iv.4.21) will not conflict with this position. For, according to Rāmānuja, this Sūtra is not an independent one; but one that is syntactically connected with जगद्व्यापारवर्जम् * * * (iv.4.17).[3] The term *mātra* in '*bhogamātra*' here has been explained by him *not* in the sense of the entirety of the *bhoga* (कात्स्न्यर्थे) but in the sense of emphasis (अवधारण) intended to restrict the equality with Brahman (ब्रह्मसाम्य) to the aspect of *bhoga* or *ānanda* alone and prevent its extension to the cosmic activities (जगद्व्यापार) of Brahman and Its other characteristics. On the basis of this Sūtra भोगमात्रसाम्यलिंगाच्च then, as interpreted by Rāmānuja, it cannot be decided whether the equality in the enjoyment of bliss between the Jīvas and Brahman is just in respect of its general aspect of *bhoga* (भोगसामान्य एव) or whether it applies to each and every aspect of Brahman's enjoyment (भोगविशेष).

The same suffix *mātra* in *bhogamātra* cannot bear two separate senses of emphasis and entirety; nor has Rāmānuja made any such suggestion, in his commentary. Hence, the Sūtra भोगमात्रसाम्यलिंगाच्च will be of no use to the Viśiṣṭādvaitin in establishing the thesis of complete equality of Mukta-Jīvas with Brahman in the enjoyment of *all its bhogas* extending to each and every aspect of it.

The cosmic activities of Brahman are indeed an expression of its inner joy (जगद्व्यापारस्यापीश्वरगतभोगत्वेन) and it must stand to reason that the Mukta Jīvas who do not engage in such activities cannot be enjoying that bliss of Brahman which will be an expression of such activities.

The Rāmānuja school recognizes further that the Goddess Lakṣmī also occupies the position of Śeṣi to all the Jīvas (including the Mukta Jīvas) and also that certain superior souls like Viṣvaksena, who are given the special status of "Nityasūris", exercise control over the other Jīvas *in release. This is a clear and unambiguous acceptance of the principle of Jīvasvarūpa-tāratamya in the Rāmānuja school*, notwithstanding its supposed denial on the ground that all difference among Jīvas is due to Karma alone. This special status given to Lakṣmī and the "Nityasūris" in the

3. ब्रह्मयाथात्म्यानुभवरूपभोगमात्रे मुक्तस्य ब्रह्मसाम्यप्रतिपादनाच्च लिंगात्, जगद्व्यापारवर्जमित्यवगम्यते । (Rāmānuja, *BSB*)

Viśiṣṭādvaita hierarchy gives solid support to Madhva's doctrine of Svarūpa-Tāratamya among Muktas. From Svarūpa-tāratamya to "Svarūpānanda-tāratamya" it is but a single logical step forward.

The Hindu Scriptures refer to an ascending order of Mukti : Sālokya, Sāmīpya, Sārūpya and Sāyujya, in which each succeeding stage includes the joy of the preceding one. This would certainly imply an intrinsic gradation of bliss in Mokṣa. As Sāyujya carries with it an element of Sārūpya also, it cannot be equated with *aikyam* or identity of being. This is evident from the Upaniṣadic text : चन्द्रमसः सायुज्यं सलोकतामाप्नोति, where the knower who has attained Sāyujya with the moon is again referred to as enjoying the benefits of Salokatā. The etymology of the word Sāyujya सयुजोः भावः also disproves the sense of "identity". The gradations of the four kinds of Mukti accepted by the Rāmānuja school also make it incumbent upon it to accept the principle of Tāratamya in Mokṣa.

Though the Svarūpānanda of each individual Mukta Jīva is a single unit of atomic dimension, it is conceivable that there can be gradations in their Svarūpānanda in regard to their quality, range, intensity etc. Since Mokṣānanda is *ex hypothesi* trans-empirical, it will be difficult to clarify the exact nature of its inner gradations in clear and precise terms *from the empirical level.* We can only say in the words of Rāmānuja that the Svarūpānanda of the Jīvas, in Mokṣa is like the very Svarūpa of the Jīvas, "*Svasamvedya*" and "*Vācām agorarah*" *sui generis* and that, *their gradations too are* similarly knowable only by one's own self and beyond the power of words to be expressed finally ! Vyāsatīrtha has made the point clear by means of an analogy, viz. the different levels of joy and satisfaction derived from the tasting of water and nectar.[4]

He has also argued in his *Nyāyāmṛta* that the principle of parity between means and ends, if applied to the two different types of Sādhanas accepted by the Rāmānuja school, viz. Bhakti and Prapatti, will inevitably lead to the acceptance of gradation of Svarūpānanda in Mokṣa among the released souls. The

---

4. स्वरूपसुखानां प्रत्येकमेकत्वेनाणुत्वेन च संख्यापरिणामकृतवैषम्याभावेऽपि जलसुधापानसुखयोरिव मधुरमधुरतरत्वादिवत् स्वरूपकृतवैषम्यं युक्तम् (*Nym* iv. 5)

validity of the principle of parity of means and ends is not weakened, as Sādhanas in both the systems merely help to manifest (*abhivyakti*) the Svarūpānanda of the Muktas and *not* to produce (*janaka*), as has already been made clear.

Prapatti is trustful surrender of self to God (*bhara-nyāsa*)[5] and Bhakti is continuous flow of contemplative thinking of God without break.[6] These two are conceived as separate and *independent means of release* and *not complementary*.

Cf. भक्त्यादौ शक्त्यभावः प्रमितिरहितता शास्त्रतः पर्युदासः
कालक्षेपाक्षमत्वं त्विति नियतिवशादापतद्भिः चतुर्भिः ।
एकद्वित्र्यादियोगव्यतिभिदुरनिजाधिक्रियाः संश्रयन्ते
सन्तः श्रीशं **स्वतंत्र प्रपदनविधिना** मुक्तये निर्विशङ्कम् ॥

(Vedānta Deśika : *Rahasyatrayasāra*)

According to the Rāmānuja school, the way of Bhakti calls for the faithful performance of the duties of Varṇāśrama and Śrauta-Smārta dharmas[7] in order to fit the mind for *nididhyāsana*. It is such Upāsanā of God with the help of anyone of the Vidyās taught in the Śrutis that earns the love and grace of God on oneself.[8]

The two ways of Bhakti and Prapatti are thus different.[9] Bhakti needs repetition of Upāsanā and requires adherence to the Śrauta and Smārta Karmas and Varṇāśrama dharmas. Prapatti, on the other hand, is free from the obligations of such Karma and needs no repetition (*āvṛtti*). It is enough to offer Prapatti but once with all one's heart. *The way of Bhakti is thus the more arduous one and long-drawn out.* It is also burdened with the

---

5. **अनन्यसाध्ये स्वाभीष्टे महाविश्वासपूर्वकम् ।
तदेकोपायतायाच्ञा प्रपत्तिः शरणागतिः ॥**

(quoted by Desika, *RGB* xviii. 66)

6. ध्यानं च तैलधारावदविच्छिन्नस्मृतिसन्तानरूपम् । वक्ष्यति च 'आवृत्तिरसकृदुपदेशात्' इति तस्यैव वेदनस्योपासनारूपस्यासकृदावृत्तस्य ध्रुवानुस्मृतित्वम् ।

(*Śrībhāṣya* i. 1. 1)

7. एवंरूपाया ध्रुवानुस्मृतेः साधनानि यज्ञादिकर्माणि (ibid)

8. उपासनापरपर्यायत्वात् भक्तिशब्दस्य । (ibid)

9. "Prapatti is an old doctrine in Southern Vaiṣṇavism. In the *Nyāsatilaka-Vyākhyā* great emphasis is laid on the fact that Prapatti as a path of approach to God is *different from the path of Bhakti and superior to it.*" (Dasgupta, *I. Phil.* iii, p. 380, fn. 2)—Italics mine.

obligations of Śāstric Karma.[10] In view of this *structural and other differences between them*, as Sādhanas, one will have to accept a corresponding difference in the nature of the *ānanda* which they will help to manifest in release.[11]

Vyāsatīrtha argues that they cannot be equalized in respect of their final fruit by our proposing to invest Prapatti with a greater measure of trust in God (*viśvāsādhikya*) and attributing less of such trust in God to the discipline of Bhakti.[12] On the contrary, there would seem to be a better case for holding that there will be a greater measure of trust in God created by Bhakti on account of constant and repeated practice by Upāsanā which is defined as : वेदनस्योपासनारूपस्य असकृदावृत्तस्य, than in Prapatti *which it is enough to offer but once*. It would lead to the fallacy of interdependence, if one should still disregard the disparity between the two Sādhanas and assert that they are both on a par and that their results also would be the same. For, unless their parity as Sādhanas is first established on satisfactory grounds, the equality of their fruits cannot be taken for granted and unless the equality of fruits is first proved the equality of Sādhanas cannot also be established.

It is therefore futile to deny that Bhakti and Prapatti are not on the same par as Sādhanas. The former must be accepted as the more arduous one and the latter as the easier one. The Śāstras would be violating the principle of equity, if they allow the same fruit as is attained by those who practise the more arduous means to others who practise the easier ones. A God who rewards the different types of Sādhakas who seek Him through such admittedly unequal means to the same extent and degree would also be liable to the charge of partiality and cruelty. The principle of equity in regard to efforts and results

10. "In the *Nyāsatilakavyākhyā* it is said that the chief difference between Bhakti and Prapatti is (i) that the former is of the nature of unbroken meditation while the latter has to be done *once for all*; (ii) the former needs varying accessory methods of worship and continual action, whereas in the latter we have *excessive faith*" (*ibid*). (Italics mine).

11. त्वद्रीत्या प्रत्येकं मोक्षहेत्वोः निरंतरचिन्ताभरन्यासरूपयोः भक्तिप्रपत्त्योः स्वरूपतः कर्मापेक्षानपेक्षाभ्यां आवृत्त्यनावृत्तिभ्यां च विषमत्वात् (*Nym* iv. 5)

12. न च तयोरुक्तरीत्या अधिकाल्पत्वेऽपि विश्वासाल्पत्वाधिकत्वाभ्यां 'साम्यमिति वाच्यम् (*Nym* iv.5)

established in *BS* ii.1.34 would also be flouted by such a view.[13]

In his commentary on Rāmānuja's *GB* (xviii.66) Vedānta Deśika introducing an alternative explanation of the verse given by Rāmānuja refers to Prapatti-Mārga as intended for the benefit of those who for social and other disabilities are unable or not competent to follow the more arduous course of Bhakti coupled with Upāsanā and the Varnāśrama and other Karmas.[14] In other words, the disparity of the Sādhanas is to be reconciled with the final result achieved by both the Mārgas and types of Adhikārins being the same, on account of the difference in the competence and capacity of the Adhikārins.[15] But then, it appears from Deśika's further comments in this connection, that he is viewing "Prapatti" not so much as an independent means on a par with the Vedic Upāsanā Mārga based on Karma and Bhakti, but as an *aid* to overcome the obstacles and 'sins' which come in the way of one's putting the regular Bhakti-Yoga into practice :

एवं सकलाभिमतसाधनतया भगवच्छास्त्रादिषु प्रसिद्धं भगवत्प्रपदनमिह प्रकृतभक्तियोगारम्भविरोधिपापनिबर्हणरूपोदाहरणविशेषे प्रदर्शितम् । 'सुदुष्करेण शोचेद्यो येन येनेष्टहेतुना । स स तस्याहमेव' इति चरमश्लोकसंग्रहः । **अत एव अत्रत्यभाष्याग्रन्थस्य गद्यस्तुतेश्च अविरोधः ।**

The view referred to by Vyāsatīrtha in his *Nyāyāmṛta* very probably represents the position of the *Tengalai school of Śrīvaiṣṇava thought*, which has given *special prominence to Prapatti as an independent Sādhana of Mokṣa* which can be practised by all without social and other restrictions, i.e., to say *as an alternative to Bhakti in its Vedic aspect*.[16]

---

13. विश्वासस्यावर्तनीयायां भक्तावेव यावदावृत्त्यपेक्षितत्वेन अनावर्तनीयप्रपत्तितोऽधिकत्वात् । यदि च फलसाम्येन साधनसाम्यार्थं प्रपत्तावधिकविश्वासः कल्प्येत, तर्ह्यन्योन्याश्रयः साधनवैषम्येऽपि साध्यसाम्ये चाधिकविधात्र्याः श्रुतेरनुपादेयत्वं, फलदातुरीश्वरस्य वैषम्यादिकं च स्यात् । (*Nym* iv.5)

14. 'सर्वधर्मान् परित्यज्य' इति स्वरूपत्याग एवास्यां योजनायाम्। न च तावता नित्यनैमित्तिकलोपप्रसंगः । दुरनुष्ठानप्रायश्चित्तादिविषयत्वोक्तेः। तुल्यन्यायतया तु नित्यनैमित्तिकेष्वपि यानि दुरनुष्ठेयानि तत्रैवं स्यात् । शक्तमधिकृत्यैव शास्त्रप्रवृत्तेः । अशक्त्या अकरणे दोषाभावात् ।
(Deśika, *RGB*. xviii. 66)

15. इह च मुख्याशक्तस्य सर्वप्रकारमुख्यानुकल्पतया एकस्यैव भगवत्प्रपदनस्य विधानात्, शक्ताशक्ताधिकारिभेदाच्च मुख्यानुकल्पयोः सर्वत्र **फलाविशेषोपपत्तेः ।**

16. "The older school thinks that the person who adopts the path of Prapatti should give up all Scriptural duties assigned to the different stages

Vyāsatīrtha says that there is no warrant in the Śāstras for making any such distinction or dichotomy in the field of Sādhanas. Even conceding that there are two different levels of Sādhakas, they must necessarily involve a corresponding difference in the nature of the result achieved by them. The principle of parity of means and ends can on no account be set aside. That is why Kumārila Bhaṭṭa himself in his *Tantra-Vārtika* recognizes :

कर्मणामल्पमहतां फलानां च स्वगोचरः ।
विभागः स्थानसामान्यादविशेषेऽपि चोदिते ॥

(i. 2. *Sūtra*. i, 2.7)

that even though there are no express statements to the effect in the Śrutis it is accepted in principle that lesser rites have lesser fruits and bigger rites have higher fruits.[17]

Vyāsatīrtha further points out that the religious duties, meditations and other spiritual activities performed by Aparokṣa Jñānins like Śuka, who may be Bhaktas or Prapannas, cannot be regarded as accessories to the acquisition of Jñāna, as in the case of unenlightened Adhikārins, by way of creating a zest for knowledge in them; or by way of putting an end to their sins arising in the event of non-performance of those duties, because persons like Śuka are already Aparokṣajñānins. Such religious activities carried out by them cannot also be taken to contribute directly to the fruit of Mokṣa, as that would entail the accepance of the Jñānakarmasamuccayavāda by the Viśiṣṭādvaitin. If the Samuccaya of Jñāna and Karma is admitted, then the diversity of Karmas after Jñāna is attained would have to be accepted as producing a diversity in the result to that extent, which would not be acceptable to the Viśiṣṭādvaitin. Such activities in which Jñānins, Bhaktas and Prapannas engage in (after attaining Jñāna) can obviously have no other goal except Mokṣa, because they would care for no other fruit. Their acti-

---

of life (*āśrama*); for it is well evidenced in the *Gītā* text that one should give up all one's religious duties and surrender oneself to God". (Dasgupta, *His- of I. Phil.* iii. p. 91). See in this connection the views of the Teṅgalai sect such as those of Pillai Lokācārya Azhagiya Maṇavāla Muni.

17. यदि ह्यल्पान्महतश्च कर्मणः समफत्वं ततो 'अक्के चेत्' इत्मनेनैव न्यायेनाल्पेन सिद्धः स इति न कश्चित् प्रवर्तेत । तत्र विधिशक्तिबाधः स्यात् अविहतशक्तिस्तु सन् अर्धाद्वा कल्पनैकफलसद्भावप्रमाणाभावात् । एवमिह तद्विशेष इति । (*Commentary*)

vities cannot be explained away merely as activities performed for the benefit of the world or its improvement (*lokasaṅgraha*) or as commandments of God. None of these can be ends in themselves. If it is supposed that they are performed by them merely to earn the love of God for themselves, we will have to point that they have already earned such love of God by rising to the level of Jñānins, Bhaktas and Prapannas. If they wish to achieve a greater measure of God's love for themselves by such activities, there will be no point in striving for it, if by such a fresh measure of God's love being showered on them, their joy in Mokṣa *is not enriched* to any appreciable extent. Nor can their activities be mere sportive activities as in the case of God Himself. For the Śrutis do enjoin upon the Aparokṣa Jñānins such performance of actions in all seriousness:

'आचार्याद्विद्यामवाप्य एतमात्मानमभिपश्य शान्तो भवेत्, दान्तो भवेत्'
(Madhva in *BSB* iii. 4.24)

"मत्कर्मकृन्मत्परमो मद्भक्तः संगवर्जितः ।
मन्मना भव मद्भक्तो मद्याजी मां नमस्कुरु ।"
इत्यादिना भक्तिप्रपत्तिमतश्च **तद्विधानात्** । (*Nym* iv. 5)

We cannot therefore escape the conclusion that all spiritual activities of Aparokṣa Jñānins, whether they take the form of Karma, Bhakti or Prapatti, *must have their own rewards in Mokṣa.* As there is no possibility of any other kind of reward in Mokṣa than realizing and enjoying one's own innate bliss, some kind of a fresh welling up of this Svarūpānanda will have to be admitted as an indisputable certainty. There is thus a very strong case for accepting the thesis of Svarūpānanda-Tāratamya in Mokṣa.

The nature and degree of bliss enjoyed by each soul should thus be in proportion to its natural fitness (*yogyatā*) and amount of preparation (*sādhana*) including its qualitative and other differences. As between them and God there is already this wide difference that they could not take part in the cosmic functions of the Supreme (*BS* iv. 4.17), there must be a wide difference in the bliss of the Supreme and that of the released. This is accepted by the Śruti text : एतस्यैवानन्दस्यान्यानि भूतानि मात्रामुपजीवन्ति,

whose implications need not necessarily be restricted to the state of bondage. This limitation between the Supreme Being and the Jīvas is not impracticable in Mokṣa as there is a God to control the latter. It is of course needless for Him to issue a command to the effect, for His wish is law unto them.[18]

परमेश्वरकामाद्यविभागेनैव तेषां सत्यकामत्वम्—
'कामेन मे काम आगात्'
(*TA* iii. 15. 2a) [*BSB* iv. 2. 26]

As in an ideal Communist State, the released can be expected to know what is good and best for them and they can be trusted to carry on their way without encroaching upon one another's province or the liberties of God. They neither do nor *can* will what is impossible of achievement or beyond their deserts. While it remains true that all their desires come true, Madhva would explain, that on no account would they entertain a low and unholy desire or one beyond their powers of achievement or jurisdiction :

स्वाधिकानन्दसंप्राप्तौ सृष्ट्यादिव्यापृतिष्वपि ।
मुक्तानां नैव कामः स्यादन्यान्कामांस्तु भुंजते ॥
तद्योग्यता नैव तेषां कदाचित्क्वापि विद्यते ।
न चायोग्यं विमुक्तोऽपि प्राप्नुयान्नैव कामयेत् ॥
(*BSB* iv. 4.18)

न च, संकल्पादेव समस्तसंभवात्सृष्ट्यादिसमस्तकार्यसंभवः—
न हि सुवर्णं शुद्धमपि वन्हिकार्यकरं भवेत् ।
अयोग्यशक्तितस्त्वेव नाधिकानन्दसंभवः ॥
न हि कश्चित्सुशक्तोपि चकाराचेतनं चितिम् ।
न च कामस्तथा भूयात् ततः स्यात्सत्यकामता ॥ (*NV* iv. 4.9)

The rights and liberties of the freed are thus constitutionally defined and properly safeguarded by the principle of undictated harmony (*satyakāmatā*) of their nature. There is no room for discord or jealousy there. Each one has his reward and each feels happy and full to the brim : like bowls and pitchers, rivers and seas filled to capacity

18. Cf. "Thy Will be done on Earth, as it is in Heaven."

यथोदंचनकुंभादेः सरित्सागरयोरपि ।
अल्पेन महता वापि **पूर्तिर्योग्यतया भवेत्** ॥
(Quoted in the Com. of *BrhUp* iii. 4. 10)

Each is so much absorbed in his own contentment and has no thoughts to give to the disparity between him and the others. He sees nothing more than that every other person also is likewise happy and contended and full to the brim. Madhva's Mokṣa is thus a Philosophical Communism come true.

One of the familiar objections to the admission of multiplicity with gradation (Tāratamya) in Mokṣa is that if there are differences and inequalities there, they would inevitably lead to jealousy and strife among the released and reduce the released state to the level of our own world.

An obvious reply to this is that difference is consistent and compatible with cooperation and good-will also—not necessarily with conflict. Madhva goes a step further and argues that inequality by itself cannot lead to strife. It is the feelings of jealousy and other bad passions that are ultimately responsible for it and as these are *ruled out* in Mokṣa, differences or inequalities by themselves connot do any harm.

For, there is no assurance that such discord will be completely eliminated, if absolute 'equality' is accepted. Instances are not wanting within our own experience (at the domestic, national and even international levels) of persons, communities and nations harboring jealousy, hatred and evil designs against their own equals :

भवेयुर्यदि चेर्ष्याद्याः समेष्वपि कुतो न ते ?
तप्यमानाः समान् दृष्ट्वा द्वेषेर्ष्यादियुता अपि ।
दृश्यन्ते बहवो लोके, दोषा एवात्र कारणम् ।
यदि निर्दोषता तत्र किमाधिक्येन दूष्यते ? *AV* iii. 4. 16)

Such tendencies, in the last analysis are traceable to defects in the human character. But inasmuch as Mokṣa is by definition a state of blessedness free from all such imperfections and bad passions of embodied existence, there can be no possibility of any strife or discord arising among the released souls. Hence, the presence of gradation in the Svarūpa and Svarūpānanda of

Jīvas in Mokṣa would not in any way disturb the peace and harmony of the released state.

Precisely the same line of argument has been adopted by Aristotle in defence of private property against the alluring pleas in favor of community of property :

"Such legislation may have a specious appearance of benevolence. Men readily listen to it and are easily induced to believe that in some wonderful manner everybody will become everybody's friend, especially when someone is heard denouncing the evils now existing in the States (suits about contracts, etc.), which are said to arise out of possession of private properity. These evils, however, are due to a very different cause —*the wickedness of human nature.* Indeed, we see that there is much *more* quarrelling among those who have all things in common—though there are not many of them, when compared with the vast number who have private property" (Aristotle's *Politics*, Tr. Jowett, Oxford, 1931, p. 63). [Italics mine.]

Madhva silences such frivolous objections against the presence of differnce and gradation in Mokṣa by quoting the words of the Sūtrakāra: अक्षरधियां त्वविरोधः[19] सामान्यतद्भावाभ्यां औपसदवत् तदुक्तम् (*BS* iii. 3. 34). The released souls are fully attuned to the Imperishable Brahman (*akṣara-dhi*). They are, as such, absolutely free from all evil and other disturbing passions of embodied existence. Hence, they will all be mutually well-disposed to one another. Those in a higher status will be extending their help and friendship to others below them. The humbler among them would look upon those above them with love and reverence like true *disciples* (*aupasada*)[20] looking upon their Gurus with unbounded love and regard. This is indeed a refreshingly new and original interpretation of this important Sūtra from the Sādhanādhyāya of the Brahmasūtras. It completely disarms all

---

19. Madhva reads अविरोधः as against अवरोधः of Śaṅkara and Rāmānuja here. Their interpretation of the term "*aupasada*" also is different.

For comments see my *BSPC* III. pp. 356-57; 362-65.

20. For the etymology of the word in the sense of a 'disciple' see my *BSPC* III. p. 358, 362-65.

objections to the doctrine of Ānandatāratamya among souls, in Mokṣa.

Such is the edifying picture of complete mutual harmony and goodwill prevailing in Mokṣa, according to Madhva. It shows how absurd and ridiculous it would be to judge the trans-empirical state from the standpoint of the passions and prejudices of our earthly life. The state of Mokṣa as a state of blessedness precludes by its very nature all disturbing passions and psychological complexes. The freed souls there lead a life of unalloyed happiness in blissful mutual fellowship and communion with the Lord. It is a state above strife and disharmony, which are left behind once for all.[21]

Thus does Madhva conclude his exposition of the subject of Mokṣa, with a dignified and spirited defence of the concept of Svarūpānandatāratamya therein. Every released soul is perfect in its own way; but the perfection (*pūrṇatva*) of each is distinctive, *sui generis*. *It is an expression of its selfhood.* The significance of this unique doctrine lies as much in its logical trenchancy as in its Mystic inwardness. It is a conception which applies to spiritual life the principle of peaceful co-existence and fellowship to the whole community of the released souls and guarantees to each one of them the fundamental right to exist *sui juris* and to be in a position to have the complete and distinctive enjoyment of its own selfhood and Svarūpānanda in communion with Brahman.

21. अश्व इव रोमाणि विधूय पापं, चन्द्र इव राहोर्मुखात् प्रमुच्य धूत्वा शरीरमकृतं कृतात्मा ब्रह्मलोकमभिसंभवामीति । (*Chan Up* uiii. 13).

Cf. "The world obviously is not one. It may be all one within the body of God. But I am not you and you are not me and I don't see why when I achieve complete Mokṣa I should completely merge in you and I don't think that I want to be. I don't see logically why I should. I might feel that my soul is linked with God. But if I lose my individuality completely, I don't see how I can enjoy the presence of God"

Prof. A.L. Basham interview with Subhananda Swami *Back to Godhead*- Vol. 18, no. 5. May 1983. (ISKCON).

CHAPTER LVIII

CONCLUSION

AS the intrinsic value and significance of the many seminal contributions of Madhva and his eminent commentators to the solution of the various problems of Indian Philosophy in general and of the Vedānta in particular, with special reference to the main divisions of the subject matter of Philosophy, such as Epistemology, Ontology, Logic and Metaphysics as well as the domain of spiritual effort (Sādhana) and its goal (mokṣa) have all been pinpointed in the preceding Chapters dealing with them and in Chapter IV also, it is hardly necessary for me to recapitulate them here.

I would however like to make one point clear before closing. The philosophers of the Mādhva school have often been glibly accused of confusing between the Vyāvahārika and the Pāramārthika standpoints in Advaita philosophy and giving an unfair account of the Śaṅkarite position in regard to the world's "Mithyātva" or unreality. "In not appreciating this difference and in equating the Pāramārthika with the Vyāvahārika, the Mādhva philosophers have fallen a prey to a gross misunderstanding about the Vedanta position" (Dr. Narain, *Op. cit.* p. 338). The distinction of the two standpoints may be an important fundamental of Advaita philosophy; but it is not good logic to take it for granted and build a superstructure on its foundation. For the knowledge of "Pāramārthikatvam" as involving the idea of "Abādhyatvam" uncontradictability with reference to all three periods of time presupposes the knowledge of what is "Vyāvahārika" or subject to such contradictability. Similarly, knowledge of the "Vyāvahārika", as defined above presupposes knowledge of "Pāramārthikatva" as *not* subject to such contradictabilty. There is thus a clear and unavoidable mutual interdependence here.[1] It is therefore no use playing hide and seek with the pair of Vyāvahārika and Pāramārthika. The external world and its experiences cannot be established to be Vyāvahārika and therefore but "mithyā" without a knowledge of the noumenal as its contradictory and the latter cannot be known as "*a-bādhya*" or uncontradictable without knowing the contradictable. Neither is thus capable of being established independently of the other. The only other way left of breaking through this stalemate is to define the negation of the world with reference to the three periods of time as envisaged in "mithyātvam" as a negation of the subject in essence (*svarūpeṇa traikālikaniṣedhaḥ*) instead of negation in its noumenal or Pāramārthika aspect (*pārmārthikatvākāreṇa niṣedhaḥ*). That would reduce the world to a nullity.

It is not that the Dvaita and the Viśiṣṭādvaita thinkers who have rejected the bifurcation of reality into Vyāvahārika and Pāramārthika have ignored or have been oblivious of the distinction made by the Advaita philosophers. They have shown themselves in their writings to be fully aware of the Advaita stand and have given the fullest consideration to the grounds on which it has been taken and have found them wanting in probative value. Hence their disagreement on this question. But it is not a disagreement due to any want of correct understanding of the other point of view. That is the bare truth of the matter.

It is my sincere hope that a close study of this work will once for all lay to rest the false view aired by some writers on Indian philosophy that Vedānṭa philosophy reached its culmination in the Advaita of Śaṅkara and that, in any case, after the work done by Śaṅkara and Rāmānuja in the history of Vedānta Darśana, there has been no forward march, no fresh development and no original contribution to Vedānta thought worth mentioning for centuries.

भाष्यटीकादिसद्ग्रन्थानुपजीव्य मया कृतम् ।
इमं प्रबन्धं सुधियो विमृशन्तु सकौतुकम् ॥

॥ श्रीकृष्णार्पणमस्तु ॥

---

1. नापि पारमार्थिकत्वाकारेण त्रैकालिकनिषेधप्रतियोगित्वमिति। अबाध्यत्वरूपपारमार्थिकत्वस्य बध्यत्वरूपमिथ्यात्वनिरूप्यत्वेन अन्योन्याश्रयात्। (*Nym* i. 1)

SELECT BIBLIOGRAPHY

Works in English

C.R. Krishnarao *Śrī Madhva, His life and Doctrine*, Prabhakara Press, Udipi, 1929.

R. Nagaraja Sarma *Reign of Realism in Indian Philosophy*, National Press, Madras, 1937.

H.N. Raghavendrachar *Dvaita Philosophy, Its Place in Vedānta*, Mysore University, 1941.

B.N.K. Sharma *Catussūtrībhāṣya of Madhvācārya* (with three commentaries, Introduction and Notes), Law Journal Press, Madras, 1934.

Svatantrādvaita or Madhva's Theistic Realism, G.S. Press, Mount Road, Madras, 1942.

Brahmasūtras and Their Principal Commentaries (of the Śaṅkara, Rāmanuja and Madhva Schools) in three Vols., Bharatiya Vidya Bhavan, Bombay, 1971-1978.

Lectures on Vedānta, Karnataka University, Dharwad, 1979.

Madhva's Teachings in His Own Words (3 rd edn.), Bharatiya Vidya Bhavan, Bombay, 1979.

History of Dvaita School of Vedānta and Its Literature (2nd edn.), Motilal Banarsidass, Delhi, 1981.

S.N. Dasgupta *A History of Indian Philosophy* (Vols. 2 to 4), Cambridge University Press, 1922-49.

S. Radhakrishnan *Indian Philosophy* (Vols. 1 and 2), George Allen and Unwin, London, 1929.

D.M. Datta *The Six Ways of Knowing*, London, 1926.

Chandradhar Sharma *A Critical Survey of Indian Philosophy*, Rider and Co., London, 1926.

V.S. Ghate *The Vedānta*, Bombay Govt. Sanskrit Series, 1926.

K. Narain *An Outline of Madhva Philosophy*, Udayana Pub., Allahabad, 1962.

A Critique of Mādhva Refutation of Śaṅkara School of Vedānta, Udayana Pub., Allahabad, 1964.

G. Trumbull Ladd *Philosophy of Knowledge*.

Pereira, Jose *Hindu Theology—A Reader*, Doubleday and Co. New York, 1976.

Ayer, A.J. *Problem of Knowledge*, Macmillan and Company, London, 1956.

Carpenter, E. J. *Theism in Mediaeval India*, London, 1921.

Ewing, A.C. *Fundamental Questions of Philosophy*, Routledge and Kegan Paul, London, 1953.

Dawes Hicks *Philosophical Bases of Theism*, Hibbert Lectures, 1937.

Alexander Campbell Fraser *Philosophy of Theism*, Gifford Lectures, 1894-96.

Russell, *Problems of Philosophy*,

Pringle Pattison *Idea of God*, 1917.

James Ward *Pluralism and Theism*, Cambridge, 1912.

Herbert Spencer *Fundamental Principles*.

Albert Schweitzer *Indian Thought and Its Development*, Adam and Charles Black, London, 1952.

D.N. Shanbhag *Some Problems of Dvaita Philosophy in Their Dialectical Setting*, Sri Rama Prakashan, Dharwad, 1982.

Hindi

Krishnakant Chaturvedi *Dvait Vedānt kā Tāttvik Anuśīlan*, Vidyaprakashan Mandir, Delhi, 1971.

Sanskrit Texts

DVAITA-VEDĀNTA

Madhvācārya *Brahmasūtrabhāṣya*, *Anuvyākhyāna*, *Nyāyavivaraṇa* and *Aṇubhāṣya* on Brahmasūtras

(Daśa-Prakaraṇas) *Tattvasaṅkhyāna*, *Tattvaviveka*, *Tattvodyota*, *Karmanirṇaya*, *Viṣṇutattvanirṇaya*, *Upādhikhaṇḍana*, *Māyāvādakhaṇḍana*, *Mithyātvānumānakhaṇḍana*, *Pramāṇalakṣaṇa*, *Gītā-Bhāṣya* and *Gītātātparya* (on *Gītā*)

Bhāgavata-Tātparya

Mahābhārata-Tātparyanirṇaya

Ten *Upaniṣad Bhāṣyas*

Dvādaśa Stotra

(All the above have been published as Collective Works of Madhvācārya and edited by T.R. Krishnacharya, Nirnayasagar Press, Bombay).

Padmanābha Tīrtha *Sannyāyaratnāvali* (Commentary on *AV*) Ed. G R. Savanur, Pune, 1937.

Trivikrama Paṇḍita *Tattvapradīpa* (Commentary on Madhva's *BSB*) ABMM, Udipi, 1958.

Jayatīrtha *Tattvaprakāśikā*, N.S. Press, Bombay, 1902.

Nyāyasudhā (Commentery on AV), 1895.

Prmāṇa-Paddhati, Chitrasala Press, Pune, 1931.

Vādāvali, N.S. Press, Bombay, 1904.

Commentaries on Daśa-Prakaraṇas of Madhva, N.S. Press, Bombay, 1897.

Viṣṇudāsācārya *Vādaratnāvali* (MS).

Vyāsatīrtha *Tātparyacandrikā*, N.S. Press, Bombay, 1913.

Nyāyāmṛta ......1910.

Tarka-Tāṇḍava, Oriental Library, Mysorc, 1943.

Mandāramañjari on Khaṇḍanatrayaṭīkās, N.S. Press, Bombay, 1896.

Vyāsa-Rāmācārya *Nyāyāmṛta-Taraṅgiṇi*, N.S. Press, Bombay, 1910.

Vijayīndra Tīrtha *Madhvādhva-Kaṇṭakoddhāra*, G.R. Savanur, Pune, 1934.

Vādirāja Tīrtha *Tattvaprakāśikā-Gurvarthadīpikā*, Udipi, 1954.

Rāghavendra Tīrtha *Gītāvivṛti*, *Candrikā-Prakāśa*, *Tattvaprakāśikā-Bhāvadīpa* (NS. Press, Bombay).

Nyāyadīpikā commentary on *Tarkatāṇḍava* Mysore Uni., 1943.

Jagannātha Tīrtha *Bhāṣyadīpikā* (commentary on Madhva's *BSB*), Bangalore, 1965.

ADVAITA

Gauḍapāda : Kārikās with commentary of Śaṅkara, Anandashrama Press, Pune, 1928.

Śaṅkara: *Brahmasūtrabhāṣya* (with commentaries), Ed. Anantakrishna Sastri, N.S. Press, Bombay, 1917.

Maṇḍana Miśra *Brahmasiddhi*, Madras GO Mss. Lib. 1936.

Sureśvara *Bṛhadāraṇyakopaniṣadbhāṣyavārtika*, Anandashrama, Pune, 1892-94.

Vācaspati Miśra *Bhāmati*, Bombay, 1917.

Vimuktātman *Iṣṭasiddhi*, GOS, Baroda.
Ānandabodha *Nyāyamakaranda*, Chowkhamba, 1907.
Sarvajñātman *Sankṣepaśārīraka*, Banaras Sanskrit Series, 1897.
Prakāśātman *Vivaraṇa*, Viz. Sanskrit Series, 1892.
Śrīharṣa *Khaṇḍanakhaṇḍakhādya*, Chowkhamba, Varanasi, 1914-21.
Citsukha *Tattvapradīpikā* with *Nayanaprasādinī*, Bombay, 1915.
Madhusūdana Sarasvatī *Advaitasiddhi*, ed. by Anantakrishna Sastri, N.S. Press, Bombay, 1917.
Śrīdhaiasvāmin Commentary on *Bhāgavata*, Brindavan edn., 1905
Brahmānanda Sarasvatī *Brahmānandīya* (Laghucandrikā), Bombay 1905

VIŚIṢṬĀDVAITA

Yāmunācārya *Siddhitraya*, Chowkhamba, 1900.
Rāmānuja *Śrībhāṣya*, *Vedārthasaṅgraha*, *Gītābhāṣya*, Kanchipuram, 1956.
Vedāntadeśika *Tattvamuktākalāpa*, Medical Hall Press, Banaras, 1910.
Commantary on Gītābhāṣya, Ananda Press, Madras, 1910
Rahasyatrayasāra.
Nārāyaṇācārya *Nītimālā*, Annamalai University, 1940.

OTHER SYSTEMS

Nāgārjuna *Madhyamaka Kārikās*, Calcutta, 1894-97.
Vātsyāyana *Nyāyasūtrabhāṣya*, Viz. Skt. Ser., 1986.
Īśvarakṛṣṇa *Sāṅkhya Kārikās*, Banaras, 1897.
Kumārila Bhaṭṭa *Ślokavārtika* Chowkhamba, 1898-99.
Tantravārtika, Banaras Skt. Ser., 1903-04.
Śrīdhara *Nyāyakandalī*.
Udayanācārya *Nyāyakusumāñjali*.
Ātmatattvaviveka.

MARĀTHI

Jñānadeva *Jñāneśvarī*, Govt. of Maharashtra, Bombay.

GERMAN

H. Glasenapp *Madhva's Philosophie des Vishnu-Glaubens*, Leipzig, 1923.

FRENCH

Mmle Suzanne Siauve *Madhva's Anuvyākhyāna* Tr. (1957-59) *Le Doctrine de Madhva*, 1968. Institute of French Indological Studies, Pondichery.

INDEX

T

U

V